THE LAST MESSENGER
THE FINAL PROPHET

BY

DR. AHMAD JAVID SARWARI QADERI

بِسْمِ ٱللَّهِ ٱلرَّحْمَٰنِ ٱلرَّحِيمِ

مَّا كَانَ مُحَمَّدٌ أَبَآ أَحَدٍ مِّن رِّجَالِكُمْ وَلَٰكِن رَّسُولَ ٱللَّهِ وَخَاتَمَ ٱلنَّبِيِّنَ ۗ وَكَانَ ٱللَّهُ بِكُلِّ شَىْءٍ عَلِيمًا

Muhammad is not the father of any of your men but rather the
Messenger of God and the seal of the prophets.

(Quran 33:40)

THE LAST MESSENGER

THE FINAL PROPHET

BY

DR. AHMAD JAVID SARWARI QADERI

Dedication

To Sara, my wife and life companion, who is an amazing person. Her love, kindness, generosity, and strength of path have always inspired me.

To Cyrus (Navid) and Alexander (Omid), our sons, it is difficult to find words that truly describe how much I love you both. Thanks for making us a family that reflects Allah's grace and love.

Acknowledgment

I would like to express my sincere gratitude to Khalifa Mushtaq Salee and Khalifa Riaz Cassim of Johannesburg, South Africa, for their loving embrace of this work, patronage, and generous support of this auspicious project. I would also particularly like to thank my editor, Harlan Moore, for his tireless work in editing this book and for his help and many suggestions regarding the publication of this book.

In pursuing this project, I have incurred many debts that I can only repay with gratitude. I am deeply grateful to my translator and editor, Muhammad Zubair of River View Society, Lahore, an inspiring man full of understanding, support, and gentle encouragement.

To my wife and children, I offer my deepest and most heartfelt thanks. You are, beyond all else, the inspiration behind my strivings and the center from which I draw my strength.

Contents

Preface

"Everything in the heaven and earth glorify God, the King, the Holy, the Exalted,
and the Wise."

Al-Jumma (62:1)

"He is God, One God, the Self-Sufficient." (Quran 112:1-2)

In the name of Him who is One and Unique, One in Essence and peerless in attributes, separate from defects and worthy of Lordhood. His existence is the beginningless, and His fixity is the Endless. No moment precedes Him, and no term encompasses His Majesty. He is solitary, single, beautiful, majestic, and equal to Him is none. He is splendorous, generous, praiseworthy, and lovingly kind, caresser of servants, caretaker, worthy of every laudation. His beautiful doing is eternal, His command exalted, His covenant gentle, His kingship without annihilation. He is the help of the grieved, the rock of the weak, the support of the disobedient, the aid of the prisoner, and the backing of the poor. The hope of the destitute is in Him, the remedy of trials comes from His generosity, and the happiness of the poor is in His Majesty and beauty.

Happy is the heart that is bound to Him, blessed is he whose companion is His name, exalted is he whose vocation is remembering Him, and pure is the tongue that is mentioning Him. He is the Lord whose love is the repose of the hearts, whose remembrance is the adornment of the ears, whose seeing is the celebration of the eyes, whose assurance is the promise of caresses, whose face-to-face vision is the ease of the spirits, and from whose direction blows the breeze of union. "All is from Him; all is in Him, and indeed all is He."

Peace and blessings of Allah (Exalted is He) be upon the most special of the special ones, the master of the messengers, the chosen of the chosen ones, the most eminent of creation, His most praiseworthy beloved Hazrat Muhammad Mustafa (May God bless and cherish him), His most glorious emissary, His dearest beloved, and His noblest friend. May God bless and cherish all his family, all progeny, all companions, and all the righteous men and women. May the Lord give them eternal peace and exalt them. Indeed, all lights are from Him and through Him.

The life of the world's paragon is known to us from different sources. Countless biographies of the Holy Prophet Hazrat Muhammad (May God bless and cherish him) already exist, ranging from classical sources such as "Sira Ibn Ishaq" which was later edited by Ibn Hisham, to works such as "The Life of Prophet Muhammad" (As-Sirah an-Nabawiya) by Imam Ibn Kathir, "Sharaf al-Nabi" by Abu Saeed Khargushi, "Muhammad Messenger of Allah" (Ash-Shifa) by Qadi Iyad, "The Path of Muhammad" by Imam Birgivi to numerous recent accounts of the life of God's messenger including, "The Sealed Nectar" (Ar-Raheeqal Makhtum) by Saifur-Rahman Al-Mubarakpuri, "Muhammad" by Martin Lings as well as other renowned works by Muslim scholars over the last millennium. Clearly, every minute detail of the beloved of Allah must have already been preserved repeatedly, and the subject matter must have been exhausted. The Noble Quran itself contains allusions to events in his life and the life of his young Muslim community. The Quran is the earliest and most important source of the life of the Holy Prophet (May God bless and cherish him) and, therefore, the best witness to the religiosity and sociocultural milieu of his earliest followers.

It has been my cherished desire from early to write in the praise and veneration of the Holy Prophet Hazrat Muhammad Mustafa (May God bless and cherish him), whose love runs in the veins of my family. My fascination with the pre-eternal and mystical figure of the Holy Prophet (May God bless and cherish him) developed through the study of Sufi writers and poets of the Indo-Pakistan subcontinent, especially Allama Muhammad Iqbal, the philosopher of Islam. The famous Persian poet Nur ad-Din Abd ar-Rahman Jami, in a poem, wrote about the pre-existence of the Holy Prophet's (May God bless and cherish him) essence. According to him, the message of any prophet who ever lived was nothing but a fragment of the Holy Prophet's (May God bless and cherish him) comprehensive message.

His light appeared on Adam's forehead,

So that the angels bowed their heads in prostration.

Noah, in the dangers of the flood,

Found help from him in his seamanship.

The scent of his grace reached Abraham,

And his rose bloomed from Nimrod's pyre.

Yusuf was for him, in the court of kindness,

(Only) a slave, seventeen dirhams worth.

His face lighted the fire of Moses,

And his lip taught Christ how to quicken the dead.

(Haft Aurang by Jami)

The description of the pre-existence (eternal) of the Holy Prophet (May God bless and cherish him) has been given by the mystics in prose and poetry. In this regard, Hazrat Sheikh Abdul Qadir Jilani, the founder of the Qadiriyya Sufi order, is quoted in Bahjat al-Asrar:

"He has been glorified by all glorious qualities; he was granted all words. By his noble nature, the props of the whole of existence stay firmly placed; he is the secret of the word of the book of angels, the meaning of the letters "creation of the world and heavens." He is the pen of the Writer who has written the growing of created things; he is the pupil in the eye of the world, the master who has smithed the seal of existence. He is the one who suckles at the teats of revelation and carries the eternal mystery; he is the translator of the tongue of eternity. He carries the honor and keeps the reins of praise; he is the central pearl in the necklace of Prophethood and the gem in the diadem of messengers. He is the first, according to the cause and the last in existence. He was sent with the Greatest *Namus* to tear the veil of sorrow, to make the difficult easy, to push away the temptation of the hearts, to console the sadness of the spirit, to polish the mirror of the souls, to illuminate the darkness of the hearts, to make rich those who are poor in heart and to loosen the fetters of the souls." (Bahjat al-Asrar)

In my first book "Sufi Light: The Secret of Meditation," I wrote a comprehensive chapter on the Holy Prophet (May God bless and cherish him) called "Mercy unto the World," and in my subsequent books, "The Spirit of a Sultan," "Sufi Prayer and Love" and "Sufi experience of God" I have continued to write inspired by a deep trusting love of the beloved of God and our Holy Prophet Hazrat Muhammad Mustafa (May God bless and cherish him). This book is thus the result of the material collected from my previous writings, which I have expanded into a book about the veneration of the Holy Prophet Hazrat Muhammad (May God bless and cherish him).

This is, of course, a great responsibility and a momentous undertaking that fills my heart with trepidation. This work calls for the evaluation of the primary sources, examination of the secondary sources, deep knowledge of Prophethood and special qualities of this sublime rank. It is my hope and prayer that the following account brings out the sublime character of the Holy Prophet (May God bless and cherish him) and highlights his special status among all creation.

The Holy Prophet (May God bless and cherish him) is the worthiest of all mankind, the greatest in position and most perfect in character and virtue. His noble being is an inestimable treasure of perfection of physique, physical beauty, strength of intellect, soundness of understanding, eloquence of tongue, and nobility of lineage, as well as knowledge, forbearance, patience, thankfulness, justice, humility, chastity, generosity, courage, modesty, mercy, good manners, and companionship.

The Holy Prophet Hazrat Muhammad (May God bless and cherish him) is a reflection of Divine Light, and it is said for a fact that he did not cast a shadow. Every moment of his life was a miracle: the gazelle spoke to him, trees and stones would greet him with peace, the handkerchief with which he wiped out his saliva would not burn in fire, and the poisoned meat of lamb would not harm him. On many occasions, water would flow and pour out from between his fingers to quench the thirst of hundreds of people.

The story of the palm trunk, *hannana*, which the Holy Prophet (May God bless and cherish him) used as a pulpit in his early days of preaching, is quite moving. When the real stage was made for the Holy Prophet (May God bless and cherish him) and the palm trunk was thus discarded, it began to moan and groan, filled with grief, as it longed for the touch of the beloved Prophet. Rumi expressed this idea in his work "Masnavi" when he said,

Should the human heart be less loving than a seemingly dead piece of wood?

How can a philosopher who denies this miracle find his way to the saints?

The Holy Prophet Hazrat Muhammad (May God bless and cherish him) performed miracles. "And the moon was split" (Quran 54:2) refers to the Prophet's (May God bless and cherish him) miracle when he was able to split the moon. He performed this miracle to highlight the truth of his message. He not only split the moon, but the two halves were so apart that Mount Hira could be seen in between them.

It is narrated in a legend that King Shakrawati Farmand of South India did indeed witness the splitting of the moon at the same time. When he learned and verified what had happened in Makkah on that very night, he converted to Islam, along with his people. This miracle apparently resulted in the first Muslim settlement in India. It is also fascinating to know that an old painting showing the splitting of the moon with all its details was displayed at the court of a Rajput in Kotah, India.

The Holy Prophet (May God bless and cherish him) was proud of only one miracle, and that was the miracle of the Quran. The Noble Quran is the uncreated living word of God, verbally rendered from the blessed lips of the trustworthy Prophet Hazrat Muhammad (May God bless and cherish him) to become the Scripture of one of the greatest faiths on earth. The word of God is so beautiful, concise, rich, and vast in meaning that no one, till the end of time, will be able to write a single verse like it. In fact, God Himself has guaranteed the safeguarding of the Quran in the following words,

"Surely, We Ourselves have sent down this exhortation, and We will most surely safeguard it." (Quran 15:10)

All the authorities unanimously agree that the Noble Quran is word for word exactly as Hazrat Muhammad (May God bless and cherish him) gave it out to the world. It has not changed since then, nor will it become corrupted until the Day of Resurrection.

The Holy Prophet Hazrat Muhammad (May God bless and cherish him) has been called *ummi*, which usually means "unlettered" in the Noble Quran (7:157). His heart was not polluted by worldly knowledge and learning but was a pure vessel ready to receive the Divine revelation. His knowledge is directly derived from the First Intellect, the source of all wisdom.

One of the greatest miracles of the Holy Prophet Hazrat Muhammad (May God bless and cherish him) was the night journey, his ascent to meet the Lord of the universe. According to tradition, this happened in the body and in an awakened state in the company of Archangel Gabriel. He first went from the Kaaba to the Al-Aqsa Mosque in Jerusalem. There, he led the souls of all previous prophets in prayer before ascending to the very presence of God. Gabriel could not accompany the Holy Prophet (May God bless and cherish him) beyond the Lote tree, which marks the furthest limit of creation.

"If I would go one step further, my wings would become burned," sighed Gabriel on the night of ascension. It was there that he met the Lord in a realm where no one else had ever entered. None has ever seen God in life, nor will anyone ever see Him. The Holy Prophet Hazrat Muhammad (May God bless and cherish him) had an intimate encounter with God alone, which he described as such:

"I have had a time with God in which no created being has access, not even the Archangels." He exchanged ninety thousand words with God. When he returned, his bed was still warm, and the leaf he had brushed upon rising was still moving. The opening of Sura seventeen relates to his ascension:

"Limitless in His glory is He who transported His servant by night from the inviolable House of worship (at Makkah) to the remote House of worship (at Jerusalem)."

In this regard, he is superior to all prophets. Even Prophet Moses (May God bless and cherish him), who requested God for a vision, could not even look at the reflection through the burning bush without fainting. The ascension of the Holy Prophet and his time with God has become the model of spiritual journey for mystics. The experience of the moments when they reached the presence of God has been described by many. Abu Yazid Bistami was the first to describe his spiritual flight through the Heavens.

The quality of character that is particularly emphasized in the Holy Prophet

(May God bless and cherish him) is his humility and kindness. In this context, Qadi Iyad, a distinguished advocate of deep reverence for the Holy Prophet (May God bless and cherish him), writes in Ash-Shifa:

"God has elevated the dignity of the Prophet and granted him virtues, beautiful qualities, and special prerogatives. He has praised his high dignity so overwhelmingly that neither tongue nor pen is sufficient to describe them. In His Book, He has clearly and openly demonstrated his high rank and praised him for his qualities of character and his noble traits. He asks His servants to attach themselves to him and to follow him obediently. It is God, great in His Majesty, who grants honor and grace, who purifies and refines. It is Allah who lauds, praises and grants perfect recompense. He places before our eyes his noble nature, perfected and sublime in every respect. He grants him perfect virtues, praiseworthy qualities, noble habits, and numerous preferences. He supports his message with radiant miracles, clear proofs, and apparent signs."

Allah, the Mighty and Majestic bestowed Hazrat Muhammad (May God bless and cherish him) with Prophethood, bearing the message, close friendship with Allah, His love, being chosen for the ascension, vision of Him, nearness, proximity, revelation, intercession, all the virtues, the praise worthy station, being sent to all mankind, leading the prophets in prayer, witnessing for him of the prophets and their communities, mastery over the descendants of Prophet Adam, bearer of the Banner of Praise, bringing good news and warning, bearing the trust, being listened to, the expanding of his breast, the removing of his burden, the elevation of his name, being helped by a mighty victory, the sending down of *Sakineh*, supported by angels, his bringing the Book and wisdom and the Immense Quran, Allah's swearing by his name, his supplication being answered, inanimate objects and animals speaking to him, the dead being brought to life for his sake, water pouring from between his fingers, the splitting of the moon, the sun going back, the clouds shading him, the glorification of the pebbles and so on. This is just a brief account of what Allah honored him.

In short, this is not a comprehensive biography of the Holy Prophet (May God bless and cherish him) but rather a humble attempt to open new paths of curiosity and to lay a groundwork for future comprehensive accounts of him as the paragon of the world.

God bless the son of Amina, who,

Brought him for the open-handed and generous.

Say to those who hope for Ahmad's intercession.

Bless him and wish him great peace.

Dr. Ahmad Javid (Sarwari Qaderi)

Aldie, Virginia, USA

November 2023

CHAPTER 1
NUR-UL-ANWAR

Allah is the King, the owner of the kingdom, and the possessor of the kingdom. The first thing God created was the light of Prophet Hazrat Muhammad (May God bless and cherish him) (his spirit) from the light of His beauty. As He said,

"I created the spirit of Muhammad (May God bless and cherish him) from the light of my countenance." (Hadith)

Then, after that, God created the heavenly Throne from the light of Prophet Muhammad's (May God bless and cherish him) eyes, and from the heavenly Throne, He created all the rest of the existing entities.

Sheikh Abdul Qadir Jilani (May God sanctify his secret), in his book, "Sirr al-Asrar," and quoting Prophet Hazrat Muhammad (May God bless and cherish him), said, "The first thing God created was my spirit and light. God also created Pen and Intellect as the first objects." This means that they are all the same. They are all the Muhammadan Reality, collectively called the light because it is pure and pristine. The creation began with Nur-e-Muhammad (Light of Muhammad), and the Lord brought that Nur from His own heart.

Farid ud Din Attar, a Persian poet and scholar, wrote,

"The origin of the soul is the absolute light, nothing else.

That means it was the light of Muhammad, nothing else."

As God says,

"There has now come to you from God a light and a clear Book." (Quran 5:15)

This light is also called intellect because it comprehends universal truths. It is called pen as well because it is the instrument of transmission of God's knowledge in the realm of letters.

The light of Prophet Hazrat Muhammad (May God bless and cherish him) is thus the origin of all entities that exist, the first of all beings, and the highest manifestation of God's attributes. The Holy Prophet (May God bless and cherish him) said, "I am from God, and the believers are from me."

Sheikh Abdul Qadir Jilani further explained, "God created all spirits from him (Prophet Muhammad, may God bless and cherish him), in the realm of divinity in the best of molds. As a matter of fact, Muhammad (May God bless and cherish him) is the name of all perfect human beings in that realm, and he is the original home."

"It has been said that when the Exalted Lord created the light of Prophet Muhammad (May God bless and cherish him) from His own light, He kept it in the presence of His Exaltedness as long as He wanted. It remained before God for one hundred thousand years. It has also been said that for two hundred thousand years, He was gazing at it seventy thousand times a day, and with each gaze, He would drape it with a new light and a new generosity. He kept the light of Prophet Muhammad (May God bless and cherish him) for thousands and thousands of years, and each day, He would look upon it with the attribute of favor. With each gaze, it would gain another knowledge and understanding.

In those gazes, the secret core of his disposition was told that the level of the Quran's exaltedness would preserve the level of his sinlessness, and this awareness was firmly rooted in his disposition. When his very clay, along with the secret core of his disposition, was brought into this world, the revelation sent down from the exalted Throne turned towards him. He was saying, "I hope that this is the realization of the promise given to me at that time."

To soothe his heart and confirm this thought, the Lord of the worlds sent down this verse: "Alif Lam Mim." Alif alludes to God, Lam alludes to Gabriel, and Mim alludes to Muhammad (May God bless and cherish him).

He is saying, "By My divinity, Gabriel's holiness and your splendor, O Muhammad, this revelation is the Quran that We promised would be the keeper of your prophecy's level and the miracle of your good fortune. (Rashid ud Din

Maybudi, Kashf al-Asrar)

"Wherein is no doubt, from the Lord of the worlds."

Hazrat Sultan Bahu (May God sanctify his secret) writes in "Mehakul-Faqr," "When Allah whose essence is everlasting and whose attributes are eternal wanted to declare His divinity and lordhood, He separated a light from His brilliance and gazed at it in the mirror of His own love, Beauty, and marifa (knowledge). He fell in love with it and named His own light the light of Muhammad (Nur-e-Muhammad) and called him "beloved." The eternal Enactor then commanded the light of Muhammad to move and talk to Me." The light of Muhammad went into ecstasy and called out, "Ya Allah." The name of Allah was thus first uttered by the light of Muhammad. The Mighty and Majestic Lord kept the light of Muhammad in front of His sight and gazed at it intently for one million and seventy-three thousand years. The Exalted Lord, whose love is the repose of the hearts, commanded (to bestow honor and eminence) "To be" the spirit of Muhammad. By the command of the All-Compelling God, the light of Muhammad became the spirit of Muhammad (May God bless and cherish him). The Exalted Lord then addressed the spirit of Muhammad (May God bless and cherish him), "Speak to Me, O Muhammad." The spirit of the paragon of the world said, "I testify that there is no god but Allah, the One without peer." Hearing this, the Lord of the world affirmed, "I testify that Muhammad is the servant and Messenger of Allah."

The Exalted Lord commanded again, "O Muhammad, move and speak to Me."

The spirit of the Holy Prophet Hazrat Muhammad (May God bless and cherish him) proclaimed, "There is none worthy of worship except Allah." Upon this, the greatest Lord honored him and said, "And Muhammad is the Messenger of Allah."

Hazrat Sultan Bahu further writes, "Know that when God (Exalted is He) wanted to create spirits, He first separated a light from His own light and from that light He created the spirit of the Holy Prophet Muhammad Mustafa (May God bless and cherish him). The Lord of Beauty was infatuated and attracted by His own light (Nur-e-Muhammad) and called him "Beloved." After that, Allah created eighteen thousand creations, angels, Jinn and all the spirits from the Ruh-e-Muhammad.

Hazrat Sultan Bahu (May God be pleased with him) writes in the "Book of Soul" (Risala-Ruhi-sharif),

"The essence is the wellspring of Reality in the domain of divinity (Huwiat). The

Lovingly Kind Lord held His heavenly court and adorned His Throne beyond the limits of all creation. As an admonition, His pure essence cannot be reached by thousands of intellects. Praise belongs to Allah (Exalted is He); the entire cosmos and all that it contains reflect the stunning beauty of its creator. He created the universe as a shining mirror to behold His divine countenance in it. From the beginningless, He is engaged in the game of love with Himself. He Himself is the sight, the seer and the sought. He Himself is (the source of) love, the lover, and the beloved.

"O chevalier, if you remove the veil of ego (yourself), you will witness the One (single Reality). Duality exists because of the illusion of your eyes."

"Know that when the One (Allah) wanted to reveal His light from the chamber of unity, He displayed His ravishing beauty in the multiplicity of the creation. His beauty, a world-burning fire, attracted both worlds like moths and burned them. He then put on the mask of mim-e-Ahmadi and manifested Himself in the face of Ahmad (Muhammad Mustafa)."

Therefore, the Holy Prophet (May God bless and cherish him) said, "I am Ahmad blia mim, which means Ahad (the One)." The Prophet (May God bless and cherish him) also said, "I am Arab without ain (A), which means Rabb."

According to Sufis, m is the letter of humanity, and if you take it out, Ahad or the "One" will remain as He was, He is, and will be. The veil of m is lifted only for the lovers who can see God through the prophet. Therefore, Prophet Hazrat Muhammad (May God bless and cherish him) had expressly said, "Who has seen me has seen Allah."

It is narrated in a tradition that once Abu Hurrayrah was strolling through the streets of Medina shouting, "I have seen Allah (Exalted is He) walking in the streets of Medina." Hazrat Umar (May God be pleased with him) passed by and was distressed by his declaration. He went to the Prophet's Mosque and told the paragon of the world what Abu Hurrayrah was saying. The Holy Prophet (May God bless and cherish him) replied, "Abu Hurrayrah is telling the truth, who has seen me has seen Allah."

According to Rumi, for believers, the Prophet (May God bless and cherish him) is "The window through which one sees the creator."

The Holy Prophet Hazrat Muhammad (May God bless and cherish him) is reported to have stated,

"Allah has created me from His light, and He created that light a thousand years before the creation of Prophet Adam (Peace be upon him)." The Holy Prophet, created from divine light, did not cast a shadow. This divine light, Allah's first creation, serving as a source for further creation is identified with the pre-existent light of Hazrat Muhammad (May God bless and cherish him). From this light, all existences have been successively created.

Another tradition maintains that "Hazrat Ali's (May God be pleased with him) essence was the first to be created from the light of Muhammad Mustafa (May God bless and cherish him). It elaborates that on the night of Miraj, Allah revealed to the Holy Prophet Muhammad (May God bless and cherish him) that He had created him from His light, and then He created Ali from Muhammad Mustafa's light."

The Holy Prophet (May God bless and cherish him), it is reported, said to Salman Farsi that Allah created him from the purity of His light, and then He created Ali from Muhammad's light and from Muhammad's and Ali's light, He created Fatima. Thus, He created from them all Al-Hassan and Al-Hussayn, as well as the rest of the Imams. It is likewise related that the Holy Prophet (May God bless and cherish him) proclaimed: "I was created from the light of Allah, and Ahl al-Bayt was created from my light."

According to another hadith, Allah created the light of Hazrat Muhammad (May God bless and cherish him) two thousand years before creating the world. The light of Hazrat Ali (May God be pleased with him) ramified as a ray from that light. The cherubim asked Allah about the light and its ray; the Lord of the worlds answered, "This is a light out of My light; its main part is Prophethood, and its ray is the immama. The Prophethood is for Muhammad (May God bless and cherish him), My servant and Messenger, and the immama is for Ali, My hujjah and My partisan. Were it not for them, I would not have created any creatures."

There is a tradition recorded in Ithbat that runs as follows: The Prophet Hazrat Muhammad (May God bless and cherish him) said, "I and Ali were light on Prophet Adam's forehead. We wandered from the pure loins into purified, immaculate wombs till we reached the loins of Hazrat Abdul Muttalib. Then, the light was divided into two parts: one part was transmitted to Hazrat Abdallah and one part to Hazrat Abu Talib. I emerged from Hazrat Abdallah, and Ali emerged from Hazrat Abu Talib."

It is narrated that Hazrat Ali, as well as his family (Ahl-e-Bayt), existed before Prophet Adam's creation as primordial luminous reflections of their corporeal bodies. These reflections are called Ashbah-e-Nur. (Bihar). The Ashbah appeared to Prophet Adam; it is said that Allah commanded the celestial veils to be raised so that Prophet Adam could see five forms before His Throne. They were the Ashbah of Prophet Muhammad (May God bless and cherish him), Hazrat Ali, Hazrat Fatima, al-Hassan and al-Hussayn. Adam and Eve saw, according to another tradition, the image (sura) of Hazrat Fatima. It was a body of light with a crown on its head, which stood for Hazrat Ali, its earrings symbolized al-Hassan and al-Hussayn. (Suyuti, Dhahabi-Mizan, Lisan al-Mizan)

It is also related that when Hazrat Imam Hussayn (May God be pleased with him) was asked what Muhammad Mustafa's family was prior to Adam He said, "We were Ashbah of light, encircling the Throne of the Merciful, teaching angels how to praise Allah and to laud Him." (Ilal, qala: Kunna ashbaha nurinnadurahawlaarshs l-rahmani fa-nu allium l-malaikata l-tasbihawa-l-tahliawa-l-tahmida)

On the night of Miraj, the angels of the Throne informed the Holy Prophet (May God bless and cherish him) that his family had been created as luminous ashbah prior to their own creation. When the angels were finally created, they learned the words of Allah's glorification from that ashbah. (Bihar- Tafsir Furat)

The creative force of Muhammad's (May God bless and cherish him) light, in its circular motion, went through the various cosmic spheres, which are called hujub (veils). The Holy Prophet (May God bless and cherish him) said, "Allah created my light, first of all things. He drew it out of His light and Majesty. It moved around the veil called qudra for eighty thousand years till it reached the veil of Al-Azama (veil of Majesty), which is beneath the veil of Al-qudra. Then it prostrated itself to Allah (Exalted is He), and the light of Ali ramified from it. Thus, my light was circling about the azama, and Ali's light circled around the qudra." From these two lights, Allah created the rest of His creatures. The Holy Prophet (May God bless and cherish him) also said,

"Allah created me and Ali from a common light, forty thousand years prior to Prophet Adam. He placed us before His gaze, and we praised Him together."

Sufi master Al-Tustari relates that when Allah wanted to create Prophet Muhammad (May God bless and cherish him), He diffused light out of His own light throughout His kingdom. When this light reached the veil of Izma, it prostrated itself to Allah. Allah (Exalted is He) created from this prostration a column of dense light, transparent like glass, wide like seven heavens. The Holy Prophet (May God bless and cherish him) worshiped Allah there for a million years, not as a body, but as a nature of faith and knowledge of what was hidden. After that period, Allah created Prophet Adam from the light of Muhammad Mustafa (May God bless and cherish him). From the light of prophet Adam, He created the muradun, and from their light, He created the muridun. Ibn al-Arabi declares likewise that Allah drew out of the "first father" (Adam) the lights of the aqtab as suns and the lights of the nujuba as stars. Many traditions emphasize the Holy Prophet's (May God bless and cherish him) superiority over other prophets and maintain that the latter was created from his light. It is related that Allah took a handful of the light of His face and looked at it, and it began to sweat. From each drop, He created a prophet. This handful of light was the Holy Prophet Hazrat Muhammad (May God bless and cherish him). The knowledge and the religious conviction of the prophets also emanated from the light of Muhammad Mustafa (May God bless and cherish him).

A hadith narrated by al-Qastalani states that when Allah created the light of the Holy Prophet (May God bless and cherish him), He commanded it to look at the lights of other prophets. It covered them, and by his light, Allah bestowed upon them the ability to talk. He then took a covenant from them to believe in Muhammad Mustafa (May God bless and cherish him).

The light of Prophet Muhammad (May God bless and cherish him) is regarded as a source for the creation of the cosmos. It is identified with the cosmological pearl, which, according to tradition, was the first creation of Allah. This pearl was greater than heaven and earth. Allah, the Mighty and Majestic, looked at it, and it became water. Then He looked at the water, and it bubbled and foamed and vaporized. From the vapor, He created the heavens, and from the foam, He created the earth.

On the authority of Abd al-Razaq, the following hadith is reported that Jabir Ibn Abdallah asked the Holy Prophet (May God bless and cherish him), "O Messenger of Allah, my father and mother be sacrificed for you, tell me of the first thing Allah created before all things." The Holy Prophet (May God bless and cherish him) told him that Allah had created the light of Muhammad (May God bless and cherish him) from His own light prior to all things. This light moved around Allah, being subordinate to Him. When Allah wanted to create the world, He divided the light of Muhammad (May God bless and cherish him) into four parts. From the first part, He created the Pen (Al-Qalam), from the second, He created the Tablet (Al-Lawh), and from the third – the Throne. The fourth part was subdivided into four. From the first of the four parts, He created the angels who carry the Throne, from the second, the Chair (Al-Kursi), and from the third, the rest of the angels. The fourth was divided again into four. From the first, Allah created the heavens; from the second, the continents; from the third, He created Paradise and Hell. Out of the fourth, He again made four parts. From the first, He fashioned the light of the believer's eyesight; from the second – the light of their hearts that is the knowledge of Allah; from the third – the light of their faith in Allah's unity. This tradition lays a special emphasis on the priority of the light on other entities, such as Pen and the Throne.

Abu Saeed Khargushi, in his book, "Sharaf al-Nabi," writes that the light of Prophet Muhammad (May God bless and cherish him) was created nine thousand years before all things. It moved around Allah, worshiping Him with various verses. Then, a pearl was created from it, then water was created from the pearl. The water billowed for a thousand years. The light of the Holy Prophet (May God bless and cherish him) was split into ten parts, out of which the heavenly world was created; that is, the Throne, the Pen, the Tablet, the moon, the sun, the stars, the angels, the light of the believers, the Chair, and Prophet Muhammad (May God bless and cherish him) himself. Prophet Muhammad (May God bless and cherish him) was thus created along with the celestial world and remote from the earthly world that came into being later.

The luminous essence of the Holy Prophet (May God bless and cherish him), out of which all existences emanated, is called by Sufis "Al-haqiqa al-Muhammadiya." It is the essence of all essences; it comprises all of them within itself and is compared to each of them, like every whole that is imminent within each of its components."

Ibn Arabi emphasizes the central role of the light of Muhammad (May God bless and cherish him), stating, "The first light appeared out of the veil of unseen, and from knowledge to concrete existence, it is the light of our Prophet Muhammad (May God bless and cherish him)." He is the 'Siraj Munir'. The intelligences (uqul), the spirits (arwah), the intuitions (basa' ir), and the essences (dhawat) are nourished by the luminous essence of Mustafa, the Elect, who is the sun of existence." Ibn Arabi further asserts that the Holy Prophet (May God bless and cherish him) is "Like the seed (bidhr) of the human race." He maintains that Prophet Muhammad (May God bless and cherish him) is prior to Prophet Adam in essence, though outwardly his descendent.

In the same vein, al-Qastalani states that haqiqah emanated from the divine light and that the upper and lower world was derived from it according to the divine command. Al-haqiqa Al-Muhammadiya is also the origin of the essence of all spiritual entities.

Abu Saeed Khargushi recorded a prophetic tradition on the authority of Abdallah b. Mubarak which incorporates the concept of the Holy Prophet's (May God bless and cherish him) primordial creation, his wandering substance (taqallab), and his cosmic creative light. It states that Allah Az o wa Jal (Mighty and Majestic) created the light of Prophet Muhammad (May God bless and cherish him) four hundred and twenty-four thousand years prior to the creation of heaven, earth, Throne, the Kursi (Chair), the Tablet (Al-Lawh), the Pen (Al-Qalam), Paradise and Hell, as well as the creation of Prophet Adam, Prophet Noah, Prophet Abraham, Prophet Ismael, Prophet Isaac, Prophet Jacob, Prophet Moses, Prophet Jesus, Prophet David and the rest of those who believed in Allah's unity. Alongside the light of Prophet Muhammad (May God bless and cherish him), the Exalted Lord created twelve cosmic veils (hujub). Allah screened that light in the veil of qudra for twelve thousand years, and during that time, it glorified Allah with various verses. Then He covered it in the veil of the azama for eleven thousand years and in the veil of minna for ten thousand years. After having gone through all the twelve veils, glorifying Allah, the Mighty and the Majestic, in each of them, Allah made that light manifest on the Tablet in the form of Muhammad's name (May God bless and cherish him). There, it was shining for four thousand years. Then, it glowed on the pillar of the Throne for seven thousand years. The tradition goes on to say that the Holy Prophet's light was shining till Allah deposited it in the loins of Prophet Adam. Then Allah transferred it to the loins of Prophet Noah, then from loins to loins, till it appeared out of the loins of Hazrat Abdallah, the Holy Prophet Muhammad's father (May God bless and cherish him). The light of Prophet Muhammad (May God bless and cherish him) came from the celestial world of light, moving through cosmic spheres till its emergence in the earthly domain.

THE LIGHT OF MUHAMMAD

The Holy Prophet Hazrat Muhammad Mustafa's (May God bless and cherish him) emergence in the corporeal world is represented as a light, to the extent that "light" serves as his name. Interpretation of the Noble Quran verses maintains that the word "Nur" (Light) mentioned in it stands for the Holy Prophet.

"Qadjaakum mina Allah e nurun wa kitabun Mubeen."

"And now there has come unto you from God a light, and a clear divine writ." (Quran 5:15)

The idea of the light of Prophet Muhammad (May God bless and cherish him) is complex and, at the same time, fascinating. It was Muqatil who first idealized the person of the Holy Prophet (May God bless and cherish him) and interpreted the "Verse of Light" (Ayat-e-Nur) Sura 24:35 as a reference to Hazrat Muhammad (May God bless and cherish him) whose light shines through other messengers. This was further elaborated by later mystics, as mentioned earlier.

The Quran says,

Allah is the light of heaven and earth.

The parable of His light is,

As it were, that of a niche containing a lamp.

The lamp is enclosed in a glass,

The glass is like a radiant star.

Lit from a blessed tree – an olive tree,

That is neither of the East nor of the West,

The oil of which will always give light,

Even though the fire has not touched it,

Light upon light,

Allah guides to His light whomever He pleases.

And Allah sets parables for men.

And Allah has full knowledge of all things.

In the house which God has allowed to be raised.

So that His name be remembered in them.

And to extol His limitless glory at morning and evening."

The verse of light, Ayat al-Nur, is famous and popular among awliya. In this verse, Allah is called the light of heaven and earth. He has ordained them by bringing them into existence. Faqir Nur Muhammad Sarwari Qaderi, in his book "Irfan," writes that the word "Allah" in this verse does not apply to the essence of God, but rather it refers to His personal name "Allah." His personal name, "Allah," is like a lamp (divine light) placed on a raised pillar in order to illuminate the entire world. God has protected this lamp by enclosing it in glass. The name "Allah" is the divine light that cannot be put out as God has said,

"They desire to extinguish God's (guiding) light with their utterances: but God will not allow (this to pass), for He has willed to spread His light in all its fullness, however hateful this may be to all who deny the truth." (Quran 9:32, 61:8)

The blessed olive tree is the symbol of Islam, from which the light is emanating and spreading to far-off places in the East and West, fulfilling the prophecy that it will eventually transform all humanity. Sufi mystics refer to the word "Nur" (Light) to the person of the Holy Prophet Hazrat Muhammad (May God bless and cherish him), in whose heart God the Most High has placed the bright lamp of His personal name "Allah." Even before he received the divine revelation, "Read in the name of thy Lord," he was a source of light for all mankind. When the light from Allah, the Exalted, came to him, it was as though 'light upon light' had been revealed to him. Divine light will eventually overcome all the hearts and illuminate the entire world.

According to Muqatil's interpretation, it is the lamp (Misbah) that stands as a symbol for the Holy Prophet (May God bless and cherish him). Through him, the divine light should shine in the world, and through him, mankind was guided to the origin of light. "Neither of the East nor of the West" is a reference to the Holy Prophet's (May God bless and cherish him) comprehensive nature, which is not restricted to one specific person or race and which surpasses the boundaries of time and space. The Holy Prophet (May God bless and cherish him) is also called Nur-al-Huda, the light of right guidance. His famous prayer of light highlights his luminous essence, which is most precious to his faithful followers.

O Lord, grant me light in my heart.

Grant me light in my speech, hearing, and sight,

O Lord, grant me light above me and light below me,

Grant me light on my right side and on my left side,

Light in front of me and light behind me.

O Lord, grant me light in my body and my soul,

Grant me light and make me light.

O Lord, increase me in light, increase me in light,

And grant me light upon light.

Even the contemporary poets of the Holy Prophet (May God bless and cherish him) described the Prophet as a light guiding the believers. Among them, Hassan b. Thabit, Kaab b. Zubayr, and Abdallah b. al-Ziba maintains that the Holy Prophet Muhammad's name (May God bless and cherish him) – "Moon of moons" – was inscribed upon the moon, whereas another name of his, "light of lights," was written on the sun. (Ibn Hisham, Ibn Sharashub)

In the same vein, Sufi mystic Mansur Hallaj, who was a disciple of al-Tustari, elaborated in his book, "Kitab at-Tawsin" in the first chapter "Tasin as-Siraj" "He was a lamp from the light of invisible – a moon radiating among moons, whose mention is in the spheres of mysteries; the Divine Truth (God) called him ummi because of the collectedness of his noble aspiration (himma).

The light of the Prophethood – from his light did they spring forth, and their lights appeared from his light, and there is no light among the lights more luminous and more visible and before pre-existence than the light of this noble one.

Allah (Exalted is He) said in a hadith qudsi,

"You are My light among My servants, My messenger to My creatures, and My hujjah upon them." (fa innakanuri fi ibadi, warasuliilakhalqi, wahujjati ala bariyyati).

The most exalted expression of the Holy Prophet's (May God bless and cherish him) primordial substance is light, which also represents his prophetic mission. It is said in a tradition about his luminous body that "wherever he went in darkness, light was shining around him like moonlight." Another tradition runs as follows,

"Dark houses were lit by his presence."

According to a tradition quoted by Imam Suyuti, "Mother of faithful" Hazrat Aisha (May God be pleased with her), who lost her needle while sewing at dawn, found it easily by the light of the Holy Prophet Muhammad (May God bless and cherish him) who had entered the home."

The Noble Quran mentions the miracle of Prophet Moses (May God bless and cherish him), who drew out his hand in front of pharaoh for it to be glowing white in the following verses: Sura al-Ahzab 7:108, Sura Taha 20:22, Sura Ash-Shuara 26:33, Sura An-Namal 27:12 and Sura Al-Qasas 28:32. Similarly the luminescence of the Holy Prophet Hazrat Muhammad (May God bless and cherish him) shown as a bright light on his right and left when he sat down. All his companions saw his light, and it is believed to be glowing on his grave till the Day of Resurrection. The brilliance of Prophet Hazrat Muhammad's (May God bless and cherish him) face strengthened the faith of his warriors in hard battles. It is narrated that in the battle of Hunayn, while the Holy Prophet (May God bless and cherish him) was standing in the darkness, he turned his face towards his followers, and it showed like a full moon.

It is specifically quoted in many traditions that the blessed fingers of Prophet Muhammad (May God bless and cherish him) were an excellent source of light. They used to glow in the dark night for him and his companions. His forefingers were particularly brighter than the sun and the moon and brightened the way for al-Hassan and al-Hussayn whenever they approached his house or left it (Ibid). It is also related that anytime the Holy Prophet was (May God bless and cherish him) standing in sunshine or moonlight or near a lamp, his light was brighter than all.

The prophetic light of the Holy Prophet Hazrat Muhammad (May God bless and cherish him) has been mentioned in many traditions even prior to his birth. The central figure in these traditions is Hazrat Abdallah, the Prophet's father. Hazrat Abdallah is said to have transmitted to his wife his divine prophetic sperm that, in due time, brought about the sacred birth of the Holy Prophet Hazrat Muhammad (May God bless and cherish him). A blaze shone on his forehead as long as this prophetic sperm dwelt in his loins.

In his sira (edited by Ibn Hisham), Ibn Ishaq narrated a detailed account of this subject. Obviously, Hazrat Abdallah was the most handsome man in Makkah, and the prophetic blaze on his forehead attracted hundreds of women who hoped to obtain the virtue of becoming the Holy Prophet's (May God bless and cherish him) mother.

A tradition quoted by Marmar B. Rashid on the authority of al-Zuhri is that one day, Hazrat Abdallah came across a group of Qurayshi women. One of them said, "Women of Quraysh, which one of you will marry this handsome man and seize the light resting between his eyes." And indeed, there was a light resting between his eyes. Hazrat Amina (May God be pleased with her), bint Wahab of the clan of Zuhra, married Hazrat Abdallah, and in due time she conceived the Messenger of Allah.

Ibn Ishaq related that one day, Hazrat Abdul Muttalib took Hazrat Abdallah by his hand and went away, and as they were passing, a woman named Qutaylah b. Asad b. Abdul Uzza b. Qusayy b. Kilab b. Murra b. Kab b. Luayy b. Ghalib b. Fihr, who was the sister of Waraqa b. Nawfal b. Assad b. Abdul Uzza was standing at the threshold of her house. She knew from her brother, who was a scholar well versed in the scriptures and had embraced Christianity, that a prophet was about to emerge among the Arabs. Waraqa b. Nawfal was one of the few who maintained the full purity of Abrahamic worship. He had realized that far from being traditional, idol worship was an innovation and a danger to be guarded against. He called himself Hanif, had nothing to do with the idols in Makkah, and looked at them as profanation and pollution. He was also the son of Hazrat Abdul Muttalib's second cousin, Nawfal. Qutaylah was very close to her brother and knew from him that the promised prophet was about to emerge in Makkah. After seeing Hazrat Abdallah's light, she was certain that the future prophet was hidden in his loins. As Hazrat Abdul Muttalib and Hazrat Abdallah passed the dwellings of Bani Asad, she watched both. Hazrat Abdul Muttalib was now over seventy years old, but he was still remarkably young for his age and attractive. Hazrat Abdallah was now in his twenty-fifth year of life and at the peak of his youth. Young Hazrat Abdallah was for his beauty, the Joseph of his times. Qutaylah was struck by the radiance that lit his face, and that seemed to her to shine from beyond this world. She thought, could it be that Hazrat Abdallah was the promised prophet? Or was he to be the father of the future prophet?

As they passed her, she was overcome by a sudden irresistible impulse and said, "O Abdallah." His father let him talk to his cousin. She asked him where he was going. "With my father," said Hazrat Abdullah. She proposed to him, "Take me here and now as thy wife, and you shall have as many camels as those that were sacrificed in thy stead." He replied, "I am with my father; I cannot act against his wishes, and I cannot leave him."

Hazrat Abdul Muttalib took Hazrat Abdallah to Wahab b. Abd Manaf b. Zuhra b. Kilab b. Murra b. Kab b. Luayy b. Ghalib b. Fihr, who was the leading man of the Zuhra clan in birth and honor, married him to his daughter Hazrat Amina as she was the most excellent woman among Quraysh in birth and position at that time. Her mother was Barra b. Abdul Uzza b. Uthman b. Abdul Dar b. Qusayy b. Kilab b. Murra b. Kab. Luayy b. Ghalib b. Fihr. Barra's mother was Umm Habib b. Asad b. Abdul Uzza b. Qusayy b. Kilab b. Murra b. Kab b. Luayy b. Ghalib b. Fihr. Umm Habib's mother was Barra. Auf. Ubayd b. Uwayj b. Adiy b. Kilab b. Luayy b. Ghalib b. Fihr.

Hazrat Abdallah stayed there with Hazrat Amina and consummated his marriage. He transferred his light to her on that very day, and she conceived the Messenger of Allah (May God bless and cherish him). When he returned to Waraqa's sister the next day, her eyes searched his face with such earnestness that he stopped beside her, expecting her to speak. When she remained silent, he asked her why she did not say to him that she had said the day before. She answered him, saying: "The light had left thee that was with thee yesterday. Today you do not fulfill the need I had of you." (Bayhaqi)

The marriage took place in AD 569, and the year following this has been famous as the Year of the Elephant.

The light that persisted as a blaze on the forehead of Hazrat Abdallah was a prophetic symbol of Hazrat Abdallah's future son. Therefore, it attracted the women who endeavored to be the Prophet's mother. Instead, he proceeded to marry Hazrat Amina. Yunus b. Bukayr, one of Ibn Ishaq's rawis, had attributed verses to Waraqa's sister. In these verses, she states that the light had gone from Abdallah, coming to rest with the clan of Zuhra, i.e., Hazrat Amina's clan. She also describes the emissary of God to be born as one who is guided, with light leading his way.

Ibn Sa'd has narrated a tradition on the authority of al-Waqidi that states that a woman could read the future in people's faces and thus predicted the meaning of Hazrat Abdallah's blazing light. Other traditions mention that the woman who wanted Hazrat Abdallah's light was Fatima bint-e-Murr. According to al-Tabari, she was a Kahina of Khatham, a Jew from the people of Tabala. According to tradition, she was extremely beautiful, young, modest, and well-versed in the scriptures. She discovered the light of prophethood on Hazrat Abdallah's forehead. According to Ibn Sa'd, it beamed up to the sky. Ibn Sa'd also has related some verses ascribed to Fatima, in which the light is described as lightning in the clouds shining like dawn. Hazrat Amina is said to have taken it from Hazrat Abdullah after marriage. She declares that it was predestined as such, independent of man's activity. Ibn Sa'd also related that a Jewish scholar had already foreseen this marriage through his scriptures. When Hazrat Abdul Muttalib was in Yemen, this scholar saw and examined him and found in him the signs of Prophethood and kingdom. He urged him to marry a woman of Zuhra. Hazrat Abdul Muttalib heeded his advice and took one Zuhra woman for himself and one – namely Hazrat Amina for his son Hazrat Abdallah.

Thus, the transmission of the prophetic light to Hazrat Amina was predestined by the Lord of the worlds. After transmitting his divine light to Hazrat Amina, Hazrat Abdullah saw the disappointed woman who said, "I have seen the light that was with you yesterday, and I wanted it to be with me. However, Allah has determined to put it only where He wanted it to be." It is said that because of this marriage, all the disappointed women of Quraysh became sick, and two hundred of them died of grief. (Ithbat, Zurqani, Khargusi)

The transmission of the prophetic light from prophet to prophet and from generation to generation affirms that Hazrat Muhammad (May God bless and cherish him) is the chosen of the Real and the best of creatures. He is God's beloved, and his beauty and perfection passed beyond the limits of understanding and imagination.

It is said that the moment the prophetic light was transmitted to Hazrat Amina, the gates of heavens and paradise opened, and the tidings about the Holy Prophet Muhammad's (May God bless and cherish him) light were sent down. From the Presence of Exaltation and Majesty, this tiding was given to the world of angels, "Surely, I am setting in the earth a vicegerent." The Magnanimous King thus laid the foundation of Hazrat Muhammad's (May God bless and cherish him) exaltation and tremendousness. As soon as the master of the messengers (May God bless and cherish him) was born, fourteen battlements fell from the castle of Caesar. In the Kaaba, there were three hundred and sixty idols, and all of them fell on their faces, and all idols of the Quraysh, as well as all over the world, were turned upside down. From four corners of the world, the call arose, "The truth has come, and falsehood has vanished away." Quran (17:81). Iblis was thrown out of his seat and took refuge in the mountains of Abu Qubays, where he announced the news to demons about the near appearance of the Prophet and their own destruction and ruin. (Ithbat, Zurqani, Khagushi, Bihar, Suyuti, Ibn al-Jawzi)

It is related to the authority of Ibn Abbas that on the first night of Hazrat Amina's pregnancy, all the beasts of Quraysh could suddenly talk. They conveyed to one another the sacred news of Hazrat Amina's pregnancy, announcing that "The safeguard and the shining lamp of all mankind" were about to be born. Fortune tellers were bewildered and cut off from their demonic sources of information. The thrones of all kings were turned over, and the tidings of the near appearance of Hazrat Abul Qasim Muhammad (May God bless and cherish him) were announced throughout the heaven and earth. (Ibn Kathir, Suyuti, Khargushi, Halabi, Zurqani)

The Messenger of God, Hazrat Muhammad (May God bless and cherish him), was the noblest of his people in birth and greatest in honor both on his father's and his mother's side. When Hazrat Amina, daughter of Wahab, the mother of the Holy Prophet (May God bless and cherish him), was pregnant, it is said that a voice told her (from unseen), "You are pregnant with the lord of this people, and when he is born say, 'I put him in the care of the One from the evil of every envier and name him Muhammad.'

While she was pregnant with the Holy Prophet (May God bless and cherish him), Hazrat Amina saw a prophetic vision. In this vision, she saw that a bright light was emerging from her body, and it illuminated the palaces of Busra in Syria (Ibn Hisham). In fact, at the time of the birth of the Holy Prophet (May God bless and cherish him), a dazzling light emerged from Hazrat Amina, and it reached the eastern and the western ends of the earth. (TarikhTabari, Zurqani, Bihar)

Similarly, other traditions frequently report in the name of Hazrat Amina. She said that the Holy Prophet (May God bless and cherish him) left her body with light that illuminated the castles of Syria and its markets till she was able to see the necks of the camels in the markets of Busra (Ibn Sa'd, Yaqubi, Ibn al-Jawzi, Suyuti). It is also narrated that the light illuminated the entire region between Syria and al-Yemen or even the whole world to its eastern and western ends. And that light was shining so intensely that it almost frightened her (Suyuti, Abu Nuaym, Ibn Sa'd, Yaqubi).

Some of the mothers of the Companions of the Holy Prophet Hazrat Muhammad (May God bless and cherish him) shared the vision of light at the time of his birth. In one of the traditions related (By Tabari, Bayhaqi and Suyuti), the mother of Uthman b. Abi al-As was present at the time of the Holy Prophet's birth. She saw a dazzling play of light bursting from every corner of the room; even the stars of heaven descended so low till she feared that they would come down on her.

According to another tradition, the Holy Prophet (May God bless and cherish him) came out of his mother directly into the hands of Abd-al-Rahman b. Awf's mother. She heard heavenly voices greeting the newborn and saw blinding light that reached the palaces of Byzantium. She also heard the salutations of the angels carrying the newborn all over the world. It is noteworthy that she was among the first to embrace Islam. (Suyuti, Abu Nuaym, Ibn al-Jawzi, Halabi, Zurqani)

In a hadith recorded by Ibn Ishaq, the Holy Prophet said:

"I am the prayer of my father Prophet Abraham and the tiding of Jesus, and my mother saw when she was pregnant with me a light coming out of her body, illuminating the palaces of Busra in Syria." (Tabari, Bayhaqi, Suyuti)

The prophetic light of Hazrat Muhammad (May God bless and cherish him), the beginning of its wandering (taqallub) – in Prophet Adam's loin – and its final emergence on his birth is narrated in a tradition. "The Prophet said, 'I was a servant of Allah and the seal of the prophets when Prophet Adam was still just clay. I shall inform you about it; the prayer of my father Abraham, the good tidings of Jesus about me, and the vision that my mother has seen, all mothers of prophets see (such visions)'." (Ibn Sa'd, Bayhaqi, Ibn al-Jawzi, Suyuti, Zurqani, Halabi)

"Our Lord! Raise up amidst them a messenger from among them who will recite Thy signs to them, teach them the Book and wisdom, and purify them. Surely, Thou art the Exalted, the Wise." Quran 2:129

It was said to Prophet Jesus, "O Spirit of God! Will there be a community after this one? He said yes. He was asked which community, and he said the community of Ahmad (May God bless and cherish him). He was asked what the community of Ahmad is (May God bless and cherish him). He said, "Knowers, wise, pious, and God-wary, as if, in their knowledge, they are like prophets. They will be content with little provision from God, and He will be content with few deeds from them. He will take them into the Garden by their witnessing that there is no god but God."

One thousand years before the birth of the Holy Prophet (May God bless and cherish him), Tubba, the king of Himyar, said to his diviner, "Do you find any kingdom whose kingdom is greater than mine?" the diviner said, "Yes, there is a prophet on the way whose kingdom will be greater than the kingdom of world's folk. He will be a master, a paragon, a leader; on his forehead will be the light of prostration, on his eyebrows the light of humility, on his hair the light of beauty, in his eyes the light of heedfulness, in his face the light of mercy, between his shoulder the light of prophecy, in his heart the light of recognition, in his secret core the light of love, in his speech the light of wisdom, in his wisdom the light of jealousy, in his jealousy the light of presence. He will be pious and blessed and aided by triumph. He is described in the psalms, and his community is considered the most excellent in the scriptures. He will dispel the darkness with light. He is Ahmad (May God bless and cherish him), the Prophet. Blessed will be his community when he comes."

And when Prophet Jesus, the son of Mary, said,

"O children of Israel! Behold, I am an apostle of God unto you, to confirm the truth of whatever still remains of the Torah, and to give you glad tidings of an apostle who shall come after me and shall be called the "Praised one." (Quran 61:6)

Prophet Hazrat Muhammad (May God bless and cherish him) is the apostle whose coming was predicted in the Christian scripture: the promise of God to humanity that a highly praised one would be sent for salvation and guidance in the fulfillment of this biblical saying.

Early Islamic poets have explained the eternal course of the prophetic light of Hazrat Muhammad (May God bless and cherish him) and its wandering as a primordial entity starting with Hazrat Adam. The following verses are attributed to al-Abbas b. Abdul Muttalib, the prophet's uncle. He composed these verses when the Holy Prophet (May God bless and cherish him) was on his way back from Tabuk. (Ibn Qatayba, Suyuti, al-Hakim, al-Tabarani, Ibn al-Jawzi)

Before your appearance on earth, you dwelt well among shadows (of paradise),

Deposited where leaves were stitched (loins of Adam).

Then you descended to earth, not as a human being,

Nor as a morsel or congealed blood,

But as a drop (within Adam's loins)

You sailed in the Ark while the flood had reached the mouth of "Nas"
and his followers.

You were transmitted from loins to loins.

When people of one generation passed away, there came a new generation.

You entered the fire of Abraham, hidden?

Till your trustworthy clan dwelt within Khindis,

On high mountains with wide areas beneath.

When you were born, the earth was lit.

And the horizon beamed with your light.

We are guided by this brightness,

And light, and in the right direction (path).

The primordial substance of the Holy Prophet (May God bless and cherish him) was displayed openly as a light long before his emergence in this world. It is recorded that not only his father, Hazrat Abdullah, but all his former ancestors had the prophetic blaze on their foreheads. Al-Waqidi has reported the light of Abd Manaf, stating, "On him was the light of the Messenger of God, and in his hand was the banner of Nizar and the bow of Ismael." (Zurqani)

The same light has been mentioned by several other traditions as seen on Khuzayma's forehead (Tarikh al-Kahmis) as well as on Mudrika's and Nizar's. (Suhayl, Halabi)

As a matter of fact, the blaze is reported to be shining on the foreheads of Prophet Muhammad's (May God bless and cherish him) ancestors as early as Hazrat

Adam. Traditions about the wandering of this shining light through all Prophet Muhammad's forefathers are written in detail in a book by Al-Masudi, "the Ithbat al-Wasiyya li-Imam Ali b. Abi Talib". The same traditions are also narrated by Abu Saeed al-Khargushi in his sira, "Sharaf al-Nabi".

Prophet Hazrat Muhammad's (May God bless and cherish him) ancestors were thus successive vehicles designed for continuous transmission of light through their bodies. The light was forwarded from one generation to another generation without leaving a trace in the body of the former light carrier. The actual transmission of this prophetic light and substance took place only during intercourse that brought about the birth of the forthcoming carrier.

It is recorded in Ithbat concerning Hazrat Adam that he used to ask Eve to wash and clean herself whenever he intended to lie with her, lest his light would come to rest within an impure body. When she conceived Seth, the light left Hazrat Adam's forehead and dwelt in her own body. Subsequently, when Seth was born, that very light shone on his forehead (Khargushi), whereas on the birth of Seth's elder brothers, the light kept on shining on Hazrat Adam's forehead. In the same way, the light did not leave Kedar's forehead before his wife conceived his successor, Hamal. The same is said about Hashim, who transferred his light to his wife only when she conceived Hazrat Abdul Muttalib (Bihar, Abu al-Hassan al-Bakri). Similarly, Hazrat Abdul Muttalib begot Hazrat Abu Talib and al-Zubayr, transmitting his light to neither of them. Only when his wife Fatima conceived Hazrat Abdullah did she absorb the whole light into her body.

The purity of both the male and female light carriers is emphasized in prophetic traditions. Ibn Ishaq writes in his Sira that both Hazrat Abdallah and Hazrat Amina came of the noblest status of all Quraysh. The Holy Prophet's (May God bless and cherish him) ancestors were all pure in race, and its preservation is a divine command, committed already to Hazrat Adam. In a tradition, Allah (Exalted is He) promised Hazrat Adam:

"Take this light together with My covenant and contract so that you will deposit the light only within pure wombs."

Hazrat Adam forwarded the same command to his successor, Prophet Seth. Hazrat Adam said,

"My son, Allah has ordered me to impose on you a covenant and a compact for the sake of the light on your face, to the effect that you will deposit it only within the purest of the woman of all mankind. Let it be known to you that Allah has put upon me a rigid covenant concerning it." Gabriel and seventy thousand angels witnessed this commandment being written. It was written with a pen brought from paradise and was sealed with Gabriel's seal. Prophet Seth was dressed in two purple robes of light. The covenant was placed in a box (Taboot) that had two doors, locked with golden chains, and sealed. The box (Taboot-e-Adam) was adorned with glittering precious stones, and both ends of it were studded with bright green emeralds. Prophet Seth, in due course, passed the same command (wasiyya) and the Taboot on to Prophet Enoch. When Enoch was born, his father noticed that the light of Muhammad Mustafa had been transferred to him. When he reached adulthood, Prophet Seth took a covenant from him, and he accepted. Prophet Enoch passed the same covenant and the box (Taboot) to Prophet Nuh and Nuh to Prophet Sam. When Prophet Hud was born, it was announced in the heavens and earth that he would break all the idols with the help of God and would destroy all the infidels. After Prophet Hud, the box was inherited by Prophet Ibrahim Khalil Allah. So, the Mighty and Majestic Lord informed Prophet Ibrahim, "I would bring a prophet out of your progeny, his name will be Muhammad and who is My beloved (Habib), and I have made him superior to all My creation. I moved him in the heaven and earth and showed him to the angels of the dominion." Prophet Ibrahim informed Sara about it, and she earnestly waited and expected the light of Muhammad to come to rest in her body. But when Hagar got pregnant with Prophet Ismael, she was disappointed and deeply saddened until God the Most High gave her tiding of Ishaq through Prophet Ibrahim.

When Prophet Ibrahim was near his death, he summoned his sons, who were six in total. He commanded to bring the box (Taboot-e-Adam), broke the seal, and opened it in front of his sons. He told them to look inside the box. When they did so, they noticed boxes inside that Taboot corresponding to the number of prophets. The last box was of Prophet Hazrat Muhammad Mustafa (May God bless and cherish him) made of red ruby, in which the image of the Holy Prophet Muhammad (May God bless and cherish him) was visible, standing in prayer. On the right side of the Prophet Muhammad (May God bless and cherish him), Hazrat Abu Bakr Siddique was standing, and it was written on his forehead, "The sincerely truthful, who would be the first to follow the Prophet among his community and whose hallmarks are self-purification and truthfulness." On his left side, Hazrat Umar Khattab was standing, and it was written on his forehead, "With his harshness and awesomeness he would subdue the enemies of God and Islam." At the back of the Prophet Muhammad (May God bless and cherish him) was Hazrat Uthman Affan, and on his forehead was written, "Allah will spread the carpet of his dignity and honor in seven heavens and in his time the light of Islam will light up in the regions of east and west." In front of the Holy Prophet (May God bless and cherish him) was Hazrat Ali Murtada, and on his forehead was written, "The Lord of the worlds will unveil the realities of the Shariah and the marks of Tariqah through his conduct and secret core. In relation to the Holy Prophet (May God bless and cherish him), he is like Aron to Prophet Moses, except that there will be no prophet after Hazrat Muhammad Mustafa (May God bless and cherish him)."

When the sons of Prophet Ibrahim looked inside the box, they all knew that the Holy Prophet Hazrat Muhammad (May God bless and cherish him) would emerge in the progeny of Hazrat Ismael. Prophet Ibrahim congratulated his son, Prophet Ismael and said, "I take a firm covenant from you regarding the light of Muhammad Mustafa, the way my forefathers took from me." Prophet Ismael kept the covenant until he married the daughter of Harith, and Kedar was born. He noticed the light of Muhammad Mustafa in him, took a covenant from him, and handed to him the box "Taboot-e-Adam". (Abu Saeed Khargushi, Sharaf al-Nabi)

The spiritual purity of the light carriers was preserved by divine decree. Prophet Seth, for example, was veiled and hence protected from Iblis on his birth by several veils of light put around him by Almighty Allah. Therefore, Iblis had no access to the boy until he was seven years old. During his entire childhood he was shielded by a cosmic column of light that was towering between heaven and earth. It is also related that a similar amud (column) of light was erected on the birth of Prophet Abraham, preserving the righteousness of the newborn. The beauty of his light evoked the praise of angels. When Kedar's son Hamal was born, it is said that the gates of heaven opened, and the rays of light, like those of the moon, were shining between heaven and earth. Accompanying the light, angels descended with blessings and salutations.

The Arab ancestors of the Holy Prophet (May God bless and cherish him) also preserved their sanctity. They used to write down a covenant for their successors to the effect that they would marry only the purest women of their time. It was customary to hang the covenant in the Kaaba since the days of Hazrat Ismael up to the year of the elephant. (Abu Saeed Khargushi)

The prophetic light brought tremendous honor for its carriers and was a source of divine blessings for the entire community. It is said that the Holy Prophet's (May God bless and cherish him) grandfather, Hazrat Abdul Muttalib, had the light of Prophet Muhammad (May God bless and cherish him) blazing on his forehead that made him a praiseworthy leader and was an intermediary between his tribe and the providence. On his intercession, he managed to bring down rain on Makkah after a period of heavy drought.

An outstanding feature of the light of Prophet Muhammad (May God bless and cherish him) and its wandering is part of the divine design aimed at the Holy Prophet's emergence at a predestined time and place. It is stated in a hadith qudsi that the entire world was created for this purpose only. "Laulaka ma khalaqtal-aflaka", "If you had not been (but for your sake), I would not have created the spheres."

Allah revealed to Prophet Adam that Muhammad (May God bless and cherish him) was the only cause for his own creation, as well as the creation of heaven, earth, paradise, and hell. The same was revealed to Prophet Jesus as well as to the Holy Prophet Muhammad (May God bless and cherish him) himself through Gabriel. (Zurqani, Khargushi)

All the carriers of the prophetic light (Nur-e-Muhammadi) had a revelation by which they came to know who their destined women (wives) were, meriting their light. These revelations were usually in the form of a dream. It is related to a tradition that Kedar, the son of Prophet Ismael, thought that his destined woman was one of the daughters of Prophet Isaac. Therefore, he married eighty of them, but the prophetic light did not forsake his body for two hundred years. During that time, none of them became pregnant. One day, he went hunting, and all the creatures that passed by him started talking to him; "O Kedar, you have grown old, and your life is near its end. But you are still busy with worldly pursuits and wasting time hunting and playing. Has not the time arrived that you do something about the light of Muhammad (May God bless and cherish him) that has been trusted to you?" When Kedar heard those words, he was very sad and swore not to eat or drink until he figured out the meaning of these words. He went to the desert and sat in deep thought. Allah (Exalted is He) sent an angel in a human form. Kedar had not seen such a handsome person. The angel sat beside him and said, "You have conquered many cities and accumulated great wealth. If you would sacrifice for Allah's sake and implore His guidance, maybe He will guide you by His grace and show you which woman to marry. If you do so, it will be better for you." The angel said those words and disappeared into the air. Kedar owned thousands of cattle, camels, and sheep. He sacrificed seven hundred sheep for God's sake. Every time he sacrificed a sheep, smokeless flame would appear and take the sacrifice towards heaven until he heard a voice from the unseen, "Allah the Most High has accepted your sacrifice and granted your petition. Go and rest under the shade of that tree, and whatever you see in a vision, act on that." Kedar did the same; he was told in his dream to marry a woman from among the Arabs — by the name of al-Ghadhira. He traveled in search of her to the land of Jerhum. She was the daughter of Zuhair Amir b. Qahtan. He asked her hand in marriage from her father, and the light did depart from Kedar and came to rest in her womb and, from thus was conceived his son Jamil (Hamal). (Khargushi). This tradition highlights the superiority of Prophet Muhammad's (May God bless and cherish him) Arab ancestors, emphasizing that his primordial prophetic substance was destined to pass only through Arabs, after Prophet Ismael and Kedar.

Hashim was also informed in a vision about the identity of his pure-chosen wife after having turned down several proposals coming from both Arabs and non-Arabs. Hazrat Abdul Muttalib was also told in a dream to marry Fatima bint Amr, the mother of Hazrat Abdullah.

Prophet Adam was the first primogenitor of the Holy Prophet Muhammad (May God bless and cherish him), who had the light of the prophet shining on his forehead like a full moon. It is narrated that Prophet Adam and Eve were clad in the "clothes of light" in paradise. (wa-Kana libas Adam wa-Hawwa thiyaban min nur). (Yaqubi)

The same tradition is quoted by Wahb b. Murabbih that Allah adorned Prophet Adam with a very beautiful bright substance like a nail that shone like the sun. After Prophet Adam disobeyed God, this coating was reduced, surviving only on his fingertips (Maarif).

Allah (Exalted is He) says in a tradition, "I covered Adam with the clothes of paradise, adorned with various ornaments, with light emerging from their folds like sunshine and the light of the prophet beaming from his forehead."

CHAPTER 2
THE STORY OF INVASION OF MAKKAH

During the attack on Makkah by Abraha, the Abyssinian in the year of the elephant, his encounter with Hazrat Abdul Muttaalib clearly highlights the exalted status of the blaze on the forehead of the Prophet's grandfather. Abraha was Christian by faith, and he became the ruler of Yemen after killing his opponent, Aryat. To please King Negus, who was filled with rage due to his actions, Abraha built a grand cathedral (house of worship) in San'a, the like of which was not seen in any part of the world. It was constructed with precious marbles brought from the palaces of the Queen Sheba, decorated with golden and silver crosses and pulpits of ivory and ebony. He told the king, "I have built a magnificent church for you; I shall not rest until I have diverted the Arab's pilgrimage to it." When this was known to all, Arab tribes throughout the Hijaz and Najd were greatly angered. One of the Arab calendar adjusters, B. Fuqaym b. Adiy b. Amir b. Thalaba b. al-Harith b. Malik b. Kinana b. Khuzayma b. Mudrika b. Ilyas b. Mudar decided to defile the church deliberately. He secretly went to San'a and managed to get into the cathedral and smeared it with filth. After that, he was able to escape and return to his own country. When Abraha found out, he made inquiries and came to know that this act was committed by an Arab who came from the House (Kaaba) in Makkah, where the Arabs went on pilgrimage. He had done this in anger because of the threat to divert the Arab pilgrimage to the cathedral. Abraha was enraged and swore that he would go to Makkah and destroy the Kaaba. Abraha summoned his magnificent army, which consisted of elephants, along with his famous elephant named Mehmood, and marched towards Makkah to destroy the House of God, Kaaba. Some Arabs joined Abraha for bounty as well.

The news of the advancing army of Abraha reached Arab tribes who decided to fight against him to defend the House of God (Kaaba) because they heard that Abraha was determined to destroy it. Dhu Nafr was the leader of his tribe. He called his people, and some of the Arabs followed him to fight Abraha to stop him from attacking the Kaaba. After a fierce battle, Dhu Nafr was defeated and put to flight but later was taken as a prisoner and brought to Abraha. Dhu Nafr pleaded for his life and told Abraha that he would be more useful to him alive than dead. Abraha pardoned him but kept him in chains.

Abraha continued his march towards Makkah until he reached Khatham. There Nufayl b. Habib al-Khathami, along with his two tribes, Shahran and Nahis, fought bravely against Abraha. He, too, was defeated and taken prisoner. When Abraha wanted to execute him, Nufayl implored him, "Spare my life, O king, for I will be your guide in the Arab country." Abraha let him live. He served him as a guide until they reached Taif, where Masud b. Muttib b. Malik b. Kaab came out with the men of Thaqib. They said to him, "O king, we obey your command. We have no quarrel with you, and our sacred house of al-Lat is not the temple you seek. You are after the Temple of Makkah. We will give you a man who will guide you there. Abraha agreed and left them unharmed. They sent him to Abu Righai to guide him to Makkah. When he had brought them as far as al-Mughammis, Abu Righai died there, and in the later days, Arabs stoned his grave.

Abraha sent his Abyssinian commander al-Aswad b. Mafsud, along with soldiers, plundered the people of Tihama, the Quraysh and others. They took two hundred camels belonging to Hazrat Abdul Muttalib b. Hashim, who was the noble and leader of the Quraysh. The people of Quraysh, Kinana, and Hudayl gathered at the Kaaba (House of God) and decided to fight the invaders but realized that Abraha had a stronger army, so they gave up the idea of battle.

Abraha sent his emissary Hunata (the Himarite) to meet the leader of the Quraysh to tell him that the king had not come to fight but only to destroy the Temple (Kaaba). If he wished to avoid war, he should return with him. To this, Hazrat Abdul Muttalib replied,

"Kaaba is Allah's sanctuary and the temple of His friend Prophet Abraham. It is His temple and sanctuary, and He knows how to defend it against the enemies."

Hazrat Abdul Muttalib, accompanied by one of his sons, came to the encampment of Abraha to meet him. He first asked for Dhu Nafr, who was a friend of his. Dhu Nafr was a prisoner by then and said, "I am a prisoner in the hands of Abraha. I cannot help you except that Unays, the elephant keeper, being a friend of mine, may be able to get you permission to see the king. He would intercede for you if he could." So Dhu Nafr told Unays, "The king has taken two hundred camels belonging to Abdul Muttalib, Lord of Quraysh and master of the Makka, who feeds men in the land and wild creatures on the mountains, and that he is now here. So, as far as you can, help him to get permission to see the king."

Hazrat Abdul Muttalib met the keeper of the elephant, who noticed the blaze beaming from his forehead. The elephant was also nearby; it was also affected by the light of Muhammad (May God bless and cherish him) and prostrated itself to Hazrat Abdul Muttalib, greeting the light resting in his loins. After their meeting, Unays talked to the king and repeated the words of Dhu Nafr. He added that Hazrat Abdul Muttalib wished to see him regarding a pressing issue.

Hazrat Abdul Muttalib was a most impressive, handsome, and dignified man. Abraha was informed about the blaze of light on the forehead of Hazrat Abdul Muttalib and that this light had been shining on the foreheads of all his ancestors. Abraha recognized that Hazrat Abdul Muttalib belonged to a race of people exceeding all kings in honor and celebrity. Abraha magicians explained to him that the elephant had prostrated itself to the light of a prophet who was about to emerge from the loins of Hazrat Abdul Muttalib. They all showed great respect to Hazrat Abdul Muttalib and kissed his knees. The king saw him and treated him with great reverence so that he would not let him sit beneath him. He could not let the Abyssinians see him sitting beside him on his throne. Therefore, he got off his throne and sat on the carpet and made Hazrat Abdul Muttalib sit beside him there. Then he asked him what he wanted through his interpreter. Hazrat Abdul Muttalib replied that he wanted his two hundred camels, which he had taken, to be returned. At this, Abraha answered, "You pleased me much when I saw you; then I was much disappointed with you when I heard what you said. Do you wish to talk to me about your two hundred camels, which my army has taken, and say nothing about your religion and the religion of your ancestors, which I have come to destroy?"

Hazrat Abdul Muttalib boldly replied, "I am the owner of the camels, and the temple has an owner who will defend it." At this, the king boasted that no none could defend it against him," Hazrat Abdul Muttalib brazenly answered, "That remains to be seen." Abraha, however, returned to Hazrat Abdul Muttalib the camels which he had taken.

Hazrat Abdul Muttalib went back to his people and informed them about Abraha's intention to destroy the House of God (Kaaba). He ordered them to withdraw from Makkah and take defensive positions on the peaks and passes of the mountains to be safe from the Abyssinian army. Hazrat Abdul Muttalib himself proceeded to Kaaba and took hold of the metal knocker of the House of God. He was accompanied by several notables as well. They stood and started praying to Allah, imploring His divine help against Abraha and his army.

While he was holding the metal knocker of the door to Kaaba, Hazrat Abdul Muttalib said, "O God, a man protects his dwelling, so protect Thy dwelling. Let not their cross and craft tomorrow overcome Thy craft." Hazrat Abdul Muttalib then let go of the knocker of the door and went with his people to take defensive positions on the mountain tops. There, they waited to see what Abraha and his army would do when they entered Makkah. The next day, the king prepared his army, along with the elephant, to march toward the holy city of Makkah with the intention of destroying the Kaaba and returning to Yemen.

When they made the elephant (its name was Mehmood) stand in the direction of Makkah, Nufayl b. Habib came close to the elephant, took hold of its ear, and said, "Prostrate Mehmood, you are in the holy land of God, or go back straight whence you came." He let go of its ear, and the elephant knelt in prostration. Nufayl ran away towards the top of the mountain. No matter how much the soldiers beat the elephant to make it get up, it would not; they beat its head with iron bars; they stuck hooks into its underbelly and tortured it, but it would not move. Then they made him face Yemen, and immediately, it got up and started running. When they set it towards the north or the east, it did the same, but as soon as they directed it towards Makkah, it knelt.

Then suddenly, Allah (Exalted is He) unleashed upon them flights of birds that came from the direction of the sea like swallows and starlings. The western sky grew black as if a wave of dark clouds swept over them. Each bird carried three stones, like peas and lentils, in its beak and two between its claws on each foot. The birds pelted them (men of elephant) with stones. The birds swooped to and fro over ranks. The pebbles were so hard and came down with such velocity that they pierced through their armor. Everyone who was hit died. The entire army withdrew in flight by the way they came, crying out for Nufayl to guide them on the way to Yemen. When Nufayl saw what punishment God had brought down upon them, he recited the following couplet:

Where can one flee when God pursueth?

Al-Ashram is the conquered, not the conqueror.

(Abraha was called Al-Ashram (Split-face) because he was hit in the forehead by an enemy's spear that split his face.)

As the army of Abraha was retreating, they were continuously falling by the wayside, dying miserably. Abraha was also hit in his body, and as they took him away from the battlefield, his fingers fell off one by one. He developed sores on his hands, oozing pus and blood. When he returned to Sana, he was in a miserable state. It is said that as he died, his heart burst from his body. After that incident, the Quraysh were called "the people of God" by other Arabs, and they were held in greater respect than before because Allah the Mighty and Majestic saved them and the Kaaba from destruction.

When the Holy Prophet Hazrat Muhammad (May God bless and cherish him) emerged in Makkah, the Mighty and Majestic Lord recounted to the Quraysh His goodness and favor in turning back and destroying the Abyssinian army to save their land and sovereignty.

"Have you not considered the way in which your Lord dealt with the Men of the elephant? Did He not reduce their guile to sheer terror? And did He not unleash upon them flocks of birds, pelting stones upon them, making them as blades of corn that have been devoured?" (Quran 105)

The Majestic Lord says in the Quran,

"For the security of Quraysh" -This means for the safety sought by Quraysh for their two journeys)

"Their security during the winter journey" -To Syria and the journey of winter to Yemen. We destroyed the army of Yemen thus. It is as if He were saying to the Prophet (May God bless and cherish him), "Remind the Quraysh of the blessing that I bestowed on them before I sent you to them.

"Let them worship the Lord of this House, Kaaba".

"Who has fed them from hunger for many years and secured them from fear of the Negus."

(Quran 106)

COVENANTS OF ALLAH

The Lord of the worlds made two covenants with His creatures concerning His Godhood and Lordship as He said,

"When your Lord brought forth the children of Adam, and from their loins their offspring, and made them bear witness concerning themselves, asking I am not your Lord? They said, "Yes indeed."

"Lest you should say on the Day of Resurrection, "We forgot about it." Quran (7:172)

Ibn Abbas's interpretation as transmitted through Saeed b. Jubayr is that after having created Adam, Allah took out of his loins all the spirits that He was about to create till the Day of Resurrection. He then made them bear witness that He was their Lord. Hence, the spirits recognized Allah's Lordship prior to the creation of their bodies. Mujahid reportedly said that they expressed their faith in One God through the words of *Talbiya* (the response to Allah's call uttered by the believers on their pilgrimage). This *Talbiya* was taught by Allah to Prophet Abraham, who initiated the pilgrimage to Kaaba. Another version of the same interpretation says that Prophet Adam's descendants were shown to him in the form of small ants. Some of these primordial entities are said to have been invested with lights. The prophets were distinguished not only by their light. It is stated that on that day, the prophets were among Adam's descendants, shining like lamps, and Allah singled them out by a special covenant.

The other is the compact He took with the angels and the prophets concerning Hazrat Muhammad's (May God bless and cherish him) Prophethood and helping him, as He says,

"And when God took compact of the prophets, I have given you of the Book and wisdom. Then, a messenger will come to you, confirming what is with you. You shall surely have faith in him, and you should surely help him." Quran (3:81)

Rashid ud Din Maybudi, in "Kashf al-Asrar," wrote, "In the whole Quran, there is no verse more complete in explaining the excellence of Muhammad Mustafa (May God bless and cherish him), to whom this verse is devoted without the association of anyone else." This is an utmost bestowal of eminence and a perfect acknowledgment of excellence, for He made his name great with His own name and lifted his measure with His measure."

Several thousand years before the birth (existence) of Muhammad Mustafa (May God bless and cherish him), a command came, "O Gabriel! I will have a friend whose name is Muhammad (May God bless and cherish him). He will be praised and caressed by Me, his name will be placed next to My name, his measure will be lifted by My bounty, his being obeyed will be obedience to Me, his words will be My revelation, and following him will be friendship with Me. O Gabriel! You make a covenant with Me to have faith in him and help him." This was when He said, "You shall surely have faith in him, and you should surely help him."

Gabriel said, "O Lord, I make a covenant that my hand will be one with his hand, I will help, and I will have faith in him." God said, "O Gabriel! Keep to this covenant and do not oppose it." Gabriel said, "O Lord, who would have the gall to oppose you?"

Then He said, "O Michael! You be a witness to Gabriel's covenant." Then, in the same way, He made a covenant with Michael, and He told Gabriel to be a witness to Michael's covenant. He made the same covenant with Seraphiel and Azrael. After that, He created Prophet Adam. He made the same covenant with him, and Prophet Adam accepted it. After Prophet Adam, He spoke to Prophet Seth, and Prophet Seth accepted – and so on and so forth, generation after generation. Here, you have nobility and excellence! Here, you have level and rank! Who else has bounty so complete? Who else has his work so well arranged? This is heavenly exaltation and divine blessings.

Quran in Sura Al-Ahzab (33:7) mentions a prophetic covenant,

"When We took from prophets their covenant, from you (Muhammad) and Noah and Abraham and Moses and Jesus the son of Mary. We took from them a rigid covenant." This covenant, too, was taken while the prophets still dwelt within Prophet Adam's loin, according to Mujahid.

An important feature of the interpretation of this verse is the stress laid on the superiority of Hazrat Muhammad's (May God bless and cherish him) primordial substance to that of the other prophets. Above all, the substance of the Holy Prophet Hazrat Muhammad (May God bless and cherish him) was the first prophetic entity created by Allah. This is based on the Quranic verse just mentioned where Hazrat Muhammad (May God bless and cherish him) is mentioned prior to Prophet Noah and the rest of the prophets.

Qatada used to recite this verse with a tradition according to which the Holy Prophet Hazrat Muhammad (May God bless and cherish him) said,

"I was first of the prophets to be created (as a primordial substance) and the last of them to be sent."

Another version of the *hadith* says, "I was the first Prophet to be created and the last of them to be sent; therefore, Allah began with me. (I was the first of those from whom He took the covenant)."

According to a *hadith* narrated by Ibn Sa'd, the Holy Prophet's (May God bless and cherish him) covenant was taken from him as soon as Prophet Adam had been formed in clay and before Allah breathed the spirit of life into him. It is said that the Holy Prophet (May God bless and cherish him) was asked, "When did you become a prophet?" He answered, "When Prophet Adam was still between spirit and body as soon as the covenant was taken from me."

Stating this *hadith,* Al-Qatallani said that the Holy Prophet (May God bless and cherish him) was drawn out of Prophet Adam's loins as soon as the latter was formed in clay. He was made a prophet, and the covenant was taken from him. Then, he was infused back into Prophet Adam's loins, thus being the first prophet in creation. The rest of the Prophet Adam's descendants were taken out of him after the spirit had been breathed into his body. Ibn Sa'd has a further version of the same *hadith*, "I was a prophet as soon as Prophet Adam was between spirit and body."

The first created prophet, The Holy Prophet Hazrat Muhammad (May God bless and cherish him), is entitled "The First and the Last, the Manifest and the Hidden." Although those attributes belong, according to the Quran (57:3), to Allah alone, in some *ahadith,* they are related to the Holy Prophet (May God bless and cherish him). Thus, he is the first prophet in the world (as a hidden entity) and the last prophet to be sent to it.

Due to his divine primordial substance, the Holy Prophet is regarded as the best of Prophet Adam's offspring; hence, Prophet Adam was surnamed after him, Abu Muhammad. This *kunya* was granted to Prophet Adam by Allah (Exalted is He) upon breathing the spirit of life into him. He also saw among his future descendants a shining light. Allah explained to him that it was the light of Muhammad (May God bless and cherish him), who was the first and the last.

The creation of the primordial substance and body of the Holy Prophet Hazrat Muhammad (May God bless and cherish him) is written in detail in *"Sharaf al-Nabi"* by Abu Saeed Khargushi and in *"Qisas al-Anbiya"* by al-Thalabi. This substance was created long before Allah (Exalted is He) breathed the spirit of life into his body when Prophet Adam was still between clay and soul. The substance of the Holy Prophet (May God bless and cherish him) on its creation is identified in these traditions with a cosmic pearl, possessing independent creative powers.

Al-Thalabi's account runs as follows: When Allah (Exalted is He) wanted to create Prophet Adam, He commanded Gabriel to fetch Him dust from the earth. After it was taken from the four corners of the earth, it was plunged into water and became clay. Then Allah, the Mighty and Majestic, ordered Gabriel to descend one more time and bring Him a handful of pure and luminous dust for the creation of Hazrat Muhammad (May God bless and cherish him) the Beloved. Gabriel brought this dust from the place of Prophet Muhammad's (May God bless and cherish him) future grave at al-Madina. Allah mingled that pure dust with the water of *Tasnim* and kneaded it till it became a white pearl. The pearl was plunged into the waters of all heavenly rivers. When it was ready and pulled out, the Creator looked at it, and it dripped a hundred and fourteen thousand drops; from each drop, Allah (Exalted is He) created a prophet. Then it was set in motion throughout the heaven and earth, so that all the angels came to know Muhamad Mustafa (May God bless and cherish him) before knowing Prophet Adam. Afterwards, Allah kneaded the pearl into the clay of Prophet Adam. When Allah breathed a soul into Prophet Adam's body and accomplished his creation, the light of the pearl of Hazrat Muhammad (May God bless and cherish him) appeared on his forehead. It was transmitted through the loins of his ancestors till the Holy Prophet Muhammad Mustafa (May God bless and cherish him) himself was born. The luminous primordial substance of the Holy Prophet (May God bless and cherish him) is thus, in fact, a cosmic entity.

PROPHET MUHAMMAD'S TAQALLUB THROUGH HIS ANCESTORS

"Wa Taqallubaka Fi Sajidin." Quran (26:219)

The spirit of the Holy Prophet Hazrat Muhammad (May God bless and cherish him) existed as a distinct prophetic entity in the world before his blessed birth. It was being transmitted from father to son until its visible manifestation on earth through the corporeal Muhammad Mustafa (May God bless and cherish him). It is important to note that the substance (spirit) of the Holy Prophet (May God bless and cherish him) was the first prophetic entity created by Allah (Exalted is He).

Due to his divine primordial substance, the Holy Prophet Hazrat Muhammad (May God bless and cherish him) is regarded as the best of Prophet Adam's offspring. The primordial (May God bless and cherish him) (spermatic) substance of the paragon of the world was set in motion by the procreation of Prophet Adam's descendants. The course of this motion was predetermined by the Lord of the worlds to include only the most excellent of all mankind. In a hadith quoted by al-Tirmidhi, the Holy Prophet (May God bless and cherish him) says,

"When Allah created the descendants of Prophet Adam, He put me within the best of fathers of them all, when He divided them into tribes, He put me within the best tribe of them all, and when afterward He made them into houses, He put me in the best house of them all."

In the same way, a hadith quoted by Ibn Sa'd says, "Allah divided the earth into two halves, putting me in the best one; that half He divided into three, and I was in the best third."

In another hadith narrated by Ibn Sa'd, the Holy Prophet (May God bless and cherish him) proclaimed, "I was sent through the best generation of mankind, from generation to generation, till I was sent out of the generation in which I live."

The same hadith is recorded by Al-Bukhari in his Sahih, which is regarded by Al-Suyuti as proof that the Holy Prophet's (May God bless and cherish him) ancestors were each the best of his generations. Yet in another version of the same hadith, it is said, "I was carried through the loins of the best generations, from generation to generation, till I emerged from my own generation."

Al-Masudi, a well-known historian, wrote a detailed tradition in his book "Marujudh-Dhahab" on the authority of Amir ul Momineen Hazrat Ali (May God be pleased with him), stating that when the Ever-Merciful Lord created, first of all, the light of Prophet Muhammad (May God bless and cherish him), He said to it, "You are My chosen one and the trustee of My Light and Guidance. It is because of you that I am going to create the earth and the heavens, lay down reward and punishment, and bring into being the Garden and the Fire." Then the account goes on to speak about the family of the Holy Prophet Hazrat Muhammad (May God bless and cherish him), about the creation of angels, of the souls, of the world, of the covenant taken from the souls which combined the belief in One God (Tawhid) with the acceptance of Prophet Muhammad's (May God bless and cherish him) Prophethood.

The Holy Prophet Hazrat Muhammad's (May God bless and cherish him) light adorned the 'Arsh' (throne) of God, and when eons later, Prophet Adam was created, that light was put on his forehead. It continued its journey, generation after generation, through numerous prophets and their successors till it came to Prophet Ibrahim. From Prophet Ibrahim, it came to his eldest son, Prophet Ismail.

The Holy Prophet (May God bless and cherish him) said, "Verily Allah chose Ismail from the progeny of Ibrahim, and chose Banu Kinanah from the progeny of Ismail, and chose Quraysh from Banu Kinanah, and chose Banu Hashim from Quraysh, and chose me from Banu Hashim."

Abul Fida quotes in his Tarikh (history) a tradition wherein the Holy Prophet (May God bless and cherish him) says, "Gabriel said to me: "I looked at the earth from the east to the west, but I did not find anyone superior to Muhammad (May God bless and cherish him) and I looked at the earth from the east to west but did not find any progeny superior to the progeny of Hashim."

The significance of the mothers (women) in maintaining the pure genealogical origin of the Holy Prophet (May God bless and cherish him) is of paramount importance. Several ahadith emphasize the pure matrimony of his grandmothers as well. The Holy Prophet (May God bless and cherish him) said,

"An impure woman has never given birth to me since I came out of Prophet Adam's loins; the nations have never ceased to transmit me from father to son till I emerged from the best two Arab clans —Hashim and Zuhra (his mother's clan)."

On one occasion, the Holy Prophet (May God bless and cherish him) told ibn Abbas that when Prophet Adam was in paradise, he, Muhammad (May God bless and cherish him), was in his loins. Prophet Adam descended to earth with him in his loins. He was on the Ark in Prophet Noah's loins and was thrown into the fire with his father, Prophet Abraham's loins. His ancestors have never coupled in fornication. Allah (Exalted is He) has never stopped transmitting him, refined from pure loins into clean wombs; two branches had never ramified without his being in the best one. (Ibn al-Jawzi, Suyuti, Zurqani)

Muhammad b. al-Saib al-Kalbi recorded that he had gone through a list of five hundred women who had given birth to Hazrat Muhamad's (May God bless and cherish him) ancestors and did not come across one who had born a child according to Jahili customs. A similar account is attributed to the Holy Prophet (May God bless and cherish him) himself,

"I emerged from pure matrimony and not from fornication. No fornication of the Jahiliya has ever touched me since Prophet Adam. I came out of purity."

The following hadith is also ascribed to the Holy Prophet Hazrat Muhammad (May God bless and cherish him), "I am the purest of you all in lineage, nuptials, and ancestry. There has not been any fornication among my ancestors since Prophet Adam. We are all maintaining pure matrimony." (Suyuti, Zurqani, Halabi)

Hence, the pure marriages of the Prophet's ancestors distinguish them completely from jahiliya and bring them closer to the Islamic spirit. "I was never born," says the Holy Prophet (May God bless and cherish him), — "from jahiliya fornication; what gave birth to me was indeed pure Islamic matrimony." (Suyuti, Zurqani)

The common notion according to which the sons of Prophet Adam married their sisters (each marrying his brother's twin sister) is refuted in Bihar and Ithbat. It is recorded in a tradition that Prophet Seth, unlike his preceding brothers, was born without a twin sister. He married in due course a woman descended from paradise (Hawa), whereas Cain got his wife from among the demons (Jinn).

The substance of the Holy Prophet Hazrat Muhammad (May God bless and cherish him) was invested with miraculous properties, especially the ability to utter the talbiya. According to a tradition, when the substance of the Holy Prophet (May God bless and cherish him) dwelt in the loins of al-Yas (one of the Prophet's Arab ancestors) – the call of glorification of Allah could be heard from within his body.

It is stated in a tradition that Allah ordered the hell fire not to touch a back (loins) from which Muhammad Mustafa (May God bless and cherish him) descended to a womb, a belly that carried him, a breast that suckled him, and a lap that covered him. The lap is interpreted to be of Hazrat Abu Talib and his wife.

The Holy Prophet's (May God bless and cherish him) ancestors were no less than true Muslims, according to early Islamic sources. It is stated that the descendants of Prophet Abraham (including the Holy Prophet's ancestors) always preserved the faith of Prophet Abraham, that is, the recognition of Allah's unity (Tawhid) and embracing of Islam.

The jahili customs of Makkah are said to have been first introduced by an Arab who did not belong to the line of Holy Prophet Hazrat Muhammad's (May God bless and cherish him) forefathers. Amr b. Luhayy of Khuza was the Arab leader who ruled Makkah in the early times and who introduced the jahili customs.

The Quran Alludes to these customs in Sura 5:103.

Another Quranic verse (9:28) declares that the unbelievers are impure.

(Innama l-mushrikuna najasun)

Therefore, Fakhr al-Din Razi writes that the ancestors of the Holy Prophet Hazrat Muhammad (May God bless and cherish him) could not possibly have been unbelievers, referring to Sura Ash-Shuara 26:219 (WaTaqallubalak Fi Sajidin). According to his interpretation, the word Sajidin stands for Hazrat Muhammad's (May God bless and cherish him) ancestors who are introduced as worshipers, hence believers. Taqallubaka means the wandering of Hazrat Muhammad's (May God bless and cherish him) primordial substance through the Sajidin.

Ibn Sa'd has narrated many traditions (Ahadith) stating that the Holy Prophet's (May God bless and cherish him) ancestors were all proper Muslims. One of them warns,

"Do not curse Mudar," says the Holy Prophet (May God bless and cherish him), "For he embraced Islam." In another hadith, a similar claim is made concerning al-Yas.

Abu al-Baqr's book "al-Manaqib al-Mazyadiyya" contains many such traditions. They proclaim, "Do not curse Ma'add, for he held the hanifiyya of Ibrahim." It further states that Ma'add feared Allah and glorified him constantly. (Ibil) Allah once ordered Prophet Jeremiah to take Ma'add to his own country, lest the troops of Nebuchadnezzar who were about to invade Arabia would harm him. Ma'add was thus saved for the sake of Prophet Muhammad (May God bless and cherish him), his future offspring. Ma'add returned to Makkah to perform a pilgrimage accompanied by several Israeli prophets. It is also said that Allah (Exalted is He) revealed to Moses that the descendants of Ma'add were worshipers and that a prophet would emerge from among them. Moreover, Ma'add urged his children to fear Allah and thank and glorify Him. Similarly, Nizar also advised his offspring to have a reverential fear of God and be cognizant of Him.

Prophethood, honor, and purity were the hallmarks of Ma'add descendants. Mudar also commanded his son al-Ya's to be God-wary. Khuzayma was the first to declare, "There is no god except Allah." He, too, commanded his son to be fearful of Allah and to uphold the faith of Prophet Abraham and Prophet Ismael.

Many Arab sources have reported similar traditions. It is reported about Kinana that he foresaw the emergence of a prophet in Makkah and hence strongly advised his people to obey and follow that prophet. Another ancestor of the Holy Prophet Hazrat Muhammad (May God bless and cherish him) namely Ka'b b. Luayy also talked about the appearance of a prophet in his preaching. He came to know about him in the Jewish and Christian scriptures.

The Arab forefathers of the Holy Prophet (May God bless and cherish him) were northern descendants of Hazrat Ismael. They, too, were upright believers and had true Islamic faith. The Holy Prophet (May God bless and cherish him) stated in a tradition,

"Do not curse Tubba, for he was a believer." Or else: "Do not curse Tubba, for he already embraced Islam."

The Quran (50:12-14) authenticates this assumption, where "The people of Tubba" is mentioned along with the people of Prophet Noah, as well as with other people who disobeyed their prophets. The interpreters deduced that Tubba, like Prophet Noah, belonged to those believers who tried in vain to spread the true faith among their people. The name of the Tubba mentioned in the above hadith, who passed near Yathrib and Makkah during an expedition to the north, was the Himyrite King Tubba n Asad Abu Karib. Regarding Tubba, the Holy Prophet Hazrat Muhammad (May God bless and cherish him) said, "Do not curse Asad of Himyar, for he was the first to supply the coat of the Kaaba." There are verses ascribed to him in which he foresees the Holy Prophet's (May God bless and cherish him) emergence and expresses his desire to join him. These verses were combined with the text of certain testaments, in which the readers are urged to transmit from generation to generation the tidings of Hazrat Muhammad's (May God bless and cherish him) future appearance. (Maarif)

Some traditions relate that the first Tubba already knew about the Prophet Hazrat Muhammad's (May God bless and cherish him) emergence and believed in him. He, too, was in the Hijaz, passing across the future place of Yathrib (Medina). During his return from the north, when he reached Yathrib, some notables and scholars whom he had brought along with him from several countries decided to stay and settle there. They knew from their holy scriptures the importance of that place as the future city of the Prophet. Tubba left a letter for the Holy Prophet Hazrat Muhammad (May God bless and cherish him), the messenger of God with them, in which he recognized his Prophethood. The first Tubba also has some verses ascribed to him, in which he foresees the appearance of the Holy Prophet (May God bless and cherish him).

The descendants of the Tubba were, hence, true believers awaiting the emergence of Hazrat Muhammad (May God bless and cherish him). It is reported that in Sana, a grave was found in which were Tubba's daughter's bodies, along with a golden inscription announcing their faith in the unity of God. It is also stated that Saif b. Dhi Yazan, one of the last kings of Himyar, conveyed the tidings of Hazrat Muhammad's (May God bless and cherish him) forthcoming appearance to Hazrat Abdul Muttalib, who had come to congratulate him on his victory against the Abyssinians. This secret knowledge was handed to him through the chain of preceding Tubbas.

Prophet Hazrat Muhammad's (May God bless and cherish him) ancestors who carried his primordial substance were all pure figures and true Muslims, and some of them were regarded as prophets as well. An early interpretation of the verse "WaTaqallubaka Fi Sajidin" (2:219) recorded by Ibn Sa'd on the authority of Ibn Abbas, through Ikrama where Sajidin is interpreted not as mere Muslim believers but as prophets carrying the substance of Prophet Hazrat Muhammad (May God bless and cherish him). It specifically states:

"Allah saw your (Muhammad's) wandering from prophet to prophet and from prophet to prophet till He drew you out as a prophet."

Al-Bazzar and some other authors narrated an outspoken interpretation, mentioning the word 'Loins' (Aslab), explaining the word "prophets" referring to his ancestors, who transmitted his substance through their bodies. Quoting Ibn Abbas, who said: "This verse means his (Muhammad's) wandering from the loins of a prophet to the loins of another prophet, till He made him emerge from the loins of his father, out of matrimony, pure since Prophet Adam."

In the same vein, the following version of Ibn Abbas's tradition clearly highlights this issue, "The Prophet (May God bless and cherish him) has never stopped wandering through the loins of the prophets, till his mother gave birth to him." (Suyuti, Al-Bazzar, Al-Tabarani, Zurqani, Halabi)

These various interpretations of the same verse by Ibn Abbas exceed the common outlook regarding this verse. He draws a clear distinction between those ancestors of the Holy Prophet Hazrat Muhammad (May God bless and cherish him) who were prophets (All of them biblical figures), and the rest of his Arab ancestors, who are supposed to carry the prophetic heritage only as 'Awsiya.' This applies mainly to the Prophet's (May God bless and cherish him) Arab ancestors descending from Hazrat Ismael, who were successors to the preceding prophets and the forthcoming ones. This implies that the Holy Prophet's (May God bless and cherish him) Arab ancestors linked Hazrat Ismael (the last prophet among his forefathers) with him.

In his book, Bihar Al-Majlisi gives a detailed explanation of this view.

"Believers are unanimous that the Holy Prophet Hazrat Muhammad's (May God bless and cherish him) parents, as well as his ancestors till Prophet Adam, were upright Muslims; moreover, they were righteous – whether sent as prophets or infallible awsiya."

The interpretation of the verse "Taqallabaka Fi Sajidin" by Ibn Abbas that distinguishes between prophets and awsiya among the Holy Prophet's (May God bless and cherish him) ancestors has been quoted by many authorities. It clearly states that not all the carriers of Prophet Muhammad's (May God bless and cherish him) substance were prophets. In one version, it is recorded that the verse means, "You're wandering through the loins of the prophets, from prophet to prophet, till He made you emerge as a prophet in this nation (among the Arabs)." It is thus concluded that Hazrat Muhammad (May God bless and cherish him) was the first to emerge as a prophet among the Arabs, while his Arab forefathers were not.

The same conclusion is found in al-Zurqani's work, "Ibn Abbas". It means the wandering of Hazrat Muhammad (May God bless and cherish him) was through the loins of the prophets, though it was through the loins of intermediaries as well." Some interpreters have stated,

"Ibn Abbas said: it means that the Holy Prophet (May God bless and cherish him) wandered through the loins of the ancestors, Prophet Adam, Prophet Noah, and Prophet Abraham, till Allah (Exalted is He) made him manifest as a prophet." (Qurtabi)

Yet another interpretation runs as follows:

"Ibn Abbas said, 'Through the loins of Prophet Adam, Prophet Noah and Prophet Abraham till you emerged'."

Prophet Adam is also said to be the first man who was chosen by Allah to be above all mankind. (Quran 3:33)

"Behold, God raised Adam and Noah and the house of Abraham, and the house of Imran above all mankind."

It is narrated that Abu Dharr asked the Holy Prophet Hazrat Muhammad (May God bless and cherish him) who was the first prophet, and the Holy Prophet (May God bless and cherish him) replied that it was Prophet Adam to whom Allah spoke. (Ibn Sa'd, Tabarani, Ibn Ishaq)

Wahb b. Munabbih wrote in Maarif that Prophet Adam was the first of messengers while Hazrat Muhammad (May God bless and cherish him) was the last of them all."

CHAPTER 3
THE BIRTH OF LIGHT

The marriage of Hazrat Abdullah and Hazrat Amina took place in the year AD 569. The year following this has been famous for the invasion of Makkah by Abraha, known ever since as the year of the Elephant. This was because the Abyssinian army's march was led by a big elephant as a symbol of power. Before the invasion of Makkah by Abraha's army, Hazrat Abdullah went to trade in Palestine and Syria with one of the caravans. On his way home, he fell severely ill and stayed in Yathrib with his grandmother's family. The rest of the caravan proceeded to Makkah without him. When Hazrat Abdul Muttalib knew about his illness, he sent Harith to take care of him and bring him back as soon as he was able to travel. But when Harith arrived in Yathrib, he was informed that his brother had passed away to the mercy of God. The sad news of his death brought great sorrow to Makkah. Hazrat Amina was devastated by the loss of her beloved husband. His death cut her to the heart, and as her only consolation was the unborn child of her dead husband, her solace increased as the time of her delivery drew near. She was conscious of a divine light within her, and from time to time, it showed so intensely that she could see as far as the castles of Busra in Syria. When Hazrat Amina was six months pregnant with Muhammad Mustafa, she heard in a vision, "Thou carry in thy womb the paragon of the world, and when he is born, then name him Muhammad."

The Holy Prophet stayed for a full nine months in his mother's womb. When his father, Hazrat Abdullah, died, the Holy Prophet was still not born. The angels of the Throne asked Allah the glorious and exalted, "O Lord, your beloved and chosen messenger is an orphan and without a father." The Lord of the worlds responded, "I am his guardian and caretaker."

Hazrat Amina narrated, "I was alone in the house, and no one was present. Hazrat Abdul Muttalib had gone to Kaaba and was busy circumambulating the sanctuary and praying. I heard a strange noise that scared me. I was trembling with fear. Somebody gently stroked me and calmed me. Then, I was given a white drink, which I drank. I saw a group of tall women surrounding me; they looked like the daughters of Abd-e-Manaf. I was wondering how they knew about my condition. The pains of labor started, and I was uncomfortable and heard a lot of commotion. I noticed that a white curtain was drawn between the heaven and the earth. I witnessed a group of angels floating in the air, holding golden trays in their hands. I was drenched in sweat, but it smelled sweeter than musk. At that time, I wished that Hazrat Abdul Muttalib was there. I noticed flocks of birds that flew in and gathered above my room; their beaks were emerald, and their wings were made of rubies. I could see as far as east and west, and flashes of light were ablaze in the east and west and at the top of the Kaaba. The pain of delivery became stronger. My back was resting against some women. I noticed that a lot of people were helping in the house, but I could not see their faces. Soon after, the Holy Prophet was born, and it was an easy birth. When I looked at my babe, he was in a state of prostration and pointing with his index finger towards heaven. Meanwhile, a cloud came down from the sky; it covered me and concealed my son from my vision. I heard a voice that said, "Take Muhammad and move him in the east and west and across the oceans so that all creation can recognize his features and character. I have named him Muhammad to dispel the darkness through him." Suddenly, the cloud cleared up, and I saw my son wrapped in a white silken cloth on a green brocade. He was holding a set of three keys that looked like pearls in his hand. A caller said, "These are the keys to success, fame, and Prophethood." Then another cloud brighter than the first one enveloped me, and I heard hooves of horses, flapping of wings and human voices. My son was concealed from my vision for the second time but for a longer duration than the first one. Once again, I heard a caller saying,

"The Holy Prophet Muhammad is moved in the east and west, shown to sons of all prophets, spirits of all men and Jinn and all the creatures. He is adorned with the purity of Adam, the limpidness of Noah, the dignity of Ibrahim, the obedience (tongue) of Ismail, the beauty of Joseph, the tiding of Jacob, the voice of Dawood, the patience of Ayyub, the piety of Yahya, the forgiveness of Jesus and all the good characters of all prophets."

The caller further proclaimed, "Congratulations, Muhammad Mustafa will conquer the entire world, and by the command of the Lord of the world, all the nations will be under his authority."

Hazrat Amina continued, "I was amazed to behold all that was happening. At the same time, I saw three figures whose faces were shining like the sun. One of them was holding a silver tray in his hands that was full of musk; another one was holding a tray made of green emerald decorated with white pearls around it. A caller said,

"O Beloved of God, the entire world is here from east to west and all that it contains oceans and continents. Take whatever you please. "He further said, "Allah the Glorious and Exalted has honored Kaaba by making it the qibla for His beloved." The third person had a green silk cloth that was folded and emitted light, he took out a shining ring that bedazzled the eyesight. He dipped and washed it seven times in that tray and then stamped it between the shoulder blades of the Holy Prophet (May God bless and cherish him). He then wrapped the stamp (signet) in the silken cloth and sealed it."

Ibn Abbas narrated, "It was Ridhwan, treasurer of the paradise." Hazrat Amina said, "The angel whispered into the ear of the Holy Prophet and said many things. He kissed him in between his eyes on the forehead and said, "O Muhammad, I give you the glad tidings that Allah, Glorious and Exalted, has bestowed you the banner of all prophets, increased you in knowledge above all, and made your heart brave and valiant. Allah, the All-Powerful, has given you the keys to the kingdom. Therefore, you should have no fear. Anyone who hears your name, Allah will put your love in his heart."

Hazrat Amina further added, "I saw a dignified man who came forward and put his lips on the mouth of the baby where he fed him like a pigeon feeds its baby. The Holy Prophet was asking for more by his gestures. He congratulated the Holy Prophet and took him away. The Holy Prophet once again disappeared from my sight. I was in anguish and said to myself," O people of Quraysh, I have given birth to my son tonight, and I see strange things and rituals done to my newborn of which none of you have any idea. I was deep in those thoughts when they returned my baby. His face was shining like a full moon, and he smelled better than musk." I heard them say, "Muhammad was taken over to east and west, was shown to all prophets and their sons. At this hour, he was with his father, Prophet Adam, who kissed him on his forehead and said, "Glad tidings be to you. You are the best of my progeny from the first to last. Allah the Exalted has granted you good fortune in both worlds; whoever is on your religion will be resurrected under your banner on the Day of Judgement."

Hazrat Abdul Muttalib narrated, "I was at the sanctuary (Kaaba) that night when Muhammad was born and was repairing the Kaaba. I witnessed that the four corners of the Kaaba prostrate near Maqam-e-Ibrahim and then stand up straight. I heard a voice glorifying Allah and offering gratitude, saying, 'The Lord of the worlds will get rid of infidelity through Muhammad Mustafa'. All the idols in Kaaba trembled and fell on their faces – Hubbal, the biggest of all, was lying in the dust. A caller announced that Hazrat Amina has given birth to Muhammad Mustafa, and a tray is brought from paradise to bathe Muhammad in it."

Hazrat Abdul Muttalib added, "When I saw Kaaba in such a state and all the idols of Quraysh lying on the ground, I was awestruck and rubbed my eyes for I thought it was in a dream. But I found myself wide awake. I came out of the precincts of Kaaba and saw the mountains of Safa and Marwa were shaking. I decided to go to Amina's house to see the newborn. I noticed that the mountains of Makkah stood tall. When I reached her room, I saw flocks of birds had gathered on the top of her room, and a white cloud was hovering over them. I once again thought to myself that perhaps I was dreaming. I rubbed my eyes again, but I was awake. Bright light was emitting from the room, and the sweet fragrance of musk was wafting in the air. I struggled to approach the room. I gently knocked on the door, and Hazrat Amina replied in a soft voice. I waited till she opened the door for me. The first thing I noticed was that the light of Muhammad was gone from the forehead of Hazrat Amina. I was afraid, and I told her that I didn't see the light in her eyes. She replied, "I have given birth to my son Muhammad, and he is the light. All the creation wants him; the birds that have gathered over my roof want to take him to their nests, and the cloud hovering over the roof wants the same." Abdul Muttalib hurriedly said, "Show me your son Muhammad."

"You can't see him tonight," said Amina. "Why?" asked Abdul Muttalib. Amina continued, "As soon as I gave birth to Muhammad, a very dignified, tall and awesome man came and told me, "O Amina, do not let anybody see this child for three days." When Abdul Muttalib heard this, he drew his sword and said, "I need to see Muhammad right now," and entered the room where Muhammad was sleeping on a green silk blanket wrapped up in white linen. Abdul Muttalib decided to enter the room, but at that very moment, an awesome-looking swordsman came out of the room. Abdul Muttalib had never seen such a fearsome person in his life. He asked

Hazrat Abdul Muttalib as to where he was headed. "To see my son, Muhammad," replied Abdul Muttalib. "Go back; you are not allowed to see him at this time until all the angels in heaven have seen his beautiful and blessed countenance." Abdul Muttalib trembled with fear, and his sword fell from his hand on the ground. He left the house, remained silent for seven days and did not mention this to anybody.

It was a tradition of all noble families among Arabs who lived in towns to send their newborns into the desert in the care of a wet nurse to be reared and to spend their childhood among the Bedouin tribes. Makkah's weather was harsh and prone to epidemics with a high infant mortality rate. In contrast, the desert air was fresh and pure, and it had a lasting impact on the soul of the child as well. The nomadic way of life of tent dwellers, often on the move, was considered a nobler one. Nobility and freedom were inseparable; hence, the nomads were free as a result. In the desert, a man was the owner of the space and free from the domination of time.

Since Qusayy told his tribe to build houses around the sanctuary in Makkah, Quraysh had taken to the sedentary lifestyle of towns. Towns were places of corruption, sloth, and avarice. Hypocrisy was rampant in the walls of the city. Everything decayed there, even language - one of the Arab's precious possessions. Arabs, in general, were illiterate, with only a few of them able to read, but the beauty of speech was a virtue that all Arab parents desired for their children. A man's worth was largely assessed by his eloquence, and the pride of eloquence was poetry. To have an eloquent speaker and a great poet in the family was indeed something to be proud of, and the best poets were nearly always from one or another of the desert tribes, for it was in the desert that spoken language was close to poetry.

The bond with the desert was an integral part of life among Arabs, with fresh air to inhale, pure language to speak, and freedom for the soul; hence, many children of the Quraysh were kept in the desert until eight years of age, so that it might make a lasting mark upon them. Some of the tribes had a high reputation for nursing and rearing children, and among these were the Bani Sa'd ibn Bakr, a branch of Hawazin, who were settled to the south of Makkah.

It was destined by the Lord of the universe that Bibi Halima, daughter of Abu Zaib Al-Sadiyah, would nurse and rear the young Muhammad (May God bless and cherish him). It so happened that a great famine and severe drought hit the entire Arabian Desert area near the vicinity of Makkah. Halimah narrated, "The famine struck the Arabs, and people were in great difficulty. Among all, I was from a destitute family. We were extremely poor. Every day, I used to wander in the desert and nearby mountains in search of edible herbs and green plants that sprouted from the ground. I collected them and brought them home and cooked them to nourish ourselves. Men and women of our tribe were going through the same situation. They also searched the desert for plants and green leaves. Those days, I was pregnant and later delivered a baby boy. I resumed my duty of collecting green herbs and endured significant hardship. One day, I went out but found nothing to bring home and returned in despair. For the next seven days, I had nothing to eat and was suffering from hunger pains. I was weak from childbirth and so debilitated that I did not know whether I was on earth or up in heaven. One night, I was in a deep sleep, and a man appeared and woke me up. He took me with him and dipped me in a stream of pure water as white as milk and sweeter than honey. He told me to drink from that water to quench my thirst and satisfy my hunger and that it would increase my milk. I drank a lot of that water. He told me to drink more of that water, and I drank more. He said, again, drink to your fill. I was fully satiated. He then asked me, "Do you know me?" I replied, "No." He said, "I am the virtue of your patience that you had at the time of your distress and hardship and the thanksgiving to the Lord of the world." That person instructed me, "Now get ready to travel to the precincts of Makkah, Allah Mighty and Majestic has ordained to provide you relief, abundance, and good fortune. Hurry, get the 'light' brilliant like the full moon and keep this a secret." Then he patted me and said, "God's favors be with you, by His grace, your milk should flow in abundance." Halima reported, "I woke up from my dream full of vitality and had more energy than any woman of Bani Sa'd. My breasts were engorged, and milk was dripping from my nipples like water flows from a goatskin."

The people of Bani Sa'd, and all my neighbors, were experiencing extreme hardships. All were suffering from poverty and hunger to the extent that their faces were pale and their bodies emaciated. Nothing grew on the ground or the mountains. The fear of death was imminent. All the women gathered around me and were in awe by my rosy appearance and breast full of milk. They exclaimed, "You look like a queen; yesterday, you were pale and frail, but today, you are fresh and lively." I said nothing because I was told in the dream not to reveal my secret.

The next day, I went out near the vicinity of Makkah in search of herbs for our livelihood. Suddenly, I heard a voice that announced that Almighty Allah has decreed that every woman in the east and west shall not bear a girl but a male due to the birth of a blessed son in Quraysh, who is like a blazing sun in the day and a full moon in the darkness of night. Blessed is the breast that shall suckle him. O women of Bani Sa'd, hurry and seize the fortune. When the women heard that call, they came down from the mountains, went to their homes, and informed their husbands of what had transpired. They decided to go to Makkah and seek a newborn to nurse. I also decided to travel to Makkah.

I had a she-ass; it was so frail and weak that its ribs were visible through the skin. All the women of Bani Sa'd mounted their rides and were moving fast except me, for my ride was moving slowly. It was dragging its feet along the path. During this journey, everything - trees, stones, hills, earth, and animals - were speaking and giving me glad tidings. Suddenly, I saw a tall, bronzed-colored man who came out from the valley between two mountains along our path. He was holding a staff in his hand that emitted bright light. He patted the donkey with his right hand on its belly and said, "O Halima, Allah the exalted gives you glad tidings and has commanded me to protect and safeguard you from demons and all evil." My husband was with me, and I asked him if he saw and heard what I saw and heard. He replied, "What is wrong with you? You look nervous and afraid?" I hesitated to tell the truth and said, "I am afraid we may not catch up with other women from our tribe."

All the women had entered the city of Makkah earlier than me, and every one of them was able to find a newborn to nurse and rear. I was late and did not find a baby to nurse. I asked my husband, "Who is the most respectable and generous person of Makkah?" He said, "Bani Makhzoom." He then left, went to the city, and found that Abdul Muttalib bin Abd Manaf was the most respectable and rich person in Makkah. As I entered the city, I saw all women of Bani Sa'd were returning with a newborn. I was disappointed and said to myself it would have been better for me to have stayed at home. However, I went to every home and inquired about a newborn that needed a wet nurse. As I was going from door to door, I saw Abdul Muttalib, who called in a loud voice, "Is there any wet nurse to take care of a newborn?" I was determined to do so. Therefore, I went forward and said, "Yes, I intend to do so." As per Arab custom, he asked me, "Who are you?" I said, "I am a woman from Bani Sa'd." He asked, "What is your name?" I said, "Halima." When Abdul Muttalib heard my name, he said, "Your name means patience and good fortune, it is a good omen." He then said, "O Halima, I have an orphan baby; his name is Muhammad. I offered him to the women of Bani Sa'd, but no one accepted to be his wet nurse. They refused because he was an orphan and nursing him was not of any benefit. Are you willing to take him and nurse?" I replied, "Let me consult my husband." Abdul Muttalib said, "I am sure you will return. I don't see any sign of unwillingness in you." I said, "If Allah decrees, I will return." I went to my husband and talked to him about it. He had a good feeling about it and said, "It is your destiny to accept this baby. If you refuse, I am afraid you will regret it." I was undecided. My nephew was with us during this journey, and he advised, "Each woman of Bani Sa'd found a baby for themselves to nurse, and their parents who will compensate them are affluent. But you want to take care of an orphan, and it will only increase your burden."

I decided not to accept Muhammad and turned back. Then I told my husband, "I hate to return in the company of women of Bani Sa'd without having taken a babe to nurse. I shall go and take that orphan to nurse. It may be that God will bless us through him." So, I swore that I would suckle Muhammad even though he was an orphan. Abdul Muttalib is his grandfather, and he is the best of men in Makkah. I also remembered my dream and it encouraged me to do so. Hence, I returned and went back to Abdul Muttalib; he was pleased to see me and asked, "Are you here to do your job?" I said, "Yes." He took me inside the house of Hazrat Amina (mother of the Holy Prophet). Her face was shining like a full moon, and her forehead resplendent with a brilliant light. When she saw me, she welcomed me (Ahlan wa sahlan bek ya Halima). She held my hand and took me to where her baby Muhammad was sleeping like an angel, wrapped in a white cloth on a green silken blanket. The sweet smell of musk was wafting from him. When I saw his beautiful face, I hesitated to wake him up. I came close to him and gently placed my hand on his chest. He opened his eyes and smiled. The light was beaming from his eyes that lit the entire place. I could not take my eyes off him. I kissed him between his eyes and picked him up. I offered him my right breast, and he latched onto it. I then offered him my left breast, but he did not latch and turned his face away. (Ibn Abbas narrated; the Holy Prophet did not latch on the left breast because Halima's son Zamrah used to suck on that side. God inspired Muhammad to latch only on the right side. Zamrah also did not eat unless Muhammad at first.)

Halimah narrated, "I took Muhammad and went to my husband. As soon as he saw Muhammad, he prostrated on the ground and praised the Lord of the world. He then said, "O Halima, by God, this is a blessed child that you have taken. We are the fortunate among our tribe." Hazrat Amina called me and said, "Do not take Muhammad out of Makkah until I tell you to do so because I have been warned about it." So, I carried him back to where our mounts were stationed, and as soon as I put him on my bosom, my breasts overflowed with milk for him. He drank to his fill, and his foster brother drank likewise his fill. They both slept peacefully. My husband went to the old she-camel that we had brought with us, and lo! Her udders were full. He milked her and drank her milk, and I drank with him until we could drink no more, and our hunger was satisfied. We spent the best of nights after a long time. Baby Muhammad was with me for three days and three nights. On the third night, I woke from my sleep and saw a man dressed in green sitting by the head side of Muhammad, kissing him between his eyes. I woke my husband quietly and said, "Look at this strange scene." He said, "Stay quiet and do not mention this incident to anyone. From the time of Muhammad's birth all the Jewish scholars are awake and alert. They are forbidden to rest for nine days."

Finally, it was time to say goodbye to Hazrat Amina. Halima narrated, "I wrapped Muhammad and got on my she-ass holding Muhammad in front of me. The she-ass prostrated towards Kaaba three times and then raised its head to heaven. The mount moved swiftly and soon overtook all the other animals. Women of Bani Sa'd were surprised to see my frail she-ass coming back to life and moving faster than all other mounts. They called me, "O daughter of Abu Zaib, it is the same animal you rode before that was dragging its feet and falling behind all others? What has changed today that it is moving so fast?" They were talking to me, and I heard the she-ass talking back, "Yes, something great has transpired and what a wonder. God has resurrected me and made me strong after I was frail and weak. Alas! You know nothing. You are dwelling in darkness. The one riding on my back is the first and the last of prophets, the best of all creation, and the beloved of Allah." The she-ass said this and moved on. On the way back home, wherever we stopped, green grass was growing in abundance.

From the moment Halima took Muhammad home, their lives changed. Their household was blessed with abundance and baraka. Halima herself confirmed that she brought the Holy Prophet to her home during a terrible drought. Her she-camel could not give a drop of milk prior to the arrival of Muhammad. Her child would cry the whole night out of hunger. With the child so distraught, Halima and her husband Harith found it hard to sleep at night.

Things changed for Halima suddenly after she brought Muhammad Mustafa home. Her household appeared to be untouched by the drought, although they lived in the most drought-stricken spot in the region. The family's goats would return from grazing with their stomachs full of grass and their udders bursting with milk. Husband and wife would milk their goats often while others failed to get even a small amount.

Halima narrated, "Our neighbors would tell their shepherds to graze their flocks where he grazes his," yet still their goats came home hungry, yielding no milk." "We enjoyed Allah's bounty for two years, and I weaned Muhammad from the breast after that. He was growing well." She continued, "None of the other boys could match him for growth. By the time he was two years of age, he was a well-built child. When he started talking, I heard something strange from him." He said, 'Allah-o-Akbar, Allah-o-Akbar, Alhamdo Lillahe Rab-i-Alamin.' The generous Lord showered our family with His bounties, and we shared our blessings with others. '

Every six months, Halima and Harith would take Muhammad to Makkah to visit his mother and other family members. They would then return with him to Dayar Banu Sa'd. By the time Muhammad was weaned from the breast, it was time for him to go back to his mother, but Halima was eager that he should stay with them longer for the blessings he brought. So, she begged Amina, "Leave my little son with me until he grows stronger, for I fear lest he be stricken with the plague of Makkah." She insisted on it until she gave him once more into her custody.

Halima narrated, "While the Holy Prophet was growing older and getting stronger, he used to go out of our tent to play with other children, but they would leave him alone. One day, he came to me with tears in his eyes and said, "Where are my brothers, I don't see them." I said, "May I be your sacrifice? They take goats for grazing all day and come back at sunset." He cried and said, "Mom, what am I doing here while my brothers are out there? Send me with them tomorrow?" I asked, "Would you like to accompany them?" "Yes," he said. The next day, I made him ready, dressed him in a new shirt, anointed his hair with oil, and applied collyrium to his eyes. I adorned him with a Yemeni charm to ward off evil eyes. He took a staff and was very happy. He went with his brothers and returned before sunset."

One day, he left with his brothers to graze the goats in the pasture close to our dwelling. Zamrah, his brother, came running to us and said, "Three men clothed in white have taken that Qurayshite brother of mine and laid him on the ground and opened his chest, and they were reaching it with their hands. I am afraid you will not find him alive." So, I and his father ran to the spot, and we found him sitting on a hilltop, looking towards heaven and he had a beautiful smile on his face. I hugged him tightly and started kissing his forehead between eyes and said, "May I be your sacrifice? What has befallen my son?" he replied, "I am fine. I was playing with my brothers. Suddenly, three men appeared out of nowhere; one of them was holding a silver tray, another was holding a green tray, and the third one had snow in his hands. They took me to the mountaintop and made me lie down gently on my side. They opened my chest in the middle. I was watching what they were doing, but I experienced no pain or discomfort. Then one of them put his hand inside my chest and took out my organs and washed them with the snow and replaced them. The second person stood and said to the first one, "You have performed your job as commanded by Allah; now stand back." He came close to me and took out my heart from the chest. He cut my heart open in two halves. He took out a black clot from it and said, "This was the portion of the devil in your bosom." He then placed something in my heart, which he was holding in his hand, and sealed my heart with a ring that emitted light. Since then, I have felt peace in my heart and body. After that, the third person came and said to the second one, "You have performed your duty." He then placed his hand on my chest, and the wound in my chest was closed in front of my eyes. He then asked his companions to weigh Muhammad against ten people of his ummah. They weighed me, and I was heavier. Then he said, weigh him against a hundred and then a thousand and at last against the entire ummah, but I was heavier and superior to all. After that, he held my hand and raised me to my feet. They gathered around me, kissed my forehead, and said, "Do not be afraid, you are extraordinarily blessed by God if you only knew." They left me here and flew in the air in front of my eyes.

(Ans bin Malik related that one day as Prophet Muhammad (May God bless and cherish him) was playing with some children near Halima's house, Jibriel (Gabriel) came with angels and made Muhammad lie down. Then he opened the boy's chest, took out his heart, extracted a lump of flesh from it, and said, "This is the portion of Satan in you." He then put Muhammad's heart in a golden tray filled with Zamzam water, washed it, and replaced it.)

Halima and Harith looked around but did not see any men, nor was there blood or any wound to bear out what the two boys were describing. No amount of questioning would make them change their story or modify them in any respect. Yet there was not even a trace of a scar on the breast of Muhammad nor any blemish on his perfect little body. The only unusual feature was in the middle of his back between his shoulder blades, a small but distinct oval mark where the flesh was slightly raised, but that had been the birthmark he had since birth.

Halima continued her story, "I took Muhammad and went to a house of Bani Sa'd. People over there advised me to take Muhammad to a soothsayer (Kahin) so that he could look at him and find out what had possessed him. They thought that perhaps Muhammad had been affected by magic and possessed by demons. Muhammad said, "I am fine and healthy, and my heart is at peace, but I shall do whatever you (Halima) want me to do." I was influenced by people's opinions and took Muhammad to the old Kahin (Soothsayer) and told him about the entire incident. Kahin said, "Let me ask the child who has experienced this, for he knows better." He asked Muhammad, "Tell me about this matter." Muhammad (May God bless and cherish him) narrated the entire incident as it happened. When he heard the story, he sprang to his feet, clutched at Muhammad, and shouted, "Beware, O Arabs, a great danger awaits you. Kill this boy and kill me along with him. If you let him live until he is a grown-up man, he will proclaim your religion as false and destroy it totally. He will call you to worship a God you do not know and invite you to a religion you do not believe in." Halima said, "When I heard his words, I grabbed my son out of his grip and said, "You are insane, if I knew you would utter such nonsense, I would not have brought Muhammad here. Call someone to kill you, I will not allow any harm to Muhammad. I took Muhammad with me home. Every home in our village emitted the smell of musk. I noticed that every day, two angels of light would come and enter Muhammad's clothing and disappear.

People of Bani Sa'd gave me advice to return Muhammad to Abdul Muttalib, who entrusted him to me. I decided to do so. Then I heard a voice, "Glad tidings be to Makkah, today, the paragon of the world is returning; for his sake, Makkah and its surroundings will be safe forever from drought, famine, destruction, and diseases."

Halima went on, "I sat on my she-ass and held Muhammad (May God bless and cherish him) in front of me and traveled to Makkah until I reached the main entrance of the city. People were gathered over there. I wanted to take care of my shabby dress, and Muhammad (May God bless and cherish him) was sitting with me. In the meantime, I heard a noise, and I looked toward the side of the noise, and as I turned back, I did not see Muhammad (May God bless and cherish him). I asked people, "Where is my boy?" They replied, "Which boy?" I said, "Muhammad Ibn Abdul Allah Ibn Abdul Muttalib; for his sake, God blessed me with abundance and baraka. I took him for nursing, reared him for four years, and now I brought him back to hand over to his grandfather Abdul Muttalib. He has been taken away from me even though he did not step his feet on the ground. I swear by Lat and Uzza if I do not find him, I will drop myself from the mountain, or will I tear apart myself." The crowd said, "What sort of game is this? We have not seen Muhammad with you." I said, "He was with me this very moment." They replied, "We have not seen him at all." I was heartbroken and started wailing, calling my son 'O Muhammad, O Muhammad' and crying loudly. People were sympathetic towards me and joined me in my search. I saw an old man who was walking with the help of a staff, he approached me and said, "O Sa'diya, why are you crying, I will send you to someone who knows where Muhammad is, and if he wishes, he will return him to you." I said, "Who is that person?" He replied, "The great idol Hubbal - He has the knowledge about Muhammad (May God bless and cherish him). Let us go to him." I shouted at him, "Don't you know what happened to Lat and Uzza the night Muhammad was born?" The old man said, "You do not know what you are saying. I'll go to Hubbal and ask him to return Muhammad to you." He then left and circumambulated seven times around the statue of Hubbal, kissed its head, and said," O Hubbal, you have been gracious towards the Quraysh from eternity. This woman, Sa'diya, states that her son is lost. She is in great distress, and her son Muhammad cannot be found." As soon as the old man uttered "Muhammad," Hubbal and all the other idols fell on their faces, and a voice said, "We all will be destroyed by the hand of Muhammad, what do you want from us?" The old man hurriedly came out, trembling and angry. He threw his staff down and cried, "O Sa'diya, by God, your son has a powerful Lord who will protect him. Call upon him silently, and He will answer your prayer."

I was afraid that Hazrat Abdul Muttalib would soon come to know about the disappearance of Muhammad and would be extremely upset. However, I decided to go to him. When he saw me, he asked, "Are you the bearer of good news or bad news?" I said, "Worse, a great misfortune has befallen me." He said, "Did you lose your son?" I replied, "Yes, I lost him." Hazrat Abdul Muttalib had the suspicion that some of the Quraysh may have killed the boy. He drew his sword, and no one dared to stand before him. He loudly shouted, "Yal ghalib, yal ghalib," which meant help in times of Jahiliya. The Quraysh heard his call and gathered around him. They asked what had befallen him. He told them that his son was missing. They made a pact to ride with him through the valleys and mountains until they found Muhammad and swore that they would not eat, wash their hair, or use perfume until they found the boy. Moreover, they took an oath to kill a thousand Arabs and one hundred of the Quraysh if they had harmed Muhammad. Their party went through all the valleys and mountains of Makkah but did not find Muhammad. Hazrat Abdul Muttalib left the party, put on his cloak, and went to Kaaba. He circumambulated the sanctuary seven times and implored the mighty God. He heard a call that said, "Do not despair, Muhammad has an All-Powerful Lord that will protect him from all evil." When Hazrat Abdul Muttalib heard this, he asked the caller, "Where is my son Muhammad?" The caller replied, "He is in Tahama under the shade of the Yemeni tree." Hazrat Abdul Muttalib put on his armor and rode towards that place. On the way, he met Waraqa Bin Nawfal, and they went together. Abu Masood Saqafi was ahead of them, and he saw Muhammad sitting under the tree. He went towards him and asked, "Who are you?" Muhammad (May God bless and cherish him) answered, "I am Muhammad Ibn Abdul Allah Ibn Abdul Muttalib." Abu Masood went back and gave the good news to Hazrat Abdul Muttalib and his Qurayshi companions. Hazrat Abdul Muttalib approached Muhammad and asked, "Who are you?" The Prophet Muhammad replied, "I am your son." Hazrat Abdul Muttalib then asked, "Tell me your ancestry?" Hazrat Muhammad (May God bless and cherish him), who was thirty-six months of age at that time, recounted his entire ancestry. Hazrat Abdul Muttalib took Muhammad and made him sit on his mount and started toward Kaaba. When he reached Kaaba, he circumambulated seven times for thanksgiving and praised the Lord of the worlds. He then rode to the city of Makkah, and the Quraysh were satisfied. Halima added that Hazrat Abdul Muttalib showered me with wealth and honored me with his hospitality, and then I returned home.

CHAPTER 4
CHILDHOOD

Hazrat Muhammad (May God bless and cherish him) was back in Makkah with his mother for the next two years. He enjoyed the affection of his family, especially his grandfather, his uncles and aunts, and his cousins with whom he grew up. Hamzah and Safiyyah, the children of Hazrat Abdul Muttalib from his last marriage, were very close to him. Hamzah was his age, while Safiyyah was younger. They had a very powerful and lasting bond between them. At the age of six his mother took him to Yathrib to visit his kinsmen. His beloved father was also buried in Yathrib. A caravan from Makkah was going to Yathrib, and they joined it. On this journey, his mother's slave girl, Baraka, was riding with them. Hazrat Muhammad (May God bless and cherish him) and Baraka were riding on one camel while his mother rode another. During their stay in Yathrib, the Holy Prophet learned how to swim in a pool that belonged to his Khazarjite kinsmen. He also learned how to fly a kite from the boys in the town.

After some time, they began the long journey back to Makkah. On their return, Hazrat Amina fell ill, and they were obliged to stop their journey. Hazrat Amina's condition worsened rapidly, and after a few days, she passed away at the mercy of Allah. She was buried at Abwa, not far from Yathrib. Baraka took care of the grieving Muhammad and consoled him during that difficult time. Hazrat Muhammad (May God bless and cherish him) had lost both his parents and was now twice an orphan. He returned with Baraka in the company of some travelers to Makkah.

His grandfather, Hazrat Abdul Muttalib, now took complete charge of him. He had a special love for his orphaned grandson, who had recently lost his mother. Hazrat Abdul Muttalib was more compassionate and kinder towards Muhammad (May God bless and cherish him) and felt great tenderness in his heart that he had never even felt for his own sons. Hazrat Abdul Muttalib loved to sit near the Kaaba. His sons used to spread a carpet for him in the shade of the Holy Sanctuary, and out of respect for their father, none of his sons would sit on it, not even Hamzah, but little Muhammad was exempt from such custom. When one of his uncles told him to sit somewhere else, Hazrat Abdul Muttalib would tell them, "Let my son be, I swear by Allah the exalted this son of mine will achieve greatness." He always used to keep him by his side and would caress him and took pride in whatever he did. The bond between the two was so great that every day, both could be seen hand in hand at the Kaaba or elsewhere in Makkah. Hazrat Abdul Muttalib always took him when he went to attend the assembly of the chiefs of the town to discuss various matters. Hazrat Abdul Muttalib did not refrain from asking the opinion of the seven-year-old boy on tribal matters. When other Arab elders objected, he would say, "By God, a great future awaits my son."

When Hazrat Muhammad (May God bless and cherish him) was eight years, two months, and ten days old, his legendary and beloved grandfather passed away in Makkah, and once again, he suffered a great loss at such a tender age. At the time of his death, Hazrat Abdul Muttalib entrusted his grandson to Hazrat Abu Talib, who was full brother to the boy's father, Hazrat Abdullah. Hazrat Abu Talib extended his affection, kindness, and protection towards his nephew and preferred him over his own sons. Hazrat Abu Talib's wife, Fatima bint Asad bin Hashim did her best to replace his mother and showered all her love on him. In later years, the Holy Prophet Hazrat Muhammad (May God bless and cherish him) narrated that she would have let her own children go hungry rather than him.

THE GREATEST COMPANION AND PROTECTOR, HAZRAT ABU TALIB

According to Sira and hadith literature, Hazrat Abu Talib bin Abdul Muttalib b. Hashim was unwavering in his protection of his nephew when the Prophet began his mission, despite the numerous attempts of the chiefs of the Quraysh to persuade him otherwise. The Holy Prophet (May God bless and cherish him) and Hazrat Abu Talib are portrayed in the hadith literature as dearly loving one another. There is a wealth of reports that testify to his lifelong belief in God and the Prophethood of Hazrat

Muhammad (May God bless and cherish him).

Al-Sayyid Muhammad b. Abdul Rasul al-Barzanji al-Hussayni (d.1103/1691) wrote a comprehensive treatise defending the faith (Iman) of Hazrat Abu Talib in response to the objection of others. A large group of Sunni scholars and hadith transmitters agree with him on the matter. Literary evidence suggests that earlier Sunni scholars upheld the faith (Iman) of Hazrat Abu Talib before al-Barzanji wrote his text in 1088 AH. (Al-Barzanji Sadad al-Din page 488). For example, Ahmad Zayni Dahlan and Abdul Husayn al-Amini (d. 973/1565), as part of a circle of Sunni scholars in the Sunni tradition, upheld the conversion of Hazrat Abu Talib to Islam. Taj al-Din al-Subki (d.771/1370) did indeed consider Hazrat Abu Talib to have believed in the Prophethood of Hazrat Muhammad (May God bless and cherish him). He cites Hazrat Abu Talib's poetry as clear proof that he accepted the prophetic claims of his nephew (Al-Subki Tabaqat vol 1. Pp 87-91). He confirms that Hazrat Abu Talib seems to have possessed faith in his heart.

Al-Qarafi also acknowledged that Hazrat Abu Talib believed in the Prophethood of his nephew manifestly and in his heart (Al-Qarafi, Sahrah p. 163). It is clearly established that Hazrat Abu Talib admitted his faith in his prose and poetry. This fact is transmitted by narrators of Sira and history in addition to his obvious aid of the Prophet and the sacrifice of his children, family, wealth, and self for him, public declaration of believing him, and urging others to follow him. A Sunni tradition establishes the faith of Hazrat Abu Talib through his words and actions. For example, Hazrat Abu Talib wrote to Najashi, the king of Ethiopia, asking him to treat the Muslims well and praising Hazrat Muhammad (May God bless and cherish him) as someone "Who came with guidance just as Moses and Jesus once did." Hazrat Abu Talib, in one of his verses, articulates his faith, which includes the words,

"Did you not know that we discovered Muhammad to be a messenger like Moses?"

It is reported that Hazrat Ali expressly said, "My father was a believing Muslim who hid his faith out of fear for what the Quraysh would do to the Hashimis." It is narrated that when the Abbasid caliph Al-Mutawakkil (232-247/846-861) asked the tenth Imam Ali b. Muhammad (Al-Hadi) (d.254/868) and questioned the faith of Hazrat Abu Talib. Imam Al-Hadi (Naqi) said, "Woe to you! If the faith of Hazrat Abu Talib were placed on a scale and the faith of all men were put on another, the faith of Hazrat Abu Talib would outweigh them all." (Al-Bahrani, Madina al-Maajiz vol 7. P 535)

Prominent Sunni scholars believed that faith (Iman) is an affirmation (tasdiq) in the heart of all that Hazrat Muhammad (May God bless and cherish him) preached to be true. Many throughout history have affirmed the truth of Shahadatayn (double testimony of faith) but were unable to make it public. In this regard, it is permissible to keep from outwardly identifying with Islam due to fear of an oppressor who may inflict unbearable pain or death upon the person, one of his children or his relatives. There is no doubt that Hazrat Abu Talib was forced into this position, as the person whom he struggled to protect from the assaults of Quraysh was none other than the Holy Prophet. To continue his protection of the Holy Prophet (May God bless and cherish him), Hazrat Abu Talib had to maintain his position as a chief of Quraysh, which would have been impossible with a public declaration of faith. However, Hazrat Abu Talib expressed his faith in monotheism and the divine inspiration of Hazrat Muhammad (May God bless and cherish him) in his life and poetry.

"Have you not learned that we have found Muhammad,

a messenger in the similitude of Moses?

This has been verified in scriptures.

And I have learned that the religion of Muhammad is the best religion for mankind.

And He derived his name from His own to exalt him,

For the possessor of the Throne is Mahmud, and this is Muhammad."

Hazrat Abu Talib.

All Sunni and Shia scholars agree that Hazrat Abu Talib used to love the Prophet (May God bless and cherish him), aid him, protect him, help him in conveying the message, affirm what he would say as truth, order his sons Jafar and Ali to follow him and help him, and praise him in poetry and testify to the truth of his religion.

According to Ibn Hajar al-Asqalani (d. 852/1449), Abd al-Rahman al-Suhayli (d. 581/1185) referred to a book by al-Masudi (d. 345/956) that Hazrat Abu Talib became a Muslim. Ibn Hajar also narrated that he had, in fact, seen that Hazrat Abdul Muttalib, the Prophet's grandfather, had died a Muslim in al-Masudi's famous extant work of history. (Al-Azhari, Bulugh, al-Barzanji, Sadad al-Din, al-Masudi, Muruj)

Nonetheless, al-Suhayli and Ibn Hajar are correct in concluding that Hazrat Abdul Muttalib's death as a Muslim would also imply Hazrat Abu Talib's conversion since the latter publicly claimed on his death bed to follow the religion of his father. In any case, the earliest recension of Hazrat Abu Talib's conversion in the Sunni community exists in the Sira of Muhammad b. Ishaq (d. 150/767) is a text which predates al-Masudi's work by two centuries.

The Umayyad era text, Kitab Sulaym b. Qays depicts Hazrat Abu Talib as a powerful aid to the Holy Prophet (May God bless and cherish him) who would order his nephew to deliver the revelation from his Lord and diligently defend him from any harm. While this image of Hazrat Abu Talib also appears in later Sunni sources, it is not contradicted by any indication that he ever repudiated the message of the Prophet of Islam (May God bless and cherish him). On one occasion, the Holy Prophet (May God bless and cherish him) specifically orders him to recognize Ali as his successor, "O Abu Talib, listen to your son Ali and obey him. For indeed God has made his rank in proximity to His Prophet that of Aaron onto Moses." (Kitab Sulaym Ibn Qays al-Hilali p313). Obviously, such advice would not be given to someone who rejected the Prophethood of Muhammad (May God bless and cherish him), Moses, or Aaron. Also, Hazrat Abu Talib is mentioned as a carrier of the sacred light that was passed on from Adam to Ali. God would not have selected individuals guilty of polytheism or any other major sin to convey divine light in their loins and wombs.

When the elders of Quraysh agreed to boycott the clans of Hashim and Muttalib, they signed a covenant and placed it inside the Kaaba for its sanctification and safekeeping. During the boycott, the Prophet (May God bless and cherish him) received a revelation that the parchment describing the conditions of the boycott had been eaten by insects except for the words "In your name, O God". When the holy Prophet (May God bless and cherish him) informed Hazrat Abu Talib of this revelation, he had no doubt in the Holy Prophet's words and succeeded in using the information to end the boycott. He went to the chiefs of the Quraysh and publicly challenged them to end the boycott if the parchment was in the condition that Muhammad (May God bless and cherish him) described. They agreed to the challenge and removed the parchment from the Kaaba to find it eaten away except for the name of God. It was shortly after this incident the boycott came to an end. (Dahlan, Asnad p 46)

It is my conviction that the Holy Prophet Hazrat Muhammad (May God bless and cherish him) was simply too committed to Allah, the Glorious and Exalted, to blemish his allegiance to Him with love for someone who rejected faith. It does not befit the Holy Prophet and his famous offspring to possess unbelieving ancestors. All the famous Sufis agree that the Holy Prophet (May God bless and cherish him) and his Household descended from an unbroken chain of monotheists that extended back to Prophet Adam. The belief in the prophetic light of Hazrat Muhammad (May God bless and cherish him) descending through the loins of his ancestors is an evident motif in the explanation of this belief.

On his deathbed, when asked by the Holy Prophet (May God bless and cherish him), Hazrat Abu Talib apparently refused to say the testimony of faith in front of the chiefs of the Quraysh to keep those individuals from harming the Holy Prophet after his death. However, after the Holy Prophet (May God bless and cherish him) left Hazrat Abu Talib's bedside, those individuals were appeased and left as well. Only after the unbelievers had left, Hazrat Abu Talib, in the presence of his brother Abbas b. Abdul Muttalib began to move his lips. Abbas moved near him and heard him reciting the Shahadatayn (Double testimony of faith) to himself. Abbas is consistently portrayed as the only one who heard this statement. He informed the Holy Prophet (May God bless and cherish him) after the event by swearing, "By God, he said the words which you commanded him to recite." (Al-Bahaqi, Sunan vol 2 p 346; Ibn Asakir, Tarikh vol 66 p331; Ibn Hajar al-Asqalani, Isaba vol 7 p198; Ibn Ishaq, Sira vol 4 p233; Al-Tusi, al-Amali pp 2651)

In his final testament, Hazrat Abu Talib told the clan of Abdul Muttalib and informed them that they would be guided if they followed Muhammad (May God bless and cherish him). The Holy Prophet ordered Hazrat Ali Ibn Abu Talib to administer Hazrat Abu Talib's last rites and burial. He also stressed Hazrat Ali to maintain ritual purity throughout the entire procedure.

CHAPTER 5
BAHIRA THE MONK

Hazrat Abu Talib took complete guardianship of the Holy Prophet Hazrat Muhammad (May God bless and cherish him) after his grandfather died and took care of him in the best way. He treated him with love and respect and preferred him even to his own children. Hazrat Abu Talib diligently protected and cherished him for forty years and extended all possible support to him and his divine mission. His relations with others were primarily determined in the light of the treatment they showed to the Holy Prophet (May God bless and cherish him).

It is narrated by Ibn Kathir on the authority of Jalhamah b. Arfutah said, "I came to Makkah when it was a rainless year, so the Quraysh said, "O Abu Talib, the valley has dried up, and the people are hungry. Let us go and pray for rainfall. Hazrat Abu Talib went to Kaaba with a young boy who was as beautiful as the sun and had a black cloud covering his head. Hazrat Abu Talib and the boy stood by the wall of the Kaaba and prayed for rain. As soon as they prayed, thick clouds gathered from all directions, rain fell in torrents, and water flowed in springs. Grass and plants grew all over, and prosperity was restored."

Hazrat Abdul Muttalib did not leave much wealth for each of his sons. Hazrat Abu Talib was the poorest and supported a large family. As a young boy, the Holy Prophet (May God bless and cherish him) took to pasturing sheep and goats for the people. Therefore, he would spend days alone in the hills and valleys of Makkah. His uncle, Hazrat Abu Talib, would go on trade trips to Syria and Yemen to make some profit.

When the Holy Prophet (May God bless and cherish him) was twelve years, two months, and ten days old, Hazrat Abu Talib decided to join a trade caravan heading for Syria. They both feared a long separation from each other. At the time of departure, the Holy Prophet (May God bless and cherish him) held the reins of the mount of Hazrat Abu Talib and said, "Dear uncle, are you going to leave me here alone?" Hearing these words, tears welled up in the eyes of Hazrat Abu Talib and he said, "No, my son, I am taking you with me." He made the Holy Prophet sit on the mount and started his journey. Once the caravan reached the border of Syria, they halted at a spot where caravans always rested. Near that place was a Christian monastery that had been lived in by a monk for generation after generation. When one died, another replaced his spot and inherited all that was in the monastery, including old scriptures. Among these manuscripts was one that contained the tidings of the coming of a prophet among Arabs. Bahira, the monk who now lived there, was fully aware of the contents of this book. He was convinced that the coming of the Prophet would be in his lifetime. He used to stand on the roof of his cell a couple of times a day and watched Makkan caravans that approached and halted not far from the monastery. One day, he noticed something the like of which he had never witnessed before; a small cloud moved slowly over the heads of some travelers in the caravan and shielded them from the intense heat of the scorching sun. The caravan stopped near a tree, and the travelers sat to rest under its shade. To his amazement, the cloud ceased to move as soon as they halted. The tree itself lowered its branches over them so they were doubly in the shade. In his heart, he knew that such an event was of high significance, and only the presence of a prophet could explain it. He immediately thought of the expected prophet and wondered if it could be that he had at last come and was amongst these Arab travelers.

Bahira sent his servant to the caravan and said, "I love the people of Quraysh. Whenever a caravan passes by my monastery, I invite them and serve them food. Now, I would like you to come to my cell, every one of you, young and old, slave man and freeman, and leave no one behind." The servant delivered the message, and all of them came to his cell. Hazrat Abu Talib left young Muhammad (May God bless and cherish him) with a servant to look after their camels and belongings. When all the people in the caravan were present at the monastery, Bahira went to the roof and noticed that the cloud was still over the tree, covering it with its shade. He scanned their faces intently one by one, but he could not see which corresponded to the description in the book. He did not see anything extraordinary. Perhaps they had not all come. He asked, "Men of Quraysh, let none of you stay behind." "There is not one that has been left behind." They answered, "Save only a boy, the youngest of us all." Bahira said, "Call him to come, and let him be present with us at this meal." They reproached themselves. Bahira insisted on sending someone and bringing the boy and the servant. When Hazrat Muhammad (May God bless and cherish him) was coming to join them, the cloud was still over his head, covering him with its shadow. One glance at the boy's face was enough to explain this miracle. Bahira was looking at him attentively throughout the meal and noticed all the features of both face and body that corresponded to what was in his book. After the meal, Bahira said, "Whose boy is this?" They replied that this boy belonged to the sheikh, referring to Hazrat Abu Talib. "What kinship has this boy with thee?" asked Bahira. Hazrat Abu Talib replied, "He is my son." "He cannot be thy son. It cannot be that this boy's father is alive." Said Bahira. "He is my brother's son," replied Hazrat Abu Talib. "What happened to his father?" said the monk. "He died when the boy was still in his mother's womb," replied Hazrat Abu Talib. "That is the truth," Bahira said. He then went to the young guest and asked him questions regarding his life, sleep and, in general, about his affairs. The Holy Prophet (May God bless and cherish him) readily answered his questions and did not hesitate to draw his cloak when the monk asked if he could see his back. When Bahira saw the very mark, he expected to see between his shoulders, as described in his book, the seal of Prophethood, he felt certain. He then turned to Hazrat AbuTalib and said, "Let me inform you, this boy of yours is a prophet of God, and the seal of Prophethood is between his shoulders on the back. Hurry and take thy brother's son back to his country and guard him against the Jews, for by God, if they see him and know of him that which I know, they will contrive evil against him. Indeed, God has great things in store for him."

MARRIAGE TO HAZRAT KHADIJAH

The Holy Prophet (May God bless and cherish him) had now passed his twentieth year, and with time, he engaged in joining merchant caravans to the neighboring countries. He came to be known throughout Makkah as al-Amin (Trustworthy), Reliable and Honest. This was due to the reports of those who had entrusted him with their goods and merchandise on various occasions. His uncle Hazrat Abu Talib had to support a large family and was financially in a weak position. One day, he told the Holy Prophet (May God bless and cherish him) hesitantly,

"Both of your parents passed away and left no inheritance. I wish I could arrange a suitable marriage for you, but my financial situation is not so good. I know Hazrat Khadijah is a rich woman of honor and dignity, she hires men to travel on her behalf and trade her merchandise. If you desire, I can take you to her, and she may agree to employ you. In this way, you may earn a handsome amount. As a result, I will be able to find you a suitable wife, and it will make me a happy man." The Holy Prophet (May God bless and cherish him) agreed and said, "O uncle, do whatever pleases you."

Hazrat Khadijah al-Kubra, daughter of Khuwalid Ibn Asad ibn Abdul Uzza Ibn Qusayy, belonged to the clan of Banu Hashim of the tribe of Banu Asad. Hazrat Khadijah's father died around 585 AD. Like many other Qurayshis, he was a rich merchant and a successful businessman whose vast wealth and business talents were inherited by Hazrat Khadijah, after whom the latter succeeded in faring with the family's vast wealth. It is said that when trade caravans used to embark upon their lengthy and arduous journey either to Syria during the summer or to Yemen during the winter, Hazrat Khadijah's caravan equaled the caravans of all other traders of Quraysh put together. She was a distant cousin of the Holy Prophet (May God bless and cherish him) Hazrat Muhammad Ibn Abdullah Ibn Abdul Muttalib Ibn Hashim ibn Abd Manaf Ibn Qusayy. Qusayy is, therefore, the ancestor of all clans belonging to Quraysh. Quraysh's real name was Fahr, and he was the son of Malik, son of Madar, son of Kananah, son of Khuzaimah, son of Mudrikah, son of Ilyas son of Mazar, son of Nazar, son of Ma'ad, son of Adnan, son of Ismaeel, son of Ibrahim (Abraham), son of Sam, son of Noah, may God bless and cherish them all.

Hazrat Khadijah was famous as Ameerat of Quraysh, Princess of the Quraysh, and at-Tahira, the Pure One, due to her impeccable personality and virtuous character, not to mention her honorable descent. She used to feed and clothe the poor, assist her relatives financially, and even provide for the marriage of those of her kin who could not otherwise have had the means to marry.

Hazrat Abu Talib took Hazrat Muhammad Mustafa (May God bless and cherish him) with him and went to the house of Hazrat Khadijah. He knocked at the door, and one of her servants came out. Hazrat Abu Talib told him to inform Hazrat Khadijah that Abu Talib wanted to see her regarding a matter. Hazrat Khadijah welcomed them when they entered her home. She was sitting on a comfortable couch surrounded by seventy of her maids, who were fanning her. Hazrat Khadijah politely asked, "My dear uncle, what brings you here, and what can I do to please you?" Hazrat Abu Talib said, "O Khadijah, Allah the Glorious and Exalted has granted you wealth and dignity, and I have come to ask you a favor." Hazrat Khadijah replied, "I will do whatever you ask me." Hazrat Abu Talib continued, "Muhammad (May God bless and cherish him) is my nephew, Abdullah's son, and I brought him here so that you can hire him to trade on your behalf. You have lots of men working for you; let him also get his share."

Hazrat Khadijah had already heard much good about him from different sources and was impressed by his amiable manners, honesty, and truthfulness. She had already been married twice before, and since the death of her second husband, it had been her custom to hire men to trade on her behalf. She agreed to the proposal of Hazrat Abu Talib and said, "I will do so. His wages would be the double of the highest she had ever paid to a man of the Quraysh." She offered him the services of her servant named Maysarah for the journey. She instructed Maysarah to serve and obey him in all matters. The Holy Prophet Hazrat Muhammad (May God bless and cherish him) did not have any practical trading experience, but he had twice accompanied his uncle Hazrat Abu Talib on his trips and keenly observed how he traded, bartered, bought, and sold and conducted business. After all, the people of Quraysh were famous for their involvement in trade more than in any other profession. When Hazrat Khadijah hired Hazrat Muhammad (May God bless and cherish him) to trade on her behalf, he was only twenty-five years old.

Before embarking on his trip as a businessman representing Hazrat Khadijah, the Holy Prophet (May God bless and cherish him) met with his beloved uncle Hazrat Abu Talib for last minute briefing and consultation. Soon after, Hazrat Muhammad (May God bless and cherish him), accompanied by Maysarah, set off with merchandise towards Syria. As soon as they left, a cloud appeared in the sky and covered Hazrat Muhammad (May God bless and cherish him) with its shadow. They followed the desert road, passing through Wadi al-Qura, Midian, and Diyar Thamud, places with which he was familiar because of having seen these at the age of twelve in the company of his uncle Hazrat Abu Talib. The Holy Prophet carried with him merchandise of hides, raisins, perfumes, dried dates, woven items, probably silver bars, and some herbs. When they reached the border of Syria, they took shelter beneath the shadow of a tree not far from the monastery of the same monk, Bahira. It was the same tree under which he had sheltered some fifteen years previously on his way to Syria with his uncle. Bahira came out of his cell and saw the cloud over the Prophet's head. He was pleased beyond measure. He asked Maysarah,

"Who are you folks?" "I am Khadijah's servant and traveling to Syria for trade," said Maysarah.

Bahira came near Hazrat Muhammad (May God bless and cherish him), kissed his head, and declared his faith,

"I testify that there is no god save Allah, and I declare that you (Muhammad) are His messenger. Jesus, son of Mary (Isa Ibn Maryam), the servant of Allah, stated that after me, no one will sit under this tree except the Hashimi and Makkan prophet, who will proclaim, "There is no god but God" (La Ilaha Illallah). He will own the banner of praise (Lawa-e-Hamd) on the Day of Resurrection and be the owner of the fountain of Kauthar and the owner of the crown and throne. You are the one God has mentioned and praised in the Torah, and I find all that has been described in the book about you to be true except one thing that is between your shoulder blades." The Holy Prophet (May God bless and cherish him) uncovered his back. Bahira saw the seal of Prophethood and kissed it. He then told Maysarah, "None other than a prophet is sitting beneath that tree. Guard him against the Jews, who are his enemies, and Allah the exalted will not make them successful in their evil intentions."

As they continued their journey into Syria, the words of Bahira sank deep into the soul of Maysarah, but they did not greatly surprise him, for he had noticed throughout the journey that he was in the company of a man unlike any other he had ever met. This was further confirmed by something he saw on his way home: He had often noticed that the heat was strangely not oppressive. One day at noon, he clearly saw two angels shading Prophet Muhammad (May God bless and cherish him) from the sun's rays with their wings. Maysarah further added that he had been traveling and trading for the last forty years and had never seen so much profit as he had that year in the company of Hazrat Muhammad (May God bless and cherish him).

As they came near Makkah, Maysarah advised the Holy Prophet (May God bless and cherish him) that he must rush and inform Hazrat Khadijah about the profits he made during this journey. He added that this might please her, and she might increase his wages. The Holy Prophet (May God bless and cherish him) mounted his camel and rode swiftly towards Makkah.

In the evenings on hot days, Hazrat Khadijah used to sit on the balcony of her three-story mansion on a cozy couch. She would sit on the couch, and her servants would carry her upstairs. She had seventy maidens who would fan her with their perfumed tresses. While reclining on the couch, she suddenly saw the Holy Prophet (May God bless and cherish him) riding a camel and approaching her house. He had a red Yemeni turban on his head. An angel with a drawn sword was watching over on his right side and on his left side as well. A cloud was covering him under its shade, and birds of air were fanning him with their wings. At first, Hazrat Khadijah did not recognize the Holy Prophet (May God bless and cherish him). She said to herself, "O God, who is this person coming towards my house?" When the holy Prophet came much closer to the house, she jumped from her couch and ran down to the gate. She saw the Holy Prophet (May God bless and cherish him), who dismounted his camel. Hazrat Khadijah could not believe it and was still in doubt. The Holy Prophet Hazrat Muhammad (May God bless and cherish him) gave her the good news of the profits they had made from the trade. Hazrat Khadijah was now more interested in the Holy Prophet (May God bless and cherish him) than the profits. She asked, "Where is Maysarah?" "He is still in the desert and will soon arrive here," replied Hazrat Muhammad (May God bless and cherish him). Hazrat Khadijah said, "Go back and tell Maysarah to come quickly." The Holy Prophet mounted his camel and rode back. Hazrat Khadijah went back to the balcony and waited eagerly for their return. She was in deep thought until they returned. (Khargushi)

Hazrat Khadijah asked Maysarah in private, "Tell me everything in detail about Hazrat Muhammad (May God bless and cherish him)." Maysarah said, "O Khadijah, Bahira, the Christian monk, informed me that Muhammad (May God bless and cherish him) is a prophet of God, and he told me to guard him against the Jews, who are his enemies. However, God will not make them succeed in their evil intentions." When Hazrat Khadijah heard this prophecy, she said to Maysarah, "Keep this a secret and do not tell anyone. You and your family are free from bondage now. I give you ten thousand dirhams as a reward."

Hazrat Khadijah was by then convinced that she had finally found a man who was worthy of her, so much so that when they sat to discuss all the business transactions in which he became involved on her behalf, the wealthy and beautiful Princess of Quraysh was thinking more about him than about those transactions.

Prophet Muhammad (May God bless and cherish him) was the most handsome person among all of God's creations. He was of medium stature, inclined to slimness with a bigger head and broad shoulders, and the rest of his body perfectly proportional. His hair and beard were thick and black, not altogether straight but slightly curled. His hair reached midway between the lobes of his ears and shoulders, and his beard was of a length to match. He had a broad forehead and large and wide-set eyes with exceptionally long lashes and thick brows that were slightly arched but not joined. His eyes were said to have been black, but some accounts say they were dark brown. His nose was aquiline, and his lips were finely shaped. Although he let his beard grow, he never let the hair of his mustache protrude over his upper lip. His skin was white but tanned by the sun. There was a light on his face, a glow, the same light that had been shown by his father, but it was more, much more intense, and it was especially apparent on his forehead and in his eyes, which were remarkably luminous.

Hazrat Khadijah simply fell in love with the Holy Prophet (May God bless and cherish him) just as the daughter of the Prophet Shuayb had fallen in love with Prophet Moses, as told in the Noble Quran, Sura al-Qasas (28:25-26).

Hazrat Khadijah then came to the Holy Prophet Muhammad and said, "Go and tell Hazrat Abu Talib to see me first thing in the morning." The Holy Prophet (May God bless and cherish him) left and informed Hazrat Abu Talib about Hazrat Khadijah's request. Hazrat Abu Talib got worried and said, "O my son, what does Khadijah want from me? Maybe she has some complaints and wants to bring them to my attention." The Holy Prophet (May God bless and cherish him) said, "O uncle, do not worry, Allah is the best disposer of all affairs."

The next morning, Hazrat Abu Talib, along with the Holy Prophet (May God bless and cherish him), went to Hazrat Khadijah's house. Standing behind the curtain, she greeted and told Hazrat Abu Talib, "Go to my uncle Umro b. Nawfal and ask my hand in marriage for your nephew Muhammad." Hazrat Abu Talib was surprised to hear this and said, "O Khadijah, are you mocking, you will not even marry your maid to Muhammad." Hazrat Khadijah replied, "By the will of Allah, it may be so; go to my uncle and do as I tell you."

Hazrat Abu Talib, along with ten respectable personalities of Quraysh went to the house of Umro b. Nawfal. They greeted him and paid their respects. Umro b. Nawfal welcomed them and said, "O Muhammad, I always loved you, and today, my love for you has increased beyond measure. Whatever you ask me today, I shall oblige you." He treated the entire party with respect. Hazrat Abu Talib said, "I have come to show my respect and ask the hand of your niece Hazrat Khadijah in marriage for my nephew Muhammad (May God bless and cherish him), who is here today with us."

Umro b. Nawfal said, "O chiefs of Quraysh, be witness that I give Hazrat Khadijah bint Khuwyalid in matrimony to Muhammad bin Abdullah bin Abdul Muttalib for a specific amount of dowry." After that, Hazrat Abu Talib got up and recited the sermon of marriage as follows,

"All praise is due to Allah Who has made us the progeny of Ibrahim (Abraham), the seed of Isma'el (Ishmael), the descendants of Ma'ad, the substance of Mudar, and Who made us the custodians of His House and the servants of its sacred precincts, making for us a House sought for pilgrimage and a shrine of security, Who also gave us authority over the people. This nephew of mine, Muhammad, cannot be compared with any other man: If you compare his wealth with that of others, you will not find him a man of wealth, for wealth is a vanishing shadow and a fickle thing. Muhammad is a man whose lineage you all know, and he has sought Khadijah, daughter of Khuwaylid, for marriage, offering her such-and-such of the dower of my own wealth."

Hazrat Muhammad (May God bless and cherish him) stayed that night at Hazrat Khadijah's house, and both were very pleased with their bond. When Hazrat Abu Talib returned home, he was content as if a heavy burden had come off his shoulders. He slaughtered camels and gave a feast on this happy occasion.

After the marriage, the Holy Prophet (May God bless and cherish him) left his uncle's house and went to live with his bride. Hazrat Khadijah (Mother of the faithful) proved to be not only a faithful wife but a friend and a strong supporter to her husband. She believed in him and shared his faith and ideals to a remarkable degree. Their marriage was blessed with happiness. She gave birth to his six children, two sons and four daughters. Their eldest son was Al-Qasim, and the Holy Prophet (May God bless and cherish him) came to be known as Abu Qasim (Father of Qasim), but he died in infancy. Their other children were four daughters, Zaynab, Ruqayyah, Umm Kulthum and Fatima. They had another son, Abdullah, who was called Tahir and Taiyab, but he also passed away.

As mentioned earlier, Hazrat Khadijah was married twice before and had lost both husbands to the ravaging wars with which Arabia was afflicted. Her first husband was Abu Halah (Father of Halah), namely Hind Ibn Zara'h, who belonged to Banu Adiyy, and the second was Ateeq Ibn Aai'th. Both men belonged to Banu Makhzoom. From her first husband, she gave birth to a son who was named after his father, Hind, who came to be one of the greatest Companions of the Holy Prophet (May God bless and cherish him). He participated in the Battles of Badr and Uhud, and he is also famous for describing the Prophet's physique. He was martyred during the Battle of Camel (Jamal), in which he fought on the side of Hazrat Ali Ibn Talib.

Baraka was a faithful slave of the Holy Prophet (May God bless and cherish him), whom he had inherited from his mother, but he set her free on the day of his marriage to Hazrat Khadijah. They married Baraka to a man from Yathrib. She had a son from the marriage, after whom she came to be known as Umm Ayman, the mother of Ayman. Hazrat Khadijah owned many slaves herself. Her nephew Hakim, the son of her brother Hizam, had bought a few young slaves at the great fair of Ukaz. Hakim presented his slaves to Hazrat Khadijah to choose one for herself. She picked a young slave named Zayd and then gifted him to the Holy Prophet Hazrat Muhammad (May God bless and cherish him). Zayd belonged to a noble family. His father was of the great northern tribe of Kalb, whose territory lay between the plains of Syria and Iraq; his mother belonged to the famous neighboring tribe of Tayy, one of whose chieftains at that time was Hatim Tayy, famous throughout Arabia for his chivalry and fabulous generosity. Zayd's mother had taken him to visit her family, and the village they were staying in was raided by some horsemen of Bani Qayn, who carried the boy off and sold him into slavery.

His father Harith searched for him everywhere but in vain, nor had Zayd seen any travelers from Kalb who could inform his parents about his situation. After a couple of months, pilgrims came from all over Arabia to visit Kaaba, and during that time, he saw some men and women of his tribe in the streets of Makkah. If he had seen them the previous year, his excitement would have been very different. He had prayed for such an occasion, yet now that it had come, it placed him in a quandary. He was wondering what message he should send his folks. He composed a poem that expressed his mind. He then told the pilgrims who he was and said, "Speak unto my family these verses, for I know well that they have sorrowed for me." The pilgrims returned home and gave the tidings to Zayd's parents. His father, Harith, along with his brother Ka'b at once set off for Makkah. They went straight to Hazrat Muhammad (May God bless and cherish him) and requested him to allow them to ransom Zayd, far as high a price as he might ask. The Holy Prophet said, "Let him choose, and if he chooses you, he is yours without ransom, and if he chooses me, I am not the man to set any other above him who chooses me." Then he sent for Zayd and asked him if he knew the two men. "This is my father, and this is mine uncle," said Zayd. "You know me and my companionship; therefore, you are free to choose between me and them," said the Holy Prophet (May God bless and cherish him). But Zayd had already made his choice and at once said, "I would not choose anyone in preference to thee; you are like my father and mother."

"Out upon thee, O Zayd!" Shouted the men of Kalb. "Would you choose slavery above freedom and above thy father, uncle, and family?" "It is so," said Zayd, "For I have seen from this man such things that I could never choose another above him." The Holy Prophet Hazrat Muhammad (May God bless and cherish him) bade them. He then took Zayd with him to Kaaba, and standing in the Hijr, he announced in a loud voice to the crowd, "Bear witness that Zayd is my son, I am his heir, and he is mine."

The father and uncle of Zayd returned home without achieving their purpose. However, they told their tribe of the deep mutual love that ended up in the adoption of their son by the Holy Prophet (May God bless and cherish him), which meant that Zayd was now free and established in honor. This was considered a high standing amongst the people of the Sanctuary. They were thus reconciled and without bitterness. From that day on, Zayd was known as Zayd Ibn Muhammad in Makkah.

The Holy Prophet's (May God bless and cherish him) youngest aunt was Safiyyah, who was married to Hazrat Khadijah's brother. She frequently visited their home and would bring her little son Zubayr, whom she had named after her elder brother. Zubayr was thus well acquainted with his cousins, the daughters of the Holy Prophet (May God bless and cherish him), from his earliest years. Safiyyah had a faithful servant, Salma, who had delivered all Hazrat Khadijah's children and was considered part of the family.

As days went by, the Holy Prophet's (May God bless and cherish him) foster mother, Hazrat Halimah, visited them occasionally, and Hazrat Khadijah was always generous and kind to her. One of those visits was a time of severe drought throughout Arabia that had depleted Hazrat Halimah's flocks. Hazrat Khadijah, therefore, made her a gift of forty sheep and a camel with howdah. This same drought resulted in a widespread famine in Hijaz.

Hazrat Abu Talib had a large family and more children than he could easily support, and the famine heavily weighed upon him. The Holy Prophet was aware of his financial situation and felt that something should be done about it. His wealthiest uncle was Abu Lahab, but he was somewhat remote from the rest of the family.

Hazrat Muhammad (May God bless and cherish him) preferred to ask for help from Abbas, who was able to afford it. He was a successful merchant who was close to him as well because they had been brought up together. Abbas's wife, Umm al-Fadl, was very kind-hearted, and she loved the Holy Prophet (May God bless and cherish him) dearly and always made him welcome at their home. So, he went to them and suggested that each of their two households should take custody of one of Hazrat Abu Talib's sons until his circumstances improved. They readily agreed, and the two of them went to Hazrat Abu Talib. He said," Do as you will, but leave me, Aqil and Talib." Jafar was now fifteen years old and was no longer the youngest of the family. His mother, Fatima, had given birth to another son to Hazrat Abu Talib, some ten years younger, and they had named him Ali. Abbas agreed to take charge of Jafar, whereas Hazrat Muhammad (May God bless and cherish him) agreed to do the same for Ali. It was about this time that Hazrat Khadijah had borne her last child, a son named Abdullah, but the babe died at an earlier age than Qasim. Ali was about the same age as Ruqayyah and Umm Kulthum, somewhat younger than Zaynab and somewhat older than Fatima. These five, together with Zayd, formed the immediate family of the Holy Prophet (May God bless and cherish him) and Hazrat Khadijah.

CHAPTER 6
THE LAST MESSENGER

From his early childhood, the Holy Prophet (May God bless and cherish him) was exceptionally intelligent and chaste and was highly regarded for his honesty, valor, justice, piety, patience, modesty, loyalty, and hospitality. Hazrat Abu Talib described his beloved nephew in the following words,

"He is fair and handsome. From his visage, mercy falls like rain. He is a shelter for orphans and a protector of widows."

The powerful attraction that centered on Al-Amin (as he was so often called) went far beyond his own family, and Hazrat Khadijah was with him at the center, loved and honored by all who came within the wide circle of their radiances. Hazrat Khadijah was very close to her sister Halah, whose son Abu l-As was a handsome youth, and she loved this nephew a lot. When Halah asked Hazrat Khadijah to find a wife for him, she consulted the Holy Prophet (May God bless and cherish him), and in due time Zaynab was married to him.

The hopes of the two tribes, Hashim and Muttalib, were set upon Hazrat Muhammad (May God bless and cherish him) for the recovery of their waning influence. Without doubt, the Holy Prophet (May God bless and cherish him) was considered by the chiefs of Quraysh as one of the most capable men of the generation who would succeed them and who would have after them the task of restoring the honor and the power of the tribe throughout Arabia. The praise of the Holy Prophet was continuously upon the men's lips; it was perhaps because of this that Abu Lahab came to his nephew with the proposal that Ruqayyah and Umm Kulthum should be betrothed to his sons Utbah and Utaybah. Hazrat Muhammad (May God bless and cherish him) agreed to the proposal, and the weddings took place.

The Holy Prophet had an inherent hatred for idolatry and polytheism of his time, and in his future role, he would outlaw all aspects of paganism. Although he was an integral part of his society, the Holy Prophet never attended any festivals and fairs that revolved around idol worship and drinking. He was also careful not to eat the flesh of any animals slaughtered in the name of someone other than Allah and avoided touching or even coming close to idols. He especially detested hearing oaths sworn upon the two famous idols, Lat and Uzza.

REBUILDING OF KAABA

When the Holy Prophet was thirty-five years old, the Quraysh decided to rebuild the Kaaba. The entire structure of the Kaaba was a low building made of white stones, approximately no more than nine arm's length. There had been no roof since the days of Hazrat Ismail, which meant that even when the door was locked, thieves could access it easily. About that time, there had been a theft of some of its treasure which was stowed in a vault that had been dug inside the Kaaba. It was built so long ago and had taken the brunt of the wearing forces of nature. As a result, its walls were cracked and weak. There had been a great flood in Makkah five years before the Prophethood of Hazrat Muhammad (May God bless and cherish him) that had almost demolished the Kaaba. Therefore, Quraysh was obliged to rebuild it to safeguard its holiness and position. For construction, the chiefs of the Quraysh decided to only use licit money in rebuilding of Kaaba. So, all the money derived from illicit means, such as usury or unjust resources, was excluded. They already had obtained wood; a Greek merchant ship had driven ashore and wrecked beyond repair at Jeddah, so they had secured its timber for the roof.

The Quraysh were so fearful of Kaaba that they hesitated to lay hands on it. Their plan was to raze its walls altogether, which were built of loose stones, and to rebuild it from the beginning. At the same time, they were afraid of incurring the guilt of sacrilege. Their hesitation was greatly increased by the appearance of a large snake that would come out every day from a hole and rest in the sun against the wall of Kaaba. If someone came close, it would open its jaw, hiss, and attack, and terrify all. Then, one day, while it was resting, God sent an eagle, which seized it in its claws and flew away with it.

This was a sign of God's approval, and Quraysh was happy. Each tribe was responsible for building a part of the Kaaba. They collected stones to start the work. There happened to be a Roman mason called Baqum, who was responsible for the building. The first man to lift a stone from one of the walls was Abu Wahab, the brother of Hazrat Muhammad's (May God bless and cherish him) grandmother. As soon as he lifted the stone, it leaped from his hand and returned to its place. Seeing this, everyone withdrew from the Kaaba, scared to proceed with the construction. Then the chief of Makhzum, Walid, son of Mughirah, said, "I will begin the razing for you." He proceeded towards Kaaba and said, "O God, fear not, we intend naught but good." Thereupon, he knocked down part of the wall between the Black Stone and the Yemenite corner, that is, the south-easterly wall. The rest of the people held back. They said, "Let's wait and see. If he is smitten, we will raze no more of it, but restore it even as it was; but if he is not smitten, then is God pleased with our work, and we will continue our work." That night passed without any harm to Walid, and he started working the next morning. Others joined him and razed all the walls down as far as the foundation of Abraham. They came upon large greenish stones like the humps of a camel. One of the men put a crowbar between two stones to lever one of them out, and with the first movement of the stone, a sudden quaking shudder ran through the entire Makkah, and they took it as a sign that they must leave the foundation undisturbed.

While they were busy rebuilding the Kaaba, they found a piece of writing in Syriac inside the corner of the Black Stone. They kept it and did not know what it was until one of the Jews read it to them. It said,

"I am God, the Lord of Kaaba. I created her the day I created the heavens and the earth, the day I formed the sun and the moon, and I placed around her seven inviolable angels. She should stand so long as her two hills stand, blessed for her people with milk and water."

Similarly, beneath the station of Ibrahim (Maqam Ibrahim) near the door of Kaaba, which bears his footprint, another piece of writing was found, a small rock. It read,

"Kaaba is the Holy House of God. Her sustenance comes from three directions. Let not her people be the first to profane her."

Quraysh brought more stones to increase the height of the building. They worked, tribe by tribe until the walls of the Kaaba were high enough for the Black

Stone to be built once more into its place. Each of the clans wanted the honor of lifting it into its place. This led to a violent disagreement among them. Swords were on the point of being drawn, and great bloodshed seemed imminent. The deadlock lasted for four to five days, and tensions were on the increase. Luckily, the oldest among the chiefs, Abu Umaiyah Bin Mughirah al-Makhzumi, suggested, "O men of Quraysh, take an arbiter between you about your dispute, the first person who shall enter in through the gate of this Mosque (Masjid)." All of them agreed to follow the old man's council. It was thus Allah's will that the Messenger of Allah, who had just returned to Makkah after an absence, should be the first to enter the Masjid. The sight of him produced an immediate and spontaneous recognition that he was the right person for this task, and his arrival was greeted with satisfaction. "It is Al-Amin, it is Muhammad, and we accept his judgment," they said. When they explained the matter to him, he asked for a mantle, and when they brought it, he spread it on the ground, and taking up the Black Stone, he laid it in the middle of the mantle. He then asked the representatives of the different tribes among them to lift the stone together. When it reached its proper place, the Holy Prophet (May God bless and cherish him) laid it in its position with his own hands. In this way, a very tense situation and danger were averted by the wisdom of the Holy Prophet (May God bless and cherish him).

The Quraysh ran out of the licit money they collected, so they had to eliminate an area covering six arm's length on the northern side of Kaaba, which is called Al-Hijr or Al-Hateem. The Black Stone rests about one and a half meters above the ground, with the Kaaba door about one-half meter above the Black Stone. The Quraysh did not lower the door because they wanted to let in only the people they desired. They also doubled the height of the walls from nine to eighteen cubits, added a roof, and six columns in two rows inside Kaaba to support it. The building of Kaaba assumed a square shape when it was completed.

PROPHETHOOD

The Holy Prophet Hazrat Muhammad (May God bless and cherish him) had a strong aversion to the superstitious practices of Makkan society and preferred to spend his time in seclusion away from the noisy festivals and crowded markets. At the same time, he felt the need to guide and save his people from all the repulsive and evil practices of Jahiliyyah. Before the start of his divine mission, he began to experience powerful inward signs in addition to those of which he had already been conscious. When questioned about these premonitions, he described them as "True visions" that came to him in his sleep, and he described them as "Like the breaking of the light at dawn." These visions resulted in his inclination towards solitude, and he started going for spiritual retreats to a cave in Mount Hira on the outskirts of Makkah. Solitude and retreat had been a traditional practice amongst the descendants of Hazrat Ismael, and in each generation, there had been people who would withdraw to a solitary place from time to time to meditate and worship God. In accordance with the sacred tradition, the Holy Prophet (May God bless and cherish him) began to seek refuge in the Cave of Hira. Here, he would spend long periods alone and worship the One God —Allah. He would take provisions with him and dedicate certain nights to doing so. Then he would return to his family; sometimes, on his return, he would take more provisions to spend longer periods of time. Following in the footsteps of his forefathers Hazrat Ibrahim and Hazrat Ismael, every year for three consecutive years, he spent the entire month of Ramadan in the Cave of Hira. After returning to Makkah, he would circumambulate the Kaaba and then go home. During this time, it often happened that after he had left the town and was approaching the Cave of Hira, he would hear clear voices, "Peace be upon thee, O Messenger of Allah." When he looked for the speaker, no one could be seen, as if the words had come from a tree or a stone. The trees and the stones would greet him with clear words.

Abu Saeed Khargushi narrated that when the Holy Prophet Hazrat Muhammad (May God bless and cherish him) reached the age of forty, God sent him in compassion to mankind as a Messenger to all men. One day, he came out of his home and went to a place called Jiyad al-Asfar on the outskirts of Makkah. Gabriel, the archangel of revelation, called him "O Muhammad." The Holy Prophet looked around but did not see the caller. Such was the awe of the caller that the Holy Prophet Hazrat Muhammad (May God bless and cherish him) fainted. Some passersby helped and brought him to the house of Hazrat Khadijah, where he told her sarcastically that she had married a madman. Hazrat Khadijah jumped from her seat and took the Holy Prophet (May God bless and cherish him) in her embrace and laid his head on her lap. She kissed between his eyes and said, "I have married a prophet of God." When Hazrat Muhammad (May God bless and cherish him) returned to his usual self, she asked, "My parents be your sacrifice; what has befallen you? What did you see that made you upset?" The Holy Prophet said, "I heard a voice that called my name, and I was awestruck." Hazrat Khadijah was pleased to hear that and said, "Go back to the same place tomorrow, if the caller was an angel, he will come back, but if it was a demon, it won't return." The next day, the Holy Prophet (May God bless and cherish him) returned to the same place. Once again, the Archangel Gabriel called his name 'Muhammad' but did not appear before him. The Holy Prophet fainted one more time. A group of men escorted him to the house of Hazrat Khadijah. The Quraysh were happy about it and said Khadijah's husband was a madman. They told Hazrat Khadijah the same, but she insisted that she had married a prophet of Allah. When the Holy Prophet (May God bless and cherish him) was calm and recollected, Hazrat Khadijah asked, "What did you notice today?" The Holy Prophet narrated what he had experienced. Hazrat Khadijah was satisfied and said, "Go back to the same place tomorrow." The Holy Prophet (May God bless and cherish him) went to the same spot the next day. This time, the Archangel Gabriel appeared to him in the best form and said,

"O Muhammad, thou art the Messenger of Allah, and I am Gabriel. Allah sends His peace and blessings upon you and says, "You are My Messenger to all mankind and Jinn and invite them to declare 'La Ilaha Illalah' (There is no deity except Allah)." Gabriel then asked him, "Do you know me." "No," replied the Holy Prophet (May God bless and cherish him). The Holy Prophet (May God bless and cherish him) raised his eyes toward the sky, and there was his visitant, clearly an angel, filling the whole horizon. The angel addressed him again, "O Muhammad, thou art the Messenger of Allah, and I am Gabriel. You are God's last Messenger, and no messenger will come after you." The Holy Prophet (May God bless and cherish him) continued gazing at the angel. He then turned away from him, but whichever way he looked, the angel was always there across the horizon, whether it was to the north, to the south, to the east, or to the west. After that, Gabriel stamped his foot on the ground, and a spring of water gushed forth. He told Hazrat Muhammad (May God bless and cherish him) to make ablution with that water and showed him how to make wudu. Gabriel got up and performed Salat (Prayer) and taught the Holy Prophet (May God bless and cherish him) how to pray. Gabriel led the Salat (Prayer), and the Holy Prophet followed him. Gabriel then disappeared, and Hazrat Muhammad (May God bless and cherish him) returned home. On his way, all the trees and all the stones he passed by greeted him with the words, "Peace be upon you, O Messenjer of Allah."

The Holy Prophet Hazrat Muhammad (May God bless and cherish him) informed Hazrat Khadijah that the Lord of the worlds had honored him with prophethood and a mission to call men and women to the unity of God. Hazrat

Khadijah was extremely happy and ecstatic and passed out. The Holy Prophet laid her down and sprinkled water on her face. When she recovered her senses, she declared her Shahadah, "There is no deity worthy of worship except Allah, and Muhammad is His Messenger."

From that day on, the Holy Prophet (May God bless and cherish him) started praying with Hazrat Khadijah at home. One day, when they were praying, Hazrat Ali, while he was still a young lad, came and asked, "O Muhammad, what religion is this that you preach and practice?" The Holy Prophet (May God bless and cherish him) replied, "This is the religion of God that He has chosen for His messengers and mankind, and He will not accept any other religion except this (Islam)." Hazrat Ali spontaneously said, "I testify that there is none worthy of worship except Allah, and I testify that Muhammad is the Messenger of Allah." After that, Hazrat Abu Talib came and saw the three of them praying together. He said, "O Muhammad, which religion is this?" The Holy Prophet (May God bless and cherish him) replied, "This is the religion of God, Who chose it and will not accept any other religion save this one; join us; otherwise, keep our affair secret." Hazrat Abu Talib turned towards Hazrat Ali and said, "Did you hear what Muhammad is saying." Hazrat Ali replied, "O father, Muhammad is speaking the truth, and I testify that God is One and Muhammad is His Messenger." Hazrat Abu Talib said with conviction, "Stay firm in your faith. None will be able to harm you." In this way, Allah revealed His religion, and Islam took root and became strong.

It is narrated that the Holy Prophet (May God bless and cherish him) went to the mountain of Thabir to meditate and worship God. When he decided to ascend the mountain, it spoke to him and said, "Do not climb this mountain, it is inhabited by scorpions and snakes." Therefore, he went to the mountain of Hira, and it said, "There are neither scorpions nor snakes on this mountain." So, he climbed the mountain of Hira, entered a cave, and went into seclusion to meditate and worship God. Whenever he went into the cave and would return home, every stone and tree on his path would greet him with these words, "Peace be upon thee, O Messenger of God."

Ibn Ishaq wrote in his Sira by the authority of Wahab b. Kaissan that Ubayd b. Qataba said to him, "The Messenger of Allah would pray in seclusion in the Cave of Hira in the month of Ramadan as was the custom of Quraysh in the old days. He would give food to the poor that came to him. When he completed the month, on his return, he would go to Kaaba first and walk around it seven times; then, he would go back to his house until the next year. Allah thus desired to bestow grace upon him and endowed him with Prophethood. It was one night towards the end of Ramadan in his fortieth year when he was alone in the cave that God honored him with his mission and showed mercy on His servants. Thereby, Gabriel brought him the command of God. The Messenger of Allah said,

"Gabriel came to me in the form of a man while I was asleep with a parchment of brocade whereon was some writing and said, "Read!" I said, "What should I read?" I am not a reader." The angel took me and pressed me in his embrace until he had reached the limit of my endurance. Then he released me and said, "Read." I said, "I am not a reader," and again he took me and overwhelmed me in his embrace, and again, when he reached the limit of my endurance, he released me and said, "Read," and again I said, "I am not a reader," he pressed me the third time so that I thought it was death and said, "Read," I said, "What then I shall read?" He said,

"Read in the name of thy Lord who created!

Who created man from a clot of blood.

Read, and thy Lord is the most Bountiful,

He who taught by the Pen,

Taught man what he knew not."

(Quran 96:1-5)

So, I read it, and he departed from me. It was as though the words were written on my heart."

The Holy Prophet Hazrat Muhammad (May God bless and cherish him) at that time feared that he might have become possessed or a Jinn-inspired poet. So, he fled from the cave, and when he was halfway down the slope of the mountain, he heard a voice above him saying, "O Muhammad, thou art the Messenger of God, and I am Gabriel." The Holy Prophet (May God bless and cherish him) stood still, moving neither forward nor backward while gazing at the angel. Then he turned his face away from him, but towards whatever region of the sky he looked, he saw him as before. The Holy Prophet (May God bless and cherish him) continued standing there for a while, neither moving forward nor turning back.

In the meantime, Hazrat Khadijah sent her men in search of him. They searched the mountains above Makkah and returned to her while the Holy Prophet (May God bless and cherish him) was still standing at the same place. Gabriel then left, and the Holy Prophet returned home. The Holy Prophet (May God bless and cherish him) came to Hazrat Khadijah, sat by her side, and drew close to her. "Cover me! Cover me!" he said, and his heart was still pounding. She was alarmed but did not ask any questions. She quickly brought a cloak and covered him. When the intensity of the awe decreased, Hazrat Khadijah said, "O Abul-Qasim, where thou have been? By God, I sent my messengers in search of thee, and they looked for you in the mountains of Makkah and returned to me." The Holy Prophet said, "Woe is to me, a poet or man possessed?" She said, "O Abul-Qasim, I take refuge in God from that. God would not treat you thus since He knows your truthfulness, your great trustworthiness, your fine character, and your kindness. This cannot be." "Tell me what you saw?" She asked. The Holy Prophet (May God bless and cherish him) told her what he had seen and experienced. She said with conviction, "Rejoice, O son of my uncle, and be at peace, verily by Him in whose hand is Khadijah's soul, I hope that you will be the prophet of this people." Then she got up, collected herself and went straight to her cousin Waraqa b. Nawfal b. Asad b. Abdul Uzza b. Qusayy, who had converted to Christianity, had read the Scriptures, and acquired the knowledge of the Torah and the Gospel. When Hazrat Khadijah related to him what the Holy Prophet (May God bless and cherish him) had told her of what he had seen and heard. Waraqa cried, "Holy! Holy! Verily by Him in whose hand is Waraqa's soul, if what you said is truth, O Khadijah, there has come unto him the greatest Namus (Gabriel) who came to Moses (Pbuh) and behold, he is the prophet of this people."

After completing his period of seclusion, the Holy Prophet (May God bless and cherish him) returned to Makkah, while circumambulating around the Kaaba, he met Waraqa, who said to him, "O son of my brother, tell me what thou have seen and heard." The Holy Prophet (May God bless and cherish him) told him and Waraqa b. Nawfal said, "Surely, by Him in whose hand is my soul, thou art the prophet of this people. There has come unto thee the greatest Namus, who came unto Moses." Then he added, "Thou wilt be called a liar and ill-treated, and they will cast thee out and make war upon thee, and if I live to see that day, God knoweth I will help His cause." Then he leaned toward him and kissed his forehead, and the Holy Prophet (May God bless and cherish him) returned home.

It is narrated by Ismail b. Abu Hakim, on the authority of Hazrat Khadijah, said to the Holy Prophet (May God bless and cherish him), "O son of my uncle, can you inform me about your visitor (angel) when he comes to you?' the Holy Prophet (May God bless and cherish him) replied that he could, and she asked him to inform her when he came. So, when Gabriel came to him, the Holy Prophet (May God bless and cherish him) said to Hazrat Khadijah, "This is Gabriel who has just come to me." "Get up, O son of my uncle and sit on my left thigh," she said. The Holy Prophet did so, and she asked, "Can you see him?" "Yes," he replied. She said, "Come and sit on my right thigh now." He did the same, and she enquired, "Can you see him?" When he said yes, she asked him to sit on her lap. When the Holy Prophet had done that, she again asked if he could see him; when he replied "yes," she removed her veil while the Holy Prophet was sitting in her lap. Then she asked, "Can you see him now?" and the Holy Prophet (May God bless and cherish him) replied, 'No.' she said at once, "O son of my uncle, rejoice and be at peace, by God he is an angel and not a Satan."

The first revelation descended on the Holy Prophet Hazrat Muhammad (May God bless and cherish him) in the month of Ramadan on the "Night of Power." In the words of God,

"The month of Ramadan in which the Quran was brought down as a guidance to men, and proofs of guidance and a decisive criterion." (Quran 2:185.)

God says, "Verily, We have sent it down on the Night of Destiny, and what has shown you what the Night of Destiny is? The night of destiny is better than a thousand months. In it, the angels and the spirit descend by their Lord's permission with every matter. It is peace until the rise of dawn." (Quran 97:1-5)

And again, "Had you believed in God and what We sent down to our servant on the day of decision, the day on which the two parties met." (Quran 8:42). This refers to the meeting of the Messenger of Allah with the polytheists in Battle of Badr. It is narrated by Abu Jafar Muhammad b. Ali b. al-Husayn that the Messenger of Allah met the polytheists in Badr on the morning of Friday, the seventeenth of Ramadan.

The second revelation descended on the Holy Prophet (May God bless and cherish him) at the time when he returned home after worshiping in the Cave of Hira and encountered Gabriel and asked Hazrat Khadijah to cover him up. She put a cloak around him and sprinkled water on his face, and the following Sura was revealed to him:

"O you, wrapped in garments! Arise and warn. Magnify your Lord, and your clothing purify! Shun idols and false worship! And give not a thing to have more (or consider not your deeds of obedience to Allah as a favor to Him). And be patient for the sake of your Lord."

(Quran 74:1-7.)

Hazrat Muhammad (May God bless and cherish him) was appointed as a prophet with the first revelation. With the second revelation, he was made Allah's messenger and entrusted with two tasks. The first task was to 'Arise and warn.' He was commanded to preach divine unity, invite people to worship Allah alone and warn them about the consequences of their wrongdoings. His second task was to obey the commands of Allah and act as a model for others. The Holy Prophet (May God bless and cherish him) accepted his duties as a prophet and messenger with resolute obedience. He answered his Lord's call by inviting members of his household to worship Allah in keeping with His commandments. Hazrat Khadijah believed in him and accepted as true what he brought from God and helped him in his work. She was the first to believe in God and His Messenger and in the truth of his message. By her, Allah has lightened the burden of His prophet. He never met with contradiction and charges of falsehood, which grieved him, but Allah comforted him with her when he went home. She consistently strengthened him, lightened his burden, proclaimed his truth, and belittled men's opposition.

Hisham b. Urwa related to the authority of his father, Urwa b. al-Zubayr from Abdullah b. Jafar b. Abu Talib that the Holy Prophet (May God bless and cherish him) said, "I was commanded by Allah (Exalted is He) to give Khadijah the good tiding of a house (in paradise) of qasab wherein would be no clamor and no toil."

The divine revelation paused for some time so that the Holy Prophet Hazrat Muhammad (May God bless and cherish him) was distressed and grieved. Ibn Hajar said, "The pause of the revelation for some time was to relieve the Holy Prophet (May God bless and cherish him) of the awe he experienced and to make him long for the divine inspiration."

Al-Bukhari reported on the authority of Jabir bin Abdullah that he had heard the Messenger of Allah speak about the period of pause as follows, "While I was walking, I heard a voice from heaven. I looked up, and surely enough, it was the same angel who had visited me in the Cave of Hira. He was sitting on a chair between the earth and the sky. I was in awe of him and knelt on the ground. I went home and asked Hazrat Khadijah, "Cover me, cover me," and Allah revealed to me the following verse."

"O you enwrapped in garments, arise, and warn! And your Lord magnify! And your garment purifies! And keep away from idols." (Quran 74:1-5.)

After these first messages had come, there was a pause for some time until the Holy Prophet (May God bless and cherish him) began to fear that he had incurred in some way the displeasure of Allah. Then, at last, the silence was broken, and Gabriel brought him the Sura of the Morning, in which his Lord, who had honored him, swore that He had not forsaken him. God said,

"By the morning brightness, and by night when it is still, thy Lord has not forsaken thee nor hate thee, and the last shall be better for thee than the first, and thy Lord shall give unto thee, and thou shall be satisfied. Has He not found thee an orphan and sheltered thee, and found thee astray and guided thee, and found thee needy and enriched thee? So as far the orphan, oppress him not, and for the beggar repel him not, and for the beautiful grace of thy Lord proclaim it." (Quran 93:1-11.)

CHAPTER 7
QURAN

THE UNCREATED WORD OF GOD

Magnanimous and beautiful is the Quran that Gabriel brought down from the All-Merciful. It is the repose of the spirits of the friends, the healing of the hearts of the ill, and mercy to the faithful. This is why God says, "He it is who sent it down upon thy heart." Elsewhere, He says,

"Brought down by the trustworthy spirit upon thy heart." (Quran 26:193-194).

When Gabriel conveyed the pure revelation, sometimes he came in the form of a mortal man, sometimes in the form of an angel. Whenever he brought verses about permitted and forbidden and the explication of the Shariah and rulings, he would be in human form, and there was no talk of the heart. Thus, He says, "He it is who sent down upon thee the Book." (Quran 3:7). "Does it not suffice that We sent down upon thee the Book." (Quran 29:51).

Then again, whenever there was talk of love, the attributes of passion, and the intimations of friendship, he would come in the form of an angel, spiritual and subtle, and he would join with Muhammad Mustafa's (May God bless and cherish him) heart. He would convey the revelation of the Quran secretly to his secret core, and no one else was aware of him. When he returned and left behind the realm of his heart, the Holy Prophet (May God bless and cherish him) would say, "He broke away from me while I was aware of him."

It is said that when he was inundated by contemplation in his speech, the revelation would first descend to his heart, for He said to him, "Who sent it down upon thy heart." Then, it would turn away from his heart to his understanding and his hearing. Then, it would descend from the summit of companionship to the low land of service for the sake of people's share. This is the level of elect of the elect, the Holy Prophet Muhammad Mustafa (May God bless and cherish him).

The Holy Quran, according to the most fundamental doctrine of Islam, is the "Uncreated word of God," manifested in the Arabic language. Through its verses, knowledge of the One and the path leading to Him is made possible. The word of God was revealed through Archangel Gabriel to the Holy Prophet Hazrat Muhammad (May God bless and cherish him) in the cave of Hira on the mountain of light (Jabl al-Noor) and continued piece by piece during the next twenty-three years of his prophetic mission. The Holy Quran is the last of divine scriptures, its meaning is infinite and forever. It contains Allah's commands, judgments, and laws that pertain to all His creation. His words are the most powerful and the root cause of all that exists.

The Glorious Quran is a manifest light and guide, full of wisdom, mercy, and clear argument – and a covenant of Allah. It is full of hope, promise, and truth in every word. Its verses remind one of one's original home and, at the same time, accompany one in one's return to God, it reverberates through all cosmic levels to the divine presence. For believers, the recitation of the Quran has been throughout their lives their chief means of concentration upon God, which is the essence of every spiritual path.

The word of God is a life-renewing light. Every Sura, every Ayah, and every word contains an ocean of meaning. If you listen and pay heed, you will witness the unfolding of the truth within yourself. The light of God will make itself manifest through the recitation of His word. If we open our hearts to its possibilities, the power of these words is eternal and never diminishing.

The Quran is the healing of the hearts of the ill, Quran is the lamp of the breasts of Tawhid voicers, Quran is the light of the heart of the familiars and the balm of the burnt.

Laylat al-qadr is the night on which the archetypical divine book miraculously descended in the form of oracular verse (Ayats) in Arabic or rather the night on which Archangel Gabriel, speaking with the voice of Allah, placed the "recitation"

(Quran) in the heart of the Prophet Muhammad (peace be upon him) during one of his retreats in a cave on Mount Hira.

The great master Ibn al-Arabi (1165–1240) boldly claims the night of destiny (Laylat al-qadr) is none other than the Prophet Hazrat Muhammad (May God bless and cherish him) himself, the perfect man, cast in the image and likeness of God. The perfect man as the form of Prophet Muhammad (peace be upon him; al-surat al-Muhammadiya), whose nature is the archetypical Quran, is called a copy (nuskha) of Allah by Sufis and described as the pole (qutb) on which the spheres of existence revolve. Therefore, he embodies both the path of descent and the path of ascent. Thus, Laylat al-qadr is both the symbolic date of the last message, and also for humanity itself, the date of second birth through which humanity becomes that which it was from all eternity. This correspondence between the Quran and the Insan Kamil (perfect man) is strengthened by the fact that the descent of one and the ascension of the other came under the sign of the same number. This number is twenty-seven since the descent of the Quran is celebrated on the twenty-seventh of Ramadan and the ascent of the Prophet (peace be upon him) on the twenty-seventh of Rajab, thus symbolically forming two semicircles whose conjunction constitutes the whole circle, tantamount to the completed divine year.

The word of God is most beautiful, rhythmic, and lyrical in character, rich in meaning and content, and perfect in composition. Apart from its apparent outer meaning, it has seven thousand different successive layers of deeper meanings, each one superior to the preceding. At the same time, it applies to the past, relates to the present, and is a road map for the future. With the passage of time, it unfolds its deeper mysteries. It is powerful, illuminating, comforting, healing, and reassuring to the ailing hearts of humanity. It is a manifest light and guide full of wisdom, mercy, clear argument, and a covenant of Allah. It is full of hope, promise, goodness, and truth in every word.

The recited Quran is the prototype of divine music. It is the sacred sound that reminds one of one's original home, and at the same time accompanies one in one's return to God; it reverberates through all cosmic levels to the divine presence. The melody of the Quran penetrates the listener's body and soul even before it appeals to his or her mind. The sacred sound of the Quran can cause spiritual rapture even in a person who knows no Arabic. In a mysterious way, this sacred quality is transmitted across the barriers of human language.

The greatest miracle of the Prophet Muhammad (peace be upon him) is the living word of God, the Quran. Its beauty does not reside so much in the melodious rhyming and powerful poetic utterances but the inspiration it instills in the hearts of those who love to recite it.

The Arabic language in which the Quran is rendered is a miracle in its sublime eloquence, and no human or jinn can compose anything like it. Labid, the great Arabic poet, was the last of the reputed poets of the Seven Odes (al-Muallaqat as-Sab). In recognition of his poetic excellence, all contemporary poets bowed in homage when he recited a couplet in the fair of Ukaz, and according to the prevalent Arab tradition, his ode was duly honored by being hung on the Kaaba. Later, Labid embraced Islam and stopped composing poetry. People were naturally surprised, for he was their most distinguished poet and publicly honored by the entire body of poets. He was the master of Arabic poetry and eloquence. When asked why he had not continued composing poetry, he replied, "What! Even after the revelation of the Quran?" There was, in the opinion of this poet laureate, no use or need for his poetry after the revelation of Allah's Book since he could neither produce anything better nor match its sublime beauty. This expression of utter helplessness and surrender to the beauty and grandeur of the Quran—the symbol of the beauty and eloquence of the Arabic language—by the greatest poet of his age signified, in fact, the surrender of all Arabic poetry to the beauty and language of Quranic eloquence.

Abu Hurayra reported Allah's Messenger (May peace be upon him) as saying, "The truest word spoken by an Arab (pre-Islamic) poet is this verse of Labid:

'Verily, everything except Allah is perishable.'"

Charles Le Gai Eaton, British Muslim, and diplomat beautifully describes the Noble Quran in his book, "Islam and the destiny of man." He writes, "Even though Quran is basically an Arabic scripture, it is essential to know how meaning and language, essence and form are married in the text of the Quran. It is as though each individual word emerged from a matrix which contains, potentially a variety of meanings that are all subtly interrelated, or as though, when one string is plucked, many others vibrate in the background; and it is precisely through such interrelationship that Tawhid the 'unity' which is the basic principle of Islam – finds expression amid limitless diversity."

He further writes, "And if all the trees on the earth were pens, and the sea – with seven seas added – (were ink) yet the words of Allah could not be exhausted."

(Quran 31:27). For the Quran to contain more than a thimbleful of the message it must rely upon images, symbols and parables which open windows on to a vast landscape of meaning, but which are inevitably liable to misinterpretation. The Prophet's wives once asked him which of them would be the first to die. 'The one with the longest arm!' he said. They set about measuring each other's arms with great seriousness, and not until long afterwards did they understand that he meant the one who extended her arm further in acts of charity. There have always been Muslims who, like the Prophet's wives, have taken figures of speech literally and others who have maintained that the inner meaning of the text will be revealed to us only on the Last Day, when the secrets of hearts are exposed together with the secrets of the Book; others, again, have regarded the literal meaning as a veil covering the majesty of the content and protecting it from profane eyes. The disputes which have arisen on this subject lead nowhere and are therefore of no consequence. Each man must follow his way according to his nature.

But in whatever sense it may be understood—superficially or in depth—a scripture such as the Quran provides a rope of salvation for the people of every kind, the stupid as well as the intelligent, and limited interpretations do not diminish its efficacy, provided they satisfy the needs of particular souls. No book of human authorship can be 'for everyone', but this is precisely the function of a revealed scripture, and for this reason it cannot be read in the way that works of human origin are read. The sun and the moon are for everyone – the rain too – but their action in relation to each individual is different and ultimately, to some they bring life and to some death. It could be said that the Quran is 'like' these natural phenomena, but it would be more exact to say that they are 'like' the Quran (they have one and the same 'author') and are, as it were, illustrations inserted between the pages of the Book.

It is an article of faith in Islam that the Quran is 'inimitable': try as he may, no man can write a paragraph that is comparable with a verse of the revealed Book. This has little to do with the literary merit of the text; in fact, a perfect work of literature could never be 'sacred' precisely on account of the adequacy of its language to its content. No conjunction of words, however excellent, could ever be adequate to a revealed content. It is the adequacy of the words – their transforming and saving power – that is inimitable, since no human being can provide others with a rope of salvation made from strands of his own person and his own thoughts. The Quran, set on a shelf with other books, has a function entirely different to theirs and exists in a different dimension. It moves an illiterate shepherd to tears when recited to him, and it has shaped the lives of millions of simple people over the course of almost fourteen centuries; it has nourished some of the most powerful intellects known to human record; it has stopped sophisticates in their tracks and made saints of them, and it has been the source of the most subtle philosophy and of an art which expresses its deepest meaning in visual terms; it has brought the wandering tribes of mankind together in communities and civilizations upon which its imprint is apparent even to the most casual observer. The Muslim, regardless of race and national identity, is unlike anyone else because he has undergone the impact of the Quran and has been formed by it.

Other books are passive, the reader taking the initiative, but revelation is an act, a command from on high – comparable to a lightening flash, which obeys no man's whim. As such, it acts upon those who are responsive to it, reminding them of their true function as vicegerents of God on earth, restoring to them the use of faculties which have become atrophied – like unused muscles – and showing them, not least by the example of the Prophet, what they are meant to be. To say this is to say that revelation, within the limits of what is possible in our fallen condition, restores to us the condition of fitrah. It gives back to the intelligence its lost capacity to perceive and to comprehend supernatural truths, it gives back to the will its lost capacity to command the warring factions in the soul, and it gives back to sentiment its lost capacity to love God and to love everything that reminds us of Him."

The Quran possesses a mysterious presence that might be called magical. This presence is untranslatable and can only be experienced in the language of revelation. It is felt by the listener and results in peace and protection. Divine lovers find the same protection by remembering God's name, Allah, in their hearts through constant dhikr. As the hadith says, "He who protects the Name of God in his heart, God protects him in this world."

The whole Quran is dhikr Allah, remembrance of God, and a commentary upon the truth of unity (Tawhid). The Quran is a reminder of God's truth and presence, and all its doctrine can be summed up in "La Ilaha Illalllah" ("There is no god but God"). The Quran is an in-depth explanation of the oneness of divine principle and, therefore, dhikr Allah. The Quran is the grand theophany of Islam, and to recite it is to invoke and remember the name of Allah. Hence, "La Ilaha illallah" is the greatest dhikr in Sufism, called "Afzal- ul-Azkar."

110

The formula of faith Shahadah, "La Ilaha Illallah," is revealed in the Quran (37:35, 47:19) as the supreme statement of divine unity and transcendence. It assigns all positive qualities to Allah. In the context of Shahadah, God is the only reality that exists. This means that there is nothing absolute except God, the Absolute, and that there is no reality outside of God, the Real. This affirmation of faith declares the complete transcendence of the Supreme Being; it also implies that all reality as such is dependent upon an underlying Reality—the Reality of Allah.

The Quran is both the source of shariah and tariqah. Islamic spirituality goes back to the Prophet (peace be upon him), who is the source of all spiritual virtues to be found in a believer. The soul of the Prophet Hazrat Muhammad (peace be upon him) was itself illuminated by divine light as revealed in the Quran; in other words, the Quranic revelation itself is the origin of Sufism.

The Quran consists of 6,200 verses (Ayats) grouped into 114 chapters or suras. Each sura is of different length—varying from as little as 3 verses to as many as 268 verses. Each verse is called an Ayah, which means miracle. Quran literally means recitation and is called the Book (Al-Kitab). It has many names, such as Al-Furqan (The Criterion) and Al-Huda (The Guide). It is also called Al-Quran-al-Majid (The Glorious Quran; 50:1 and 88:4) and Al-Quran-al-Karim (The Noble Quran; 56:7). The reality of the Quran existed with Allah on the level of reality beyond time in "the Guarded Tablet" (Al-Lawh al-Mahfuz) and was sent down through the archangel (85:22) to the soul of Prophet Hazrat Muhammad (May God bless and cherish him).

The Quran also reveals the "Most Beautiful" divine names and qualities that are means of not only knowing God but also connecting to Him. They play a central role in Islamic metaphysics. The Quran itself commands the believers to call upon Him through the names (7:180). His names, qualities, attributes, and acts are displayed in the cosmos as God's self-knowledge through self-manifestation and self-determination. Allah has Himself revealed His names in the scripture; therefore, He is mysteriously present in His names that also reflect His love and mercy, as well as His justice and judgment.

The Quran not only accepts and affirms the truth about the sacred books revealed prior to it but also verifies all previous scriptures: "And We have sent thee the Book full of truth, confirming the truth of whatever there still remains of earlier revelations and determining what is true therein" (5:47). For instance, the Noble Quran says,

"Sure, We have sent down Torah full of guidance and light" (5:45). The Quran further states, "We caused Jesus son of Mary to follow in the footsteps of those earlier prophets, fulfilling that which was revealed before him in Torah, and We gave him Scripture as a guide and light affirming the truth which was revealed prior to it in Torah as a guidance and reminder for the believers" (Quran 5:47).

The verses of the Quran were memorized by many of the Companions and gradually set to writing by such Companions as Hazrat Ali (May God be pleased with him), Hazrat Abu Bakr (May God be pleased with him), and Zayd Ibn Thabit. Hazrat Abu Bakr was the first to complete a written manuscript of the Quran during the lifetime of the Prophet (peace be upon him). During the time of Hazrat Usman (May God be pleased with him), the definitive text of the Quran based on the copy from the manuscript of Hazrat Abu Bakr and the confirmation of those who had heard the verses from the mouth of the Prophet (peace be upon him) was copied and sent to the four corners of the Islamic world. The Quran is truly safeguarded from all alterations as promised by Allah Himself: "Surely, it is We Ourselves who have revealed step by step this reminder, and surely it is We who shall truly guard it from all corruption" (Quran 15:9).

The Quran is an infinite source of knowledge and wisdom and is limitless and vast in meaning and guidance. It is also brief, concise, simple, and clear.

The entire Quran and all its chapters except one begin with the name of God: "In the name of Allah, the Most Compassionate, the Most Merciful" ("Bismillahi-r-Rahmani-r-Rahim"). This verse is not a simple statement of fact, nor does it merely convey information. It is like sura Al-Fatihah, a prayer, and a supplication. One cannot think of any other combination of words to match the beauty of "Bismillahi-r-Rahmani-r-Rahim," which so adequately articulates our innate human needs and emotions. When one sincerely calls upon Allah's help in these words, one should be conscious that whatever one intends to do must accord with Allah's will. When supplicating to Allah in these words, one uses two of His most important and beautiful names: ar-Rahman and ar-Rahim. An appeal to Allah's grace and mercy ensures that Allah will bless the supplicant and aid the supplicant in making his or her work flourish. The Messenger of Allah (peace be upon him) said, "Any undertaking embarked upon without pronouncing 'Bismillahi-r-Rahmani-r-Rahim' is deprived of all blessings." Therefore, it is important that, before starting any worthwhile human undertaking, one recites the eloquent and succinct words of God. Historically, this prayer formed the very earliest teachings received by human beings from Allah.

The Quran tells us that when Prophet Nuh (peace be upon him) asked the believers accompanying him to board the ark, he said, "Embark on it. In the name of Allah shall be its course and its berthing. Surely, my Sustainer is Most Gracious, the Ever Merciful" (Hud 11:41). The letter sent by Prophet Sulayman (peace be upon him) to the Queen of Sheba also began with these blessed words. When the queen read the letter, she said to her council, "A truly distinguished letter has been delivered to me. It is from Sulayman, and it reads, 'In the name of Allah. The Most Gracious, the Ever Merciful'" (An-Namal 27:29–31). This verse contains three of the asma al-husana—the most beautiful names of Allah—ar-Rahman and ar-Rahim. Allah is the supreme and all-comprehensive name of God. All Arab-speaking followers of the Abrahamic faith—both Jews and Christians—used the name Allah in reference to God. The Arabs of the pre-Quranic period used it in this very sense, in reference to the one and true Creator of human beings and the universe. Even the idolaters among them did not consider any of their so-called gods in any way rivaling or comparable to Allah. They admitted that Allah alone is the creator of the heavens, the earth, and all other things; that He alone created the sun and the moon and made them subservient to certain laws; and that He alone sends down the rain and cherishes and sustains life and creation.

The word Allah is derived from Al-Ilah, meaning "The One God," Who is unique, omnipotent, the Creator of the cosmos, and the All-Powerful. The word Allah can be found in Syriac, Aramaic, and Hebrew languages in the form of Aloho, Elaha, Allaha, or Elohim. The word Allah is reserved only for Him. It is not derived from any other name or root. God has truly said, "Do you know anyone worthy of the same name as He" (Quran 19:65).

The Blessings of Bismillah

Apart from its general blessings touching all areas of human activity, this supplication has a special significance in relation to reciting, understanding and gaining insight into the Quran. Pronouncing Bismillah reminds us that the faculty of intelligence and articulate speech is the greatest gift of Allah to human beings. It is this human faculty of comprehension and expression that qualified humanity to be the recipient of Allah's unique blessing—the Quran. The Quran explicitly states that Allah is ar-Rahman, "the Most Gracious," and out of His grace, He created humans, endowed them with the faculty of speech, and then taught them the Quran.

"The Most Gracious—ar-Rahman—He taught the Quran.

He created the human being,

And taught him clear speech." (Ar-Rahman 55:1–4)

Bismillah also reminds us of ar-Rahman which is prominently reflected in His revelation, and His grace alone holds the key to its inexhaustible treasures. It is through His mercy and grace alone that fresh avenues of knowledge will constantly open, unraveling its mysteries and wisdom. Whatever difficulties a seeker might experience on this path of knowledge, these will be resolved by His grace as it guides the seeker's steps and helps, supports, and sustains the seeker along the path. Ar-Rahman is the One Who showers His mercies and favors on the entire creation without distinction between good and bad, faithful and rebel, the beloved and the hated. He pours upon all creation infinite bounties. God says in the Quran, "My Mercy encompasses everything" (Araf 156). Rahman is the al-iradat al-khayr, divine will toward total good. Some believe that Rahman, like Allah, is a proper name of the creator and cannot be attributed to others. God Most High says, "Call upon Allah or call upon the Compassionate (ar-Rahman): by whatever name you call upon Him, to Him belong the most beautiful names" (Isra 110). Ar-Rahim is the source of infinite mercy and beneficence, Who rewards with eternal gifts those who submit to His will. God (Exalted is He) says, "He is compassionate and beneficent towards (only) to the faithful" (Ahzab 43). Ar-Rahim indicates beneficence toward those who have a choice and who use it according to Allah's will for His pleasure. A hadith proclaims, "Rahman belongs to the people of this world; Rahim belongs to those in the hereafter." That is why Sufis pray, "Ya Rahman ad-Dunya wa Rahim-al-Akhira" ("O Rahman of the world, and Rahim of the hereafter"). Rahman is mercy upon the nafs and gives us sustenance in this world. Rahim is mercy upon the heart and gives eternal salvation in the hereafter.

Allah did not, in an outpouring of grace, merely create a world and then forget all about it or leave its sustenance and provision to others. He is, in fact, continuously sustaining it, and His beneficence continuously watches over its well-being. His servants call upon Him. He listens and responds to their supplications. Furthermore, His blessings are not confined to this earthly life but also extend far beyond—to the life hereafter. Those who follow His commandments shall continue to receive his blessings even in the eternal life hereafter. Therefore, for believers, both divine attributes—ar-Rahman and ar-Rahim—are indispensable. It is related to a tradition attributed to Hazrat Ali Ibn Talib, the Prophet's cousin and the fourth Caliph of Islam, that "the whole of the Quran is contained in the Fatihah, the whole of the Fatihah in the Bismillah (In the name of God, the Compassionate, the Merciful), the whole of the Bismillah in the 'ba' (the opening letter), and the whole of the 'ba' in the diacritical point under the 'ba.'" This point can be understood to represent the first drop of ink from the divine pen (al-Qalam) with which God wrote the archetypes of all things upon the preserved tablet (al-lawh al-Mahfuz) before their descent into the realm of creation. In this sense, just as the Bismillah marks the beginning of the Quran, so too does it mark the beginning of creation.

The Opening

Al-Fatihah

The first sura of the Book (the Quran), *al-Fatihah* ("The Opening"), is considered by most scholars to be the first sura to have been revealed in Makkah. *Al-Fatihah*, which is the synopsis and mission statement of the Quran, truly reflects characteristics of divine wisdom. The primary meaning of *al-Fatihah* is "The Opening," which indicates the sura's function as "the Opening of the Book" (*Fatihat-al-Kitab*) and as the first sura to be recited in each cycle of all the ritual prayers as well. This sura also can open one's breast to faith in God.

Fatihah has been given the name of *Umm al-Kitab* ("Mother of the Book"). It is also known as the "Mother of the Quran," because, according to Sufis, the entire Quran is condensed and contained in the opening chapter. Therefore, because it serves as a foundation for the whole of the Quran, it is named "the Foundation" (*al-Asas*). Other titles are "the seven oft-repeated," "the Cure" (*al-Shifa*) because of its healing powers for the body and soul, "The Chapter of Praise" (*surat al-hamd*), and "the Chapter of Prayer" (*surat al-Salah*).

Al-Fatihah

In the name of Allah, the Most Gracious, the Ever Merciful.

Praise be to God, Lord of the worlds,

The Compassionate, the Merciful,

Master of the Day of Judgment,

Thee we worship, and from Thee we seek help.

Guide us upon the straight path,

The path of those whom Thee hast blessed, not of those.

Who incur wrath, nor of those who are astray.

Imam Jafar al-Sadiq (May God be pleased with him) said the bi of bism (In the name) alludes to His eternal subsistence (Baqa-uhu), the sin is for His names (Asma-uhu), and the mim is His sovereignty (Mulk-uhu). The faith of the believer is his recollection of His eternal subsistence, and the service of the spiritual seeker is his recollection of His names, while the extinction (Fana) of the lover from the kingdom is through the King (Allah).

Imam Jafar Al-Sadiq (May God be pleased with him) also said that the word bism has three letters, ba, sin, and mim. The ba is the gate (Bab) of Prophethood, the sin is the secret (Sirr) of Prophethood, which the prophet (May God bless and cherish him) confided to the elite of his community, and the mim is the kingdom (Mamlakah) of faith which embraces the white and black.

It is related by Imam Jafar al-Sadiq (may God be pleased with him) that he was asked about, "Bismillai l-Rahman l-Rahim (In the name of God, the Gracious, the Merciful)". He said: the ba is the brilliance (baha) of God, the sin is His resplendence (sana), and mim is the glory (majd). Allah is the God of everything, the gracious (Al-Rahman) to all His creation, the Merciful (Al-Rahim) to believers in particular.

Ibn Abbas said, "When in the name of God, the All-Merciful, the ever-Merciful descended, the winds were stilled, the oceans threw up waves, the beast gave ear, the Satan fled the heaven, and the Exalted Lord swore His oath, "His names will not be pronounced over anything without its being blessed."

Hazrat Aisha said in this vein, "When in the name of God, the All-Merciful, the Ever Merciful descended, the mountains made a noise such that their droning was heard by the folks of Makkah. They said, "Muhammad has worked sorcery on the mountains."

According to Ibn al-Arabi, the mercy of Al-Rahman is all-encompassing and indiscriminate, while that of Al-Rahim is discriminating, singling out those who believe in God and do good deeds which merit reward.

Imam Ali Ibn-e-Musa Raza (May God be pleased with him) said, "When the servant says, 'In the name of Allah,' its meaning is, "I have branded myself with the brand of my Lord." O Lord, I have your brand, and I am happy with it, but I lament at my own being. O Generous One, remove my being before me so that Your being may set all my work aright."

People may ask, 'In the texts of the Book and Sunnah, God's name are many, and all of them are great, beginningless, pure, and beautiful. What wisdom is there in beginning the tremendous Quran with these three? Of all of them, why did He choose these and not add any others?' The answer is, "He combined the meanings of those names in these three names. Their meanings are of three sorts: one sort belongs to majesty and awe, another to blessing and nurture, and the third to mercy and forgiveness. All that is majesty and awe is placed in the name 'Allah,' all that is blessing, and nurture is in the name "Al-Rahman" (All-Merciful), and all that is mercy and forgiveness is in the name "Al-Rahim" (Ever-Merciful).

"Praise belongs to God, the Lord of the worlds."

Imam Jafar al-Sadiq (May God be pleased with him) narrated concerning God's words Alhamdu lillah; praise be to God, he added, "The one who praises God through His qualities, even as He has described Himself, has truly praised Him. For praise (hamd) is a ha, a mim, and a dal. The ha is from wahdaniyah, God's oneness, the mim is for mulk, God's sovereignty; the dal is from daymumiyah, God's permanence. Whoever knows Him through His oneness, sovereignty, and permanence truly knows Him.

This is the praise of the lovingly kind God, who provides daily provisions, the one in name and mark. He is powerful, self-standing, and transcendent in essence and attributes, without beginning and end, described by the description of majesty and attributes of beauty.

"The owner of the Day of Judgment."

This alludes to the permanence of His kingship. In other words, the day of every king's empire ends and disappears, but God's kingship is permanent today and tomorrow, for it never comes to an end. Judgement here means reckoning and reward. God is saying,

"The power and caretaker of calling the servants to account am I."

Thus, no one else will become aware of the servants' defects, lest they be shamed. Even though calling to account is severe, not lifting the veil during the accounting is nothing but generosity. This is the way of God; whenever, He strikes a blow of severity, He places on it the balm of generosity.

"Thee alone we worship, and Thee alone we ask for help."

This alludes to salat (prayer), which is the core of religious and spiritual life and the basis of the inner relationship of the lover with the beloved on the mystical path. This is to adorn the soul through worship and self-purification. "Adornment" alludes to everything in the shariah that ought to be, and "purification" alludes to everything in the shariah that ought not to be. In this way, a worshiper seeks to realize the truth in his or her life, and God reveals Himself in the hearts of those who pray. This mystical experience (union) is the goal of all in this world. Worship is a believer's response to the perpetual outpouring of love by which Allah lays siege to every soul.

Thee alone we worship is sheer Tawhid, and that it is the belief that nothing other than God is worthy of worship. The worshiper knows that lord-hood is fitting for Allah and that He alone is the object of worship without peers.

"Guide us to the straight path."

This is the essence of worship and obedience. It is the supplication, asking, pleading, and imploring of the believers. It is seeking firmness of faith in Allah. It means, "O God show us your path, make us travel upon it, and make us firm in it." Showing is what the Exalted Lord says in, "He it is who shows you, His signs." (Quran 40:13).

Traveling is what He says in, "You shall surely ride stage by stage." (Quran 84:19).

Being pulled is what He says in, "We brought him near as a confidant." Quran (19:52).

"The path of those whom Thou hast blessed, not of those who incur wrath, nor of the misguided."

It has been said, "Those whom Thou has blessed with submission and the Sunnah." He tied the submission (shariah) and the Sunnah together because, if the two are not joined, the servant will not have the straightness of the religion.

Fatihah is the most important prayer in the whole of the Quran that one can offer. It is taught directly by the Creator and is the best form of adoration, glorification, and supplication. Its seven often-repeated verses form the basis of every Muslim's prayer, spoken five times daily. This sura expresses our passionate feeling of gratitude to Allah. This feeling overwhelms all believers who are willing to reflect upon His providence and His infinite compassion, mercy, and justice—manifest all around us. From this intense sense of gratitude, there springs a desire in the human being to adore and worship Allah alone and to call upon Him alone for help and guidance.

Many ahadith attribute an exalted status to the Fatihah. In one, the Prophet (May God bless and cherish him) told a man that he would teach him the greatest sura; when he asked what it was, the Prophet (peace be upon him) responded, "It is praise be to God, the Lord of the worlds, the seven oft repeated, and the Mighty Quran, (Quran 15:87) that I was given." A famous Hadith Qudsi—that is, a non-Quranic saying of God reported by the Prophet (peace be upon him)—states, "I have divided Fatihah between Myself and My servant, and My servant shall have that for which he prays. When the servant says, "Praise be to God, Lord of the worlds," God says, "My servant has praised Me." When the servant says, "The Compassionate, the Merciful," God says, "My servant has magnified Me." When the servant says, "Master of the Day of Judgement," God says, "My servant has glorified Me"—this is My portion, and to him belongs what remains."

The Fatihah thus has a threefold structure: the first three verses deal with the nature of God, the middle verse deals with the relationship between God and His servants, and the last three verses deal with various states of human beings.

The Holy Prophet Hazrat Muhammad (May God bless and cherish him) considers this sura to be of great power and importance, saying, "By Him in Whose Hand lies my soul, in neither the Torah, the Psalms, the Gospel, nor the Quran was the like of it revealed." In another hadith narrated by Mujahid, the Prophet (May God bless and cherish him) said, "Satan was frightened four times; when he was cursed by God: when he was expelled from the Garden, when Muhammad was sent (as a Messenger); and when the Fatihah was revealed." Thus "Bismillahi-r-Rahmani-r-Rahim" should be employed by all believers to consecrate all licit actions, since from a Quranic perspective all things should be performed for the sake of God and in His name. In this regard, the Prophet (May God bless and cherish him) said, "Any important matter not begun with the name of God shall be cut off."

CHAPTER 8
THE FIRST BELIEVERS

Hazrat Khadijah was the first to believe in God and His Messenger and who accepted as true what he brought from God and helped him in his prophetic mission. Hazrat Ali Ibn Talib was the first male to believe in the Messenger of Allah, to pray with him, and to believe in his divine message. Zayd b. Harith, the freedman of the Holy Prophet Hazrat Muhammad (May God bless and cherish him) was the one to accept Islam after Hazrat Ali. Then Abu Bakr b. Quhafa, whose name was Atiq converted to Islam at the invitation of the Holy Prophet (May God bless and cherish him). His father's name was Uthman b. Amir b. Amr b. Ka'b b. Sa'd b. Taym b. Murra b. Ka'b b. Luayy b. Ghalib b. Fihr.

It is narrated that the Messenger of Allah said, "I have never invited anyone to accept Islam, but he has shown signs of reluctance, suspicion, and hesitation, except Abu Bakr, and when I told him of it, he did not hold back or hesitate." Hazrat Abu Bakr was widely liked and respected due to his vast knowledge, amiable personality, and agreeable presence. When he converted to Islam, he showed his faith openly and called all whom he trusted to God and His Messenger. Those who accepted Islam at his invitation, according to Ibn Ishaq were, Uthman b. Affan, Abdul Rahman b. Auf, Sa'd b. Abu Waqas, and Talha b. Ubaydullah b. Uthman. He brought them to the Holy Prophet (May God bless and cherish him) after they responded to his invitation, and they accepted Islam and converted.

Some of the earliest conversions took place by motives that could not be ascribed to any human persuasion; rather they were divinely inspired. Hazrat Abu Bakr was famous throughout Makkah for his ability to interpret dreams. One day, he had an unexpected visit from Khalid b. Said Ibn al-As. He had a terrifying dream that upset him, but he knew that it must be significant. Therefore, while he was still remarkably distressed by that experience, he came to Hazrat Abu Bakr to tell him the meaning of it. He dreamt that he was standing at the edge of a great pit in which was a vast raging fire that seemed to have no end to it. Then his father came and tried to push him into it. As they were struggling at the brink at the same time, he felt around his waist the firm grip of two hands which held him back despite his father's pushing. When he looked around, he saw that it was Al-Amin, Hazrat Muhammad (May God bless and cherish him), the son of Hazrat Abdulah, and at that time, he woke up from his dream.

"Rejoice, this man who saved you is the Messenger of God, so follow him, and enter Islam, which should safeguard you against falling into the fire," said Hazrat Abu Bakr. Khalid went straight to the Holy Prophet (May God bless and cherish him) and having told him of his dream, he asked him what his message was, the Holy Prophet (May God bless and cherish him) instructed him, and he embraced Islam.

At about the same time, a merchant friend of Hazrat Abu Bakr from the tribe of Abdu Shams was returning home from Syria from a business trip. One night, he was awoken from a deep sleep by a screaming voice in the desert that said:

"Sleepers awake, for verily Ahmad has come forth in Makkah." This was Uthman b. Affan, and grandson through his mother of one of Hazrat Abdul Muttalib's daughters, Umm Hakim al-Bayda, and the Holy Prophet's aunt. These words deeply impacted his heart, though he did not understand what was meant by "coming forth," nor did he recognize that the meaning of Ahmad "most glorified' stood for Muhammad, "glorified." During his journey, he met Talha from the tribe of Taym, a cousin of Hazrat Abu Bakr. Talha had been to Bostra, where he had been asked by a monk if Ahmad had yet appeared amongst the people of the sanctuary (Kaaba). "Who is Ahmad?" Talha inquired. The monk replied, "The son of Abdul Muttalib's son Abdullah. This is his month in which he shall come forth, and he is the last of the prophets."

Talha told this to Uthman, who told him of his own experience. They decided to go to Hazrat Abu Bakr, who was known to be a closest friend of the Holy Prophet (May God bless and cherish him) on their return so that they could relate their story. After repeating the words of the monk and the words of the desert voice in front of the Holy Prophet (May God bless and cherish him), they took shahada and entered Islam.

Another remarkable conversion that took place was that of Abdullah Ibn Mas'ud. He himself narrated, "I was at that time a youth just grown into adulthood, and I was pasturing the flocks of Uqbah Ibn Abi Muyat, when one day the Holy Prophet (May God bless and cherish him) and Hazrat Abu Bakr passed by me. The Holy Prophet (May God bless and cherish him) asked me if I had any milk to give them to drink. I replied that the flocks were not mine but entrusted to my care, and I could not give of them to drink. The Holy Prophet (May God bless and cherish him) said, "Is there a young ewe that no ram has ever leaped?" I said I have and brought her to them. The Holy Prophet (May God bless and cherish him) put his hand to her udder and prayed, where upon the udder swelled with milk, and Hazrat Abu Bakr brought a rock that was hollowed like a cup. The Holy Prophet (May God bless and cherish him) milked her into it, and we all drank. Then he commanded the udder to dry, and it dried." After that incident Abdullah Ibn Mas'ud went to the Holy Prophet and accepted Islam.

Among the early Muslims were Az-Zubair bin Awwam Al-Asadi, a friend of Hazrat Abu Bakr, Bilal bin Rabah (The Abyssinian), Abu Ubaidah Amir bin Al-Jarrah from Bani Harith bin Fihr, Abu Salamah bin Abdul Asad, Al-Arqam bin Abdul Arqam from the tribe of Makhzum, Uthman bin Mazoun and his two brothers Qudamah and Abdullah, Ubaidah bin Al-Harith bin Al-Muttalib bin Abd Manaf, Sai'd bin Zain Al- Adawi and his wife Fatimah, daughter of Al-Khattab (the sister of Umar bin Khattab), Khabib bin Al-Aratt, and many others.

Ibn Ishaq in his Sira counted forty of them who were the first believers that belonged to various clans of the Quraysh. After that people entered the folds of Islam in hosts, men, and women so that the new faith could no longer be kept secret. The new converts took the commands addressed to the Holy Prophet (May God bless and cherish him) as applying to themselves. As to the ritual prayer, they were now careful not only to perform the ablution in preparation for it but also to make sure that their clothes were kept clean. The divine revelation now began to come more frequently. They were immediately transmitted by the Holy Prophet (May God bless and cherish him) to those who were with him, then passed from mouth to mouth, memorized, and recited as part of their worship. The Noble Quran so eloquently described the ephemeral nature of all things, of death and of the certainty of the Resurrection and the Day of Judgment and Paradise and the Hell. But above all, the Noble Quran told of the glory of God, of His oneness, His truth, wisdom, goodness, mercy, bounty, and power.

The Holy Prophet (May God bless and cherish him) was distinguished among the people of Makkah for his modesty, virtuous behavior, and graceful manners. He possessed a spotless character. He was the most obliging to his fellow Makkans, the most honest in talking, and mildest in temper. He was kindhearted, generous, and hospitable. He always impressed others by his piety, truthfulness, and keeping his promises. The Holy Prophet (May God bless and cherish him) detested idols and could never tolerate someone swearing by Al-Lat and Al-Uzza.

Hazrat Ali Ibn Abu Talib reported that Allah's guidance always protected the Holy Prophet (May God bless and cherish him) from practicing the rites of Jahiliyyah. In this regard, the Holy Prophet (May God bless and cherish him) said,

"I have never tried to do anything the people of ignorance did except for two times. Every time Allah safeguarded me from doing so, and I never did that again. Once, I told my fellow shepherd to take care of my sheep when we were in the upper part of Makkah. I wanted to go to down to Makkah and entertain myself as the young men did. I went down to the first house in Makkah, where I heard flute and tambourine. I entered and asked, "What is this?" someone said, "It is a wedding party." I sat down to listen but was soon overtaken by a deep sleep. The next day I was awakened by the heat of the sun rays. I went back to my fellow shepherd and told him about that. I did one more time the same thing, but I slept again till the sun was in the sky. After that I never did it again."

It is narrated by the authority of Ibn Abbas that once, Hazrat Abu Talib was repairing the well of Zamzam. At that time, the Holy Prophet (May God bless and cherish him) was a young child. Hazrat Abu Talib took the loincloth of his nephew and carried stones in it. As soon as he did that, the Holy Prophet (May God bless and cherish him) fell to the ground and lost consciousness. People told Hazrat Abu Talib that his son had become unconscious. When he recovered his consciousness, his uncle asked him, "What has befallen you, my son." He said a man dressed in white garments approached me and said, "Cover yourself." Ibn Abbas continued that the first command the Holy Prophet received as a prophet was, "Cover yourself." After that incident in childhood, nobody ever saw him again in such a state.

Jafar bin Sulaiman Al-Zabiy narrated that someone asked Abdul Rahman bin Jaysh, "How did the Holy Prophet (May God bless and cherish him) get rid of the devil's plot?" He replied, "When the devil wanted to harm the Holy Prophet (May God bless and cherish him), demons came down from the mountain and valley and intended to do mischief. One of the demons had a big flame in his hand and sought to hurl it towards him. The Holy Prophet was alarmed to see that. In the meantime, Gabriel came and said to the Holy Prophet (May God bless and cherish him), "Recite." "What should I recite?" Gabriel said,

تعويز رسول عليه الصلوت والسلام

آعوذ بكلما ت الله التا مات التى لا يجاوز هن بر ء ولا فا جر من شر ما خلق و ذرا ء و برا ء و من شر ما ينزل من السما ء و ما يعرج فيها و من شر ما ذراء فى الأرض و من شر ما يخرج منها و من شر كل طارق الا طارقآ يطرق بخير يا رحمن ـ

As soon as the Holy Prophet recited after the Gabriel, the fire died, and the demons retreated.

SHAMAIL MUHAMMAD MUSTAFA

"And when Jesus the son of Mary said, "O Children of Israel! Behold, I am an apostle of God unto thee, to confirm the truth of whatever remains of Torah, and to give you glad tidings of an apostle who shall come after me, and he shall be called the 'Praised one."

(Quran 61:6)

The Holy Prophet Hazrat Muhammad (May God bless and cherish him) is the apostle who's coming was predicted in the Christian Scripture: the promise of God to humanity that "a highly praised one" would be sent for salvation and guidance in the fulfillment of this Biblical saying.

Today, more than a billion people (one in every five human beings) follow his faith, sing his praises, and invoke God's peace and blessings upon him and his family. His behavior, his acts, and his words serve as models for the faithful, who try to imitate him even in the smallest details of his *Sunnah*. He indeed was sent as a mercy unto the universe, "The helper of the two worlds," and the one who was the goal and meaning of all earlier divine religions. As he was also the goal and cause of creation, the following *hadith* refers to him.

"But for thee, but for thee, I would not have created the spheres." God proclaimed with love, "*Laulaka, Laulaka, ma khalaqt al Aflaka.*" The Holy Prophet Hazrat Muhammad (May God bless and cherish him) is God's first and best creation. "The first creation that Allah created was the light of your prophet from His light."

(Bukhari, Sahih). He was the first of all prophets as he said, "I was a prophet when Hazrat Adam was between water and clay." (Bukhari, Sahih). He was also the last and the seal of all prophets as he proclaimed, "I was first of prophets in creation and the last of them in resurrection" (Abu Hurrayrah). The Holy Prophet Hazrat Muhammad (May God bless and cherish him) is the cause of creation. He manifests the divine presence and serves as a connection between all the worlds of creation. There is no other way to experience God in Islamic thought or religion but through him. If you want (love) Allah, follow the Holy Prophet Hazrat Muhammad (May God bless and cherish him).

Each prophet was sent to a particular people at a certain time, but Hazrat Muhammad (May God bless and cherish him), 'the chosen one', was sent to all humanity until the end of time. The love of the Holy Prophet Hazrat Muhammad (May God bless and cherish him) is a pre-requisite of faith, as he has said,

"As long as you do not love me more than anything else, your faith is not complete" (Bukhari). God Himself says, "If you love Me, follow the Prophet." And the Holy Prophet (May God bless and cherish him) said, "Whosoever loves God, loves me."

The faithful simply love the Holy Prophet (May God bless and cherish him), for the love of the prophet leads to the love of God. Hence, the Holy Prophet (May God bless and cherish him) is the true embodiment of divine love.

When your heart is filled with the love of Ahmad,

Then, know with certitude that you are safe from fire.

(Sanai)

According to Rumi, for believers, the Holy Prophet Hazrat Muhammad (May God bless and cherish him) is "The window through which one sees the Creator."

One of the Holy Prophet's (May God bless and cherish him) name is Dhikr Allah, and sending blessings on him is synonymous with remembering Allah. Sufi master Ibne Ata Ullah wrote in one of his treatises that there is a deep connection between remembering Allah and remembering the Holy Prophet (May God bless and cherish him), as God says to the Holy Prophet (May God bless and cherish him), "O Muhammad, I have made you one of the remembrances of Me. Those who remember you remember Me, and those who love you love Me."

The Holy Prophet Hazrat Muhammad (May God bless and cherish him) is, above all men, unique among the prophets. According to the Noble Quran, Hazrat Muhammad (May God bless and cherish him) is he who must be obeyed. Allah (Exalted is He) says,

"Whoever obeys the Messenger obeys Allah." (Quran 4:80)

Imam Jafar ibn Muhammad (AS-Sadiq) said, "Allah knew that His creatures would not be capable of pure obedience to Him, so He told them this in order that they would realize that they would never be able to achieve absolute purity in serving Him. He placed between Himself and them someone (His beloved) of their own species, clothing him with His own attributes of compassion and mercy. He brought him out as a truthful Messenger to creation and made it such that when someone obeys him, they are obeying Allah, and when someone agrees with him, they are agreeing with Allah.

Hazrat Muhammad (May God bless and cherish him) to Allah is like the light is to the sun and proves that Hazrat Muhammad's (May God bless and cherish him) light is as the "Light from God's light."

The Holy Prophet (May God bless and cherish him) was not only a Messenger of Allah but much more. He was the instrument through which God worked. The following Quranic verse is frequently quoted to affirm this belief: "And you, O Prophet, did not cast pebbles when you cast them, but it was Allah the Almighty Who cast them." (Quran 8:17). In another place, God the Most High says, "Those who swear allegiance to you do not but swear allegiance to Allah, the hand of Allah is over their hands." (Quran 48:10). Therefore, Hazrat Muhammad (May God bless and cherish him) is an aspect of God's activity.

Islamic faith is primarily based on the doctrine of unity of being and the universal man. The Holy Prophet Hazrat Muhammad (May God bless and cherish him) is the perfect man (Insan-e-Kamil) in whom all the possibilities of cosmic existence are realized. For believers, he is the perfect mirror reflecting and emanating all of God's names and attributes in his inner reality, which is referred to as Muhammadan Reality. For believers, he is the most perfect model in all respects, to be imitated even in the minutest details. They have deep trust in the promise of the Holy Prophet (May God bless and cherish him), who said, "O my son, who has cherished my Sunnah without doubt has cherished me and who cherishes me will be with me in paradise."

The faithful see their beloved Prophet Hazrat Muhammad (May God bless and cherish him) in the verses of the Noble Quran, which is in fact, a commentary on his character, miracles, beauty, and high rank. Some of the passages in the Glorious Quran are expressions of the Holy Prophet's (May God bless and cherish him) unparalleled beauty and majesty. "By the sun" is therefore the story of Hazrat Muhammad's (May God bless and cherish him) face, and "By the night" is the tale of his beautiful black hair. God the Most High has time and again taken oath by the eternal loveliness of His beloved the Holy Prophet Hazrat Muhammad (May God bless and cherish him) in sura 91 and 92. In the beginning of sura 93, "By the morning light," is used as an allusion applied to his sun-like radiant face.

In the Noble Quran, there are many verses in which Allah, the exalted, bestows eminence and honor upon His beloved messenger. Allah, the Mighty and Majestic, says, "Remember thy Lord." (7:205). "And worship thy Lord." (15:99). "And when thy Lord said." (2:30). "And for thy Lord be patient." (74:7). "And thy Lord magnify." (74:3). "And thy Lord creates." (28:68). The Real is the Lord of All creation but He singled out Muhammad Mustafa (May God bless and cherish him) by mentioning him to make him great in the hearts of the servants.

The Holy Prophet Hazrat Muhammad (May God bless and cherish him) was not only of high moral and exalted character, but all the spiritual qualities were physically manifested in his body. He was "Beauty from head to toe," and according to a Sufi master, "God has created Hazrat Muhammad's (May God bless and cherish him) body in such unsurpassable beauty as has neither before him nor after him been seen in any human being. If the whole beauty of the Holy Prophet (May God bless and cherish him) were unveiled before our eyes, they could not bear its splendor." That is why the Holy Prophet (May God bless and cherish him) said, "Joseph was beautiful, but I am more handsome."

In Islamic spirituality, the soul of the Holy prophet Hazrat Muhammad (May God bless and cherish him) is the first creation and emanation from the essence (Being) of Allah where beauty per se (real beauty) is found in its fullness. If the One (Allah) is the king, beyond beauty, then the Prophet Hazrat Muhammad's (may God bless and cherish him) soul is the queen, the epitome of beauty. From the illuminative aspect, divine emanation is to be understood as the "absolute light" (Nur-i-Mutlaq). It is the light of God which is attached to everything. The absolute light is in fact, the "Light of Muhammad" which is the first emanation.

According to a prophetic saying, "Allah is beautiful and loves beauty." He indeed is the most beautiful of all things, situated in pure light and pure radiance, included within itself the nature of all beings. It is also recommended to do what is beautiful.

"Surely God loves the beautiful doers." The Holy Prophet Hazrat Muhammad Mustafa (May God bless and cherish him) said, "Beautiful doing is that you worship (contemplate) God as if you see Him, for if you do not see Him, surely He sees you." Doing the beautiful is that you worship God in wakefulness and awareness as if you are gazing upon Him, and you serve Him as if you are seeing Him. This hadith alludes to the heart's encounter with the Unseen and the spirit's contemplation of the Beloved. It is an incitement to self-purification in deeds, curtailment of wishes, and loyalty to what was accepted on the First Day (Day of Alast).

The beauty of form and the perfect proportion of his body are related in many famous traditions by Hazrat Ali (May God be pleased with him), Ans ibn Malik, Abu Hurrayrah, Al Bara ibn Azib, Hazrat Aisha, Ibn Abi Halah, Abu Juhayfa, Jabir ibn Samura, Umm Ma'bad, Ibn Abbas, Mu'arrid ibn Mu'ayqib, Abu Tufayl, Al-Ida ibn Khalid, Ibn Hizam and others.

The Holy Prophet (May God bless and cherish him) is the worthiest of all mankind, the greatest of them in position and most perfect of them in character and virtue. His noble being is an inestimable treasure of perfection of physique, physical beauty, strength of intellect, soundness of understanding, eloquence of tongue, and nobility of lineage as well as knowledge, forbearance, patience, thankfulness, justice, humility, chastity, generosity, courage, modesty, mercy, good manners, and companionship.

When the Holy Prophet (May God bless and cherish him) was granted permission to emigrate (the Hijra) from Makkah to Medina, he was accompanied by his companions Hazrat Abu Bakr and his freed slave Amr Ibn Fuhairah alongside their guide Abdullah Ibn Uraiqit (who was polytheist). During their journey, they rested at a camp in Qudaud at a time of drought. They requested some food and drink from Umm Ma'bad but there was unfortunately nothing to offer them. The Holy Prophet Hazrat Muhammad (May God bless and cherish him) noticed an emaciated goat, which he requested to milk. Miraculously, the milk started flowing at the blessed hand of the Holy Prophet (May God bless and cherish him), and they all drank, and the Holy Prophet left plenty of milk for Umm Ma'bad and her family. When her husband, Aktham Ibn Abu al-Jawn al-Khuzai returned from herding his sheep, he saw all the milk. He asked his wife where this had come from, and she explained a 'blessed man' had passed by us. He asked her to describe him, and what she said is an incredible description of the Messenger of Allah (May God bless and cherish him).

The story of Umm Ma'bad 'Atikah bint Khalid al-Khuzaiyyah' attests to the physical beauty and overwhelming presence of the Holy Prophet (May God bless and cherish him). She said,

"I saw a man of visible radiance and purity, beautiful appearance, bright faced, with neither protruding ribs nor a small head, handsome and fair. He was graceful and elegant, with intensely deep black and large eyes, and his eye lashes were lush. His voice was mellow and soft. The whiteness of his eyes was bright. His eyebrows were beautifully arched but not connected. His neck was long and his beard densely full. When silent, he was dignified, and when he spoke, glory rose and overcame him. He was from afar the most beautiful of men and the most glorious, and up close, he was the sweetest and the loveliest. He was sweet of speech and articulate, his words precise, neither too little nor too much. His speech was like a string of cascading pearls. Among the three, he was the most radiant in appearance and the finest of them in stature." (Al-Baihaqi and Al-Hakim).

"Shamail al Mustafa," the physical and celestial beauty of the Holy Prophet Hazrat Muhammad (May God bless and cherish him), has been described by Hazrat Ali, the son-in-law of the Holy Prophet and the fourth caliph of Islam, as follows,

"Hazrat Muhammad was neither excessively tall nor short, but rather was of a medium stature among (his) people. His hair was neither extremely curly nor straight, but rather it was wavy and flowing. The plaits of his hair were parted. His hair reached beyond the lobe of his ear. His complexion was azhar (bright, luminous). He was neither corpulent nor was his face completely circular, but it was slightly rounded. His eyes were black and his lashes long. When he walked it, was as though he went down a declivity. When he turned to look at someone or something, he would turn his whole body. He had the seal of prophethood between his shoulder blades, and he is the seal of the prophets. His face shone like the full moon in the night. Hazrat Muhammad had a wide forehead and long arched eyebrows, which did not meet. Between his eyebrows, there was a vein that swelled when he was angry. The upper part of his nose was prominent. He was thick bearded, had smooth cheeks, a full mouth, and his teeth were set apart. He had thin hair on his chest. His neck was like the neck of an ivory statue, with the shine of silver. Muhammad was proportionate, broad-chested and broad-shouldered. His heart was the soundest and most generous of hearts. His speech was the most truthful of speech. He was the gentlest of people and the kindest of them in companionship. Whoever saw him for the first time would be awe-stricken. Whoever came to know him would love him. Whoever described him would say, "I saw neither before him nor after him anyone like him."

HIND IBN ABU HALAH'S DESCRIPTION OF THE HOLY PROPHET

It is narrated that the most comprehensive description of the Holy Prophet Hazrat Muhammad (May God bless and cherish him) was told by the Companion, Hind Ibn Abu Halah, who is Hazrat Khadijah's son from a previous husband and the Holy Prophet's stepson. This hadith is mentioned in Imam al-Tirmidhi's Ashamail an-Nabawiyah (The prophetic traits) and Qadhi Iyadh's Ash-Shifa (The Healing)

It is narrated by the authority of Imam al-Hassan Ibn Hazrat Ali (May God bless and cherish him), who said, "I asked my maternal uncle Hind ibn Abu Hala to describe the features of the Messenger of Allah (May God bless and cherish him) because he had the unique ability to describe them fully. It was my cherished wish that he would do so for me. He said,

"The Messenger of Allah was imposing and majestic. His face looked like the full moon. He was somewhat taller than medium height and a little shorter than what could be described as tall. His head was large, and he had hair that was neither curly nor straight. If his hair parted, he would leave it parted, and it did not go beyond the lobes of his ears if he allowed it to go long. He was very fair skinned with a wide brow and had thick eyebrows with a narrow space between them. He had a vein there, which throbbed when he was angry. He had a long nose with a shine of light over it, which someone might mistakenly consider to be his nose. His beard was thick and full. He had black eyes, firm and high cheeks, a full mouth, and white teeth with slight gaps between his front teeth. The hair of his chest formed a thin line. His neck was like that of a statue made of pure silver. His physique was proportionate. His body was firm and full. His belly and chest were equal in size. His chest was broad, and the space between his shoulders was wide. He had full calves. He was luminous (the parts of his body that were visible while he was clothed shone a brilliant light). Between his neck and naval there was a line of hair, but the rest of his torso was free of it. He had hair on his forearms and shoulders and the upper part of his chest. He had thick wrists, wide palms, thick hands, and feet. His fingers were long. His body was strongly formed. He had high insteps, and his feet were so smooth that water ran off them. When he walked, he walked as though he were going down a hill. He walked in a dignified manner and walked with ease but swiftly. When he turned to address somebody, he turned his whole body. He lowered his gaze, looking downwards more than upwards. He restrained his gaze. He would lead his Companions, who walked behind and was the first to greet any person he met."

Imam al-Hassan said, "Tell me how he spoke."

Hind Ibn Abu Halah replied, "The Messenger of Allah was always subject to grief and was always reflective. He had no rest, and he only spoke when it was necessary. He spent long periods in silence. His speech was comprehensive, and his words neither superfluous nor inadequate. He was kindhearted and never harsh. He valued gifts and blessings, even if they were small. He did not censure anything nor criticize or praise the taste of food. Worldly affairs did not make him angry. He showed concern for the people's rights and helped them to attain it. He did not try to strive for his own due, nor did he get angry about it, and never sought to avenge himself. When he pointed, he did so with his whole hand. When he was surprised about something, he turned his palms upside (facing upwards). During conversation, he would place his right hand on his left hand. When he was angry, he turned away his face. And when he was happy, he would close his eyes. His laughter generally consisted of a smile, but when he did so, his teeth showed as white as raindrops."

Imam al-Hassan said, "I refrained from mentioning these details from my younger brother Imam Hussayn for a while. Then, at last I spoke to him and found that he had already beaten me to it. He had asked our father, Hazrat Imam Ali, about how the Messenger of Allah (May God bless and cherish him) behaved at home and when he was outside of home, his assemblies, and about his physical features. He had not omitted anything to ask."

It is narrated that Imam al-Hussayn said, "I asked my father how the Holy Prophet (May God bless and cherish him) was at home. Hazrat Ali replied,

"The Holy Prophet (May God bless and cherish him) entered home as if he had been granted permission. When at home, he divided his time into three parts, one part for Allah the Mighty and Majestic, one part for his family, and one part for himself and the people. He preferred those who were knowledgeable and keen to learn the matters of religion. Some people needed one thing, some needed two, and some had many needs. The Holy Prophet (May God bless and cherish him) concerned himself with them and did what was needed. He used to tell them that what he was saying were the rules of religion and Shariah, and those who were present should convey these to those who were absent, and they should let him know about what was needed by those who could not convey their needs to him. On the Day of Judgement, Allah (Exalted is He) would make firm the feet of a person who conveys to a ruler the need of someone who cannot convey it himself." The Companions will not leave his holy company until they have eaten something.

"The Holy Prophet Hazrat Muhammad (May God bless and cherish him) held his tongue except regarding what concerned people. He brought people together and did not split them. He honored the nobles of every people and appointed them over their people. He was conscious about his Companions and constantly watched them but was never discourteous. He cared about his Companions and asked how other people were doing. He praised what was beautiful and good, disliked what was ugly and bad, and discouraged such behavior. He was not negligent so that his Companions would also be not negligent. He turned every situation into good and did not neglect what was right. The best and the most preferred in his eyes were those who had good counsel for all the Muslims. Those he most loved were the people who supported and helped their fellow believers."

Imam al-Hussayn then asked his father, Hazrat Ali, about the Holy Prophet's assembly and how he behaved in it. Hazrat Ali replied,

"The Messenger of Allah (May God bless and cherish him) did not sit or stand up without mentioning the name Allah. He did not reserve a special place for himself and forbade others to do so. When he came to an assembly of people, he sat down at the edge of the gathering and told his Companions to do the same. He gave everyone who sat with him his due share so that no one thought that anyone was honored more than he was. If anyone sat with him or stood close to him to ask something, the Holy Prophet (May God bless and cherish him) gave him full attention until that person turned away. When someone asked him for something he needed, he either departed with it or received kind words. He had the kindest and best behavior of all people, being like a father to them. They all had equal rights and respect with him.

His assembly was one of mercy, modesty, patience, and trust. In his presence, voices were not raised, nor shortcomings were made public. His Companions were humble and strived for piety. They respected the elderly and showed compassion to the young. They helped those in need and were kind to strangers.

The Holy Prophet Hazrat Muhammad (May God bless and cherish him) was always cheerful, easygoing, and never harsh with his Companions. He was never rough, did not raise his voice, nor utter obscenities. He did not find fault with people nor over-praise anyone. He ignored what was redundant and never disappointed anyone. The Holy Prophet   (May God bless and cherish him) avoided three habits: pretention, useless talk, and what did not concern him. He also avoided three things in respect of others: he did not censure anyone; he did not scold them nor try to find out their faults. He only spoke about those matters which he expected would benefit others. When he spoke in an assembly, people sitting with him were as quiet as if birds were sitting on their heads. When the Holy Prophet finished talking, his Companions would ask questions but did not behave disorderly. When someone talked in his presence, he kept quiet until he had finished and agreed with what was said. He laughed at what they laughed at and was surprised at what surprised them. He was patient with a stranger who had a coarse language.

The Holy Prophet told his Companions, "If you see someone in need of something, then give it to him." He did not look for praise except from someone who had spoken ill before. The Holy Prophet was silent for four reasons: forbearance, caution, appraisal, and reflection. As for his appraisal, he looked at all with equality and listened to them fully. As for reflection, he weighed upon what would endure and what would vanish. He was cautious in adopting something good so that his Companions would follow him and avoid something bad, which then would be abandoned by his followers. He constantly strived to determine what would benefit his Ummah (Nation) that would do good in this world and in the hereafter."

Abu Hamzah Ans bin Malik, the slave of the Holy Prophet (May God bless and cherish him), said, "The Holy Prophet Hazrat Muhammad (May God bless and cherish him) was the most handsome of all people, the most kind and affectionate in temperament, the most fragrant in smell, and had the softest hands of all. I have never smelled any perfume more fragrant than the smell of the Holy Prophet (May God bless and cherish him) and have never found any silk or brocade softer than the hands of the Beloved of Allah."

Ali-Bara said, "I did not see anyone with a more beautiful lock of hair resting on a red robe than the Messenger of Allah (May God bless and cherish him)."

Abu Hurarayra said, "I have not seen anything more beautiful than the Holy Prophet Hazrat Muhammad (May God bless and cherish him). It was as if the sun was shining on his face. When he laughed, it reflected from the wall."

Jabir ibn Samura was asked, "Was his face like a sword." He replied, "No, it was like the sun and the moon. It was round."

In her description, Umm Ma'bad said, "From afar, he was the most beautiful of people, and close up, he was the most handsome."

Ibn Abi Hala said, "His face showed like the full moon." At the end of his description, Hazrat Ali said, "Anyone who saw him suddenly was filled with awe of him. Those who kept his company loved him."

According to a tradition, the Holy Prophet Hazrat Muhammad (May God bless and cherish him) told his close Companions, especially his four friends, to remember his features and attributes and promised that anyone who stitched the description of his features in his shroud would be followed by a thousand angels on the last day of life who will recite the funeral prayers for him and ask for forgiveness on his behalf until the Day of Judgment.

The Holy Prophet Hazrat Muhammad was famous among his people as al-Amin, or "Trustworthy," and al-Sadiq or the "Truthful." People trusted him with their valuables, and he never told a lie. He was a man of truth and honesty. He had the best moral character, was well-spoken, and loved to help people. He was very compassionate, extremely gentle, and kindhearted. God the Most High describes his beautiful manners in the following words.

"Indeed, you are of a great moral character." Quran (68:4). And,

"Indeed, in the Messenger of Allah, you have an excellent example to follow for whoever hopes in Allah and the Last Day and remember Allah unceasingly." Quran (33:21)

His cousin, son-in-law, fourth Caliph of Islam, and the commander of the believers, Hazrat Ali (May God be pleased with him), described the Holy Prophet

(May God bless and cherish him) in the following way:

"He was the last of the prophets, the most truthful, the best of them in character, and the most loving. Whoever saw him for the first time would stand in awe, and whoever got to know him would love him. Everyone would attest to the fact and say, I have never seen anyone before or after him who was comparable to him."

Even his enemies attested to his trustworthiness, truthfulness, and greatness —as did Abu Sufyan, the archenemy of Islam, in front of Heraclius, the emperor of Rome.

Michael Hart, in his book, "The 100 Most Influential Persons in History," wrote that the Holy Prophet Hazrat Muhammad (May God bless and cherish him) was the greatest man who ever lived on the face of the earth. He ranked him higher than Prophet Moses (May God bless and cherish him), Prophet Jesus (May God bless and cherish him), the Buddha, and Lao Tzu, for this unlettered man of the desert bedazzled the whole Muslim world with sublimity and majesty of his message. "He founded one of the greatest religions of the world and forever changed the history of civilization," Michael Hart writes.

Professor Hassan Ali, in his magazine, 'Nur al Islam' quoted a Brahman friend who wrote as follows,

"I recognize and believe that the Messenger of Allah (May God bless and cherish him) is the greatest and most mature man in human history. No man possessed the characteristics, mannerisms, and ethics that he possessed at one time. He was a king under whom the entire peninsula was unified. Yet he was humble. He believed that the dominion belonged to God alone. Great riches would come to him, and yet he lived in a state of poverty; fire would not be lit in his house for many days, and he would stay hungry. He was a great leader. He had small numbers in battle against thousands, and yet he would decisively defeat them. He loved peace agreements and would agree to them with a firm heart, even though he had thousands of his brave Companions by his side.

"He was deeply concerned about the affairs of the Arabian Peninsula, yet he did not neglect the affairs of his family, household, or the poor and needy. In general, he was a man concerned with the betterment and well-being of mankind, yet he did not indulge in amassing worldly fortunes. He even prayed for his enemies and would warn them of the punishment of God."

Similarly, Alphonse de La Martaine in 'Historic de al Turquie' wrote,

"Never has a man set for himself, voluntarily or involuntarily, a more sublime aim, since this aim was superhuman, to subvert superstitions that have been imposed between man and his creator, to render God unto man and man unto God, to resolve the rational and sacred idea of divinity amongst the chaos of the material and disfigured gods of idolatry then existing. Never has a man undertaken a work so far beyond human power with such feeble means, for Hazrat Muhammad (May God bless and cherish him) had in the conception as well as in the execution of such a great design, no other instrument than himself and no other aid except a handful of men living in a corner of the desert.

"Finally, never has a man accomplished such a huge and lasting revolution in the world because, less than two centuries after its appearance, Islam in faith and in arms reigned over the whole of Arabia and conquered in God's name Persia, Transoxiana, western India, Syria, Egypt, Abyssinia, all known continents of Africa, numerous islands of the Mediterranean Sea, and Spain. If greatness of purpose, smallness of means, and astonishing results are the three criteria for a human genius, who could alone compare any great man in history with Prophet Muhammad (May God bless and cherish him). Regarding all standards by which human greatness can be measured, we may even ask, is there any man greater than him?"

Poverty (faqr) was an attribute of the Holy Prophet (May God bless and cherish him). According to a tradition, he said, "Faqri Fakhri," 'Poverty is my pride.' He slept on a mat of hay and a pillow stuffed with coarse date fibers. Hazrat Umar ibn Khattab once came to visit his house and found him sitting on a hay mat, which had left marks on his body. He had a pot of water by his feet, and there was some cloth hanging on the wall. This was all he had at the time when the Messenger of Allah (May God bless and cherish him) had the Arabian Peninsula under his control. When Hazrat Umar ibn Khattab saw this, he wept bitterly, for he could not control his emotions. At this, the Messenger of Allah (May God bless and cherish him) said, "Why are you crying, O Umar?" he replied, "Why should I not cry? Khosro of Persia and Caesar of Rome enjoy the best of this world, while you are in this state of poverty that I see.' The Holy Prophet (May God bless and cherish him) replied, "O Umar, aren't you happy that they enjoy this world, and we will enjoy the eternal life in the hereafter?"

At the time of the conquest of Makkah, when the Holy Prophet (May God bless and cherish him) led his Companions numbering ten thousand, Abu Sufyan was standing on a hill alongside al-Abbas, the uncle of the Holy Prophet (May God bless and cherish him). He was amazed by the vast numbers of Muslims marching towards Makkah like a storm is unstoppable in its course. On seeing this, Abu Sufyan said to al-Abbas, "O al-Abbas, your nephew has become a great king." Al-Abbas said in reply, "This is not kingship but rather prophethood, and this is a message from the Lord."

He conquered Makkah without fighting and was very humble and forgiving. He gathered the people who had abused, harmed, and tortured him and his followers and drove them out of the city. On this occasion he said to them, "What do you think I will do to you?" They replied, "You are kind and generous, and you will only do good for the sake of God." He pardoned them all and said, "Go, you all are free and safe."

One of the Companions, An-Numan Basheer said, "I saw the Holy Prophet (May God bless and cherish him) one day when he was unable to buy low-quality dates to satisfy his hunger" (Muslim). In this vein, Abu Hurrayrah said, "The Holy Prophet (May God bless and cherish him) never filled his stomach for three consecutive days until his death" (Bukhari). Such accounts attest to the fact that the Holy Prophet (May God bless and cherish him) was a simple and humble person. He would not only serve himself but would serve others as well. Hazrat Aisha, the wife of the Holy Prophet (May God bless and cherish him), said, "I was asked how the Messenger of Allah (May God bless and cherish him) behaved in the house." She said, "He would help in the house with daily chores. He was like any other man; he washed his clothes, mended his shoes, milked his sheep, and served himself."

When all the Arabian Peninsula was under his control and great fortunes and riches would pile up into the Mosque, he would give it away to the poor and needy. His wife, Hazrat Aisha, said that the Holy Prophet (May God bless and cherish him) borrowed some food from a Jew and agreed to pay him later and gave him his armor as collateral. The Holy Prophet Hazrat Muhammad (May God bless and cherish him) strongly disliked the riches of this world because he knew the world's reality. He said, "The likeness of this world to the hereafter is like a person who dipped his finger in the ocean – let him see what would return." (Muslim)

The Holy Prophet (May God bless and cherish him) was concerned about his people. He would visit the sick, whether he or she was Muslim or non-Muslim.

If he knew that a Companion was sick, he would rush to visit him or her, along with those who were present with him. In this regard, it is narrated by the authority of Ans bin Malik that, "Once a Jewish boy who used to serve the Holy Prophet (May God bless and cherish him) became sick. So, he told his Companions, "Let us go and visit him." The Holy Prophet (May God bless and cherish him) went to visit him along with his companions and found the father of the boy sitting by his head. The Messenger of Allah (May God bless and cherish him) looked at the boy and said, "Proclaim that there is no true god worthy of worship except Allah alone, and I will intercede on your behalf because of it on the Day of Resurrection." The boy looked at his father. The father said, "Obey Abul Qasim." Therefore, the boy announced, "There is no true god worthy of worship except Allah alone and Muhammad (May God bless and cherish him) is his last messenger." The Holy Prophet (May God bless and cherish him) said, "All praise belongs to Allah, Who saved him."

The Holy Prophet (May God bless and cherish him) has the eminence of prophethood, the rank of messengerhood, the beauty of mediation, the praiseworthy station (Quran 17:79), and the visited pool. He said,

"My pool extends from Adan to Amman. Its wine is more intensely white than milk and sweeter than honey. Anyone who takes and drinks it will never thirst again. The first to enter it will be the destitute among the emigrants."

He is the seal of prophets, the master of the messengers, the interceder for the sinners, and the candle of the earth and heaven. The rein of his steed has passed beyond the heavens, and the courtyard of the splendorous Throne was made the place for the soles of his feet.

CHAPTER 9
CALL TO ISLAM

The religion was now firmly established based on ritual purification and prayer, and with the revelation of Sura Mudathir, "Arise and warn," came the first command related to his mission. The first person to embrace Islam was Hazrat Khadijah and after her were Hazrat Ali, Zayd, and the Holy Prophet's friend Hazrat Abu Bakr. Steadily, there was an ever-increasing group of devout believers and worshipers of both men and women, most of them young.

The first adherents of the new faith took God's commands revealed in the Scripture seriously and applied them to themselves and would keep vigils. As to the ritual prayer (Salat), they were careful not only to perform the wudu (Ablution) in preparation for it but also to make sure their clothes were clean and free from all defilement. They were also quick to learn by heart all that had been revealed of the Noble Quran, so that they might read it as part of their prayers. Divine revelation began to pour on the Holy Prophet's (May God bless and cherish him) heart. They were immediately transmitted to those close to the Holy Prophet (May God bless and cherish him), then passed from person to person, memorized, and recited.

SECRET CALL

The Holy Prophet (May God bless and cherish him) carried out his sacred mission privately and in secret during the first three years of his prophethood. He started his call from home and then moved to the people closely associated with him. He called unto Islam whomsoever he thought would attest the truth which had come from the Lord of the worlds. As a matter of fact, there was an ever-increasing group of sincere believers and intense worshipers, both men and women.

The Holy Prophet (May God bless and cherish him) used to meet and teach the new converts in privacy because the call to Islam was still spreading on an individual and secret basis. The believers greeted each other with the words given to the Holy Prophet (May God bless and cherish him) by Archangel Gabriel as the greeting of the people of paradise, "Peace be upon you" (Asalm o Alaikum), to which the answer is, and on you be peace, (Walaikum-as-Salam), the plural being used to include the two guardian angels of the person greeted.

Ibn Ishaq mentioned in his Sira that when there was time for prayers, the Holy Prophet (May God bless and cherish him) and his Companions would go into the mountain valley to pray secretly. Hazrat Abu Talib once saw the Messenger of Allah and Hazrat Ali praying, he asked them what they were up to. When he was informed that it was obligatory prayer, he told them to stay constant in their practice. (Ibn Ishaq)

The Holy Prophet (May God bless and cherish him) and his Companions conducted their religious activities in a private manner and on individual basis. The news leaked to the Quraysh, but they paid little attention to it since the Holy Prophet (May God bless and cherish him) was not attacking their religion nor speaking about their idols. The secret stage continued for three years, and as a result a group of strong believers emerged stamped by the spirit of brotherhood with one definite aim in their mind: propagating and firmly establishing the religion of God. Until then, the Holy Prophet (May God bless and cherish him) was content to teach within a rather narrow circle of believers. The time, however, had come to preach the new faith of the Lord of the worlds openly. Then, the first revelation regarding the preaching descended, giving Allah's Messenger the duty of publicizing it for his people to confront them, invalidate their falsehood, and crush down their idolatrous practices.

"And warn thy family who are thy nearest of kin." (26:214)

In obedience to Allah's command, the Holy Prophet (May God bless and cherish him) called Hazrat Ali to him and said, "God has commanded me to warn my family, my nearest of kin, and this task is beyond my strength. But make ready food with a leg of roasted lamb, and fill a cup with milk, and gather the Bani Abd al-Hashim and Bani Abd al-Muttalib that I may tell them that which I have been commanded to say." Hazrat Ali obeyed the Holy Prophet's (May God bless and cherish him) orders and did exactly as he had been told, neither more nor less, and most of the clans (about forty men) responded to the invitation. "When they were assembled," said Hazrat Ali, "The Holy Prophet (May God bless and cherish him) told me to bring in the food which I had made ready. Then, he took a piece of meat, bit upon it, and put it again into the dish, saying, "Take it in the Name of God." The men ate, several of them at a time, until not one of them could eat anymore." Said Hazrat Ali, "I could see no change in the food, except that it had been stirred by men's hands; and by my life, if they had been but one man, he could have eaten all of that I had put before them." Then the Holy Prophet (May God bless and cherish him) said, "Give them to drink, so I brought the cup, and each drank his fill, though one man alone could have emptied that cup. But when the Holy Prophet (May God bless and cherish him) was about to address them, Abu Lahab immediately took the initiative and addressed the Holy Prophet (May God bless and cherish him), "These are your uncles and cousins, speak to the point, but first, you have to know that your kinsmen are not in a position to withstand all the Arabs. You must bear in mind that your relatives are sufficient for you, if you follow their tradition, it will be easier for them to face the other clans of Quraysh supported by other Arabs. Verily, I have never heard of anyone who has incurred more harm on his kins people than you." Then he told the gathering, "Your host has placed a spell upon you." Whereas they dispersed before the Holy Prophet (May God bless and cherish him) could even speak. The Messenger of God kept silent and did not speak in that meeting.

The Holy Prophet (May God bless and cherish him) invited them to a second meeting and told Hazrat Ali to do exactly as he had done for the previous meeting. So, another similar meal was prepared, and everything went as before. The Holy Prophet (May God bless and cherish him) then stood up and said,

"I celebrate Allah's praise. I seek His help. I believe in Him. I put my trust in Him. I bear witness that there is no god to be worshiped but Allah with no associate. A guide could never lie to his people. I swear by Allah that there is no god but He, that I have been sent as a Messenger to you and to all the people in general. I swear by Allah that you will die just as you sleep, you will be resurrected just as you wake up. You will be called to account for your deeds. It is then either Hell forever or the Garden forever."

The Holy Prophet (May God bless and cherish him) then said, "O sons of Abd al-Muttalib," he continued, "I know of no Arab who hath come to his people with a nobler message than mine. I bring you the best of this world and the next. Allah, the Mighty and Majestic, has commanded me to call you unto Him. Which of you, then, will help me in this and be my brother, mine executor, and my successor amongst you?"

There was silence throughout the clan. Jafar and Zayd could both have spoken, but they knew that their Islam was not in question and that the purpose of the gathering was to bring in others than themselves. But when the silence remained unbroken, the thirteen-year-old Hazrat Ali stood up and said, "O Prophet of God, I will be thy helper in this." The Holy Prophet (May God bless and cherish him) laid his hand on the back of Hazrat Ali's neck and said,

"This is my brother, my executor, and my successor amongst you. Hearken unto him and obey him." The men rose to their feet, laughing and saying to Hazrat Abu Talib, "He has ordered thee to hearken unto thy son and obey him." Hazrat Abu Talib stood up and firmly said to the Holy Prophet (May God bless and cherish him), "We love to help you, accept your advice, and believe in your words. These are the kinspeople whom you have gathered, and I am one of them, but I am the fastest to do what you like. Do what you have been ordered. I shall protect you and defend you, but I am on the religion of my forefathers Hazrat Ibrahim and Hazrat Ismael."

Abu Lahab then said to Hazrat Abu Talib, "I swear by Allah that this is a bad thing. You must stop him before the others do." Hazrat Abu Talib however answered; "I swear by Allah to protect him as long as I am alive."

None of the Holy Prophet's (May God bless and cherish him) four uncles showed any inclination to follow him except Hazrat Abu Talib who made no objection to the conversion of his two sons Hazrat Jafar and Hazrat Ali, and he also vowed to protect and help his nephew. His uncle Hazrat Abbas was evasive and Hazrat Hamzah uncomprehending at that time, though both assured him of their unfailing affection and support. Abu Lahab clearly showed his dislike, turned against him, and labelled him a deceiver.

As to the Holy Prophet's aunts, Safiyyah had no hesitation in following him as her son Zubayr had done, but her five sisters could not bring themselves to make any decision. On the other hand, his aunt by marriage, Umm al-Fadl, the wife of Hazrat Abbas was the first woman to enter Islam after Hazrat Khadijah (Mother of the faithful), and she was soon able to bring three of her sisters to the Holy Prophet (May God bless and cherish him) Maymunah, her full sister, and two half-sisters Salma and Asma. It was in the household of Umm al-Fadl that Hazrat Jafar had been brought up, and it was there that he had come to know and love Asma, whom he had recently married; Hazrat Hamzah had married her sister Salma.

In those early days of Islam, the Holy Prophet (May God bless and cherish him) and his Companions practiced their new faith in private and would gather outside Makkah to pray. Divine revelation continuously enjoined patience upon them.

"Bear with patience what they say, and part from them with a courteous farewell." (Quran 73:10)

"Deal gently with the disbelievers; give them respite for a while." (Quran 86:17)

In several other places in the Noble Quran, the Holy Prophet (May God bless and cherish him) is commanded to have patience, for patience is the antidote of the poison of trial.

"We indeed know that thy breast is straightened by what they say." (Quran 15:97)

"And be patient with beautiful patience." (Quran 70:5)

"Be patient with thy Lord's decree, for surely thou art in Our eyes." (Quran 52:48)

After some time, the Holy Prophet (May God bless and cherish him) became sure of Hazrat Abu Talib's strong commitment to his protection while he called the people unto Allah. One day, he stood up on Mount As-Safa and called out loudly, "Ya Sahahah" (This is an Arabian expression used when one needs dire help or intends to draw the attention of others to a great ordeal). Al-Bukhari reported on the authority of Ibn Abbas that the Messenger of Allah ascended Mount As-Safa and started to call, "O Bani Fihr! O Bani Adi (Two tribes of Quraysh)." A group of people gathered below, and those who could not, sent somebody to report to others. The Holy Prophet's (May God bless and cherish him) uncle, Abu Lahab was also present. The Holy Prophet (May God bless and cherish him) proclaimed, "You see, if I were to tell you that there were some horsemen in the valley planning to attack you. Would you believe me? They said, "Yes, we have only heard the truth from you." The Holy Prophet (May God bless and cherish him) then continued, "I am a warner to you before a severe torment." The Holy Prophet (May God bless and cherish him) gave them a general warning, then he made a particular reference to certain tribes and said, "O Quraysh, rescue yourselves from the Fire; O people of Bani Kaab, rescue yourselves from the Fire; O Fatima daughter of Muhammad, rescue yourself from the Fire, for I have no power to protect you from Allah in anything except that I would sustain a relationship with you" (Sahih Muslim, Sahih al-Bukhari). It was a bold call unequivocally to the closest people that belief in Allah and His religion constituted the basis of any future relation between him and them and that blood relation on which the whole Arabian life was based, had lost its relevance in the light of that Divine command.

The Holy Prophet (May God bless and cherish him) kept on disseminating the religion of God until the following verse was revealed.

"Therefore, proclaim that which you are commanded, and turn away from al-Mushrikun (Polytheists)." (15:94)

The Holy Prophet (May God bless and cherish him) began to proclaim the invitation to Islam openly at the gatherings and assemblies of the idolaters. He would recite the verses of the Noble Quran, "O people! Worship Allah. You have no god but Him." (7:59)

The Quraysh saw that the Holy Prophet's (May God bless and cherish him) teachings were directed against their gods, their principles, and their religious practices. They realized the danger of the new faith. Therefore, some of their leading men went in a group to Hazrat Abu Talib, to insist that he should restrain his nephew's activities. He put them off with a conciliatory answer, but when they saw that he had done nothing to stop his nephew, they came to him again and said, "O Abu Talib, you are one of our honorable chiefs and we have great respect for you. By God, we will not tolerate our gods, our ways, and our fathers to be insulted. Either make him desist or we will retaliate against both of you."

Hazrat Abu Talib was greatly disturbed and sent for his nephew, and having told him what they had threatened, he said, "O son of my brother, spare me and spare thyself. Lay not upon me a burden greater than I can bear." The Holy Prophet (May God bless and cherish him) answered him, "I swear by God, if they put sun in my right hand and the moon in my left hand on condition that I abandon this course before He hath made it victorious, or I have perished there in, I would not abandon it." Then, with tears in his eyes, the Holy Prophet (May God bless and cherish him) rose to his feet and turned to go, but Hazrat Abu Talib called him back; "Son of my brother, go thou and say what thou wilt, for by God, I will never forsake thee on any account."

When the Quraysh came to know that their meeting with Hazrat Abu Talib had achieved nothing, they still hesitated to take direct action against the Holy Prophet (May God bless and cherish him). As a chief of clan, Hazrat Abu Talib had the power to grant inviolate protection, and it was in the interest of every other chief of clan in Makkah to see that the rights of chieftaincy were duly respected. So, they started to organize a widespread persecution of all those adherents of the new faith who had no one to protect them.

The Holy Prophet (May God bless and cherish him) was determined. He started practicing the new religion right before the eyes of the Quraysh, praying aloud in the Holy Sanctuary of Kaaba during the day while the idolaters watched. He then started disapproving of the superstitious practices of idolatry, revealing its worthless reality and utter uselessness. All of this resulted in increased acceptance of the call, and people were entering the religion of God one after the other. Soon, it was the season of pilgrimage, and Arabs started to come to Makkah from all over Arabia. The people of Quraysh had a high reputation for hospitality, not only regarding food and drink, but also because they made every man welcome, both him and his gods. The Quraysh agreed to come up with a plan to keep away the Arab pilgrims from the new faith preached by the Holy Prophet (May God bless and cherish him). It was therefore decided that the visiting Arabs should be told that the Holy Prophet Muhammad (May God bless and cherish him) in no way represented the Quraysh. Something needed to be said, and here lay their weakness, for some had taken to saying that he was a soothsayer (Kahin), others that he was possessed (Majnun), others that he was a poet, yet others that he was a sorcerer. In this regard, they consulted Al-Walid, the son of Mughirah, who was the most influential man of the tribe at that time, as to which of these accusations would be best likely to convince, but he rejected them all. Later, he decided that although Prophet Muhammad (May God bless and cherish him) was not a sorcerer, his words had the power to separate a man from his father, or from his brother, or from his wife or from his family. He advised them, therefore, to let their unanimous accusation be along those lines namely that the Holy Prophet (May God bless and cherish him) was a dangerous sorcerer, to be avoided at all costs. They decided that outside the city of Makkah, all the roads must be manned, and that visitors must be warned to be on their guard against the Holy Prophet (May God bless and cherish him), for they knew from their own experience how winning he could be.

The Quraysh carried out their plan thoroughly and appointed men everywhere to warn the pilgrims. Hazrat Abu Dharr, who belonged to the clan of Bani Giffar lived to the northwest of Makkah, not far from the Red Sea. He had already heard of the Holy Prophet (May God bless and cherish him) and of the hostilities of the Quraysh. Like most of his tribesmen, Hazrat Abu Dharr was a highwayman, but unlike them, he was a firm believer in the Oneness of God and never worshiped idols. His brother Unays went to Makkah for business and on his return, he told Hazrat Abu Dharr that there was a man of Quraysh who claimed to be a prophet of God and who proclaimed that there is no god, but Allah and his people were against him. Hearing this, Hazrat Abu Dharr was overcome by a strange curiosity and deep conviction that here was a true prophet. He immediately set off for Makkah, and though he met with members of Quraysh on his arrival, he did not pay attention to them. Soon, he found his way to the Holy Prophet's (May God bless and cherish him) house. The Holy Prophet (May God bless and cherish him) was lying asleep on a couch in the courtyard, and his face was covered with a cloak. Hazrat Abu Dharr woke him up and greeted him. "On thee be peace," said the Holy Prophet (May God bless and cherish him). "Tell me about what you proclaim and teach?" said the Bedouin. "I am no poet," said the Holy Prophet (May God bless and cherish him), "But what I utter is the Quran, and it is not I who speak but God who speaketh." "Recite for me." Said Abu Dharr and the Holy Prophet (May God bless and cherish him) recited a Sura, whereupon Abu Dharr said, "I testify that there is no god but God, and that Muhammad is the Messenger of God."

"Who are thy people?" The Holy Prophet (May God bless and cherish him) asked and at the man's answer he looked at him in amazement and said, "Verily God guides whom He will." The tribe of Giffar were mostly highway men. The Holy Prophet (May God bless and cherish him) instructed him in Islam and told him to return to his tribe and await his instructions. So, he returned to his tribe, and many of them entered Islam through him. In the meantime, he continued his calling as a highway man with special attention to the caravans of Quraysh. But when he had despoiled a caravan, he would offer to give back what he had taken on the condition that they would testify to the oneness of God and the prophethood of Hazrat Muhammad (May God bless and cherish him).

A similar encounter with the Holy Prophet (May God bless and cherish him) was by Tufayl, a man of Daws that resulted in bringing Islam to the Bani Daws, an outlying western tribe. Tufayl was warned on his arrival in Makkah by Quraysh against speaking to the sorcerer Hazrat Muhammad (May God bless and cherish him) or even listening to him lest he should find himself separated from his people. Tufayl himself was a poet and a man of considerable standing among his people. He was so afraid of being bewitched that before entering the Kaaba, he stuffed his ears with cotton balls. The Holy Prophet (May God bless and cherish him) was present in the Mosque, having just taken up his stance to pray between the Yemeni corner and the Black Stone. His recitation of the Quranic verses was not very loud however, some of it nonetheless penetrated Tufayl's ears. "God would not have it," he said later, "but that He would make me hear something of what was recited, and I heard beautiful words. So, I said to myself, I am a man of understanding, a poet, and not ignorant of the difference between the fair and the foul. Why then should I not hear what this man has to say? If it is fair, I will accept it, and if foul, reject it. I stayed in the Holy Sanctuary until the Holy Prophet (May God bless and cherish him) left, whereupon I followed him, and when he entered his house, I entered after him and said, "O Muhammad thy people told me this and that, and they so frightened me about you that I stuffed my ears so that I should not hear thee. So, tell me the truth of what thou art." The Holy Prophet (May God bless and cherish him) explained to him and recited the Noble Quran, and Tufayl made his profession of faith. Later, he returned to his people, determined to preach Islam, and convert them. His father and wife followed him into Islam, but the rest of his tribe hesitated. Tufayl went back to Makkah in great disappointment and requested the Holy Prophet (May God bless and cherish him) to put a curse on them. Instead, the Holy Prophet (May God bless and cherish him) prayed for their guidance and said to Tufayl, "Return to thy people, call them to Islam, and deal gently with them." Tufayl did exactly what he was instructed, and as years passed, more and more of Daws entered the fold of Islam.

In Makkah, the steady increase in the number of believers corresponded with the increase in hostility of the disbelievers. Whenever a new convert came to the Holy Prophet (May God bless and cherish him) and pledged his or her allegiance, it was often a slave, a freed slave, or a member of the Quraysh of the outskirts, or else a young man from the Quraysh of the hollow, with little influence in the Arab society. On the contrary, their conversion would increase tenfold of the hostility of their relatives and kinsmen.

The Quraysh very well understood that the Holy Prophet (May God bless and cherish him) could never be prevented from his call. They reverted to cheap means to suppress the spread of Islam. As for Allah's Messenger, he would earnestly go to the people who gathered during the pilgrimage season, visit them in their camps, and invite them to One God, Allah. Abu Lahab, the Holy Prophet's (May God bless and cherish him) uncle, would shadow him shouting aloud, "Do not listen to him for he is a liar; he is an apostate."

The Quraysh put all their efforts into degrading the Holy Prophet (May God bless and cherish him) as a madman possessed by a Jinn or an insane person.

"And they say, O you (Muhammad) to whom the dhikr (The Quran) has been sent down; verily, you are a mad man." (15:6). The Holy Prophet was labelled a liar practicing witchcraft.

"And they (Arab Pagans) wonder that a warner has come to them from among themselves! And the disbelievers say: "This (Prophet Muhammad) is a sorcerer, a liar." (38:4)

The Quraysh used all sorts of abusive language, calling him a madman or one possessed by an evil spirit, and so on.

"And verily those who disbelieve would almost make you slip with their eyes through hatred when they hear the Reminder (The Quran), and they say, verily he (Muhammad) is a madman." (68:51)

However, the Holy Prophet (May God bless and cherish him) continued to proclaim what God had ordered him to proclaim, concealing nothing and hence inciting their dislike by forsaking their idols and religion. Among the early believers, there was a group who had no strong clan at their back to support and protect them. These innocent men and women were abused, ridiculed, and humiliated openly daily. It was at the beginning of the fourth year of the call that the polytheists realized that they could not stop the spread of Islam without persecuting the converts and torturing them. The leaders of Quraysh convened a meeting and decided to persecute anyone in their tribe found to be following the new faith.

One of the staunch enemies of Islam was Abu Jahl. Whenever he heard of the conversion of a man of high birth and powerful clan, he would undermine his judgement by questioning his intellect and threatening him with terrible consequences if he was a merchant. If the new convert was weak without any strong family connections, he would physically beat him and put him to unspeakable torture.

The uncle of Hazrat Uthman bin Affan used to imprison him in a dark room, wrap him in a mat of palm leaves, and set fire underneath him. When Umm Musab bin Umair heard of her son's conversion, she put him to starvation and then expelled him from her house. He was used to a luxurious life, brought up in affluence and with much delicacy. As a result of the hardships, he had to bear in way of Allah's religion, his skin was covered with wrinkles, and signs of suffering reflected from his face.

Hazrat Bilal, the slave of Umayyah bin Khalaf, was severely beaten by his master when the latter came to know of his conversion to Islam. Sometimes, a rope was put around his neck, and young boys were made to drag him through the streets and even across the rocky areas of Makkah. He was also subjected to hunger and starvation. Once, he was bound during the hottest part of the day and placed on burning sands under the scorching sun in Makkah. His master had a great stone brought and placed upon his chest. He said, "By God, I will not stop until you are dead or until you reject the new faith and worship Lat and Uzza." While Hazrat Bilal was suffering extreme torture, he only chanted, "Ahad, Ahad (The One Lord, the One Lord). In the meanwhile, Hazrat Abu Bakr was passing by, his heart melted at his condition. Harzat Abu Bakr said to Umayyah, "Have you no fear of God that you treat this poor fellow like this? How long is it to go on?" He replied, "You are the one who converted him, so save him from his plight that you see." "I will do so," said Hazrat Abu Bakr, "I have got a black slave, tougher and stronger than he, who is a heathen. I will exchange him for Bilal." The transaction was carried out, and Hazrat Abu Bakr took him and freed him.

Hazrat Ammar bin Yasir was another victim of the cruelty of Quraysh. He was a freed slave of Bani Makhzum. He, along with his mother and father, embraced Islam in the very beginning. They were constantly tortured, made to lie on the hot sand, and were beaten brutally. Ammar himself was at times thrown into fire. The Holy Prophet (May God bless and cherish him) once passed while he saw his family was tortured and said, "O family of Yasir! Be patient; you will certainly find your place in Paradise." Ammar's father died due to severe torture. His mother, Bibi Sumaiyah, was bayoneted to death by Abu Jahl himself. She was given the title of first woman martyr in Islam (May Allah's peace and blessings be upon her). Hazrat Ammar himself was subjected to unspeakable torture and continuously harassed and threatened with severe punishment unless he forsakes his new religion. During extreme torture, in a weak moment, he uttered a word that was interpreted as his withdrawal, though his heart never wavered for a moment. When he came back to the Holy Prophet (May God bless and cherish him) who consoled him for his suffering and confirmed his faith. The Divine Command came, and the following verse was revealed.

"Whoever disbelieved in Allah after his belief except him who is forced (to renounce) and whose heart is at rest with faith." (16:106)

Abu Fakih Aflah—a freed slave of Bani Abdud Dar, was another of those helpless victims. The Makkan Polytheists used to lay him on hot sand and place a huge stone on his back so that he couldn't move, leaving him like that until he lost consciousness. They also used to tie his legs with rope and drag him around until they thought he was dead. Hazrat Abu Bakr also passed by him while he was being tortured, and he purchased his freedom for the sake of Almighty God.

Khabbab bin Al-Aratt was a slave of Umm Ammar bin Saba Al-Khuzaiyah. He was another poor fellow and subjected to the same brutality on every possible occasion. They would take him by his hair and drag him in the streets. They would twist his neck and throw him into the fire and drag him until his back would be burned.

Many women converts were maltreated in the similar way. Zarinah An-Nahdiyah and her daughter Umm Ubays, and many others had experienced their full share of persecution at the hands of polytheists.

Hazrat Abu Bakr was a wealthy believer before emigration to Medina, and he freed six slaves in Islam, Bilal being the seventh, namely Amir b. Fuhayr, Zarinah and Umm Ubays. Zarinah lost her sight when he freed her, and the Quraysh said, "Al-Lat and Al-Uzza are the ones that have taken away her sight." But she said, "By the House of God, you lie. Al-Lat and Al-Uzza can neither harm nor heal." So, Allah, the Lord of the worlds restored her sight. Al-Nahdiyah and her daughter belonged to a woman of B. Abdul Dar. Hazrat Abu Bakr passed by them when their mistress had sent them to grind wheat for her and she was saying, "By God, I will never free you." Hazrat Abu Bakr said to her, "Free yourself from your oath." She said, "It's free; you corrupted them, so you free them." They agreed upon the price, and he said, "I will take them, and they are free."

In another instance, Hazrat Abu Bakr passed by a slave girl of B. Muammil, a clan of B. Adiy b. Kab, who converted to Islam. Ummar b. al-Khattab was mercilessly beating her to make her renounce her faith. At that time, he was a polytheist. He beat her until he no longer could and said, "I have only stopped beating you because I am tired." She replied, "May God treat you in the same manner." Hazrat Abu Bakr came forward, bought her, and freed her.

Ibn Ishaq narrated on the authority of Muhammad b. Abdullah b. Atiq from Amir b. Abdullah b. al-Zubayr that Abu Qahafa told his son Hazrat Abu Bakr, "My son, I witness that you are freeing weak slaves. If you intend to do what you are doing, why don't you free powerful men, who could defend you and protect you." Hazrat Abu Bakr replied, "I am only trying to do what I am attempting for God's sake." The following verses were revealed in reference to him and what his father said to him.

"He who gives (from) his wealth to purify himself. And not for anyone who has done him a favor to be rewarded. But only seeking the countenance of his Lord, Most High." (92:18-21)

Makkan polytheists used all sorts of atrocities against some of the Companions. They imprisoned them in animal enclosures and then dragged them into the hot sun. Some were clothed in iron armor and then tied on hot boulders to fry in the scorching sun. The new converts concealed their faith to avoid torture and suffering. As for the Holy Prophet (May God bless and cherish him), it was not easy for the Quraysh to lay hands on him because he had such significance, nobility, and matchless perfection of character. Moreover, he had the protection of his great uncle Hazrat Abu Talib, who came from noble descent and had a great clan behind his back. For Makkan polytheists the situation was extremely worrisome, and they had reached the limits of their patience.

Abu Lahab, the Holy Prophet's (May God bless and cherish him) uncle, was at the forefront of those who committed atrocities and countless acts of hatred against the Holy Prophet (May God bless and cherish him). To damage his reputation and cause him pain, Abu Lahab forced his two sons to divorce their wives, Hazrat Ruqayyah and Hazrat Umm Kulthum, the Holy Prophet's (May God bless and cherish him) daughters. Abu Lahab also showed delight upon his second son's death and called him the man cut off with offspring. (Tafsir Ibn Kathir, Surat Al-Kawther)

It is not certain whether the marriages had already taken place, or whether they were still betrothed, but Abu Lahab's satisfaction at this action was ruined when his wealthy Umayyad cousin, Hazrat Uthman bin Affan asked for the hand of Hazrat

Ruqayyah and married her. This marriage was most pleasing to the Holy Prophet (May God bless and cherish him) and Hazrat Khadijah. Their daughter was happy, and their new son-in-law was devoted to them. Hazrat Ruqayyah was the most beautiful of their daughters and one of the most beautiful women of her generation throughout all of Makkah, and Hazrat Uthman was a remarkably handsome man. To see the two of them together was a reason for rejoicing.

"Verily, God is beautiful, and He loves beauty." Not long after their marriage, when they were both absent from Makkah, the Holy Prophet (May God bless and cherish him) sent a messenger, who returned considerably later than he was expected. When he began to offer his excuses, the Holy Prophet (May God bless and cherish him) said, "I will tell thee, if thou wilt, what hath kept thee; thou did not stand there gazing at Uthman and Ruqayyah and marveling at their beauty."

Abu Lahab would shadow his steps during the pilgrimage season, pronounce him a liar, and persuade the pilgrims against him and his call. Tariq bin Abdullah al-Muharabi narrated that he would not stop merely ridiculing him, but rather he would throw stones at him until his ankles bled (Kunzul-Umal). Abu Lahab's wife, Umm Jamil bint Harb, the sister of Abu Sufyan, who was another archenemy of Islam, was not less than her husband in enmity and hatred she had for the Messenger of Allah (May God bless and cherish him). She used to gather thorns and tie them in bundles with twisted palm leaf fiber and scatter them in the path of the Holy Prophet (May God bless and cherish him). She was truly an ill-mannered woman with abusive language. On every occasion she enkindled the fire of enmity and hatred against the Holy Prophet (May God bless and cherish him). She was deservedly labelled as 'The carrier of firewood' in the Noble Quran.

When Umm Jamil heard the Sura 'Tabat-Yada', she swiftly proceeded to the Holy Sanctuary with a handful of pebbles to throw at the Holy Prophet (May God bless and cherish him). The Mighty Lord put a curtain over her sight, and she saw only Hazrat Abu Bakr, who was sitting next to the Holy Prophet. She then shouted at him, threatening to break his companion's mouth with her handful of pebbles, and recited verses full of insult and disrespect.

"We have disobeyed the dispraised one, rejected his call, and alienated ourselves from his religion."

When she left, Hazrat Abu Bakr turned to the Holy Prophet (May God bless and cherish him) in disbelief and asked with surprise about the matter. The Holy Prophet

(May God bless and cherish him) said, "She did not see me. Allah prevented her from being able to see me."

Abu Lahab and his wife lived next door to the Holy Prophet (May God bless and cherish him). Despite having blood relations, they inflicted much pain on him and constantly harassed him. Similarly, other neighbors of the Holy Prophet (May God bless and cherish him) would also torture him in his own house.

Ibn Ishaq narrated, "The group of people who used to harm the Messenger of Allah in his house included Abu Lahab, Al-Hakam bin Al-As bin Umayyah, Uqabah bin Abu Muait, Adi bin Hamra, Al-Thaqafi and Ibn Al-Asda al-Hudhail. They were all his neighbors, and he was not safe from their transgressions except for Al-Hakam bin Abdul As. One of them would throw intestines of sheep on him while he was praying another would throw it in his pot of food. The Holy Prophet would use a rock to screen himself from them when he prayed. When they would do so, he would remove it with a piece of wood and put it away by the door then say, "O Bani Abd-Manaf! what kind of neighborly treatment is this?"

Al-Bukhari narrated on the authority of Ibn Masud, "Once the Holy Prophet (May God bless and cherish him) was praying inside the Mosque in the Holy Sanctuary where Abu Jahl was sitting with some of his friends. One of them said, "Who among you would bring the guts of a camel of Bani so and so and put it on the back of Hazrat Muhammad (May God bless and cherish him) when he lowers his head in prayer?" The most wicked of them Uqbah bin Abi Muait stood up and hence brought forth the animal's gut. He waited until the Holy Prophet (May God bless and cherish him) prostrated, and then he placed those filthy organs on his back between his shoulders. One of the Companions said, "I was watching all this incident but could not do anything about it. I wished that I had some men with me to prevent all this insult." They started laughing and falling on each other. The Holy Prophet (May God bless and cherish him) was in prostration and did not lift his head till little Hazrat Fatima (The Holy Prophet's daughter) came and removed the filth with her small hands.

The Messenger of Allah (May God bless and cherish him) raised his head and said three times," O Allah! Destroy the infidels of Quraysh." When Abu Jahl and his companions heard what the Holy Prophet (May God bless and cherish him) said, they were frightened as they believed that the prayers and invocations were accepted in the Holy Sanctuary in the city of Makkah. The Holy Prophet (May God bless and cherish him) invoked Allah Azo wa Jal, "O Allah! Destroy Abh Jahl, Utbah bin Rabia, Shaybah bin Rabia, Al-Walid bin Utbah, Umayyah bin Khalaf and Uqbah bin Abi Muait." And he mentioned a seventh person whose name I cannot recall. By Allah, in whose hand is my life, I saw the dead bodies of those persons who were counted by the Holy Prophet (May God bless and cherish him) in the one of the wells of Badr. (Sahih Bukhari, the book of Ablution). The seventh person was Umarah bin Al-Walid. (Ibn Hisham)

Umayyah bin Khalaf was a wretched soul who, whenever he saw the Holy Prophet (May God bless and cherish him), would slander and use foul language about him. In the Noble Quran, Allah revealed about him in Sura al-Humaza,

"Woe to every slanderer and back biter." (104:1)

Ibn Hisham narrated, "Al-Humaza is the one who publicly mocks a person, and Al-Humaza is the one who secretly declares the defects of people and defames them."

Uqbah bin Abi Muait once attended a gathering of the Holy Prophet (May God bless and cherish him) and listened to his teachings. A close friend of his, Ubay bin Khalaf, came to know about this. He was infuriated by this action and strongly condemned Uqbah and ordered him to spit in the face of the Holy Prophet (May God bless and cherish him), and he shamelessly did it. Ubay did not spare any thinkable way to humiliate the Holy Prophet (May God bless and cherish him). He once ground old, decomposed bones and blew the powder on the Holy Prophet (May God bless and cherish him) (Ibn Hisham). It is about him that Allah revealed,

"But no, he will be thrown into the crusher." (104:4)

Rashid-ud-Din Maybudi explained in Kashf-al-Asrar, "It will not be like what they fancy and will not be as they hope. In truth, at the resurrection, they will be thrown into Hell. They will be held captive in humiliation and misery in the depths of the Crusher, their hands and feet fettered, stretched with a chain of seventy yards, without hope for the mercy of the Real."

"And what will thee know what the Crusher is?" (104:5). And how would you know how hard are the depths of the Crusher? And how burning is its fire?

At times, Abu Jahl would come to listen to the Holy Prophet (May God bless and cherish him) recite the Quran, and then he would leave without believing its truth nor taking any heed to its warning. He would inflict harm on the Messenger of Allah by his speech and take every opportunity to negate the message of the Lord. He would then go around arrogantly and boast about what he did. The Mighty and Majestic Lord revealed about him,

"So, he (the disbeliever) never believed (in this Quran, in the message of Muhammad) nor prayed." (75:31)

Abu Jahl also wanted to stop the Holy Prophet (May God bless and cherish him) from praying inside the Holy Sanctuary. Once, the Holy Prophet (May God bless and cherish him) was inside the Mosque praying when Abu Jahl approached him, threatening and using abusive language. The Holy Prophet (May God bless and cherish him) admonished him strongly. Abu Jahl retaliated rudely, claiming that he was the most powerful in all Makkah, and pointed out that he could summon the largest council of men to support him. Allah then revealed,

"Then let him call upon his council of helpers." (96:17)

It is also related that the Holy Prophet (May God bless and cherish him) took Abu Jahl by his neck, shook him back and forth severely, and said, "Woe to you (O man) and then (again) woe to you! Again, woe to you (O man) and the woe to you."

Despite this, Abu Jahl never regretted his behavior, nor did he realize his foolish ways. On the contrary, he was determined to go to extremes and swore he would dust the face of the Holy Prophet (May God bless and cherish him) and step on his neck. No sooner had he proceeded to fulfill his wicked intention than he was seen turning back in terror, shielding himself with his hand (as if something horrible was in his pursuit). His companions asked him what the matter was. He said, "I saw a ditch of burning fire and some wings flying." Later, the Holy Prophet narrated: "If he had proceeded further, the angels would have plucked off his limbs one after another." (Sahih Muslim)

In the light of such inhuman treatment, the Holy Prophet (May God bless and cherish him) deemed it wise to advise his followers to conceal their faith in both words and deeds. He decided to meet them secretly so that the Quraysh would not become aware of his goals. He also wanted to avoid any open confrontation with the polytheists because it was not in the interest of the new religion at this early stage. Once, the Muslims were on their way to the hillocks of Makkah to hold a secret meeting with the Holy Prophet (May God bless and cherish him), when a group of polytheists observed their suspicious movement and started abusing and fighting them. Sa'd bin Abi Waqqas hit a polytheist and shed his blood, and thus it was the first bloodshed in the history of Islam.

DAR AL ARQAM

The Holy Prophet (May God bless and cherish him), despite the disgraceful treatment of the Makkans, continued to preach the Islamic faith candidly and openly with deep devotion and strong conviction. But for the welfare of the new believers and the strategic interest of the new faith, he decided to meet the faithful secretly to instruct them in the Quran and Islamic faith at the estates of Al-Arqam bin Abdul-Arqam Al-Makhzumi which were situated on As-Safa.

So far, the clan of Makhzum was strongly against the new faith and seemed to have much hatred of the Holy Prophet (May God bless and cherish him). However, the Holy Prophet (May God bless and cherish him) had at least the devotion of Abu Salamah, the son of his aunt Barrah. By the grace of Almighty Allah, there came unexpected help and strength for the religion of Allah. Abu Salamah had a rich cousin on his father's side named Arqam-the Makhzumite, whose grandfathers were brothers. Arqam came to the Holy Prophet (May God bless and cherish him) and pronounced the declaration of faith, and uttered the two shahadatayn, La Illaha illallah (There is no god but God) and Muhammadan Rasulallah (Muhammad is the Messenger of God). He placed his large house near the foot of Mount Safa at the service of Islam. As a result, the believers took refuge in the center of Makkah, where they could meet and pray together without fear of being seen or disturbed.

HAZRAT HAMZAH COVERTS TO ISLAM

With the constant trickle of new converts in the fold of Islam, there was a corresponding increase in hostility of the Quraysh. Once some of the important men of the Quraysh were gathered in the Hijr, plotting against the Holy Prophet (May God bless and cherish him). At the same time the Holy Prophet (May God bless and cherish him) entered the Holy Sanctuary. He went to the east corner of the Kaaba, kissed the Black Stone, and began to make (Tawaf) around the Kaaba. As he passed the Hijr, the Quraysh raised their voices, abusing and condemning him. The Holy Prophet (May God bless and cherish him) heard what they said but remained calm. He passed them again in his second round, and they slandered him again. But when they did the same on the third round, the Holy Prophet (May God bless and cherish him) stopped and addressed them, "O Quraysh, hear me. Verily, by Him who holds my soul in His hand, I bring you slaughter!" the Holy Prophet's (May God bless and cherish him) words and the way he said them seemed to bind them as by a spell, and not one of them moved or spoke until one of them said, "Go thy way, O Abu l-Qasim, for by God thou art not an ignorant fool." They were all embarrassed by their momentary weakness.

One of the strongest enemies of the new faith was Amr, also called Abu l-Hakam from the clan of Makhzum, which the believers were quick to change to Abu Jahl (The father of ignorance). He was the grandson of Mughirah and nephew of the now-elderly Walid, who was chief of the clan. Abu Jahl was sure to succeed his uncle and had already used his wealth and influence to establish his position in Makkah. He was famous for his ruthless behavior and his readiness to take revenge on anyone who opposed him. He was one of the strongest enemies of the new faith and most vocal in his denunciation of the Holy Prophet (May God bless and cherish him). He was very brutal in persecuting the helpless believers of his own clan and urged other clans to follow suit.

One day, the Holy Prophet (May God bless and cherish him) was sitting outside the Holy Sanctuary near the Safa gate, so named because the pilgrims go out through it to perform the rite of making seven trips between the Hill of Safa and the Hill of Marwah. The Holy Prophet (May God bless and cherish him) was alone in this hollowed place and in deep contemplation. By chance Abu Jahl happened to pass that way. Finding the Holy Prophet (May God bless and cherish him) alone, he found the opportunity to revile him with all the abuse he could muster. The Holy Prophet (May God bless and cherish him) remained calm and quiet during this episode. After insulting the Messenger of Allah, Abu Jahl left and entered the Mosque to join his fellow Quraysh who were gathered in the Hijr. The Holy Prophet (May God bless and cherish him) rose to his feet and returned to his house.

As soon as the Holy Prophet (May God bless and cherish him) left, Hazrat Hamzah came from the opposite direction on his way from the hunt with his bow slung over his shoulder. It was his custom whenever he came from outside Makkah to do honor to the Holy Kaaba before he joined his family. A woman of the house of Abdullah ibn Judan of Taym, rushed out of her house near the Safa gate when she saw Hazrat Hamzah approaching Kaaba. The Judan family were cousins of Hazrat Abu Bakr. She herself was sympathetic to the Holy Prophet (May God bless and cherish him) and his teachings. She was outraged by Abu Jahl's insults, every word of which she had overheard. "Abu Umarah," she said to Hazrat Hamzah, "If only you had seen how Hazrat Muhammad (May God bless and cherish him), your brother's son, was treated even now by Abu Hakam, the son of Hisham. He found him sitting here alone and ferociously reviled him and abused him. Then he left." She pointed towards the Mosque to indicate where he had gone, "and Muhammad answered not a word." Hazrat Hamzah was the most stalwart man of the Quraysh, and when angry, he was the most formidable and the most unyielding. His mighty frame shook with anger, and something stirred in his soul. He was inclined towards the religion of God, and this event brought to completion an already half-formed resolve. He made straight for Abu Jahl, and standing over him, he raised his bow and brought down with all his force on his back. "How dare to insult Muhammad," he said, "Now that I am of his religion, and now that I proclaim what he proclaims. Strike blow for blow if you can." Abu Jahl was taken by fear and surprise and felt that it was better that the matter should be closed. So, when his friends rose to their feet as if to help him, he motioned them to be seated, saying, "Let Abu Umarah be, for by God I reviled his brother's son with an ugly reviling."

Hazrat Hamzah faithfully followed the religion of Islam, and because of his conversion, the Quraysh were now more hesitant to abuse the Holy Prophet (May God bless and cherish him) directly. Hazrat Hamzah was now there to protect the Holy Prophet (May God bless and cherish him). This unexpected event made the Quraysh change their tactics to stop the spread of Islam. In view of this danger, the Quraysh agreed to follow a suggestion that was made in the meeting by one of the leading men of Abdu Shams, Utbah bin Rabia. He said, "Why should I not go to Muhammad (May God bless and cherish him) and make certain offers to him, some of which he might accept? And what he accepts that will we give him, on the condition that he leaves us in peace." Utbah was of a less violent and more conciliatory nature than most of the Quraysh, and he was also known for his intelligence. He was a grandson of Abdu Shams, the brother of Hisham, the clan named after these two sons of Abdu Manaf, son of the great Qusayy, who was influential among Quraysh.

In the meantime, the Holy Prophet (May God bless and cherish him) was sitting alone in the Mosque beside Kaaba. Therefore, Utbah left the assembly of Quraysh and went straight to the Mosque. "Son of my brother," he addressed the Holy Prophet (May God bless and cherish him), "You are a noble person of the tribe, and your esteemed lineage assures you a place of honor among Quraysh. And now you have created a matter of grave concern for thy people, because of which you have rifted our community, declared their way of life to be foolish, spoken against our gods and religion, and called our forefathers infidels. I have come to you to propose something and see if any of it is acceptable to you. If it is wealth that you seek, we will gather a fortune for you from our properties so that you may be the richest man amongst us. If it is honor that you seek, we will make you our overlord and take no decision without your consent, and if you seek kingship, we will even make you, our king. And if you cannot get rid of this affliction that had haunted you, we will find you a physician and spend our wealth until your cure is complete." When Utbah finished talking, the Holy Prophet (May God bless and cherish him) said to him, "Now listen to me, O father of Walid." "I will," replied Utbah. Therefore, the Holy Prophet (May God bless and cherish him) recited to him part of a revelation which he had recently received from Allah.

Utabah was hoping to win over the Holy Prophet (May God bless and cherish him) by making sound offers, but as he listened to the verses of the Quran, his thoughts had changed to wonderment at the beauty of the words themselves. He sat there with his hands behind his back and was amazed at the divine music that flowed into his ears. The signs (Ayahs) that were recited spoke of Revelation itself and of the creation of the earth and Heaven. Then it related the story of the prophets and of the peoples of old, who, having rejected them, had been destroyed and doomed to Hell. Then came a verse that spoke of the believers, promising them the protection of the angels in this life and the bliss of the hereafter. The Holy Prophet (May God bless and cherish him) concluded his recitation with the words,

"And His signs are the night and the day and the sun and the moon. Bow not down in adoration unto the sun nor unto the moon, but bow down in adoration unto God their creator, if Him indeed ye worship." (Surah Sajda:37).

The Holy Prophet (May God bless and cherish him) then placed his forehead on the ground in prostration. Then he said, "O Abu l-Walid, thou had heard what thou had heard, and all is now between thee and that."

Utabah was awestruck by the divine revelation, and his facial expression showed signs of amazement. When he returned to his companions, they exclaimed, "What has befallen thee, O Abu l-Walid?" He replied, "I have heard an utterance the like of which I have never yet heard. It is not poetry by God, neither is it sorcery nor soothsaying. People of Quraysh pay attention and do as I say. Come not between this man and what he is about, but let him be, for, by God, the words that I have heard from him will be received as great tidings. If the Arabs strike him down, ye will be rid of him at the hands of others, and if he overcomes the Arabs, then his victory will be your victory, and his might will be yours might, and you will be the most fortunate of men."

At this, the Quraysh ridiculed him and said, "Muhammad has bewitched him with his tongue." "I have given you my opinion," he answered, "Now it is up to you to do whatever pleases you," Utabah said nothing else; moreover, the effect of the Quranic verses was short-lived. The Quraysh did not get the results they were expecting. So, they decided to go to the Holy Prophet (May God bless and cherish him) directly and argue with him. They sent him a message, "The nobles of thy people are gathered together that they may have a word with you." The Holy Prophet (May God bless and cherish him) rushed to meet them, thinking they must have had a change of heart. The Holy Prophet (May God bless and cherish him) desired to guide them to Allah but he was disappointed as soon as they began repeating their offers already made to him. However, the Holy Prophet (May God bless and cherish him) listened patiently. When they finished talking, the Holy Prophet addressed them, "I am neither possessed, nor do I seek honor for myself. I do not desire kingship over you. Allah has sent me to you as a Messenger and revealed to me a Book and commanded me to be a teller of good tidings and a warner. I have conveyed to you the message of my Lord, and I have given you good counsel. If you heed to what I have brought you, that is your good fortune in this world and the hereafter, but if you deny me, then I will patiently await God's judgment between us."

They challenged by saying, "If you do not accept our offers, then do something that would prove that you are a messenger from God. Ask your Lord to remove those mountains that have surrounded us and instead flatten out for us our land and make rivers flow through it like the rivers of Syria and Iraq. And to raise for us some of our forefathers, Qusayy amongst them, that we may ask him if what you say be true or false. But if you are unable to do so, then ask for favors for yourself. Ask God to send an angel with you, who shall confirm your words. And ask Allah to bestow you gardens and palaces and treasures of gold and silver that we may know your rank with your Lord."

The Holy Prophet (May God bless and cherish him) answered, "I am not the one to ask Allah for such things, nor I was sent for that, but God has sent me to warn and give good tidings." The Quraysh refused to listen to his divine message and said, "Then make fall the sky in pieces on our heads." The Holy Prophet (May God bless and cherish him) replied, "That is for God to decide; if He will, He will do it."

The infidels went on to criticize another point. One of the most puzzling features of the Quranic verses was the recurring mention of the strange name 'Rahman', apparently related to the source of the Holy Prophet's (May God bless and cherish him) inspiration. One of the Surah began with the words, "The infinitely good (Ar-Rahman) taught the Quran." And because the Quraysh believed the rumor that the Holy Prophet (May God bless and cherish him) was taught his utterances by a man in Yemen called Rahman, they said, "We will never believe in Rahman." The Holy Prophet (May God bless and cherish him) remained silent as they continued their assault. "We have justified ourselves before you, and we swear by God that we will not leave you in peace until we destroy you or until you destroy us." One of them further said, "We will not believe you until you bring God and the angels as proof."

The Holy Prophet (May God bless and cherish him) was hurt and disappointed, and he rose to his feet. As he was about to leave, Abdullah, the son of Abu Umayyah of Makhzum, also got up and said to him, "I will never believe in you, nay, not until you take a ladder and I see you climbing to heaven, and until you bring us four angels to testify that you indeed are a messenger of God and even then I think I would not believe." Abdullah, on his father's side, was first cousin to Abu Jahl but his mother was Atikah's daughter of Abd al-Muttalib, and she had named her son after her brother, the Holy Prophet's father. When the Holy Prophet (May God bless and cherish him) heard such words from so near a kinsman, he went home filled with sadness.

The followers of the new faith were continuously growing, but almost all the new converts came from ordinary members of the Quraysh with no strong connections or influence. Abd-ar-Rahman, Hazrat Hamzah and Arqam had been exceptions, but even they were far from being leaders, and the Holy Prophet (May God bless and cherish him) was hoping to win some of the chiefs, not one of whom had shown any interest to join him and support the religion of God.

CHAPTER 10
EMIGRATION TO ABYSSINIA

The new faith "Islam" was proclaimed to be one with the monotheism first taught by Prophet Hazrat Ibrahim (May God bless and cherish him), the venerable patriarch of the Hebrew Bible and the common ancestor of the Arabs and Jews. The Holy Prophet (May God bless and cherish him) openly denounced the idolatry practices surrounding the Holy Sanctuary, the Kaaba, and the dissolute lives of its patron tribe, the Quraysh, as pagan, idolaters, and morally corrupt. The Holy Prophet (May God bless and cherish him) was thus at odds with those who benefited both economically and politically from the status quo. Therefore, the Quraysh considered the prophetic message a serious threat to their way of life and power and started persecuting and torturing the Holy Prophet (May God bless and cherish him) and his earliest followers, which took them to the brink of despair.

The series of persecutions started late in the fourth year of the prophethood, slowly at first but steadily increased and worsened day by day. In the fifth year, the situation got so grave that it was no longer tolerable, and Muslims began to seriously think of ways to avert the painful treatments.

Abu Jahl, as mentioned earlier, was at the forefront of the oppressors. It was through him that his clansmen tortured the three poorer believers, Yasir and Sumayyah, and their son, Ammar. They refused to renounce Islam, and Sumayyah died under the suffering they inflicted on her. It was said to them, "Are not al-Lat and al-Uzzah your gods?"

They would reply, "Rabi Allah ul Ahad, wa dinehi din-e-Muhammmad" (Our

Rab is Allah, who is One, and our religion is the religion of Muhammad).

But some of the victims of Makhzum and other clans could not endure what they were made to suffer. It was at those desperate times that Allah informed them that the earth was too restricted for them, alluding to emigrating.

"God is for those who do good in this world, and Allah's earth is spacious. Only those who are patient shall receive their reward in full, without reckoning." (39:10).

The Holy Prophet (May God bless and cherish him) knew that Ashamah, who was known as Negus, King of Abyssinia (Ethiopia), was a fair ruler and would not wrong any of his subordinates, so he said to his followers, "If you went to the country of the Abyssinians, you would find there a king under whom none suffered wrong. It is a land of sincerity in religion until such time as God shall make for you a means of relief from what you now are suffering.

The believers emigrated in great numbers, some emigrating with their families and others by themselves, and they eventually arrived at Abyssinia. Al-Zuhri said: Hazrat Jafar Ibn Abi Talib emigrated with his wife Asma bint Umays al-Khathamiyyah, and so did Hazrat Uthman ibn Affan with his wife Hazrat Ruqayyah, the daughter of the Holy Prophet (May God bless and cherish him). Khalid Ibn Said ibn al-As also left with his wife, Umm Salamah, the daughter of Abu Umayyah ibn al-Mughirah. The Holy Prophet (May God bless and cherish him) said with respect to Hazrat Uthman and Hazrat Ruqayyah, "They are the first people to emigrate in the cause of Allah after Hazrat Ibrahim and Hazrat Lot."

They left Makkah under the darkness of the night and headed for the sea, where two boats were ready for sailing to Abyssinia (Ethiopia). The news of their emigration reached Quraysh, so some men were sent to follow them, but the converts had already left Port of Shuaybah towards their destination, where they were received and accorded due hospitality. Abdullah ibn Jafar was born in Abyssinia. Born there, too, was the slave girl of Khalid ibn Said's daughter, the mother of Amr ibn al-Zubayr and Khalid ibn Zubayr. Amongst the people of Quraysh, born there was also al-Harith ibn Habib.

Al-Zuhri said: Urwah ibn al-Zubayr reported to me that Hazrat Aisha said:

"There is not a moment I can recall that my parents did not practice the true faith (Islam), and not a day would pass that the Messenger of God (May God bless and cherish him) did not visit us twice a day, in the morning and the evening. When pagans started persecuting Muslims, many people emigrated with their families to Abyssinia. Hazrat Abu Bakr also intended to leave Makkah to emigrate to Abyssinia. When he reached Birk al-Ghimad, Ibn al-Dughunnah, who was the chief of his tribe, met him and asked, "Where are you headed." Hazrat Abu Bakr replied, "My tribe has exiled me, so I intend to journey throughout the land and worship my Lord." Ibn al-Dughunnah replied, "O Abu Bakr! A man such as you should not be exiled— indeed, you succeed where others fail. You cultivate the bond of kinship and carry the weary; you act hospitality towards guests and aid your kinsmen in times of their distress. I will act as your protector, so return to your tribe and worship your Lord in your homeland."

Ibn al-Dughunnah accompanied Hazrat Abu Bakr on the return journey to Makkah. Ibn al-Dughunnah visited Quraysh and his allies and told them, "Indeed, Hazrat Abu Bakr has been exiled, but no one should exile a man such as him. Will you exile a man who finds success where others fail, who cultivates the bonds of kinship and bears all, who acts with hospitality towards guests and aids his kinsmen in times of their need.?" The Quraysh acknowledged the protection of Ibn al-Dughunnah and granted Hazrat Abu Bakr a haven. They said to Ibn al-Dughunnah, "Tell Abu Bakr to worship his Lord in his home and to pray there as he wishes, but also order him neither to trouble us nor to seek to make his prayers and Scripture reading known anywhere outside his home." Abu al-Dugunnah did the same.

After these events, it occurred to Hazrat Abu Bakr to build a Mosque inside the courtyard of his home. There, he used to pray and recite the Noble Quran, but Pagan women and children would gather and stumble over one another to see and watch him in amazement. Hazrat Abu Bakr was a man much given to weeping, and he could not control his tears while reciting the word of God. These instances frightened the notables of Quraysh, so they sent a message to Ibn Dughunnah. When he arrived, they said to him, "We agreed to provide Hazrat Abu Bakr a safe place on the condition that he worships God in his house, but he has transgressed that condition by building a Mosque in the courtyard of his house and thus brought attention to all his praying and Scripture reading. Indeed, we are afraid that he is misguiding our women and children, so go to him and order him as follows: if he is content with going no further than worshiping God in his home, then he may do so; if he refuses to avoid bringing attention to this, then ask him to release you of your covenant. For we have come to loathe your protection and will not allow Hazrat Abu Bakr to bring attention to his faith."

Hazrat Aisha said: "Ibn al-Dughunnah then came to Hazrat Abu Bakr and said, "O Abu Bakr, you know the conditions on which I swore an oath to you; either choose not to go beyond their stipulations, or else relieve me of my pact. Indeed, I do not wish for the Arabs to hear that I violated an undertaking that I have granted to anyone." Hazrat Abu Bakr replied, "In that case, I relieve you of your oath of protection. I shall be content with the protection of God and His Messenger."

That day, the Messenger of God (May God bless and cherish him) was in Makkah, and he said to the believers, "Today, I have seen the land of your emigration; indeed, I have been granted a vision of a marshy land full of date palms between the black fields —meaning the two fields of lava rock."

In the month of Ramadan of the same year, the Holy Prophet (May God bless and cherish him) went into Kaaba, where a large gathering of Quraysh was assembled, including some notables and elders. Suddenly, the Holy Prophet (May God bless and cherish him) began reciting Sura An-Najm (Chapter 53, The Star). The awe-inspiring words of Allah descended unexpectedly upon the polytheists, and they were instantly stunned by them. It was as if they were shocked for the first time by the divine revelation. In the past, they used to ignore the word of God by not listening to it but also to talk loudly and rudely when the Quran was recited.

When the unspeakably beautiful words of Allah came in direct contact with their hearts, they were spellbound and listened intently to such an extent that when the Holy Prophet (May God bless and cherish him) reached the heart-rendering ending:

"So, fall you down in prostration to Allah and worship Him alone." (Quran 53:62)

The entire gathering unconsciously and with full obedience prostrated themselves as if they were helpless. It was a moment of truth and utter amazement when they realized that the words of God had conquered their hearts. When the Quraysh heard about this incident, they accused their fellow Quraysh. Consequently, they began to fabricate lies, alleging that the Holy Prophet (May God bless and cherish him) had attached to their idols great respect and ascribed to them the power of intercession. All of these were excuses to justify their prostration with the Holy Prophet (May God bless and cherish him) on that day.

The news of this incident was misreported to the Muslim emigrants in Abyssinia. They were informed that the whole of Quraysh had converted to Islam. Therefore, they made their way back home. They arrived in Makkah in the month of Shawal of the same year. When they were in the vicinity of Makkah, they discovered the truth. Some of them returned to Abyssinia, while others entered the city secretly, and some sought the protection of notables.

SECOND EMIGRATION OF MUSLIMS TO ABYSSINIA

The believers were continuously tortured, persecuted, and humiliated in many ways. When the Quraysh heard the news that the emigrant Muslims were accorded good hospitality and warm welcome in Abyssinia, they were very angry and increased their dreadful treatment of the believers. Thereupon, the Holy Prophet (May God bless and cherish him) deemed it imperative to allow the helpless Muslims to seek asylum in Abyssinia (Ethiopia) for a second time. The Quraysh were however, on the alert, and emigration this time was not an easy task. However, the Muslims managed to travel to Abyssinia before the Quraysh were able to block their exodus. The group of emigrants this time consisted of eighty-three men and nineteen women.

The Quraysh could not tolerate the prospect of a haven available to the believers in a Christian kingdom. Hence, they made a last-ditch effort to get those Muslims extradited to Makkah and sent two of their strongest envoys to demand their return. They were Amr bin Al-As and Abdullah bin Abi Rabia (before they embraced Islam). They took with them precious gifts for the king and his clergy and were able to win some of the courtiers over to their side. The Quraysh envoys demanded that the Muslim emigrants should be extradited and handed over to them on the basis that they had abandoned the religion of their ancestors, and their leader was propagating a new religion different from theirs and from that of the king. On hearing the claims against the Muslims presented by the envoys, the Christian king summoned the Muslims to his court. He asked them to explain the teachings of their new faith. The Muslim refugees gathered and selected Hazrat Jafar bin Abi Talib to speak on their behalf. Not for all the emigrants had the exile been a necessity. Hazrat Uthman bin Affan's family had given up trying to make him recount, but the Holy Prophet (May God bless and cherish him) nonetheless allowed him to go and take with him Hazrat Ruqayyah. Their presence was a source of strength to the community of exiles. Another couple very pleasant to look upon was Hazrat Jafar bin Abi Talib and his wife Asma. They had the full protection of Hazrat Abi Talib, but the refugees needed a spokesperson and Hazrat Jafar bin Abi Talib was an eloquent speaker. He had a commanding presence and was winning in person. The Holy Prophet (May God bless and cherish him) said to him on one occasion, "Thou art like me in looks and in character." It was Hazrat Jafar bin Abi Talib he had chosen to preside over the community of exiles, and his qualities of leadership and intelligence were unmatched.

Hazrat Jafar bin Abi Talib stood up in the court of Negus and addressed the king and his courtiers; "O king, we were plunged in the depth of ignorance and barbarism, we worshiped idols, and we ate dead animals. We were accustomed to lewd behavior, we disregarded humanity, breaking the ties of kinship and ignoring hospitality and the rights of neighbors. We were lawless, and the strong among us exploited the weak. This is how we lived until Allah sent us a messenger, one of our own people, whose lineage, truthfulness, trustworthiness, and integrity were well known to us. He called us to worship Allah alone and to renounce the stones and the idols which we and our forefathers used to worship beside Allah. He also commanded us to be truthful in speech, fulfill covenants, nurture ties of kinship, be kind to our neighbors, and refrain from spilling blood unlawfully. He forbade us from obscenities and false witness and not to consume an orphan's property nor slander chaste women. He commanded that we worship Allah alone without associating any partner with him. He taught us to perform Salat (Prayer), give charity, and fast in the month of Ramadan." The king and the entire court were listening intently. Hazrat Jafar bin Abi Talib continued,

"So, we trusted him and believed in him and followed the religion of Allah that he preached. We began to worship Allah alone, we did not associate any partner with Him, and we forbade what Allah made unlawful for us, and adopted what He made lawful for us. Therefore, O king, our people turned against us and began torturing and persecuting us to make us renounce our faith and revert to the old immorality and worship of idols. The Quraysh oppressed us, made life intolerable for us and prevented us from observing our religion. So, we left for your country, choosing you before anyone else, seeking your protection and hoping to live in peace and that, O king, you will not wrong us."

The Negus was impressed by his speech and eager to hear more. He asked Hazrat Jafar bin Abi Talib, "Do you have with you something of what your prophet brought concerning God?"

Hazrat Jafar bin Abi Talib, in his rich and melodious voice, recited the opening verses of Sura Maryam (Chapter 19), wherein, is told the story of the birth of both Prophet John and Prophet Jesus Christ, down to the account of Mary having been fed with the food miraculously.

"And made mention of Mary in the Book, when she withdrew from people upon a place towards the east and secluded herself from them; and We sent unto her Our Spirit, and it appeared unto her in the likeness of a perfect man. She said, "I take refuge from thee in the Infinitely Good if any piety thou hast. He said: I am none other than a messenger from thy Lord, that I may bestow on thee a son most pure. She said: how can there be for me a son, when no man hath touched me, nor am I unchaste? He said, even so, shall it be thy Lord saith: it is easy for Me that We may make him a sign for mankind and a mercy from Us, and it is a thing ordained." (Maryam:16-21)

On hearing the verses of the Noble Quran (The word of God) the king, along with his clergy, were moved to tears. They rolled down his cheeks, wetting his long beard. The king addressed the Muslims and said, "It is obvious that these words and those which were revealed to Jesus are the rays of the light which have radiated from the same source."

Turning to the envoys of the Quraysh, the king said, "I am afraid I cannot give you back these refugees. They are free to live and worship in my kingdom as they please."

The envoys of the Quraysh were disappointed, but when they came back from the court, Amr said to his companion, "Tomorrow, I will tell him something that shall make the king upset. I will tell him that they believe that Prophet Jesus, the son of Mary, is a slave." So, the next day, he went to the king and said, "O king, they utter an enormous lie about Jesus the son of Mary. Do but call them and ask them what they say of him."

Therefore, the king sent them word to come back and tell him what they said of Jesus. The believers were troubled by this situation. They consulted each other as to what they should reply. They all knew that they had no choice but to say what God had said. When they entered the royal court, they were asked about Prophet Jesus.

Hazrat Jafar ibn Abi Talib answered boldly, "We say of him what our Holy

Prophet (May God bless and cherish him) brought unto us, that he is a slave of God and His messenger and His Spirit and His word which He cast unto Mary the blessed virgin."

The Abyssinian king Negus was impressed; he took a piece of wood and said, "Jesus the son of Mary exceeded not what thou have said by the length of this stick." At this, the clergy around him grumbled, and he added, "For all your grumbling." The king then addressed Hazrat Jafar ibn Abi Talib and his companions, "Go your ways, for you are safe in my land. Not for mountains of gold would I harm a single man of you." Then he pointed towards the envoys of the Quraysh and told his attendant, "Return unto these two men their gifts, for I have no use for them." So, Amr and Abdullah returned to Makkah disgracefully.

The news of what the Abyssinian king had said about Prophet Jesus reached his people, and they were angry and turned against him, demanding an explanation. They accused him of having left their religion. He sent word to Hazrat Jafar ibn Abi Talib and his companions and made ready boats for them and told them to embark and leave if necessary. Then he took a parchment and wrote on it, "I testify that there is no god but God, and that Muhammad is His slave and His messenger and that Jesus the son of Mary is His slave and His messenger and His Spirit and His word which He cast unto Mary."

He put that parchment beneath his gown and went out to confront his people. He addressed them, "Abyssinians, have I not the best claim to be your king?" They said that he had. "Then what do you think of my life amongst you?" "It has been the best of lives," they answered. "Then what is it that bothers you?" he said. "Thou have left our religion," they answered, "and has claimed that Jesus is a slave." "Then what you say of Jesus?" he asked. "We say that he is a son of God," they replied. Then he put his hand on his breast, pointing to where the parchment was hidden, and testified to his belief in 'this' which his people took to refer to their words. So, his people were satisfied and dispersed, for they were happy under his rule. He then sent word to Hazrat Jafar ibn Abi Talib and his companions that they could disembark and live in peace and comfort.

UMAR CONVERSION TO ISLAM

The two Quraysh envoys failed on their mission to extradite Muslims from Abyssinia. This dismayed Quraysh, and they were livid. Therefore, they intensified their efforts to suppress and persecute the believers under the leadership of Abu Jahl, whose nephew Umar was one of the most violent towards the converts. He was a young man of twenty-six, headstrong, and not easily deterred, and of great resolution. He was feared and respected in Makkah, but at the same time, he was a strong opponent of the new religion.

Those whom God willed to do so answered the Holy Prophet's (May God bless and cherish him) call, namely, the young and the destitute, and eventually, the number who believed in him increased greatly, even though the infidel Quraysh rejected what the Holy Prophet preached. They would point to him whenever he passed by them in their gatherings and say, "This boy from the sons of Abd al-Muttalib hears a voice, as they allege, from heaven."

The beginning of Hazrat Umar's conversion to Islam after many had already become Muslims before him was as follows: It was after the unsuccessful return of the envoys from Abyssinia that he was seized by anger that aggravated him to action, and so taking up his sword he set out from his house. On his way, he came face to face with Nuaym ibn Abdullah, who was a member of his clan. Nuaym had accepted Islam already, but he kept his conversion secret in fear of Umar and others of his people. The facial expressions on Umar's face alarmed him, and he asked him where he was headed. "I am going to Muhammad, who has split Quraysh into two," replied Umar, "and I shall kill him." Nuaym tried to stop him by convincing him that he might himself be killed as well. But when he noticed that Umar was determined and would not listen to his argument, he thought of another way by which he might at least delay him so that he could inform the Holy Prophet (May God bless and cherish him) of his intentions. Even though it meant betraying fellow Muslims who, like himself, were concealing their faith, he knew that it was necessary and that they would forgive him. "O Umar," he said, "Why not first go back to the people of thine house and set them right." "What people of my house?" Umar asked. "Thy brother-in-law Sa'id bin Zayd bin Amr b, Nufayl and thy sister Fatima, umm Jamil bint al-Khattab," said Nuaym. "They are both followers of Muhammad in his religion." Umar was also told that she no longer ate the carrion from which he ate. Without a word, Umar turned and made straight for his sister's house. Another newly convert by the name of Khabab bin Aratt, who belonged to the clan of Zuhrah, used to come to recite the Noble Quran to Said and Fatima, and he was with them at that moment with some pages of the Sura Taha that had just been revealed, and they were reciting it together.

They heard Umar's voice, who was shouting his sister's name as he approached; Khababa hid in a corner of the house. Fatima took the manuscript and put it under her dress. But Umar had already heard their reading, and when he came in, he said to them, "What was that sound I heard?" Both his sister and her husband replied, "You heard nothing." "Nay," he said, swearing, "I have heard that you have become followers of Muhammad and have turned from your religion." Then, he attacked his brother-in-law Sa'id and grappled with him. Fatima went to the defense of her husband; Umar struck her on her head and split her scalp in two places. The husband and wife could not contain themselves and shouted, "We are Muslims, and we believe in God and His Messenger, so do what you will." Fatima's head was bleeding, and when Umar saw the blood on his sister's head and face, he felt sorry for what he had done. A change came over him, and he said to his sister, "Give me that script that I even now heard you reading, that I may see what it is that Muhammad has brought." Umar could read like them, but when he asked for the script, she replied, "We fear to trust you with it." "Don't be afraid," he said. He then laid his sword on one side and swore by his gods that he would give it back when he had read it. She realized that he was softened, and she desired that he could enter Islam. She said to him, "O my brother, thou art impure in thine idolatry, and only the pure can touch it." Umar listened to his sister, and he went and washed himself. She gave him the page on which the opening verses of Sura Taha were written. He began to read it until he reached,

"Verily, I am Allah! La Ilaha Ana (none has the right to be worshiped but I), so worship Me and maintain prayer (Salat), for My remembrance." (20:14)

Umar read the verses with great interest and was very fascinated with them. "How beautiful and how noble are these words!" When Khabab, who was hiding from Umar heard this, he came out and said to him, "Umar, I have hope that God has chosen you through the prayer of His Prophet (May God bless and cherish him), whom yesterday I heard pray, "O God, strengthen Islam with Abu l-Hakam, the son of Hisham or with Umar, the son of Khattab."

"O Khabab," said Umar, "Where will Muhammad now be, that I may go to him and enter Islam?" Khabab told him that he was at the house of Arqam near the Safa gate with many of his Companions. Umar reached that place with the sword hanging from his arm. He knocked at the door. The Companions of the Holy Prophet (May God bless and cherish him) were alarmed and turned to see who the intruder was. One of them peeped through a hole in the door and said in a worried voice, "It is

Umar with his sword." Hazrat Hamzah was there, and he said in a commanding voice, "Let him in. As a friend he is welcome. As a foe, he will have his head cut off with his own sword." The Holy Prophet (May God bless and cherish him) agreed and asked his Companions to open the door. They had been warned by Nuaym, so that his coming was not unexpected. The Holy Prophet (May God bless and cherish him) went forward to meet him; he seized him by the belt and pulled him into the middle of the room, Saying, "What has brought you here, O son of Khattab? I cannot see thee desisting until God sends down some calamity upon thee."

Umar replied, "O Messenger of God, I have come to thee to declare my faith in God, and His Messenger and in what he hath brought from God."

Allah-o-Akbar (God is most great) said the Holy Prophet (May God bless and cherish him), in such a way that every man and woman in the house knew that Umar had entered Islam, and they all rejoiced.

Ibn Hisham narrated in his Sira on the authority of Abdullah b. Abu Najih, his companion Ata and Mujahid and others that Umar's conversion to Islam, according to what he used to say himself, happened in the following way.

"I was far from Islam. I was a wine drinker in the Jihaliya period and used to love and enjoy it. We used to gather at a place called al-Hazwara, near the houses of the family of Umar b. Abd b. Imran al-Makhzumi. One night, I went out to seek my boon companions, but when I got there, there was no one present, so I thought it would be better if I went to the so and so, who was a famous wine seller in Makkah at that time. I was hoping to get something to drink from him, but I could not find him either. So, I thought it would be better to go around Kaaba seven or seventy times. Therefore, I came to the Mosque to circumambulate around the Kaaba, and there I noticed that the Holy Prophet (May God bless and cherish him) was standing in prayer. During his prayer, he faced Syria, putting the Kaaba between himself and Syria. He was standing between the Black Stone and the southern corner. When I saw him, I was curious and thought it would be a good thing if I could listen to what Muhammad said. If I came near to him, I might scare him, so I came from the direction of the Hijr, got underneath its coverings, and began to move slowly. Meanwhile, the Holy Prophet (May God bless and cherish him) was standing in prayer, reciting the Quran until I stood in his qibla facing him, there being nothing between us but the covering of the Kaaba. I overheard him reciting the beginning of Sura Al-Haqqah (69) of the Noble Quran. I said to myself, "By God! This is poetry, as the Quraysh have said." Then the Holy Prophet (May God bless and cherish him) recited,

"That this is verily the word of an honored messenger (Gabriel or Muhammad) which he has brought from Allah. It is not the word of a poet. Little is that you believe." (69:42-43)

So, I said to myself, "He is a soothsayer."

The Holy Prophet then recited,

"Nor is it the word of a soothsayer (or a foreteller), little is that you remember! This is the Revelation sent down from the Lord of the universe (mankind, Jinns and all that exists)." (Quran 69: 42-43) up to the end of the Sura.

When I heard the Quran, my heart was softened, and I wept, and Islam entered my heart, but I ceased not to stand in my place until the Holy Prophet (May God bless and cherish him) had finished his prayer. Then he went away. The Holy Prophet (May God bless and cherish him) used to go past the house of the son of Abu Hussayn, which was on his way, so he crossed the place where pilgrims run. Then he went between the house of Abbas Abd Ibn Azhar b. Abu Auf al-Zuhri, and after that, he passed by the house of Al-Akhnas b. Shariq until he entered his own home. I followed him, until when he got between the house of Abbas and Ibn Azhar, I overtook him. When he heard my voice, he recognized me and thought that I had followed him only to ill-treat him. He was upset and said, "What has brought you at this hour?"

I replied that I had come to believe in God and His Messenger and what he had brought from God. He gave thanks to God and said, "God has guided you." Then he rubbed my chest and prayed that I might be steadfast. After that, I left, and the Holy Prophet (May God bless and cherish him) went inside his house. But God knows what the truth is.

There was no question of Hazrat Umar's keeping his faith secret. He wished to tell everyone, especially those who were most hostile to the Holy Prophet (May God bless and cherish him). Ibn Ishaq narrated on the authority of Hazrat Umar,

"When I embraced Islam, I remembered the archenemy of the Holy Prophet (May God bless and cherish him) was Abu Jahl. So, the next day, I went and knocked at his door, and Abu Jahl came out and said, "The best of welcome to my sister's son! What hath brought thee here?" I answered, I came to tell you that I believe in God and in his Messenger Muhammad, and I testify to the truth of that which he has brought."

"God curse thee," he said, and then he slammed the door in my face.

Once Hazrat Umar had become a Muslim, he left to visit al-Walid ibn al-Mughirah. He said, "O uncle! I bear witness that I believe in God and His Messenger, and I testify that there is no god, but God and that Muhammad is His servant and Messenger! So, go inform your people of this."

But Al-Walid said, "My nephew! Remain firm in your stance towards Muhammad. Your stature among the people is well known. Will a man rise amid his people in the morning in one state and begin the evening in another?"

"By God," replied Umar, "The matter has become clear to me, so inform your people that I have converted to Islam."

"I will not be the one to tell them this about you," said al-Walid. Hazrat Umar then entered the elder's assemblies, and once he ascertained that al-Walid did not mention anything about him, he went to Jamil ibn Mamar al-Jumahi and said, "Spread the news, I testify that there is no god, but God and that Muhammad is His servant and Messenger."

Jamil ibn Mamar stood up, picked up his cloak, and the group of the Quraysh followed him. "Umar ibn Khattab has abandoned his religion," declared Jamil, but the Quraysh said nothing in reply, for Umar was an esteemed leader of his tribe, and they were afraid to denounce him. When Hazrat Umar saw that they did not denounce him because of his faith, he headed straight to their assemblies, which were as well attended as they had ever been. He then entered the walled enclosure of the Kaaba, pressed his back up against the Kaaba, and shouted aloud,

"O people of Quraysh! Do you not know that I testify that there is no god but God, and Muhammad is His servant and Messenger." The Quraysh rose in fury, and some of the men attacked him fiercely. He spent most of that day fighting them off, and eventually, they left him alone. Thus, he was able to publicly announce his acceptance of Islam, walking back and forth in their midst and testifying that there is no god, but God and that Muhammad is His servant and Messenger. Hazrat Umar's conversion had a tremendous impact in Makkah. Mujahid, on the authority of Ibn Abbas, related that he asked Hazrat Umar bin al-Khattab why he had been given the epithet of Al-Farooq (he who distinguishes truth from falsehood), and he replied, "After I entered Islam, I asked the Holy Prophet (May God bless and cherish him), "Aren't we on the right path here and in the Hereafter?"

The Holy Prophet (May God bless and cherish him) answered, "Of course you are! I swear by Allah in whose hand my soul is that you are right in this world and in the Hereafter." I therefore asked the Holy Prophet (May God bless and cherish him), "Why then do we have to conduct our religious activities in secret. I swear by Allah, who has sent you with the Truth, that we will leave our hiding places and proclaim our noble faith openly." We then went out in two groups, Hazrat Hamzah leading one and I the other. We headed for the Mosque in broad daylight and when the polytheists of Quraysh saw us, their faces went pale and got nervous and resentful. On that very occasion, the Holy Prophet (May God bless and cherish him) attached to me the epithet of Al-Farooq.

Ibn Masud related that they were never able to pray at the Kaaba until Hazrat Umar embraced Islam. (Tarikh Umar bin Al-Khattab)

Suhaib bin Sinan ar-Rumi, in the same vein, said that it was only after Hazrat Umar's conversion that they started to proclaim the call, assemble around, and circumambulate the Holy Sanctuary freely.

Ibn Masud also reiterated, "We have been strengthened a lot since Hazrat Umar embraced Islam."

CHAPTER 11
THE BAN

When the Muslims increased in number, and the faith became manifest, the pagans from the infidel Quraysh began to deliberate on the matter of what to do with the members of their own tribes who believed in the new faith, for they desired to force them to abandon their religion. The Quraysh, under pressure from Abu Jahl, decided that the best solution to this problem would be to place an interdiction on the entire clan of Hashim who, except for Abu Lahab, were resolved to protect their kinsmen whether they believed him to be a prophet or not. A document was drawn up according to which it was decided that no one would marry a woman of Bani Hashim and Bani Muttalib or give his daughter in marriage to a man of Hashim and Muttalib, and no one was to sell anything to them or buy anything from them. This boycott was to continue until the clan of Bani Hashim themselves outlawed the Holy Prophet (May God bless and cherish him) or until he renounced his claim to prophethood. The writer of the document was Mansur b. Ikrima b. Amir b. Hashim b. Abdu Manaf b. Abdul Dar b. Qusayy and the Holy Prophet (May God bless and cherish him) invoked Almighty Allah against him, and his fingers withered. Almost forty leaders of the Quraysh set their seal to the ban, though not all of them were equally in favor of it. The clan of Muttalib stood by their Hashemite cousins, and they were included in the ban. The ban document was hung in the middle of the Kaaba to remind them of their obligations.

When the ban was enforced, the two clans of Bani Hashim and Bani Muttalib gathered around Hazrat Abu Talib in that quarter of the hollow of Makkah where he and most of the clan lived. The Holy Prophet (May God bless and cherish him) and Hazrat Khadijah and their household arrived to live among their clan. Abu Lahab and his wife moved away and went to live in the house that he owned elsewhere and thus showed his solidarity with the Quraysh.

Ibn Ishaq said that Husayn b. Abdullah told me that Abu Lahab met Hind d. Utba when he had left his clan and joined the Quraysh against them, and he said, "Haven't I helped al-Lat and Al-Uzzah, and haven't I abandoned those who have abandoned them and assisted their opponents."

She said, 'Yes, and may God reward you well O Abu Utba.' Among the other things that he said were, "Muhammad promises me things which I do not see. He alleges that they will happen after my death; what he has put in my hands after that?" then he blew on his hands and said, "May you perish."

It was not possible to enforce the ban strictly, because a woman was still a member of her own family after marrying into another clan. Abu Jahl was always on the watch, but even he could not always impose his will. One day, he met Hazrat Khadijah's nephew Hakim bin Hizam with a slave carrying a bag of flour, and they were heading for the dwelling of Bani Hashim. Abu Jahl accused them of taking food to the enemy and threatened to denounce Hakim before the Quraysh. While they were arguing, Abu l-Bakhtari, a man of Asad clan, came and inquired what was the matter. When he came to know, he said to Abu Jahl, "It is his aunt's flour, and she has sent to him for it. Let the man go on his way." Hakim and Abu l-Bakhtari both were non-Muslims but the passing of this bag of flour from one member of the clan of Asad to another could concern no one outside that clan. The interference of Makhzumite was outrageous and intolerable, and when Abu Jahl was adamant Abu l-Bakhtari picked up a camel's jawbone and brought it down on his head with such a force that he was half dazed and fell to the ground, whereupon they trampled him heavily under foot to the gratification of Hazrat Hamzah, who happened to pass by at that moment.

Hisham ibn Amr of Amir had a close marriage relationship with the clan of Bani Hashim. He would often bring a camel laden with food to the entrance of Shib Abu Talib under the cover of night. Then he would take off its halter and strike a blow on the flank so that it would go past their houses, and on another night, he would load it with clothes and other gifts.

Despite all the odds, the Holy Prophet (May God bless and cherish him) and the believers persevered, and their determination never weakened. During the sacred months, when they could go about freely without fear of persecution, the

Holy Prophet (May God bless and cherish him) frequently went to Kaaba, and the leaders of Quraysh would take any chance to insult and mock him. Sometimes, when the Holy Prophet (May God bless and cherish him) recited the Revelations warning Quraysh of what happened to former peoples, Nadr of Abd ad-Dar would rise to his feet and say,

"By God, Muhammad is no better as a speaker than I am. His talk is but tales of the men of old. They have been written out for him even as mine have been written out for me." Then, he would tell them tales of Rustam and Isfandiyar and the kings of Persia. In this connection, the following verses were revealed,

"When Our revelations are recited unto him, he saith: tales of the men of old. Nay, rather stain has covered their hearts of that which they were earning." (Quran 83:13-14)

The boycott of Hashim and Muttalib lasted two or more years and showed no signs of having any of the desired effects. It brought further attention to the Holy Prophet (May God bless and cherish him) and caused the new religion to be talked of more than ever throughout Arabia.

This unfair ban ultimately resulted in disagreement among the various Makkan factions, especially those who had close relations with the victims. The first person to stand against the boycott was the same Hisham, who had so often sent his camel with food and clothes for the Hashemites. But he alone could not do it by himself. So, he went to the Makhzumite Zuhayr, one of the two sons of the Holy Prophet's (May God bless and cherish him) aunt 'Atikah,' and said to him,

"How can you be content to eat and wear clothes and marry women when your mother's kinsmen are suffering? They can neither buy nor sell, neither marry nor give in marriage, and I swear by God that if they were related to the mother of Abu l-Hakam (Abu Jahl), and you asked him to do so what he had asked you to do, he would never have done it."

Zuhayr said, "What can I do? I am but a single man. If I had with me another man, I would not rest until I had annulled this ban." "I have found a man," said Hisham. "Who Is he?" "Myself." "Find us a third." Said Zuhayr. So Hisham went to Mutim Ibn Adi, one of the leading men of the clan of Nawfal, who was a grandson of Nawfal and brother of Hisham and Muttalib.

"Is this what you want," he said, "That the two sons of Abdu Manaf should perish while you approve of the Quraysh? By God, if you allow them to do this, you will soon find them doing this to you." Mutim asked for a fourth man, so Hisham went to Abu l-Bakhtari of Asad, the man who had struck Abu Jahl before, and when he asked for a fifth man, Hisham went to another member of the Asad clan, Zamah Ibn al-Aswad, who agreed to be the fifth without asking for a sixth person. They all agreed to meet that night on the outskirts of Hajun above Makkah and undertook not to drop the matter of the ban until they had had it annulled.

The next morning, they joined the gathering of the Quraysh in the Mosque and, Zuhayr, dressed in a long robe, went round the Kaaba seven times. Then he turned towards the people and said, "O people of Makkah, are we to eat food and wear clothes, while the sons of Hashim perish, unable to buy and unable to sell? By God, I will not stop until this unjust ban be torn up." Abu Jahl shouted at Zuhayr, "You lie!" "It shall not be torn up."

"Thou art the better liar," said Zamah, "We were not in favor of its being written when it was written."

"Zamah is right," said Abu l-Bakhtari, "We are not in favor of what is written in it, neither do we hold with it."

"You are both right," said Mutim, "and he that said no is a liar. We call God to witness our innocence of it and of what is written in it." Abu Jahl began to accuse them of having plotted it all overnight.

Hazrat Abu Talib was sitting in a corner of the Mosque. He came forward and announced that a Revelation had been sent to his nephew, the Holy Prophet Hazrat Muhammad (May God bless and cherish him), to the effect that worms had eaten away all their declaration that had points of injustice except the opening word that bore the name of God, in Thy Name, o God. He proposed that he would be ready to give Muhammad up to them if his words proved untrue, otherwise, they would have to withdraw and cancel the boycott. The Quraysh agreed to his proposal. Al-Mutim went into the Kaaba to see the parchment and there he discovered that it was eaten by worms, and nothing was left except the part bearing the Name of Allah.

Most of the Quraysh has been already won over, and this unquestionable sign was a final and altogether a decisive argument. Therefore, the ban was formally revoked, and the body of Quraysh went to give the good news to the Bani Hashim and the Bani Muttalib.

When the ban was lifted, there was temporary relief of hostilities against the Muslims. The news of this soon reached Abyssinia. This resulted in the hasty return of some of the Muslims to Makkah while others decided to remain there for a while.

Hazrat Abu Talib was now eighty years of age but still keenly protected his nephew. He became ill and developed extreme weakness. Meanwhile, the leaders of the Quraysh concentrated their efforts on trying to persuade the Holy Prophet (May God bless and cherish him) to agree to a compromise. Therefore, their delegation came to see Hazrat Abu Talib to discuss the issue with him. The delegation of the Quraysh comprised twenty-five men, including notables like Utbah bin Rabia, Shayba bin Rabia, Abu Jahl bin Hisham, Umayyah bin Khalaf, and Abu Sufyan bin Harb. They first paid tribute to him and confirmed his exalted status among the Arabs. They then proposed that they would refrain from intervening in his religion if he did the same.

Hazrat Abu Talib called for his nephew and informed him of the summary of the meeting and said, "My dear nephew, these are the nobles of our people. They have come to propose a compromise and a peaceful co-existence that they should all practice both religions."

The Holy Prophet (May God bless and cherish him) turned to the delegation and said,

"I will guide you to the means by which you will gain control over both the Arabs and non-Arabs."

In another version, it is narrated that the Holy Prophet (May God bless and cherish him) addressed Hazrat Abu Talib and said, "O uncle, why don't you call them unto something better?" Hazrat Abu Talib asked him, "What is it that you invite them to?"

The Holy Prophet (May God bless and cherish him) replied, "I invite them to hold fast to a message that is bound to give them access to kingship over the Arabs and non-Arabs."

Ibn Ishaq narrated in his Sira, "It is just one word that will give you supremacy over the Arabs and non-Arabs."

The leaders of the Quraysh were taken by surprise and wondered what sort of word was that which would benefit them to that extent. Abu Jahl asked, "What is that word? I swear by your father that we will surely grant you your wish, followed by ten times as much."

The Holy Prophet (May God bless and cherish him) answered, "I want you to testify that there is no god worthy of worship except Allah and then dissociate yourselves from any sort of worship you harbor for any deities other than Allah."

The Quraysh were angry and said, "How is it possible to combine all the deities in One God. It is really something unheard of." They looked at one another and said, "By God, this man will never give up, nor will he offer any concessions. Let us hold fast to the religion of our forefathers, and Allah will in due course deliver judgement, and settle the dispute between us and him."

After that incident, the Lord of the Worlds revealed the following verses,

"Sad. By the Quran endowed with remembrance. Nay, those who disbelieve are steeped in self-glory. How many generations before them did We destroy? In the end they cried for mercy when there was no longer time to be saved. So, they wonder if a warner has come to them from among themselves! And the unbelievers say, "This is a sorcerer telling lies. Has he made the gods (All) into one God? Truly, this is a remarkable thing." And the leaders among them impatiently said, "Walk ye away, and remain constant to your gods! For this is truly a thing designed against you." "We never heard (the like) of this among the people of these later days. This is nothing but a made-up tale." (Quran 38:1-7)

THE YEAR OF HEARTBREAK

Not long after the annulment of the ban, the Holy Prophet (May God bless and cherish him) suffered two great losses, one after the other, that cut him to the heart. It was the death of his affectionate and protecting uncle Hazrat Abu Talib, and the passing away of his beloved wife Hazrat Khadijah to the mercy of Allah, the Mighty and Majestic.

Hazrat Abu Talib fell ill in the tenth year of the prophethood, and his condition worsened over a period of six months till he breathed his last in Ramadan. On the authority of Al-Musaiyab when Hazrat Abu Talib was on his deathbed, the Holy Prophet (May God bless and cherish him) came to him, where some of the leaders of the Quraysh, including Abu Jahl and Abdullah bin Abi Umayyah, were sitting. He requested, "My dear uncle, say the words that through them I may intercede for thee on the Day of the Resurrection."

Abu Jahl and Abdullah bin Abi Umayyah said to him, "Abu Talib, would you abandon the religion of Abdul Muttalib?" the Holy Prophet (May God bless and cherish him) repeated his request, and the same thing was said to him by (Abu Jahl and Abdullah bin Abi Umayyah). But Hazrat Abu Talib was hiding his faith and said, "I am on the religion of my forefathers, Hazrat Ibrahim and Hazrat Ismael." There is no doubt that Hazrat Abu Talib was a fortress that protected Islam and Muslims from the offenses of the tyrants and ignorant.

Ibn Ishaq narrated in his Sira that when death drew near to Hazrat Abu Talib, Hazrat Abbas saw him moving his lips, and he put his ear close to him and listened, and then he said, "My brother hath spoken the words you wanted him to speak."

The Holy Prophet (May God bless and cherish him) had not fully recovered from the trauma of losing his most beloved uncle Hazrat Abu Talib, when his most beloved wife, Hazrat Khadijah, fell ill. When the Holy Prophet (May God bless and cherish him) saw her in severe illness, he became tearful, he said, "O my beloved, the time of separation has arrived, O queen of heaven, heaven is eagerly waiting for you."

Hazrat Khadijah was not afraid of death but was heartbroken about parting ways with the love of her life. Hazrat Khadijah requested the Holy Prophet (May God bless and cherish him) to sit with her for one last time so that by looking at his divine countenance, she should be at peace. Hazrat Khadijah then requested the Holy Prophet (May God bless and cherish him) to use the cloth as a shroud which he used to put on his holy shoulders during the time of revelation. The paragon of the world could not control the tears that flowed down his cheeks. He took the cloth off his shoulders and gave it to Hazrat Khadijah.

At the same time, Hazrat Jibreil (Gabriel) appeared to the Holy Prophet (May God bless and cherish him) and said, "The Lord of Glory and Generosity said that whatever Khadijah has, she sacrificed it all on My way. Now, her shroud is upon Me. She will be gifted with the cover of blessings from Me and a shroud from Heaven." (Rozatal Shohoda)

At the time of her passing away to the mercy of Allah, she was about sixty-five years old, while the Holy Prophet was nearing fifty. They had lived in great harmony for 25 years. She had been not only his wife but also his intimate friend, his supporter, his wise counsellor, and mother to his whole household including Hazrat Ali and Zayd. Her four daughters were filled with grief but the Holy Prophet (May God bless and cherish him) consoled them by saying that Gabriel came to him and said to tell Hazrat Khadijah that the Lord of the worlds sends greetings of peace, and that He had prepared for her a lofty palace in paradise.

CHAPTER 12
THE NIGHT JOURNEY AND ASCENSION

The story of the Holy Prophet Hazrat Muhammad Mustafa's (May God bless and cherish him) night journey and ascension has fascinated devout Muslims since the dawn of Islamic history, and the Muslim mystics were among the first to recognize its rich potential for spiritual and theological enlightenment. This story depicts how the Holy Prophet (May God bless and cherish him) was led by Archangel Gabriel, who came with an angelic steed Buraq, and took the Holy Prophet (May God bless and cherish him) in the middle of the night from a location in Makkah to a remote holy location, which came to be identified with Jerusalem, where he led the souls of all prophets (124,000 in number) in salat (prayer) before ascending towards the divine throne. Then, he was taken to seven celestial heavens where he met with prophets and angels. He was shown both Hellfire and Paradise. Finally, at the end of the Lote-Tree, Archangel Gabriel asked to pardon him as he could go no farther without his wings burning off.

"If I would go farther, my wings would become burned," sighed Gabriel on the night of ascension.

Most Muslim scholars turn to two main passages in the Noble Quran for proof-texts of the Holy Prophet's night journey and ascension to meet the divine beloved. The first of these passages is known as the "Night journey verse" because of its explicit albeit brief allusion to a journey by night. It describes how one of God's servants (The Holy Prophet, May God bless and cherish him) was taken on a mysterious journey and shown some of God's signs:

"Glorified be the One who caused his servant to journey by night from the sacred place of ritual prayer to the furthest place of ritual prayer, whose precincts We have blessed, to show him some of Our signs. Indeed (God) is the One who hears, the One who sees." (Quran: 17-1)

Muslim commentators who interpret this verse are virtually unanimous that it describes a pivotal event in the life of the Holy Prophet (May God bless and cherish him), a time when he was introduced to some of his pious predecessors and was shown some of God's signs in the universe.

Similarly, some early Quranic interpreters understood a different set of verses from another chapter of the Quran as providing further details about the Holy Prophet's otherworldly journeys. These two passages in the Quran reveal details of the events that took place. In this passage from the chapter (Sura) of the Quran known as "The Star" (Al-Najm), the Holy Prophet (May God bless and cherish him) is shown God's signs and marvels:

"By the star when it sets,

Indeed, your companion is not astray,

Nor does he speak vainly.

It is nothing less than a revelation revealed,

Taught to him by a being of intense power,

Possessing strength. He straightened up.

While he was on the highest horizon.

Then he drew near and descended,

And was a distance of two bows or closer.

He revealed to His servant what he revealed.

The heart did not lie in what it saw.

Will you then argue with him about what he saw?

He saw Him another time.

At the Lote-Tree of the boundary,

Next to the garden of refuge,

When the Lote-Tree was covered by what covered

His vision did not stray, nor was it excessive.

He saw some of the greatest signs of his Lord."

(Quran 53:1-18)

These opening verses from "The Star" describe how the Holy Prophet (May God bless and cherish him) witnessed God's signs in a series of visions. After the death of the Holy Prophet (May God bless and cherish him), Muslim scholars agreed that the portion of it which describes a vision near "The Lote-Tree of the boundary" refers to the night of heavenly ascension. Regarding the events described in these two key Quranic passages, the night Journey, and the opening of the chapter of 'The Star', Muslim scholars from a variety of backgrounds have composed oral and written commentaries on these verses to explain their meaning and significance.

One sound hadith on the night journey and ascension is recorded in the Sahih of Muslim b. Hajjaj al-Qurayshi, who died in (261/875), that has gained wide popularity throughout the Islamic world in the centuries following the death of the Holy Prophet (May God bless and cherish him). This hadith combines the basic elements of the night journey, and ascension accounts from the Quran.

Shayban b. Farruj heard from Hammad b. Salama, who heard from Thabit Bunani, who heard from Anas b. Malik that the Messenger of God said,

"I was brought the Buraq, which is a tall white mount larger than a donkey and smaller than a mule. It places its hoof as far as the eye can see. I rode it until I came to the house of the Sanctuary (Jerusalem). I tied it up to the ring that the prophets tied to it. I entered the Mosque and prayed two cycles in it. Then I exited, and Gabriel came to me with a vessel of wine and a vessel of milk. I chose milk, and Gabriel said,

"You chose natural disposition (al-Fitra)."

"Then he ascended with us to the first heaven. Gabriel sought to open the gate, and someone said, "Who is it?" He said, "Gabriel." "And who is with you?" he replied, "Muhammad." "Has he been sent for?" He replied, 'Yes, he has been sent for.' The gate was opened, and I found Hazrat Adam, who greeted me and said,

مرحبا با لا بن الصالح والنبئ الصالح

"Welcome, O righteous prophet and righteous son." Then we went up to second heaven. Gabriel sought to open the gate. A voice said, "Who is it?" He replied, "Gabriel." It said, "Who is with you?" He replied, "Muhammad." It said, "Was he sent for?" He replied, "He was," and the gate was opened for us. There, I found my cousins, Prophet Jesus and Prophet John (Yahya ibn Zakariya). They greeted me and said,

مرحبا بالا خ ا لصالح والنبئ الصالح

"Welcome, O righteous Prophet and righteous brother." Then he ascended with us to third heaven, and Gabriel sought to open the gate. It was opened for us, and then I found myself with Joseph. He has been given half of all beauty. He greeted me and said,

مر حبا با لا خ الصالح والنبئ الصالح

"Welcome, O righteous Prophet and righteous brother." Then he ascended with us to the fourth heaven, and Gabriel sought to open the gate. It was opened for us. I found myself with Prophet Idris (Enoch). He said, "Welcome. O righteous Prophet and righteous brother."

مرحبا با لا خ الصالح والنبئ الصا لح

God said, "We raised him to an exalted station." (Quran 19:56).

Then he ascended with us to the fifth heaven, and Gabriel sought to open the gate. It was opened for us, and then I found myself with Prophet Aaron (Haroon), who greeted me and said, "Welcome, O righteous Prophet and righteous brother."

مرحبا با لا خ الصالح و النبئ الصا لح

Then he ascended with us to the sixth heaven, and Gabriel sought to open the gate. It was opened for us, and I found myself with Prophet Moses, who greeted me and said, "Welcome, O righteous Prophet and righteous brother."

مرحبا با لا خ الصالح والنبئ الصا لح

Then he ascended with us to seventh heaven, and Gabriel sought to open the gate. It was opened for us, and then I found myself with Prophet Abraham leaning against the Frequented House (Al-Bayt al-Mamur). Every day, seventy thousand angels enter it and do not return to it."

"Then he took me to the Lote-tree of the Furthest Limit (boundary); its leaves are like the ears of elephants, and its fruits are like large vessels. When a command from Allah covers it, what is covered undergoes a change which no creature can describe due to its sublime beauty. Then God revealed to me what He revealed, and He made fifty prayers every day and night obligatory for me. I came down to Moses, and he said to me, "What did your Lord impose upon your community." I replied, "Fifty prayers." He said, "Return to your Lord and ask Him to lighten it. Your community cannot bear that. I tested the Israelites and tried them with less, and they failed." So, I went back to my Lord and said, "O my Lord, lighten it for my community." So, He eliminated five. I returned to Moses and said, "He eliminated five for me." He said, "Your community will not be able to do that, so go back and ask Him to lighten it."

"I kept going back and forth between my Lord and Moses until Allah said, "Muhammad, they are five prayers each day and night. For each prayer is worth ten, which makes fifty prayers. For one who intends to do good deeds but does not do it, one good deed is written (in the book of deeds); if one does it, ten are written. One who intends to do an evil deed but does not do it, nothing is written; if one does it, one is written."

Then, I went down to Moses and told him about it. He said, "Go back to your Lord and ask Him to lighten it." The Messenger of Allah said, "I have gone back to my Lord so often that I am ashamed to do so (again)."

In another version of the same hadith narrated by Abu Sa'id Khudri the Holy Prophet (May God bless and cherish him) said, "Gabriel sought to open the gate of the heaven. A voice said, "Who is with you?" He said, "Muhammad." "Was he sent for?" asked the voice. He said, "Yes he was." The gate was opened for us. I saw an angel whose name was Ismael. He was accompanied by a group of seventy-thousand angels. Each one of them had seventy-thousand angels under their command. They were guarding the gate of the heaven of this world. They all greeted me with salutations and prayers for my exaltation."

It is narrated by Wahab bin Manbah, who heard from Abu Usman al-Nahdi, who quoted that Salman Farsi said, "The heaven of this world is called *Barqima* (برقيم). God created it from a green emerald. The inhabitants of this (Worldly) heaven glorify Allah (Exalted is He) by reciting,

سبحان ذ ى الملك والملكوت

Whoever glorifies God with these words will get the reward of the inhabitants of this heaven.

Wahab bin Manbah also narrated from Abu Usman al-Nahdi, who heard from Salman Farsi that the Holy Prophet (May God bless and cherish him) was taken to the second heaven. Its name is *Arfalmun* (ارفلمون). God the Mighty and Majestic created it from white silver. Its guardian angel is *Rafyalil* (رفيالیل), and the inhabitants of this heaven glorify Allah by reciting,

سبحان ذ ى العز ة والجبروت

Whoever glorifies Allah with these words will get a reward equal to the inhabitants of the second heaven.

Wahab bin Manbah narrated from Abu Usman al-Nahdi, who heard from Salman Farsi that the third heaven is called *Faidun* (فيدون) and its guardian angel is Kababael (كبا باعيل) Its inhabitants glorify God with the tasbih of,

سبحان الحى الذى لا يموت

Whoever glorifies Allah with this recitation will get a reward equal to that of the inhabitants of this heaven.

It is narrated that Prophet Joseph is in the third heaven, and Prophet Jesus, son of Mary, and Yahya, son of Zakaria, are in the second heaven. The Holy Prophet (May God bless and cherish him) said, "I saw two men sitting on a throne studded with rubies. Both were very close to one another. I asked Gabriel, "Who are these two men?" He said, "They are cousins, Jesus, son of Mary, and Yahya, son of Zakariah." The Holy Prophet (May God bless and cherish him) added that Prophet Jesus closely resembles Urwah bin Masud al-Thaqafi. It is reported in a hadith that the Holy Prophet (May God bless and cherish him) said, "I saw Jesus, who was young and tall with straight hair and a brilliant red face."

The Holy Prophet (May God bless and cherish him) narrated, "I was taken to the fourth heaven. Its name is *Maoon* (ماعون)." Wahab bin Manbah narrated that the fourth heaven is called (ماعون), and Allah created it from brilliant white jewels. Its guardian angel is Mominyael (*مومن يائيل*). The tasbih (glorification) of its inhabitants is,

سبحان القدوس رب الملائكته والروح

Whoever glorifies God with these words will have the reward of the inhabitants of this heaven. The Holy Prophet said, "I saw a dignified person and asked Gabriel, "Who is this man?" He said, "Your brother Idris, Allah has granted him an exalted station."

رفعه الله مكانا عليا

Abu Sa'id Khudri said that when the Holy Prophet (May God bless and cherish him) met Idris. He greeted him and said, "Welcome to the righteous brother and righteous prophet."

مرحبا با لاخ الصالح والنبئ الصالح

The Holy Prophet (May God bless and cherish him) continued, "I saw Maryam bint Imran in this heaven, and Allah had granted her seventy lofty palaces made of white pearls. The mother of Moses was granted seventy palaces made of green emerald. Asiyah was granted seventy palaces made of coral, and Fatima Zahra was granted seventy palaces made of red rubies. Then we ascended to the fifth heaven."

Wahab bin Manbah narrated that the fifth heaven is called *Deqa* (ديقا). God the Mighty and Majestic created it from pure red gold. Its guardian angel is *Saftialeil* (*ليل سفطيا*). Its inhabitants glorify Allah constantly. Whoever glorifies Allah with these words will get the reward equal to the inhabitants of this heaven.

سبحان من جمع بين الثلج والنار

The Holy Prophet Hazrat Muhammad Mustafa (May God bless and cherish him) said, "Then we ascended to the sixth heaven; Gabriel sought to open the gate and it was opened. There, I saw an elderly person, who was very graceful and was surrounded by his companions. He had long tresses and was conversing with his followers. I asked Gabriel, "Who is this man?" He said, "Haroon (Aaron) bin Imran and the people around him are Bani Israel." I greeted him and he responded with salutations of peace.

Wahab bin Manbah quoted that the sixth heaven is called "Dafna" (دفنا), and Allah created it from yellow sapphire. Its guardian angel is Rooyabil (رويابيل). The inhabitants of this heaven glorify Allah (Exalted is He) by saying,

سبحان القدوس رب كل شيء وخالق كل شى

Whoever glorifies Allah with these words will get a reward equal to the reward of inhabitants of the sixth heaven.

It is narrated in another hadith that the Holy Prophet (May God bless and cherish him) said, "Afterwards we ascended to the seventh heaven. God created it from light, and it is called Arbia (عربيا). The inhabitants of the seventh heaven glorify Allah with the tasbih of (Glory be to the creator of light),

سبحان خالق نور

Whoever recites these words to glorify Allah will get the reward of the inhabitants of seventh heaven. Wahab bin Manbah narrated that Allah (Exalted is He) will increase their reward by seven times.

This hadith contains elements from the night journey verse and from the passage from the beginning of "The Star" chapter, connecting the two allusions with a rich narrative. Nevertheless, this hadith recorded by Muslim gives a short but relatively complete account of the combined night journey and ascension narrative, presenting a framework.

It is narrated from Al-Hassan al-Basri that the Holy Prophet (May God bless and cherish him) said, "While I was sleeping in the Hijr, Gabriel came to me and prodded me with his foot. I sat up, but I did not see anything, so I lay back down again." That happened three times. He said, "Then, he grabbed me by the arm and pulled me to the door of the Mosque. There was the riding animal, the Buraq."

It is narrated that on the night of the Miraj (Ascension), when the Holy Prophet (May God bless and cherish him) wanted to place his feet in the stirrups, Buraq shied away from him. Why did Buraq shy away from him? The answer is that when Buraq saw that he would be the steed of the Master, he lifted his head, rejoiced, and strutted. He said, "O Master! I have hope from you. Afterwards, a day will come when you strut into paradise, just as today you are going to Jerusalem.

On that day also I want to be your mount, for the habit of noble men is that whoever seeks an intimate at night will have in the day the rejoicing of a close friend."

The paragon of the world verified this covenant for him and, with the clemency of prophethood and the tenderness of messenger-hood, said, "At the resurrection, you will be my mount."

Then the Buraq said, "O Paragon of the world, nonetheless, I still want a token from you so that I may bind it around my neck as a collar and make it a necklace for myself."

The Mater answered his request and gave a strand of his black hair to him. Buraq bound that to his neck with the hand of need and until the coming of the Hour will remain in the giddiness of that wine and the revelry of that union.

The collection of hadiths assembled by Abu Isa al-Tirmidhi (d.279/892) details the intimate conversation between the Holy Prophet (May God bless and cherish him) and his Lord.

Ibn Abbas said that the Messenger of God said, "During that night, my Lord came to me in the most beautiful form."

He said, "Muhammad, do you know what the heavenly host debate?"

I said, "No." So, He put his hand (palm) between my shoulder blades until I felt its coldness between my nipples," or he said, "between my collarbones." "Then, I knew what was in heaven and what was on the earth. He said, "Muhammad, do you know what the heavenly host debate?" I said, "Yes, about the penitential acts (Kaffarat) and the steps (Darajat)."

It is important to know that various popular traditions attributed to Ibn Abbas (d.68/687) (a famous early scholar and Companion of the Holy Prophet (May God bless and cherish him)), offer a wealth of detail from the description of the angels encountered to the account of the seas and mountains crossed beyond the seventh heaven.

Most importantly, Ibn Abbas's narrative mentions explicitly that the Holy Prophet (May God bless and cherish him) sees His Lord during his ascension; it also reports in detail the intimate conversation between the Holy Prophet (May God bless and cherish him) and God (Exalted is He) at the climax of the narrative, and lastly, it often describes at length the Holy Prophet's (May God bless and cherish him) visit to Paradise and Hellfire during his ascension.

The following is an early version of the Ibn Abbas ascension narrative:

"I saw a great matter, which tongues cannot discuss, and imaginations cannot reach. My sight was bewildered beside it to the point that I feared blindness, so I closed my eyes and put trust in God. When I closed my eyes, God returned my vision to me in my heart, and I began to gaze with my heart at what I had been gazing at with my eyes. I saw a dazzling light. I was forbidden to describe to you what I saw of His grandeur. I asked my Lord (Exalted is He) to favor me with the steadiness of vision towards Him in my heart to complete His blessing of me. My Lord did that and favored me with it, and I gazed upon Him in my heart until He made it easy.

When He inclined towards me from His dignity (Exalted is He), he placed one of His hands between my shoulder blades, and I felt the coldness of His fingers upon my heart for some time. With that, I felt His sweetness, His beautiful fragrance, cool pleasure, and generous vision. All the terror that I had encountered vanished.

My Lord (Glorified and praised be He) spoke to me, saying.

"Muhammad, do you know what the heavenly host debate is?" I said, "My Lord, You are most knowing in that and in all things. You are the one who knows unseen." He said,

"They debate about the steps and goodness."

Allah (Exalted is He) said, "O Muhammad, speak so that I may listen! Ask so that I may bestow!"

I said, "My Lord, you took Abraham as a bosom friend and gave him an immense kingdom. You spoke to Moses directly (Quran 4:164). You gave David (Daud) the Psalms and a tremendous kingdom and made iron malleable for him and subjected the mountains to him. You bestowed on Solomon a kingdom not befitting to anyone after him (Quran 38:35) and subjugated to him men, jinn, devils, and the winds. You raised Idris to a high place (Quran 19:57). You taught Jesus the Torah and the Gospel (Quran 3:48), and You made him heal the blind and leper and give life to the dead with Your permission (Quran 3:49). What is there for me, my Lord?"

Allah, the Mighty and Majestic, said, "I took thee as a beloved just as I took

Abraham as a bosom friend; written in the Torah is, "Muhammad is the beloved of the Merciful." I spoke to thee just as I spoke to Moses directly. I have sent you to all people on earth, the white, the black, and the red, the jinn and humans. I have never sent a prophet before to them all. I have made your community such that none will be permitted to speak until they have testified that you are My slave and My Messenger. I made you the first of the prophets to be created and the last of them to be sent. I gave you the Opening of the Book and the 'seal' of Sura al-Baqarah, which were from the treasuries of My Throne. I have not given them to a prophet before you. I have made the earth, its land, and its seas virtually pure and a place of prayer for you and your community."

"Outside of these, I honored you with three traits. With these three traits, I made you more excellent than the folk of heaven and earth. I expanded for thee thy breast, I lifted from thee thy burden, and I raised up for thee thy mention, so I will not be mentioned without thy being mentioned along with Me."

"And lift from thee thy burden: the burden of the community's sins was weighing down upon your back and making you weak, and you were unsettled and without ease in sorrow for the disobedient. We put aside that burden from you. We forgave all their sins, and We gave your heart stillness and quiet."

"And raise up for thee thy mention: We lifted high your name, mention, and fame, for We bound it to Our name and paired it with the formula of Tawhid. O Muhammad, whenever the sun of your having been raised up shown on someone, he took a portion. From your status and being raised up, Adam, the chosen, found the rank of closeness. Because of you, Idris found the rank of chieftainship. In relation to you, the Bosom friend found the good fortune of bosom friendship. Through your love, Moses found the exaltedness of speaking with God. By being your doorkeeper, Jesus found confirmation and help."

"Then, after that, He informed me of matters about which He did not permit me to tell you."

"He revealed to His servant what He revealed" (Quran 53:10)

Even though He said these words with the lid on and left them obscure to declare the magnificence of Muhammad Mustafa's (May God bless and cherish him) measure, it has been mentioned in some books that a group of the Companions asked the Holy Prophet (May God bless and cherish him) what this revelation was. The

Holy Prophet (May God bless and cherish him) explained as much as their capacity was able to bear. He said that the Lord of the Worlds complained about his community, saying,

"O Muhammad, in holding to the covenant I, who am the Lord, did not create of the depths of hell for your community. But they, in breaking the covenant, are trying to throw themselves into hell. O Muhammad, I am the Exalter and the Abaser. He is exalted whom I exalt, and he is abased whom I abase. They are seeking exaltation from elsewhere, and they see abasement coming from elsewhere. O Muhammad, I do not ask them today for tomorrow's deeds, but today they seek from Me tomorrow's provision. O Muhammad, the provision that I have put in their name I will not give to another, but they give the deeds that are My rightful due and fitting for Me to others through eye service. O Muhammad, the blessings come from Me, and they show gratitude to others. O Muhammad, nonetheless, I am seeking for pretexts to forgive your community. O Muhammad were it not that I love to rebuke them and talk with them I would not call them to account for anything. O Muhammad, I did four things with previous communities that I will not do with your community: I took a people into the earth, I changed a people's form, I rained down stones on a people, and I destroyed a people with flames of fire. Because of your eminence and rank, I will not do any of these with your community. O Muhammad, I secluded you with Me to show people who you are and to show you who I am."

When God's Messenger saw all this honoring and exalting from the Exalted Threshold, he said, "Lord God, bestow all of my community on me!"

The command came, "O Muhammad, tonight you came alone. As a favor for your coming to this feast, I bestow upon you a third of that. Tomorrow, at the resurrection in the Greatest Gathering, I will bestow the rest on you. Then the world's folk will know your level and rank with Me."

The hadith narrative by Ibn Abbas confirms the Holy Prophet's (May God bless and cherish him) vision of God, drawing upon the Quranic verses from the Sura of The Star,

"The heart did not lie in what it saw" and "his vision did not stray, nor was it excessive." The idea of seeking steadiness (Thibat) of vision becomes an important subject for divine lovers. This hadith also incorporates the details from the "Heavenly host debate," God touching the Holy Prophet (May God bless and cherish him) and the intimate conversation between the Holy Prophet (May God bless and cherish him) and his Lord (Exalted is He) on the night of ascension.

Yunus narrated from Ibn Shihab from Anas that Abu Dharr said that the Messenger of Allah said, "The roof of my house was split open, and Gabriel descended and opened my breast. Then he washed it with the water of Zamzam. Then he brought a golden dish filled with wisdom and belief, and he poured it into my breast and then closed it up. He took me by hand and ascended with me to heaven." (Muslim and Al-Bukhari)

In the hadith of Ibn Shihab, it is narrated, "Every prophet said to me, "Welcome to the righteous prophet and righteous brother," except Adam and Abraham who said, "A righteous son."

Ibn Abbas also narrated, "Then he went up with me until I came to a level plan where I heard the squeaking of the pens." Anas reported, "Then he went up with me until I came to the Lote-Tree of the furthest Limit. It was covered in colors that I did not recognize. Then, I was brought into the garden."

Malik Ibn Sa'sa'a narrated a hadith, "When I passed Prophet Moses, he wept. He was asked, "Why are you weeping?" He replied, "Lord, this is a young man who was sent after me, and more of his community will enter the Garden than those of my community." (Ibid).

In a tradition, Abu Hurayrah narrated, "Then, he traveled until he came to Jerusalem and dismounted. He tied his mount to the rock and prayed with angels. When the prayer was over, they asked, "Gabriel, who is this with you?" He said, "This is Muhammad, the Messenger of Allah and the seal of the prophets." They asked, "Had he been sent already?" He said, "Yes." They said, "May the Lord give him a long life as a brother and a Khalif. An excellent brother! An excellent Khalif!" Then, he met the spirits of prophets who praised their Lord, and he mentioned what each of them said. They were Abraham, Moses, Jesus, David, and Solomon.

He continued, "The Holy Prophet (May God bless and cherish him) praised his Lord, the Mighty and Majestic, saying, "All of you have praised your Lord, so, I will praise Him. Praise be to Allah who has sent me as a mercy to the world and as a bringer of good news and a warner to all people. He sent down the Furqan (Quran) on me, which makes all things clear. He has made my community the best community, and He has made my community a middle community. They are the first, and they are the last. He opened my breast for me, removed my burden from me, elevated my renown, and made me an opener and a seal. Prophet Abraham said, "This is why Muhammad is better than you."

In the version of Abu Hurayrah, we also find, "I was told, this is the Lote-Tree of the furthest Limit. Each member of your community who treads your path will reach it. It is the Furthest Lote-Tree, from its roots, issues rivers of sweet water, rivers of unaltered milk, rivers of wine to delight the drinkers, and rivers of pure honey. This tree is so huge that it would take a rider seventy years to ride across its shade. A single leaf from it could shade the creation. Light covers it, and angels cover it." Abu Hurayrah said that this refers to the His words,

"What covers the Lote-Tree covers it."

It is narrated in a hadith, "The Messenger of Allah was given three things, he was given the five prayers, he was given the seal of Surat al-Baqarah, and he was given a pardon for the major wrong actions of every one of his followers who did not associate anything with Allah."

Al-Bazzar narrated that Hazrat Ali Ibn Abi Talib (May God be pleased with him) said, "When Allah (Exalted is He) wanted to teach His Messenger the Adhan (call for prayer), Gabriel came to him with a riding beast called the Buraq. He went to mount it, and it shied away from him. Gabriel said, "Be still. By Allah, no one more honored with Allah than Muhammad Mustafa (May God bless and cherish him) has ever ridden you." So, he mounted it and rode until it brought him to the veil just below the Merciful. Then an angel came out of the veil, and the Messenger of Allah asked, "Gabriel, who is this?" He said, "By the One who sent you with the truth, I have the closest station of all creatures to Allah, but I have not seen this angel from the time I was created until this very moment. The angel said, "Allah o Akbar" (Allah is greater), Allah o Akbar." A voice came from behind the veil, "My slave has spoken the truth. I am greater! I am greater! The angel said, "I testify that there is no god but Allah." A voice from behind the veil said, "My slave has spoken the truth. There is no god but Me," and the rest of the Adhan is mentioned, although he did not mention the response to the words, "Come to the prayer, come to success."

He said the angel took the Holy Prophet Hazrat Muhammad (May God bless and cherish him) by the hand and pushed him forward so that he was the imam of the inhabitants of the heavens, including Prophet Adam and Prophet Noah."

Abu Jafar Muhammad Ibn Ali Ibn Al-Husayn said, "Allah honored Muhammad

(May God bless and cherish him) above the inhabitants of the heavens and earth."

Most Muslim scholars believe that the Holy Prophet (May God bless and cherish him) went on the night journey in his physical body while he was awake. This statement has been attested by Ibn Abbas, Jabir, Anas, Hudhayfa, Abu Hurayrah, Malik Ibn Sa'sa, Abu Habba al-Badni, Ibn ad-Dahhak, Said Ibn Jubayr, Qatada, Ibn al-Musayyab, Ibn Shihab, Ibn Zayd, Al-Hassan al-Basri, Ibrahim, Masruq, Mujahid, Ikrima, and Ibn Jurayj. It is also what has been stated by at-Tabari, Ibn Hanbal, and many other scholars.

The words of Allah are clear evidence for this,

"Glory be to the One who traveled with His slave by night from the Masjid al-Haram to the Furthest Mosque." (Quran 17:1)

The Holy Prophet (May God bless and cherish him) saw his Lord (Exalted is He) on the night of ascension. Ibn Abbas said, "He saw Him with his eyes." Abu l-Aliyya said that he saw Him with his heart twice.

Ibn Abbas narrated that the Holy Prophet (May God bless and cherish him) said, "I saw my Lord in the most beautiful form." In the narrative of Abu Usman Bahili, the Holy Prophet (May God bless and cherish him) said, "My Lord was shown to me in the most beautiful form. He said, "O Muhammad," and I said, "Here I am, obeying Thee." "About what are the Higher Plenum disputing?"

The narrative of Jabir Ibn Samura is this, "Surely God disclosed Himself to me in the most beautiful form."

The narrative of Anas goes like this, "My Lord came to me in the most beautiful form." Anas also said, "Among the favors God will bestow on Adam on the Day of Resurrection is that He will say, "Did I not bestow upon you, My form?"

Ibn Ishaq mentioned that Ibn Umar sent to Ibn Abbas to ask whether the Holy Prophet (May God bless and cherish him) had seen his Lord. He replied, "Yes." This statement is related to him by various paths of transmission. He said that Allah singled out Prophet Moses for direct speech, Prophet Abraham for close friendship, and Muhammad Mustafa (May God bless and cherish him) for direct vision. The proof of it lies in the words of Allah, the Mighty and Majestic.

"The heart did not lie about what it saw. What will you dispute with him about what it sees? He saw Him another time." (Quran 53:11-13)

Abu l-Fath ar-Razi and Abu l-Layth as-Samarqandi narrated this from Ka'b al-Ahbar, and Abdullah Ibn al-Harith said, "Abbas and Ka'b agreed on this point. Ibn Abbas said, "As for us, the Banu Hashim, we say that Hazrat Muhammad (May God bless and cherish him) saw his Lord twice." Ka'b said, "Allah o Akbar (Allah is greater)!" until the mountains echoed him. He further said, "Allah divided His vision and His speech between Hazrat Muhammad (May God bless and cherish him) and Prophet Moses. He spoke directly to Prophet Moses, and Hazrat Muhammad (May God bless and cherish him) saw Him with his heart."

Sharik relates that when Abu Dharr commented on this verse, he said, "The Holy Prophet (May God bless and cherish him) saw his Lord."

Malik Ibn Yakhamir related from Mu'adh Ibn Jabal that the Holy Prophet (May God bless and cherish him) said, "I saw my Lord, and He asked me, "Muhammad, about what did the higher Assembly disagree?" (Ibn Hanbal, at-Tirmidhi).

Abdul Razzak Ibn Hammam narrated that Hassan al-Basri used to swear by Allah that Hazrat Muhammad Mustafa (May God bless and cherish him) saw his Lord.

An-Naqqash related that Ahmad Ibn Hanbal said, "I say that the hadith of Ibn Abbas means that he saw Him with his eye. He saw Him. He saw Him." He kept repeating that until he ran out of breath.

Abu Abd al-Rahman Sulami, in his book, "The Subtleties of the Ascension" (Lataif ul Miraj), emphasizes the night journey and ascension as proof of the unique status and favor that the Holy Prophet (May God bless and cherish him) enjoyed. It depicts the Holy Prophet's (May God bless and cherish him) status as being beyond the status enjoyed by anything in God's creation. He compares the Holy Prophet's station with other prophets, especially that of Prophet Moses. The latter merely spoke with God through a state of separation from Him. The Holy Prophet (May God bless and cherish him) was able to both speak to and witness the divinity in intimate proximity. Similarly, he compares the Holy Prophet's (May God bless and cherish him) station with that of the angels, even the most exalted of angels, such as Gabriel. He drew upon the popular hadith that Gabriel would have burned up had he approached the divinity to the degree that the Holy Prophet (May God bless and cherish him) was able to approach during the ascension, illustrating the Holy

Prophet's superiority to Gabriel in the eyes of God.

Muhammad b, Musa Ibn Farghani (Wasiti) was asked, "How was his (Prophet Muhammad's, May God bless and cherish him) state on the night of ascension?" He said,

"He clothed him in clothes of His attributes, He permitted him the witnessing, and He addressed him face to face." And the meaning of this is that He clothed him in the clothes that are (suited) to his attributes and that are (suited) to the truthful witness of his description." It means, "He strengthened him and steadied him for what he specified exclusively for him and his family."

Wasiti was also asked, "What was the wisdom of ascension?" He said,

"God (Exalted is He) wanted to lift up the state of the beloved from the station of servanthood to the station of eternity, and from the station of eternity to the station of lordship."

Wasiti explained, "He showed the Holy Prophet (May God bless and cherish him) in the station of servanthood to teach the proprieties of servanthood to the community. Then, He moved him to the station of eternity to teach through it the propriety of who he is in that station. Finally, He moved him to the station of lordliness (namely the ascension), to which he was caused to journey by night. At that, the station and traces were eliminated from him. He was moved to the station, which was created out of approach and nearness."

The Holy Prophet Hazrat Muhammad Mustafa (May God bless and cherish him) went alone and met God (Exalted is He) in a realm where no one else has ever entered. None has ever seen God in life, nor will anyone ever see Him. The Holy Prophet (May God bless and cherish him) had an intimate encounter with the divine beloved alone, which he described as such,

"I had a time with God in which no created being has access, not even the Archangels."

This narrative of the Holy Prophet's (May God bless and cherish him) night journey to the divine throne implies certain secret revelations received by him. This may be regarded as the central expression of Islamic spirituality and establishes the image of the Holy Prophet (May God bless and cherish him) as the paradigm of sainthood or "Friendship" (walayah). In this sense, the walayah of the wali can only be participation in the walayah of the Holy Prophet (May God bless and cherish him).

Thus, the Holy Prophet's (May God bless and cherish him) ascension becomes a road map and paradigm for the return of devoted servants of God to the state of intimate friendship with the divine, which is based on sincere worship, devotion, and following in the footsteps of the Holy Prophet (May God bless and cherish him). The path to God describes the outward activity as a reflection of the inner journey, an ascent that goes by way of the soul, spirit, heart, secret core, and beyond. The paradigm of the journey is provided by the Holy Prophet's (May God bless and cherish him) Miraj, which literally means "ascending ladder."

The Holy Prophet (May God bless and cherish him) provided the model to be emulated, for he is the only one who actualized all possible perfections. He traveled up through the spheres of the macrocosm while simultaneously traveling the depths of his own secret core. Therefore, Sufis describe the ascending levels of the self as seven subtleties because the Holy Prophet (May God bless and cherish him) climbed through the seven spheres in his journey to Allah. In this respect, the Holy Prophet's (May God bless and cherish him) ascent to God fulfills the promise of the Quran's descent from God. The Book was sent down so that through it people could climb up. The Holy Prophet (May God bless and cherish him) forged the path for his ummah to follow. When Sufis describe the ascending stations on the path, they are mapping out the levels through which the soul must travel in its voluntary journey back to the One.

The Holy Prophet's (May God bless and cherish him) ascent, on the one hand, delineates the stages of the path (tariqah) to God, and on the other hand, it is the counterpart to Prophet Hazrat Adam's fall. As the Prophet Adam's creation marks the beginning of the story of love, the Holy Prophet Hazrat Muhammad's (May God bless and cherish him) ascension is its culmination. Allah created human beings because He loves them, and He wants them to love Him in return. He created Prophet Adam in the most beautiful stature as the prototype of all his children. He created the Holy Prophet Hazrat Muhammad (May God bless and cherish him) as the beautiful exemplar (33:24) for his community to follow in his footsteps. Allah made the Holy Prophet (May God bless and cherish him) actualize the fullness of human perfections by placing within him the individual perfections scattered throughout all the previous prophets. The sign of his perfection is that during Miraj (ascension), he reached the station of two bow's length or closer. (Quran 53:9)

Famous Sufi scholar Samani explains Sura Najm, that is taken as referring to the Miraj (ascension), highlighting the nature of the Holy Prophet's (May God bless and cherish him) entrance into the Divine Presence. In this vein, he explains the verse, "The eye did not swerve." (Quran 53:17) as a reference to the Holy Prophet's (May God bless and cherish him) perfect love for Allah, which prevented him from gazing on others, the obstacle for one pointed vision.

Regarding the verse,

"Then he drew closer, so he came down until he was two bow's length away, or closer." (Quran 53:8-9)

Hazrat Imam Jafar al-Sadiq said, "When the beloved Prophet approached in utmost nearness, the utmost awe overcame him, so his Lord was gentle with the utmost gentleness, for the utmost awe can be endured only with the utmost gentleness."

"He heard the mysteries, tasted the wine of union, reached contemplation, fled from the two worlds and took ease with the Friend. Then He revealed to His servant what He revealed" (Quran 53:10); in other words, there was what there was, and there happened what happened, and no one is aware of those mysteries.

It has been reported that on the morning of the day after the night of Miraj, the Holy Prophet (May God bless and cherish him) reported about the beginning of his journey on earth to Jerusalem. The Companions were happy and accepted that, and the report was spread in Makkah. Hazrat Abu Bakr Siddiq was absent that day and had not seen the Holy Prophet (May God bless and cherish him). When Abu Jahl heard the report, he said to himself, "If it is possible to turn Abu Bakr away from the followers of Muhammad (May God bless and cherish him) through some cause, the cause may be this absurd report." Hence, he got up and set off on the road of Abu Bakr. He said to him, "O son of Abu Qahafa! This companion of yours, Muhammad (May God bless and cherish him), is talking about an absurdity that no intelligent man would ever accept. He says that last night, he left his Mosque and went to Jerusalem and returned the same night. O Abu Bakr, do you believe that someone can in one night go from Makkah to Jerusalem and return on the same night? That is one month for a caravan or a man who goes on foot. If you believe this absurd report, there is no doubt whatsoever that your intelligence is defective."

The sincerely truthful Abu Bakr gave him a prudent answer and said, "If he said that, he is telling the truth." Abu Jahl despaired of him, and Hazrat Abu Bakr hurried to the Messenger of Allah and, before sitting down, said to him, like someone truthful and in love, "O Messenger of Allah! Tell me about your journey last night."

He said, "O Abu Bakr, last night Gabriel came bringing Buraq and took me to Jerusalem. I saw the pure spirits of the prophets and the chieftains of the Higher Plenum, and I led them in prayer. From there, I journeyed to the realm of the Dominion and arrived at the Highest Horizon. I saw the greatest signs and returned to the region of Makkah while it was still night."

Hazrat Abu Bakr said, "You have spoken the truth, O Messenger of God! By the exaltedness of the Lord who sent you with the truth, just as you were awake and taken on this journey in your form and person from place to place, my spirit was also taken in companionship with and service to you. Your journey was in the form and frame, and my journey in serving you was in spirit and secret core. I saw myself in a dream in your service, and you were shown in wakefulness by the confirmation of the Real." Just as he was saying these words, trustworthy Gabriel came and revealed this verse,

"And he who brought truthfulness and he who assented to it." (Quran 39:33)

From that day on, Hazrat Abu Bakr's title became "The sincerely truthful," and until the coming of the Hour, the folk of the Sunna and the Jama'a will emulate him in assenting to the truthfulness of the Miraj.

It is narrated in a sound report from Hazrat Ali, who said, "Whenever I heard something from God's Messenger, God gave me benefit from it. From that, I came to the certainty of knowledge and the worthiness of deeds. But if someone narrated it to me, I would make that person swear an oath. When he swore it, I would rely on him. One day, Abu Bakr Siddiq narrated to me, but I did not make him swear an oath to the truthfulness of his words because he always spoke the truth. He said,

"I heard God's Messenger saying, "Whenever a servant with faith does a sin and after that sin, makes ablution and washes fully, then after finishing, he performs two cycles of prayer, God will pass over that sin from him and will pardon him." The explication of this report is the Noble Quran, "Whoever does something ugly or wrongs himself and then asks forgiveness of God, he will find God forgiving and Ever Merciful." (Quran 4:110)

CHAPTER 13
DESTINATION YATHRIB

In the season of Hajj that followed the Year of Sadness, the Holy Prophet (May God bless and cherish him), according to his usual practice for the last several years, visited the various groups of tents in the valley of Mina. Here, the pilgrims camped for five days. The Holy Prophet (May God bless and cherish him) proclaimed his message to anyone who would listen, reciting for them the beautiful verses of Revelations as he felt moved to recite. Aqabah is the nearest point of Mina to the Holy City of Makkah, and it was this year at Aqabah that he came upon six men of the tribe of Khazraj from Yathrib. The Holy Prophet (May God bless and cherish him) did not know any of them, but they had heard of him and of his claim to prophethood. As soon as he told them who he was, their faces beamed with interest, and they listened to him attentively. All of them had heard from the Jews in Yathrib and were familiar with their threats,

"A prophet is now about to be sent. We will follow him, and we will slay you as Ad and Iram were slain."

When the Holy Prophet (May God bless and cherish him) was done speaking, they looked at each other and said, "This is indeed the prophet that the Jews promised us would come. Let them not be the first to reach him!" Then they asked some questions and the Holy Prophet (May God bless and cherish him) answered them. Without hesitation, each of the six men accepted Islam and promised to fulfill the conditions of the new faith which he laid before them. They unanimously said, "We have left our people, for there is no people so torn by enmity and evil as they, and it may be the will of Allah to unite them through thee. We will now go to them and invite them to accept thy religion even as we have accepted it, and if God gathers them together about thee, then no man will be mightier than you."

On their return to Yathrib, these six men delivered the message of Islam to as many of their people as they could. The following year, in AD 621, five of them performed their pilgrimage again, bringing with them seven others, two of them from Aws. At the same place of Aqabah, these twelve men pledged themselves to the Holy Prophet (May God bless and cherish him), and this pledge is known as the first Aqabah. In the words of one of them,

"We pledged our allegiance to the Messenger of Allah on the night of the first Aqabah, that we would associate none with Allah, that we would neither steal, nor commit fornication, nor slay our offspring, nor utter slanders; and that we would not disobey him in that which was right. And he said to us, "If ye fulfill this pledge then Paradise is yours; and if ye commit one of these sins and then receive punishment for it in this world, that shall serve as expiation. And if ye conceal it until the Day of Resurrection, then it is for Allah to punish or forgive, even as He will."

This group of men comprised five of the six who had met the Holy Prophet (May God bless and cherish him) the year before, and the sixth man who stayed behind was Jabir bin Abdullah bin Riab. The other seven were Muadh bin Al-Harith ibn Arafa, Dhakwan bin Abdul Qais, Ubaidah bin As-Samit, Yazeed bin Thalabab, Al-Abbas bin Ubaidah bin Nadlah (from Khazraj), Abul Haitham bin At-Taihan and Uwaim bin Saidah from Aws.

After the pledge in the form of an oath, the Holy Prophet (May God bless and cherish him) sent with them Musab bin Umair of Abd al-Dar (who by that time had returned from Abyssinia as an instructor) to teach them the tenets of Islam and recite the Quran to them. He was given the task of propagating Islam among those who had not professed faith. He lodged with Asad bin Zurarah in Yathrib. Musab was also to lead the prayers because in their Islam, neither Aws nor Khazraj could yet endure to give one another precedence. The new converts were so zealous, and the ground was so prepared that the message of Islam spread like wildfire from house to house and from tribe to tribe. The rivalry between the two tribes of Aws and Khazraj had been long-standing. But at the same time, there had been frequent intermarriages between the two sides. Therefore Asad, the Khazrajite host of Musab, was the first cousin of Sa'd ibn Muadh, chief of one of the clans of Aws. Sa'd was against the new religion. He was upset and embarrassed to see his cousin Asad in the company of

Musab and some newly converted Muslims sitting one day in a garden near his dwellings. He decided to put an end to such gatherings, but he did not wish to be directly involved because of Asad. So, he went to Usayed who was his assistant and said, "Go to these men who have come to our territory to make fools of our innocent brothers. Drive them out forcefully and forbid them to come to our territory again. If Asad were not my kinsman, I would have saved thee this trouble, but he is the son of mu mother's sister, and I can do nothing against him."

Usayd took his spear and went to the place where the believers were gathered. He stood over their heads and shouted with the entire strength he could muster. He said, "What brings the two of you here to make fools of our weaker brothers? Leave this place if you care for your lives." Musab looked at him and gently invited him to sit down and said, "Listen to what I say. Then, if it pleases you, accept it, and if not, keep thyself clear of it." "That sounds fair," said Usayd. He liked Musab's appearance and the way he spoke. Striking his spear in the ground, Usayd sat beside them on the ground. Musab spoke to him about Islam and recited the verses of the Noble Quran to him. His face beamed with satisfaction so that those who were present could see the light of faith in his expression.

"How excellent are these words and how beautiful!" he said when Muasb finished speaking. "What do you do if you wish to enter this religion?" They told him that he must wash himself first from head to toe to purify himself. And he must purify his garments and then perform the prayer. There was a well nearby, so he washed himself and purified his garments, and uttered Shahada, "There is no god but Allah, and Muhammad is the Messenger of Allah." They taught him how to pray, and he prayed. Then he said, "There is a man behind me, who if he follows you, you will be followed by every man of his people, and I will send him to you now." Usayd went straight to Sa'd bin Muadh. Sa'd was sitting with his companions and waiting for Usayd. When he saw him coming, he said to his friends, "I swear he is not coming the same way as he left." When Usayd arrived, they asked him hastily, "What did you do?" Usayd answered that he had encountered no problem. "By God, I spoke with those two men. I saw no harm in them. First, I rebuked them. Then they said, "We will do as you please." Usayd intended to have Sa'd and Musab see each other, so he was trying to convince him about their innocence. He told him that he could go and speak to the men if he so wanted. Sa'd was angry, he took the spear from his hand and headed to where the believers were sitting. He argued with his cousin Asad and accused him of taking advantage of their kinship. He was threatening and shouting at Muasb for a while. But there was no change in Musab's attitude. He was calm and gentle. He spoke to Sa'd just as he had spoken to Usayd. Sa'd agreed to listen. He put aside his spear, sat down, and began to listen to Musab. He was in awe at the very start with the invocation, "In the name of Allah, the All-Merciful, the All-Compassionate," that Musab had spoken. His face lit up with amazement. Even, before Musab had finished speaking, he started to ask questions like Usayd, "What does one need to do when one wants to submit and enter this religion?"

Musab told him the same thing he had told Usayd. When Sa'd had performed prayer, he went back to join Usayd and those who were with him. From there, they went to the assembly of their people. Sa'd addressed his men and said, "What would you say of my standing among you?" "You are our esteemed Lord," they answered, "And the best of us in judgement and knowledge." Then he said, "I swear that I would not speak either to your men or women until you believe in Allah and His Messenger." And by nightfall, there was no man or woman of his clan who had not entered Islam except for one, Al-Usairim, who embraced Islam on the Day of Uhud. On that day, he fought valiantly against the polytheists but was martyred before observing any prayer. The Holy Prophet (May God bless and cherish him) said about him, "He had done a little, but his reward is great."

Yathrib was a very fertile place for the new religion. Musab stayed there, carrying out his mission steadily and successfully. He went from house to house, sharing the baraka of the faith. In a short time, there was no household left in Yathrib that had not converted to Islam. Only one family refused the call of Islam; they were under the influence of the poet Qais bin Al-Aslam, who managed to hold them back until the year five AH.

The light of faith could not be contained within Yathrib and had started to spread to its outskirts. Musab went to the surrounding tribes, delivering the message of Islam. One day, Musab wrote a letter to the Holy Prophet (May God bless and cherish him) requesting further instruction as to how he should act. In his reply, the Holy Prophet (May God bless and cherish him) described the Jumma prayer to him and thence the Muslims in Yathrib gathered in the house of Sa'd ibn Haysama and performed the Jumma prayer. Musab stayed with Asad for about eleven months and many people embraced Islam during that time.

It was pilgrimage season once again, and there was a flow of people towards Makkah. Musab had returned to Makkah to give tidings to the Holy Prophet (May

God bless and cherish him) of how he had fared among the various clans of Aws and Khazraj. The Holy Prophet (May God bless and cherish him) was shown in a vision the well-watered land between two tracts of black stones, and he was sure that it was Yathrib. He knew that this time he, too, would be of the emigrants. There were few people in Makkah whom the Holy Prophet (May God bless and cherish him) trusted so much as his aunt by marriage, Umm al-Fadl. He was also certain his uncle Hazrat Abbas, although he had not entered Islam, would never betray him. So, he told them both that he hoped to go and live in Yathrib and that it all depended on the delegation that was expected from the oasis for the coming pilgrimage. On hearing this Hazrat Abbas said that he felt it his duty to go with his nephew to meet the delegates and speak with them, and the Holy Prophet (May God bless and cherish him) agreed.

There were seventy people, including two women, who came to Makkah after a long, arduous journey. They were eager to meet the Holy Prophet in person, but it was impossible for this many people to meet the Holy Prophet (May God bless and cherish him). Therefore, they chose Ka'b ibn Malik and Bara ibn Marur among them and sent them to Kaaba. Bara had a dream earlier that he was performing his prayer facing the direction of the Kaaba. His friends censured him, for this meant dissension from the Holy Prophet's (May God bless and cherish him) practice, who faced Masjid al-Aqsa. He was looking forward to asking the Holy Prophet (May God bless and cherish him) about his dream. Neither of them had seen the Messenger of Allah before, and they did not know what he looked like. They were wondering how they would recognize him. They asked a Makkan, who replied, "Do you know his uncle Abbas ibn Abdul Muattalib?" "Yes," they replied because Hazrat Abbas frequently came to Yathrib for trade. "Then it is easy. He is the man who sits next to Hazrat Abbas in the Kaaba. Go there, and you will find him," said the Makkan. The two men entered Kaaba where Hazrat Abbas was sitting down and the Holy Prophet (May God bless and cherish him) was beside him. They greeted him. When the Holy Prophet saw how warm and sincere, they were, he turned to his uncle and said, "Do you know these men?" "Yes," said Hazrat Abbas, "This is Bara ibn Marur, chief of his clan, and this is Ka'b ibn Malik."

The Holy Prophet was extremely delighted to see those two men because there were seventy more people like them behind them, and they had come to pledge their allegiance to him. They asked how they were going to meet. It was once again decided to meet at Aqabah in Mina secretly at night during the middle of Tashreeq

Days (11th, 12th, and 13th day of Dhul-Hijjah).

Ka'b ibn Malik gave an account of this historic meeting that changed the course of Islam: "We set out for pilgrimage and had a meeting with the Messenger of Allah (May God bless and cherish him) secretly planned at night. We were accompanied by Abdullah bin Amr bin Haram, one of the most notable and respected among our people. We said to him, "O Abu Jabir, you are certainly one of the most respected and one of the most notable of our people. We do not want you to be fuel for the fire tomorrow. Then we invited him to accept Islam and told him of the meeting we had already planned with the Holy Prophet (May God bless and cherish him) at Al-Aqaba. He entered Islam and attended Al-Aqaba, and he was our chief representative." Ka'b continued, "That night, we slept with our companions in our camps. After a third of the night had elapsed, we started to leave quietly, and we gathered in a hillock nearby. We were seventy-three men and two women, Nusaibah bint Ka'b (Umm Umarah) from the Bani Mazin bin Najjar and Asma bint Amr (Umm Muni) from Bani Salamah. We waited for the Holy Prophet (May God bless and cherish him) until he came accompanied by his uncle Hazrat Abbas bin Abdul Muttalib, who at that time had not converted to Islam. Yet he wished to be present for the matters of his nephew to make sure that the promises made to him were reliable. When the Holy Prophet (May God bless and cherish him) arrived, Hazrat Abbas was the first to speak,

"O people of Khazraj, you know the esteem in which we hold Muhammad (May God bless and cherish him), and we have protected him from his people so that he is honored by his tribe and safe in his country. However, he has decided to join himself with you. So, if you think that you will keep to what you promised him and that you will protect him against all that shall oppose him, yours be that burden which you have taken upon yourselves. But if you think you will betray him and fail him after he has gone out unto you, then leave him now."

Ka'b replied, "We have heard your words, and now O Messenger of Allah, it is for you to speak and take from us any pledge that you want regarding Allah the exalted and yourself." (Ibn Hisham)

After reciting the Noble Quran and pronouncing a summons to God and to Islam, the Holy Prophet (May God bless and cherish him) said,

"I want absolute obedience both at times of difficulty and at times of ease, both when you have little to eat and in times of abundance. I want you to give to charity.

You will not hold anything equal to Allah, perform prayer, and give alms. You will do good and forbid evil. I make with you this pact on condition that the allegiance you pledge me shall bind you to protect me even as you protect your women and children."

Bara ibn Marur stood up, held the Messenger of Allah by the hand, and said,

"I swear by He who has sent you with Truth that we will protect you as we protect our children and women. We promise you, and we swear allegiance to you, O Messenger of Allah! By Allah, we are men of war and reliable in combat. This characteristic we have inherited from our ancestors."

Then Abul Haitham bin At-Taihan interrupted and said, "O Messenger of Allah, there are ties between us and the Jews, which we are willing to cut. But might it not be that if Allah grants you power and victory, should we expect that you would not leave us and return to thy people?"

The Holy Prophet (May God bless and cherish him) smiled and replied, "Nay, it would never be, your blood will be my blood. In life and death, I will be with you and you with me. I will fight whom you fight, and I will make peace with those with whom you make peace" (Ibn Hisham). Asda ibn Zurara came to the front, held the hand of the Holy Prophet (May God bless and cherish him), and said, "O people of Yathrib, we have not come except because we have had a deep belief that he is the Messenger of Allah. We are already convinced that following him means a departure from the pagan Arabs even if it were at the risk of our life. Should you give a pledge, hold fast to it, and your reward is with Allah, but if you fear, then I advise you to leave him now."

Ibn Ishaq narrated, "When they gathered for the pledge. Al-Abbas bin Ubaydah bin Wadlah asked, "Do you know the significance of the pledge that you are making with this man? You are, in fact, affirming that you will fight against various enemies. If you fear that your property will be at risk or the lives of your nobles will be in danger, then leave him now, because if you do this after the pledge, it will be degrading for you both in this world and the world to come. But if you think you can carry out what you are called upon to undertake, the heavy burden, I swear by Allah that here in lies the good of this world and that of the next."

Those gathered at Aqabah replied with one voice, "We have already considered the loss of our property and the lives of our nobles, yet we pledge him allegiance.

But what's our reward if we do so." The Holy Prophet (May God bless and cherish him) firmly replied, "Paradise is in store for you." After that, everyone began to give the pledge. Jabir said, "So man by man we stood before the Holy Prophet (May God bless and cherish him) taking the pledge so that by that we could be granted paradise." (Musnad, Ahmad)

TWELVE DELEGATES

The Holy Prophet (May God bless and cherish him) asked them to form a committee of twelve delegates; each one would represent his tribe and be responsible regarding the articles of the pledge and his people. The delegates from Al-Khazraj were nine: Asad bin Zurarah bin Ads, Sa'd bin Ar-Rabi, Abdullah bin Rawadah, Rafi bin Malik, Bara bin Marur, Abdullah bin Amr, Ubaidah bin Samit, Said bin Ubaidah and Al-Mundhir bin Amr. The other three were from Aws, Usayd bin Hudair, Sa'd bin Khaithamah, and Rifah bin Abdul Mundhir. They came one by one and swore allegiance to the Holy Prophet (May God bless and cherish him). Two women from Yathrib, Nasibah bint Ka'b and Asma bint Amr, who had come with the group pledged to the Holy Prophet (May God bless and cherish him) orally.

The second Aqabah pledge, also known as the Great Aqabah pledge, was an unprecedented breakthrough in the history of Islam. It laid the foundation for a future Muslim state in a vast desert surging with disbelief and ignorance. At the very last moment, a devil in Mina stood on the highest ground and shouted to get the attention of the Quraysh, "O people of Quraysh, Muhammad and his Companions have conspired for war against you." The Holy Prophet (May God bless and cherish him) heard his voice and said, "This is Azab (the Jinn) of Al-Aqabah. O enemy of Allah, we are leaving you now." Then he commanded his men to go to their camps. Al-Abbas ibn Ubaydah heard the devil's voice, and he came to the Holy Prophet (May God bless and cherish him) and said, "By Allah, who has sent you with Truth, we are powerful enough to put the people of Mina to our swords tomorrow if you desire." The Holy Prophet (May God bless and cherish him) replied, "We have not been commanded to follow that course. Now go back to your camps in peace."

As soon as the Quraysh heard about the pact between the Holy Prophet (May God bless and cherish him) and the people of Yathrib, they were infuriated, and the news of this historic event spread in all directions. The Quraysh fully realized that such an allegiance would have far-reaching consequences that would uproot their society. A large delegation of Makkan leaders set out for the camp of Khazraj in

Mina. They addressed them, "O people of Khazraj, it has been brought to our attention that you have come to make a pact with Muhammad and invite him to Yathrib. By Allah, we would really hate to have any fight between us and you."

The polytheists of Yathrib had no knowledge of the secret pact between the Holy Prophet (May God bless and cherish him) and some of the people of Yathrib. They swore by Allah and said that there was no truth in this matter. Abdullah ibn Salul, who was a polytheist, refuted the allegations, denouncing them null and void. He said that his people would never do anything unless he gave them such instructions. The Muslims among them, however, remained silent, neither denying nor attesting such claims. The leaders of the Quraysh seemed to be convinced by the reassurances of the Khazraj pilgrims, however, they were frustrated and not entirely satisfied. Some of them pursued the pilgrims but failed in catching them. However, some of the horsemen from Quraysh caught up with Sa'd ibn Ubaydah and Mundhir ibn Amr, who had been left a little behind, and took them as prisoners. But Mundhir somehow managed to escape, making use of a negligent moment. They tied up Sa'd and dragged him into Makkah. Sa'd was the chief of Khazraj, and here he was with his hands and arms tied and a rope around his neck. They were pulling his hair and throwing insults at him. In the meantime, Mutim ibn Adiyy and Harith ibn Harb heard of the situation and came to rescue him. Sa'd had helped both by giving them protection as they passed through Yathrib with their caravans, aiding them to reach their destination safely. This favor of his done earlier proved fruitful at a time when he needed it badly.

FIRST EMIGRANTS

The Holy Prophet (May God bless and cherish him), now by the permission of Allah, (Exalted is He), encouraged his followers in Makkah to emigrate to Yathrib. One of them had already done so. After the death of Hazrat Abu Talib, his nephew Abu Salamah had no protector, and he felt compelled to take refuge from his own clan. So, he set off for Yathrib, mounting his wife on a camel with their young son Salamah in her arms. He was leading the camel. But Umm Salamah was from the other branch of Makhzum, the Bani l-Mughirah, and the first cousin of Abu Jahl. He and some of her family members followed them and snatched the camel's rope from Abu Salamah's hand. He was far outnumbered and knew it would be futile to resist. So, he told her to return with them and said he would find a way for her to join him. Their son was taken hostage. Umm Salamah, after the departure of her husband, and the loss of her son spent a year by herself weeping and lamenting. A relative of hers eventually had pity on her and convinced others to release her son and let her join her husband. She then set out on a journey of five hundred kilometers with no help whatsoever. After a short journey on the road, she met a man of Abd ad-Dar Uthman ibn Talha, who was not yet a believer. He insisted on escorting her to the end of her journey. They had heard that Abu Salamah was in Quba, a village at the most southerly point of Yathrib full of palm trees. So, when they came within sight of Quba, Uthman said to her, "Thy husband is in this village, so enter with God's blessings." And then he turned back towards Makkah. Umm Salamah never forgot his kindness and never ceased to praise him for his nobility.

After the pledge of the second Aqabah, the Muslims in Makkah began to emigrate in considerable numbers, amongst the first to go were some of the Holy Prophet's cousins, sons and daughters of Jahsh an-Umayma, Abdullah with his blind brother Abu Ahmad, and their two sisters Zaynab and Hamnah. With them were many others of Bani Asad who had ties with Abdu Shams. Hazrat Hamzah and Zayed went, leaving their wives in Makkah for the time being. But Hazrat Uthman took his wife Hazrat Ruqayyah with him, and Hazrat Umar took his wife Zaynab, their daughter Hafsah, and their young son Abdullah. Hafsah's husband Khunays of Sahm was also with them.

There were numerous instances of atrocities by Makkan polytheists against the emigrants. Suhaib bin Sinan Ar-Rumi wanted to emigrate but was ridiculed by the polytheists, who said that he had come to Makkah as a worthless beggar, but that their town had been gracious enough, and he had managed to make a lot of fortune. They declared that he would not leave Makkah. Seeing this, he offered to give away all his wealth to them. They eventually agreed to release him on that condition. The Holy Prophet (May God bless and cherish him) heard about him and said, "Suhaib has profited, Suhaib has profited."

صهيب صهيب، ربح ربح

The story of Umar ibn Al-Khattab, Aiyash bin Abi Rabia, and Hisham bin Al-Asi bin Wail is a clear example of treachery and torture done by the Makkan polytheists towards the believers. The three of them agreed to meet at a certain place one morning to emigrate to Yathrib. Hazrat Umar and Aiyash came to the appointed meeting place, but Hisham was held by the Makkans. After the two had made it to Yathrib, Abu Jahl and his brother Al-Harith came to Yathrib to see their brother

Aiyash. They tricked him by exploiting his weakness regarding his love for his mother. They told him that his mother had sworn she would not comb her hair nor shade herself if the sun of Makkah became too hot for her until she set eyes on him again. Aiyash was very troubled by this, but Hazrat Umar said to him, "They want to trick you, by God. If lice troubled your mother, she would use her comb, and if the heat of Makkah oppressed her, she would take shelter." But Aiyash would not listen, and he insisted on returning to Makkah to release his mother from her oath. When they were halfway between Yathrib and Makkah, Abu Jahl and Harith fell upon him, bound his hand and feet, and brought him home as a prisoner, saying, "O people of Makkah, do with your fools as we have done with this fool of ours."

Like Hisham, Aiyash was forced to renounce Islam. After a while, they felt so guilty that they thought no atonement was possible for such a great sin. But then the following revelation came,

"O My slaves who have acted unwisely against yourselves, despair not of God's mercy. Verily, God forgives sins in their entirety. He is the All-Forgiving, the All-Merciful. And turn unto your Lord in repentance and surrender unto Him before there came unto you the punishment when ye shall not be helped." (Quran 39:53-54)

Hazrat Umar wrote these verses and found a way of sending the inscription to Hisham, who said, "When it came to me, I raised it close to my eyes and lowered it away from them, but I could not understand it, until I said, 'O God, make me understand it.' Then God put it into my heart that it had been revealed for our very sakes about what we had done." Hisham showed the verses to Aiyash and they both renewed their faith, and repented.

Despite all the pressure and obstacles, there was a steady stream of emigrants towards Yathrib, which the Quraysh were unable to control. Three months had passed since emigration began, which had started with Abu Salamah. In the city, which had seemed so prosperous and harmonious only ten years ago, everything had changed. Among the Muslims, only slaves and imprisoned ones, along with the Holy Prophet (May God bless and cherish him), Hazrat Abu Bakr and Hazrat Ali remained in Makkah. If they went and settled in Yathrib, the Quraysh would have serious trouble with Aws and Khazraj, who were skilled warriors. Their trade on the route to Damascus and Yemen, both in winter and summer, would be in jeopardy.

The leaders of Quraysh gathered in Daru Nadwah, their assembly place, for an important meeting. The participants in this secret meeting were Abu Jahl, Jubayr ibn Mutim, Tuayma ibn Aliyy, Harith ibn Amir, the brothers Utba and Shyba ibn Rabia, Abu Sufyan, Nadr ibn Harith, Abul Bakhtari, Zam'a ibn Aswad, Hakim ibn Hizam, the brothers Nubayh and Munabbih ibn Al-Hajjaj and Umayya ibn Khalaf.

A devil in the form of an old man with rugged clothes whom they did not know came to them and said, "I am an old man from Najd, I am one of your uncle's sons. I heard that you have gathered here to discuss an important business. I thought that perhaps I may be of some help. But I will leave if you don't want me." "If he is our uncle's son, then he is from us. He would not come from Najd to conspire against us," they said and let him in.

Abu Jahl was presiding over the meeting. He started the discussion by saying, "You know the situation of this man of yours; if he leaves us and goes somewhere else, he will gather followers and attack you, and this will cause you more harm. Tell me what you suggest we should do to avoid this situation and come up with a strategy. Abul Bakhtari stood up and said, "We should tie him up in chains and imprison him for life until he grows old and dies like other poets." The old man from Najd intervened, "I am not of your opinion. This will never solve the problem. If you imprison him, the news of his capture will spread beyond the walls you build around him and will reach his friends. They will come for him and attack you and take him away. This is not a reasonable solution; you should think of something else."

Aswad ibn Rabia then spoke, "We should exile him from our community, kick him out of Makkah, and let him go wherever he wants. We should not care where he goes after we have gotten rid of him." This idea did not please the old man, who took the stage and said, "I swear this is not a solution. Do you not see the beauty in his words, truth in his message, and grace in his actions? These will win the hearts of the people, and they will attack you in your own city."

All the eyes were on Abu Jahl, who agreed with the old man's statements. He said, "I also have an opinion on this matter that you are trying to solve." "What is it, O Abul Hakam?" they asked. He continued, "I believe the ultimate solution lies in forming a group of young men from each tribe who are strong and good swordsmen. They should attack him simultaneously with swords and kill him at once. In this way, we will be able to get rid of him forever. When he is killed his blood will be on the hands of all the tribes, and the sons of Abd Manaf won't be able to fight all these tribes. They will only have the option of demanding the blood money, which we will pay, and the issue will be solved." The old man from Najd nodded his head in agreement and said, "The words spoken by this friend are right. I cannot think of any better solution."

The infidels had then made their decision and plotted to kill the Holy Prophet (May God bless and cherish him). They left Daru Nadwa in secrecy just as they had gathered there. Everyone went home.

Allah the exalted sent Gabriel to the Holy Prophet (May God bless and cherish him) and informed him what he should do. It was noon, which was an unusual time for visiting when everybody was relaxing at home. The Holy Prophet (May God bless and cherish him) came and knocked on Hazrat Abu Bakr's door, asking permission to enter. Hazrat Abu Bakr at once knew as soon as he saw him at that hour that something important had happened. Hazrat Aisha and her older sister Asma were with their father when the Holy Prophet (May God bless and cherish him) came in. Hazrat Abu Bakr said, "May my father and mother be sacrificed for him! By Allah he is not coming at this hour except for something important." The Holy Prophet (May God bless and cherish him) said to him, "Tell those with you to leave." Hazrat Abu Bakr replied, "O Messenger of Allah, they are my daughters; they are like your family. Have no fear."

The Holy Prophet (May God bless and cherish him) announced, "Allah has given me permission to leave Makkah and emigrate." "Together with me?" asked Hazrat Abu Bakr. "Together with thee," replied the Holy Prophet (May God bless and cherish him). Hazrat Abu Bakr was overjoyed, unable to control his emotions, and started crying out of joy. For the last four months, he had been feeding two camels for this trip. This was the start of the new era that would change the course of history. There could not be a greater fortune than being a Companion to the Holy Prophet (May God bless and cherish him) on this historic journey. Hazrat Aisha was, at that time, a young girl, probably in her ninth year. She used to say afterwards, "I knew not before that day that one could weep for joy until I saw Abu Bakr weep on that occasion."

When they had made their secret plans, the Holy Prophet (May God bless and cherish him) returned to his house and told Hazrat Ali that he was about to leave for Yathrib, bidding him stay behind in Makkah until he had given back to their owners all the goods that had been deposited in their house for safekeeping. The Holy

Prophet (May God bless and cherish him) had never ceased to be known as Al-Amin, and there were still many disbelievers who would trust him with their valuables as they would trust no one else. He told Hazrat Ali what Gabriel had told him about the plot the Quraysh had made against him.

The chief of Makkah had chosen eleven men to implement their doomed plan to assassinate the Holy Prophet (May God bless and cherish him). These men were Abu Jahl bin Hisham, Hakam bin Abdul As, Uqbah bin Abu Muait, An-Nadr bin Al-Harith, Umayyah bin Khalaf, Zama'h bin Al-Aswad, Tuaimah bin Adi, Ubai bin Khalaf, Nabih bin Al-Hajjaj and his brother Mubih bin Al-Hajjaj. They had agreed to meet outside the house of the Holy Prophet (May God bless and cherish him) after nightfall. But while they were waiting until their numbers were complete, they heard women's voices coming from the house, the voices of Sawdah, Umm Kulthum, Hazrat Fatima, and Umm Ayman. This made them think, and one of them said that if they climbed over the wall and broke into the house their names would be forever held in dishonor among the Arabs because they had violated the privacy of women. So, they decided to wait until their intended target came out.

The Holy Prophet (May God bless and cherish him) used to rise early in the morning and go to Kaaba to offer prayers. The Holy Prophet (May God bless and cherish him) and Hazrat Ali were aware of the assassin's presence. The Holy Prophet (May God bless and cherish him) took out his cloak in which he used to sleep and gave it to Hazrat Ali, saying, "Sleep on my bed and wrap yourself in this green Hadrami cloak of mine. Sleep in it, and no harm should come to you from them." The Holy Prophet (May God bless and cherish him) then came out of the house, threw a handful of dust on the enemies, and began to recite Sura Yasin,

"And We have put before them a barrier and behind them a barrier, and We have covered them so that they see not." (Quran 36:9)

Allah the exalted took away their sight so that they did not see him, and he passed through their midst and went on his way. It was the twenty-seventh of Safar (Islamic month) during the fourteenth year of prophethood. He went straight to the house of Hazrat Abu Bakr, his most trusted Companion, and left with him hastily before the beginning of the Fajr (daybreak). Hazrat Abu Bakr had saddled two camels and was waiting. The Holy Prophet (May God bless and cherish him) mounted one of them, and Hazrat Abu Bakr the other with his son Abdullah behind him. They knew that the Quraysh would mobilize all their resources to find them. Therefore, instead of taking the road to Yathrib on the north side of Makkah, they went along the road south of Makkah towards Yemen. When they had gone a little way, the Holy Prophet (May God bless and cherish him) stopped his camel, and looking back said, "Of all God's earth, thou art the dearest place unto me and the dearest unto God and had not my people driven me out from thee I would not have left thee."

Amir ibn Fuhayrah, the shepherd whom Hazrat Abu Bakr bought as a slave and then set free and put in charge of his sheep, had followed behind them with his flock to cover up their tracks. Soon they made for a cave in the Mount of Thawr on the way to Yemen. When they reached the cave, Hazrat Abu Bakr sent his son Abdullah to Makkah along with the camels, telling him to listen to what was going on in Makkah regarding the absence of the Holy Prophet (May God bless and cherish him). Amir was to pasture his sheep as usual with other shepherds during the day and bring them back to the cave at night so that they could drink the milk.

It was Hazrat Abu Bakr, who entered the cave first to make sure it was safe for the Holy Prophet (May God bless and cherish him). He tore his shroud and plugged all the holes inside the cave. However, two big holes remained to be covered. After inspection of the cave, he invited the Paragon of the world inside. While inside, the Holy Prophet (May God bless and cherish him) put his glorious head on the thigh of Hazrat Abu Bakr to get some rest. Hazrat Abu Bakr put his feet in the two remaining holes as well. After some time, a poisonous snake bit Hazrat Abu Bakr's foot. The pain was very intense, and he was writhing in agony but remained still to not to disturb his beloved Companion. Tears ran down his cheeks and cold sweat was pouring from his forehead. This alerted the Holy Prophet (May God bless and cherish him), and he asked, "What is wrong with you, O Abu Bakr." "May my mother and father be sacrificed for you, O Messenger of Allah, a snake has bitten me, "Abu Bakr said. The Holy Prophet (May God bless and cherish him) applied his saliva gently on his wound and then prayed to his Lord to heal his faithful Companion. Suddenly, his pain vanished as if nothing had happened.

They confined themselves to the cave of Thawr for three nights: Friday, Saturday, and Sunday (Fathul Bari). Abdullah, son of Hazrat Abu Bakr, returned to the cave with his sister, Asma, bringing food. They brought the news that the Quraysh had offered a reward of a hundred camels to anyone who could find the Holy Prophet (May God bless and cherish him) and bring him back to Makkah. Horsemen were already following every route from Makkah to Yathrib, hoping to overtake them. They were sure that Hazrat Abu Bakr was with the Holy Prophet

(May God bless and cherish him) since he had also disappeared.

The Quraysh were very upset when they came to know that the two companions had escaped. They got hold of Hazrat Ali, brought him to Kaaba, and tortured him brutally to make him reveal the secret of their disappearance. But he said nothing. They went to Hazrat Abu Bakr's home and saw Asma, Abu Bakr's daughter, to find out the whereabouts of the two friends. She refused to tell them anything, and Abu Jahl slapped the girl so hard that her earring broke up. (Ibn Hisham)

Some of the Quraysh thought they must be in hiding in one of the numerous caves in the hills around Makkah. Arabs were good trackers, even when a flock of sheep had followed in the wake of two or three camels. The reward of capturing the fugitives was so generous that the bounty hunters tried every possibility of finding them.

On the third day, the silence of their mountain sanctuary was broken by the sound of men's voices at some distance below them that gradually grew louder as the men were climbing up the side of the mountain. They were not expecting Abdullah until after nightfall. The voices were now not far off—five or six men at least, and they were coming closer. The Holy Prophet looked at Hazrat Abu Bakr and said, "Grieve not, for verily God is with us." And then he said, "What do you think of two when God is their third?"

They could now hear footsteps, and soon, the men were standing outside the cave. They spoke decisively that there was no need to enter the cave since no one could possibly be there. They returned the way they had come. After the Quraysh left, the Holy Prophet (May God bless and cherish him) and Hazrat Abu Bakr went to the mouth of the cave. They found an Acacia tree, about the height of a man, which had not been there that morning, covering the entrance of the cave. Over the gap left between the wall of the cave and the tree, a spider had woven its web. Right at the entrance of the cave was a hollow rock where a rock dove had made a nesting place and was sitting as if she had eggs with her mate perched on a ledge not far above.

Soon after, Abdullah and his sister approached at the expected time. They came out of the cave without disturbing the dove to meet them. Amir had also come; he had brought the Bedouin to whom Hazrat Abu Bakr had entrusted the two camels he had chosen for their journey. The Bedouin was still a polytheist, but he could be relied on to keep their secret and to guide them to their destination by such an unusual path that only a true man of the desert would know. He was waiting for them in the valley below with the two camels and had brought a third camel for himself. Hazrat Abu Bakr took Amir behind him to serve them during their journey.

Asma had brought a bag full of provisions but had forgotten to bring a rope. So, she took off her girdle and divided it into two lengths, using one to tie the bag, securing her father's saddle and keeping the other for herself. For this reason, she earned the title "She of the two girdles."

When Hazrat Abu Bakr offered the Holy Prophet (May God bless and cherish him) the better of the two camels, he said, "I will not ride a camel that is not my own." "But she is yours, O Messenger of Allah," said Hazrat Abu Bakr. "Nay." Said the Holy Prophet (May God bless and cherish him). "But what price did you pay for her?" Hazrat Abu Bakr told him, and the Holy Prophet (May God bless and cherish him) said, "I take her at that price." Hazrat Abu Bakr did not insist further. It was the Holy Prophet's Hijrah, cutting all ties with his homeland for the sake of Allah, the exalted. Therefore, his offering, the act of emigration, must entirely be his, not shared by another in any respect. The camel on which the act of Hijrah was to be accomplished must be his own since it was part of his offering. The camel's name was Qaswa, and she remained his favorite camel.

The small caravan departed for Yathrib, and their guide was Abdullah bin Uraiqit. It was Rabi ul-Awwal, 1st year AH. They travelled through many villages on their way to Quba. At one point in their journey, the Holy Prophet (May God bless and cherish him) received a revelation that told him,

"Verily He who hath made binding upon thee the Quran will bring thee home once more." Quran (28:85).

Even though many people had already given up trying to get the reward money for the Messenger of Allah, some still persevered. Suraqa bin Malik was one of them who said, "While I was sitting in one of the gatherings of my tribe Banu Mudlij, a man from them came to us and stood up while we all were sitting. He said, "O Suraqa! Without doubt I have just seen some people far away on the seashore, and I think they are Muhammad and his Companions." Suraqa continued, "I, too, realized that it must have been them. But I said to him, 'No, it is not them, you may have seen some other folks." I stayed in the gathering for a while and then got up and left for my home. Immediately, I ordered my slave girl to get my horse, which was behind a hillock and get it ready for me. I took my spear and left the house by the back door. I mounted my horse and went in pursuit of the two men."

It had been three days since the travelers had left Thawr. After a short while they saw a cloud of dust approaching fast from behind. Hazrat Abu Bakr was extremely worried and said, "O Messenger of Allah, the man following us is about to catch up with us." The Holy Prophet (May God bless and cherish him) reassured him and said, "Do not worry, Allah is with us." Hazrat Abu Bakr was concerned for his beloved friend, and tears were rolling down his face. The Holy Prophet saw his state and said, "Why are you crying O Abu Bakr?" Hazrat Abu Bakr replied, "I swear by Allah, I am not crying for myself. I fear he will harm you in some way, O Messenger of Allah."

As soon as Suraqah approached them, his horse stumbled, and he fell from it. Then he stood up, got hold of his quiver and took out the divining arrows, and drew lots as to whether he should harm them or not. But the lot came out to his dislike. He ignored the divining arrows, mounted his horse, and charged towards his target. Suraqah heard the recitation of the Noble Quran by the Holy Prophet (May God bless and cherish him) and as he prayed, "O my Lord, concerning this man who is approaching us, give us succor the way You see fit." The Holy Prophet (May God bless and cherish him) was intently looking at Suraqah. Suddenly, the forelegs of Suraqah's horse sank into the sand up to its knees, and he fell from it. He dusted himself, got up, and tried to take out the horse legs out of the sand but could not do so. Eventually when the horse stood up again, it kicked up so much dust that it rose in the sky like smoke. Once more Suraqah drew lots with the divining arrows, and this time as well, it was to his dislike. When he noticed how he had been stopped from harming them, it came to his mind that the cause of Messenger of Allah would be victorious. They stopped, and Suraqah mounted his horse and approached them. He said to the Holy Prophet (May God bless and cherish him), "Your people have announced a reward equal to the blood money for your head." Then, he told him all the plans the Quraysh had made concerning them. He offered them some food and provisions, but the Holy Prophet (May God bless and cherish him) refused to take anything. The Holy Prophet said to him, "Do not tell others about us." Suraqah then requested the Messenger of Allah to write for him a statement of security and peace. The Holy Prophet (May God bless and cherish him) told Amir bin Fuhairah to do so, and he inscribed it on a piece of skin.

In another version by Hazrat Abu Bakr, he said, "We emigrated while the Quraysh were in pursuit of us. None caught up with us except Suraqah bin Malik on a horse. I said, "O Messenger of Allah, this one has caught up with us." The Holy Prophet (May God bless and cherish him) replied, "Do not grieve; verily Allah is with us." (Quran 9:40). The traces of submission were evident from Suraqah's face. Then the Holy Prophet gave him the following good tiding,

"I wonder how you will be when you take possession of the two bracelets of Chosroes of Persia, O Suraqah!" (Ibn Abdulbar, Istiab). "You mean Chosroes, the son of Hurmuz?" Suraqah tried to clarify. The Holy Prophet (May God bless and cherish him) replied, "Yes."

Suraqah, who had set off with the intention of killing the Holy Prophet (May God bless and cherish him), had now submitted in his presence and was returning to Makkah as a new man. (Ibn Hisham)

THE STORY OF UMM MABAD

The party of the Holy Prophet (May God bless and cherish him) continued its journey until it reached two small tents (in the land of sons of Huza) belonging to a woman called Umm Mabad Al-Khuzaiyah. She was a gracious, elderly, and heavy-set woman who used to sit in front of her tent with a mat spread out for travelers and offer food and drink to them. The Holy Prophet and his Companions approached her tent and asked for food and some milk. But unfortunately, Umm Mabad had nothing on hand to offer them, for no rain had fallen for a long time, and all the greenery had dried up. There was a great drought in the area. She told them that the herd was out in the pasture, and the only goat left behind was almost dry. The Holy Prophet (May God bless and cherish him) asked, "Does it have milk?" Umm Mabad replied, "It can hardly stand; how can it have milk?" "Will you let me milk it?" the Messenger of Allah asked. She answered, "May my mother and father be sacrificed to you, if you find a drop of milk in it, do milk it."

The Holy Prophet (May God bless and cherish him) touched its udders, reciting over it the name of Allah, supplicated, and to their joy, there flowed plenty of milk out of them. The Holy Prophet (May God bless and cherish him) first offered it to the lady of the house, and she shared what was left with the members of the party. They all drank to their fill. Before he left, he milked the goat, filled the container, and gave it to Umm Mabad.

When her husband came back from herding the sheep that had not found anything to eat, he was astonished to see the bucketful of milk and asked, "O Umm

Mabad, what is this bucketful of milk? The sheep were not here; even if they were, none have milk." His wife replied, "I swear by Allah that someone very holy came here today." And then she narrated the entire story. Abu Mabad was intrigued, "Can you describe him to me?" Umm Mabad started to describe the beauty of the Messenger of Allah in a way as if an artist was making a portrait.

"He was a man whose beautiful face shone with divine light. His figure was graceful and charming. His belly was flat and not protruding, his head was neither small nor large, and he was of medium build. His eyes were black with fine eyebrows and long lashes. There was a velvety quality to his voice. His shoulders were broad, his beard full and thick. He was dignified when silent, and there was a great sense of bonding when he spoke. He would start his conversation with the name of Allah and would continue exalting Him. When one looked at him from afar, he was the most handsome and charming of men; when one approached him, he was the embodiment of beauty and love. He spoke calmly in a way so as not to annoy one's ears, not too much and not too little. His reason flowed like a poem. He was not tall enough to look down on people nor short enough to be lost in a crowd. In appearance, he was like a third branch between two branches. He would shine out in the company of the three, and he would be the most handsome of them. His Companions would rush around him like a mother; when he speaks, they listen to him with great attention, and when he asks for something, they run to get it. They hover around him, and they never show the slightest reluctance when seeing to his needs; they seem to race each other to serve him."

Abu Mabad was mesmerized by the description of the stranger who visited his tent in his absence. He said to his wife, "I wonder if this is the man of the Quraysh that we have heard about," and then he continued, "I wish I had seen him, I wish I could be friends with him! If one day I have the power, I will stop by in Makkah and shout at the top of my lungs and tell the people about his virtues. It does not matter if they do not understand where this voice comes from, for what matters is not who the voice belongs to but what that voice says." Then he composed verses of poetry in admiration of the Holy Prophet (May God bless and cherish him) that echoed all over Makkah to such an extent that the people of Makkah thought it was a Jinn whispering words in their ears. These verses opened with the praise of Almighty Allah, the exalted who gave them the felicity to host the Messenger of Allah for a short while. It then gave an account of the delight that would settle in the heart of his Companions, and it closed with an invitation to all mankind to come and see for themselves Umm Mabad, her goat, and the container of the milk that would testify to the truthfulness of the Muhammad Mustafa (May God bless and cherish him).

On hearing those lines, Asma, the daughter of Hazrat Abu Bakr, got to know that the Messenger of Allah and his loyal friend Hazrat Abu Bakr were making their way to Yathrib. During their journey to Yathrib, the Holy Prophet (May God bless and cherish him) met Buraydah bin Al-Husaib Al-Aslami along with eighty other people. The Holy Prophet asked him, "From which people are you?" He replied, "From Aslam." The Holy Prophet looked at Hazrat Abu Bakr and said, "Then we are safe." Then he asked him, "From which branch?" He answered, "From Banu Sahm." So, the Holy Prophet said to Abu Bakr, "Your victory has come." Buraydah and all his men accepted Islam at the invitation of the Messenger of Allah. The Holy Prophet (May God bless and cherish him) prayed the night prayer, and they all prayed behind him.

The small caravan of the Holy Prophet (May God bless and cherish him) was passing through a place called Arj, and they knew that they were near Quba and the arduous journey was coming to an end. But the camels they were riding were exhausted, and their pace had become slower. Hazrat Abu Bakr was riding the same camel with the Messenger of Allah so that the other camel might get its strength back. Between Juhfa and Harsha, they met a person named Abu Aws Tamim ibn Hajar. He realized the situation and offered them a camel at once. He also gave his slave Masud to attend them and instructed him to stay by their side till they reached their destination. "Go with them and keep to this road which no one else knows. Never leave them for a second." Later, Abu Aws became Muslim after the Holy Prophet (May God bless and cherish him) arrived in Yathrib. He would send the same Masud on foot to Yathrib to inform them about the Quraysh army that was coming towards Yathrib from Makkah before the Battle of Uhud.

One morning, when they were close to a place called Rim, they saw a small caravan approaching from the opposite direction. They were so happy to see that it was Zubayr ibn Awwam with his friends who were returning from Damascus, where they went for trade. The joy was mutual because Zubayr was also the Holy Prophet's (May God bless and cherish him) aunt's son. The Messenger of Allah's (May God bless and cherish him) arrival in the oasis, he told them, was awaited with the greatest eagerness. Before bidding them farewell, he gave them each a change of clothes from out of the fine white Syrian garments (Bukhari). Zubayr also intended to return there as soon as he had disposed of his wares in Makkah.

It was twelve days after leaving the Cave of Thawr that they reached the valley of Aqiq up the rugged slope on the other side. The sun was well up, and the heat was intense. Usually, they would make a stop to rest until the heat of the day had passed, but they now decided to continue, and when at least they came within sight of the plane below, there could be no question that it was Quba. The place was lying before them with palm groves, orchards, and gardens within three miles of the slope they had to ascend. Most of the emigrants from Makkah had first stayed here, and many of them were still there.

The Holy Prophet instructed his guide, "Lead us straight to Bani Amr at Quba, and draw not yet near the city." That city was soon to be known throughout Arabia and thence elsewhere as "The City of the Holy Prophet" in Arabic Al-Medina.

In the meantime, there was a great sense of excitement in anticipation of the arrival of the Holy Prophet (May God bless and cherish him) in Quba and Medina. The people of Quba were expecting him any minute, for the time of his arrival was overdue. Therefore, with the first light of the day, some of Bani Amr would go out to look for him along with the men of other clans and those of the emigrants who were still there. They would go into the desert and wait until the heat of the sun was unbearable, then they would retire to the shade and wait there till the afternoon. They had gone out that morning but had already returned by noon and were no longer looking expectantly in that direction. When they were near Quba, the sun shone on the white clothes of the Holy Prophet (May God bless and cherish him) and Hazrat Abu Bakr. At the same time, a Jew happened to be on the roof of his home and caught sight of them. He immediately knew who they were. So, he called out at the top of his voice, "O sons of Qaylah, here the friend you have been waiting for has come."

So, men, women, and children hurried from their houses and streamed once more onto the strip leading to the desert. The entire crowd was overtaken by a wave of excitement. Their faces were lit with joy, and they were running to welcome their beloved guest. The Holy Prophet (May God bless and cherish him) briefly addressed the enthusiastic crowd,

"O people, give unto one another greeting of peace, feed those who are hungry, honor the ties of kinship, and pray in the hours when men sleep. Even so, shall you enter Paradise in peace."

The Holy Prophet (May God bless and cherish him) decided to stay with

Kulthum, an old man of Quba who had previously hosted both Hazrat Hamzah and Zyad in his house on their arrival from Makkah. However, Hazrat Abu Bakr lodged with a man of Khazraj in the village of Sunh so that both tribes could share the honor of hospitality. After a day or two, Hazrat Ali ibn Abi Talib arrived from Makkah on foot. He had been given the duty to return all the entrusted belongings to their owners and then to emigrate. Hazrat Ali mostly travelled by night and sustained an open wound on his feet. When the Holy Prophet (May God bless and cherish him) saw him, he opened his arms and embraced him with tears in his eyes. Then he rubbed his saliva on his wounds that were bleeding and prayed to Allah for his cure. Before long, Hazrat Ali's wounds were healed completely (Ibn Hisham, Sira). The Holy Prophet (May God bless and cherish him) and Hazrat Abu Bakr stayed in Quba for four days, and they built a mosque there. Later, this mosque was known as the Quba Mosque, and it was the first Mosque in Islam.

COVERSION OF ABDULLAH IBN SALAM

Many people came to greet the Holy Prophet (May God bless and cherish him), and among them were some Jews. Abdullah ibn Salam was a great Jewish scholar. His ancestry went back to Prophet Joseph and Prophet Jacob. He was born among the children of Israel in one of the three big Jewish tribes around Medina, called the Banu Qaynuqa. His father, Salam, and his grandfather, Harith, were both Jewish scholars and known for their piety and good character. Abdullah ibn Salam was well versed in the knowledge of the Torah and knew that the last Messenger of Allah would come in Makkah and, therefore, eagerly anticipated his arrival. He also knew that the last prophet, after appearing in Makkah, would emigrate to Medina and was looking forward to the coming of the Messenger of Allah with enthusiasm. When the news of the Holy Prophet's (May God bless and cherish him) arrival in Quba reached him, he was picking up dates in a tree while his aunt Khalidah bint Harith was sitting under that tree. Upon hearing the glad tidings, he started praising Allah loudly. His aunt was surprised at his enthusiasm and said, "Woe unto you. You would not have shouted so loud had you heard the coming of Moses, the son of Imran." He replied, "My dear aunt, I swear by Allah the exalted that he is the brother of Moses. He is of the same religion as him. Whatever he was sent with, Muhammad (May God bless and cherish him) has been given the same mission." She then asked, "O son of my brother! Is this the last messenger who will appear before the end of the world, whose coming we have been waiting for?" He said without a doubt, "Yes."

Abdullah ibn Salam immediately went to the presence of the Holy Prophet (May God bless and cherish him). When he saw his resplendent face shining with divine light, he said, "I swear by Allah that there is no lie in this face." The Holy Prophet (May God bless and cherish him) was surrounded by his Companions, and the first words that Abdullah ibn Salam heard were these,

"Let greetings and peace spread among you, feed the hungry, visit your relatives, when people sleep at night perform prayers and thus enter Paradise" (Ahmad Ibn Hanbal, Al-Masnud). Abdullah ibn Salam was mesmerized by the truth and beauty of his words. The blessed face he saw could only belong to the prophet. He murmured his testimony of faith on the spot, "And I bear witness that you are the true Messenger of Allah, and there is no doubt that you have come with the truth." When he became Muslim, the Holy Prophet (May God bless and cherish him) changed his name to Abdullah from Husayn, and from then on, he was known as Abdullah ibn Salam. (Bukhari, Sahih)

SALMAN FARSI

On the second or third evening during the Holy Prophet's (May God bless and cherish him) stay in Quba, there came a man who was different in appearance from any of the others. It was Salman Al-Farsi from Persia, born to Zoroastrian parents in the village of Jay near Isfahan. He had become a Christian and gone to Syria at a very young age. There, he had served a saintly priest, who, on his death bed, told him to go to the Bishop of Mosul, who was old as well but knew all the scriptures. He also, on his death bed, told him that the time was now at hand when the last prophet would appear. He will be sent with the religion of Prophet Ibrahim (May God bless and cherish him) and will appear in Makkah, where he will emigrate from his homeland to a place between two lava tracts, a country of palms. His three major signs are that he will eat of a gift but not if it was given as alms, and between his shoulder blades is the seal of prophecy. If you have the ability, go and wait for him. Thus, the priest inspired a new zeal in Salman, and he decided to go to Medina.

Before long, he found a caravan of the tribe of Kalb and gave them his fare in return for a trip to Medina. But during the journey, when they reached Wadi l-Qura near the Gulf of Aqabah, he was deceived, and they sold him to a Jew. Later, the Jew sold him to a cousin of his of Bani Qurayzah in Medina. As soon as he reached Medina, he knew beyond doubt that here was the place to which the last Messenger of Allah would emigrate.

Salman's new owner had another cousin who lived in Quba, and on the arrival of the Holy Prophet (May God bless and cherish him), he left for Medina with the news. He came running to his cousin, who was sitting under one of his palms while Salman was working on the top of the tree. Salman heard him say, "May God curse the sons of Qaylah! I have just visited them a while ago. Everyone is gathered around a man who has come from Makkah and who they claim is the Messenger of Allah, and they are listening to him eagerly." These words filled Salman with certainty that his search for the Messenger of Allah had come to an end. He was seized by a wave of joy, and his whole body was trembling now. He was afraid that he would fall out of the tree. He quickly came down the tree and started questioning the Jew from Quba. But his master shut him off and ordered him to go back to work. Salman was helpless, and so he climbed the tree once again. That evening, somehow, he managed to slip away, took some dates he had saved and went to Quba. The Holy Prophet (May God bless and cherish him) was surrounded by his Companions. Salman approached the paragon of the world and offered him the dates, specifying that it was alms. Salman was watching very closely. The Holy Prophet (May God bless and cherish him) did not touch what he had brought. He turned to his Companions and said, "Eat in the name of Allah." Since the Holy Prophet (May God bless and cherish him) did not eat from the alms, in Salman's mind, the first sign of prophethood was present. The following day, Salman returned with some food, and this time, he said, "I see that you do not take alms. This time, I have brought you a gift." The Holy Prophet (May God bless and cherish him) took it in his hand and ate from it along with his Companions.

CHAPTER 14
MEDINA, THE CITY OF THE PROPHET

The people of Medina were joyful and impatient for the arrival of their beloved prophet. The Holy Prophet (May God bless and cherish him) stayed in Quba for a full three days, and during this time, he laid the foundation of the first Mosque in Islam. On Friday morning, he set out from Quba at noon time. He and his party took a break in the valley of Ranaia to pray with the Khazrajite clan of the Banu Salim, who were expecting him. This was the first Friday prayer, prayed in a land that from now onward was to be his home. There was a congregation of up to a hundred men, including some of his kinsmen from Bani An-Najjar and some of the Bani Amr, who escorted him from Quba.

After the Friday prayer, the Holy Prophet (May God bless and cherish him) mounted Qaswa, and Hazrat Abu Bakr and his other Companions mounted their camels and set off with him in a grand procession for the city of Medina.

On both sides of them, dressed in armor with their swords drawn, rode young men of Aws and Khazraj as a guard of honor. In this way, they showed that they were sincere and their pledge of protecting the Holy Prophet (May God bless and cherish him) was no empty word.

There had never been such a day of great celebration in Medina. Men, women, and children had lined up the route to Medina. They were rejoicing, and their joyous cries went up to the sky,

"Come is the Prophet of God! Come is the Prophet of God."

They were singing the following song,

طلع البدر علينا من ثنيات الوداع

وجب الشكر علينا ما دعا للـه داع

أيها المبعوث فينا جئت بالأمر المطاع

جئت شرفت المدينـة مرحبا يا خير داع

The full moon rose over us from the valley of Wada. '

And it is incumbent upon us to show gratitude.

For as long as anyone in existence calls out to Allah.

Oh, our Messenger amongst us,

Who comes with the commands to be heeded?

You have brought to our city nobility.

(Ibn Kathir Al-Bidaya wa'n Nihaya, Muhibbat-Tabari, Al-Riyadu'n Nadira)

The entire Medina was echoing with celebratory songs and melodies. Some of the girls were playing daff (Tambourine) and singing,

"We are all neighbors of the sons of Najjar.

How fortunate we are that Muhammad is our neighbor."

The Holy Prophet (May God bless and cherish him) would respond, "Allah knows that I love you too." (Ibn Majah, Sunan)

Qaswa set the slow and stately pace of the procession as it passed amid the gardens and palm groves to the south of Medina. The houses were still few and scattered, but gradually, they approached the main city. Everybody was eagerly inviting the Holy Prophet (May God bless and cherish him), "Alight here, O Messenger of Allah, for we have the strength and protection for thee, and abundance." Some would take hold of Qaswa's halter, but each time, the Holy Prophet would bless them and respond gently, "Let her go her way, for she is under the command of Allah."

The Holy Prophet's (May God bless and cherish him) mount passed by the houses of Utbah bin Malik, Abbas ibn Ubaidah, Ziyad bin Walid, Farwa ibn Amr, Sa'd ibn Ubaidah, Munzir ibn Amr, Sa'd ibn Rabi, Harija ibn Ziyad, Abdullah ibn

Rawaha, Aliyy ibn Najjar, Salit ibn Qays and his father. But Qaswa moved forward and then stopped in a place and looked around it. Then, she moved and continued to walk. Qaswa then turned back to where she had first stopped. It was a large, walled courtyard which had in it a few date palms and the ruins of a building. Qaswa knelt there and flattened her chest against the ground. The Holy Prophet (May God bless and cherish him) alighted and said, "This, if God wills, will be the dwelling."

This place was inhabited by Banu An-Najjar, a tribe related to the Holy Prophet (May God bless and cherish him) from the maternal side. It was his wish to honor his maternal uncles and live among them. Meanwhile, Abu Ayub Ansari, who lived close by, had untied the baggage, and carried it into the house. Others of the clan came forward and begged the Holy Prophet (May God bless and cherish him) to be their guest, but he said, "A man must be with his baggage." Abu Ayub Ansari had been the first of the clan to pledge himself at the second Aqabah. He vacated the ground floor for the Holy Prophet (May God bless and cherish him) and stayed with his wife in the upper part of the house.

The Holy Prophet (May God bless and cherish him) asked who owned the courtyard where Qaswa had stopped. Muadh, the brother of Awf, told him that it belonged to two orphan boys, Sahl, and Suhayl. They were under the guardianship of Asa'd. The Holy Prophet asked him to bring them to him. They came and stood before the Holy Prophet (May God bless and cherish him). He asked them if they would sell him the courtyard and told them to name their price, but they said, "Nay, we give it to you, O Messenger of Allah." He would not take it as a gift and the price was fixed with the help of Asa'd.

THE BLESSED HOUSE OF ABU AYUB ANSARI

Abu Ayub Ansari considered himself the most fortunate man in the world, for the Holy Prophet (May God bless and cherish him) stayed as a guest with him for seven months (Ibn Hisham). This house had a historical and spiritual significance about it. It was the house that had been built by the King of Tubba, Abu Karib As'ad. He was a powerful and mighty king. When he first came to Yathrib with his army to lay siege to it, he was confronted by two Jewish men who said to him, "You cannot lay siege to this city because this is where the awaited Messenger of Allah will emigrate." This statement had such an effect on his heart and soul that he left his throne and kingdom in Yemen and settled in Yathrib, which he knew was to be the place that the last Messenger of Allah would emigrate to. He sincerely believed in the last Messenger of Allah. When he arrived in Yathrib, he noticed that he was not the only one who knew about his coming but there were many sincere hearts that were waiting for him there. Therefore, he decided to stay there. Before long, he had a house built with the intention of hosting the last Messenger of Allah, whom they knew would be coming. They told him, "We see in our scripture that the last Messenger Muhammad that Allah the Exalted will send will emigrate here, and we are waiting here to welcome him." When the king saw their sincerity, he built a house for each one of them and saw to their needs. King Tubba's intentions were pure, his efforts sincere, but his life was short. On his deathbed he called the man he held to be the most wise and trustworthy to his side and left a letter. He wanted him to give the letter to the last Messenger whom he would not live long enough to see. If that man should fail as well, he wanted him to give it to another trustworthy man, and to leave this as a will to the generations to come. However, both of his sons, Lamis and Wahabi, were not quite so devoted as their father, and they sold this house that their father had passed on to them. The house kept changing hands through wills, and at last, it had ended up in the hands of Abu Ayub Ansari. The King of Yemen had not been able to host the last Messenger of Allah, but Allah the Mighty and Majestic had not let his sincere efforts go to waste, and now he was in a way hosting the last Messenger in the same house that he had built long ago.

It is narrated by Salihi in his book that the letter written by King Tubba was brought to the Holy Prophet (May God bless and cherish him) by a messenger called Abu Laila. When the Holy Prophet (May God bless and cherish him) met Abu Laila, he said, "Are you Abu Laila who brings the letter of the King of Tubba?" Abu Laila asked, "And who are you?" The Holy Prophet (May God bless and cherish him) replied, "I am Muhammad. Bring me that letter." And he gave it to the Holy Prophet (May God bless and cherish him). On it was written,

"To the Messenger of the Lord of the worlds, the last in the line of prophets, Muhammad, the son of Abdullah, from the ruler of Tubba." The king showed his respect for the Messenger of Allah in the opening sentence by writing the name of the Messenger of Allah before his name is striking. The letter continued the following words,

"O Muhammad, I have submitted in faith to you, to your Lord, who is the Lord of everything and all that you have brought from your Lord. I have done this so that when I reach you on the Day of Judgment, you may not forget me. Know that I am of the first ones who believed in you even before you came, even before Allah sent you. I am of your religion, and the religion of Ibrahim."

When the Holy Prophet (May God bless and cherish him) read the letter, he said three times emphasizing the fact that all things in their beginning and in their end belong to Allah, "Greetings be to you as well, O my true brother in the land of Tubba." (Halabi, Seerah)

THE DAWN OF THE NEW ERA FOR GOD'S RELIGION

The new community of Muslims in Medina was made of two groups. Those who escaped Makkah were called *Muhajirun* or Emigrants. The native converts of Medina were called *Ansar* or Helpers, for the assistance they had given to Islam. After the Holy Prophet (May God bless and cherish him) gave orders, the entire community of believers joined hands to build their much-anticipated religious center along with some apartments for the Holy Prophet (May God bless and cherish him) and his family.

The construction of the Mosque took about seven months, during which time the Holy Prophet (May God bless and cherish him) joined in the work and laid bricks with his Companions. The simple structure was made of mud bricks, wooden poles, and a roof of palm leaves, though most of the walled in courtyard was left open to the sky. In the middle of the northern wall, that is, the Jerusalem wall, they put stones on either side of the prayer niche. As they worked on the Mosque, they chanted two verses that one of them had made up for that occasion.

"O God, no good is but the good hereafter,

So, help the Helpers and the Emigrants."

And they also sang.

"No life there is but the life of the hereafter,

Mercy O God on Helpers and Emigrants."

During the construction of the Mosque, the Holy Prophet (May God bless and cherish him) caught sight of Ammar. While everyone carried the mud bricks one at a time, he was carrying two pieces of mud bricks on his back. He had lost his mother as the first martyr of Islam and had endured unspeakable torture at the hands of the polytheists. The Holy Prophet approached him, and stroked his head, and then dusted off the dirt from his clothes. Ammar did not stop working as the Holy Prophet (May God bless and cherish him) of Allah was doing all these. Suddenly, the Holy Prophet (May God bless and cherish him) saw the future unfold before his eyes, and looking at Ammar with affectionate gaze, he said; "Have pity for Ammar, the son of Sumayya for he will be martyred by a most furious crowd" (Muslim, Sahih; Hakim, Al-Mustadrak; Ibn Sa'd, Tabaqat). (Ammar would be martyred thirty-seven years later from that day, on the day of Saffin, as he fought on the side of Hazrat Ali (commander of believers). He became a symbol for fighting for the righteous side, and even in his death, he served the unity of Islam).

Medina was the new home of the Holy Prophet (May God bless and cherish him) and his Companions. A group of the people had started to gather at the Mosque where the Holy Prophet (May God bless and cherish him) would share the verses that were revealed to him and would discuss deeds that would be most pleasing to Allah, the exalted. While the rest of the community was engaged in trade or attending to their gardens, the only goal of these people was to make sure that the teachings of the new religion were preserved and not lost. These people were destitute and would faint for not having eaten for a long time. They used the Mosque of the Holy Prophet (May God bless and cherish him) as their home, for they had no roof under which they could live nor any relatives who could help them. They were called the People of the Bench (*Ashab as-Suffa*), and they never asked for help from anyone and were content with whatever circumstances they found themselves in. Their top priority was to obey Allah and to obey the Holy Prophet (May God bless and cherish him). The Messenger of Allah would advise his Companions to look after these people and would assign their sustenance among them.

Allah the Exalted says in the Quran:

"That (which you spend) is for the poor, who, having dedicated themselves to Allah's cause, are in distressed circumstances. They are unable to move about the earth (to render service in Allah's cause and earn their livelihood). Those who are unaware (of their circumstances) would think them to be wealthy because of their abstinence and dignified bearing, but you will know them by their countenance — they do not beg of people importunately, and whatever good you spend, surely Allah has full knowledge of it." (Al-Baqarah 2:273)

Among the *Ashab as-Suffa* were Abu Hurayra, Abu Dhar al-Gaffari, Kaa'b Ibn

Malik, Salman al-Farsi, Hanzalah Ibn Masood, Suhaib Ibn Sanan Rumi, and Bilal Ibn Ribah. Abu Hurayrah said, "I saw seventy *Ashab as-Suffa* in such a condition that none of them had a complete dress for himself. Each one of them had one sheet that he tied up with his neck. Some of them had their sheets reach near their ankles while others reached just below their knees. Each of them used to hold the partition of his sheet with his hand lest his body is exposed."

The Mosque (Masjid Nabawi) was large enough to accommodate a good-sized crowd and remained unaltered for the next nine years. The Holy Prophet's (May God bless and cherish him) apartment was built as a separate structure attached to the Mosque and was connected to it by a doorway. A place (bench) was dedicated for poor or homeless Muslims to sleep in at night.

While the construction of the Mosque was going on, the Holy Prophet (May God bless and cherish him) stayed in the house of Hazrat Abu Ayub Ansari, by whose door Qaswa (the camel) had stopped before finally settling in the empty lot. At the same time, Hazrat Abu Ayub Ansari had already unloaded the Holy Prophet's (May God bless and cherish him) baggage and had it stored in his home. His spacious house had two floors, with the master bedroom on the upper level. Hazrat Abu Ayub Ansari insisted that his guest sleep on the second floor, but the Holy Prophet (May God bless and cherish him) wanted to sleep on the first floor, making it easier to always meet people.

That night Hazrat Abu Ayub Ansari and his wife could not sleep and were worried. They felt uneasy about sleeping above the Holy Prophet (May God bless and cherish him) and were afraid of coming between him and any revelation that might descend upon him from heaven. The next day, they told the Holy Prophet (May God bless and cherish him) their fears and begged him to sleep on the second floor, insisting they would never want to sleep above the Messenger of God. The Holy Prophet (May God bless and cherish him) reassured them that it was alright and that he also preferred the first floor. For some time, Hazrat Abu Ayub Ansari and his wife remained nervous but finally began to ease.

Then, one-night Hazrat Abu Ayub Ansari accidentally broke a pitcher of water, and it spilled all over the floor. He and his wife quickly mopped up the water. They were worried that it might leak through the floor onto the Holy Prophet (May God bless and cherish him) who was sleeping directly below. The next morning, they asked him if he had noticed any dripping during the night. He smiled and assured them he had not. Hazrat Abu Ayub Ansari again begged that he would not feel at ease unless they switched floors. Finally, the Holy Prophet (May God bless and cherish him) agreed to sleep upstairs, and Hazrat Abu Ayub Ansari and his wife were relieved. In later years, Hazrat Abu Ayub Ansari related that he had never had a better and more pleasant sleep when he was sleeping on the first floor under the Messenger of God.

The Emigrants were generally poor, given that many of them had escaped Makkah with little more than clothes on their backs. Many of the men slept in the Mosque at night or in the streets while the women and children congregated in the homes of sympathetic Helpers. The Holy Prophet (May God bless and cherish him) himself shared in the deprivation of his followers. When the Mosque had been completed, the Friday prayers were being performed there. To deliver his sermon and be able to connect with Companions, the Holy Prophet (May God bless and cherish him) would stand up on the stump of a palm tree, which served as a pulpit and address his audience. One day, a companion came from outside Medina and saw the Holy Prophet on a simple pulpit addressing his followers. He turned to Ansar (Helpers) and said, "If the Messenger of Allah should allow it, I would like to make him a pulpit, that he can stand on it if he likes or lean on it as he delivers his sermon." The Holy Prophet (May God bless and cherish him) was informed about this, and he spoke to that person. He offered his services and said, "O Messenger of Allah! Shall I make you a pulpit so that you can get on to deliver your message on Fridays? In that way everyone would be able to see you and you will have conveyed your divine teachings to all."

The Holy Prophet accepted his offer. He started working on the new pulpit and hence built a large pulpit with a few steps. As a result of this the old palm stump was set aside. During the Friday prayer, the Holy Prophet (May God bless and cherish him) was about to mount the new pulpit when suddenly a voice was heard by all those present in the Mosque. It was like the sigh and moan of a camel. It seemed like the old stump was crying due to sadness. The Holy Prophet (May God bless and cherish him) turned to where the voice was coming from. It was clear that it was (Hannanah) the palm stump that had been set aside and could no longer experience the closeness of the Messenger of Allah. The sound of moaning would not stop, so the Holy Prophet (May God bless and cherish him) sat near the stump and stroked it gently with his blessed hands. Then suddenly, the sighing stopped, and the stump was silent. The Holy Prophet (May God bless and cherish him) knelt a little and whispered, "If you like, I can put you back where you were, or I can plant you somewhere in Paradise so that you may be watered by its springs, so that you may flourish new greens and the servants of Allah may eat from your fruits." It looked like the stump had accepted the second offer. The Holy Prophet (May God bless and cherish him) then turned to his Companions and said, "It preferred to be planted in Paradise" (Darimi, Sunan). With the passage of time, when the Mosque needed to be expanded, Ubayy Ibn Ka'b took that stump as an important relic belonging to the Holy Prophet (May God bless and cherish him). (Ibn Sa'd, Tabaqat)

One day Hazrat Abu Bakr left his small, rental house and was walking towards the Mosque. Hazrat Umar Ibn al-Khattab came out from his quarters as well and saw his friend passing by. He asked him where he was going. Hazrat Abu Bakr replied, "I am hungry, and I don't have any food in my house." "The same reason got me out of my house," said Hazrat Umar. Just then, they both saw the Holy Prophet (May God bless and cherish him) coming out of his apartment. He came up to them and asked, "Why are you both outside on such a hot day?" After they told him the reason. The Holy Prophet (May God bless and cherish him) replied, "By God, the same thing got me out of my house. Come on, let us see Abu Ayub." They went to his home and were graciously given a simple meal. The Holy Prophet said with tears in his eyes, "Dates, bread, and meat! This is an indulgence that you will be asked about on the Day of Judgment. So, when you eat, say, "Praise be to God who has satisfied our hunger."

THE CALL FOR PRAYER

The atmosphere in Makkah was very hostile and violent, and the believers could not freely and openly pray in the congregation. But Medina was much more welcoming, and Islam was now finally established over there. Divine Revelations came pouring into Medina, and Allah (Exalted is He) had ordained the giving of alms and the fast of Ramadan and had laid down what was forbidden and what was allowed. The five daily prayers were regularly performed in congregation at the Mosque (Masjid e Nabawi). But there was yet no system to call people out of their homes to perform their prayers at the Mosque. Everyone judged the prayer time by the position of the sun in the sky, either by the first sign of light on the eastern horizon or by the dimming of its glow in the west after sunset. The Holy Prophet and the Companions felt the need for a means of summoning people to prayer when the right time had come. At first, they discussed blowing a horn as the Jewish people did, but then they decided against it. Then, they entertained the possibility of a bell (*Naqus*) or wooden clapper like Christians, but this idea was rejected as well. They were exploring a new way of calling. The next day, when they were discussing this issue, Abdullah Ibn Zayd, who had been at the second Aqabah, had a dream which he recounted to the Holy Prophet (May God bless and cherish him). "O Messenger of Allah! I dreamt of a man who passed by me wearing two green garments, and he had a *naqus* (bell) in his hand. So, I said to him, "O servant of God, will you sell me that *naqus?*" He asked me, "What will you do with it?" "We will summon the believers to prayer with it," I replied. "Shall I not tell you a better way?" he asked. "What way is that?" He told me to call people with the following words,

"God is most great (Allah o Akbar) and he repeated this glorification four times, then each of the following words twice. I testify that there is no god but God. I bear witness that Muhammad is the Messenger of Allah. Come unto prayer, come unto salvation, Allah is most great, there is no god but God."

Hearing these words, the Holy Prophet (May God bless and cherish him) said that this was a true vision. He told Abdullah, "Go and teach these words to Bilal, who has a powerful, melodious voice. Let him call people to prayer with these words." At the same time, Hazrat Umar was leaving his house to pray with the Holy Prophet (May God bless and cherish him) and wanted to share with him a dream he had the previous night. Just as he was thinking of that, he heard Bilal's voice. He was surprised because Bilal was repeating the very same words that had been spoken to him in his dream. When he came to the presence of the Holy Prophet (May God bless and cherish him), he said, "O messenger of Allah! I swear by He who has sent you with Truth that I dreamt of the very same words." This practice that became the symbol of prayer came to be known as the Adhan.

The Muslims of Medina had been given the title of *Ansar* by the Holy Prophet (May God bless and cherish him), which means "Helpers." Whereas the Muslims of Quraysh and other tribes who left their homes and emigrated to Medina were called "*Muhajirun.*" But Medina had also been inhabited by Jews for a long time, and they were a sizeable party as well. To have peace and harmony in Medina, the Holy Prophet (May God bless and cherish him) made a pact of mutual obligation between his followers and the Jewish community. According to that pact, Muslims and Jews were to have equal status at the same time, allowing each party to pursue its own religion. If a Jew were wronged, then he must be helped to his rights by both Muslims and Jews, and the same if a Muslim were wronged. In case of war against the polytheists they must fight as one people, and neither Jews nor Muslims were to make a separate peace. The Jews accepted this agreement for political reasons. The

Holy Prophet (May God bless and cherish him) was by far the most powerful man in Medina, and his influence was increasing. They had no choice but to accept, they yet did not believe that God would send a prophet who was not a Jew.

To unite the community of believers still further, the Holy Prophet (May God bless and cherish him) now instituted a pact of brotherhood between the Helpers and the Emigrants so that each of the Helper would have an Emigrant brother who was nearer to him than any of the Helpers, and each Emigrant would have a Helper brother who was nearer to him than any Emigrant. But the Holy Prophet (May God bless and cherish him) made himself and his family an exception, so he took the Hazrat Ali by the hand and said, "This is my brother," and he made Hazrat Hamzah the brother of Zayd.

DEATH OF ASAD IBN ZURARA

Asad Ibn Zurara (Abu Umama), who was one of the Helpers who had come to the Aqaba allegiances and had been chosen as the representative of the Najjar, fell seriously ill at the time the Mosque of the Prophet was built. Before long the news of his death came. This was the first incident of its kind after emigration. Medina was engulfed in deep sorrow. The Holy Prophet (May God bless and cherish him) was also deeply grieved. However, the hypocrites were looking for an excuse to raise doubts and this was an opportunity to do so. They said, "Had Muhammad (May God bless and cherish him) been a real prophet, would his Companion not die?" This, in fact, was a strange statement. Were they implying that the Companions of the previous prophets were immortal and had lived forever? They very well knew that Prophet Moses and Prophet Aron were also mortals, and that the children of Israel all had passed. Their only intention was to sow seeds of contention and doubt when they could. It was only Allah the Exalted who gave both life and death and those who said so also knew this very well. The men from the sons of Najjar after the burial of Asad Ibn Zurara came to the presence of the Holy Prophet (May God bless and cherish him) and said, "O Messenger of Allah! You know Abu Umamah was our representative; now that he has died, please choose another man among us as representative."

The Holy Prophet (May God bless and cherish him) looked at them with great affection and embraced them. Then he said, "You are the sons of my uncle; I am one of you. From now on, I will be your representative." The tribe of Bani Najjar was overjoyed. They had lost their most honorable man, but Allah the Exalted gave them the paragon of the world as his successor. (Ibn Hisham, Sira; Ahmad Ibn Hanbal, Al-Musnad; Hakim, Al-Mustadrak)

Kalthum Ibn al-Hadam, who was a Companion, had also died. The Holy Prophet (May God bless and cherish him) was in the graveyard attending his burial. Salman Farsi was also with him. He was curious and looking for the third sign of prophethood, having known that he did not accept alms but received gifts. The Holy Prophet (May God bless and cherish him) was dressed in two pieces of garment. He had put one piece on top of the other so that his right shoulder and neck could be seen. This was the opportunity Salman Farsi had been hoping for – the seal of prophecy that his last master had talked about. He slowly approached from behind to see the mark. The Holy Prophet (May God bless and cherish him) noticed that Salman was looking for something. The Holy Prophet (May God bless and cherish him) gently uncovered his back so that Salman could see the seal. Now, the seal of prophethood was clearly visible, just as his previous master had described. Salman Farsi was in a state of ecstasy. He could not contain himself and started crying with joy. He turned around and started kissing the Holy Prophet's (May God bless and cherish him) head. Tears were rolling down his cheeks because this was the moment he had been dreaming of for years.

The Holy Prophet (May God bless and cherish him) called him and made him sit in front of him. Salman Farsi talked about his quest for the Truth and his journey to find him in detail. How he left Persia, how he came to Damascus, his search in Mosul, his story in Nusaybia, the priest he met in Ammuriya, and what hardships he had been through. He then shared with the Holy Prophet (May God bless and cherish him) what his last master had told him. His dedication and faith pleased the Holy Prophet (May God bless and cherish him) so much that he asked him to tell his account once more to the Companions. (Ahmad Ibn Hanbal, al-Musnad; Ibn ul-Athir)

Allah, the Mighty and Majestic, says in the Quran,

"Yet they are not alike; among the people of the Book there is an upright community, reciting Allah's Revelations in the watches of the night and prostrating (themselves in worship). They believe in Allah and the Last Day and enjoin and promote what is right and good and forbid and try to prevent evil and hasten to do good deeds as if competing with one another. These are righteous ones. (Al-Imran 3:113-114)

AN ATMOSPHERE OF JEALOUSY

Among the polytheists and the people of the Book (Jews and Christians) in Medina, there were those who knew the Holy Prophet (May God bless and cherish him) and were inclined towards him, and there were those who were against him and plotted secretly to kill him. During the first year in Medina, the enemies of Islam did not form an organized opposition but acted clandestinely.

Among the chief adversaries to the new religion were two cousins, the sons of two sisters, but of Aws and Khazraj through their fathers. Each one had great influence in his tribe. The man of Aws, Abu Amir, was also known as a monk because he was an ascetic and wore garments of wool. He claimed to be of the religion of Prophet Ibrahim, and the people of Yathrib showed him great respect. He visited the Holy Prophet (May God bless and cherish him) to ask about the new religion. The Holy Prophet (May God bless and cherish him) recited the verses of the Quran, which had more than once defined the new religion as the religion of Prophet Ibrahim.

"They say, 'Be Jews or Christians (so) you will be guided.' Say, "Rather (we follow) the religion of Ibrahim, inclining towards truth, and he was not of the polytheists." (2:135)

Abu Amir said, "I am Hanif (Ibrahimic faith)," and he accused the Holy Prophet (May God bless and cherish him) of having falsified the Ibrahimic faith. "I have not," the Holy Prophet (May God bless and cherish him) answered, "In fact, I have brought it white and pure."

"May God let the liar die lonely and outcast in exile." Said Abu Amir. "So be it," replied the Holy Prophet (May God bless and cherish him) "May God do this to him who is lying." (Ibn Hisham, Sira)

Abu Amir soon realized that his authority was rapidly waning, and he was also upset by his son Hanzalah's devotion to the Holy Prophet (May God bless and cherish him). He therefore decided to take his remaining followers, ten in all, to Makkah, and hence, this was the beginning of his own exile.

Abdullah Ibn Ubayy was the chief of Khazraj and cousin of Abu Amir. He had prepared himself for the leadership in Medina to bring people together who were living in chaos. He was thus frustrated by the coming of the Holy Prophet (May God bless and cherish him), and as a result, robbed of his authority. He likewise had the bitterness of seeing his own son Abdullah as well as his daughter Jamilah won over by the Holy Prophet (May God bless and cherish him). When one of the chiefs of Khazraj Sa'd ibn Ubaydah got ill, the Holy Prophet (May God bless and cherish him) went to see him. All the influential men of Medina had their houses built as fortresses, and on his way, he passed by the fortress of Ubayy, who was sitting with his people outside it. Out of courtesy, the Holy Prophet (May God bless and cherish him) stopped, greeted him, and sat with him for a while. Then the Holy Prophet (May God bless and cherish him) recited the Quran and invited him to Islam. Ibn Ubayy rudely turned to him and said, "Nothing could be better than this were it to be true. Stay at home, and whoever comes to you, preach to him this. But who so does not come to you, do not burden him with your talk nor enter people's gatherings which they don't like."

Soon after, a voice said, "Nay, come unto us with it, and visit us in our gatherings and our homes, for that we do love that Allah has given us bounty and has guided us." The speaker was Abdullah ibn Rawahah. The Holy Prophet was deeply hurt despite Abdullah's tribute. When the Holy Prophet (May God bless and cherish him) visited the sick Sa'd ibn Ubadah, he immediately asked him what was troubling him. The Holy Prophet (May God bless and cherish him) told him about Ibn Ubayy's disbelief. Sa'd replied, "Deal gently with him, O Messenger of Allah, for before you came to us, we were preparing to crown him as our king. Your arrival has robbed him of a kingdom."

Ibn Ubayy soon realized that his influence was slowly diminishing, and if he did not enter Islam, it would be gone altogether. He thought that a nominal acceptance of Islam would strengthen his authority once more, for Arabs were averse to breaking their old ties. It was therefore, not long, before he decided to enter Islam. However, the believers were not sure about his sincerity. There were others about whom they were equally doubtful.

One day Hazrat Abu Bakr met a man by the name of Finhas and had a long conversation with him. This gave hope to Hazrat Abu Bakr because he was a person who knew the Torah and the Gospel and taught children the stories of Prophet Moses in the synagogue. If he were to become a Muslim, many people around him would also enter Islam. Hazrat Abu Bakr met Finhas the next day and started to preach about the new faith. He spoke about the unity of God and the afterlife and said, "O Finhas, fear Allah and be a believer. You know well that Muhammad is the Messenger of God and has been sent with the Truth. You will find this in the Torah and Gospel as well."

Finhas did not agree and started mocking the teachings of Islam. He said, "I swear by Abu Bakr that we do not need Allah! We do not ask of Him as much as He asks of us. We are richer than Him. Look, if He were richer than us, He would not ask of our wealth as your friend (Muhammad) preaches. He forbids interest for you but gives us interest. If He were richer than us, He would not give us interest."

Finhas was interpreting the verse, "Who is it that would loan Allah a goodly loan." (Quran 2:245). He was insulting Allah the Exalted and this infuriated Hazrat Abu Bakr, who was by nature a gentle natured person. Hazrat Abu Bakr slapped him across the face even before he could finish what he was saying. Hazrat Abu Bakr then said, "O you enemy of God, I swear by He who holds my life in His hands that had there not been a treaty between you and us, I wouldn't let you live." It was well known that Hazrat Abu Bakr was the most refined man with a mild temper, but in the matters of faith, his stance was those of the most valiant of men.

Soon, the words of Finhas reached Hazrat Umar, and he too was enraged. He drew his sword and went on to finish Finhas. At the same time, Gabriel came to the Holy Prophet (May God bless and cherish him) and let him know what had transpired. He brought the following Revelation.

"Say, O Muhammad, to those who have believed that they should forgive those who expect not the days of Allah so that He may recompense a people what they used to earn." (45:14)

This implied that one had to stay calm and not waste time with the deniers, for their judgement would be delivered on the Day of Resurrection by Allah, the greatest of all judges. Hazrat Umar did not know this verse. The Holy Prophet (May God bless and cherish him) sent someone to him to inform him. Before long, a Companion caught up with Hazrat Umar and told him that the Holy Prophet (May God bless and cherish him) has sent for him for an urgent matter. Hazrat Umar came to the presence of the Holy Prophet (May God bless and cherish him) at once. The messenger of Allah said, "Put your sword down O Umar," and then read him the new verse that Gabriel had brought. Hazrat Umar had now calmed down and said, "I swear by He who sent with Truth that I will not be provoked like this again and never lose my temper."

The Jewish man Finhas, who had been slapped by Hazrat Abu Bakr, came to the Holy Prophet (May God bless and cherish him) and made a complaint. He told him that Hazrat Abu Bakr had attacked and pounded him without telling him what he had said and was asking for retribution. The Holy Prophet (May God bless and cherish him) called Hazrat Abu Bakr and asked, "Why did you do such a thing?" To clarify the situation, Hazrat Abu Bakr said, "O Messenger of Allah! This man is the enemy of Allah and has committed a sin against the Creator. He spoke words that the believers would not tolerate. I fear to say it, he said that Allah is poor and that he is rich. I was enraged, and I hit him for Allah's sake." When Finhas heard that he denied, and said, "I did not say those things." He was now accusing Hazrat Abu Bakr of lying. The Holy Prophet already knew the truth about what had transpired. In the meantime, Gabriel brought the following verses of the Quran.

"Allah has certainly heard the statement of those (Jews) who said, "Indeed, Allah is poor, while we are rich." We will record what they said and their killing of the prophets without right and will say, "Taste the punishment of the Burning Fire." (Al-Imran 3:181)

Medina was populated by three distinct groups with ethnic and religious differences. At that time, Medina had a population of ten thousand people. There were around fifteen hundred Muslims, four thousand Jews, and four thousand five hundred Arab polytheists. The Holy Prophet was able to form alliances through divine wisdom. The wars between different groups that had continued for hundreds of years had weakened the social bonds. Just as there were conflicts between different groups, there were also conflicts within the groups themselves. There were enmities between Aws and Khazraj, and among Jewish tribes, the Bani Qaynuqa, the Bani Nadir, and the Bani Qurayza. The situation in the city was almost chaotic, and there was no sense of safety. Commerce was almost at a standstill because of this disorder. The people of Medina were looking towards the Holy Prophet (May God bless and cherish him) to bring the people together and establish peace. The Holy Prophet (May God bless and cherish him) was able to forge alliances between different factions. "Your religion unto you, and our religion unto us" was the mandate the Holy Prophet (May God bless and cherish him) proposed so that different groups can live in harmony and peace without resorting to violence. According to this system, whatever their language, religion, race, or tribe, people were going to share the town if they respected each other. Nobody was going to have to change their religion, nor would any member of any religion be under oppression.

The situation in Medina was stable and peaceful. The potential problems that Muslims may have had to face in the new city of Medina had thus been taken care of one by one by the Holy Prophet (May God bless and cherish him). Now, it was time to send for the members of families who had been left behind. The *Muhajirun* had gone on hijra without taking their families with them. All they had cared about was that they had been told to emigrate, and they hastened to comply with the divine command. They did not worry that they would be leaving their homes back in Makkah, and their families might be left without food and protection. They were focused on faith, and when there was a command, they would move mountains to comply with that command.

When the Mosque (Masjid e Nabawi) was nearly complete, the Holy Prophet (May God bless and cherish him) gave orders to build two small dwellings attached to its eastern wall, one for his wife Hazrat Sawdah, and the other for his betrothed, Hazrat Aisha. The Holy Prophet (May God bless and cherish him) sent Zayd to Makkah to bring Hazrat Sawdah, and with her Hazrat Umm Kulthum and Hazrat Fatima. At the same time, Hazrat Abu Bakr sent word to his son Abdullah to bring Umm Ruman, Asma and Aisha. Zayd also brought his own wife, Umm Ayman, and their small son Usamah. Talha also travelled with them and having disposed of all his immovable property he embarked on his own hijra.

Zubayr ibn Awwam had married Hazrat Abu Bakr's daughter Asma, and she was pregnant with Abdullah. When the command for hijra came, she set off on the journey even though the birth of her child was close. She travelled five hundred kilometers and reached Quba, where her labor pain started, and they took a break there. Soon, she gave birth to a boy. This birth brought a lot of joy and excitement because it was the first child to be born since the emigrant's arrival in Medina.

Without wasting time, they brought the baby to the presence of the Holy Prophet (May God bless and cherish him). He took the baby in his arms and named him Abdullah. The Holy Prophet (May God bless and cherish him) then asked for a date. He took the date, and after chewing it a little, he gave the sap to the baby and prayed for him.

The Holy Prophet (May God bless and cherish him) and his daughters went to live with Hazrat Sawdah in her small new dwelling. After a few months had passed, it was decided that Hazrat Aisha's wedding should take place. The Holy Prophet (May God bless and cherish him) had long been very near and very dear to the family of Hazrat Abu Bakr, and Hazrat Aisha had been accustomed to seeing him every day, except during the few months when he and her father had already emigrated, while she and her mother were still in Makkah. From her childhood, she had seen her father and mother treat the Holy Prophet (May God bless and cherish him) with such great reverence and love which they gave to no one else.

Little preparations were made for the wedding – not enough at any rate. Hazrat Abu Bakr had brought some fine red striped cloth from Bahrain, and it had been made into a wedding dress. She was clothed in that dress. Then her mother took her to a nearby built house where some women of the *Ansars* (Helpers) were waiting for her outside the door. They greeted her, combed her hair, and adorned her with ornaments. Unlike his other marriages, there was no wedding feast. The occasion was as simple as possible. A bowl of milk was brought, and having drunk from it himself, the Holy Prophet (May God bless and cherish him) offered it to her. She shyly refused it, but when he pressed her to drink, she did so. She then offered the bowl to her sister Asma, who was sitting beside her. Others also drank it.

Medina was well known throughout Arabia as a place where, in certain seasons, there was a great danger of fever, especially for those who were not native to the place. The Holy Prophet (May God bless and cherish him) himself did not get the fever, but it severely affected many of his Companions, including Hazrat Abu Bakr and his two freedmen, Amir, and Bilal. Their illness even forced them to perform their prayers in a sitting position. Prayers that they had never abandoned their prayers, even in the face of fierce pressure from Makkan polytheists. Seeing them suffering, the Holy Prophet (May God bless and cherish him) said, "Know this well: those who pray sitting will get only half the reward of someone praying standing." Thus, encouraging them to pray while standing (Ibn Kathir, Al-Bidaya wan-Nihaya). The three of them shared the same space, and they spent the time of illness together. The verses concerning the head covering (Hijab) of the women had not been revealed, so Hazrat Aisha would regularly come to visit her father and ask, "O father, how are you?" The state they were in spoke for itself, for they were burning with fever and delirious about the longing for Makkah. Hazrat Abu Bakr, during the height of his fever would say everybody is staying alive among his people, yet death is nearer to him than his shoelaces.

Hazrat Abu Bakr did not recognize his daughter nor hear what she had said. So, she said to herself, "I swear my father does not know what he says," and then she turned to Amir ibn Fuhyara and asked him the same question. "How do you feel, O Amir?" He wasn't quite himself either. He was speaking of gardens and orchards, saying that he had been introduced to death without having a chance to look at the world with different eyes. "I swear Amir does not know what he is speaking of either." She spoke. She was unable to get a reasonable answer from her father and Amir, so she went to see Bilal. But Bilal looked even worse; he was lying on the floor with a fever, trying to lift his head and mumbling the following,

"Would that I could ever walk in a valley where I would be surrounded by the grass of I*dhkhir* and *Jelil?* (Two good-smelling grasses). Would that I could drink one day the water of *Majannah and* would that *shamah* and *Tafil* (two mountains of Makkah) I will be able to see again."

They were in a desperate situation filled with the longing for their homeland, the memories of its mountains, the air of its highlands, the scent of its grasses, and the freshness of its springs. The illness had brought back all these memories. Hazrat Aisha was deeply sad and informed the Holy Prophet (May God bless and cherish him) of their condition. The Holy Prophet (May God bless and cherish him) lifted his hands in prayer and supplicated,

"Dear Lord! I leave unto you the judgement of Utbah ibn Rabia, Shayba ibn Rabia, and Umayya ibn Khalaf. They forced us to leave our land and come to this place. You take care of them," then he supplicated again, "O Lord of the worlds, let the Medina be dear to us, as dear as you made Makkah to our hearts! Let this place be a place of health and let there be *baraka* in its measurements and weights! O Lord, take this illness from us and hurl it somewhere in the direction of Al-Juhfa." (Bukhari, Sahih)

Allah, the Exalted granted his prayer. That night, when the Holy Prophet (May God bless and cherish him) went to bed, he had a dream. There was a black woman with disheveled hair, and she had left Medina and was going towards Juhfa, a place which is also named Mahay. This was a clear sign that their illness was going to disappear and would leave Medina. From that day on, the Emigrants were free of fever and became healthy.

There was the dawn of the new civilization in Medina based on the Islamic faith. The Holy Prophet (May God bless and cherish him) laid the foundation of the new society. Social relations were revised from the beginning. He enjoined the believers to observe righteousness and praiseworthy manners and infused into them the ethics of good traits, honor, nobility, and divine worship. In this context, obedience to Allah (Exalted is He) was the primary goal. One day, a Companion approached the Holy Prophet (May God bless and cherish him) and asked,

"What deed is better in Islam?" the Holy Prophet (May God bless and cherish him) replied, "That you offer food and extend greetings to one whom you know or do not know." (Bukhari, Sahih)

In this regard, Abdullah ibn Salam reported, "When the Holy Prophet (May God bless and cherish him) arrived in Medina, I went to see him, and I immediately recognized by looking at his blessed countenance that he would never be a liar. The first thing he said was, "O people! Extend the greeting of peace among yourselves, provide food to the needy, maintain the ties of kinship, observe prayer at night while people are asleep and then you will peacefully enter the Garden." (Tirmidhi, Ibn Majah)

The Holy Prophet emphasized,

"He will not enter Paradise, whose neighbor is not safe from his wrongful conduct." (Muslim)

"The Muslim is the one from whose tongue and hands the Muslims are safe." (Bukhari, Sahih)

The Holy Prophet (May God bless and cherish him) reiterated, "As long as you do not wish for your brother what you wish for yourself, your faith has not reached maturity. (Ibid)

The Messenger of Allah said, "The believers in their mutual love are like the human body where when the eye is in agony, the entire body feels the pain; when the head hurts, all the body will experience pain. (Muslim, Mishkat al-Massabih)

Abu Dawood in Sunan narrated that the Holy Prophet (May God bless and cherish him) said, "Show mercy to people on earth so that Allah will have mercy on you in heaven."

"He is not a believer who goes to bed full and knows that his neighbor is hungry." Mishkat al-Masabih)

The Holy Prophet (May God bless and cherish him) also said. "Abusing a Muslim is an act of disobedience and fighting him is disbelief." (Bukhari, Sahih)

The Messenger of God added, "To remove something harmful from the road is charity, and it is a part, from the parts of faith." (Mishkat al-Masabih)

"Charity erases sins just as water extinguishes fire." (Ibid)

It is narrated that the Holy Prophet proclaimed, "Clothing an under-clad believer gets you a garment from Paradise, feeding a hungry believer will make you eligible for the fruits of heaven, and if you provide water to a thirsty Muslim, Allah will provide you with a drink from the sealed nectar." (Mishkat al-Massabih)

The Holy Prophet stressed, "Try to avoid Fire even by half a date (in charity) if not by uttering a good word." (Bukhari, Sahih)

Those were the qualities and attributes on basis of which the Holy Prophet (May God bless and cherish him) wanted to build a new community, the most wonderful and honorable society ever known in history. In this way he established a new community (Ummah), united not by tribal affiliations and genealogy but by faith and loyalty to the Holy Prophet's (May God bless and cherish him) message. Therefore, Yathrib becomes Medina, "The Prophet's City" (*Medinat-al-Nabi*).

Most of the population in Medina was Jewish, but there were also Christians in the town. When Muslims interacted with either community, the subject would inevitably turn to religious issues, and hence, there would be a mutual exchange of ideas. In this vein, Allah (Exalted is He) revealed in the Quran:

"O people of Book (Jews and Christian)! Why do you dispute concerning Abraham (Whether he was a Jew or a Christian) when both Torah and Gospel were not sent down save after him? Will you ever not use your reasons?" (Al-Imran 3:15)

One day, the Jewish and Christian scholars of Najaran came to visit the Holy Prophet (May God bless and cherish him). When the subject discussed came to the commandments of Allah, the Holy Prophet preached about Islam and invited them to truth.

"Do you mean, O Muhammad, that we should worship you like the Christians worship Jesus?" was their reply, although, the Holy Prophet (May God bless and cherish him) had invited them to worship Allah (Exalted is He) only, who is one in essence and attributes. Just then, another Christian scholar came forward and said, "Do you have such a request when you invite us to Him?" "Absolutely not," the Holy Prophet (May God bless and cherish him) added, "I seek refuge in Allah from worshiping or calling others to worship any other power than Him. This is not what Almighty Allah sent me for, that is not what I have been commanded to do."

It was hard to believe that these religious scholars who claimed to be men of God should utter such words. Allah, the Mighty and Majestic revealed the following verse:

"It is not for a human (prophet) that Allah should give him the Scripture and authority and prophethood and then he would say to the people, "Be servants to me rather than Allah," but (instead, he would say), "Be pious scholars of the Lord because of what you have taught of the Scripture and because of what you have studied." (3:79).

Adiyy ibn Hatam was present as well and said to the Holy Prophet (May God bless and cherish him), "O Messenger of Allah! They do not worship Allah at all." At this, the Holy Prophet (May God bless and cherish him) said, "Of course, they do not worship! But they consider halal as haram, and haram as halal, they preach their own desires, and their followers accept what they tell them. For them this constitute worship." (Ibn Kathir, Tafsir)

CHAPTER 15
THE PERMISSION TO FIGHT IN THE CAUSE OF ALLAH

The Holy Prophet (May God bless and cherish him) received a Revelation not long after his arrival in Medina. It said,

"Unto those who are attacked, permission to fight is given, unto those who fight because they have been wronged; and God is able to give them victory. They are those who have been evicted from their homes without right – only because they say, our Lord is God." (Quran 22:39-40)

The Holy Prophet (May God bless and cherish him) knew that permission to fight was a command, and the obligation of war had also been stressed in the covenant with the Jews. Although the Lord, in an early revelation, said,

"Deal gently with the disbelievers, give them respite for a while." (Quran 6:17)

But now the time had come, and Allah the exalted had declared war on the Quraysh (polytheists). The Holy Prophet (May God bless and cherish him) was therefore obligated to take tough measures to establish peace and security not only in Medina but outside Medina as well. To that end, he organized groups of armed men to scout the outskirts of Medina to ensure security and to gather information about the movements of the Quraysh. They were especially watching caravans that might travel through Medina, hence preventing them from attacking the people of Medina. In this way, the Holy Prophet (May God bless and cherish him) wanted to make it clear that Arabia would no longer be safe for them until they submitted to the divine command. This was soon confirmed by another revelation,

"Fight them until persecution is no more, and religion is all for God. And if they cease – then indeed, Allah is seeing of what they do." (Al-Anfal 8:39)

The Holy Prophet (May God bless and cherish him) took measures aimed at establishing a security zone around Medina and succeeded in making alliances with Bedouin tribes at strategic points along the coast of the Red Sea. The Quraysh were vulnerable regarding their caravans, and it was in the spring and early summer months, when their trade with Syria was most active, that they were at risk of attack from Medina. In the autumn and winter months, their caravans travelled to Yemen and Abyssinia.

The first campaign undertaken was the Sariyya mission under the command of Hazrat Hamzah. A force of thirty fighters was dispatched for this expedition. It took place seven months after the Hijra. A caravan of Quraysh consisting of three hundred men, including Abu Jahl, was returning from trade. The goal of the Muslim mission was to show the polytheists that Muslims were strong enough to not only defend themselves but to confront any threat. When the fighters of Hazrat Hamzah reached the place called Saiful-Bahr, they came across the caravan. There was a brief encounter between the two groups. However, with the efforts of Majdi ibn Amr, who was friendly with both parties, the situation was handled calmly. Therefore, the fighters of Hazrat Hamzah returned to Medina. This mission was carried out in the month of Ramadan.

Soon after, in the month of Shawwal, the Holy Prophet gave a mission to his cousin Ubayda ibn Harith, as the head of sixty armed men to confront a Qurayshi force of two hundred men led by Abu Sufyan. The two rival parties met at the place called Rabigh, and after firing a few arrows, they left the field.

A month later, in Dhu al-Qadah, a task force of twenty men was formed under the command of Sa'd ibn Ubada, and they marched all the way to a place called Hurrar in pursuit of a Qurayshi caravan.

When the Holy Prophet (May God bless and cherish him) went out himself on an expedition, he appointed one of his Companions in charge of Medina during his absence, and the first to have this honor was the Khazrajite chief Sa'd ibn Ubadah. The Holy Prophet (May God bless and cherish him) did not take part in any of the missions until it was eleven months after the Hijra. But on each occasion when he remained in Medina, he would give the leader a white banner mounted on a lance.

During the first year, the Holy Prophet (May God bless and cherish him) sent only those of his Companions who were Emigrants. But then the news came that a rich Makkan caravan was returning from north under the escort of Umayyah, with a hundred-armed men. The caravan had merchandise loaded on as many as fifteen hundred camels. In this case, the Emigrants alone were no match for a hundred Quraysh. Therefore, the Holy Prophet (May God bless and cherish him) sent out two hundred men, over half of whom were Helpers. On this occasion, the information was inadequate, and therefore, no encounter took place.

Three months later, they missed another caravan, which was less heavily guarded. Abu Sufyan was leading this party to Syria for trade, but the news came too late. When the Holy Prophet (May God bless and cherish him) and his men reached Ushayrah in the valley of Yanbu, which is close to the Red Sea towards southeast of Medina, the caravan had already passed. However, Abu Sufyan would soon be returning from Syria.

So far, no military encounter had taken place between the Muslims and the Quraysh. The Makkans were already vigilant about the danger of having a formidable enemy established in Medina. Nevertheless, it occurred to them that this would not affect their trade with the South. This presumption would soon be proved to be wrong when the Holy Prophet (May God bless and cherish him) received the news of a caravan that was on its way from Yemen. He sent his cousin Abdullah ibn Jahsh with eight other Emigrants to intercept it near Nakhlah, between Taif and Makkah. It was one of the sacred months of Rajab, and the Holy Prophet (May God bless and cherish him) gave Abdullah no instructions to attack the caravan but simply bring him news of it.

While their party was waiting in Nakhlah, they came upon a caravan passing by. This caravan belonged to the Quraysh and was carrying provisions for war. Abdullah and his companions were in a dilemma. It was the last day of Rajab, and it was considered a sin to fight in that month. On the other hand, the Holy Prophet's (May God bless and cherish him) only definite instructions had been to bring him the news, but he had not forbidden them to fight either, or had he made mention of the sacred month. They also remembered the verse,

"Permission to fight is given unto those who fight because they have been wronged – those who have been unjustly driven from their homes." (22:39)

They were at war with the Quraysh and had recognized at least two of the merchants as men of Makhzum, which of all the clans of Makkah had shown most hostility to Islam. Had they waited for the end of the month (which was not a sacred month), their enemies would be protected for they would have reached the sacred precinct (Haram). One of them took out his bow and arrow and shot an arrow towards the caravan. The arrow hit Amr ibn al-Hadhrami, and the man died on the spot. In the fight that ensued, Uthman ibn Abdullah and Hakam ibn Qaysan were taken captive, and Nawfal ibn Abdullah fled.

Abdullah and his men took the prisoners, the camels, and the merchandize back to Medina. He set aside one-fifth of the spoils for the Holy Prophet (May God bless and cherish him), dividing the rest among his companions and himself. The Holy Prophet (May God bless and cherish him) did not accept the spoils and said, "I did not bid you to fight in the sacred month." Abdullah and his companions were extremely embarrassed. The believers in Medina also blamed them for their violation of Rajab, while the Jews said it was a bad omen for the Holy Prophet (May God bless and cherish him). The Quraysh set about spreading the news far and wide that the Holy Prophet (May God bless and cherish him) was guilty of sacrilege.

During all this chaos, a divine revelation came from heaven.

"They question thee about the sacred month and fighting therein. Say, to fight therein is a grave offense; but having men from God's path and sacrilege against Him and the Holy Mosque and driving out His people there from are graver with God. And torturing is graver than killing." (Quran 2:217)

The Holy Prophet (May God bless and cherish him) interpreted this as confirming the traditional ban on fighting in the sacred month but making an exception in this case. Because forcing people out of their homeland, confiscating their possessions and wealth, and torturing people were all graver sins. The Holy Prophet (May God bless and cherish him) accepted a fifth of the spoils and relieved Abdullah and his friends of the fear that lay so heavily upon them. The clan of Makhzum sent ransom for the two prisoners, but Hakam accepted Islam and remained in Medina.

Now that the blame had become clear, Abdullah ibn Jahsh came to the Holy Prophet (May God bless and cherish him) and said, "O Messenger of Allah! Will we be able to partake the merit that the fighters have gained with this battle?" the Holy Prophet (May God bless and cherish him) remained silent, for the answer to this question was already clear from the verse that had come. The verse said,

"Surely those who believe, those who emigrate and strive in Allah's cause – they are the ones who may hope for the mercy of Allah. Allah is All-Forgiving, All-Compassionate." (Quran 2:218)

THE CHANGE OF QIBLAH

After *Isra* (night journey) and *Miraj* (the ascension to Heaven) both the obligatory prayers and supererogatory prayers had, all been performed facing the direction of al-Quds (towards the city of Jerusalem), a place blessed by Allah the exalted. But the heart of the Holy Prophet (May God bless and cherish him) was longing for Kaaba, and he sincerely wished that one day he would turn his face towards Kaaba. Some of the Companions of the Holy Prophet (May God bless and cherish him) also desired to turn towards Kaaba in their prayers. In fact, the Qiblah had been towards the direction of Kaaba since the creation of Hazrat Adam. Prophet Ibrahim and Prophet Ismael had both performed their prayers turning their faces towards the Kaaba. Many prophets from Prophet Moses to Prophet Saleh had done the same. So, it was natural that the Kaaba would ultimately be the Qiblah of the Last Messenger of God as well. The Jews of Medina claimed superiority, boasting of the fact that the Muslims were praying towards their Qiblah.

One day, when the Archangel Gabriel visited the Holy Prophet (May God bless and cherish him), he said to him, "O Gabriel, I ask my Lord to turn my face away from Qiblah of the children of Israel and towards Kaaba." "Verily, I am but a subject myself; you ask for it yourself from your Lord," answered Gabriel. Allah, the Exalted, responded to the request of his beloved. It was Monday, sixteen months after Hijrah, that Angel Gabriel came down with the following verses from the Lord of the worlds:

"Certainly, We have seen you (O Messenger) often turning your face to heaven (in expectation of a revelation. Do not worry), for We will surely turn you in a direction that will please and satisfy you. (Now the time has come so) turn your face towards the sacred Mosque. And you, O believers, turn your faces towards it wherever you are." (Al-Baqarah 2:144)

A mihrab was forthwith made in the south wall of the Mosque, facing towards Makkah, and the change was accepted with great joy by the Holy Prophet (May God bless and cherish him) and his Companions. Since that day, Muslims have turned in the direction of the Kaaba for the performance of the ritual prayer. There are various reports about the circumstances of the revelation of this verse. One report says that when the revelation came, the Holy Prophet was performing the noon prayer with his Companions, and that he changed his direction after the third cycle and concluded the prayer in that direction. (Ibn Sa'd, Tabaqat)

The Jews of Medina started criticizing this change openly, creating doubts and *fitna* (sedition). But Allah the exalted took care of their objection by the following revelation.

"The foolish among the people will say, "What has turned them away from their Qiblah, which they used to face?" Say, 'To Allah belongs the east and the west, He guides whom He wills to a straight path. And thus, we have made you a just community that you will be witness over the people, and the Messenger will be a witness over you. And We did not make the Qiblah which you used to face except that We might make evident who would follow the Messenger from who would turn back on his heels. And indeed, it is difficult except for those whom Allah has guided. And never would Allah have caused you to lose your faith. Indeed, Allah is to the people kind and merciful." (Quran 2:142-143)

This verse was a great relief for all believers, for the God of the world clearly announced all the questions raised by hypocrites. The Jews, however, continued their mischief and said that the Holy Prophet (May God bless and cherish him) was diverging from the Qiblah of previous prophets. They said, "Had he been a real prophet, then he would not have left the Qiblah of the prophets before him." The Makkan polytheists, on the other hand, were saying,

"It is good that he is retracting and changing his views. Look, he has changed his Qiblah and has turned towards ours soon, he will also change his religion and come to our side." The hypocrites, those who were outwardly Muslims but inwardly did not believe in Islam, started their gossip and said,

"Muhammad does not know where to turn! Had it been the right Qiblah before, why has he given it up? And if the second Qiblah is the correct one, why has he been turning towards the false one till today?"

The Noble Quran spoke of those who guessed about the reasons for the change of Qiblah even though they knew deep inside that such an important event could have happened for no other reason than as a command from Allah, the exalted.

"Even if (O Messenger) you were to bring those who were given the Book (before) every sign, they would not follow your Qiblah nor will you be a follower of their Qiblah, nor would they be followers of one another's Qiblah. So, if you were to follow their desires after what has come to you of knowledge, indeed, you would then be among the wrongdoers." (Quran 2:145)

After one month, Allah revealed to the Holy Prophet (May God bless and cherish him) to fast in the month of Ramadan. Allah (Exalted is He) addressed the believers,

"O you who believe! Prescribed for you is the fast, as it was prescribed for those before you, so that you may deserve Allah's protection (against the temptation of your carnal soul) and attain piety." (Quran 2:183)

Fasting was not an unfamiliar type of worship for the Companions. They had already started to fast on certain days of the month. They had learned that the prophets before them had fasted, and they were expecting this to become their prescribed mode of worship as well. In a *hadith Qudsi*, Allah has said,

"Fasting belongs to Me, and with it I recompense."

Ramadan is a month of revelation during which the Noble Quran was revealed. The Quran laid the foundation of a new heavenly code of life that contains every commandment, full of wisdom and knowledge for all humanity. Ramadan is a month of mercy and compassion, during which God showers His blessings on mankind and multiply the rewards of good deeds. Fasting illuminates the heart, purifies the soul, and leads the spirit into the presence of God. Therefore, the Holy Prophet (May God bless and cherish him) said,

"Make your bellies hungry, livers thirsty, and leave the world alone, then perhaps you may see God with your hearts."

Hazrat Umar ibn Khattab narrated that once the Holy Prophet (May God bless and cherish him) and a few of his close Companions were sitting in the prophet's Mosque when a young man wearing white clothes and with black hair appeared and asked him several questions. There were no signs of travel on him, and we did not recognize him. The young man knelt before the Holy Prophet (May God bless and cherish him) with extreme reverence, put his hands on his thighs and asked, "O Messenger of Allah, please teach me what Islam?" the Holy Prophet (May God bless and cherish him) replied, "To bear witness that there is no god but God and that Muhammad is His Messenger, to perform daily prayers, to pay the alms (Zakat), to fast during Ramadan, and to go on the pilgrimage to Kaaba if you can find the means to it is. Islam is the complete and exclusive surrender of the faithful to God's will and his perfect acceptance of the injunctions as preached in the Quran." The man said, "You have spoken the truth."

The young man then asked, "What is Iman (Faith)?" the Holy Prophet (May

God bless and cherish him) replied, "To have faith in Allah, His angels, His scriptures, His messengers, and the Last Day, and to have faith in measuring out, both the good of it and the evil of it." The man said, "You have spoken the truth." The young man asked again, "What is Ihsan?"

To this the Holy Prophet (May God bless and cherish him) said, "Ihsan is to do the beautiful with the meaning that you worship Allah as if you see Him, for even though man does not see God, God always sees man." The young man said again, "You have spoken the truth." He then asked, "Tell me about the final hour?' The Holy Prophet (May God bless and cherish him) said, "The one asked does not know more than the one asking." The man said, "Tell me about its signs?" The Holy Prophet (May God bless and cherish him) replied, "The slave-girl will give birth to her mistress, and you will see barefoot, naked and dependent shepherds compete in the construction of tall buildings." Then the man left. The Holy Prophet (May God bless and cherish him) said to me, "O Umar, do you know who he was?" I said, "Allah and His Messenger know best." The Holy Prophet (May God bless and cherish him) said, "Verily, he was Gabriel who came to teach you your religion." (Muslim, Sahih)

The entire Islamic doctrine, its spiritual and moral ideas and 'authentic religious experience' can be summed up in the above hadith (Hadith of Gabriel). The Quran states that "Mercy is with those who practice Ihsan (*Al-Muhsinun*) those who do well." (Quran 7:56). The believer must feel that he or she must behave with awe and respect and must never forget the all-embracing divine presence.

Islam (submission) and Iman (faith) are known to all Muslims. They constitute the "five pillars" and its "three principles" or the Shariah (Divine law) and the creedal teachings. The five pillars are mentioned in the hadith of Gabriel. The three principles are divine unity, prophecy (*Nabuwat*) and eschatology (Muad).

What needs to be noted is that the third category mentioned in the hadith – doing the beautiful –is just as important from the point of view of the Holy Prophet (May God bless and cherish him). "Surely God loves the beautiful doers." Doing the beautiful is that you worship God in wakefulness and awareness as if you are gazing upon Him, and you serve Him as if you are seeing Him. This hadith alludes to the heart's encounter with the unseen and the spirit's contemplation of the Beloved. It is an incitement to self-purification in deeds, curtailment of wishes, and loyalty to what was accepted on the Day of *Alast*.

It has come in the traditions that in one of the battles, Hazrat Ali was struck by an arrow. The arrowhead was so stuck in his bone that as much as they tried, it could not be removed. They said, "Unless the flesh and skin are taken away and the bone is broken, the arrowhead cannot be taken out." His elders and young ones said, "If this is the case, we must wait until he is praying, for we always see that in the devotion of the prayer, it is as if he has no awareness of the world."

They waited until he was finished with the obligatory acts and customs of prayer and began with the supererogatory and additional acts. The physician came, opened the flesh, broke the bone, and took out the arrowhead while Hazrat Ali remained as he was in the state of prayer. When he gave the greeting to complete the prayer, he said, "My pain has eased."

They told him what had happened to him while he was unaware. He said, "When I am in whispered prayer with God, the world might turn upside down, or they might strike me with swords and spears, but I would not be aware of the bodily pain because of the pleasure of the whispered prayer.

CHAPTER 16
MARCH TOWARDS BADR

The Quraysh were making great preparations for war in Makkah. They had taken hold of all the possessions of the Emigrants. They intended to transport their belongings to Damascus and sell them for profit. The caravan that was carrying their valuables was led by Abu Sufyan and was estimated to be worth fifty thousand dirhams. This trade would give Quraysh an overwhelming superiority in conflict with the Muslims in Medina.

The time was now at hand for Abu Sufyan to return with all the wares which he had acquired in Syria. The Holy Prophet (May God bless and cherish him) sent Talha ibn Ubaydullah and Said ibn Zayd to Hawra on the seashore towards the west of Medina to bring him news as soon as the caravan arrived. This information would help them to intercept the caravan further down the coast. The two scouts were housed by a chief of Juhayrah, who hid them in his house until the caravan had passed. But someone in Medina - probably a Jew or a hypocrite - had already sent word of the Holy Prophet's (May God bless and cherish him) plan to Abu Sufyan. After getting his information, Abu Sufyan immediately hired a man of the Ghifari tribe named Damdam to go to Makkah with all speed and urge Quraysh to mobilize an army and march out to their rescue. He himself pressed forward along the coastal route, traveling both day and night.

The Holy Prophet (May God bless and cherish him) gave orders that fighters among believers be gathered. At this important junction, he took it upon himself to inspect the fighters and was meticulous about who was to accompany him. All the believers, both grown up and young, were very enthusiastic about joining him on this expedition. But the Holy Prophet (May God bless and cherish him) singled out

Abdullah ibn Umar, Usama ibn Zayd, Rafi ibn Hadij, Bara ibn Azib, Usayd ibn Thabith, and Umayr ibn Abi Waqas to return home because they were too young. When the other young men saw that they were turned down, they started walking on their toes so that they would appear taller and not be rejected. The ones who had to return were very disappointed, went to a corner, and started to sob. When his brother Sa'd ibn Abi Waqas saw his brother's condition, he asked him, "What is bothering you, my dear brother?" Umayr replied, "I fear that the Messenger of Allah will see that I am young as well and tell me to return home." He further said, "I am hoping that Allah may grant me the gift of martyrdom, and that is why I want to go." His sincerity paid off, and upon the insistence of his brother, he was allowed to join the Muslim army. He had a long sword, and he found it difficult to carry it. His older brother helped him with his sword. When he put the sword on his belt, the end of it was dragging on the ground (Bukhari, Sahih; Ibn Athir). On that day, Umayr was sixteen years old.

Some of the Companions stayed in Medina due to valid reasons. Hazrat Uthman, the Holy Prophet's (May God bless and cherish him) son-in-law, was one of them. He stayed behind because his wife, Hazrat Ruqayyah, was seriously ill. The Holy Prophet (May God bless and cherish him) asked Abdullah Ibn Makhtum to lead the prayers in his absence.

In previous expeditions, the Ansar (Helpers) had not taken part, but now the situation was very different and delicate indeed. This caravan of Abu Sufyan strengthened the foundation of the Makkan army that was going to attack Medina. There were some people who also wanted to be with the Holy Prophet (May God bless and cherish him), although they had not yet accepted Islam. Hubayb ibn Isaf was one of them. He was famous for his power and skill in warfare. But this was a matter between the Quraysh and the Holy Prophet (May God bless and cherish him) himself. There had been an agreement between the polytheists of Medina regarding security, pledging that they would defend the city together with the Muslims. But there was not yet a threat that could necessitate the participation of the polytheists. Therefore, the Holy Prophet (May God bless and cherish him) turned down such offers by polytheists due to strategic reasons. However, Hubayb ibn Isaf came back saying that he had become Muslim and thereby would not leave the side of the Holy Prophet (May God bless and cherish him). (Ibn Abd el barr, Istiab; Salhi, Subulu l-Huda wa-Rashad; Suhaili, Rawdu l-unf)

The Holy Prophet (May God bless and cherish him) appointed Qays ibn Abi

Sasaa as the commander of the foot soldiers, and when they left the place called As-Suqya, he told him to count the combatants. The number of the Companions at the well of Abu Inaba was three hundred and thirteen. This number made the Holy Prophet (May God bless and cherish him) very happy, and he said with joy, "As many as the Companions of Talut." (Tabari, Tarikh; Salihi)

It is reported that the Companions at Badr were three-fifths Ansar and two-fifths Muhajirun. This number, as our Holy Prophet (May God bless and cherish him) pointed out, was the same number as the number of the men in the army of Prophet David against the army of Goliath. The Holy Prophet (May God bless and cherish him) set off from As-Suqya on Sunday evening. The Muslim army had only two horses and seventy camels with them. They marched forward by taking turns riding the camels. The Holy Prophet (May God bless and cherish him) rode the camel with Hazrat Ali and Hazrat Abu Lubaba, taking turns. Hazrat Ali and Abu Lubaba would offer their turn by saying, "O Messenger of Allah, you mount, and we will walk alongside you." But the Holy Prophet (May God bless and cherish him) would decline their offer and say, "You are not stronger than me in walking."

When the army reached Rawha, the Holy Prophet (May God bless and cherish him) sent Abu Lubaba back to Medina and appointed him as deputy to look after the affairs of the town. Abu Lubaba was sad to be returning. Before his return, he left the shield he was wearing with the Holy Prophet (May God bless and cherish him). Along this entire journey, the Holy Prophet (May God bless and cherish him) was praying to Allah, "My Lord, these people are barefooted, give them strength to endure against the difficulties of the road. They have no clothes on their back, to clothe them! They have nothing to eat, feed them! These are poor people; make them rich with your grace." (Ibn Sa'd, Tabaqat)

When they reached Turban, the Holy Prophet (May God bless and cherish him) turned toward Sa'd ibn Abi Waqas and called out to him, "O Sa'd." He was pointing to a gazelle in the distance and told Sa'd to prepare his bow and arrow. Sa'd did as the Holy Prophet (May God bless and cherish him) ordered him and took aim at the gazelle. The Holy Prophet (May God bless and cherish him) put his blessed cheek on his shoulder and said, "Release now." At the same time, he prayed, "My Lord! Allow him to hit the target." The arrow pierced through the neck of the animal. The gazelle was cut, and food was prepared for the entire army.

On the other hand, Abu Sufyan had returned with his caravan from Damascus.

He had received information from his sources in Medina and had changed his route to reach Makkah. He had also hired Damdam ibn Amr by paying him twenty mithqal of gold as a messenger to the Quraysh to let them know what was happening on the road. Close to Makkah, Damdam cut the nose and ear of his camel and ripped his saddle apart to further incite the Makkans. He tore his clothes to show the gravity of the situation.

As Abu Sufyan was passing Badr, he was on high alert. He asked Majdi ibn Amr, "Have you seen anyone here? Has there been anything out of the ordinary?" "I don't think there is anything serious to worry about. I have only come across two horsemen. They stood on that hill for a while, got some water from the well, and then left." said Majdi. These two men were Babas ibn Amr and Adiyy ibn Abi Zaghba. They, too, had come to gather information about the caravan. When they met Majdi, they speculated that the caravan would pass that point in a day or two. Majdi was of the same opinion. Then they left that place and reported it to the Holy Prophet (May God bless and cherish him). (Ibn Hisham, Sira)

Abu Sufyan was alarmed by this information. He at once proceeded to the place that was pointed out; when he came to the hill, he saw camel droppings. He was curious and started to pick at it. He found some date stones in it. "By God," he said, "This is the fodder of Yathrib." He immediately rushed back and directed his caravan away from the road and marched at full speed along the shore by the sea, leaving Badr on their left.

ATIKAH BINT ABDUL MUTTALIB'S DREAM

Shortly before the arrival of Damdam, the Holy Prophet's (May God bless and cherish him) Aunt Atikah bint Abdul Muttalib had a dream that terrified her and left her with a conviction of impending doom for Quraysh. She sent for her brother Hazrat Abbas and told him what she had seen; she said, "O my brother! I have seen such a dream that I fear some great disaster will befall your tribe." Hazrat Abbas noticed that she was nervous and turned pale while recounting her dream. He asked, "What did you see?" she answered, "I will not tell you until you promise me that you will not share it with anyone else. If people should hear it, they will ridicule us and speak of unpleasant things." She narrated, "I saw a man riding a camel, and he halted in the valley and shouted at the top of his voice, "listen O people, a devastating disaster shall lay you prostrate in these days." I saw a great crowd gathered around him. Then he entered the Mosque (Kaaba) with the people following him, and from out of their midst, his camel carried him up to the roof of the Kaaba, and again he shouted out the same warning. Then his camel took him to the top of Mount Abu Qubays, and there again, he cried out the same warning to people. Then he took a rock from the Mount Abu Qubays and hurled it down the slope, and as it reached the foot of the mount, it broke into many pieces, nor was there any house or any dwelling in the city but was smitten with a piece of it."

Hazrat Abbas told his sister's dream to Utbah's son Walid, who was his friend, and Walid told his father. Thereby, the news spread like wildfire through the entire city. The next day Abu Jahl exclaimed in the presence of Hazrat Abbas, with gleeful mocking, "O son of Abdul Muttalib, since when hath this prophetess been telling her prophecies amongst you? It is not enough for you that your men should play the prophet. And must your women do the same?"

Abu Jahl further continued, "There is Atikah, she says that some great evil will befall us in three days' time. If what she says does not come to pass, then we will pass judgement on your family as a family of liars among the Quraysh, and you will not be able to escape this shame as long as you live."

Atikah was very upset with her brother Hazrat Abbas for letting her secret out into the open. But Abu Jahl had his answer the next day, when the valley of Abu Qubays resounded with the powerful voice of Damdam. The people poured out of their homes and out of the Mosque to where Damdam was shouting in the valley. Abu Sufyan had paid him handsomely, and he played his role very well. He had turned around his saddle and was seated with his back to his camel's head. Moreover, blood was dripping from camel's nose and ears, "Men of Quraysh." He shouted, "The caravan, the camels, and your goods with Abu Sufyan! Muhammad and his fighters are upon them, rush to help."

The town of Makkah was instantly in an uproar. The news was like a spark that ignited the fire of war. This presented an excellent opportunity for the likes of Abu Jahl. The rich were providing the means to those who were not equipped to fight, telling everyone that they had to participate in the war. People like Suhayl ibn Amr, Zama ibn Aswad, Tuayma ibn Adiyy, and Hanzalah ibn Abu Sufyan, who were well versed in poetry, were inciting people, "Will you turn a blind eye to Muhammad and those inexperienced little children who have left you for him? Do you not see that the people of Yathrib are taking hold of this caravan and confiscating your goods? For those considering taking part in this war, we will give money to those who want money and power to those who want power."

Nawfal ibn Muawiya was also one of those visiting the rich of Quraysh, asking them to provide those who could not afford to fight with provisions. Abdullah ibn Abi Rabia responded promptly to his request, "Take these five hundred dinars and spend them as you see fit." Nawfal had already taken three hundred dinars from Huwaytib ibn Abduluzza. Thayma ibn Adiyy had given him twenty camels and had taken upon himself the expenses of the men who would fight on those camels. (Waqidi)

The Quraysh were deliberately forcing people who they thought were Muslims or those who had the potential to become Muslims to go to the battle. Hazrat Abbas, Hazrat Ali's brother Aqil, and Talib, and another nephew of the Holy Prophet (May God bless and cherish him), and Nawfal ibn Harith were among these people.

The Quraysh were certain that Abu Lahab was on their side. Without doubt, he was a staunch denier of the Holy Prophet's (May God bless and cherish him) message. But on this occasion, Abu Lahab said that he was not able to participate in war, however he said that if As ibn Hisham went to war in his place, he would cancel his entire debt of four thousand dirhams that Hisham owed him. As ibn Hisham accepted his offer. It is also said that he was afraid to join the battle because of Atikah bint Abdul Muttalib's dream. (Tabari, Tarikh; Waqidi, Maghazi)

On the other hand, people like Umayya ibn Khalaf, brothers Utbah and Shayba, Zama' ibn Azwad, Umayr ibn Wahab, and Hakim ibn Hizam who had expressed their fear over Atikah's dream came to the idol Hubal and drew arrows. The first arrow they drew pointed to 'no' while deciding whether they should join the war. But before long, Abu Jahl had heard of the matter and accused them of being cowards. This gave them no choice but to join.

Umayyah ibn Khalaf was an elderly man of excessive corpulence. He had even difficulty moving because of his weight. Therefore, he preferred to stay in Makkah rather than go to war. He was sitting near the Kaaba among the Quraysh when Uqba ibn Abi Muayt approached him with a censer of incense, which he placed before him, saying, "Scent thyself with that Abu Ali for you are now as good as a woman." "May God curse you," said Umayyah and got ready to set out with the others.

Two days had passed since the arrival of Damdam, who had brought the news of the caravan. An army of about a thousand men was quickly mustered, ready for

270

the battle. They were sure of their strength and were marching ceremoniously towards the battlefield. The Makkan forces were led by Abu Jahl, consisting of one hundred horses and seven hundred camels. For them, the trade caravan was of secondary importance, and instead they wanted to finish Islam and the Muslims once for all. They had arranged to feed the army among themselves. The day they left Makkah, Abu Jahl had slaughtered ten camels to feed the army. When they had reached Usfan, it was Umayyah ibn Khalaf's turn, and he had nine camels slaughtered. When they reached Kudayd, the famous poet Suhayl ibn Amr slaughtered ten camels. In the following days, ten camels were slaughtered by Utbah ibn Rabia and another ten by Munabbih and Nubayh from the sons of Hjjaj.

When the Makkan army reached the place called Juhfa, Juhaym ibn Salt turned to his friends and said, "Have any of you seen the horseman who rode beside me a minute ago?" No one had seen anything. They said, "You must have gone mad. The devil is playing with you." Juhaym had seen a vision, which he was unable to shake off. In his vision, a horseman from afar rode towards him and told him that many of the prominent people of the Quraysh, including two sons of Rabia, Utbah and Shaybah, Abdul Hakam ibn Hisham (Abu Jahl), Umayya ibn Khalaf and Abul-Bakhtari had been killed. He then cut the head of Juhaym's camel and sent it rolling toward the Makkan fighters, and the blood spurting from its neck stained all the tents that were there. When the fighters started to recount the dream among themselves, and finally it reached Abu Jahl, he said, "There you go, another prophet from among the sons of Muttalib."

In the meantime, Abu Sufyan had sent another messenger named Qays ibn Imru al-Qays, who caught up with the Makkan army in Juhfa and conveyed the following message,

"You set out thinking about your goods in the trade caravan and your men with them, now Allah has saved both your goods and your lives from harm, so then return." Conveying to them the message that the war was now unnecessary. People like Harith ibn Amr, Umayyah ibn Khalaf, Rabi's sons Utbah and Shaybah, Hakim ibn Hizam, Abul Bakhtari, Ali ibn Umayya, and As ibn Munabbih, who did not want to fight in the first place started their preparation to return.

Abu Jahl was calling this cowardice, and Uqba ibn Abi Muayt and Nadr ibn Harith were helping him to humiliate those who planned to return. They said,

"We swear we will not return until we have reached Badr! Then we will stay there for three days, slaughter camels, eat and drink, and will entertain ourselves with dancing women! Thus, the Arabs will know that we have gathered and have come all the way here, and then they will have nothing to say against us! Come, let us continue until Badr."

But not everyone was of the same opinion. Ahmad ibn Sharik called out to the sons of Zuhra, telling them that the caravan was now safe and that there was no need to fight, and thus they were returning. The sons of Zuhra were followed by the sons of Adiyy, and no one was left to continue to Badr from these two tribes. Abu Sufyan, who heard that Abu Jahl was leading the Quraysh into battle despite all efforts said, "Woe to my tribe! This is undoubtedly nothing but the selfish ambition of Amr ibn Hisham (Abu Jahl)."

The Holy Prophet (May God bless and cherish him), who had been fasting since the day they had set off, told his Companions who had not yet broken their fast, "I have broken my fast here, break your fast as well." Thus, from that day on, it was allowed not to fast in case of travel and war. When their party came to a place called Safra, the Holy Prophet (May God bless and cherish him) asked the name of the mountain that stood before them and the name of the tribe that lived there. He did not like the answer, and changed his route, keeping Safra on his left and marched towards the valley of Zafiran to the right.

When making strategic decisions, the Holy Prophet (May God bless and cherish him) always asked the opinion of his close Companions. His chief Companions Hazrat Abu Bakr and Hazrat Umar had given their advice. Miqdad ibn Amr then spoke, "O Messenger of Allah! Continue your quest as Allah has asked you; we will always be with you! I swear by Allah that we will not say as the children of Israel said to Prophet Moses, "Go forth then, you and your Lord, and fight both of you, we will be just here." (Quran 5:24). We won't say, "you and your Lord go and fight, but we will fight with you on your right and on your left, in front of you and behind you to death. We swear by He who has sent you with Truth, even if you should tell us to walk all the way to Bark al-Ghimad, we will come with you without any hesitation."

This honest and humbling statement made the Holy Prophet (May God bless and cherish him) very happy. His beautiful face lit up like a full moon. He prayed for them and then addressed the rest of his Companions. He also wanted to listen to the opinions of the Ansar. For when the Ansar had given their word of allegiance at Aqaba, they had meant providing the *Muhajirun* with security only within the bounds of Medina.

Now, the situation was beyond Medina, and a bloody conflict was soon going to happen. That is why the Holy Prophet (May God bless and cherish him) repeated his request,

"Tell me your views and advise me."

Sa'd ibn Muadh stood up, saying, "Let me speak on behalf of the Ansar, for it seems to me that your question is directed at us, O Messenger of Allah." "Yes," the Holy Prophet (May God bless and cherish him) replied. Then Sa'd started speaking,

"You look worried that Ansar will protect you only in their homeland, O Messenger of Allah! Verily, I now speak on behalf of them. I will tell you, go as far as you like, get in touch with anyone you see fit, and cut ties with those you want. Take as much from our possessions as you like, leave to us as much as you wish, and know that the amount you take from us will make us happier than the amount you leave us. We are always at your command, and we will always obey your orders. We will always be on your side. We have submitted to you in faith, bear witness that what you bring is Truth, and we have sworn allegiance to you. So, lead us wherever you will O Messenger of Allah. We will always be with you. We swear to Allah, who sent you with Truth, that should you ride your horse into the sea, we too will ride our horses there and plunge in after you. And rest assured that not even one of us will stay behind! If you should encounter the enemy tomorrow with us, none of us will turn back. You will see that Allah will enlighten your eyes and give you cause for joy through us, with the blessings of His Messenger. I believe that Allah the Exalted has given you a mission that you had not been expecting. Walk with us with the blessings of Allah. We will always be walking on your right and left, front and back, and will fight along with you to the death."

In the meantime, Angel Gabriel revealed the verses of glad tidings that Allah has promised one of the two groups—that is the trade caravan and the Makkan army —would fall (Al-Anfal 8:7-8). The Holy Prophet (May God bless and cherish him) turned towards his Companions and said, "Come walk with the blessings of Allah, for Allah the exalted promises one of the two groups to me. I swear I could almost see enemy topple and fall one by one." And therefore, with strong conviction and determination, they made their way towards Badr.

Badr was situated at the crossroad where Arabs would come together, trade, and organize fairs. In short, Badr was a place well-known to both Makkans and the people of Medina. The Holy Prophet (May God bless and cherish him) arrived with his

Companions at Badr on a Friday. They decided to stay there overnight, and hence, the battle would take place the next day. (Ibn Sa'd, Tabaqat; Ibn Abdulbarr, Istiab)

To get information about the position of the enemy, the Holy Prophet (May God bless and cherish him) sent Hazrat Ali, Zubayr ibn Awwam, Bashas ibn Amr and Sa'd ibn Abi Waqas to Badr for a scouting mission. They set off in the dead of night, and when they reached the wells of Badr, they came upon two men sent by the Quraysh, Aslam and Arid. They two had come to inspect the area and collect information. After a short battle, the Muslims overpowered them, took them captive, and brought them to the presence of the Holy Prophet (May God bless and cherish him). The Holy Prophet (May God bless and cherish him) was performing his prayers at that time. Without waiting until he had finished his prayer, they began to interrogate the two men, who said that they were the army's water carriers. But some of their inquisitors presumed that they were lying, for they hoped that it was Abu Sufyan who had sent them to get water for the caravan. They continued beating them until they said, "We are Abu Sufyan's men." And then they left them. The Holy Prophet made the concluding prostrations to his prayer, gave the greetings of peace, and said, "When they told the truth, you beat them, and when they lied, you let them be. They are indeed from the army of the Quraysh." Then the Holy Prophet (May God bless and cherish him) asked the prisoners, "Where is the Quraysh army?" "Behind that hill, you see," they replied. "And how many are they?" "Many." "What is their number?" "We don't know," they said. "How many camels do they slaughter in one day?" asked the Holy Prophet (May God bless and cherish him). "Sometimes nine, sometimes ten." Upon which the Holy Prophet (May God bless and cherish him) said, "They must be around nine hundred or one thousand men." (Ibn Sa'd, Tabaqat)

"And what leaders of the Quraysh are among them?" asked the Holy Prophet (May God bless and cherish him) again. They named fifteen leading men, and those included of Abu Shams, the brothers Utbah and Shaybah; of Nawfals, Harith and Tuaymah; of Abd ad-Dar, Nadr, who had pitted his tales of Persia against the Quran; of Asad, Hazrat Khadijah's half-brother Nawfal; of Makhzum, Abu Jahl; of Jumah, Umayyah; of Amir, and Suhayl. Hearing those names, the Holy Prophet said, "Verily, Makkah has offered before you today her most precious."

The two armies were very close, and now it was clear that Badr would be the place where they would battle. It was the seventeenth of Ramadan, on Friday evening, that the Holy Prophet (May God bless and cherish him) came to Badr with his Companions and gave orders to set up their camp. Hubab ibn Munzir approached him and asked, "O Messenger of Allah! Is your choice of place due to a divine command that we cannot change or is it a personal choice you made after assessing the entire battlefield." "It is a choice made as a result of considering all the conditions on the ground," replied the Holy Prophet (May God bless and cherish him) Hubab hesitantly and gently said, "O Messenger of Allah! Where we are now is not a favorable place to fight; it would be better if you commanded us so that we may go closer towards that well down there. I know this place and the wells thoroughly. Down there is a well I know of with replenishing and sweet water. We can make a reservoir there, collect more water, fulfill our needs, and close off the other wells."

Hubab's suggestion was strategically accurate. At the same time, Angel Gabriel descended and brought the good news that Hubab's suggestion was correct. The Holy Prophet (May God bless and cherish him) the said, "What Hubab points to is right." He made his way to the place that Hubab had suggested and set camp by the noted well.

Another advantage of this place was that the Muslim army was stationed facing the direction of Damascus and was not directly facing the sun, while the Quraysh army had taken up their position on the Yemen side, which this meant they had to fight facing the sun.

A command tent was set up for the Holy Prophet (May God bless and cherish him). The Messenger of Allah went to inspect the field and the well along with his Companions. He then called out the names of the leading men of the Quraysh and showed with his blessed hands one by one where they would fall and die. He then entered the command tent along with his close Companion, Hazrat Abu Bakr. Suddenly, the Holy Prophet (May God bless and cherish him) felt the presence of someone standing outside the tent. When he stepped outside, he saw that it was S'ad ibn Muadh. His face reflected anxiety, it was obvious he feared that polytheists might inflict some harm to the Holy Prophet (May God bless and cherish him). He was holding his sword in his hand, ready to protect the Messenger of Allah. The Holy Prophet (May God bless and cherish him) turned to him and said, "It seems to me, O Sa'd, that you fear the threat these people present." "By Allah, yes, O Messenger of Allah! This is the first battle we will engage in with the polytheists." The Holy Prophet (May God bless and cherish him) applauded Sa'd's loyalty. That night, he pleaded to his Lord, asking Him to grant victory to the handful of believers who only wanted to uphold the cause of Allah. While praying, he supplicated,

"O my Lord! Here are the Quraysh who have come with all their might and arrogance. They challenge Your authority and call Your Messenger a liar. O my Lord! I ask You to give me the victory You have promised against them! O my Lord! Early tomorrow morning, bury their arrogance in the dust."

Soon after, light sprinkles of rain started at Badr. The Holy Prophet (May God bless and cherish him) rejoiced it as a sign of favor from God. It was like an outpouring of mercy before the coming victory. It refreshed the men and laid the dust and made firm the soft sand of the valley of Yalyal where now they were marching. But it slowed the enemy who had yet to climb the slopes of Aqanqal, which lay over to the left of the Muslims.

That night, God sent a pleasant sleep (Sakinah) upon the believers, and they woke up fully refreshed. It was Friday, the seventeenth of Ramadan, in the year AH 2. As soon as it was dawn, the Quraysh marched forth and climbed the hill of Aqanqal. The sun was directly up when they reached the top. They made their camp at the foot of the slope. It appeared to them that the Muslims were fewer than they had anticipated. They sent out Umayr of Jumah on horseback to estimate their number and to see if they had any reinforcements in the rear. He reported that there was no sign of any further troops other than those who were now facing them on the other side of the valley. But he also warned them and said,

"O men of Quraysh! Do not think that any man of them will be slain but he shall first have slain a man of you; and if they slay of you a number that is equal to their numbers what, good will be left in life thereafter?" Umayr was also known as a diviner throughout Makkah, and this made his statement worrisome.

As soon as he spoke these words then Hakim of Asad, Hazrat Khadijah's nephew, seized this opportunity and went on foot through the camp until he came to one of Abdu Shams and said, "Father of Walid (Utbah), you are the leader of the Quraysh and the one they obey. Do you want to be remembered with praise amongst them until the end of the time?" "How shall that be?" said Utbah. "Lead the men back," said Hakim. "And take upon thyself thy slain confederate Amr." He meant that Utbah should eliminate one of the strong reasons for fighting and pay the blood money to the kinsmen of the man who had been killed at Nakhlah, for whose brother Amir had in fact come to take his revenge. Utbah agreed to do all that but urged him to go and speak to Abu Jahl, the man insisting on war. Meanwhile, he addressed the troops saying, "Men of Quraysh, you will gain nothing by fighting Muhammad and his Companions. If you lay them low, each man of you will forever look with loathing on the face of another who has slain his uncle or his cousin or someone yet nearer kinsman. Therefore, turn back and leave Muhammad to the rest of the Arabs. If they slay him, that is what you desire, and if not, he will find that you have shown restraint towards him."

Abu Jahl acted quickly and rebuked Utbah with cowardice, of being afraid of death for himself and for his son Abu Hudhayfah. Then he turned to Amir and urged him not to let slip his opportunity of revenge for his brother. Amir leapt to his feet and started ripping of his clothes and began to utter cries of lamentation at the top of his voice. This kindled the fire of war, and the Quraysh were filled with rage and violence. While the two parties were preparing for the battle, it provided a chance for Suhayl's son Abdullah to make his way silently across the uneven sands to the Muslim camp, where he went straight to the presence of the Holy Prophet (May God bless and cherish him) where joy was on both their faces.

That morning, the Holy Prophet (May God bless and cherish him) arranged his combatants in rows, ready for battle. He passed in front of each man to give them good heart and to straighten their ranks. He corrected the combatants that were standing a little to the front or back and made them stand in a straight line. He then saw someone standing half a body's width forward in one of the rows. He approached the Companion standing out of line, gave him a slight poke with his arrow in the belly and said, "Keep in line, O Sawad."

Sawad ibn Ghaziyya stepped back in line and then called out, "O Messenger of Allah! You have hurt me. God has sent thee with Truth and justice, so give me my requital." The Holy Prophet (May God bless and cherish him) turned toward Sawad and said, "Take it," laying his own belly bare and handing the arrow to Sawad. Everyone was watching Sawad closely, but what Sawad did next leave everyone stunned. He stooped forward and imprinted a kiss on the Holy Prophet's (May God bless and cherish him) belly and then wrapped his arms around him, hugging him tightly. "What made you do this?" asked the Holy Prophet (May God bless and cherish him). "O Messenger of Allah, we are now faced with the battle, and I desire that at my last moment with you – if so, it be – my skin should touch your skin, so I may go to divine presence with such a blessing." The Holy Prophet (May God bless and cherish him) prayed for him and blessed him.

Suddenly, a strong wind blew, and after a while it stopped. Before long, a second wind blew, and then a third, and then it ceased. With the first wind Archangel Gabriel, with the second wind Archangel Michael, and with the third wind Archangel Israfil had come with a thousand angels each. They were sent down to help the believers. Archangel Michael stood on the right side of the Holy Prophet (May God bless and cherish him) with a thousand angels, while Archangel Israfil stood on the left side of the Holy Prophet (May God bless and cherish him) with a thousand angels too. The angels were wearing green, yellow, and red turbans on their heads with one end hanging down to their waist. Their horses had a woolen mark on their foreheads. (Salihi, Subulu l-Huda war-Rashad)

The Holy Prophet (May God bless and cherish him) gave a big white banner to Musab ibn Umayr to represent the Emigrants *(Muhajirun)*. Besides these, two more banners were given, one to Hubab ibn Munzir who carried the standard of Khazraj, and Sa'd ibn Muadh, who carried the standard of Aws.

The Quraysh had started their advance across the undulating dunes. The Makkan army appeared much smaller than it was. The Holy Prophet (May God bless and cherish him) then returned to the command tent with Hazrat Abu Bakr and prayed for the help that God had promised him. A slight slumber came upon him, and when he woke up, he said, "Be of good cheer Abu Bakr, the help of God has come. Here is Gabriel, and in his hand is the rein of a horse which he is leading, and he is armed for battle."

The Holy Prophet (May God bless and cherish him) had a few words of advice to give to his Companions before the battle started. He said, "I know that some people from the sons of Hisham and others have been forced to join this war, we do not need to harm them! Whoever of you come upon a man from the sons of Hisham, spare them." Of course, the Holy Prophet (May God bless and cherish him) was referring to his beloved uncle Hazrat Abbas ibn Abdul Muttalib, who had become a Muslim but was hiding it from the Quraysh just like Hazrat Abu Talib who believed in the oneness (unity) of Allah and had proclaimed his nephew a prophet of Allah like Prophet Moses in his poetry.

The Holy Prophet (May God bless and cherish him) had even freed Abu Rafi in return for the good news that he had brought – the news that Hazrat Abbas had become a Muslim along with his wife. (Ibn Sa'd, Tabaqat). Abu Rafi was a slave of Hazrat Abbas, who he had given to the Messenger of Allah as a present.

There were also others that the Holy Prophet (May God bless and cherish him) had told his Companions to spare when fighting. He said, "There are none among them except for Abul Bakhtari who has rights upon me. Whoever sees him should spare him. Do not touch him unless he attacks you first." Abul Bakhtari came to rescue the Holy Prophet (May God bless and cherish him), when after the incitement of Abu Jahl, some polytheists had thrown camel tripe on his blessed head. Abul Bakhtari was so enraged by Abu Jahl's behavior that he cracked open his head with a club. He also played a deciding role in ending the boycott that had lasted for three years. Therefore, the Holy Prophet (May God bless and cherish him) had not forgotten his acts of kindness towards him.

It was evident that the battle would start soon. The Quraysh were already near and now halted within easy reach of the water basin that the Muslims had made. It seemed obvious that their first move would be to take possession of it. Aswad ibn Asad from the polytheists came to the front and shouted, "I swear by Allah that I will either drink water from this basin of yours or destroy it." After saying this, he ran frantically towards the water. Hazrat Hamzah stepped forward to meet him and struck him with a blow that severed one of his legs below the knee. Even in that injured state he crawled towards the water reservoir to destroy it. So much so that the blood gushing from his leg stained the water, and with his other foot he destroyed part of the reservoir. With a second blow Hazrat Hamzah killed him.

While the two armies were facing each other at a very close distance, Utbah ibn Rabia stepped forward from the ranks of the enemy and gave the challenge for single combat. And for the further honor of the family, his brother Shaybah and his son Walid stepped forward on either side of him. When Abu Hudhayfa saw that his father Utbah had stepped forward and was shouting at the Holy Prophet (May God bless and cherish him), he himself wanted to come forward and fight his father, but the Holy Prophet (May God bless and cherish him) stopped him. Instead, the sons of Afra bint Ubayd from Ansar, Awf and Muadh and Abdullah ibn Rawaha stepped forward. The polytheists were shouting, "O Muhammad, put before us men from our tribe who would be equal to us."

Upon which the Holy Prophet (May God bless and cherish him) turned to his own family since it was above all for them to be the first combatants. Therefore, he said, "Arise O Quraysh," "Arise O Hamzah, arise O Ali." Ubaydah was the oldest and most experienced man in the army, a grandson of Abdul Muttalib, and he faced Utbah, while Hazrat Hamzah faced Shybah and Hazrat Ali faced Walid. Hazrat Ali came before Walid, and with two strikes, Hazrat Ali ended his life. Everyone on the Quraysh side were looking at each other in shock as Walid's lifeless body lay on the ground. This time, Utbah stepped forward, and Hazrat Hamzah stood against him. They drew their swords, and in no time, Utbah was on the ground. Now, it was Utbah's brother Shaybah's turn. He attacked with all his strength to avenge his brother. Ubaydah struck Shaybah to the ground but received from him a sweep of the sword that severed one of his legs. Hazrat Hamzah and Hazrat Ali turned their swords on Shybah, and Hazrat Hamzah gave him the death blow. Then, they carried their wounded cousin back to their camp. He had lost a lot of blood, and the marrow was oozing from the stump of his leg. He had only one thing on his mind, "Am I not a martyr, O Messenger of Allah?" he said as the Holy Prophet (May God bless and cherish him) approached him. "Indeed, you are," he answered. Ubaydah then said, "O Messenger of Allah! Had Abu Talib been living today, he would have seen me verify his prediction." With these words, Ubaydah was reminding the Holy Prophet (May God bless and cherish him) of the poem that Hazrat Abu Talib had recited in the days, implying that he, too, had fulfilled the task that had fallen upon him. (Hazrat Abu Talib had said the following in a poem.

"Today, you refute Muhammad, but I swear by the House of Allah that today we cannot say a word! The day will come when we fight with him with honor. We will not have him over to you until we have sacrificed our sons and our lives." (Ibn Hisham, Sira; Tabarani, Mujmu l-Kabir). The tense stillness between the two armies was broken by the sound of an arrow from the Quraysh, and a freed man of Hazrat Umar fell to the ground, fatally wounded. A second arrow pierced the throat of Haritha, a young man from Khazraj, while drinking water from the basin.

A full-scale war had now begun. The Quraysh were giving it their all to finish off the Muslims with one last push, while the believers were showing determination so that the oppression, they suffered for fifteen years might end, and to show the invincibility of faith, so that they might make the name of Allah the exalted reign on earth.

Just as the survivors of the war would recount later, the day had gone so fast that they had not been able to see who had struck whose head and which sword had cut whose arm. (Ibn Sa'd, Tabaqat)

The Holy Prophet (May God bless and cherish him) himself fought at the very forefront. Speaking of what he saw, Hazrat Ali would later say, "At one point when Badr became too fierce, we would seek refuge under the wings of the Messenger of Allah."

The Holy Prophet (May God bless and cherish him) exhorted his men, saying,

"Race with each other to win Paradise, which is as big as the earth and the heaven! I swear by He who holds my life in His hands, whoever falls here today fighting with patience and without the thought of returning home and with only the pleasure of Allah as his goal, Allah Almighty shall straightaway enter him into His Paradise."

At that time, Umayr ibn Numan had retired to one side to eat some dates to curb his hunger. When he heard the Holy Prophet (May God bless and cherish him), he asked, "Really, O Messenger of Allah, is it as big as the earth and the heaven?" to which the Holy Prophet (May God bless and cherish him) replied, "Yes." "You mean that what stands between me, and Paradise is only death?" he said. Then he looked at the dates in his hand and said, "You are keeping me away from embracing my Lord," and throwing the dates away, he brandished his sword and ran towards the enemy and was lost in the crowd. (Muslim, Sahih; Ahmad ibn Hanbal, Musnad; Bayhaqi, Sunan)

At one point, Hazrat Umar came close to the Holy Prophet (May God bless and cherish him) and heard him recite this verse,

"But let them know that the hosts will all be routed, and they will turn their backs and flee." (Al-Qamar 54:45). As he attacked the enemy with agility, Hazrat Umar was reassured when he heard the verse that the Quraysh were surely going to be defeated.

During the battle of Badr, the Holy Prophet took up a handful of pebbles and shouted at the Quraysh, "Defaced be those faces!" He hurled the pebbles at them, conscious that he was hurling disaster. At the same time, he encouraged his Companions to charge. The slogan of the battle the Holy Prophet had chosen was, "*Ya mansur amit*," (O thou God has made victorious, slay), and it resounded from every throat as the men surged forward.

Awf and Umayr were the first to meet the enemy, and both fought until they were martyred. Their deaths and those of Ubaydah and the two killed by arrows brought the number of martyrs up to five. Only nine of the faithful were to die that day.

A revelation that came immediately after the battle said,

"And you threw not (O Muhammad) when you threw, but it was God that threw." (Quran 8:17). Nor were the pebbles the only manifestation of divine help that flowed from the hand of the Holy Prophet (May God bless and cherish him) that day. At one point during the heat of the battle, a sword broke in the hands of a believer. He came to the Holy Prophet (May God bless and cherish him), and the Messenger of Allah gave him a wooden club saying, "Fight with this, Ukkashah." He took it and brandished it, and it became in his hand a long, strong and gleaming sword. He fought with it for the rest of Badr and in all the other battles, and it was named al-Awn (which means divine help).

ABUL BAKHTARI

During the battle, a Companion ran into Abul Bakhtari. The Holy Prophet (May God bless and cherish him) had instructed his Companions to spare his life unless he first attacked them. Mujazzar ibn Ziyad told Abul Bakhtari, "The Messenger of Allah has forbidden to kill you." On hearing this, Abul Bakhtari was relieved, but he was not alone in this war. His friend Juada ibn Mulayha had accompanied him, so, he said, "What about my friend?" Mujazzar answered, "There is no such order for your friend. It is only in your favor." Upon this, Abul Bakhtari said, "I will not leave my friend alone. Better I die with him! How can I let the women of Makkah say, 'he abandoned his friend in order to stay alive." Then he resumed his fight and swung his sword back and forth fiercely. At last, he was killed by a blow from Mujazzar. He was feeling guilty, and his head down in shame He came to the presence of the Holy Prophet (May God bless and cherish him) and informed him, "O Messenger of Allah, I swear by He who has sent you with Truth that I tried my best to take him captive and bring him to you, but he resisted and preferred to die fighting. That is why I had to kill him."

THE END OF ABU JAHL

Abdul Rahman ibn Awf was engaged in fighting in the front ranks when two youngsters, Muadh ibn Amr, and Muadh ibn Afra approached him. They were quite young but had barely escaped from being sent home by the Holy Prophet (May God bless and cherish him) when the believer's army had set off from Medina. At that moment, Abdul Rahman wished that more experienced men had come to his side. One of the youths asked him very politely, "Dear uncle, do you know Abu Jahl?" "Yes, I do." Answered Abdul Rahman ibn Awf, "And what business do you have with him, O sons of my brother?" "I heard him slander the Messenger of Allah. I swear by He who holds my life in His hands that if I see him, I will kill him." While Abu Jahl was fighting with unabated ferocity while murmuring poetry, Abdul Rahman said, "The man you seek about is right over there," pointing towards him. Both the youths quickly made their way to him. They attacked in unison on each side, and with the blows from their sword Abu Jahl was now lying on the ground and was fatally wounded. Ikrimah, the son of Abu Jahl, then struck Muadh and all but severed his arm at the shoulder. Muadh went on fighting with his good arm, while the other hung limply by its skin at his side. When it became too painful, he stooped and putting his foot on the dead hand jerked himself up, tore off the limb and continued fighting.

Most of the Quraysh escaped, but some fifty were mortally wounded or killed outright in the battle or even taken and cut down as they fled. About the same number were taken captives. The polytheists were in great numbers, and hence, the likelihood of their regrouping and returning to fight was still a possibility. The Holy Prophet (May God bless and cherish him) was persuaded to return to the shelter along with Hazrat Abu Bakr, while some of the Helpers kept watch. Sa'd ibn Muadh was standing guard while the warriors started bringing their captives. There was a strong expression of disapproval on his face, so the Holy Prophet (May God bless and cherish him) asked him, "O Sa'd, it seems what they are doing is worrying you." Sa'd strongly agreed and said, "This is the first defeat God has inflicted on the polytheists, and I would rather see their men slaughtered than left alive." Hazrat Umar was of the same opinion. But Hazrat Abu Bakr was in favor of letting the captives live, in the hope that one day they might become believers, and the Holy Prophet (May God bless and cherish him) held the same opinion. But later that day, when Hazrat Umar returned to the shelter, he found the Holy Prophet (May God bless and cherish him) and Hazrat Abu Bakr in tears on account of a revelation that had come,

"It is not for a prophet to hold captives until he hath made great a slaughter in the land. Ye would have for yourselves the gains of this world, and God would have you the hereafter and God is Mighty and Majestic and Wise." (Quran 8:67). But the revelation then made it clear that the decision to spare the captives was accepted by Allah.

The war had ended. The Companions were waiting for the order of the Holy Prophet (May God bless and cherish him) so that they could inspect the battlefield and see the dead and wounded. The Holy Prophet (May God bless and cherish him) specifically asked whether Abu Jahl was among the dead. Abdullah ibn Masud went out to the battlefield and started searching until he found the man who was one of the greatest enemies of Islam in the entire Makkah. Abu Jahl still had enough life left in him to recognize the enemy, who now stood over him. Abdullah had been the first Muslim to recite the Noble Quran aloud in front of the Kaaba and, Abu Jahl had struck him a severe blow and wounded him in the face, for he was a poor man, and his mother was a slave. Abdullah placed his foot on the neck of Abu Jahl, who said, "Thou has climbed high indeed, little shepherd." Then he asked, "Tell me, who has won the war?" "God and His Messenger have won," he answered. Then he cut off his head and took it to the camp and conveyed the news to the Messenger of Allah. The Holy Prophet (May God bless and cherish him) first said, "La Ilaha illallah," and then went down in prostration and performed two cycles of prayer and thanked Allah, who had made Islam and the Muslims victorious.

Jubayr, the son of Mutim ibn Adiyy, was taken captive and brought to the presence of the Holy Prophet (May God bless and cherish him), where he asked for forgiveness. Mutim ibn Adiyy, who had offered the Messenger of Allah protection on his journey back from Taif, had also sided with the believers and was instrumental in ending the boycott. The Holy Prophet (May God bless and cherish him) remembered his kindness and said,

"Had Mutim ibn Adiyy been living today, and if he had asked me about these captives, I would have set them free just for his sake."

During the entire battle, Hazrat Ali would, from time to time, check upon the Holy Prophet (May God bless and cherish him) to make sure that he was safe. He always found him in prostration and performing prayer. Hazrat Ali would dive again into the midst of the polytheists and start fighting. Although his mind was continuous with the Holy Prophet (May God bless and cherish him), he would come back and check on him. Eventually, when the battle ended, and Hazrat Ali was once again by the side of the Holy Prophet (May God bless and cherish him), he was still in prostration and calling out to Allah,

"O my Lord! The All-Living and Self-Subsisting." (*Ya Hayy Ya Qayum*). And he continued his supplication until every Quraysh fled Badr.

It is narrated by Jabir. "We were praying with the Holy Prophet (May God bless and cherish him) during the battle of Badr, and we realized that at one point he was smiling when he finished. We asked him, "O Messenger of Allah! We saw you smile during the prayer, why was that?" in response, he said to us, "Archangel Michael just passed by me. He had gone after an infidel and was returning with dust covering his clothes. He smiled at me, and I smiled back." (Abu Yala, Musnad; Haysami, Majma z-Zawaid)

THE ANGELS AT BADR

The battle of Badr was extraordinary in all respects. The Quraysh had left Makkah with such high hopes, and now they were fleeing, wounded, and defeated, having left almost all their leading men on the battlefield. In fact, Badr had been a battle that ended even before it started. It was as if men could not see who were coming at them and slaying them one by one.

When believers charged on that day, they did not charge alone. The Holy Prophet (May God bless and cherish him) knew, for he had been promised,

"I will help you with a thousand angels, following one another" (Quran 8:9). And the angels also had received a divine command,

"When thy Lord revealed unto the angels, "I am with you, so strengthen those who have believed. I will cast terror into the hearts of those who disbelieved, so strike (them) upon the necks and strike from them every fingertip." (Quran 8:12)

The presence of the angels was felt by all, as a strength by the faithful and as a terror by the infidels. Two men of a neighboring tribe had gone to the top of a hill to see the battle and to take part – so they hoped – in the looting after the battle. A cloud swept by them, a cloud filled with the neighing of stallions, and one of the men dropped instantly dead. "His heart burst with fright," said the one who lived to tell it. One of the believers was pursuing a man of the enemy, and suddenly, the man's head flew from his body before he could reach him, struck by an unseen hand.

Suhayl ibn Amr, one of the polytheists who had been taken as a prisoner in Badr on his return to Makkah after he was ransomed, narrated, "During the Battle of Badr, I saw such stallions between the earth and the heavens with horsemen dressed in white riding them that it seemed to me that they were either taking everyone captives or were killing them."

Saib ibn Abi Hubaysh, who had been taken captive that day, swore that it was no mortal being who had taken him captive. When he was asked who then had captured him, he answered, "When the Quraysh started to lose, I was in shock. Then suddenly, a tall man dressed in white, and a turban wrapped around his head riding a horse with white feet, whose forehead filled the sky, and the earth caught up with me and tied me up tightly with a rope. At that point Abdur Rahman ibn Awf came up to me, and seeing me in that state asked, "Who captured you?" No one answered. Then he took me to the presence of the Messenger of Allah. He asked me, "O ibn Hubaysh! Who took you captive?" "I do not know?" I answered. Upon that, he said, "It was one of the angels who took you captive."

Hazrat Abbas, the Holy Prophet's uncle, (May God bless and cherish him) was taken captive by a Companion who was of a slight build. Hazrat Abbas on the other hand, was a strong and a heavy-built man. The Holy Prophet (May God bless and cherish him) asked Abu l-Yasar, "O Abu l-Yasar, will you tell me how it is that you were able to take Abbas as captive?" he answered, "O Messenger of Allah! When taking him captive, a man I had not met before helped me." The Holy Prophet (May God bless and cherish him) said, "An angel has helped you."

That day when all had been said and done, Angel Gabriel came to the presence of The Holy Prophet (May God bless and cherish him) "O Muhammad, Allah the exalted sent me to you and told me to stand by your side until you are content with me. Are you content with me?" upon which the Holy Prophet (May God bless and cherish him) replied, "Yes, I am content," and then told him that he could leave Badr.

Abdul Rahman ibn Awf was carrying body armor, which he had taken as a bounty, and he passed by the corpulent Umayyah, who had lost his mount and was unable to escape. He was accompanied by his son Ali, holding on to his hand. Umayyah called out to his old friend, "Take me prisoner, for I am worth more than the body armor." Abdul Rahman agreed, and throwing away his possessions, he took him and his son each by hand. While he was leading them towards the camp, Bilal saw them and recognized his former master and torturer. "Umayyah," he shouted, "The head of disbelief! May I not live if he survives."

Abdul Rahman strongly protested that they were his prisoners. But still, Bilal repeated his cry, "May I not live if he survives." Bilal shouted with all his power of his voice, "O Helpers of God, the head of disbelief, Umayyah! May I not live if he survives."

Men came running from all sides and encircled the prisoners. Then a sword was drawn, and Ali ibn Umayyah was struck to the ground but not killed. Then men closed upon them and quickly made an end of them both.

THE MARTYRS

There were fourteen martyrs from the believer's side that day. Six of them were from *Muhajirun*, eight from Ansar, two from Aws, and six from Khazraj. Some reports say that the number of martyrs was eighteen (Tabarani, Majmu l-Kabir). Among the martyrs was the Holy Prophet's (May God bless and cherish him) cousin, who had lost his foot in the one-on-one combat. Ubaydah ibn Harith, Sa'd ibn Abi Waqas's younger brother Umayr ibn Abi Waqas, Akil ibn Abi Bukayr who had come to Badr with three of his brothers, Afra's sons Awf and Muadh, Umayr ibn Humam, Sa'd ibn Haysama, Dhushimalayn ibn Abdiamr, Mubashir ibn Abdul Munzir, Hazrat Umar's freed slave Mihja, Safwan ibn Bayda, Yazid ibn Harith, Rafi ibn Mualla, and Aris ibn Malik's cousin Harith ibn Suraqa. The Holy Prophet (May God bless and cherish him) did not return from Badr at once and decided to stay there for another three days. During that time, he performed burial rites and funeral prayers for his Companions who had come with him and who had been the first to become martyrs.

The polytheists, on the other hand, left seventy dead as they left and fled. Some of the Quraysh the Holy Prophet (May God bless and cherish him) had cursed in his supplication before the war were among the dead. Abu Jahl, Umayyah ibn Khalaf, Rabia's sons Utbah and Shaybah and Uqba ibn Muayt. They all were lying lifeless on the ground in the exact places where the Holy Prophet (May God bless and cherish him) had indicated before the battle had even begun.

The Holy Prophet (May God bless and cherish him) gave orders that the bodies of all the infidels slain in the battle should be thrown into a pit. He stopped by the lifeless bodies of the polytheist chiefs and addressed them,

"O son of such and such! O Abu Jahl ibn Hisham! O Utbah ibn Rabia, O Shaybah ibn Rabia! O Umayyah ibn Khalaf! Have you now seen what it means to disobey Allah and His Messenger? Have you seen that what your Lord promised you was the Truth? I have truly seen that what my Lord promised me was the Truth! No others have treated their prophets as badly as you! While people put faith in me, you refuted me! While they embraced me, you drove me out of my homeland! While others helped me, you declared war on me! And Allah punished you very badly indeed for all that you have done to me. Although I was sure of what I was saying, you accused me of lying, and you called me false, although I was loyal and true."

Hazrat Umar, who witnessed this address, said, "O Messenger of Allah! It has been three days since these people died. Why are you then speaking to their rotten lifeless bodies as if you expect a response?" The Holy Prophet (May God bless and cherish him) answered, "Do not think that you can hear what I am saying better than they do. For they can hear everything I am saying now but do not have the power to respond."

When the dead body of Utbah ibn Rabia was dragged towards the pit, the face of his son Abu Hudhayfa turned pale and was filled with sorrow. The Holy Prophet (May God bless and cherish him) felt for him and gave him a look of compassion. Abu Hudhayfa looked towards the Holy Prophet (May God bless and cherish him) and said, "O Messenger of Allah, it is not that I question thy command as to my father and the place where they have thrown him. But I used to know him as a man of wise counsel, forbearance, and virtue, and I had hoped that these qualities would lead him unto Islam. And when I saw what had befallen him, and when I remember what state of disbelief he died in after my hopes for him, it saddened me." Then the Holy Prophet (May God bless and cherish him) blessed Abu Hudhayfa and was very kind towards him.

Abu Jahl was undoubtedly the man who had pursued the Holy Prophet (May God bless and cherish him) relentlessly and who bore the greatest animosity towards him. When burying him, the Holy Prophet (May God bless and cherish him) said, "Had Abu Talib been living today, he would have witnessed how our swords came upon their heads." For Hazrat Abu Talib had recited a long poem during the Makkan years in anticipation of the future after Abu Jahl and his accomplices had attacked the Holy Prophet (May God bless and cherish him),

"The oppressors of today will see tomorrow what swords will fall upon their heads." (Hazrat Abu Talib)

Although the Muslim army was outnumbered by the polytheists, they had won a great victory by the grace of Allah. In this regard, a revelation descended from heaven,

"You (O believers) did not kill them (by yourselves in the battle), but Allah killed them, what you (O Messenger) threw (dust at them at the start of the battle), it was not you who threw, but Allah threw. (He did all this) so that he might put the believers to a test by a fair testing. Surely, Allah is All-Hearing, All-Knowing." (Al-Anfal 8:17)

THE NEWS OF VICTORY COMES TO MEDINA

The Holy Prophet (May God bless and cherish him) sent Zayd ibn Harith and Abdullah ibn Rawaha to Medina to inform them of the outcome of the war. The next day of the battle, they came to a place called Aqiq, and there they parted ways to reach Medina by different routes. Before long, the people of Medina heard Abdullah ibn Rawaha call out, "O Ansar! Good tiding to you! The Messenger of Allah is safe and sound, the Quraysh have been killed and taken captive. The two sons of Rabia and Hajjaj, Abu Jahl, Zama' ibn Aswad and Umayyah ibn Khalaf have been killed. Sufyan ibn Amr is among the prisoners."

Asim ibn Adiyy listened to Abdullah attentively and asked, "Is what you say true, O ibn Rawaha?" "Of course, it is true," Abdullah answered. "I swear it is true. Tomorrow, the Messenger of Allah will arrive here, with prisoners in fetters." There was an atmosphere of celebration among the followers of the Holy Prophet (May God bless and cherish him). Abdullah ibn Rawaha was going from door to door sharing this good news.

Zayd ibn Harith had entered Medina from a different neighborhood, riding the Holy Prophet's (May God bless and cherish him) camel Qaswa. He, too, was giving the good news of the victory in Badr, proclaiming, "Rabi's sons Utbah and Shaybah, Hajjaj's two sons, Abu Jahl, Abul Bakhtari, Zama ibn Aswad, and Umayyah ibn Khalaf have all been killed. Many of them have been taken prisoners, including Suhayl ibn Amr."

One of the hypocrites approached Abu Lubabah and said, "Your friends have been so torn apart after the war that they will not be able to collect themselves ever again after this day. Look, the chief Companions, and Muhammad has been killed. Here is his camel, we all recognize it. And this Zayd is in shock and does not know what he is talking about." Abu Lubabah looked at the man who was making these assumptions and said, "Soon, Allah the Almighty will prove that what you are saying is not true."

THE SPOILS OF WAR

The Holy Prophet (May God bless and cherish him) commanded Habbab ibn Arat to collect the spoils of Badr, consisting of one hundred and fifty camels and other goods, before leaving the battlefield. He himself rode the camel left by Abu Jahl to Medina. He would fight on this camel in his later battles, and finally, in Hudaybiya, this camel was slaughtered (Ahmad ibn Hanbal, Musnad; Ibn Sa'd, Tabaqat). He appointed the free slave Shukran to see the affairs of the prisoners of war as they were brought to Medina. Until then, there was no divine command concerning prisoners and the spoils of war. That is why the Holy Prophet (May God bless and cherish him) said, "Whoever you have killed among the polytheists, their valuables now belong to you, and whoever has taken a captive, he is that man's captive." But soon, there was discontent, for those who had stayed behind to guard the Holy Prophet (May God bless and cherish him) demanded a share of the booty, and those who had pursued the enemy and captured men and armor, and weapons were unwilling to give up what they had taken. But before the Holy Prophet (May God bless and cherish him) had time to restore harmony by ordering an equitable distribution of all that had been captured. God (Exalted is He) sent down immediately a revelation,

"They will question thee concerning the spoils of war," say, "The spoils are for God and the Messenger. (Quran 8:1). The Holy Prophet (May God bless and cherish him) therefore ordered that everything that had been taken including the captives should be brought together and no longer be considered as the private property of any individual. The command was at once obeyed without any question.

After all the work was done in Badr, the Holy Prophet (May God bless and cherish him) left for Medina with his army. Two of the most valuable captives, that is, those whose families could be relied upon to pay the full ransom of four thousand dirhams, were Nadr of Abd ad-Dar and Uqbah of Abdu Shams. At the same time, they were two of the worst enemies of Islam, and if they were allowed to return, they would immediately resume their evil activities. The Holy Prophet (May God bless and cherish him) was continually keeping an eye on them but there was no sign of any change of heart in either man. It became also clear to him that if it was not in accordance with the will of God that they should be left alive. At one of the stops, he gave order that Nadr should be put to death. It was Hazrat Ali who beheaded him. At a subsequent stop Uqbah suffered the same fate at the hands of a man of Aws.

The Holy Prophet (May God bless and cherish him) divided the remainder of the captives and the rest of the spoils between the Companions in so far as possible, an equal share to every man who had taken part in the expedition.

The most eminent among the prisoners was the chief of Amir Suhayl, cousin of Hazrat Sawdah and brother of her first husband. Others most closely related to the Holy Prophet (May God bless and cherish him) were his uncle Hazrat Abbas, his son-in-law, Hazrat Zaynab's husband Abu l-As, and his cousins, Aqil and Nawfal. The Holy Prophet (May God bless and cherish him) gave instructions that the captives should be well treated, though clearly, they had to be bound. But the thought of his uncle prevented the Holy Prophet from sleeping that night. Some of the Companions realized that and asked him the reason. He answered, "I could not sleep on account of Abbas." One of the Companions got up and went to Hazrat Abbas and untied him. A little while later, the Holy Prophet (May God bless and cherish him) asked, "Why I don't hear Abbas anymore?" The Companion who untied him, came forward and said, "O Messenger of Allah, I untied his fetters." The Holy Prophet (May God bless and cherish him) smiled. It was clear that he was very happy about what had been done. He then addressed the Companion who had untied Hazrat Abbas, "Go now and untie all the prisoners."

There were a few Companions who had not fought in Badr who were also entitled to getting some of the spoils. These were Abu Lubabah ibn Abdul Munzir, whom the Holy Prophet (May God bless and cherish him) appointed as caretaker of Medina in his absence, Talha ibn Ubaydullah, and Said ibn Zayd, whom he had sent on the road to Damascus to pursue Abu Sufyan's caravan. Hazrat Uthman, who could not come because his wife Hazrat Ruqayyah was seriously ill, and Asim ibn Adiyy, Harith ibn Hatib, Hawwar ibn Jubayr, and Harith ibn Simma, whom he had left as deputies in Quba. The Holy Prophet (May God bless and cherish him) also set aside a portion of the spoils for the relatives of those Companions who had been martyred in Badr.

FATE OF THE CAPTIVES

The Muslims were faced with the captives situation after Badr, and there were no divine commandment regarding them. That is why the Holy Prophet (May God bless and cherish him) gathered his Companions together and consulted them about what they should do with them. There are reports that at that time Angel Gabriel came and told the Holy Prophet (May God bless and cherish him) that he was free to do as he pleased with the prisoners. (Abdul Razaq, Musannaf; Nasiri, sunan l-Kubras; Ibn Sa'd, Tabaqat)

"What do you think about these prisoners?" the Holy Prophet (May God bless and cherish him) asked his Companions. He then said, "Even if they should be your brothers of yesterday, Allah the Almighty has made them look upon you and your opinion to determine their fate."

Hazrat Abu Bakr came forward, "O Messenger of Allah, even though Allah has helped you and made you victorious over them, they are still your relatives. Some of them are the sons of your uncles, some of them are members of your tribe, and some of them are your brothers! I think it would be better if you took ransom for them and set them free. Thus, with what we take from them, we will be more powerful than that of the deniers. And maybe in doing so, Allah the Exalted will soften their hearts towards you with this merciful gesture, and maybe one day they will come to you in submission."

After listening to Hazrat Abu Bakr, the Holy Prophet (May God bless and cherish him) turned towards Hazrat Umar and said, "And what do you make of it, O son of Khattab?" Hazrat Umar replied, "O Messenger of Allah, these are men who drove you out of your homeland, who declared you to be a liar, and who fought with the intention of killing you! I disagree with Abu Bakr; I think you should hand over so and so person to me so that I may finish him myself. Leave Aqil to Ali and to Hamzah, leave his brother. These are the leading men of the Quraysh. I do not like the idea of them being captives."

At that moment, Abdullah ibn Rawaha came forward and said, "O Messenger of Allah, as far as I am concerned, there are enough shrubs and firewood in this valley. I say let's burn this place while they are in it." Upon ibn Rawaha's suggestion, Hazrat Abbas said, "In doing so, you cut all ties of kinship."

After listening to the views of the Companions, the Holy Prophet (May God bless and cherish him) entered his home in Medina. The Companions waiting in the Mosque continued to discuss among themselves. Some of them shared the same view as Hazrat Abu Bakr, that they should take ransom and set the prisoners free, while others wanted to follow Hazrat Umar's idea.

After a while, the Holy Prophet (May God bless and cherish him) stepped out and said, "Verily, Allah has softened the hearts of some that they are softer than soft!

And he has hardened the hearts of some that they are harder than stone." And then he addressed Hazrat Abu Bakr,

"You, O Abu Bakr, are like Michael who descends with compassion and among prophets, like Ibrahim who says, "He who follows me is truly of me, while he who disobeys me, indeed you are All-Forgiving, All-Compassionate." (14:36). And Jesus who said, "If you punish them, they are your servants; and if you forgive them, you are the All-Glorious with irresistible might, the All-Wise" (Quran 5:118). After that the Holy Prophet (May God bless and cherish him) said to Hazrat Umar, "And you, O Umar! Among the angels, you are like Gabriel with fierceness, toughness, and the intention of punishing the enemies of Allah, and among the prophets, you are like Hazrat Noah (Nuh), who said, "My Lord! Do not leave on earth any from among the unbelievers dwelling therein." (Nuh 71:26). And Prophet Moses who said, "Our Lord! Destroy their riches, and press upon their hearts, for they do not believe until they see painful punishment." (Yunus 10:88)

The Holy Prophet addressed both Hazrat Abu Bakr and Hazrat Umar, "If you agree on a viewpoint, I will not oppose it." At the same time, Abdullah ibn Masud's voice was heard, "O Messenger of Allah, I would like you to forgive Suhayl ibn Bayda because I have heard him say beautiful things about Islam, he is about to become a Muslim." The Holy Prophet (May God bless and cherish him) agreed to set free the prisoners in return for a ransom. As for the exact price of the ransom, they agreed on four thousand uqiyyas (a measure of gold). Despite having the ransom price, the Companions were flexible, and the amount was decreased for those who could not arrange the full amount. And then there were poor captives who had no means to pay the ransom. It was decided that those who did not have the means to pay for their own ransom should teach ten young Muslims how to read and thereby gain their freedom. (Before Islam, the people of Makkah were more literate than the people of Medina. Ibn Sa'd Tabaqat; Bayhaqi, Sunan). Those who neither had the money nor knew how to read or write were set free upon the condition that they would not speak ill against Islam ever again and would not help those who opposed Islam. Amr ibn Abdullah, also known as Abu Izza, was one of those people. (Bukhari, Sahih; Ibn Hisham, Sira)

Each of the prisoners had been shared between a few of the Muslim fighters, and the group that owned Hazrat Abbas brought him to the presence of the Holy Prophet (May God bless and cherish him) and said, "O Messenger of Allah, allow us to forgo the ransom for our sister's son" 'By sister,' they meant the prisoner's grandmother, Salma. But the Holy Prophet (May God bless and cherish him) disagreed. Then he turned to Hazrat Abbas and said, "Ransom thyself Abbas and thy nephews, Aqil and Nawfal, and thine ally Utbah, for you are a rich man." Hazrat Abbas hesitantly said, "I was already a Muslim, but the people made me march out with them." The Holy Prophet (May God bless and cherish him) replied, "As to your Islam, God knows. If what you say is true, He will reward you. But obviously, you were against us, so pay the ransom." At this, Hazrat Abbas replied that he had no money, but the Holy Prophet (May God bless and cherish him) said, "Where then is the money you did leave with Umm Al-Fadl? You two were alone when you said to her, 'If I should be slain, so much is for Fadl, for Abdullah, for Qitham and for Ubaydullah." After hearing the truth, the faith truly entered the heart of Hazrat Abbas. "By Him who sent thee with the Truth, "he said, "None knew of this but she and I. Now, I know that you are the Messenger of God." (Tabari). And he agreed to ransom his two nephews and his confederate as well as himself.

The Holy Prophet's son-in-law, Abu l-As was one of the captives. His brother Amr came from Makkah with a sum of money sent by Hazrat Zaynab to ransom him, and with the money, she sent a necklace of onyx, which her mother Hazrat Khadijah (mother of the faithful) had given her on her wedding day. When the Holy Prophet (May God bless and cherish him) saw the necklace he turned pale, recognizing it at once as Hazrat Khadijah's. He was deeply moved and said to those who had a share in the prisoner, "If you should see fit to release her captive husband and return her the ransom, it is up to you to do so." They at once agreed and both the money and necklace were returned together with Abu l-As. It had been hoped that he would accept Islam while he was in Medina, but he did not, and when he left for Makkah, the Holy Prophet (May God bless and cherish him) told him that on his return, he should send Zaynab to Medina and this he promised to do. The revelation had made it clear that a Muslim woman could not be the wife of a pagan man.

As soon as Abu l-As reached Makkah, he informed Zaynab that he had promised the Holy Prophet (May God bless and cherish him) that he would send her to Medina. Both husband and wife agreed that their little daughter Umamah should go with her. Their son Ali had passed away in infancy. Hazrat Zaynab was pregnant as well and expecting her third child. When all the preparation for the journey had been completed, Abu l-As sent his brother Kinanah to escort her to Medina. All the plans were made in secret, but nonetheless, they set off in broad daylight, and the news spread fast. Some of the Quraysh followed them to bring Hazrat Zaynab back to the tribe to which she belonged by marriage. When they were close to them, a man called

Habbar galloped ahead and circled around them. He took out his spear and threatened Hazrat Zaynab. Kinanah dismounted, took his bow, knelt on the ground facing the intruders, and emptied his quiver in front of him. He shouted, "By God, if anyone comes forward, I will put an arrow into him." The men drew back as he readied to shoot. They consulted with others, and Abu Sufyan and one or two others dismounted and walked towards him. They asked him to unbend his bow and discuss the matter with them. Kinanah accepted the proposal, and Abu Sufyan said to him, "It was a mistake to bring the woman out openly in front of people when you know very well what has befallen the Quraysh and all that Muhammad had done to us. This will be considered a weakness on our part. In my life, it is not that we want to keep her from her father, nor would that serve us any purpose. Take her back to Makkah, and when the gossip has stopped about our meekness, then steal her out secretly to join her father in Medina. Kinanah agreed, and they returned to Makkah. Shortly afterwards, Hazrat Zaynab had a miscarriage, which was attributed to this incident. When she had recovered after a while, Kinanah took her out with Umamah under the cover of the night and escorted them as far as the valley of Yajaj, some eight miles from Makkah. There, Zayd was waiting for them as previously arranged, and he brought them safely to Medina.

Abdullah ibn Jabir was holding Walid, the youngest son of the now-dead Walid, the former chief of Makhzum. His two brothers, Khalid and Hisham, came to pay his ransom money. Abdullah would not agree to a lesser amount, and Khalid, the prisoner's half-brother, was unwilling to give so much. But the full brother Hisham reproached him by saying, "True, he is not your mother's son." Whereupon Khalid agreed. The Holy Prophet (May God bless and cherish him), on the other hand, was against the transaction and told Abdullah that he should ask them for nothing less than their father's famous arms and armor. Khalid once more refused, but Hisham made him accept the condition. When they had brought the armor to Medina, they left for Makkah. However, Walid, at one of the stops, managed to slip away from them and returned to Medina. He went straight to the Holy Prophet (May God bless and cherish him) and accepted Islam and pledged his allegiance to him. His brothers followed him to Medina, and then they came to know what had happened. Khalid was outraged and said, "Why did you not do this before the ransom and before our father's treasured legacy had left our hands? Why did you not become a Muslim then, if that was your intention, to begin with?" Walid answered that he was not the man to let the Quraysh say of him, "He did but followed Muhammad to escape from having to pay ransom." However, he went back to Makkah in the company of his brothers to get some of his possessions. He did not suspect that they would do anything against him. On arrival in Makkah, they imprisoned him with Ayyash and Salamah, the two Muslim half-brothers of Abu Jahl. They were tortured and ill-treated. The Holy Prophet (May God bless and cherish him) always used to pray for their escape.

Most of the captives were at least courteous towards the Holy Prophet (May God bless and cherish him), except Ubayy of Jumah, the brother of Umayyah and a close friend of Uqbah, who both had been killed during the battle. As he was leaving Medina with his ransomed son, he said, "O Muhammad, I have a horse named Awd that I feed every day on many measures of corn. I shall slay thee when I am riding him." "Nay," the Holy Prophet (May God bless and cherish him) answered, "It is I who shall slay thee if God wills." (Waqidi, Kitab Al-Maghazi)

In Makkah, Ubayy's two nephews, Safwan and Umayr, were discussing about the great loss caused to the Quraysh by the death of its finest leaders who had been buried in the pit at Badr. Safwan was the son of Umayyah and likely to become chief of Jumah now that his father was dead. His cousin Umayr was the man who had ridden around the Muslim forces at Badr and estimated its strength. "By God, there is no good in life now that they are gone," said Safwan. Umayr agreed because his son was one of the prisoners, and he was too heavily in debt to ransom his son and he was so upset that he was ready to sacrifice himself for the good of the Quraysh. "But for a debt I cannot pay," he said, "and a family I fear to leave destitute, I would ride out to Muhammad and kill him." "On me be thy debt," Safwan told him, "And thy family be as mine! I will care for them as long as they live." Umayr accepted his offer right away, and they swore to keep it a secret between the two of them until they achieved their objective. Umayr then sharpened his sword and smeared it with poison and set off for Yathrib pretending to ransom his son. When he reached Medina, the Holy Prophet (May God bless and cherish him) was sitting in the Mosque. Hazrat Umar was present at that time, and when he saw Umayr with his sword, he stopped him from entering the Mosque. The Holy Prophet (May God bless and cherish him) told him to keep a close eye on Umayr and be on guard. Umayr greeted them as per pagan custom. The Holy Prophet (May God bless and cherish him) said, "Allah has given us a better greeting than yours, O Umayr! It is peace, the greeting of the people of Paradise." Then the Holy Prophet (May God bless and cherish him) inquired why he had come. Umayr mentioned his captive son as a reason. "Why then you have come with a sword?" asked the Holy Prophet (May God bless and cherish him). "God damn swords! Have they done any good service?" said Umayr. "Tell me the truth," said the Holy Prophet (May

God bless and cherish him). "What is the purpose of your visit?" and when Umayr mentioned his son again, the Holy Prophet (May God bless and cherish him) repeated to him word for word the conversation he had with Safwan in Makkah. "So, Safwan took upon himself your debt and your family," the Holy Prophet (May God bless and cherish him) concluded. "That you should slay me, but God came between thee and that." Umayr was taken aback, "Who told you this," he said, "For by God there was no third man with him?" "Gabriel told me, "Said the Holy Prophet (May God bless and cherish him). "We called you liar," said Umayr, "When you brought us the tidings from heaven. But praise be to God who has guided me unto Islam. I testify that there is no god but God, and Muhammad is the Messenger of God." The Holy Prophet (May God bless and cherish him) turned to his Companions and said, "Instruct your brother in his religion, and recite unto him the Quran, and release for him his captive son." (Ibn Sa'd, Tabaqat). Umayr returned to Makkah and eagerly preached Islam and made many converts. After some time, he returned to Medina as an Emigrant.

AFTER BADR

The outcome of the Badr was a humiliating defeat for the polytheists and a manifest victory for the Muslims. The Quraysh forces fled in great disorder in the valleys and hillocks, heading for Makkah in panic and too ashamed to face their own people. The first person to bring the bad news was Haiysuman ibn Abdulla Al-Khuzza. At that time, the Makkans were gathered at Hijr, talking to each other. When they saw Haiysuman approach with his clothes in tatters, exhausted and looking terrified, they understood what had transpired. "What is it? What news have you brought?" they asked together. He did not know where to start. He ushered one word at a time, "Utbah ibn Rabia, Shaybah ibn Rabia, Abu l-Hakam ibn Hisham (Abu Jahl), Umayyah ibn Khalaf, Zama' ibn Aswad, and the two sons of Hajjaj, Nabih and Munnabah, and Abu Bakhtari ibn Hisham have been killed."

Safwan ibn Umayyah was present; he was outraged and cut him off in disbelief, "I swear this man is talking nonsense, he has no reason left in him! Ask him about me as well; let him tell you what has become of me." The men asked Haiysuman what had become of Safwan. He pointed towards him at the Hijr and said, "There he is sitting," and he continued, "But I swear his father and his brother have been killed." For a few moments, it seemed as if life had come to a standstill in Makkah and the city, and its people were stunned in shock.

Now, people encircled him to get the details of what exactly had happened in

Badr. The Quraysh army had left seventy of its combatants on the battlefield, along with a further seventy who had been captured. There were a considerable number of fighters that had been wounded.

At the same time, Abu Sufyan ibn Harith entered the Mosque, and when people saw him, they gathered around him to hear the news. Abu Lahab approached him and said, "Come here, my nephew! I swear by my life that you seem to bear news! What has become of our men? Come here and tell me." Abu Sufyan was distressed. He said the following, "When our forces met them, it was as if we willingly had stretched our necks before them, and they simply went about killing or capturing us as they wished! I do not blame any one of our men, for during the battle, we encountered men on horses that spanned the distance between the earth and the sky, all dressed in white. Such men who were impossible to confront or to catch up to."

Before Ibn Harith could finish his words, Abu Rafi could not contain his excitement and shouted out, "There is no doubt that they were angels of God." When Abu Lahab heard what he said, he slapped him across his face and started beating him violently. He threw Abu Rafi on the ground and continued assaulting him. Abu Rafi was a slender man who was seriously injured, lying almost lifeless on the ground.

Umm Fadl was standing thereby and watching the entire incident. She was enraged because Abu Rafi was Hazrat Abbas's slave. She took out one of the pegs of the tent and stood over Abu Lahab, "How can you beat a slave just because his master is not here?" She was very upset and brought down the wooden pole with all her might on the head of Abu Lahab. His head was split with blood spurting from it. He was stunned and did not know what had happened. His wound got infected, and within a week, his whole body was covered with pustules. He died from that wound, and his body was left for three days unburied. His sons, however, for fear of shameful rumors, dragged his body to a pit and covered him with stones and dust.

MAKKAH IN MOURNING

The entire Makkah was in a state of mourning; everyone had lost someone, and everyone was lamenting after their dead. From every family, someone had either been killed or taken captive by the Muslims. Things belonging to the people in Badr were left in the open, and women were gathering around those possessions and wailing for days. This process continued for a month. Finally, someone came forward and said, "Do not act like this! For the news of your condition will reach Muhammad and his friends, and this will make them happy." Though they did not like this suggestion at first, they later realized that the man was right, and so they stopped coming together to wail, rip their clothes and beat their faces.

The polytheists also decided not to act too hastily about the release of their captives. They presumed that by waiting longer before paying the ransom, they would be able to negotiate the amount.

The Badr was the first armed encounter between the Muslims and the polytheists. It was a decisive battle that gained the believers a historic victory acknowledged by all Arabs and dealt a heavy blow to the religious and economic structure of the Quraysh. There were also the Jews who used to regard each Islamic victory as a blow to their own entity. Both these parties were burning with rage and hatred since the Muslims had achieved that great victory.

Although victory had been won at Badr, it was obvious that matters were not fully settled, for as they fled the battlefield, the hatred of Quraysh was no less than when they had gone there in the first place. The impact of war had touched every household. Even those people who had gone to Badr reluctantly were now filled with hatred against Islam and Muslims, swearing that they would take revenge as soon as possible. People who had witnessed that day took oaths not to sleep in their beds, continuously wailed, and vowed never to touch anything new until revenge was taken.

There were those who were not pleased with the Muslim's victory in Medina. These were the polytheists who secretly wanted the Makkan army to win and the Jews who did not like to see another power arising. The Bedouin tribes scattered around Medina were also worried about this new situation. They feared that a strong state built in Medina would in the future threaten their existence.

AL-KUDR INVASION

The Holy Prophet (May God bless and cherish him) received information soon after Badr that the tribes of Banu Sulaym of Ghatafan were gathering forces to attack Medina. The Holy Prophet (May God bless and cherish him) took the initiative himself. He appointed Siba ibn Urfuta as a deputy of Medina. (Some have reported the deputy as Abdullah ibn Umm Makhtum. Ibn Sa'd, Tabaqat; Tabari, Tarikh; Suhayli, Raw du l-unf). He mounted a surprise attack on them in their own homeland at a watering place called Al-Kudr. He rode with two hundred horsemen. Banu Sulaym, who had not yet been able to organize their men, started to flee and left five hundred camels behind. After taking one-fifth for himself, the remaining camels were distributed among the horsemen, two camels per head. This invasion took place in Shawwal in year 2 AH, seven days after the event of Badr. (Ibn Hisham)

AS SAWEEQ INVASION

Abu Sufyan, due to the shame and guilt he felt at the defeat of Badr, swore that he would not oil his hair, wash himself, or come near his wives until he took revenge on the Muslims. He gathered two hundred men and resorted to the hit-and-run strategy to inflict losses on the Muslims. Abu Sufyan came as close as one or two stations away from Medina. He secretly entered Medina in the darkness of night and knocked at the door of Huyayy ibn Akhtab, the chief of the Bani Nadir tribe. When he saw that Huyayy was afraid to let him in, he went to another leader of the tribe, Salam ibn Mishkam.

Salam entertained Abu Sufyan with great hospitality and gave him the information he needed. Abu Sufyan stayed there for a while and then left. When he returned to his men, they killed the Ansar they came across, and on their way, they cut and burned some date palm trees. As soon as the Holy Prophet (May God bless and cherish him) became aware of this incident he set off with a group of two hundred men, eighty of them mounted on horses, and followed in the pursuit of Abu Sufyan and his men. (Ibn Sa'd, Tabaqat)

When Abu Sufyan heard that the Muslim army was following them, he told his men to return to Makkah as quickly as possible. Fearing that the current pace of running away was not enough, he told them to drop everything they had on the camels to lighten their load. The Muslims brought back the provisions (Saweeq, a kind of barley porridge) that the polytheists had thrown to hasten their escape. Hence, this campaign was called as-Saweeq invasion. It took place in Dhu-Hajjah 2 AH, two months after Badr.

EXPEDITION OF DHI-AMR

In Muharram, 3 A H, the Holy Prophet (May God bless and cherish him) was informed that Banu Thalabah and Banu Muharib were preparing men to launch an attack on the outskirts of Medina. The Holy Prophet (May God bless and cherish him) organized a force of four hundred and fifty horsemen and foot fighters and set out to settle this affair. This was the biggest of the military campaigns before the battle of Uhud. He left Hazrat Uthman ibn Affan in charge of the affairs of the Muslims in Medina. On the way, they captured one person who embraced Islam and acted as a guide for the army. When the enemies received the news of their approach, they hurriedly dispersed into the mountains. The Muslim army encamped at a well named Dhi-Amr for the entire month of Safar, 3 A H. The Holy Prophet wanted to impress upon the surrounding Bedouins tribes that Muslims were a force to reckon with.

DEATH OF KA'B IBN AL-ASHRAF

Ka'b ibn Al-Ashraf belonged to the Tayy tribe. He was a wealthy man and famous for his good looks, and as a poet, he lived a luxurious life in his fort south of Medina, close to Banu Nadir's dwellings. He was a strong enemy of Islam and the Holy Prophet (May God bless and cherish him) among the Jews. He was intent on harming the Holy Prophet (May God bless and cherish him). When he heard that the Muslims were victorious in Badr, he was frustrated and swore that he would prefer to die if the news were true. When it was clear that the Muslims were victorious, he wrote poems satirizing the Holy Prophet (May God bless and cherish him), praising the Makkan polytheists, and encouraging them to unite against the Messenger of Allah. He went to Makkah and started his campaign against the Muslims, instigating the Quraysh against the Holy Prophet (May God bless and cherish him). When Abu Sufyan asked him to which religion, he was more inclined, the religion of Muhammad or the faith of Makkans, he said that the pagans were better guided. In this regard, Allah revealed the following verse,

"Have you not seen those who were given a portion of the Scripture? They believe in *Jibt* and *Taghut* (superstition and false objects of worship) and say to the disbelievers that they are better guided as regards the way than the believers." (Quran 4:51)

He returned to Medina and started slanderous propaganda in the form of obscene songs and vulgar poetry to defame the Muslim women. The Holy Prophet (May God bless and cherish him) was deeply concerned with this situation and called his Companions and said, "Who will take care of Ka'b ibn Ashraf? He has spoken evil about Allah and His Messenger." To comply with his command, Muhammad ibn Maslamah, Abbad ibn Bishr, Al-Harith ibn Aws, Abu Abs ibn Jabr, and Abu Nailah volunteered to do the task.

Muhammad ibn Maslamah came forward and said, "O Messenger of Allah, do you wish that I should kill him?" He said, "Yes." He said, "Allow me to talk to him in the way I deem fit." The Holy Prophet (May God bless and cherish him) consented.

Muhammad ibn Maslamah went to Ka'b and talked to him, "This man (the Holy Prophet) has made up his mind to collect charity from us, and this has put us in a great hardship." When Ka'b heard this, he said, "By God, you will be put to more trouble by him." Muhammad ibn Maslamah answered, "No doubt, now that we have become followers, we do not like to forsake him until we see what turn his affairs will take. I want you to give me some loan." He said, "What will you put as security?" Muhammad ibn Maslamah said, "What do you want?" The cunning Jew demanded women and children as articles of security against the debt. Ibn Maslamah said, "Should we pledge our women whereas you are the most handsome of the Arabs? The son of one of us may be abused by saying that he was pledged for two wasq (unit of weight) of dates. Instead, we can pledge you, our weapons. Ka'b agreed to his proposal. After that, Salkan ibn Salamah (Abu Nailah) went to see Ka'b for the same purpose, accompanied by a few Companions. In this way, both men with their weapons could see Ka'b together.

It was the fourteenth of Rabi-ul-Awwal, the 3 A H, and they left the presence of the Holy Prophet (May God bless and cherish him) at night. They went and called upon Ka'b at night. He came down, although his wife warned him not to meet them, alleging that, "I hear a voice which sounds like the voice of a murderer." He replied, "It is only Muhammad ibn Maslamah and my foster brother Abu Nailah. When a gentleman is called at night, even if he be pierced with a spear, he should respond to the call."

Abu Nailah said to his companions, "As he comes down, I shall extend my hand towards his head to smell, and when I hold him tight in my grip, you should do your job." So, when Ka'b came down, they talked for a while. Then, they invited him for a walk in the moonlight. On the way out, Abu Nailah said, "I smell the nicest perfume from you." Ka'b said, "Yes, I have a mistress who is the most scented of the women of Arabia." Abu Nailah said to him, "Allow me to smell your head." He said, "You may smell." So, he caught his head and smelled it. Then he said, "Allow me to do so one more time." He then held his head tight and told his companions to do their job. They attacked him and killed him at once. They returned after completing their mission. One of them, Al-Harith ibn Aws, was wounded by mistake by the sword of his men. He was bleeding severely. When they reached Baqi Al-Gharad, they shouted, 'Allah o Akbar.' The Holy Prophet (May God bless and cherish him) heard their *Takbir* and realized that they had completed their mission. As they saw him, he said, "Cheerful and bright are your faces." In response, they said, "And you are O Messenger of Allah." The Holy Prophet (May God bless and cherish him) then applied his saliva to Al-Harith's wound, and it healed on the spot. (Ibn Hisham, Sira; Bukhari, Sahih; Zadul Maa'd and Sunan Dawood). This incident instilled fear in the hearts of Jews, and they remained committed to their pact with Muslims.

BANI QAYNUQA

There was a treaty between the Jews and the Muslims, and the Muslims abided by their commitment and did not violate any of its obligation. However, it was clear that the Jews did not consider the Holy Prophet's (May God bless and cherish him) covenant as binding upon them, and they preferred the Makkan idolators over them. The Jews resorted to treachery, betrayal, and covenant breaking. The Messenger of Allah's movements were regularly reported to Makkah, and if the Quraysh marched out against the Holy Prophet (May God bless and cherish him) they were ready to reinforce them with powerful Jewish contingents.

The revelations were now full of warnings against the Jews. The Holy Prophet (May God bless and cherish him) and his Companions were advised to beware of them,

"They will do all they can to ruin you, and they love to cause you trouble. Their hatred is clear from what their mouths utter, and what their breasts conceal is greater." (Quran 3:118)

The Messenger of Allah also had received a command, "If thou fear treachery from a folk, then throw back upon them their covenant. Verily God loveth not the treacherous." (8:58)

On his return from Badr, the Holy Prophet (May God bless and cherish him) went to meet the Bani Qaynuqa in their marketplace in the south of Medina. Reflecting on the miracle of Badr, he wanted them not to call down upon themselves the anger of God, which had just now fallen upon the Quraysh. They answered, "O Muhammad, do not deceive yourself by that encounter, for it was against men who had no knowledge of war, but if you want to fight us then know that we are a force to be feared and indeed you have not met up with anyone like us before."

In this regard, a revelation came to the Holy Prophet (May God bless and cherish him).

"Say (O Muhammad) to those who disbelieve, you will be defeated and gathered to Hell, and worst indeed is that place to rest. There has already been a sign for you in the two armies that met (in Badr). One was fighting for the cause of Allah, and as for the other (they) were disbelievers. They (the believers) saw them with their own eyes twice their number. And Allah supports with His victory whom He pleases. Verily, in this is a lesson for those who understand." (Quran 3:12-13)

This behavior of the Bani Qaynuqa was seen as a declaration of outright hostility. The Holy Prophet (May God bless and cherish him) turned back and advised his followers to be patient.

Ibn Hisham reported on the authority of Abu Aun that an Arab woman came to the same marketplace to sell or exchange some goods and was grossly insulted by one of the Jewish goldsmiths. While she was sitting at the goldsmith's place, he fastened the corner of her garment to the back of it without her knowledge. So, when she stood up to leave, it uncovered her body, and her private area was exposed. The Jews laughed at her. She fixed her clothes. A Muslim man came and killed the Jewish goldsmith. The other Jews attacked the Muslim man, killing him in the market. His family demanded vengeance and proceeded to rouse up the Helpers against Bani Qaynuqa.

Blood had been shed on both sides and a conflict had started. The Jews withdrew into their powerfully fortified and well-provisioned strongholds. They had an army of seven hundred men, which was more than double the Muslim army at Badr, and they relied on at least as many men from Ibn Ubayy and Ubadah ibn Samit.

On Saturday, the fifteenth of Shawwal, the Holy Prophet (May God bless and cherish him) marched out with his army. Hazrat Hamzah ibn Abdul Muttalib was carrying the standard of the Muslims and laid siege to the Jews that lasted for fifteen days. During this mission, the Holy Prophet (May God bless and cherish him) appointed Abu Lubabah ibn Abdul Mundhir in charge of Medina. At this point, Ibn Ubayy came to the Holy Prophet (May God bless and cherish him) and said, "O Muhammad treat my confederates well." The Holy Prophet (May God bless and cherish him) put him off, and he then repeated his request. Suddenly Ibn Ubayy clutched the Holy Prophet (May God bless and cherish him) by his coat of mail, thrusting his hand into the neck of it. The Holy Prophet's (May God bless and cherish him) face turned red with anger, "Let go thy hold," he said. "By God, I will not until you promise to treat them well," replied Ibn Ubayy. The Holy Prophet (May God bless and cherish him) said, "I grant thee their lives." Having decided that the Bani Qaynuqa should forfeit all their possessions and be exiled, the Holy Prophet then ordered Ubadah to escort them out of the oasis. They took refuge with a kindred Jewish settlement to the northwest of Wadi-l-Qura and eventually settled in Syria. The Muslims were greatly enriched by the armor and weapons that were divided amongst them after the Holy Prophet (May God bless and cherish him) had taken one-fifth for himself.

DEATHS AND MARRIAGES

On his return from Badr, the Holy Prophet (May God bless and cherish him) visited the grave of his daughter Hazrat Ruqayyah, and his youngest daughter Hazrat Fatima accompanied him. After the death of Hazrat Khadijah (mother of the faithful), this was the first bereavement they had suffered. Hazrat Fatima was heartbroken and extremely sad by the loss of her sister. Tears were pouring out from her eyes as she was sitting beside her father at the edge of the grave. The Holy Prophet (May God bless and cherish him) comforted her and wiped her tears with the corner of his cloak. On their return from the cemetery, the Holy Prophet (May God bless and cherish him) heard the voice of Hazrat Umar, who was forbidding women who were weeping for the martyrs of Badr and Hazrat Ruqayyah. The Holy Prophet addressed, "What cometh from the heart and from the eye that is from God and His mercy, but what cometh from the hand and from the tongue that is from Satan." By hand he meant the beating of the breast and scratching of the cheeks, and by the tongue he meant the loud noises which was custom among Arab women.

Hazrat Fatima was his youngest and most beloved daughter, and she was at this point, about twenty years of age. She had close resemblance in manners, character, and kindness to her father and was graceful like her mother. Hazrat Abu Bakr and Hazrat Umar had both asked for her hand, but the Holy Prophet (May God bless and cherish him) had put, them off saying that he must wait for the time appointed by Heavens. The Holy Prophet always was in favor of Hazrat Ali as the most befitting husband for her. One day, Hazrat Ali was grazing camels in the oasis of Medina, when Hazrat Abu Bakr and Hazrat Umar approached him and asked him why he had not asked the Holy Prophet (May God bless and cherish him) about Hazrat Fatima's hand in marriage. Hazrat Ali was also encouraged by a family member to do so. Hazrat Ali was at first hesitant on account of his extreme poverty. But he had acquired a humble dwelling not far from the Mosque. Hazrat Ali went to the presence of the Holy Prophet (May God bless and cherish him) and sat in front of him. The Holy Prophet (May God bless and cherish him) asked, "Ali, why are you here? What do you want?" Hazrat Ali was very shy and hesitantly asked for the hand of Hazrat Fatima. The Holy Prophet (May God bless and cherish him) smiled and then continued," If I accept your proposal, can you tell me what you can offer my daughter as dowry?" Hazrat Ali replied, "Nothing is hidden from you. I do not have anything apart from a horse, armor, and a sword." The Holy Prophet told Hazrat Ali to wait while he went to seek Hazrat Fatima's approval.

Abdullah ibn Masud narrated that the Holy Prophet (May God bless and cherish him) said, "Allah the exalted has commanded me to marry Fatima to Ali." He also said, "O Ans! Do you know what message Gabriel has brought me from the Lord of the Throne?" He then said, "Allah has commanded me to arrange Fatima's marriage with Ali."

The Holy Prophet (May God bless and cherish him) went to Hazrat Fatima and said, "My love, Ali has proposed for your hand in marriage. Allah desires it, and His Messenger is also happy with this bond. Now, I need your approval so that I can give good news to Ali."

Hazrat Fatima was very shy, and with a bowed head, she remained silent. The Holy Prophet (May God bless and cherish him) presumed her silence as her approval as it is a custom among Arabs. So, he returned to Hazrat Ali and said, "Congratulations, your wish has been fulfilled." He then said, "Ali, it is important for you to have a horse, and the sword is an important item to have. So, keep both. But your armor is something you can do without it. I suggest you sell it and buy items for your marriage with it." Hazrat Ali sold his armor for four hundred and eighty dirhams and presented it to the Holy Prophet (May God bless and cherish him). The Holy Prophet (May God bless and cherish him) gave some money to Hazrat Bilal and asked him to buy perfume and dry dates for the wedding.

A ram was sacrificed, and some of the Helpers brought offerings of grain. Abu Salamah, cousin to both bridegroom and bride, was keen to help. The more so since he owed so much to Hazrat Ali's father Hazrat Abu Talib, who had given him protection against Abu Jahl and other hostile members of his clan. So, Umm Salamah went together with Hazrat Aisha to make ready the house for the bridal couple and to prepare the food. Sand was brought from outside and spread over the earthen floor of the house. The bridal bed was a sheep skin, and there was a faded coverlet of stripped cloth from Yemen. For a pillow they stuffed a leather cushion with palm fibers. They laid out the dates and figs for the guests to eat in addition to food. A skin was filled with water that they had perfumed. It was overall a blessed wedding in Islam.

The Holy Prophet (May God bless and cherish him) withdrew as a sign for the guests to leave the bridal couple alone, but he told Hazrat Ali to wait until he returned, which he did shortly after the last guest had departed. Umm Ayman was still there helping with the house. The Holy Prophet (May God bless and cherish him) asked permission to enter. He asked her to bring him some water, which she did. Having taken a mouthful and rinsed his mouth, he spit it back into the vessel. Then, when Hazrat Ali came, he made him sit in front of him, and taking some of the water in his hand, he sprinkled it over his shoulders and breast and arms. Then he called Hazrat Fatima to him. He did the same to her as to Hazrat Ali and invoked blessings upon them both and upon their offspring. (Ibn Sa'd)

Hazrat Ali narrated that the Holy Prophet (May God bless and cherish him) told him, "Angel Gabriel came to me and said, O Muhammad, Allah sends peace upon you and says, I have married your daughter to Ali ibn Abu Talib in the Heavens and now you also arrange the marriage ceremony of Fatima with Ali on earth."

Next year, after the event of Badr, the family of Hazrat Umar suffered two losses. The first of these was the death of his son-in-law Khunays, the husband of his daughter Hafsah. Khunays was one of the Emigrants to Abyssinia, and it was on his return that this marriage had taken place. Hafsah was still very young when she became a widow. She was both beautiful and intelligent, having learned, like her father, to read and write. Hazrat Umar, seeing that the death of Hazrat Ruqayyah had left Hazrat Uthman so disconsolate, offered him Hafsah in marriage. Hazrat Uthman said that he would think about it, but after some time, he excused himself by saying that he should not marry for the moment. Hazrat Umar was disappointed but determined to find a suitable husband for his daughter. So, he went to Hazrat Abu Bakr, whom he counted as his best friend, and proposed the match for him. Hazrat Abu Bakr already had a wife to whom he was deeply committed. Therefore, his reply was negative. The next time, when Hazrat Umar was in the presence of the Holy Prophet (May God bless and cherish him), he gave vent to his grievance. The Holy Prophet (May God bless and cherish him) told him, "I will show you a better son-in-law than Uthman, and I will show him a better father-in-law than you." "So be it," said Hazrat Umar with a smile. Hazrat Umar soon realized that the better person referred to in both cases was none other than the Holy Prophet (May God bless and cherish him), who would take Hafsah as wife, and who would become for the second time the father-in -law of Hazrat Uthman by giving him in marriage Hazrat Ruqayyah's sister Umm Kulthum. Later, Hazrat Abu Bakr explained the reason for his silence to Hazrat Umar, namely that the Holy Prophet (May God bless and cherish him) had confided to him, as a secret not yet to be divulged, his intention to ask for the hand of Hafsah.

The wedding of Umm Kulthum and Hazrat Uthman took place first and after the legally necessary four months had passed since the death of Khunays, and when a room was added to those of Hazrat Sawdah and Hazrat Aisha adjoining the Mosque, the Holy Prophet's (May God bless and cherish him) marriage was celebrated. The arrival of Hazrat Hafsah did not affect the harmony of the household. In fact, Hazrat Aisha was pleased to have a companion near to her age, and a lasting relationship was soon developed between them.

AFTERMATH OF BADR

In the aftermath of Badr, the neighboring Red Sea tribes were now firmly allied to Medina. In this way, they effectively blockaded the coastal road to Syria for the Makkan caravans. To further reduce the power of the Quraysh, all access to north was shut down, and a similar strategy was applied on the routes to the east and west. In this regard the Quraysh had already taken measures to strengthen their alliances with Sulaym and Ghatafan, through whose territory the caravan had to pass if they took the route to the head of the Persian Gulf and thence to Iraq. The Quraysh also urged those tribes to attack Medina whenever they found an opportunity to do so.

In the coming months, the Holy Prophet (May God bless and cherish him) received warning of three possible attacks, two by Sulaym and one by Ghatafan. However, the Holy Prophet (May God bless and cherish him) took the initiative by attacking them at once, but in each instance, they had the news of his coming, and therefore they vanished before he could reach them. One of these expeditions was remarkably successful. It was against the Ghatafan tribe of Thalabah and Muharib.

The Holy Prophet, along with his fighters, followed them deep into their hiding place in the mountains to the north of Najd. This was done with the help of a man of Thalabah who accepted Islam and offered his services as a guide. As the Muslim army was ascending the hilly area, it started raining, and the army was drenched as well as the Holy Prophet (May God bless and cherish him). The Holy Prophet (May God bless and cherish him) stayed back, removed his garments, and hung them on a tree to dry. He himself lay down on the ground to rest. He was soon overcome by sleep. When he woke up, he found a man standing over him with a drawn sword. It was the chief of Muharib tribe. He shouted, "O Muhammad, who will protect you from me this day?" The Holy Prophet (May God bless and cherish him) at once answered, "God." Instantly, Angel Gabriel clothed in white dress appeared between them and placing his hand on the man's chest, he pushed him backwards. The sword fell from the hand of Dathur and the Holy Prophet (May God bless and cherish him) seized it. Angel Gabriel vanished from Dathur's sight, but he realized that it was an angel. "Who will protect you from me?" said the Holy Prophet (May God bless and cherish him). The chief of Muharib said, "Nobody." And he proclaimed, "I testify that there is no god but God, and Muhammad is the Messenger of God." The Holy Prophet (May God bless and cherish him) handed him his sword, which touched him deeply. They went to camp together and Dathur was instructed in Islam. Later, he returned to his tribe and began calling people to Islam.

The Makkans effectively lost the Red Sea caravan route. The only alternative was to use the territory of Najd for trading. They decided to send a rich caravan to Iraq using this route. It consisted of mainly silver bars and vessels worth around a hundred thousand dirhams. Safwan was leading this caravan. The Jews of Media were aware of this secret information. By chance, one of the Helpers overheard their conversation regarding this matter.

The Holy Prophet appointed Zayd at the head of a hundred-horse force to intercept this caravan near Qaradah, which was one of the watering places along the route. Zayd, with his small, swift force, was able to ambush them by surprise. This unexpected onslaught put to flight Safwan and his men. Therefore, Zayd and his force returned to Medina with all the Makkan transport camels with their rich loads of silver and with a few captives. This incident intensified the preparation that had been in progress after the Battle of Badr for a revenge attack on Medina.

HAZRAT ABBAS'S LETTER

It was a Thursday in the month of Shawwal, 3 A H, that the Holy Prophet (May God bless and cherish him) received a letter that Hazrat Abbas had sent when he was in Quba. Due to its urgent nature, the horseman had ridden from Makkah to Medina in three days. (Waqidi, Maghazi). After listening to Ubayy ibn Ka'b read him the letter, the Holy Prophet (May God bless and cherish him) told Ubayy to keep the contents of the letter a secret and then went to see Sa'd ibn Rabi.

The Quraysh had already left Makkah to take revenge on the Muslims after getting help from the neighboring tribes. The Quraysh had given all the goods that were in the caravan of Abu Sufyan that he had led to Damascus to the newly formed army. They had contributed generously in other ways as well to make it a strong force against Muslims.

The Holy Prophet (May God bless and cherish him) dispatched his Companions to different places to gather information about the Makkan army. The Makkan forces consisted of three thousand men. Seven hundred of the men had full body armor, and there was a troop of two hundred horsemen. The number of the camels was as many as the men, not counting the transport camels and those that carried howdahs for the women. Abu Sufyan was the commander in chief of this army. He had with him his wife Hind and a second wife as well. Safwan likewise brought his wives and other chiefs the same. The leader of the cavalry was Khalid ibn Walid, and Abu Jahl's son Ikrima was his second in command. They had also taken their women with them so that they would encourage the men not to flee.

Jubayr ibn Mutim remained in Makkah but sent his Abyssinian slave named Wahshi, who was an expert at throwing spear with the army. Wahshi had never missed his mark, and Jubayr told him, "If you kill Hamzah, Muhammad's uncle, in revenge for mine, you will be a free man." Hind came to know about this, and during their halts, she would encourage and incite Wahshi to fulfill his mission and promised to reward him generously.

The Muslims had a week before the Makkan polytheists would reach Medina. During this time, they had to bring all those who lived in the outlying parts of the oasis along with their cattle and belongings inside Medina for safety. This was done well. Due to the urgency of the situation, Companions such as Sa'd ibn Muadh, Usayd ibn Khudayr, and Sa'd ibn Ubadah had donned their weapons and were keeping guard over the Holy Prophet (May God bless and cherish him), not leaving him alone for a single moment, even when they prayed.

When the Makkan army reached Abwah, Abu Sufyan's wife Hind bint Utbah, who had lost all her relatives, including her father at Badr, had wanted to open the grave of the Holy Prophet's (May God bless and cherish him) mother and tear apart her heart, but fearing that this might become a custom and similar treatment might be done to their graves the Quraysh did not allow her. All the way towards the battlefield, Hind was reciting poetry to encourage the soldiers and keep them motivated.

CONSULTATION WITH COMPANIONS

The Makkan army had come to the vicinity of Uhud, which meant they were at a striking distance from Medina. All the Companions were gathered, and the Holy Prophet (May God bless and cherish him) was busy in consultation with them. The current situation was totally different from the one in Badr. A strong army of three thousand men was ready to attack. The Holy Prophet (May God bless and cherish him) had a dream, and he shared it with his Companions. He said,

"I swear by Allah that I have seen such things which I hope will turn out to be good. I saw wearing impregnable armor (shield) and I put my hand in it. I noticed a dent in my sword, and I saw some animals being slaughtered." The Companions asked him the meaning of the dream. The Holy Prophet (May God bless and cherish him) said that the slaughtered animals signified that some Companions would become martyrs, the dent in the sword meant some trouble that would befall him and the death of someone very close to him. And the strong armor (shield) is Medina, and we shall seek refuge in it."

The Holy Prophet (May God bless and cherish him) was of the opinion not to go out from the city and that they should encamp themselves within the city walls. The enemies should be left in the open to exhaust themselves, but if they attacked Medina, Muslim fighters would be ready to fight them at the city entrances, whereas the Muslim women would help from the rooftops. The Holy Prophet (May God bless and cherish him) eagerly wanted to know the opinion of his Companions. Ibn Ubayy, the head of the hypocrites, was the first to speak, and he supported the idea to stay within the city. In fact, he did not want to fight in the first place.

When the Holy Prophet (May God bless and cherish him) had spoken, most of the younger Muslims were burning with eagerness to march out against the enemy. "O Messenger of Allah," said one of them, "Lead us forth against the enemy. Let them not think we fear them or that we are too weak for them." Most of the Companions were inclined toward this view.

Hazrat Hamzah, the Holy Prophet's (May God bless and cherish him) uncle, who was a celebrated hero of the battle of Badr, was at the forefront of those eager people who urged him to go out and meet the disbelievers. He addressed the Holy Prophet (May God bless and cherish him), "By God who has sent the Book down upon you, I will not taste food till I fight them with my sword outside Medina." (As-Seerah Al-Halabiyah)

An elderly man of Aws named Khaythamah rose to speak and expressed the same arguments. His son Sa'd was one of the martyrs at Badr, and he said, "Last night in my sleep, I saw my son. His face was blazing with light, and I noticed that he was very happy amid the gardens and rivers of Paradise. He said to me, 'Come unto us and be our companion in Paradise. All that my Lord promised me, here I found to be true.' And I am an old man, and I wish to meet my creator, so pray, O Messenger of Allah that He will grant me martyrdom and the company of Sa'd in heaven."

Then one of the Helpers by the name of Malik ibn Sinan of Khazraj rose to speak, "O Messenger of Allah," he said, "We have before us one of the two good options; either Allah will grant us victory over the enemy, and that is what we would have, or else Allah will grant us martyrdom. I do not care which it may be, for indeed, there is good in both."

It was clear from the words that were spoken that most of the believers were against staying behind the city walls, and therefore, the Holy Prophet (May God bless and cherish him) decided to confront the enemy face-to-face at Uhud outside Medina.

All day, starting from the moment when morning prayer was performed, the only subject discussed was how to face the Makkan army whose presence close to the city was felt. At the Friday prayer, the Holy Prophet (May God bless and cherish him) emphasized the importance of the holy war and all that it demands of effort and patience. He told his followers that victory would be theirs if they remained steadfast. Then, he issued orders for them to get ready for the battle. After the prayer, two of the Companions were waiting to speak to him. One was Hanzalah ibn Amir. It was his wedding day – a day that had been chosen some weeks ago. He was betrothed to his cousin Jamilah; the daughter of Ibn Ubayy, and he was inclined to delay his marriage and get ready for the battle. The Holy Prophet (May God bless and cherish him) advised him to celebrate his marriage and spend the night in Medina. The next day, he would have ample time to join the army and take part in the holy war.

The other person was Abdullah ibn Amr of Bani Sulaimah, who three years ago, went on pilgrimage and had entered Islam in the valley of Mina. He had pledged his allegiance to the Holy Prophet (May God bless and cherish him) at the second Aqabah. Three nights previously, he had a dream. A man had come to him, and he recognized him to be one of the Helpers named Mubashir, who said to him, "After a few days, you shall come unto us." "And where are you?" asked Abdullah. "In Paradise," replied Mubashir, "We do all that it pleases us to do." "Were you not martyred at Badr?" Abdullah inquired. "Yes indeed," said Mubashir, "But then was I brought to life." The Holy Prophet told him, "That is martyrdom." Abdullah knew this in his heart but wanted confirmation from the Messenger of Allah. Then he left to get ready for the battle and to say farewell to his children. His wife had passed away recently, leaving him with a son Jabir and seven daughters. His son was now in his adulthood. Jabir had already returned from the Mosque and was getting ready for the fight since he had missed the battle of Badr. His father said to him, "My son, it is not appropriate that we leave our women – he meant his daughters – without a man. They are young and helpless, and I fear for them. But I shall go out with the Messenger of Allah, and if Allah grants me martyrdom, I leave them under your care."

When the afternoon prayers were performed, all the men were assembled in the Mosque. The Holy Prophet (May God bless and cherish him) took Hazrat Abu Bakr and Hazrat Umar with him into his house to help him dress for battle. In the meantime, Sa'd ibn Muadh and Usayd ibn Khudayr told the other Companions, "Even though revelation comes to him from the heavens, you have pressured him to fight outside Medina. Let us go and leave the matter to him and do as he tell us."

While the Companions were waiting outside, the Holy Prophet (May God bless and cherish him) appeared. He had put on his armor, wrapped his turban, and was holding his shield in one hand and had his sword by his side. One of the Companions said apologetically, "O Messenger of Allah, we pressured you, it was not appropriate for us to have opposed your opinion. Do as you please, O messenger of Allah."

But the Holy Prophet (May God bless and cherish him) answered them by saying, "Once a messenger has put on his armor, it would not be appropriate for him to take it off until Allah has judged what will pass between him and his enemy! Now focus on what Allah has decided for you and follow His orders. Now, be ready in the name of Allah! The victory will be yours as long as you remain steadfast." (Bukhari, Sahih; Ahmad ibn Hanbal, Musnad; Hakim, Mustadrak)

YOUTH IN UHUD

The Holy Prophet (May God bless and cherish him), just like in the battle of Uhud, wanted to send youth who were too young back to Medina. Abdullah ibn Umar, Usama ibn Zayd, Usayd ibn Zubayr, Zayd ibn Thabit, Zayd ibn Arqam, Araba ibn Aws, Amr ibn Hazm, and Abu Said Al-Khudri were among those who had been turned away that day. These young men eagerly wanted to fight against the infidels and were deeply disappointed. They were not the only ones who were sent away, as the Messenger of Allah turned down the Jews and the polytheist Arabs who offered to fight alongside the Muslims. On their way to Uhud, the Muslim army saw a well-organized group approach towards them. The Holy Prophet (May God bless and cherish him) asked who they were. When he learned that it was a group that had not yet become Muslim but wanted to fight alongside Muslims. The Holy Prophet (May God bless and cherish him) said, "We cannot get help from the people of denial to fight the people of denial,"

Some of the young men were very insistent to go to war along with the Holy Prophet (May God bless and cherish him). When he allowed Rafi ibn Khadij, who was young but looked strong and older in appearance, to come with him to fight, another young man named Samurah ibn Jundub came forward and said to the Holy Prophet (May God bless and cherish him), "O Messenger of Allah, I am stronger than Rafi, I could defeat him if we were to wrestle."

The Holy Prophet (May God bless and cherish him) was impressed by his determination, and so he let the two young men wrestle in front of the Companions. The result was as Samurah had claimed. It may be that Rafi ibn Khadij lost on purpose so that his friend would be able to join him to fight. Seeing their passion, the Holy Prophet allowed both to come to war with him.

The Holy Prophet (May God bless and cherish him) divided his Companions into three groups. Hazrat Ali was holding the banner of the *Muhajirun*, Usayd ibn Khudayr was carrying the banner of Aws, and Hubab ibn Mundhir was holding the banner of Khazraj. He had left Abdullah ibn Makhtum as his deputy in Medina. There were about one thousand Muslim fighters in the army. Only one hundred of them wore armor. Zubayr ibn Awwam was leading the cavalry, and Hazrat Hamzah was the leader of the men who were marching towards Uhud with no armor. Just as in Badr, Muslims were one-third of the enemy by way of numbers. But they were not afraid of the enemy's power on death, for martyrdom in the way of Allah was their one goal to achieve.

MARCH TO UHUD

The Muslim army reached Shaykhayn in the evening, which is halfway between Medina and Uhud. Hazrat Bilal made the call to prayer, and the men prayed after the Holy Prophet (May God bless and cherish him). The Makkan army was hoping that the Muslims would come out to fight, and hence, their greater number would be to their advantage. The Messenger of Allah knew all the facts on the ground and was determined to compensate for the disparity of numbers by taking up a position that would give his army an upper hand. To do so, he needed a guide since they would have to pass through the territory of Bani Harith. Abu Haysamah offered his services to guide them. On their way, they had to pass through an orchard belonging to a blind man who was a hypocrite. He came to know that the Messenger of Allah and his Companions had entered his orchard. He behaved badly and said, "If you are the Messenger of Allah, I do not forgive the fact that you have entered my garden. Had it been not you but someone else, I would have beaten them up." While he was saying inappropriate words, he threw dust from his garden on the Holy Prophet (May God bless and cherish him). He was abusing the Messenger of Allah. One of the Companions hit him on the head. Before the situation escalated further, the Holy Prophet intervened and said, "Leave this man alone, he is not only blind in the eye, but also in the heart."

While in Medina, Hanzalah and Jamilah had consummated their marriage. Jamilah had a dream that night. She saw that Hanzalah was standing outside of heaven, and a door opened for him, and he entered through it, and then it closed. When she woke up, she interpreted it, "This is martyrdom." They performed their ablution and prayed the dawn prayer together. Hanzalah bade farewell to her, but she clung to him and would not let him go. And again, he lay with her. But he suddenly got up, put on his armor, seized his weapons, and left home.

It was Saturday, and Bilal's heart-rendering call for prayer was heard in the valley of Uhud. The entire Muslim army performed the morning prayer in ranks behind the Messenger of Allah. Soon, there was a commotion in the army. Ibn Ubayy ibn Salul had been in consultation with some of his close followers during the night, and when it was time to advance towards the enemy, he turned his back to Medina with three hundred of the hypocrites and doubters, to the great shame of his son Abdullah who remained with the army. Ibn Ubayy did not inform the Holy Prophet (May God bless and cherish him), and when questioned by some of the Helpers, he said, "He has disobeyed me but keeps counsel with mere young men of no judgement and decides to go to war. We do not know why we are sacrificing ourselves. We do not know what we are facing."

Abdullah ibn Haram (the father of Jabir) went after them and called out, "I adjure you by Allah not to desert your people and your prophet in the very presence of the enemy." At this they answered, "If we knew you would be fighting, we would not leave you. But we do not think there will be a battle." Abdullah retorted, "Enemies of God, God will protect His Prophet beyond any need of you."

The Muslim army was now reduced to seven hundred men only. They advanced under the cover of the darkness towards the enemy's position. They moved towards the right across a volcanic tract until they reached the southeastern bed of the valley. From here, they again moved northwest, up the hill. By now the day had broken, and they could see Makkan camps ahead of them a little below. They continued until they were directly between the enemy and Makkah. The Holy Prophet (May God bless and cherish him) stopped there and dismounted. Hazrat Bilal made the call for prayer, and they all prayed behind the Holy Prophet (May God bless and cherish him).

The Holy Prophet (May God bless and cherish him) turned to his Companions and delivered a sermon, advising them to keep to Allah's Book, to know what was permitted and what was not, and was emphasizing patience and certainty and earnestness and effort. The army had taken their position and were ready for the Holy Prophet's (May God bless and cherish him) command. The Messenger of Allah gave them one last warning, "No one of you should start fighting until I tell you to do so."

When the Holy Prophet (May God bless and cherish him) finished talking, Hanzalah went forward to greet him, for he had just arrived from Medina. Meanwhile, the Holy Prophet (May God bless and cherish him) chose fifty of his best archers and appointed Abdullah ibn Jubayr as their leader. He instructed them strictly, "Keep these horsemen away from us, do not let them come from behind to surround us. Even if we should come victorious, stay where you are! Let us not receive an attack from your direction. Even if you see that we have defeated the enemy and have entered their rank, do not move from your position. Even if you see that they come upon us and have torn our flesh, do not leave your position until you receive word from me. Even if you see that we have been killed, do not try to come, and save us. Instead, shoot your arrows at them because horses cannot advance when they have arrows thrown at them. And remember that we will win if you keep your position safe." (Waqidi, Maghazi; Said ibn Mansur, Sunan.)

When the Holy Prophet (May God bless and cherish him) learned about who was carrying the banner of the polytheist, he said, "We are far better than them in matters of loyalty," and then asked, "Where is Musa'b ibn Umayr?" "Here," Musa'b said and came to the front. The Holy Prophet (May God bless and cherish him) ordered him, "You take the banner," and gave it to him. The slogan of the believers that day was "Amit – Amit" meaning "Kill".

THE MAKKAN'S ARMY ATTACK

The Makkan army was arranged for the battle, and they had come to Uhud in great pomp and show. Khalid ibn Walid was keeping the right flank with two hundred horsemen. These were the horsemen that the Holy Prophet (May God bless and cherish him) had drawn to the attention of the archers to keep them in check. The left flank of the army was kept by Ikrima, the son of Abu Jahl. The foot soldiers were led by Safwan ibn Umayya, and the enemy's archers were led by Abdullah ibn Abi Rabia. (It has also been reported that the infantry was commanded by Amr ibn Al-As. In a strange twist of fate, the most important names of the day of Uhud would later become Muslims).

The banner of the polytheists was carried by Talha ibn Abi Talha. It was Hanzalah's father Abu Amir, who had gone to Makkah with fifty of his men to join the Quraysh who started the attack. He shouted, "O you tribe of Aws,". Those who saw him responded, "O you sinful man, may your eyes go blind." With this first spark, the full-fledged war broke out. One could clearly hear the voices of the Qurayshi women reciting poems and chanting songs, encouraging their fighters against Muslims. It was especially the wife of Abu Sufyan Hind who heartened the men with her words. Hind was promising impossible things to the soldiers should they win the battle, trying to turn them into ruthless killers. Under the leadership of Hind, the Qurayshi women were beating their timbrels and drums and singing.

On, ye sons of Abd ad-Dar,

Onwards, ye that guard the rear.

Smite, with every sharp sword smite.

When the Makkan soldiers were advancing, Hind started up an old song used in ancient wars.

Advance, and we embrace you,

And soft carpets spread.

But turn your backs, we leave you,

Leave you and not love you.

When the two opponent forces almost mingled, the Muslim archers shot a volley of arrows towards the cavalry, and the neighing horses almost drowned the women's voices and their drums. The Messenger of Allah who learned of this situation prayed to Almighty Allah, "Dear Lord, I fight only in your Name, I walk on towards the enemy only in your Name, the reason I am fighting the enemy is only for your sake! You are my sole support, and what a beautiful aid You are indeed."

HAZRAT ALI'S MODESTY

Talha ibn Abi Talha, the standard bearer of the polytheists, challenged the Muslims for a single combat and shouted, "Who will fight me." A moment of silence occurred in the battlefield, and Talha repeated his challenge a second time. He said, "O you, the Companions of Muhammad! You proclaim that your dead will go to Paradise, and our dead will rot in Hell. You lie! I swear by Lat that had you really believed that you would have put a man before me." At this Hazrat Ali leaped at once in front of him. They drew swords and a fierce battle started in front of the two armies. Before long Hazrat Ali pushed Talha to the ground, just as he was about to deliver him the final blow Hazrat Ali stepped back. This was very unusual; the fight should have ended with Talha's death. After the battle they asked Hazrat Ali why he had stepped back. He answered that just as he was about to strike him, Talha's private parts had been exposed, and hence he stepped back. (That day, Talha died in the battle).

Talha's brother now took the banner, and he was cut down by Hazrat Hamzah. Then Sa'd of Zuhrah put an arrow through the neck of Talha's second brother, and his four sons were killed one after the other by Hazrat Ali, Zubayr, and Asim ibn Thabit of Aws. Two of them were carried to their mother Salafah, who was in the rear, and when she was told who had dealt their mortal wounds, and she swore that one day she would drink wine out of Asim's skull.

A SWORD WELL-USED

As the battle raged, the Holy Prophet (May God bless and cherish him) took up a sword and brandished it, saying, "Who will take this sword and do justice to it?" Immediately, Hazrat Umar went to take it, but the Holy Prophet (May God bless and cherish him) turned away from him, saying again, "Who will take this sword and do it justice?" Zubayr said he would take it, but again the Holy Prophet (May God bless and cherish him) turned away, repeating his question a third time. "What is its right, O Messenger of Allah?" said Abu Dujanah, a man of Khazraj. "It's right," said the Holy Prophet (May God bless and cherish him), "is that you should strike the enemy with it until its blade be bent." "I will take it together with it's right," he said. And the Holy Prophet (May God bless and cherish him) gave it to him. He was a valiant man, who glorified the battle. His red turban was well known and among Khazraj, it was called the turban of death. He put on his red turban, winding it around his helmet. Ansar saw it and it meant that a great slaughter would be inflicted on the enemy. The sword in hand, he strutted up and down the enemy lines. When the Holy Prophet (May God bless and cherish him) saw him, he said, "That is the gait which Allah detest save at such time and place as this." (Ibn Ishaq)

Hind was a large woman of imposing appearance. She was still amid the Qurayshi fighters urging them to fight, and she narrowly escaped being cut down by Abu Dujanah, who thought she was a man. He raised his sword above her head when she shrieked, and realizing she was a woman, he turned against the men at her side.

On the Day of Uhud, the banner of polytheists kept falling; whosoever carried it was killed by Muslim fighters. The Makkan forces were demoralized when they saw their banner kept falling. Seeing that every man who picked it up was being slain, they no longer had the heart to pick it up. The banner was left to the women to carry. Amra bint Alqama, one of the women in the rear, turned to pick it up, but it was too late. The Makkans were faced with defeat. Their women were tearing their faces to stop their men from fleeing. The wife of Abu Sufyan, Hind, was railing at the men from fleeing and was physically putting herself in front of them to keep them from running.

MARTYRDOM OF HAZRAT HAMZAH

Hazrat Hamzah was unmistakable for his powerful stature and for his style of fighting. Allah the Mighty and Majestic had, through the sword of Hazrat Hamzah, killed thirty-one polytheists from the enemy. He had killed some of the men who had been carrying the banner of the enemy and thus had played an important role in the defeat that the polytheists suffered at the beginning. Wahshi saw him from a distance, and while keeping to the edge of the fray, he was able to reach a point of relative safety but close enough to strike. Hazrat Hamzah was now fighting face to face with the last of the standard bearer of Abd ad-Dar, and when he lifted his sword to strike, he momentarily laid open his armor. Wahshi was quick to see his chance and launched his spear with perfect aim. Hazrat Hamzah staggered a few steps forward. Having already killed his man, he fell to the ground. Wahshi waited till his body was lifeless and then went and drew up his spear and returned with all speed to the camp. The martyrdom of Hazrat Hamzah made no difference to the sense of defeat that was spreading through the Makkan army. Another Abyssinian slave of the family of the seven dead standard bearers, now took up the standard himself, but he, too, was soon killed.

Although Hazrat Hamzah's ostrich feather was no longer to be seen, Hazrat Ali, Zubayr, Abu Dujanah, and others of the Emigrants and Helpers fought like lions. It seemed like none could resist them. Hazrat Ali's white plume, Abu Dujanah's red turban, the bright yellow turban of Zubayr, and the green turban of Hubab were like flags of victory that gave strength to the Muslim fighters. Abu Sufyan narrowly escaped the sword of Hanzalah, who was fighting bravely in the center and was about to cut him down, when a man of Layth came from the side and thrust Hanzalah through with his spear, dropping him down to the ground where he killed him with a second thrust.

THE MESSENGER OF ALLAH'S COMMAND NEGLECTED

That day, the cavalry of the Makkan army had attacked three times in a row, and every time they attacked, they had been pushed back by the group of archers stationed on the hill. The horses could not advance with the arrows coming directly at them. The Holy Prophet (May God bless and cherish him) had insisted that they always keep their positions. But the moment the Makkan army was defeated and started running away, some of the archers were calling out, "O you people, come to the spoils! Allah had helped you defeat the enemy, but you stay there doing nothing. Look, yours have become victorious over the enemy; go after them and collect the spoils with your brothers."

The archers obviously had forgotten the orders given by the Holy Prophet (May God bless and cherish him). Their commander, Abdullah ibn Jubair, reminded them of the strict orders not to leave their posts on any account. They replied that the battle had ended, and the enemy had been routed, so there was no need to stay behind. Forty of the archers sped down the slope in the direction of the battlefield, leaving Abdullah with only ten archers behind. When Khalid ibn Walid saw this opportunity, he led his men at full gallop for the post where the archers were stationed. Abdullah and his men tried to stop them with their arrows, till the arrows were depleted. They fought with swords and spears. None of the ten faithful was left alive. Khalid attacked the rear of the Muslim's army, and Ikrima followed him. They both made much havoc in the ranks of believers.

Hazrat Ali and his Companions now turned to face the new onslaught. Meanwhile, some of the idolaters who had been put to flight rallied and came back to fight. The tide of the battle had suddenly changed, and the Makkans were shouting, "O Uzzah! O Hubbal!" Many of the Muslims in the rear who escaped being cut down now lost their heart and fled to the mountains. The Holy Prophet (May God bless and cherish him) called them to return, but their ears were deaf to his voice. Many Muslims, however, continued to fight, but the initial impetus was lost. The Muslim fighters were driven back step by step, and the entire battle moved towards Uhud in the direction of the Holy Prophet (May God bless and cherish him).

The battlefield looked like Doomsday, but the Holy Prophet had not moved from his place and had stood his ground against the enemy. He was close to the enemy position and was shooting arrows at them. There were few people left around him. In some reports, this number is fifteen, and in some, thirty. The disbelievers realized that the circle of Companions around the Holy Prophet had weakened and started shooting arrows at him.

Abu Talha was one of the best archers in the Muslim army, and that day, three bows broke in his hands. He was aiming and shooting arrows with one hand, and with the other, he was protecting the Holy Prophet (May God bless and cherish him). At one point, he saw the Holy Prophet (May God bless and cherish him) had gone into the open field and said to him,

"O Messenger of Allah, let my mother and father be sacrificed for you! Do not go so much in the open, for the enemy may recognize you and target you by shooting arrows. Let my life perish for you."

The Companions, including two women, were shooting volley after volley of arrows into the enemy as other men joined to protect the Holy Prophet (May God bless and cherish him). Among the first to join were two of Muzaynah, Wahb, and Harith, and a small body of enemy horses now approached from the left, "Who will fight them," said the Holy Prophet (May God bless and cherish him). "I will, O Messenger of Allah." Wahb instantly replied. He shot at them with such speed and accuracy that his arrows came upon them as if from a group of archers, and they withdrew. "Who will fight those horsemen," said the Holy Prophet (May God bless and cherish him) as another body of horsemen made for them. "I will, O Messenger of Allah," replied Wahb, and again he fought as if he were not one man but many, and again they retreated. Then, a third group emerged from the lines. "Who will stand up to these?" said the Holy Prophet (May God bless and cherish him). "I will," said Wahb. "Arise then," said the Holy Prophet (May God bless and cherish him), "And rejoice for Paradise is thine." Wahb rose joyfully as he drew his sword, "By God, I give no quarter, and I seek no quarter." Then he plunged into their midst and fought his way through them and out at the other side, while the Holy Prophet and his Companions were amazed at his valor. "O God, have mercy on him!" said the Holy Prophet (May God bless and cherish him). Wahb once again entered the thick of the battle until they encircled him on all sides and killed him. His body was found with twenty lance thrusts apart from what the swords had done to him. No one who saw him fighting ever forgot it. Hazrat Umar said after years," Of all deaths, the one I would remember for bravery is Wahb's death." Sa'd of Zuhra narrated ten years later that he still remembers the voice of the Holy Prophet (May God bless and cherish him) giving Wahb the glad tidings of Paradise.

The Companions were putting their bodies as shields around the Holy Prophet (May God bless and cherish him) so that no arrow would hit him. They had formed a human shield around his body. Talha ibn Ubaydullah reached for an arrow that was coming towards the Holy Prophet (May God bless and cherish him), and it severed two of his fingers. His two fingers were gone, but he deflected the arrow that was aimed at the Holy Prophet (May God bless and cherish him).

At one point, when the disbelievers came so close to the Holy Prophet (May God bless and cherish him), he said, "Who will stand against them." It was Talha's voice that rose first, "I will, O Messenger of Allah!" it was clear that where he stood had strategic importance, so the Holy Prophet May God bless and cherish him) said, "You stay where you are." And someone from the Helpers called out, "I, O Messenger of Allah." The Helper fought valiantly, but before long, he fell martyr.

Another group of disbelievers attacked right after the first one. The Holy Prophet's (May God bless and cherish him) voice echoed through the field of Uhud, "Who will stand against them." It was again Talha who said, "I, O Messenger of Allah." "You stay where you are," replied the Holy Prophet (May God bless and cherish him). Then another Companion from the Helpers said, "I, O messenger of Allah." He fought fiercely, and he, too, was martyred. This went on until four of the Helpers were martyred and one fatally wounded. But help was at hand to replace them. Hazrat Ali, Zubayr, Abu Dujanah, and others who had been at the forefront reached the side of the Holy Prophet (May God bless and cherish him).

It was not only Talha who made himself a human shield around the Holy Prophet (May God bless and cherish him), but some of the other Companions had also fallen martyrs that day, and there was practically no one who had not been injured. Abu Dujanah had made himself a shield to protect the Holy Prophet and had received numerous arrows. Abdul Rahman ibn Awf had received more than twenty sword blows that day, and he lived the rest of his life suffering from those wounds.

Sa'd ibn Abi Waqas had entered the enemy ranks with the intention of becoming a martyr. He saw someone from afar with a red face that the Makkans were attacking mercilessly. He asked Miqdad ibn Aswad who the red-faced man was. "O Sa'd, "said Miqdad. "That is the Messenger of Allah, and he is calling you by his side." He ran to the Holy Prophet (May God bless and cherish him). When he saw Sa'd coming, he made him sit by his side and told him to shoot arrows at the enemies. Sa'd got hold of his bow and started shooting arrows, all the while saying, "Dear Lord! These are your arrows, and You defeat the enemy with these." The Holy Prophet (May God bless and cherish him), who heard this, was giving Sa'd arrows to shoot and was praying for him, "Dear Lord! Accept Sa'd prayer! Dear Lord, let Sa'd arrows hit the target!" "Shoot, and let my mother and father be sacrificed for you, O Sa'd," said the Holy Prophet (May God bless and cherish him). (Hakim, Mustadrak; Ibn Athir, Usdul Ghaba)

In the meantime, a disbeliever named Utbah ibn Abi Waqas approached the Holy Prophet (May God bless and cherish him) and threw four stones at him one after the other, and one of them hit the Holy Prophet (May God bless and cherish him) in the face. The stone had broken a lower right tooth, and his blessed lip had burst open.

The Muslim fighters were in disarray, and taking advantage of this weakness, the disbelievers kept attacking. At one point, they heard Ibn Qamia's voice, "Here! Take that, I am Qamia, "and attacked the Holy Prophet (May God bless and cherish him). The Holy Prophet turned to Ibn Qamia and said, "I leave you to Allah."

The Holy Prophet (May God bless and cherish him) was faced with a looming danger, and he called out, "Who will drive these men?" A sharp but strong voice was heard, "I, O Messenger of Allah.' When the Companions turned to where the voice was coming from, they saw that a woman was running towards the Holy Prophet (May God bless and cherish him) with bandages in one hand and a water skin in her other hand. This was Nusaybah bint Ka'b, a woman of Khazraj, who felt that her place was nonetheless with the army. Her husband Ghaiyyah and two sons were there, but that was not the reason. Other women had husbands and sons in the army and were content to stay at home. But Nusaybah had been one of the two women who had gone out with seventy men of Medina to the second Aqabah, nor could she find it in her nature to stay behind on this occasion. So, she had risen early that morning and, having filled a skin with water, set off for the battlefield. She took with her a sword, a bow, and a quiver of arrows. She reached without difficulty, not long after the battle had begun, the place at the foot of the mountain where the Holy Prophet (May God bless and cherish him) had taken up his position.

Suddenly, Ibn Qamia, a man from one of the outskirts clans of the Quraysh, who had already made much slaughter among Muslims, urging his horse, brought down his sword in a blow that he was sure no helmet could resist. But Talha was standing next to the Holy Prophet (May God bless and cherish him), he threw himself in the direction of the sword and was somehow able to deflect the blow a little, at the expense of losing the use of his fingers of one of his hands for the rest of his life. The enemy's blade narrowly missed the crown of the Holy Prophet's (May God bless and cherish him) helmet and glanced off the side of it, grazing his temple, driving two of the helmet rings into his cheek and then his mailed shoulder. The Holy Prophet (May God bless and cherish him) momentarily fell to the ground. His assailant withdrew as quickly as he had come.

Nusaybah had started fighting, trying to protect the Holy Prophet. She was wielding her sword and shooting arrows. When she heard the voice of Ibn Qamia, who was shouting at the top of his lungs, she walked over to him along with Musa'b ibn Umayr and tried to finish him off with a few blows from her sword. But that day, Ibn Qamia had worn two shields on the top of him, and Nusaybah's sword would not cut through. Musa's ibn Umayr, who was carrying the banner of the Holy Prophet, was also fighting like a lion. Ibn Qamia had sworn to kill the Holy Prophet (May God bless and cherish him), and Musa'b in his armor looked very much like the Holy Prophet (May God bless and cherish him). That is why he had become the target of the enemy that day. Then suddenly, Ibn Qamia stood in front of Musa'b. They drew their swords and started to battle it out on one. This was a fierce battle, and, in the end, Musa'b fell martyr. Even though Musa'b fell, the banner of Islam would not lie there on the ground! Miraculously, an angel in the shape of Musa'b continued carrying the banner.

Ibn Qamia thought that he had killed the Holy Prophet (May God bless and cherish him). He turned to the Quraysh and started to shout with joy, "I have killed Muhammad!" his voice echoed everywhere in Uhud. In places where his voice was heard, there were those who dropped their swords and those who were wailing from grief. Hazrat Umar was in total shock as if struck by lightning when he heard Ibn Qamia's words, he said, "Let me hear not anyone say, "Muhammad has been killed", or else I will cut off their heads,' putting such an eventuality out of his mind. That day, Hazrat Umar calmed down only after he saw the Holy Prophet (May God bless and cherish him) sitting with his Companions. (Tabari, Al-Jamiu l-Bayan)

However, the shout of "Muhammad is slain" was taken up all over the field, mingled with the glorification of the idols "Uzza and Hubbal." Muslim fighters were overcome with self-reproach and grief, while many of them still fighting were discouraged. But there were some exceptions. Malik ibn Duhshum approached

Haritha ibn Zayd, explaining what he had heard and wanted to verify the news. Haritha responded to his question in the following way, "Even if the Messenger of Allah may have been killed, Allah is alive, and He never dies. The Messenger of Allah, for his part, performed the duty he received from his Lord to communicate His messages. So, then stand up and fight to the death for His religion."

It was the sister of Anas, the son of Nadr (After whom the Holy Prophet's ,may God bless and cherish him, servant was named), the daughter of Nadr, who had been told by the Holy Prophet (May God bless and cherish him) that her son was killed by an arrow at Badr and was in Paradise. Anas came upon two of his comrades for whom life seemed to have lost its meaning and told them, "Why sit here?" he exclaimed. "The Messenger of Allah has been slain," they said. "Then what will you do with life after him?" said Anas. "Rise and die, even as he died." (Waqidi). Anas then set off and plunged into the fray. There he found Sa'd ibn Muadh, who told the Holy Prophet (May God bless and cherish him) afterward what Anas had told him, "Paradise! I smell its fragrance blowing from the other side of Uhud." "O Messenger of God, I could not fight as he fought." Later, they found his body lying dead with more than eighty wounds. He was so disfigured as to be unrecognized by anyone, save his sister who knew him by his fingers. (Bukhari, Sahih)

The Muslim fighters sought refuge on the higher ground above the plain, and it was made easier by the fact that most of the enemy fighters felt that the battle was over, and they too slackened their effort. The dead had not yet been counted, but it was evident that they amply avenged those who had died at Badr.

In the chaos that ensued in Uhud, the first Companion to see that the Holy Prophet (May God bless and cherish him) was alive and let the other Companions know was Ka'b ibn Malik. Ka'b ibn Malik was ahead of others, and he was surprised to see a man whose stature and bearing were exactly like those of the Holy Prophet (May God bless and cherish him). Then, as he came close, he saw the incomparable and unmistakable brightness of the eyes, and he turned and shouted to those behind him, "O Muslims, be of good cheer! This is the Messenger of God." The Holy Prophet (May God bless and cherish him) motioned to him to be silent, but the news spread from mouth to mouth, and men came rushing to reassure themselves that it was true. So great was the rejoicing that it was as if the defeat had suddenly been changed into victory.

The helmet of the Holy Prophet (May God bless and cherish him) was shattered by the sword of Ibn Qamia, and two of its rings were stuck into his cheek. Moreover, he had fallen into one of the trap holes that Abu Amir had dug. After falling, the Holy Prophet (May God bless and cherish him) almost fainted. Hazrat Ali at once ran and held the Holy Prophet's (May God bless and cherish him) hand. At the same time, Talha ibn Ubaydullah descended into the hole, and using his spear as a support, he helped the Holy Prophet (May God bless and cherish him) get out, even with the weight of two armors upon him. He was overjoyed when he heard the Holy Prophet (May God bless and cherish him) saying, "Today, Talha has deserved everything." Talha was beaming with delight, and he felt a divine peace he had never felt in his entire life.

The Holy Prophet (May God bless and cherish him) was now in great pain. The metal rings were deeply embedded in his flesh, so they halted for a moment. Hazrat Abu Bakr came forward to help when he saw that blood was squirting from his blessed face. At the same time, Abu Ubaydah stepped forward and said, "By God, leave that job to me," and insisted upon it. He approached the Holy Prophet (May God bless and cherish him) with great care. He first tried to pull the rings with his fingers, but it was clear that it would hurt the Holy Prophet (May God bless and cherish him). So, he tried to pull the rings with his teeth, he first bit one of them and tugged on it with all his might. The ring had come out, but so had Abu Ubaydah's tooth. When Hazrat Abu Bak saw this, he came to help, but Abu Ubaydah did not allow him. The once again pulled the ring with his teeth and tugged on it so hard that another one of his teeth fell out as well. (Hazrat Abu Bakr later narrated that among the men who have lost their front teeth, the most adorable is Abu Ubaydah. (Tayalisi, Musnad; Ibn Kathir, Al-Bidaya wa'n Nihaya)

The wound of the Holy Prophet (May God bless and cherish him) began to bleed again, and Malik ibn Sinan of Khazraj put his mouth to it, sucked out the blood, and swallowed it. The Holy Prophet (May God bless and cherish him) asked Malik, "Are you drinking my blood?" "Yes, I am O Messenger of Allah, "said Malik. The Holy Prophet (May God bless and cherish him) then stated, "Whoso would look on a man whose blood is mingled with my blood, let him look on Malik, the son of Sinan." Abu Ubaydah was also included, for while removing the rings, he had pulled out two of his own teeth, and his mouth was bleeding. The Holy Prophet (May God bless and cherish him) told them,

"Whose blood has touched my blood; him the Fire cannot reach."

One of the Companions, Hatib ibn Balta'ab, who saw that the blessed face of the Messenger of Allah had been wounded and teeth broken, was enraged, and asked, "O Messenger of Allah, who did this to you." The Holy Prophet (May God bless and cherish him) told him the name of the person," Utbah ibn Abi Waqas." Hatib then asked in which direction he went. The Holy Prophet (May God bless and cherish him) pointed to the direction Utbah had gone. Hatib ibn Balta'ab drew his sword and went after the disbeliever. He finished him off and then came back to the presence of the Holy Prophet (May God bless and cherish him). He said to him twice to express his contentment, "May Allah be pleased with you, and then prayed for him.

One of the horsemen of Quraysh was by the name of Ubayy, the brother of Umayyah, who had sworn that he would kill the Messenger of Allah from the back of his horse 'Awd', which he was now riding. Having learned that the Holy Prophet (May God bless and cherish him) was alive, he came to look for the body to see if there was still life in it. When he heard the shout of Ka'b he rode up the glen and shouted, "O Muhammad, if you live, then I may not live!" Some of the Companions around the Holy Prophet (May God bless and cherish him) wanted to attack Ubayy, but the Holy Prophet (May God bless and cherish him) told them to hold off. Then he took a spear from Harith ibn as-Simmah and stepped in front. Ubayy approached with a drawn sword, but before he could strike a blow, the Holy Prophet (May God bless and cherish him) thrust him in the neck. He bellowed like a bull, then swayed, and almost fell from his horse. After recovering his balance, he galloped down the slope and did not stop until he reached the Makkan camp. There, his nephew, and other clan members were present, and he shouted, "Muhammad has slain me," in a voice he could not control. They looked at his wound and made light of it, but he was convinced that it was mortal. "He told me that he would kill me," he said, "And by God, if he had spit upon me, he would have killed me." He was dead soon after that.

When the Holy Prophet (May God bless and cherish him) and his party climbed to the top of the glen, Hazrat Ali went to fill his shield with water from a cavity in the rocks. He held it up to the Holy Prophet (May God bless and cherish him), but its pungent smell repelled him. He did not drink from it despite his thirst, though he used some of it to wash the blood from his face. Since they were still within the enemy's reach from the plain, the Holy Prophet gave orders to move onwards to the higher ground, and he tried to raise himself onto a ledge of rock from which further ascent could be made. But he was too weak to climb. So, Talha crouched below, and taking the Holy Prophet (May God bless and cherish him) on his back, he raised him to the desired height. The Holy Prophet (May God bless and cherish him) praised him that day, "He that would behold a martyr walking the face of the earth, let him look on Talha the son of Ubaydullah." (Ibn Hisham, Sira)

As soon as they reached the top, it was noontime, and they prayed after the Holy Prophet (May God bless and cherish him). The Holy Prophet (May God bless and cherish him) performed his prayer while sitting, and the rest of the Companions followed his example. Then they lay down to rest, and many of them slept a deep sleep, while some of them kept watch.

HAZRAT HAMZAH'S BLESSED BODY

The battle had now practically ended, and the Quraysh were busy about their dead and tending to their wounded comrades. The losses had not been great. There were only twenty-two killed so far out of the three thousand. From the Muslim's side, they found about sixty-five people dead, many of the dead they did not know. Some of the dead and wounded needed their attention. Among these was Shammas, still alive but unable to move. They also searched for the body of the Holy Prophet (May God bless and cherish him) but could not find it. While the Quraysh were searching for the dead bodies, Wahshi went back to the body of Hazrat Hamzah, cut open his belly, cut out his liver and brought it to Hind. He presented it to her and said, "This is Hamzah's liver." Hind's eyes were wide open, full of hatred and rage. She took Hazrat Hamzah's liver and chewed upon it, swallowed a piece of it and spit out the rest. This was the moment when her hatred was at its zenith. Wahshi asked her, "What shall be mine for slaying the slayer of thy father?" "All my share of the spoils," was her reply. But obviously, this had not been enough to quench the feeling of revenge and hatred she was harboring inside her. She took hold of Wahshi's hand and asked him to show her where Hazrat Hamzah had fallen. When they reached the body, she cut off his nose and ears and other parts of his flesh and wore it around her neck as an ornament. She wore them until they reached Makkah. Hind then took off her necklace, pendants, and anklets and gave them to Wahshi. She then called out to other women to mutilate other dead bodies. They all made for themselves ornaments of vengeance with what they cut from the bodies of the martyrs. Triumphantly, Hind mounted upon a rock and uttered a chant of victory. Some of the other Quraysh also did the same to the dead Muslims.

Abu Sufyan was striking the side of Hazrat Hamzah's mouth with the point of his spear and said, "Taste that you rebel," when Hulays passed by the leader of one of the clans of Kinanah. He said in a loud voice so that Abu Sufyan could hear, "O sons of Kinanah, can this be the lord of the Quraysh who is doing what you see with the body of his dead cousin?" Abu Sufyan said, "Confound thyself, it was a slip, tell none about it."

Hanzalah's body was lying among the dead, when his father Abu Amir came upon him. He was grieved and lamented, "Did I not warn you against this man?" He meant the Messenger of Allah. Then he looked at Hind and other women and shouted, "O Quraysh let not Hanzalah be mutilated, even though he was an adversary to us." And therefore, they did not touch his body.

DIVINE HELP

A small disobedience and error by the archers had created such havoc. Allah, the Mighty and Majestic, was teaching a lesson that success was only possible through obedience to Allah, the exalted and His beloved Messenger. The men were now retreating to the mountain but were determined to sacrifice their lives for the sake of Allah and His Messenger and not to leave him ever again. Due to their renewed commitment and sincerity, God sent down Sakinah (peace) upon those men who had been wielding swords since early morning and risking their lives, just as in Badr. A sweet slumber came upon them, and they almost dropped their swords from their hands. Men like Abu Talha were picking up their swords again but could not help dropping them once more. Sleep enveloped them like a warm blanket and took away all their worries. Allah the exalted had promised to help the faithful with five thousand angels, but when they disobeyed the commands of the Holy Prophet (May God bless and cherish him), the angels had returned and left them on their own. (Ahmad ibn Hanbal; Musnad, Tabari, Mujmu l-Kabir; Ibn Kathir, Tafsir)

When the Holy Prophet (May God bless and cherish him) retreated to the vicinity of Mount Uhud that day, Sa'd ibn Abi Waqas saw two angels in white clothes --Gabriel and Michael -- fighting and protecting the Messenger of Allah against the enemy. When Sa'd was shooting arrows that the Holy Prophet was handing him, a handsome young man with a radiant face, and dressed in white was bringing back the shot arrows from the battlefield and saying, "Shoot, O Abu Ishaq."

Musab ibn Umayr was carrying the banner of the Holy Prophet (May God bless and cherish him). After having been killed by Ibn Qamia, it fell to the ground, but an angel had taken the appearance of Musab and was letting the flag of the Holy Prophet (May God bless and cherish him) fly high. The Holy Prophet once called him, "Musab advance forward." The angel turned towards him and said, "I am not Musab." When Abdul Rahman ibn Awf heard the Holy Prophet (May God bless and cherish him) calling out to Musab he said, "O Messenger of Allah, was Musab not martyred." "Yes," replied the Holy Prophet (May God bless and cherish him), "But an angel is carrying Musab's duty for him instead." (Ibn Sa's, Tabaqat; Ibn Abi Shyba, Musannaf; Salihi, Subulu l-Huda wa r-Rashad)

During the battle, the Holy Prophet asked Harith ibn Simma as to where Abdul Rahman ibn Awf was. He answered that he was fighting valiantly with the enemy at one corner of the field. Upon which the Holy Prophet (May God bless and cherish him) said, "There is no doubt that the angels are fighting with him." When Harith heard this, he ran straight to Abdul Rahman ibn Awf and saw seven disbelievers all around him on the ground. He asked, "May Allah increase you in might. Have you killed them all?" "I have killed these and these," he said and then added, "but I did not see who killed those?"

Both sides had suffered great losses, and Abu Sufyan, the commander of Makkan forces, found it dangerous to attack the Muslims any further. The Companions of the Holy Prophet (May God bless and cherish him) were gathered around him and were regrouping their forces. This regrouping of the Muslim forces scared the disbelievers. Besides, they did not know why the three hundred hypocrites had left before the battle had even begun. Therefore, they feared that they might return any moment. This would pose a new danger. They had not forgotten what the Muslims had done at the beginning of the Battle of Uhud. Abu Sufyan very well knew that the believers were not afraid of death but rather welcomed it.

But before the Makkan army prepared to set off, Abu Sufyan mounted his chestnut mare and rode to the foot of the mountain, close to the point where the Holy Prophet (May God bless and cherish him) and his Companions had been stationed. He shouted at the top of his voice, "War goes by turns, and this is a day for that day. Exalt thyself O Hubbal! Make prevail thy religion."

The Holy Prophet (May God bless and cherish him) told Hazrat Umar to go and answer him, saying, "God is All-Highest, Supreme in Majesty. We are not equal, our dead are in Paradise, and yours are in Hell." So, Hazrat Umar went to the edge of the precipice below which Abu Sufyan was standing and answered him as the Holy Prophet (May God bless and cherish him) had told him. Then Abu Sufyan called to Hazrat Umar, having recognized his voice, "I adjure thee by God, have we slain Muhammad?" "No, by God," said Hazrat Umar, "But he is even now listening to what you say." "I take thy word for it than the word of Ibn Qamia," said Abu Sufyan. As he was leaving, he said, "Some of your dead have been mutilated. By God, I take no pleasure therein. I forbade it not, nor did I command it." Then he added, "Badr will be your meeting place with us next year." Hearing this, the Holy Prophet (May God bless and cherish him) sent another Companion to the edge of the cliff to shout another response, "That is a binding covenant between us."

Abu Sufyan rode to where his army was waiting on the further side of the plain and set off towards the south. The Holy Prophet wanted to make sure they did not mean to cause any further harm. He feared that on the way back to Makkah they might enter Medina and attack the women and children. Therefore, he sent Sa'd of Zuhrah down to the plain to follow them and see where they were headed. "If they were leading their horses," he said, "And riding their camels, they are heading for Makkah, but if they are riding their horses and leading their camels, they are for Medina, and by Him in whose hand is my soul, if that is their aim, I will overtake them and fight them." Sa'd went down to the place where the Holy Prophet's (May God bless and cherish him) horse 'Sakb' had been tethered ever since their arrival in Uhud. He rode on it after the enemy till he was sure they were headed for Makkah. He then hastened back with the good news that their horsemen were on camelback leading their horses beside them.

THE BURYING OF THE MARTYRS

When the Quraysh left the battlefield at Uhud and did not engage in further conflict with Muslims, the Companions descended into the field and started looking for the dead and wounded. The Holy Prophet (May God bless and cherish him) sent Harith ibn Simmah ahead to look for the body of Hazrat Hamzah, but when he found it, he was so appalled at the sight that he had no courage to tell the Holy Prophet (May God bless and cherish him) and did not return for a while. Hazrat Ali was sent after him. He found Harith standing by the mutilated body, and they both returned together. When the Holy Prophet (May God bless and cherish him) saw what had been done to his beloved uncle. He said, "Never have I felt more anger than now I feel, and when next God gives me a victory over Quraysh, I will do the same with thirty of their dead." (Ibn Ishaq) But at the same time, a revelation came down,

"If they inflict punishment, then inflict only so much as you have suffered, but if you endure patiently, that is better for the patient." (16:126)

Upon receiving this command, the Holy Prophet (May God bless and cherish him) expressly forbade mutilation of the dead after every battle, and he told his Companions to respect the human face as being the most godlike part of the body, "When one of you strikes a blow, let him avoid striking the face – for God created Adam in His image." Abdullah ibn Jahsh's body was lying down not far from Hazrat Hamzah, and his body was also mutilated. But when the Holy Prophet (May God bless and cherish him) looked around for others of the dead, he saw the body of Hanzalah. None of the Quraysh had touched his body, and he lay there as angels had laid him after washing his body with his hair still wet upon the dry earth. Those who looked at him gave thanks to Allah, for in his beauty and his peace, he was a sign from Heaven. (He got married the night before Uhud and consummated his marriage the same night but left for the battle early and did not find time to make ritual ablution).

Not far away were the bodies of Khaythamah and Ibn ad-Dahdahah. Khaythamah, whose martyred son had appeared to him in his dream, bidding him to hasten to join him, and Thabit ibn ad-Dahdahah was the one who had made a gift of the palm tree to the orphan. When the Holy Prophet (May God bless and cherish him) saw Thabit, he said, "Palms with low hanging heavy-laden clusters, what a multitude of these hath the son of Dahdahah in Paradise." (Waqidi)

The Holy Prophet (May God bless and cherish him) was deeply grieved to see the horrific state of his uncle and started sobbing. He then looked around for something to cover his uncle's mutilated body. A Companion from the Helpers came forward and took off a piece of his dress. He put it on Hazrat Hamzah, but it was not enough to cover his entire body. Then another Companion took off a piece of his dress and covered the body.

People were busy looking for their dead. They found the body of a man called Usayrim, who only the day before had been rebuked for not having accepted Islam. Whenever, he was told about Islam, he would say, "If I knew it to be true, all that you say, I would not hesitate." They found him mortally wounded but still alive. "What brought you here?" they asked him. "Was it care for thy people, or was it for the sake of Islam?" "It was for Allah," he said. "All of a sudden, I believed in Allah and in His Messenger, and I entered Islam. Then I took my sword and came out early morning to be with the Messenger of Allah, and I fought until I was struck, the blow that felled me here." The Companions stayed with him until he passed away. They informed the Holy Prophet (May God bless and cherish him), and he reassured them that he was one of the people of Paradise. Later, he was known as the man who entered Paradise without having prayed one of the five daily prayers.

Then, they found the body of a stranger, which they did not recognize until one of them remembered him as Mukhayriq, a learned Rabbi of the Jewish clan of Thalabah. On the Day of Uhud, early in the morning, he summoned his people to keep their pact with the Messenger of Allah and to join him in the fighting against the idolators. They argued that it was Sabbath. He said, "You keep not Sabbath truly." Then, he took them as witnesses that Muhammad was his sole heir. "If I am slain this day," he added, "My possessions are for Muhammad to use even as God shall show him." After that, he took his sword and weapons and set out for Uhud, where he fought until he was killed. After his death, his proceeds from his rich palm grove were distributed as alms in Medina, and the Holy Prophet (May God bless and cherish him) praised him as "the best of the Jews."

When the Makkan army intended to return the way, they had come, some people (especially women) began to set out from Medina to tend to their wounded and to see for themselves what had happened. Among the first women to come were Hazrat Safiyyah, Hazrat Fatima, Hazrat Aisha and Umm Ayman. When the Holy Prophet (May God bless and cherish him) saw Hazrat Saffiyah approaching the battlefield, he called to Zubayr and said, "Help me with thy mother and let Hamzah's grave be dug right away. Go and meet your mother and take her back, lest she sees what has happened to her brother." Soon after, Zubayr went to his mother and said, "The Messenger of Allah told me to take you back." But she had already learned what the Quraysh did to Hazrat Hamzah. She said, "I have heard that my brother had been mutilated, but it was for the sake of Allah, and that which is for His sake do we fully accept. I promise that I shall be calm and patient if God will." Zubayr came to the Holy Prophet (May God bless and cherish him), and he allowed her to come. So, she came and looked at her brother and prayed over him and recited the verse.

"Verily we are from God, and verily unto him are we returning."

Then, they remembered the verses that were revealed after the battle of Badr:

"O you who believe, seek the help of God in steadfastness and in prayer, verily God is with the steadfast. And say not 'dead' of those who have been slain in God's path, for they are living, only you perceive not. And we shall surely try you with something of fear and of hunger, and loss of goods and lives and harvesting. But give good tidings unto the steadfast, who say when a blow befalls them; verily we are for God, and verily unto Him are we returning. On these are blessings from their Lord and mercy, and these are the rightly guided. (Quran 2:153-7)

The Holy Prophet's (May God bless and cherish him) aunt Hazrat Saffiyah then stood over the body of her sister Umaymah's son Abdullah ibn Jahsh and prayed for him. The Holy Prophet's beloved daughter Hazrat Fatima joined her too, and both women wept over their dead relatives, and the Messenger of Allah himself joined them in sobbing. At the same time, their cousin Hamnah, Abdullah's sister, was approaching, and with great sorrow they informed her about the death of her husband Musa'b as well as the deaths of her brother and uncle.

The Holy Prophet (May God bless and cherish him) told the believers to take the armor of the martyrs and said, "Bury them with their blood and clothes." Thus, the martyrs of Uhud were buried without being washed and with what they were wearing that day. He then addressed that all the dead should be brought and laid next to the body of Hazrat Hamzah and that graves should be dug. Hazrat Hamzah was wrapped in a mantle, and the Holy Prophet (May God bless and cherish him) prayed over him the funeral prayer, after which he prayed after each one of the dead, seventy-two prayers in all. The Holy Prophet (May God bless and cherish him) told the believers to bury two or three in a grave. Hazrat Hamzah and his nephew Abdullah ibn Jahsh were laid together in one grave. The Holy Prophet asked his Companions, "Look for Amr, the son of Jumah and Abdullah the son of Amr," he added, "They were close friends in this world, so lay them in one grave." But the wife of Amr and sister of Abdullah (The father of Jabir) had already taken the two bodies together along with the body of her son Khallad. She wanted to take them to Medina, but her camel refused to go beyond the edge of the plain. So, by Allah's will, she was obliged to bring the bodies back to the battlefield. Therefore, the three were laid in one grave, and the Holy Prophet (May God bless and cherish him) commenced their burial. "O Hind," he said, "They are all of them together in Paradise, Amr and thy son Khallad and thy brother Abdullah." She answered, "O Messenger of Allah, pray God that He places me with them."

Among the martyrs was a man of Muzaynah who had fought so valiantly, who had none of his people present, for his nephew had also fought to the death. Therefore, the Holy Prophet (May God bless and cherish him) stood beside him and said, "May God be pleased with thee, even as I am pleased with thee." They wrapped him in a green striped cloak he was wearing, and when he was put in the grave, the Holy Prophet (May God bless and cherish him) drew it up to cover his face, and his feet were uncovered. So, he told his Companions to gather some desert grass from the plain and spread it over his feet. And this was done to many of the dead so that both their faces and feet be covered before the earth was piled up over them.

The Holy Prophet (May God bless and cherish him) then addressed all the martyrs and said, "The Messenger of Allah bears witness that on the Day of Judgment you will be martyrs, witnesses in the eyes of Allah." The Holy Prophet (May God bless and cherish him) then turned to his Companions and said,

"O people, visit them and come here! Give greetings and salute them. I swear by Allah who holds my life in his hands that they will respond to the greetings of each Muslim who salutes them."

After the last martyr was laid to rest, the Holy Prophet (May God bless and cherish him) asked for his horse and mounted it, and they set off down the gorge, which was the way they had come in the dawn. When they reached the other end, he told his army to stand in line to give thanks and praise to Allah. The men formed two lines facing Kaaba, with the women behind them, fourteen women in all. They all glorified God and said,

"O God, I ask of Thy blessings and Thy mercy and Thy grace and thine indulgence. O God, I ask of Thee the eternal bliss that fades not nor passes away. O God, I ask of Thy safety on the day of fear, and plenty on the day of destitution."

Despite everything that had happened, Medina was displaying great patience in the face of such calamity. Instead, people were rejoicing in the fact that the Holy Prophet (May God bless and cherish him) was safe and was among them. A woman of Helpers who had heard the false news that the Messenger of Allah had been killed came personally to welcome him when she knew that the company of Uhud was returning. Someone had told her that her brother and father had been killed in the battle, another told her that her son and husband had become martyrs. But it was as if she did not hear their words. She was only concerned about the welfare of the Messenger of Allah and kept running to welcome him. She was asking everyone she met, "Where is the Messenger of Allah?" When she saw the radiant face of the beloved of Allah, she said, "Let my mother and father be sacrificed for you, O Messenger of Allah. Having seen that you are safe and sound, all other calamities will be easy for me."

When Sa'd ibn Muadh, who was holding unto the rein of the horse that the Holy Prophet (May God bless and cherish him) was riding on saw his mother who had come to welcome those who were returning from Uhud he said, "This is my mother, O Messenger of Allah." The Holy Prophet (May God bless and cherish him) comforted her, for her other son Amr ibn Muadh had been martyred at Uhud. But this brave woman said, "I have seen you safe and sound, what calamity can shake me now?"

HAMRAU L-ASAD

The sun was now setting as the believers were entering the city of Medina, and they went to the Mosque to pray. After the prayer, the Holy Prophet lay down to rest. He fell into a deep sleep and did not hear the call for prayer by Bilal. He prayed alone when he woke up. The Companions from Aws and Khazraj, along with two Sa'd stood guarding the door of the Mosque for there was still the possibility that the Quraysh might return and inflict further harm to the believers.

The next morning, after the prayers, the Holy Prophet (May God bless and cherish him) told Bilal to announce that the enemy must be pursued. He told them, "None should go out with us save those who were present at the battle yesterday." When people returned to their various clans, most of them had multiple gashes and arrow wounds and they were tended by their families. But when they heard that the Holy Prophet (May God bless and cherish him) was summoning them, they bandaged their wounds, and hurried to the Mosque and were ready to set off once again. Malik and Shammas were seriously injured and unable to move. Shammas had none of his family members in Medina. He was carried unconscious from the battlefield to the apartment of Hazrat Aisha. But Umm Salamah tended to his wounds because he was from her clan. Since it was obvious that he would soon pass away, the Holy Prophet (May God bless and cherish him) gave instructions that he should not be buried in Medina but with his fellow martyrs at Uhud.

The Messenger of Allah was one of the first to be ready, although he could hardly move his right shoulder. When Talha came to inquire about the time of departure, he was surprised to see the Holy Prophet (May God bless and cherish him) mounted on his horse. So, he ran to his house to get himself ready. When the Holy Prophet (May God bless and cherish him) was marching out of the city, he saw forty men of Bani Salimah waiting for him. Most of them were wounded, some with more than ten gashes, but they were determined to fight for Allah and his Messenger. The Holy Prophet (May God bless and cherish him) was pleased with them and prayed, "O Lord! Have mercy upon the Bani Salimah."

Of all the clans, only one man went out who had not fought at Uhud, and that was Jabir. He went to the Holy Prophet (May God bless and cherish him) and said, "O Messenger of Allah, I intended to be present at the battle, but my father left me in charge of my seven sisters. But God preferred him for martyrdom, though I had hoped for it. So, let me go with you now." The holy Prophet (May God bless and cherish him) allowed him to join the fighters.

The Muslim army made their halt about eight miles from Medina. The enemy forces at that time were stationed at Rawha, which was not far away. After knowing their position, the Holy Prophet (May God bless and cherish him) ordered his men to spread themselves over a wide area of ground, and to collect wood as much as they could find, and to make piles of wood. By sunset, they had prepared over five hundred beacons, and when night had fallen, every group set fire to it. The flames were seen far and wide, as if a great army were encamped there.

In the meanwhile, Mabad ibn Abi Mabad, a man of Khuzah, who was still an idolator but was friendly with Muslims, came to the presence of the Holy Prophet and said, "O Muhammad! I swear by Allah that what had befallen your Companions has made us sad as well. We would have so wanted Allah to exalt you and to defeat your enemies." He sat down and talked for a while and then asked permission to leave. The Holy Prophet (May God bless and cherish him) accompanied him on the way for a little while. When Mabad left Hamru l-Asad, he went to where the Makkan army was encamped.

The Quraysh had agreed to attack Medina even though people like Safwan ibn Umayyah insisted on going back to Makkah. The arrival of Mabad happened at a critical time. When Abu Sufyan saw Mabad, he turned to those around him and said, "Here is Mabad! He must have fresh news." And then called out to him, "What is the news, O Mabad?" What news do you bring us from over there?" upon which Mabad started to speak, "I must say that I have seen Muhammad and his Companions coming towards you with a great force that I have not seen before. They are extremely furious. Members of Aws and Khazraj who were not with him yesterday have joined him as well this time. Their only goal is to avenge themselves, and they do not intend to return before they have achieved their goal. They are enraged as to what befell them, and they regret much what happened yesterday. I have not seen such a determination before." Abu Sufyan could not hide his astonishment and said, "Woe unto you, what are you talking about." Mabad exaggerated and continued, "I swear you will see the foreheads of their horses before you leave this place." Abu Sufyan was now worried and said, "We had just decided to go back and wipe them out altogether." Mabad shook his head and said, "I would not advise that at all. Their power was so majestic that I have even composed a poem about what I have seen."

Abu Sufyan was now completely intrigued, and he asked him to recite the poem. Mabad then started to recite the poem at length. In the verses, Mabad spoke about the surprise and apprehension he felt on seeing the majesty and power of the Muslim army, expressing his worries about the Makkan forces whom they now targeted. The language he was using was very well chosen, and the expressions were very powerful. In the face of such powerful words, Abu Sufyan was speechless. He was lost in thought. It seemed to him that Safwan had been right about not attacking Medina. One could see anxiety written all over his face, and at last he decided to order his army to return to Makkah.

On the way back, they came upon a caravan and sent the following message to the Messenger of Allah, "tell Muhammad from me that we are resolved to come against him and his Companions to root them out from the face of the earth. Tell him this, and when you reach Ukaz on your return, I will load your camel with raisins." When the message was delivered to the Holy Prophet (May God bless and cherish him), he answered in the following words of recent revelation,

"Sufficient for us is Allah, and supremely to be trusted is He." (Quran 3:173)

It was clear that even though the enemy was running away, they tried not to compromise their pride and utter challenges even when they were retreating in fear. Having spent Monday, Tuesday, and Wednesday at Hamru l-Asad lighting fires every night, the Holy Prophet (May God bless and cherish him) and his Companions then returned to Medina.

Shammas passed away soon after they had set out, and he was buried at Uhud. Malik had also died during their absence, but his family had buried him in Medina. The Holy Prophet (May God bless and cherish him) gave orders that his body should be taken to Uhud and buried there.

Another crisis had been averted, and the evil plans of the polytheists had been repelled. However, the news that came from around the Medina was not encouraging. The Holy Prophet (May God bless and cherish him) and his Companions who returned from the campaign of Hamrau l-Asad, having tended to the wounds of Uhud, hardly had time to gather strength when they received the bad news. The martyrdom of the seventy Companions in Uhud and the apparent victory of the Quraysh had whetted the appetite of others who had been waiting for an opportunity to attack Medina.

CHAPTER 17
DIVINE RULING REGARDING INHERITANCE

Soon after the battle of Uhud, Amra bint Hazim, who had lost her husband Sa'd ibn Rabi in Uhud and who was now pregnant, came to the Holy Prophet (May God bless and cherish him) with her other child whom Sa'd had entrusted to her, said, "O Messenger of Allah! These are the daughters of Sa'd who fought with you and fell martyr in Uhud! Their uncle came and confiscated all his property and left nothing for his children. What can you do for us, O Messenger of Allah? For without financial means, these children won't be able to have a promising future or have a home of their own when the time comes." (Waqidi, Maghazi; Ibn Athir, Usdu l-Ghaba; Ibn Hajjar, Isaba). This was indeed a tragic situation, for here was a woman who had lost her husband, who now was faced with the Arab tradition that the brothers take over the property of a man who had fallen in war. The Holy Prophet (May God bless and cherish him) looked affectionately at the two orphans who were standing by his side and said, "I hope that Allah, the All-Merciful, will give the last ruling about this matter." Before long, angel Gabriel brought verses that spoke of Allah's final judgement on the rules of inheritance concerning those who die and leave their relatives behind. (An-Nisa 4:11).

After the revelation, the Holy Prophet (May God bless and cherish him) sent Jabir ibn Abdullah to call Sa'd ibn Rabi's brother and wife to his presence and said, "Give two-thirds of Sa'd's property to his two daughters, give one eighth to his wife and the rest is yours." This was the first time that the Holy Prophet had allocated inheritance. When Amra heard what the Holy Prophet (May God bless and cherish him) had said, she could not contain herself and shouted, "Allah is the greatest," for she could see that justice was done in her case. This clearly meant that from now on, women could receive a portion of the inheritance according to divine ruling. She was so happy that her glorification could be heard in the four corners of the Mosque.

RIGHTS OF ORPHANS AND POLYGAMY

The orphans that were left because of frequent wars and personal disputes that happened for no good reason would usually be taken under the protection of their relatives. These relatives would, therefore, be the beneficiaries of the orphan's inheritance. When the orphaned child was a girl, the situation was worse. Such girls would not be allowed to get married for fear that they would share their inheritance with others and lay claim to that property. As a result, they would be married to their guardians to keep their inheritance.

In the days of ignorance, the Arabs married as many women as they wanted and left them whenever they desired. Marriage and divorce were completely at the will of the man in that culture. Another reason for such marriages was because of the high rate of men dying in conflicts. Consequently, there were many widowed women and orphaned girls left behind.

The Lord of the universe sent down revelation to the Holy Prophet (May God bless and cherish him) addressing this issue. Allah (exalted is He) said,

"O people! Abstain from rebelling against your Lord, who created you from one man, and from that man He created a companion, and from them made many men and women. Refrain from disrespecting Allah, whose name you pronounce, to ask for something from each other, and from severing ties of kinship. Allah is the supreme protector over you."

These verses thus pointed to the fact that all of humanity was a family that had the same father and mother, and that people should obey Allah's commands that would follow:

"Give orphans their property, do not take the unclean in return for the clean, do not mix their property with yours and then eat from it. For doing so is a great sin." This verse was a great warning for people to act justly towards orphaned girls whose rights were taken away from them under various pretexts. It further says,

"If you fear that you will not be able to deal justly with the orphan girls, then marry those that please you of (other) women, two or three or four. But if you fear that you will not be just, then (marry only) one or those your right hand possesses. That is more suitable that you may not incline (to injustice)." (Quran 4:3)

Those few verses uprooted the fabric of Arab society and marked the beginning of a new era. It had two aspects, the first was the rights of orphans. It was so important that men were advised to marry other women rather than fall into the trap of old traditions of locking them into houses and not letting them marry others or simply confiscating their property. Secondly, Allah the exalted limited the number of women a man could marry and that it was advised to treat them equally was an indispensable condition to the rule.

"However, if you fear that (in your marital obligation) you will not be able to observe justice among them, then content yourselves with only one or the captives that your right hand possess. Doing so it is more likely that you will not act rebelliously." (Quran 4:3)

And then in the same Sura (An-Nisa) came the expression that everyone must pay attention to, "You will not be able to deal between your wives with absolute justice (in respect of love and emotional attachment), however much you may desire to do so." (Quran 4:129)

Thus, Allah the exalted proposed marriage to one woman as being the norm and commanded men to uphold the principle of fairness when there were exceptional circumstances to marry the second, third or fourth. Among the Companions, Nawfal ibn Muawiyah was married to five, Harith ibn Qays was married to eight, and Ghaylan ibn Salam was married to ten women. (Bayhaqi, Sunan; Ibn Kathir, Tafsir; Abu Dawood, Sunan; Tirmidhi, Al-Jami u Sahih; Ahmad ibn Hanbal, Musnad). They all came to the Holy Prophet (May God bless and cherish him) and explained their situation. The Holy Prophet (May God bless and cherish him) advised them to keep four of their wives and to part with the others. The rights of the women were not limited to merely this. An entire chapter (Sura) of the Nobe Quran titled 'An-Nisa' was dedicated to the conditions and rights of women.

"And give the women (upon marriage) their bridal gifts graciously. But if they give up willingly to you anything of it, then take it in satisfaction and love. And do not give the weak-minded your property which Allah has made a means of sustenance for you but provide for them with it and clothe them and speak to them words of appropriate kindness. And test the orphans (in their ability) until they reach marriageable age. Then, if you perceive in them sound judgement, release their property to them. And do not consume it excessively and quickly (anticipating) that they will grow up. And whoever (when acting as guardian) is self-sufficient should refrain (from taking a fee), and whoever is poor – let him take according to what is acceptable. Then, when you release their property to them, bring witnesses upon them. And sufficient is Allah as Accountant." (Quran 4:4-6)

After Uhud, there was peace in Medina for a couple of months. Then suddenly came the news that Bani Asad were planning a raid on the city of Medina even though the family of Jahsh and some other Asadites who had previously lived in Makkah had entered Islam. Much of this big and powerful tribe of Najd were still close allies of the Quraysh. After the setback of Uhud, they thought that Muslims were now weak and vulnerable and an easy target to strike. It was, therefore, imperative for Muslims to show solidarity and strength. Hence, the Holy Prophet (May God bless and cherish him) sent out a force of one hundred and fifty well-armed and well-mounted men under the command of his cousin Abu Salamah into their territory to deal with them. Abu Salamah was instructed to do all in his power to take their camp by surprise. This he succeeded in doing, and after a brief encounter with little bloodshed, the Bedouin withdrew and scattered in all directions. The Muslim forces returned to Medina after eleven days with a large herd of camels and three herdsmen. The expedition was successful, and it proved the determination and power of Muslims. Not long after this incident, Abu Salamah died from reopening a wound he had received in Uhud. (Waqidi, Maghazi)

On a Thursday in the month of Muharram, the Holy Prophet (May God bless and cherish him) received news that Khalid ibn Sufyan al-Hudhayl was preparing an army to fight against Medina. He was the chief of the Lihyanite branch of Hudhayl and a remarkably evil man. If they could get rid of him, the danger from the south would become less. The Holy Prophet (May God bless and cherish him) sent Abdullah ibn Unays, a man of Khazraj, with instructions to kill him. Abdullah ibn Unays, before leaving for his mission, asked the Holy Prophet (May God bless and cherish him), "O messenger of Allah, describe him to me that I may know him." The Holy Prophet (May God bless and cherish him) answered, "When you see him, he will remind you of Satan." It took Abdullah ibn Unays eighteen days to accomplish his mission. He was able to get very close to Khalid ibn Sufyan and was able to kill him. After his mission, the Holy Prophet (May God bless and cherish him) gave him the staff he was holding and said, "This will be greatest proof between you and me on the Day of judgment." Before Abdullah ibn Unays died, he asked that the staff that was given to him by the Holy Prophet (May God bless and cherish him) to be placed by his shroud. (Ibn Hisham, Sira; Tabari, Majmu al-Kabir, Ibn Kathir, Al-Bidaya wa n-Nihaya)

TWO TRAGIC EVENTS OF RAJI AND BIR-I-MAUNA

The Quraysh of Makkah thought that the Muslims in Medina had been weakened after the defeat in Uhud, but the expedition of Hamru l-Asad proved their assumption wrong. The two attempts that the polytheists had put into action had been averted before they even started. It was the fourth year of Hijra and the month of Safar when some men of Adal and Qura people came to the Holy Prophet (May God bless and cherish him) and said that they had become Muslims and that they needed a guide who would teach them about the tenets of the faith and religion. The Holy Prophet (May God bless and cherish him) accepted their request, for these people who had accepted Islam could not be left without a guide who would help them in matters of religion. Therefore, he selected ten companions from among the Ashab-e-Suffa (people of the bench) who had devoted themselves to learning the Quran and lived within the Mosque (Masjid-e-Nabawi). Asim ibn Umar ibn Khattab was chosen as the leader of the group. Some reports say that the leader was Marsad ibn Abi Marsad. (Ibn Hisham, Sira; Tabari, Tarikh; Ibn Sa'd, Tabaqat)

The group set off and came all the way to a well called Raji used by the Hydhayl tribe who lived in Hijaz. Suddenly, they were trapped in a blazing fire that was prepared well before their arrival. They were surrounded by one hundred archers from the sons of Lihyan who were waiting in hiding. They were attacked and confined to the fire. The Companions tried to climb to a higher ground to defend themselves. The enemy told them to surrender and said, "We promise that if you surrender, we will not kill you." The men who had told them they were Muslims and brought them all the way here from Medina now could nowhere to be seen. The Companions decided to fight till their last breath. When Asim ibn Umar saw that martyrdom was near, he started shooting arrows, praying, "Dear Lord, let the Messenger of Allah learn of our state." He had only seven arrows and, each one he shot had brought down a polytheist. When he ran out of arrows, he got hold of his spear, and with it he killed all those who attacked him. When the spear broke as well, he started wielding the sheath of his sword and said, "Dear Lord, I fought to protect your religion as long as I lived; do not let my body be dishonored in the hands of the polytheists after I have fallen martyr." When Asim ibn Umar was martyred, the enemies wanted to tear apart his body, cut off his head and take it to Makkah for a reward because on the Day of Badr, he had killed important Makkan men such as Uqba ibn Muayat. When they approached his body, they could not sever his head due to the bees that were swarming around his body. They left him and decided to come back early the next morning. When they returned the next day, they could not find his body. Heavy rain had fallen that evening and the flood water had washed Asim's body to a place they could not locate. Asim's prayer had thus been answered, and Allah had not allowed them to desecrate his body. (Bukhari, Sahih; Ahmad ibn Hanbal, Musnad; Ibn Hisham, Sira)

Seven of the Companions were martyred by the enemy forces. Only three had been left, Khubayb ibn Adiyy, Zayd ibn Dasinna, and Abdullah ibn Tariq. The sons of Lihyan repeated that if they surrendered, they would not kill them. The Companions had no choice but to surrender. They first untied the strings of their bows and bound their hands with the strings. Abdullah ibn Tariq protested and accused them of deception, upon which they killed him right away. They took Khubayb and Zayd and made for Makkah. They then sold them to the Makkan polytheists for a price. The Makkans, who had been deeply humiliated in Badr, and who had not been able to settle their accounts in Uhud were pleased to have two Muslim captives. They first imprisoned them for a couple of days and then brought them to a place called Tanim. There they met for the first time since their imprisonment, and they hugged and exhorted each other to patience. They took Khubayb a short distance away, and when he saw that they were about to bind him to a stake, he asked to be allowed to pray first. And he prayed two cycles of ritual prayer, it is said that he was the first to offer prayer before death. Then they bound him to the stake and said, "Revert from Islam, and we will let thee go free." "I will not revert from Islam, "he replied. "Don't you wish Muhammad was in your place?" they said, "And that you were sitting in your home?" "Nay, I don't wish that Muhammad should be pierced by a single thorn and that I might be sitting at home," answered Khubayb. "Revert O Khubayb, for if you don't, we will surely kill you," Quraysh persisted. "My being slain for God is but a trifle, if I die in Him," he said and then, "As to your turning my face away from the direction of the House of God (Kaaba), verily God said, wherever you turn, there is the face of God." Then he said, "O God, no man is here who will take Thy Messenger my greetings of peace, so take him Thou, my greeting of peace."

At that time the Holy Prophet (May God bless and cherish him) was sitting with Zayd and others of his Companions in Medina, and there came over him a state when revelation descended upon him. They heard him say, "And on him be peace and the mercy of God." Then he said this was Gabriel who greeted me with peace from Khubayb." (Waqidi). The polytheists had gathered around forty young boys whose fathers had been killed in Badr, and they gave each one a spear and said, "This is he who slew your fathers." They speared him but did not kill him. So, a man put his hand over the hand of one of the boys and thrust Khubayb fatally, and another did the same. As long as he lived, he continuously glorified Allah, saying, "There is no god but Allah, and Muhammad is the Messenger of Allah."

His fellow captive Zayd was then slain, and he also prayed two cycles of ritual prayer before he was martyred. He also gave similar answers to their questions. Akhnas ibn ash-Shariq, who had gone out to Tanim with others remarked, "No father loveth his son as the Companions of Muhammad love Muhammad."

BIR-I-MAUNA INCIDENT

In the same month of Safar, a man named Amir ibn Malik came to visit the Holy Prophet (May God bless and cherish him). The Holy Prophet (May God bless and cherish him) greeted him and invited him to Islam, but he did not accept it. He had some reservations; however, he asked the Holy Prophet (May God bless and cherish him), "O Messenger of Allah! Why don't you send some of your Companions to the people of Najd to speak to them about Islam? I think our people will accept the invitation." The Holy Prophet (May God bless and cherish him) replied, "I fear that the people of Najd will do my Companions some harm." But Amir ibn Malik promised, "I give you my word for them." According to Arab culture, giving one's word was like a surety, and going back on one's words meant loss of honor and dignity. The Holy Prophet (May God bless and cherish him) agreed and chose seventy people from among his Companions. (Tabari, Al Jamiul Bayan; Ibn Kathir, Tafsir). The Holy Prophet (May God bless and cherish him) instructed them to follow Amir ibn Malik and preach Islam to the people of Najd. He also gave them letters to deliver to the leaders of the various clans. Munzir ibn Amr was appointed as the head of the delegation. (Ibn Hisham). All the Companions were people of the bench (Ashab-e-Suffa) who were well-versed in the Quran and knew *Ahadith* (Prophetic traditions) of the Messenger of Allah.

They left Medina and came to a well called Mauna and set up a camp over there. They let their camels rest and graze in the area. They chose three people and sent them to Amir ibn Tufayl to deliver him the letter of the Messenger of Allah. Amir ibn Tufayl was the nephew of Amir ibn Malik. Haram ibn Milhan was one of the three delegates to hand over the messages. When they reached the destination, Haram ibn Milhan told his two companions to stay behind and said, "You both stay behind as I go to them! If they give me safe passage, you will see it, but if they try to kill me then go to your friends and inform them what has happened." Then he went to Amir ibn Tufayl and handed over the letter from the Holy Prophet (May God bless and cherish him). He even did not look at it and instead gave orders for Ibn Milhan to be killed. Upon his orders, Jabbar ibn Salma got hold of his spear and thrust it into Ibn Mjlahn's back, and it came out from his chest. Ibn Milhan was covered in blood, and he wiped his face with blood that was on his hands and shouted, "Allah-o-Akbar (Allah is the greatest). I swear by the Lord of Kaaba that I have been saved." (This statement made by Ibn Milhan also led to the salvation of the person who killed him. What Ibn Milhan said was incomprehensible to Jabbar at first. He was bewildered; how could a man whom he had just pierced with a spear could say, "I am saved." Finally, he understood that this was an expression of joy to become a martyr and be forever in peace. Jabbar acknowledged, "I swear by Allah he has been saved," and then he became a Muslim. Waqidi, Maghazi; Ibn Kathir, Al-Bidaya wa'n Nihaya)

Amir ibn Tufayl then called out to the sons of Amir ibn Malik and told them to kill the rest of the Companions. The sons of Amir, however, did not obey his order because they wanted to honor the words of their uncle Amir ibn Malik. Amir ibn Tufayl was enraged and called people from different tribes to attack the envoys of the Holy Prophet (May God bless and cherish him). The Companions decided to defend themselves but were outnumbered, and as a result they were all killed. It was only Amr ibn Umayya that had been saved that day, and he made his way back to Medina. On his way back, he came across two people who were from the tribe that had murdered his friends. So, he killed them thinking to avenge his dead Companions. But both men were in fact innocent, and loyal to Abu Bara. The Holy Prophet (May God bless and cherish him) did not approve this and insisted that the blood money should be paid to the next of kin.

When Ubaydah died after his single combat with Utbah at the Battle of Badr, he left a widow who was much younger than himself, Zaynab, the daughter of Khuzaymah of the Bedouin tribe of Amir. She was of a very generous nature, and even before Islam, she was famous as 'the mother of the poor.' A year after being widowed, she was still unmarried, and when the Holy Prophet (May God bless and cherish him) asked her to marry him, she gladly accepted the offer. A fourth apartment was made for her in the Holy Prophet's house adjacent to the Mosque.

THE FATE OF BANI NADIR

The Bani Nadir was a Jewish tribe living in Medina, and they were allies of the Bani Amir, the tribe of the two men that Amr ibn Umayya had killed not knowing that the Holy Prophet (May God bless and cherish him) had given them protection. The Bani Nadir had also signed a pact with Muslims for defending Medina and to live peacefully together, however they were secretly in contact with the Makkan polytheists and harboring enmity towards the Holy Prophet (May God bless and cherish him).

One Saturday, the Holy Prophet (May God bless and cherish him) came to Quba with a group of his Companions. He performed the afternoon prayer and visited the Bani Nadir in that area. The purpose of this visit was to seek their assistance in paying the blood money of the two men from the sons of Amir, with whom they were allies. The Holy Prophet (May God bless and cherish him) was accompanied by his Companions such as Hazrat Abu Bakr, Hazrat Umar, Hazrat Uthman, Talha, Zubayr, Sa'd ibn Muadh, Usayd ibn Khudayr, and Sa'd ibn Ubadah. The Jews greeted the Holy Prophet (May God bless and cherish him) and said, "O Abul Qasim, we will do what you ask us to do. But first, sit down and rest for a while. In the meantime, we will discuss the matter among ourselves." Seeing their positive response, the Holy Prophet (May God bless and cherish him) sat down and leaned on the wall of a house nearby and started to wait there.

At the same time, the Bani Nadir conspired among themselves, led by Huyayy ibn Akhtab, "O Jewish people! As you see, Muhammad has come to you with not even ten men with him. Climb the roof of the house he is sitting against, throw a rock over him and kill him. You will never get such a chance again. If he is killed, his friends will disperse. Those who came from the Quraysh will return to their own homeland, and those who joined him from Aws and Khazraj will return to their own business. The timing is right; how long will you wait?" Hearing this plan of action, a man called Amr ibn Jahhash stood up and said, "I will climb that roof and throw a rock over him." And he went towards the house, where the Holy Prophet (May God bless and cherish him) was resting under its shade.

Salam ibn Mishkam saw the gravity of the situation and warned his people, "O people, even if you oppose me for the rest of your life, agree with me today. I swear to Allah that if you try to do this, he will be informed of this, and he will at once realize that you are about to deceive him. This will be a violation of the treaty between us; therefore, do not do such a thing."

While they were arguing, angel Gabriel came to the Holy Prophet (May God bless and cherish him) unseen by any save him and told him that the Jews were planning to kill him and that he must return to Medina at once. So, he rose and left the place without a word, and everyone assumed that he would shortly rejoin them. The Companions waited for a while, and Hazrat Abu Bakr said, "There is no point in waiting for him over here. It is clear the Holy Prophet (May God bless and cherish him) has left for some important reason." So, they all got up and left.

Kinanah ibn Swayra came to the members of his tribe and said, "Do you know why Muhammad stood up and left?" "No, we don't," they responded. He then said, "I swear by Torah that I know the reason. The reason Muhammad left is that he was informed about the trap you set for him. Do not fool yourselves. I swear by Allah that he is no doubt the last messenger you expected him to come from the family of Aron, but Allah bestowed him as He pleased. According to the Torah, his birthplace is Makkah, and where he will emigrate to is Yathrib. As to his attributes, there is not the tiniest divergence, they are exactly as the Torah has revealed." After that, he further explained, "What he offers you is much better than fighting him. Unfortunately, I already see you leaving behind your property and homes among the cries of your children and family. At least obey me in two things, for there is nothing to gain from the third." "What are these two things?" they asked. "Become Muslims and being of the same religion as of Muhammad, and you will save your property and wealth and share the same exalted status as his Companions. In this way, you will not be exiled." "We will not leave the Torah and diverge from the covenants of Moses," they replied. "Then wait, for he will soon send you news telling you to leave his country and go somewhere else. So, say yes to his demand, for he would not confiscate your property and spare your lives, and you will be able to keep what is yours."

In Medina, the Companions went to the Holy Prophet's (May God bless and cherish him) home. He explained to them what had happened, and then he sent Muhammad ibn Maslamah to the Bani Nadir telling him about what to say to them. He immediately obeyed the orders and went to the Jewish fortresses. Some of their leaders came out and greeted him. "The Messenger of God," he announced, "has sent me to you, and he said, 'By plotting to slay me, you have violated the pact I made with you." Then he recounted to them the exact details of their plot, as the Holy Prophet (May God bless and cherish him) had told him, then he delivered his message, "I give you ten days to depart from my country. Whoever of you is seen after that shall be killed."

"O son of Maslamah," they said, "We never thought that a man of Aws would bring us such a message." "Hearts have changed," he replied. While the tribe of Bani Nadir was preparing to leave Medina, Abdullah ibn Ubayy ibn Salul sent two of his envoys with the message, "Do not leave your home and belongings. Go to your fortresses and stay there. I have two thousand men with me of my own tribe and other Arabs. They, too, will enter the fortresses with you and will fight with you to the death. The Quraysh will also help you; they will never leave you alone. Do not forget that our allies from Ghatafan will support you as well."

In the meantime, they sent news to the Bani Qurayza tribe and asked for help from their leader Ka'b ibn Asad, but he replied, "Not a single person from our tribe will violate our pact with Muhammad," and thus turned them away. However, Huyayy ibn Akhtab sent his brother to the Holy Prophet (May God bless and cherish him) with the message, "We shall not leave our dwellings and our possessions. So do what you will."

When the Holy Prophet (May God bless and cherish him) heard their message, he said, "Allah-o-Akbar" (God is the greatest), and all the Companions around him echoed the magnification. "The Jews have declared war," he said. Immediately, the Holy Prophet (May God bless and cherish him) mustered an army and gave the banner in the hand of Hazrat Ali. He set off towards the fortresses of Bani Nadir, located in the south of the city of Medina. They performed the afternoon prayer outside and then marched towards their position. An exchange of stones and arrows started between them until dark. The Jews were taken by surprise by the swift attack of the Muslims. They thought that help was at hand to come from Bani Qurayza and Ibn Ubayayy the next day and that in another 2-3 days, their allies from Ghatafan would be by their side. At the same time, Muslim army was increasing in numbers with the continuous stream of fighters. The Muslims surrounded them from all sides. At night the Holy Prophet (May God bless and cherish him) returned to Medina with ten Companions and left Hazrat Ali in charge of the Companions. They chanted "Allah-o-Akbar' all night long until it was time for morning prayer, when the Holy Prophet (May God bless and cherish him) joined them.

After a few days, the Jews were totally disappointed when no help arrived from Ghatafan, and Ibn Ubayy admitted that he could do nothing. They were completely cut off from the outside world, with no sign of help from any direction. Their morale was down, and their hopes shattered. After ten days, the Holy Prophet (May God bless and cherish him) gave orders to cut off some of their palm trees that were in sight of the walls. As soon as they started cutting the trees, loud cries were heard from the fortresses. Jewish women were crying and tearing their clothes and throwing themselves on the ground. Bani Nadir was appalled. Huyayy sent a message to the Holy Prophet (May God bless and cherish him), "O Muhammad! If you have forbidden destruction on the world, then why are you having these date trees axed?"

There was also a difference of opinion on the Muslim side. It was not long before the angel Gabriel revealed the following verse,

"Whatever (of their) palm trees you may have cut down or left them standing on their roots, it was by Allah's leave and so that He might disgrace the transgressors." (Al-Hashr 59:5)

This was a compromise, for the Holy Prophet (May God bless and cherish him) knew that the area was virtually his, but it was done by divine permission. It had the immediate effect of demoralizing the enemy's resistance. The Jews loved their palm trees and still hoped to return one day to their territory because they knew that the Quraysh were determined to eradicate Islam from the oasis. But if the palm trees were destroyed, it would take thirty years to regrow them. Therefore, Huyayy sent a message to the Holy Prophet (May God bless and cherish him) that they would leave their land. The Holy Prophet (May God bless and cherish him) replied, "Leave your land and take with you all that your camels can carry except your arms and armor." Huyayy hesitated, but his fellow tribesmen compelled him to accept. Muhammad ibn Maslamah was supervising their departure. Many of the Jews were still taking it very slowly. They were delaying by saying that some citizens of Medina owed them money. The Holy Prophet (May God bless and cherish him) learned about it and said, "Then come to some compromise by reducing the amount, and then take all your loans at once and leave."

With heavy hearts, the Bani Nadir started to leave their homeland, burning their own houses so as not to leave anything behind. They loaded their possessions on six hundred camels from the doors of their houses to the lintels. When they set off, it was one of the most magnificent caravans in the history of Medina. The women had put on their best clothes and adorned themselves with jewelry, and they drew back the curtains of their howdahs to display their wealth, gold, and precious stones. As their caravan paraded, the sound of tambourines and drums could be heard throughout the city. Many of them stopped and settled on land that they owned in Khaybar, but others went further north and settled in the south of Syria.

The Bani Nadir had left quite a large piece of land, and on it burned and destroyed houses, along with weapons like swords and armor. Since these goods had not been won as spoils in combat, the Holy Prophet (May God bless and cherish him) declared them to be the property of Allah and announced that he would disperse them as he deemed fit. (Al-Hashr 59:7)

When the situation was under control, the Holy Prophet (May God bless and cherish him) gathered all the Helpers and addressed them, "If you would like, I can divide the property of Bani Nadir that Allah has given me between you and the Muhajirun. But you know that your Muhajirun brothers do not have any property or homes to live in, they are only dependent on your help and hospitality. If you like and allow, I can give these to them, and they can leave your homes and start to live on their own."

The Helpers were worried to hear what the Holy Prophet (May God bless and cherish him) said. They feared whether they had committed any negligence in taking care of their Muhajirun brothers and sisters. At this, Sa'd ibn Muadh spoke for Aws, and Sa'd ibn Ubadah stood up and spoke on behalf of Khazraj and said, "O Messenger of Allah! Divide it among our Muhajirun brothers and sisters! If you like, you can even take it from our property and divide it among them, too. But please do not separate them from us, let them continue to live with us."

This was a very moving moment. It showed that very strong social bonds had been formed between them. This attitude of the Ansar pleased Allah and His Messenger. Soon, Allah revealed through Gabriel,

"Those who before coming had their abode (in Medina), preparing it as a home for Islam and faith, love those who emigrated to them for Allah's sake, and in their hearts do not begrudge what they have been given, and indeed they prefer them over themselves, even though poverty be their own lot. (They, too, have a share in such gains of war). Whoever is guided against the avarice of his own soul—these are the ones who are truly prosperous. (Al-Hashr 59:9)

The Holy Prophet (May God bless and cherish him) was pleased and raised both his hands and said, "Dear Lord! Have mercy on the Ansar and their children." All the spoils of what was left from Bani Nadir were divided among the Muhajirun. Two of the Ansar, including Sahl ibn Hunayf and Abu Dujana, were given a share, and that was on account of their poverty. The famous sword of Abi l-Huqayq was given to Sa'd ibn Muadh.

After the new year of AD 626, Hazrat Fatima, the beloved daughter of the Holy Prophet (May God bless and cherish him), gave birth to another son. The Holy Prophet (May God bless and cherish him) was so pleased with the name Al-Hassan that he now named the younger brother Al-Hussayn, which means the little Hassan, which is the "little beautiful one."

Soon after that, the Holy Prophet's (May God bless and cherish him) wife, Hazrat Zaynab, "The mother of the poor," fell ill and passed away. She was married to the Holy Prophet (May God bless and cherish him) for less than eight months. He led her funeral prayer and buried her in Baqi, next to the grave of his daughter Hazrat Ruqayyah. The next month, Abu Salamah also died of a wound he had received from Uhud. The Holy Prophet (May God bless and cherish him) was at his bedside when he breathed his last, and it was the Holy Prophet (May God bless and cherish him) who closed his eyes when he was dead.

Abu Salamah and his wife had been a most devoted couple, and they had vowed that if one of them died, the other would not marry again. But Abu Salamah told his wife that if he died, she should marry again. He prayed, "O God, grant Umm Salamah after me a man who is better than me, one who will keep her happy." After four months, the Holy Prophet (May God bless and cherish him) asked for her hand in marriage. She replied that she feared she was not a suitable match for him. "I am a woman whose best time has gone," she said, "And I am the mother of orphans. Moreover, I have a nature of exceeding jealousy, and O Messenger of Allah, you have already more than one wife." The Holy Prophet (May God bless and cherish him) answered, "As to your age, I am older than you, as to thy jealousy, I will pray God to take it from you, and as to your orphans, God and His Messenger will care for them.' And so, they were married.

THE SECOND BADR

After the battle of Uhud, when the Makkan troops were leaving, Abu Sufyan challenged the Holy Prophet (May God bless and cherish him) and said, "The new meeting time and place for us will be the beginning of the next year at Badr. We shall meet there and battle it out." To his challenge, the Holy Prophet (May God bless and cherish him) had Hazrat Umar to reply, "It will happen if Allah wills it to happen." The message of the Holy Prophet was relayed to the enemy. Now, the time was at hand, and the Holy Prophet (May God bless and cherish him) started to prepare his Companions for the battle, going to Badr once again. On the other hand, Abu Sufyan was feeling the weight of his challenge, even though it was his idea, and he was now trying to find an excuse not to go to war. By chance, it was a year of drought, and going to war in such circumstances meant more harm than good. He was not willing to be the one to break the challenge he had proposed, but he wanted the Holy Prophet (May God bless and cherish him) to be the one to break it. Abu Sufyan consulted some of the leaders of the Quraysh, and they planned accordingly.

Nuaym ibn Masud, one of the leading men of Ghatafan, had come to Makkah and brought the news about the army in Medina. Abu Sufyan saw his arrival as an opportunity and offered him twenty camels should he be able to convince the Holy Prophet (May God bless and cherish him) not to go to war. Nuaym agreed and departed for Medina at once. He spread the rumor that Abu Sufyan had prepared a great army ready to march towards Badr. He advised the people of Medina to "Stay and not to fight against the Quraysh. By God, I do not think any one of you will escape with his life."

Abu Sufyan was sure that Nuaym would accomplish his goal. So, he told the Quraysh, "We have sent Nuaym ibn Masud to stop the friends of Muhammad leaving for Badr. He would do his best. But let us embark on our way as well. We can stop after we have traveled for one or two nights, and then we will return. It will appear that it was not us but them who turned back on their words. But even if they come, we will tell them that it is a year of drought, and we shall postpone fighting until next year."

In Medina the Jews and the hypocrites were happy with this development and were further spreading rumors that Abu Sufyan, with his great army, had set off for Badr. This was an attempt to demoralize the Muslims. In this situation, Hazrat Abu Bakr and Hazrat Umar came to the Holy Prophet (May God bless and cherish him) and said, "O Messenger of Allah! There is no doubt that Allah will support His religion, and the believers will be victorious. And He will make His Messenger glorious. We have a commitment to battle, and we do not want to go back on our word. The enemy will consider it our cowardice. You shall lead us to the place of meeting, and we swear that we will be steadfast."

The Holy Prophet (May God bless and cherish him) was greatly pleased to hear this and said, "I swear by He who holds my life in His hands; even if no one should accompany me, I will go to the appointed place alone." The Holy Prophet (May God bless and cherish him) left Abdullah ibn Rawaha as his deputy in Medina and set off to Badr with one thousand and five hundred men. There were ten horses in the army, and Hazrat Ali ibn Abi Talib was carrying the standard.

Abu Sufyan and his two thousand army with fifty cavalrymen were also on the road. But scenes from Badr and Uhud were continuously playing in his mind. He was filled with fear, and going to Badr felt like suicide for him. The Makkan army stopped at a place called Marraz-Zahran near the water of Majanna. When they were ready to leave, he addressed them, "O people of Quraysh! Return! Do you not see that we are suffering from drought this year? Let us return now and fight in a year when our pastures are green and our animals have enough to eat. How can we fight in such conditions? I am returning, return with me."

On the contrary, the Holy Prophet (May God bless and cherish him) and his Companions spent eight days at the fair of Badr, and those who attended it reported the news far and wide that the Quraysh had broken their word but that the Holy Prophet (May God bless and cherish him) and his followers had kept theirs. This was a great moral victory for Muslims, and it established their superiority over the enemy.

The Holy Prophet (May God bless and cherish him) and his Companions returned from Badr and stayed in Medina for a month without an incident. Then, at the beginning of the fifth Islamic year, the Muslims received news from the direction of Damascus, from a place called Dumat Al-Jandal, that some tribes of Ghatafan were again planning to attack Medina. These people were also attacking caravans and confiscating their goods.

The Holy Prophet (May God bless and cherish him) set out with a sizable force into the plains of Najd, but the enemy disappeared as before when they were almost upon them. It was during this expedition that the Holy Prophet (May God bless and cherish him) received a revelation instructing him how to pray "The prayer of fear," that is how an army should conduct the ritual prayer and modify it in times of danger, while some of them should keep watch when other pray. (An-Nisa 101-2)

One of the Ansar (Helpers) who was part of this expedition was Jabir, the son of Abdullah. He narrated the following incident that happened during one of their encampments, "We were with the Holy Prophet (May God bless and cherish him) when a man brought the chick of a bird in the gathering of the Holy Prophet (May God bless and cherish him) and his Companions. They noticed that the parent of the chick was following it, flapping around it. When the man sat down, its parent threw itself upon its chick, and did not concern itself with the danger out of care towards its baby. This astonished the Companions. The Holy Prophet (May God bless and cherish him) then turned to his Companions and said, "Are you amazed at this bird? You have taken its chick, and it threw itself into danger out of mercy for the chick! I swear by God, your Lord is more merciful to you than this bird is to its chick. Then he turned to the man and asked him to put back the baby bird where he had found it." The Holy Prophet then said, "God hath a hundred mercies, and one of them has he sent down amongst the Jinn and men and cattle and beasts of prey. Thereby, they are kind and merciful unto one another, and thereby the world creatures tend unto their offspring. And ninety-nine mercies have God reserved unto Himself and there with He may show mercy unto His slaves on the Day of Judgement." (Muslim)

The example given of utmost mercy is the mercy of mothers, but God's mercy towards His servants is more than that, and His love is not like their love. Once, the Holy Prophet was passing by when a woman with a child in her arms was baking bread. They had told her that God's Messenger would be passing. She came forward and said, "O Messenger of Allah! We have heard you say that God is more lovingly kind to His servants than a mother to her child." The Messenger of Allah said, "Yes, that is so."

The woman became happy and said, "O Messenger of Allah! A mother would never toss her child into this oven." The Holy Prophet wept. Then he said, "God chastises in Fire only those who refuse to say, 'There is no god but God.'

Ka'b Ujra narrated that one-day God's Messenger said to his Companions, "What do you say about a man slain in God's path?"

They said, "God and His Messenger know best."

He said, "He is in the Garden." Then he said, "What do you say about a dead man concerning whom two just witnesses say that they knew nothing of him but good?"

They said, "God and His Messenger know best."

He said, "He is in the Garden." Then he said, "What do you say about a dead man concerning whom two just witnesses say that they never saw any good from him?"

The Companions said, "He is in Fire."

The Holy Prophet (May God bless and cherish him) said, "How badly you have spoken – a sinful servant and a forgiving Lord!" Say, "Each act according to his own manner." (17:84)

Jabir further narrated that while on their way back to Medina, the Holy Prophet (May God bless and cherish him) and some of the Companions were riding in the rear of the army. Jabir was riding an old and weak camel that could not keep up with the rest of the Companions, and hence he stayed back. In the meantime, the Holy Prophet (May God bless and cherish him) passed by him and asked him why he was so far behind. "O Messenger of Allah," he answered, "The camel I am riding cannot go faster." At this, the Holy Prophet (May God bless and cherish him) said, "Make him kneel," and made his own camel kneel as well. Then he said, "Give me that stick." Which I did, and he took it from me and gave one or two prods to the camel. Then he told me to mount it, and I mounted it. By Allah, my camel moved faster and outstripped his."

"On our way back, the Holy Prophet (May God bless and cherish him) conversed with me and said, 'Will you sell your camel to me?' I said, 'I will give him to you.' 'Nay,' he said, 'but sell him to me.' Jabir narrated that it seemed to me that the Holy Prophet (May God bless and cherish him) wanted to bargain. I asked, 'To name me a price,' and he said, 'I will take him for a dirham.' 'Not so,' I said, 'For then you would be giving me too little.' 'For two dirhams,' he said, 'Nay,' I said. And the Holy Prophet (May God bless and cherish him) went on raising the price until he reached forty dirhams, that is an ounce of gold, to which I agreed. Then he asked me, 'Are you married, Jabir?' and when I said I was, he said, 'An already married woman or a virgin?' 'One already married,' I said. I further explained, O Messenger of Allah, my father was martyred on the Day of

Uhud and left me with his seven daughters, so I married a motherly woman who would take care of them, comb their hair, and look after their needs.' The Holy Prophet (May God bless and cherish him) agreed that I had made a good choice. When we reached near Medina, the Holy Prophet (May God bless and cherish him) said that he would sacrifice camels and spend the day here, and she would have the news of our homecoming and would set about shaking the dust from her cushions.' 'We have no cushions,' I said. 'They will come,' he said. 'The next morning, I took my camel and knelt him outside the Holy Prophet's (May God bless and cherish him) house. The Holy Prophet (May God bless and cherish him) came out and told me to leave the camel and pray two cycles in the Mosque. I obeyed his command. Then he asked Bilal to weigh me out an ounce of gold, and he added a little more that tipped the scale. I took the gold and turned to go, but the Holy Prophet (May God bless and cherish him) called me back. 'Take your camel,' he said, 'He is thine, and keep the gold as well." (Ibn Ishaq)

The Holy Prophet (May God bless and cherish him) was busy with one or another campaign during the months that followed Uhud. One day, Salman Farsi came to the presence of the Holy Prophet (May God bless and cherish him) to seek his blessings and help. His master was a Jew of Bani Qurayza, who made him work hard all day on his land to the south of Medina from morning to evening, and hence, he was unable to have any contact with the Muslim community. For this reason, he was also unable to take part in any of the expeditions during the last four years. It seemed to him that there was no way out for him. He also asked his master what it would take to set him free, but his price was far beyond his means. He had to pay his master forty ounces of gold and plant three hundred palm trees. Therefore, he came to the presence of the Holy Prophet (May God bless and cherish him) and talked about his plight. The Holy Prophet (May God bless and cherish him) told him to write an agreement with his master to pay the gold and the palms for his freedom. Then he asked his Companions to help Salman with the palms. They all happily contributed, one bringing thirty palm shoots, another twenty, and so on until the full number had been reached.

The Holy Prophet asked Salman to dig the holes for the palms, and when it was ready, the Holy Prophet (May God bless and cherish him) planted the palms, which all took root and thrived. The remaining amount was forty ounces of gold that Salman needed to buy his freedom. The Holy Prophet (May God bless and cherish him) had received a piece of gold, which was the size of a hen's egg, which he gave to Salman, telling him to give it to his master. "How far will it go towards what I have to pay?" said Salman, thinking that it would not be enough. The Holy Prophet (May God bless and cherish him) took the gold from him, put it in his mouth, and rolled his tongue around it. Then he gave it back to Salman, saying, "Take it and pay him the full price with it." Salman weighed out to his master forty ounces from it, and in this way, he became a free man.

Although the Holy Prophet (May God bless and cherish him), along with his followers, spent most of the time dealing with enemies and had been engaged in confrontations, during the period of relative peace, the Holy Prophet (May God bless and cherish him) addressed the many issues relating to day-to-day business, family, and other concerns. He put forward an idea that a third of each day and night should be for worship, a third for work, and a third for family. The last third included the time spent on sleep and at meals. As to worship, much of it was done during the night. In addition to the evening (Isha) prayer and dawn prayer, they performed voluntary (*Tahajad*) prayer as well. Allah the exalted stressed that the Noble Quran should be recited and remembered, and the Holy Prophet (May God bless and cherish him) recommended various litanies and glorification. The Companions were used to lengthy night worship and vigils, and the Holy Prophet (May God bless and cherish him) himself prayed all night.

God (Exalted is He) sent a revelation to lessen the burden and said,

"Verily, thy Lord knows that thou keep vigil well-nigh two-thirds of the night, and sometimes half of it or a third of it, thou, and a group of those that are with thee, God determines the night and the day. He knows that you will not be able to come up to the full measure of it, and therefore hath He relented unto you. Recite then even so much of the Quran as is easy for you." (Quran 73:20)

However, the sincere Companions continued to pray much of the night, of which the last third was mentioned by the Holy Prophet (May God bless and cherish him) as being especially blessed by the Lord of the universe, "Each night, when a third of which has yet to come, our Lord, (Exalted is He), descends unto the nearest heaven, and He says; "Who calleth unto Me, that I may answer him? Who prayeth unto Me a prayer that I may grant him? Who asketh My forgiveness that I may forgive?" (Bukhari). It is regarding this time of the night that Allah revealed in the Quran saying,

"They arise from (their) beds, they supplicate their Lord in fear and in longing, and from what We have provided them, they spend. And no soul knows what has been hidden for them of comfort for eyes as reward for what they used to do." (Sajda 32:16-17)

"Who is it that will lend to God a beautiful loan, and He will multiply it for him many times? And God contracts and expands, and to Him, you shall be returned." (Quran 7:245)

It is narrated in a hadith, "God descends and says, "Who will supplicate Me that I may respond to him? Then He spreads His two hands and says, "Who will lend to one who is neither lacking nor wrongdoing?"

One day, Hazrat Ali Murtada went home, and Hassan and Husayn were weeping before Hazrat Fatima Zahra. Hazrat Ali said, "O Fatima, what happened to the brightness of my eyes and the joy of my heart that they are weeping?"

Hazrat Fatima said, "O Ali" it seems that they are hungry, for a day has passed, and they have eaten nothing." She had placed a pot on fire, so Ali said, "What do you have in the pot?"

She said, "There is nothing in the pot except plain water. I put it on the fire to keep the children happy, for they think I am cooking something." Hazrat Ali's heart became constricted. He had a cloak that he had put aside. He took it to the market and sold it for six dirhams and bought some food. He returned and told Hazrat Fatima Zahra. She said, "You have succeeded, O Abu l-Hassan! May you remain in good." Hazrat Ali went to go back to the Mosque of the Messenger and saw a nomad who was selling a camel. He said, O Abu l-Hassan! I am selling this camel! Buy it!"

Hazrat Ali said, "I can't. I don't have the price."

The nomad said, "O Abu l-Hassan! I will sell it to you until the time when spoils arrive, or a gift comes to you from the House of Wealth."

Hazrat Ali bought the camel for sixty dirhams and set off in front of it. Another nomad came to him and said, "O Ali, sell this camel to me."

He said, "I will sell it."

He asked, "How much?"

He answered, "For as much as you want."

He said, "I will buy it for one hundred and twenty dirhams."

Hazrat Ali said, "I have sold it to you." And took one hundred and twenty dirhams from him. He went back to his house and said to Hazrat Fatima that he would give sixty dirhams to that nomad, and they would use the other sixty. He went out looking for the nomad. He saw the Holy Prophet (May God bless and cherish him), and he said, "O Ali, where are you going?" Hazrat Ali told him the story. The Holy Prophet (May God bless and cherish him) became happy and congratulated him. He said, "O Ali, that was not a nomad. That was Gabriel who sold it and Michael who bought it. And the camel was one of the she-camels of Paradise. This is that loan you gave to God when you were kind to a poor man after God had said, 'Who is it that will lend God a beautiful loan?'"

THE BANI MUSTALIQ

The Holy Prophet (May God bless and cherish him) received the news that the leader of Bani Mustaliq, Harith ibn Abi Dirar, had gathered a large army with the help of the neighboring tribes and was planning to attack Medina. He sent one of his Companions, Burayda ibn Husayb to collect information and inspect the area. Burayda set out on the road and came close to their positions. When they saw him approach, they asked, "Who are you?" Burayda replied, "I am one of you." He continued, "I heard that you have gathered to attack that man in Medina. If you are serious about it, I will join you. I will go to my tribe and bring those who obey me, and then we can attack together." They were happy to hear that. Harith ibn Abi Dirar was excited and said, "That's the reason we have gathered here, now, go to your tribe and be quick."

Burayda left immediately and made his way to Medina. As soon as the Holy Prophet received this news, he mustered an army to meet this challenge. It was the sixth year after Hijra and the month of Shaban. He left Zayd ibn Haritha as a deputy in Medina. On this mission, the hypocrites also joined the army in the hope of receiving a share of the spoils of war. The army took a break in a place called Halaiq. There, a man from the sons of Abdul Qays approached them. The Holy Prophet (May God bless and cherish him) asked him, "Where is your tribe?" "In Rawha," he replied. The Holy Prophet (May God bless and cherish him) asked, "Where are you going?" the man replied, "I have come to submit in faith to you and bear witness that you have brought the Truth and to fight alongside you with the enemy." The Holy Prophet (May God bless and cherish him) was very happy and said, "Praise belongs to Allah, who has honored you with Islam." The man then asked, "Which act earns best the pleasure of Allah?" "The Salah (Ritual Prayer) that you pray on time." The Holy Prophet answered.

The Muslim army then came to a place called Muraysi. The enemy forces that were gathered to attack Medina learned that the Muslim army was advancing towards them. They were struck with fear and in great panic. The man they had sent to gather information was also taken captive by Muslims. The Muslim army took position and were ready for battle. The standard of *Muhajrun* was carried by Hazrat Abu Bakr, while Sa'd ibn Ubadah was carrying the banner of Ansar. Before the battle, the Holy Prophet (May God bless and cherish him) ordered Hazrat Umar to announce the following, "Come say, "La ilaha illallah" so that your property and lives may be protected." The entire valley of Muraysi echoed with the deep voice of Hazrat Umar. The enemy responded by showering arrows towards the Muslim's army, and they as well exchanged arrows. That day, as described by Hazrat Juwayriya, the enemy soldiers saw the army of Islam to be much greater than they really were, and the Muslims saw the enemy much smaller than they were in numbers. Indeed, men who were not seen before had come on their horses to help the Muslim fighters. The exchange of arrows continued for a while. The Holy Prophet (May God bless and cherish him) then ordered his Companions to attack the enemy on foot. The entire Muslim army marched forward, and Bani Mustaliq could not stand the onslaught. All the enemy fighters were taken captives, and their possessions confiscated. Ten people died on the side of the enemy and only one Companion was lost among the Muslims, Hisham ibn Subaba, and that was by mistake. The Holy Prophet (May God bless and cherish him) ordered that his blood money be paid to his brother Mikyas ibn Subaba. Mikas ibn Subaba however, attacked the Ansar and killed the Ansar who had killed his brother by mistake and then went to Quraysh.

The captives consisted of two hundred families. Burayda ibn Husayb was appointed to supervise the captives. Shukran, the freed slave of the Holy Prophet (May God bless and cherish him), was responsible to oversee the spoils of war, including the camels, sheep, and other livestock. The job of distributing the spoils was given to Mahmiya ibn Jaz. When the distribution was over, Hazrat Juwariya bint Harith, the daughter of Harith ibn Abi Dirar, the leader of the enemy, was given to Thabit ibn Qays ibn Shammas and his cousin, then Thabit took the full rights of Harith's daughter Juwariya unto himself in exchange for a date grove in

Medina. (Waqidi; Maghazi; Salihi, Subulu l-Huda wan-Rashad). It is also reported that Hazrat Juwariya's name was Barra, and the name Juwariya was given to her by the Holy Prophet (May God bless and cherish him). (Abu Dawood, Sunan; Ahmad ibn Hanbal, Musnad). But then Juwariya made a deal with Thabit to be set free for four hundred dirhams of gold.

The Muslim army treated the captives with compassion by feeding them and clothing them. Hazrat Juwariya had a dream prior to this event that a moon had been born in Medina and had come all the way to her. She had been under the spell of that vision for days but did not share it with anyone. She recited the Shahadah "*La illaha illallah, Muahmad ur Rasul Allah*" and became Muslim. She then came to the presence of the Holy Prophet (May God bless and cherish him) and said, "O Messenger of Allah! I am a Muslim woman now who bears witness that there is no god but God, and you are His Messenger. I am the daughter of Harith ibn Abi Dirar. You know what has become of my people. I have been given to Thabit ibn Qays and his cousin. But Thabit bought me in exchange for a date grove in Medina. I made an agreement with him for my freedom for an amount that I will not be able to pay. He did not force me to agree, I did it on my own accord. Because I believe you will help me with this. O Messenger of Allah, help me to gain my freedom."

The Holy Prophet (May God bless and cherish him) listened to her thoughtfully and then said, "Would you like me to offer you something that is even better than that?" She was surprised and said, "And what could that be, O Messenger of Allah?" the Holy Prophet (May God bless and cherish him) said, "I will pay for your freedom and then marry you." She said, "Yes, O Messenger of Allah, I accept."

The Holy Prophet (May God bless and cherish him) sent a word for Thabit ibn Qays, who came to his presence immediately. He told him that he wanted to pay the price for Hazrat Juwariya and then to marry her. Thabit was indeed very happy to hear that because it was a good match for him. He said, "Let my mother and father be thy ransom. She is yours for no price." But the Holy Prophet (May God bless and cherish him) paid the price, freed Hazrat Juwariya, and married her. The news of this marriage spread among the Companions. And out of respect for the blessed union and new relationship, the Companions set free more than a hundred families.

Abdullah ibn Ubayy ibn Salul, who was a hypocrite, had been with the Muslim army on this campaign. He sat with ten of his friends and started venting his anger and dissent, "I have never seen such a thing. I knew that this would happen to us at some point. My tribe ignored me, they should have made me king! Do you not see, now they prefer him over us in our own land and scorn and insult us. I swear our situation with the Quraysh is like feeding the crow so that it may come and take our eyes out! Till I had heard Jahjah's call, I had given up all hope that there was going to be such a stance against them and that I would die before hearing it. But I am sorry to say, I am still alive, and yet I have no power to answer that call. It is also true that who is greater and who deserves more respect will be made clear when we get back to Medina."

After that, Ibn Ubayy addressed his friends, "You have done this to yourselves. You accepted them into your city, and they came and settled in your land. You gave them from your possessions, and now they have the same resources as you! I swear if you had not received them with open arms, they would not have been here but somewhere else. But you see, they do not agree with what you do and even make you the target of their arrows. The truth is you fought for them, and your children are left fatherless because of them! They grew in numbers while you diminished."

A young man by the name of Zayd ibn Arqam heard him say all these words. He came to the Holy Prophet (May God bless and cherish him) immediately and told him one by one what he had heard. The Holy Prophet (May God bless and cherish him) was not happy, and his face changed color. First, he said to Zayd, "Young man, could it be that you misheard him because you were angry with him?" Zayd was sure of himself and said, "No, O Messenger of Allah! I swear, I heard exactly that from him." The Holy Prophet (May God bless and cherish him) again questioned him, "Could it be that you have misheard him?" "I swear no, O Messenger of Allah," he said. The Holy Prophet (May God bless and cherish him) once again asked, "Maybe it was not him but someone else who said it; perhaps you mistook him?" Zayd replied, "I swear it was him, O Messenger of Allah."

Some of the Companions heard what Zayd ibn Arqam said. They went to Abdullah ibn Ubayy and told him to ask forgiveness for what he had said. But he denied the allegations and said, "I swear by great Allah that I have not uttered such words," and walked over to the Holy Prophet (May God bless and cherish him) and refuted what Zayd had claimed. Hazrat Umar was also furious at what he heard. He grabbed his sword and came to the Holy Prophet (May God bless and cherish him). At that time, the Holy Prophet (May God bless and cherish him) was sitting under the shade of a tree and having his back massaged. Hazrat Umar asked, "O Messenger of Allah! Do you have pain in your back?" "Yesterday evening, the camel threw me off its back," said the Holy Prophet (May God bless and cherish him). Hazrat Umar asked, "O Messenger of Allah! Allow me to get rid of this Ibn Ubayy." "Will you really do it?" asked the Holy Prophet (May God bless and cherish him). "Yes," said Hazrat Umar, "I swear by He has sent you with Truth that I will do it."

Upon this, the Holy Prophet (May God bless and cherish him) said to Hazrat Umar, "Should I give the word in Yathrib, there are many who will kill him," Hazrat Umar said, "O Messenger of Allah! Why don't you then order Abbad ibn Bish to take his head?" (Waqidi; Salihi). The Holy Prophet (May God bless and cherish him) did not like that idea and said, "No, then people would say that Muhammad is killing his friends." After that, Hazrat Umar suggested, "Why don't you tell people to get on the road." The Holy Prophet (May God bless and cherish him) agreed to his proposal.

The leader of Aws Sa'd ibn Ubadah approached the Holy Prophet (May God bless and cherish him) and said, "O Messenger of Allah! You set off at such a strange time today. You have never set off at this time of the day before; what is the reason for this change?" The Holy Prophet (May God bless and cherish him) turned towards him and said, "I believe what your friend has said has not reached you?" Sa'd was a wise man who understood the situation well and said, "O Messenger of Allah! You will displace him if you want to! Because it is you who is in favor and he who needs favor. Glory is with God, His Messenger, and the believers. But treat him kindly! Because when Allah brought you here, his tribe was getting ready to declare him leader with a crown and a gown decorated with pearls and gems. All the gems on his crown had been put in place, except for one piece that was held by a Jew called Yusha who refused to give it to him. He was aware that Ibn Ubayy wanted that piece badly for his own glory. So, Yusha was asking a very high price for it. At the same time, Allah the Mighty and Majestic sent you, and he probably thinks that you have robbed him of what was supposed to be his."

Ibn Ubayy's son Abdullah, who heard of what Hazrat Umar said to the Holy Prophet (May God bless and cherish him), came to his presence. He was pale and upset indeed. He said, "O Messenger of Allah, if you plan to kill my father because of what he has said, then leave that business to me. I swear, I can bring him to you before you even stand up from your place. The people of Khazraj know that there is no son better than me in service to his parents. I have been preparing their food from such and such time. What I fear is that if you order someone else to kill him, I would not be able to bear to see the murderer of my father walk among us. And I am sure I will kill that man and then go to Hell! But your forgiveness is greater and more valuable." The Holy Prophet (May God bless and cherish him) gently replied, "O Abdullah! I do not wish to kill your father, nor have I ordered it done; as long as he is among us, we will treat him kindly and only wish him well." Abdullah was greatly relieved to hear that.

When the Muslim army reached Atiq, Abdullah went to the front of the army and waited for the camel of his father. When he saw him, he took the reins of his camel and made it sit on the ground and stepped on the camel's front legs. Ibn Ubayy ibn Salul did not expect this behavior from his son and said, "What are you trying to do, you son of such and such?" Abdullah answered, "I swear by Allah, you cannot enter Medina until the Messenger of Allah gives you leave! Then you will see who is held in favor and who is not." The Holy Prophet (May God bless and cherish him) was informed about Abdullah's behavior. He did not like that a son should turn against his father. So, he went to them while Abdullah's foot was still on the camel's legs. His father said, "There is no doubt now that I am out of favor even when it comes to my children. I am lower than a woman." The Holy Prophet addressed Abdullah, "Get your father free." And only then Abdullah let his father enter Medina.

The Holy Prophet (May God bless and cherish him) then set off on the road and called out, "Hal, Hal" to his camel to move faster. In the meantime, Angel Gabriel brought a revelation from God. The Holy Prophet (May God bless and cherish him) was sweating profusely. It looked like the camel he was riding would kneel at any moment. The moment the revelation had passed, the Holy Prophet (May God bless and cherish him) came towards Zayd ibn Arqam and said, "Your ears have not deceived you, young man! For Allah the Exalted has sent the revelation that verifies what you have heard."

THE DISAPPEARANCE OF QASWA

It was during the same journey that the famous camel of the Holy Prophet (May God bless and cherish him) Qaswa had been lost, and the Companions were looking for it everywhere. The hypocrites saw this as an opportunity to gossip about it. Zayd ibn ul Lusayt asked, "Why are these men running around in all directions?" somebody told him, "Qaswa, the camel of the Holy Prophet (May God bless and cherish him), has disappeared." Upon which Zayd said mockingly, "Why does not Allah tell him where his camel is?" The Companions were angry at him, "You enemy of Allah, let He take your life. What you are engaging in is clear dissent. I swear by

Allah that the Holy Prophet (May God bless and cherish him) gives us news greater than the whereabouts of his camel; he keeps bringing us news from the heaven."

Angel Gabriel descended with the news of what had happened, and the Holy prophet (May God bless and cherish him), addressed the crowd, "A man from hypocrites is making fun of the Messenger of Allah because his camel has been lost and says, "Why does not Allah tell him where the camel has gone? I swear by Allah that except for God, no one knows about the unseen. But right now, God the Great is telling me where the camel is. It is in such and such valley, and its reins are tied to a tree. Go in that direction and find it."

The companions went in the direction and found the camel as described by the Holy Prophet, with its reins tangled up in a tree.

THE NECKLESS

Whenever the Holy Prophet (May God bless and cherish him) embarked upon a campaign or a journey, he would draw lots among his wives and would take one of them with him. On the expedition of Bani Mustaliq, he took Hazrat Aisha and Umm Salamah along with the army. Hazrat Aisha (the mother of the faithful) had a very thin physique, and during the entire journey, she would be in her howdah on the camel's back. Around sunset, the army halted at a place. Hazrat Aisha was wearing an onyx necklace that her mother had given her at her wedding, and it was her most treasured possession. By chance, the necklace had unclasped and fell to the ground. Due to darkness, she was unable to find it. The halt was a brief one because the place was without water. But the Holy Prophet (May God bless and cherish him) then gave orders to wait until daylight. Some of the Companions were complaining due to lack of water for ablution and prayer. They even went to Hazrat Abu Bakr and voiced their concerns. There was no water well around, and the army had already used up all their supplies. But in the last part of the night, a revelation came to the Holy Prophet (May God bless and cherish him) that entailed and allowed earth purification when water was not accessible.

"If you find not water then purify yourselves with clean earth, wipe over your faces and your hands." (Quran 4:43). This commandment was a big relief for the Muslims in such a situation. Usayd later narrated, "This was not the first blessing that had been brought on us by the family of Hazrat Abu Bakr." The next day, the necklace was nowhere to be found but when the camel rose, the necklace was lying underneath him.

THE LIE

The next stop of the army was at a valley with a plain field that stretched across some distance. The Holy Prophet (May God bless and cherish him) was with Hazrat Aisha, and he suggested that they should have a race. Hazrat Aisha narrated afterwards, "I wrapped up my robe around me, and the Holy Prophet (May God bless and cherish him) did the same. Then we raced, and he won the race. "This is for that race," he said, "Which you won from me before." He was referring to an incident that had taken place in Makkah before emigration. Hazrat Aisha explained, "He had come to our house, and I had something in my hand, and he said, 'Bring it here to me,' and I would not and ran away from him, and he ran after me, but I was too fast for him."

At the next stop, before they reached Medina, the camel that was carrying Hazrat Aisha stopped, and her howdah had been unbound and put on the ground. The clasp of her necklace was loose, and it slipped again. In the meantime, she stepped out to satisfy a call of nature. Before her return, the men had saddled the camels and led them to the howdah, which they loaded upon the mount. They failed to notice that she was not in her howdah. So, they led away the camel to join the army. When she came back to the camp, she found out that the entire army had gone. Therefore, she went where her howdah was, thinking that when they realized her absence, they would come back for her. She sat there and was overcome by sleep. As she was lying there, Safwan, son of Muattal, passed by. He had also fallen behind the army for some reason and was not at the camp. He noticed her and stood over her but soon recognized her, and he said, "Verily, we are for God, and unto Him we are returning. This is the wife of the Messenger of Allah." His utterance of the verse woke her up, and she gathered herself. Safwan offered her his camel and escorted her on foot to the next halt. (Waqidi)

The army stopped to take a break. Hazrat Aisha's howdah was put on the ground, and when she did not emerge from it, they assumed she was asleep. But soon, to their surprise, she rode into the camp led by Safwan. That started a scandal that was to shake Medina, and hypocrites were eager to start it. The Holy Prophet (May God bless and cherish him), Hazrat Aisha, and most of the Companions were unaware of the trouble that was brewing.

It had been twenty-eight exhausting days since the campaign ended, and they returned to Medina. The slender body of Hazrat Aisha had weakened to the point of illness, and she was resting in bed. By that time, the slander that the hypocrites had whispered against herself and Safwan was being repeated throughout the city. Her own cousin, Mistab of the clan of Muttalib, was among the propagators of the rumor. She herself was unaware of these false accusations. She noticed that the Holy Prophet (May God bless and cherish him) was also a little reserved in his attention towards her. When he would come to the room where she was resting, he would just ask, 'How are you today.' She was heartbroken and asked the Holy Prophet's (May God bless and cherish him) permission to go to her parents, where her mother could look after her, and the Holy Prophet (May God bless and cherish him) agreed.

Hazrat Aisha herself narrated, "I went to my parents home without any knowledge of what was being said and recovered slowly from my illness some twenty days later. Then, one evening, I went out with the mother of Mistab (her mother was the sister of my father's mother), and as she walked beside me, she stumbled over her dress and said, 'May Mistab perish.' 'God forbid,' I said, 'That was a bad thing to say about a man of the Emigrants who fought at Badr.' She looked at me and said, 'O, daughter of Abu Bakr, can it be that the news had not reached you?' 'What news?' I said, then she told me the whole story, what the slanderers had said, and how it was being recapped in Medina. 'Can this be so?' I spoke. 'By God, it is indeed.' Was her reply, and I returned home in tears. I wept and wept until I thought my grief would split my liver. I asked my mother, 'People are talking at my back, and you did not tell me a word.' She said, 'My dear daughter, take it not so seriously, for there is seldom a beautiful woman married to a man who loveth her, but her fellow wives are full of gossip about her, and others repeat what is said.' So, I stayed awake the whole night, and my tears flowed without ceasing."

But in fact, the wives of the Holy Prophet (May God bless and cherish him) were all women of piety, and not one of them took part in spreading the slander. On the contrary, they defended her and spoke well of her. Those responsible for the gossip were Hamnah, Zaynab's sister, thinking to support her sister's interest (wife of the Holy Prophet). In addition to Mistab was the poet Hassan ibn Thabit, and behind all this were Ibn Ubayy and other hypocrites who had started everything.

Usama, who was of the same age as Hazrat Aisha, spoke strongly in her defense. "This is a lie," he said, "We know naught but good of her." His mother, Umm Ayman, was also very empathetic in praise of her.

The Holy Prophet (May God bless and cherish him) was deeply hurt by all this mischief. The next day, he went to the mosque and ascended the pulpit, and after praising God, he said, "O people, what you say of men who harm me regarding my family, reporting of them what is not true. By God, I know naught but good of my household, and naught but good of the man they speak of, who never entered a house of mine, but I am with him." No sooner the Holy Prophet (May God bless and cherish him) said that Usayd rose to his feet and said, "O Messenger of Allah, if they are of Aws, we will deal with them, and if they be of our brethren Khazraj, then give us thy command, for they deserve that their heads should be cut off." At this Sa'd ibn Ubaydah stood up and started arguing with Usayd. But the Holy Prophet (May God bless and cherish him) silenced them and sent them home.

Hazrat Aisha narrated, "I was with my parents, and I had wept for two days and nights, and while I was sitting with them when a woman from the Helpers came and asked if she could join us. I let her in, and she sat and wept with me. In the meantime, the Holy Prophet (May God bless and cherish him) entered and sat down. A month had passed, and no tidings had come to him about me from heaven. After declaring that there is no god but God, he said, "O Aisha, I have been told such and such a thing concerning thee, and if you are innocent, surely God will declare your innocence, and if you did that is wrong, then ask forgiveness of God and repent unto Him, for verily if the slave confess his sin and then repents, God forgives him." When the Messenger of Allah finished speaking, my tears ceased to flow, and I said to my father, 'Answer the Messenger of Allah for me.' And he said, 'I know not what to say.' When I asked my mother, she said the same. I was very young in age, but I said, 'I know well that you have heard what men are saying, and it has upset your soul, and if I say unto you that I am innocent - and Allah knows that I am innocent, this will not satisfy you, whereas if I say that which I know I am guiltless of, you will still not be satisfied. Therefore, I will say what the father of Joseph said: 'Beautiful patience must be mine, and God is He of whom help is to be asked against what they say." (Quran 12:18). Then I turned to my couch and lay on it, hoping that God would declare me innocent. Not that I thought He would send down a revelation on my account, but I was hoping that the Messenger of Allah would see in his sleep a vision that would prove me innocent.' 'The Messenger of Allah was still sitting among us when suddenly he was seized by the power of revelation, and pearls of sweat dripped from his face, even though it was a cold wintry day. Then, when he was relieved of the weight of revelation, he smiled and said, 'O Aisha, praise God, for He has declared thee innocent.' Then my mother said, 'Arise and go to the Messenger of Allah,' and I said, 'Nay by God, I will not arise and go to him, and I will praise none but God." (Bukhari). The verses that were revealed:

"Verily they who brought forth the lie are a party amongst you. When you take it upon your tongues, uttering with mouths that of which you had no knowledge, you counted it but a trifle. Yet, in the sight of God, it is enormous. And why, when you heard it, did you not say, "It is not for us to speak of this. Glory be to Thee (Allah). This is a great slander. God warns you, beware of ever repeating the like thereof, if you are believers." (Quran 24:15-17)

After that, there was a period of relative calm and peace in Medina. One day a Bedouin came to the presence of the Holy Prophet (May God bless and cherish him) and said, "O Messenger of Allah, when is the Hour?" Obviously, the Bedouin was burning in love for the real and an ocean of passion was boiling in his heart although he knew that the knowledge of the time of Resurrection was only with God. As the following verse was already revealed, "He has knowledge of the Hour." (Quran 31:34). But in wishing to see the divine beloved, he wanted to talk because of longing. The Holy Prophet (May God bless and cherish him) knew where his pain was coming from and asked, "What have you done for that day that you ask about it? How is it that you hope for it?" the Bedouin said, "I have not done much prayer and fasting, but I love God and His Messenger." The Holy Prophet (May God bless and cherish him) smiled and said, "A man will be with the one he loves." Tomorrow, everyone will be with the one he loves today.

A nomad came and asked the Holy Prophet (May God bless and cherish him), "Who will take care of my account tomorrow?" The Messenger of Allah replied, "God will take care of the servants' accounts." The nomad went back in happiness and joy and kept on saying, "So, I am saved! When a generous person decides, he forgives."

"Whoso brings a beautiful deed shall have ten times the like thereof, and whoso bring an ugly deed shall be recompensed only with its like." (6:160).

It is by the bounty of Allah that one beautiful deed of the servant becomes ten, and by His bounty, ugly deeds change into beautiful deeds. God says, "Those – God shall change their ugly deeds into beautiful deeds." (25:70)

Abu Dharr narrates, "I said, 'O Messenger of Allah, teach me a deed that will bring me near to the Garden and keep me away from the Fire." The Holy Prophet (May God bless and cherish him) said, "When you do an ugly deed, follow it with a beautiful deed." I said, if, "There is no god but God" one of the beautiful deeds?" He said, "It is the most beautiful of the beautiful deed."

CHAPTER 18
THE TRENCH

For about a year, the Muslims lived in Medina in peace. There were small disturbances nonetheless but the Holy Prophet (May God bless and cherish him) handled them with much wisdom. The Jews who were forced to leave Medina and were now settled in Khayber started plotting against the Holy Prophet (May God bless and cherish him). About twenty leading Jews, such as Salam ibn Abi l-Huqayq, Huyayy ibn Akhtab, Kinana ibn Abi l-Huqayaq, Hawza ibn Qays, and Abu Amir came together and went to Makkah and started provoking the Quraysh against the Messenger of Allah. They told Abu Sufyan that in war against Muhammad, they were with him. Abu Sufyan was pleased to hear this. He told them, "The dearest of men to us are those who help us against Muhammad." So, they took Jews with other chiefs of Quraysh inside Kaaba, and together, they swore a solemn oath to God that they would not fail one another until they had achieved their goal.

The Quraysh had not been able to come to the second Badr that they had made a promise to fight. This cowardly behavior had cost them a lot of humiliation. Now, they had a chance to regain their reputation with the Jews helping towards that end. The Jewish groups then left the Quraysh and went to Ghatafan and made them offers. They promised them that they would give half of their yearly produce and grains of Khayber if they joined in the war against the Holy Prophet (May God bless and cherish him). They told them that the Quraysh would be with them too. They undertook to rouse up all the nomads in the plain of Najd to help them. The clans of Fazarah, Murrah, and Ashjah also joined them against the Muslims. The Bani Sulaym contributed a seven-hundred-strong force to the army of Quraysh. Only Bani Amir remained altogether faithful to their pact with the Holy Prophet (May

God bless and cherish him).

It was the month of Shawwal and the fifth year of the Hijra when the Quraysh gathered in Darun Nadwah. They raised their standards and gave it to Uthman ibn Talha. A four-thousand-strong Makkan army started its march towards Medina under the command of Abu Sufyan. The army had three hundred horses and one thousand five hundred camels. The tribes that had agreed to fight alongside Quraysh started to join quickly. Bani Sulaym joined with seven hundred men, Bani Fazarah with one thousand men, Ashja with four hundred, and Bani Murrah with four hundred men. Before long, the total number of the Makkan army reached ten thousand men.

The confederate army marched forth from Makkah to plunder Medina. At the same time, with the help of Hazrat Abbas, several horsemen from Bani Khuzah set out with all speed for Medina to warn the Holy Prophet (May God bless and cherish him) of the impending attack and to give him details of its strength. They all reached Medina in four days, thus giving the Holy Prophet only a week to prepare for a war.

The Holy Prophet (May God bless and cherish him) immediately convened a consultation meeting with his Companions to come up with a strategy for this confrontation. The Holy Prophet (May God bless and cherish him) spoke words of encouragement, promising them victory if only they would have patience and obey orders. The Companions expressed their opinions. The memory of Uhud was still fresh in their minds. So, this time, they were carefully evaluating the situation. Suddenly, Salman Farsi rose to his feet and said, "O Messenger of Allah, in Persia, when we feared an attack of cavalry, we would surround ourselves with a trench, so let us dig a trench around Medina now." Everybody welcomed his plan with great enthusiasm. The Holy Prophet (May God bless and cherish him) also liked his idea. The decision had been made. The Holy Prophet (May God bless and cherish him) went to the outskirts of Mount Sal and set up camp over there. Then, they made the decision as to where the trenches were going to be dug. Medina was encircled by mountains, and the enemy could only come from the north, and this is where they would dig the trench.

Time was running out; therefore, every effort was to be made to finish the job before the arrival of the enemy forces. They first drew a line from the fortress of Shaikhayn to Mazad, leaving Mount Sal at the back. They started digging from Mazad, and it stretched to Dhubab and Ratij. The area was divided among the

Companions. Men were divided into groups of ten and everyone had to dig a length of forty Zira (a measure of length around one yard). These small groups worked together, the Ansar between Dhubab and the mountain of Abu Ubaydah, and the *Muhajirun* between Ratij and Dhubab.

Salman Farsi knew exactly how wide and how deep the trench would have to be, and having worked with the Jews of Bani Qurayzah, he knew they had all the equipment that was needed. So, shovels, mattocks, and pickaxes were borrowed from the Jews and date baskets were used to carry the excavated earth.

The Holy Prophet (May God bless and cherish him) worked himself from dawn to twilight. Salman was very prominent at digging, for he was not only very strong but had been an expert at this. He did the job of ten men. And a friendly rivalry started between the Companions. "Salman is ours," the Emigrants claimed. "He is one of us," the Helpers said, "We have more right to him." The Holy Prophet announced, "Salman is one of us, the people of the House."

Rocks and stones excavated from the trench were piled up on the medina side so that they might be used against the enemy. The men were stripped to the waist, and those who could not find baskets used their garments to carry the earth. Several youngsters took part in digging and carrying the stones and earth. Usama and Hazrat Umar's son Abdullah and their friends, who were teenagers, participated in this mission. Bara from the Haritha clan of Aws, in the after years, narrated about the great beauty of the Holy Prophet (May God bless and cherish him) as he remembered him at the trench, wearing a red cloak, his chest covered with dust and his long black hair touching his shoulders. "More beautiful than him, I had not seen."

The Holy Prophet (May God bless and cherish him) was working very hard, sometimes with the Emigrants, sometimes with the Helpers, and sometimes as a carrier. Despite the hardness of the work, the Companions were enjoying their time. A convert who was one of the people of the bench (*Ahl-e-Suffa*) and who lived in the Mosque was a pious man, but his looks were not very pleasing, and therefore, his parents named him Juayl (meaning a little beetle). The Holy Prophet (May God bless and cherish him) changed his name to Amr, meaning life and spiritual well-being. The Companions were singing a couplet to him,

"His name he changed, Juayl to Amr,

Today, he is the only supporter of the weak."

Slowly, the Companions made a song of it, and the Holy Prophet (May God bless and cherish him) joined in by repeating "Amr and help."

The digging continued, and as they dug deeper, Jabir was the first one to encounter a big rock that he could not loosen or break. The Holy Prophet was informed. He called for some water and spat into it, then prayed on it and sprinkled the water over the rock, and they were able to shovel it out like a heap of sand. (Ibn Hisham)

The next day, Salman and Hazrat Umar came upon a gigantic rock, and even though they were pounding on it with all their might and all the tools they were using broke, the rock stayed as it was. Hazrat Umar went to the Holy Prophet (May God bless and cherish him) and informed him. The Holy Prophet (May God bless and cherish him) came to the scene. The Companions noticed that he had tied a stone to his belly to suppress his hunger. He had not eaten a morsel of food for days. He first asked for a bowl of water and spat into it and poured it over the rock. The Holy Prophet prayed for Allah's help. Salman picked up his hammer, said *Bismiallah* and pounced upon the rock. With the first blow, a third of the rock broke away, and there was a flare of lightning that flashed back over the city and towards the south (from the direction of the Yemen). People were watching in amazement without a sound. Salman gave it another blow, and a third of the rock broke away this time, and again there was a flash but in the direction of Uhud and beyond towards the north. A third blow split the rock into fragments, and this time, the lightning flashed eastwards.

Salman saw the three flashes and knew that they must have some significance, so he asked the Holy Prophet (May God bless and cherish him) about it. The Holy Prophet (May God bless and cherish him) asked, "Did you see them, Salman?" By the light of the first, I saw the castles of Yemen and the doors of San'a, and God has opened unto me the Yemen. By the light of the second, I saw the castles of Syria, and the keys of Syria has been given to me. By the light of the third flash, I saw the white palace of the Kisra at Madain, and God opened the Persia for me. Angel Gabriel gives me the news that my Ummah will conquer these lands and so rejoice today for the good news of victory tomorrow." (Waqidi). Then the Holy Prophet (May God bless and cherish him) turned towards Salman and described to him the minutest details of the appearance of the palaces of Kisra. Salman was astonished to hear all the details. He said, "Yes, O Messenger of Allah, you spoke the truth; they are just as you described it. I bear witness, once again that you are the Messenger of

Allah."

The Holy Prophet (May God bless and cherish him) then shared another good news with Salman. He said, "These are the victories that Allah will make possible after I am gone. O Salman! Damascus will certainly be conquered, and Heraclius will escape to the end of his kingdom. You will be faced with no force as you seize Damascus. And the east will be conquered, too. The Kisra will be killed, and there will never be a Kisra again."

Most of the Companions were poor and normally did not have enough food to eat. The hard work of digging increased their hunger pangs. Jabir ibn Abdullah noted that the Holy Prophet (May God bless and cherish him) was exceedingly lean on that day. He asked his wife to cook him a meal. She said, "We have this lamb only and a small amount of barley. At the end of the day, when it was getting dark, Jabir went to the Holy Prophet (May God bless and cherish him) as he was leaving and invited him to the meal of mutton and barley bread. "The Holy Prophet (May God bless and cherish him) took my hand in his hands," said Jabir, and "Knotted his fingers through my fingers. I wanted to host him alone, but he asked a crier to call out, "Go with the Messenger of Allah unto the house of Jabir. Respond for Jabir is inviting you." Jabir uttered, '*Inna lillahi wa inna alihi rajiun*' and hurried to inform his wife. She asked him, "Did you invite them, or he did?" "Nay, he invited them," Jabir replied. "Then let them come," she said, "For he knows best."

The meal was presented to the holy Prophet (May God bless and cherish him), and he blessed it, uttered the name of Allah over it and began to eat. There were ten Companions sitting down with him, and when they had all eaten their fill, they rose and went to their homes, making room for the ten more. And so, it went on until all the diggers at the trench had satisfied their hunger, and still there remained some mutton and some bread. (Ibn Ishaq; Waqidi).

One day, while the Companions were busy digging the trench, a small girl entered the camp. She was carrying something in her hand and wanted to give it to her father and uncle. It was the niece of Abdullah ibn Rawahah. The Holy Prophet (May God bless and cherish him) saw the girl and called her. She told him that she was carrying some dates that she had brought for her father and uncle to eat. The Holy Prophet (May God bless and cherish him) asked her to give them to him, and she poured them into his hands. The dates did not fill his hands. The Holy Prophet asked for a garment to be spread on the ground and threw the dates in such a way that they were scattered over it. Then he invited the diggers for lunch. They came one by one and began to eat the dates. The dates increased in number and were overflowing from the edges of the garment, and all men were satisfied. (Ibn Hisham)

THE SIEGE

The Holy Prophet (May God bless and cherish him) left Abdullah ibn Umm Makhtum as deputy in Medina. The women and children were housed in secure places of the city and barriers were placed around them against possible danger. The Muslim army was comprised of three thousand strong men. Zayd ibn Haritha was carrying the standard of the Emigrants, while Sa'd ibn Ubada was carrying that of the Helpers. The slogan of the trench was "*Ha Min la Yunsarun,*" which meant, "They will never be helped." The army was positioned at the foot of Mount Sal with the trench in front of them and waited for the Makkan forces to arrive. Soon, the ten thousand Makkan army landed around Medina. It was as if the earth and heavens were filled with soldiers. The scene was quite impressive.

The Makkan army was sure of its strength and numbers. They had planned to enter from one end of Medina with ten thousand fighters and then come out the other side, having exterminated all the Muslims, including the Messenger of Allah. Their goal was to occupy and conquer Medina and not leave anything standing. They were shocked when they were confronted with the trench. What was this? It was something they had not seen before. They looked at each other dumbfounded and said, "This is a trick that the Arabs have not played before." One of them said, "There is a Persian among his Companions, this must have been his idea." They first thought that the trench may only be in front of them. So, they went left and right to see where it ended. But they were disappointed to see that all entry places into Medina had been blocked by the trench.

Abu Sufyan was commanding the army, Khalid ibn Walid and Ikrima ibn Abu Jahl were once again in command of the cavalry. Amr ibn Abdiwud was in Khalid's troops. Between the two armies, a broad trench lay, and the archers were lined up on both sides all the way. The enemy horses were unable to jump across the trench, and when they came closer, showers of arrows warned them that they were within the range of the Muslim fighters. Therefore, they drew back.

They spent the entire day in consultation and realized that if they could engage the Muslims on two fronts, they might be able to cross the trench. Their attention was focused on Bani Qurayzah, whose fortresses blocked the southeast entry to Medina. Huyay of Bani Nadir had come from Khaybar to join the army, and he offered his services to go to Bani Qurayzah and persuade them to break their alliance with the Holy Prophet (May God bless and cherish him). If they agreed, then Medina could be attacked from two sides at the same time.

Huyay ibn Akhtab went and knocked at the door of Ka'b ibn Asad, the leader of Bani Qurayzah, which was the last remaining Jewish community in Medina. When he heard the voice of Huyay, he did not open the door. He was afraid of Huyay and considered him as the bearer of misfortune, someone who had brought a disaster upon his own people who would do the same for them if allowed to have his way. "Woe unto you, O Ka'b, open the door!" he said and continued knocking. "I have signed a treaty with Muhammad and given him my word, and I won't break it. I have seen nothing but loyalty from him." "Confound thee, O Ka'b, and let me in," said Huyay. However, Ka'b still did not open the door. Finally, Huyay accused him of not letting him in simply because he did not want to share his food with him. This angered Ka'b, and he opened the gate. Huyay started his work and said, "I have brought you a lasting glory and an army like a surging sea. I have brought you three forces, the Quraysh and Kinanah and Ghatafan, with ten thousand men and a cavalry of one thousand strong. They have all given their word to me that they will not leave this place until they have wiped out Muhammad and his friends."

Although these words were to Ka'b's liking, he was not sure of the outcome of such actions. He had heard similar words before, but it had always been the Holy Prophet (May God bless and cherish him) who was victorious at the end. So, he said, "You have always brought me shame that will only end in a disaster. You are like a cloud without water, all thunder and lightning, and nothing else."

Finally, Huyay swore to God, "If Quraysh and Ghatafan return to their territories and have not eliminated Muhammad, I will enter with thee into the fortress, and my fate will be as thine." This convinced Ka'b that there could be no possibility of survival for Islam, and therefore he broke his covenant with the Holy Prophet (May God bless and cherish him) and openly declared it invalid. Ka'b then went to his tribesmen to inform them of this decision. They were skeptical and opposed this initiative at first. Ibn al-Hayyaban was an old scholarly Jew from Syria who had come to live with Bani Qurayzah in the hope of meeting the coming prophet. Many of them felt that Muhammad was indeed the promised one, but some could not accept a prophet who was not a Jew. Their opinion began to change when they saw the land beyond the trench surging with men and horses as far as the eyes could see.

Instantly, people in Medina were talking about how Ka'b had now declared himself to be an enemy of the Holy Prophet (May God bless and cherish him). Hazrat Umar was the first Companion to hear that the Jews were now against the Muslims. He went to the Holy Prophet, who was sitting with Hazrat Abu Bakr. "O Messenger of Allah," he said, "I have heard that Bani Qurayzah have broken their pact and are at war with us." The Holy Prophet (May God bless and cherish him) was troubled to hear that news. He sent Zubayr to find out the truth. He also called Sa'd of Aws and Khazraj along with Usayd and told them about the new development and said, "Go and see if this is true. If it is false, then say it plainly, but if it is true then tell me in a way that I can understand." When they reached the fortress of Bani Qurayzah, they became aware that, indeed, they had renounced the treaty. They tried to convince them to revert to the pact before it was too late. They answered mockingly, "Who is the Messenger of God? There is no pact between us and Muhammad." Ka'b and other Jews were so confident of the victory of Quraysh that they did not listen to them at all. When they returned to the presence of the Holy Prophet (May God bless and cherish him), they said, "Adal and Qarah." These were the two tribes who had betrayed Khubayb and his friends and were killed by Hudhayl. The Holy Prophet (May God bless and cherish him) understood and glorified God by saying "Allah-o-Akbar!" Be of good cheer, O Muslims."

There were some righteous people among the Bani Qurayzah. On that day, three brothers, Asad, Asid and Salaba, from the sons of Sane, came to the presence of the Holy Prophet (May God bless and cherish him). They told him that they were not following the decisions of Ka'b ibn Asad and that they had accepted Islam.

Soon, the news of the treason spread among the believers, and they were genuinely worried, for their children and families were at risk from an attack that could come from the inside. Therefore, the Holy Prophet (May God bless and cherish him) sent back a hundred men to the town to look after the situation. At the trench, things were difficult to predict. On the one hand, the army of Ahzab was looking for a weak point and an opportunity to cross the trench. On the other hand, Bani Qurayzah was conspiring to attack the city. Then the warning came that Huyay was urging the Quraysh and Ghatafan to send by night each a thousand men to the fortresses of Bani Qurayzah so that they could attack the center of the city and take the women and children captives. The Holy Prophet sent Zayd ibn Haritha with a troop of three hundred horsemen to patrol the streets of Medina via a different route. These soldiers glorified God throughout the night, and it was as if the city was filled with a mighty force.

The trench was to be watched day and night, and similarly, the city of Medina was protected by constant patrol. Each man was working longer and harder, and the stress was intense. But only once did they succeed in crossing it.

While Ikrima was patrolling the trench, he suddenly realized that the narrowest section of the trench was poorly guarded. He succeeded in making his horse leap across the gap. He was followed by three other riders. By the time a fourth man had crossed, Hazrat Ali and his men reached the narrow section and made it once more uncrossable. In this way, the rest of the enemy riders were cut off. One of the men who crossed was Amr ibn Abdi Wud. Amr ibn Abdi Wud was a champion of the Quraysh and a legendary fighter. He was known in Arabia to be worth a thousand soldiers. They occupied an area near the hillock of Sal. Amr challenged the Muslim fighters to single combat. Hazrat Ali volunteered to go, but the Holy Prophet (May God bless and cherish him) told him not to, as Amr was famous for being the most skilled warrior and as powerful as a thousand men. Amr's first challenge went unanswered, whereupon he repeated it. Such was the prestige of his name that no one in the Muslim camp dared to meet him in a trial of strength. Hazrat Ali again offered himself, but the Holy Prophet (May God bless and cherish him) told him to stay. Amr ibn Abdi Wud threw his insolent challenge a third time and taunted Muslims at the same time for their cowardice. He even expressed amazement that Muslims were not showing any eagerness to enter Paradise, where he was ready to send them. When Amr hurled his third challenge and no one answered him, Hazrat Ali rose and solicited the Holy Prophet's (May God bless and cherish him) permission to go out and fight him. Hazrat Ali put on the battle dress of the Holy Prophet (May God bless and cherish him). The latter gave him the Dhu l-Fiqar and prayed for his victory, saying, "O God! Thou hast called to Thy service Obaida ibn Harith on the day the battle of Badr was fought, and Hamzah ibn Abdul-Muttalib on the day the Battle of Uhud was fought. Now Ali alone is left with me. Be his protector, give him victory, and bring him safely to me."

When the Holy Prophet (May God bless and cherish him) saw Hazrat Ali going towards his adversary, he said, "He is the embodiment of all faith who is going to an encounter with the embodiment of all unbelief."

Hazrat Ali was ready for the combat, went forward, and said, "O Amr, it is believed that if any man of the Quraysh offers you two proposals, you always accept at least one of them." He said, "Yes." Hazrat Ali said, "I call you to Allah and to His Messenger and to Islam." Amr ibn Abdi Wud said, "I have no need of that." Hazrat Ali said, "Then, I call you to a duel with me." He said, "Wow, O son of my brother? I do not want to kill you. Your father was a boon companion of mine. Therefore, go back you are just a boy." At this Hazrat Ali replied, "By Allah, I want to fight and kill you." Amr became enraged at this, so he dismounted his horse and charged at Hazrat Ali. The fight started and lasted for quite a while. Mostly, Amr violently attacked Hazrat Ali, while Hazrat Ali briskly evaded him. A cloud of dust rose and hid both the fighters from sight. At one-point, Hazrat Ali overpowered him and gave him a chance, reminding him that victory and defeat depended on the will of God, and if he chose to change his ways then he would be saved in this world and the hereafter. However, Amr was determined to die by the sword.

Amr launched one last attack that shattered the shield of Hazrat Ali and inflicted a shallow wound to his head, but before he could raise his sword again, Hazrat Ali's sword, Dhu l-Fiqar, flashed in the sunlight, landing the final blow and with that he was killed. It is said that Hazrat Ali's blow cleft the most formidable warrior of Arabia into two. When people heard Hazrat Ali's voice raised in magnification, they knew that Amr was dead.

Later, when Amr's sister came to his dead body to mourn his death, she was surprised to see that his weapons and armor were intact. When she was told that it was Ali ibn Talib who had killed him, she composed some verses praising him (Hazrat Ali). (These verses have been quoted by the Egyptian historian Abbas Mahmood Al-Akkad in his book Al-Abqariyyat Imam Ali—The Genius of Imam Ali). The verses said,

"If someone other than Ali had killed Amr, I would have mourned his death all my life. But the man who killed him is a hero, and he is peerless. His father was also a lord."

In the meantime, Ikrima and his fellow horsemen took advantage of the distraction and crossed over to the other side. But Nawfal of Makhzum failed to jump the gap, and his horse fell with him into the trench. They began to stone him, but he called out, "O Arabs, death is better than this." So, they went down and finished him.

The next day, the Quraysh made multiple attempts to cross the trench, even before sunrise. The Holy Prophet (May God bless and cherish him) reassured the believers and promised them victory if they remained steadfast. The actual fighting was limited only to the exchange of arrows. Nor was anyone killed on either side. Sa'd ibn Muadh was struck in the arm by an arrow that severed a vein, and many of the horses of Quraysh and Ghatafan were wounded.

The time for the noon prayer came, but the Muslim fighters were so wary that none could pray. When time was running out, those near the Holy Prophet (May God bless and cherish him) said, "O Messenger of Allah, we have not prayed." At this, he replied, "Nor I, by God, I have not prayed." The time for the afternoon prayer came and went, marked by the setting of the sun, but the enemy kept on attacking, and it was only after dark that they moved back to their camps. The Holy Prophet (May God bless and cherish him) left the trench and left Usayd to guard it with a group of men. He then led the remainder of the four prayers that were now due. Khalid ibn Walid returned late at night in the hope of crossing the trench, but Usayd kept him at bay.

The Holy Prophet (May God bless and cherish him) was aware of the gravity of situation and he knew that his Companions were under great hardship and their endurance was near the end. Therefore, he negotiated a pact with the two chiefs of Ghatafan, offering them a third of the date harvest of Medina if they would withdraw from the battlefield. They sent back a word, "Give us half of the dates of Medina." But the Holy Prophet (May God bless and cherish him) refused to increase his offer of a third, and they agreed to it. He sent for Hazrat Uthman and told him to draw up a peace treaty between the Muslims and the clans of Ghatafan. Then he sent for the two Sa'd, and they came to his tent, the chief of Aws, with his wounded arm, and he told them of his plan. They said, "O Messenger of Allah! If this is an order that came from heaven, then do it. On our part, we listen and obey you. But if this is something that can go either way, we have nothing but the sword to give them." The Holy Prophet (May God bless and cherish him) replied, "I see that the Arabs have allied themselves against you; they have attacked you from all sides; under such circumstances, I hope that splitting their power for a while will be in our favor." Sa'd ibn Muadh stood up and said, "O Messenger of Allah! Before Islam, we used to call to gods other than Allah, and we worshiped idols. Even in those days, they had no hope of getting dates from Medina except through buying or through our hospitality. Now that Allah has honored us with Islam, and we have found the right path, and you have honored us with your presence, we would not part with our property because they tell us so. We do not need such an agreement! I swear that till Allah has decided among us, we will not give them anything but the sword." And this was the end of the affair.

LOGISTIC SUPPORT FROM BANI QURAYZAH

Bani Qurayzah was providing logistical support to the Makkan army on the other side of the trench. The supplies of the polytheists army were rapidly depleted. Hence, Abu Sufyan asked Huyay, "Fodder for our horses has finished, do you have any to give us?" "Yes, we do," he said, and he left and went to Bani Qurayzah to see to the needs of the Quraysh. The Quraysh sent twenty camels, and Bani Qurayzah loaded them with provisions for the Makkans. At the same time, twenty people from the sons of Amr ibn Awf had left the trench to observe burial rituals for some of their relatives who had died. They were making their way back to Medina when they came to the valley of Aqiq, and they came across the camels that were carrying the provisions for Makkans. They had an encounter with them and were able to seize the provisions. They brought the camels to the Holy Prophet (May God bless and cherish him) and told him what had happened. This resulted in a great celebration at the trench.

ATTACK ON WOMEN

A group of Bani Qurayzah took advantage of the absence of the Holy Prophet (May God bless and cherish him) from Medina and started to shoot arrows into the compound where his family and aunts were staying. This cowardly act of attacking unprotected and innocent women and children was to create panic among the Muslims. One of the Jews had come all the way to enter the compound. Hazrat Saffiyah saw him and called out to Hassan ibn Thabit, an old Companion to confront him. Hassan was very old and weak and did not have the strength to fight the enemy. So, he said, "May the Lord have mercy on you, O daughter of Abdul Muttalib. You know well that I am not the man for this job; had I been able, I would have gone with the Holy Prophet (May God bless and cherish him) and fought against the enemy." Hazrat Saffiyah put on her garments, grabbed a sword, and went to where the man was. The Jew who was trying to enter the compound was confronted by her. She raised her sword and finished him with one blow to his head. Then she called to Hassan, "O Hassan, come down and take out the possessions of the man." He replied, "I do not need his possessions, O daughter of Abdul Muttalib." When other intruders saw that their companion was killed, they ran away. When the Holy Prophet (May God bless and cherish him) received the news that his aunt Hazrat Saffiyah had killed the man who attacked their compound, he allocated a portion of the spoils of war to her and considered her one of the warriors. (Abu Yahya, Musnad; Haysami, Majmu Zawaid)

Nuaym ibn Masud was the man whom Abu Sufyan and Suhayl had bribed to intimidate, if he could, the Muslims from keeping their promise to meet the Quraysh at the second Badr. He was a clever man and able to manipulate people and provoke conflicts between them. He was a friend of Bani Qurayzah, and he had come all the way to fight the Holy Prophet (May God bless and cherish him). With every passing day, however, he was feeling greater unease inside and asking himself whether what he was doing was right. After a while, famine spread and caused death among men and the animals on the other side of the trench. His admiration for the men of the new religion increased because of their resolve and resistance against an army of more than three times their strength. Then came the time when he himself said, "I accepted Islam in my heart." That night he made his way to the city and went to the camp to see the Holy Prophet (May God bless and cherish him). "What has brought you here, Nuaym?" asked the Holy Prophet (May God bless and cherish him). He answered, "I have come to declare my belief in your word and testify that you have brought the truth. So bid me do what you will, O Messenger of Allah. You must command me, and I will fulfill your behest. My people and others know not of my Islam."

The Holy Prophet (May God bless and cherish him) replied, "You are one of us now; try to keep the enemy away from us as much as you can, and do not forget that war is a deception." "Then I will do so, "said Nuaym, "But O Messenger of Allah! I might have to say certain things that I don't mean; will you give me permission to do so?" His intention was sincere, and they were at war; under such circumstances, the power of word was sometimes more powerful than the sword, that is why the Holy Prophet (May God bless and cherish him) gave him the permission he was seeking.

Nuaym then went to see Bani Qurayzah, who welcomed him as an old ally. He told them, "I came here to warn you of my fears for your safety and to give you, my advice." Then he continued that if the Quraysh and Ghatafan failed in their mission to defeat the Muslims, they would return home and leave the Jews at the mercy of Muhammad and his followers. Therefore, you should not fight Muslims for the Quraysh until they have given leading men as hostages to guarantee that they would not withdraw until the enemy had been finished. His advice was greatly appreciated by Bani Qurayzah, who had the same concerns.

After this, he went to his old friend Abu Sufyan and told him and the other chiefs of Quraysh who were present that he had a serious piece of information to tell them on the condition that they would swear not to tell anyone that he was the informer. "You know very well that Bani Qurayzah regret that they have violated the agreement they had with Muhammad, and they wish to renew the treaty and return to the way things were before! They sent an envoy to him while I was with them. The message they sent was, "We will give you seventy-two men from the leaders of Quraysh and Ghatafan so that you can cut off their heads but in return you will let Bani Nadir, our brothers to go back to their lands. If you do this, we will fight along with you against those that are left. Muhammad has agreed, so if the Jews ask you for some of your men as hostages, give them none of yours." Then he went to his own people of Ghatafan and said, "O people of Ghatafan, you know I am one of you, but let this stay only between us! You must know that Bani Qurayzah has sent men to Muhammad," and repeated what he had told Abu Sufyan. He warned them, "Do not give your men to them."

Nuaym had played his role perfectly, and all three groups had taken what he said seriously. The leaders of the two invading armies decided to say nothing to Huyay, but to know the truth of the matter, they sent Ikrimah to Bani Qurayzah with the following message: "Make yourself ready to fight tomorrow so that once and for all we may rid ourselves of Muhammad." They replied, "Tomorrow is Sabbath, but in any case, we won't fight with you against Muhammad unless you give us some of your men who shall be for us as a security until we have made an end of him. For we fear that if you lose the war or sustain some damage, you will go back to your homelands and leave us here unprotected in the hands of Muhammad."

When this message reached the Quraysh, "By God, what Nuaym said was indeed the truth," they said. And they sent back a message to Bani Qurayzah that they would not give them a single man. The Quraysh insisted that they should fight, to which they said they would not strike a blow until they had received hostages.

Abu Sufyan then went to Huyay and said, "Where is the help that you promised us from your people? They have deserted us, and now they seek to betray us." "By Torah, nay!" said Huyay. "The Sabbath is here, and we cannot break the Sabbath. But on Sunday, they will fight against Muhammad and his Companions." It was only then that Abu Sufyan told him about the demand for hostages. Huyay was shocked to hear that. Abu Sufyan accused the Jews of treachery, and he left for the fortress of Bani Qurayzah.

The relations between the Quraysh and the tribes of Najd were also very fragile. Nearly two weeks had passed, and nothing had been achieved. The provisions of both armies were running out. More and more of their horses were dying every day of hunger and arrow wounds, and some camels had also died. They had participated in this mission in the hope of plundering, by which they were lured to come. Now, those hopes proved totally impossible. There was widespread discontent and distrust, and the entire expedition seemed to be failing already. And now the final blow was dealt upon them by the Lord of the universe.

THE WIND

God's help made itself felt once again. The Holy Prophet (May God bless and cherish him) had been supplicating his Lord for three days now. "O Lord! Revealer of the Book, Swift caller to account, turn the confederates to flight, turn them to flight and cause them to quake." The Holy Prophet (May God bless and cherish him) saw Gabriel, and turning to his Companions, he repeated three times, "Take care, rejoice at the news that comes from Allah."

Hardly had he finished his words and there was total chaos in the enemy's ranks. The weather had been exceptionally cold and wet for days, and now a fierce wind blew from the east with torrents of rain that forced every man to run for shelter. Tents were flying in the air; one could hardly see anything. The confederate army was already divisive and close to inner conflict. Now, they were faced with an unprecedented storm that hit their side of the trench. Their cauldrons were overturned, their fire had gone out, and their camp was destroyed. The night fell, and it was pitch dark. The Quraysh were shivering from cold, and men were huddled together for warmth.

The Muslims were somewhat protected from the wind, and none of their tents were blown over. But it was bitterly cold. The Holy Prophet (May God bless and cherish him) went to the men who were close to his tent. He asked, "Is there no one among you who will bring me news of this army?" Then he said that the person to do so would be his neighbor in Paradise. Upon this, Hazrat Abu Baker came forward, and pointing to Abu Hudayfah, he suggested: "How about if you send Abu Hudayfah?" The Holy Prophet (May God bless and cherish him) addressed Hudayfah and said, "Get up and bring us the news of these men who seem to be running this way and that way." Hudayfah was embarrassed and did not stand because a strong wind had blown his clothes, and he was wearing a dress that belonged to his wife and it only covered him down to his knees. (Hakim, Mustadrak; Bazzar, Musnad)

The Holy Prophet (May God bless and cherish him) told him: "Neither cold nor heat will touch you until you have come back to us." Hudayfah did not fear falling martyr, but he did fear falling captive. The Holy Prophet (May God bless and cherish him) reassured him: "You will not be taken prisoner either." And the Messenger of Allah prayed for him; "O Lord! Protect him from dangers that may come from behind, right, left, above and below." As Hudayfah was leaving for his mission, the Holy Prophet called him and said, "Do not do anything to them until you have returned."

Hudayfah crossed to the other side of the trench and entered the crowd that was near the fire that had been lit in the middle. A hefty man who seemed to be their commander was sitting near the fire. They were all numbed by the cold. The commotion from where Hudayfah was alerted Abu Sufyan. He was worried that a spy might have entered their ranks. Therefore, he said to those near him, "Let everyone hold the hand of the person next to him and look him in the face." This was a clever move by Abu Sufyan. So, Hudayfah held the hands of the men to his right and left and then asked the man on his right, "Who are you?" "Muawiya Ibn Abu Sufyan." Then he turned to the man on his left and asked him who he was; "Amr Ibn al-As," the man answered. In this way, he averted the danger of being caught by the enemy.

They spent the night, and then near the dawn when the strong winds began to abate, Abu Sufyan shouted in a loud voice, "O people of Quraysh, our horses and camels are dying, Bani Qurayzah have betrayed us, and now we have suffered from the wind that you see. therefore, prepare to leave, for I am going myself." After saying these words, he went to his camel and mounted it. He was in such a hurry that he forgot to untie his animal. But Ikrimah rebuked him, "You are the commander of these people, will you run so hastily, and leave the men behind?" Abu Sufyan was embarrassed, and he dismounted his camel. The polytheist army broke camp and moved on, and he waited until the army was on its way to Makkah. He also agreed with Khalid Ibn Walid and Amr that they should cover the rear with a detachment of two hundred horses.

As soon as Hudayfah saw that the Makkah forces were returning, he made his way to the camp of Ghatafan, but found the place completely deserted, for the wind had broken their resistance. Therefore, Hudayfah returned to the Holy Prophet (May God bless and cherish him). On his way back, he came upon a group of about twenty horsemen; they said to him, "Tell your friends, Allah the Exalted overpowered that multitude with the wind and armies." These were men he did not recognize. When he came to the presence of the Holy Prophet (May God bless and cherish him), he was standing in prayer wrapped in a shawl belonging to one of his wives due to bitter cold. "When he saw me," said Hudafah, "He motioned me to sit beside him at his feet and threw the end of the shawl over me. Then with me still under the shawl, he made the bowing and the prostration. When he finished prayer, I told him the news."

Now that the confederates had retreated, there was no reason to stay at the trench. That is why the Holy Prophet (May God bless and cherish him) gave orders that every man had permission to return home, whereupon most of them set off at speed for the town. The next morning, there was not a single enemy fighter left on the other side of the trench. The Holy Prophet praised and thanked God; "He is one, there is no deity beside Him. He has made His fighters victorious, and He has responded to His slave with His help. He has defeated his enemies, and He has wiped out confederates. There will be no such thing after this. From now on, it will not be them who come to fight us, we will be the determining force in the battle."

As the Holy Prophet was leaving the trench, Abu Sufyan had left the following letter for him with Abu Usama al-Jushami, "I write this letter by taking oath in the name of Lat and Uzza and in the name of Allah! I marched upon Medina with a great army; I had come here to wipe you off the face of the earth so that I may not have to face you again! I see that you do not want to face us, you seek refuge behind the trench. But there will surely be a day between you and me, a day like Uhud."

Ubayy Ibn Ka'b read the letter to the Holy Prophet (May God bless and cherish him), and he dictated the following response.

"Your message reached me. You still trust in your numbers, and you are still a slave to your pride. You had no other plan than to come straight at us and finish us.

But this is something that will be decided only by Allah, and Allah, the Mighty and Majestic has given us victory. Do not forget that Allah will show you the day when I shall topple and destroy Lat, Uzza, Isaf, Naila, and Hubbal! I warn you of that day now, O you bonehead of the tribe of Bani Ghalib."

THE BANI QURAYZAH

The Holy Prophet (May God bless and cherish him) had returned to Medina with his Companions to rest and had just retired to the room of Hazrat Aisha. He asked for some water, and washed his hands, face, and head and went to the Mosque where he prayed the noon prayer in congregation. He then returned to his humble dwelling. He saw a man who was splendidly dressed in a turban and a cloth of brocaded velvet thrown over the saddle of the mule he was riding. When the Holy Prophet (May God bless and cherish him) saw him, he hurried to see that man. Hazrat Aisha was surprised to see the Holy Prophet in such a hurry. She also wanted to know who was at the door. The Holy Prophet (May God bless and cherish him) was well pleased because it was none other than the Angel Gabriel who had come in the form of Dihyah al-Kalbi.

"O Messenger of Allah! You have laid down your arms too soon. We, the angels, have not put our weapons aside since the enemy came here! We pursued them till Himrau l-Asad and left them only when we were sure that they could inflict no harm. Verily, God in His might and His majesty commands you, O Muhammad, that you should go against the sons of Qurayzah. I am going to them even now that I may cause their souls to quake." (Ibn Ishaq)

When the Holy Prophet (May God bless and cherish him) returned to his room, Hazrat Aisha was still at the door and asked him, "Who was it that you spoke to?". "Did you see him?" asked the Holy Prophet (May God bless and cherish him). "Yes, I did," replied Hazrat Aisha. "Who did you think he resembled?" "Dihyah Ibn Khalifa al-Kalbi," she replied. "That was Gabriel! He was telling me to advance upon the Bani Qurayzah."

The Holy Prophet (May God bless and cherish him) gave orders that none should pray the afternoon prayer until he had reached the land of Bani Qurayzah. The standard that had not been rolled up after the trench was given to Hazrat Ali. He put on his armor and mounted his horse (named Luhayf because of the length of its tail) along with the three thousand men and marched out.

The siege had started that day, and by the evening Sa'd ibn Ubada sent the believers baskets full of dates. At this, the Holy Prophet (May God bless and cherish him) said, "What wonderful food is the date," thus appreciating the charity of those who helped his Companions.

The next day, the Holy Prophet (May God bless and cherish him) assigned archers to specific locations, and they engaged in exchange of arrows with the enemy. Days went by, and Bani Qurayzah felt somewhat secure as they had enough supplies and did not want to surrender. But after a while, their hopes started to dwindle, and they became very desperate. Even if they continued to resist, there was not much they could do. Therefore, they made a request to negotiate, and the Holy Prophet (May God bless and cherish him) agreed.

Nabbash Ibn Says came out of the fortress and went to the Holy Prophet (May God bless and cherish him) and said, "Give us the chance to leave with our property and our families as you let the Bani Nadir leave. We will take whatever our camels can carry except for the weapons." Their proposal was not accepted. So, Nabbash immediately came up with another offer. "Then do not touch our lives, leave our women and children to us, and let us go without taking any of our possessions." Obviously, they were not able to dictate their terms, and conditions, and it was rejected.

Nabbash returned to the fortress in desperation and told his people about the conversation he had with the Holy Prophet (May God bless and cherish him). Ka'b Ibn Asad then called out to his tribe; "O people of Bani Qurayzah! You can see now what is happening to us. I will now suggest three alternatives, and you are free to choose whichever you like?" "What are they?" they asked.

"We can follow this man and submit to him. I swear by Allah that it is already clear that he is a Messenger of God; he is the prophet whose attributes you read in your book. In this way you will have protected your lives, your possessions, and your women! I swear by Allah that you already knew that Muhammad is a prophet. The one thing that stops us from following is that he was not chosen from among the Bani Israel, but that Allah chose him from among a people He wanted. Your refusal is nothing but out of jealousy. I swear I was not against violating our agreement with him; all this trouble has been caused by this inauspicious man, Huyay Ibn Akhtab. (Inb Hisham, Sira: Tabari, Tarikh)

Do you remember what Ibn Jawwas said to you when he came here? He asked,

"Do you know why I left Damascus and came here? You had asked, 'Why?' And he answered. 'Verily, a prophet will come from this land, if he appears while I am still alive, then I will be his follower and helper. If he appears after me, do not stay indifferent to him; go to him and be his helper. Give him my greetings and tell him that I submit to him. Come, let us make our allegiance to him now."

They did not like what they heard. So Ka'b suggested his second alternative. "Well, since you did not accept my first option, let us kill our children and women and confront the Muslims till death. In doing so, we will have left nothing behind that will bother us. We will then fight him until Allah decides between us. If we all die, we will have died together and will have left no one that grieves for us. If we came out alive out of this, then we will find other women and start a new life."

Neither the first nor the second option was something they could accept. "How can we kill our children and women?" and "what meaning would life have without them?" they asked. Ka'b then shared his last suggestion, "Since you have not accepted my previous suggestions. You should listen to this one, at least. Tonight, is Saturday evening, and Muslims feel safe, let us attack them this evening." It looked like they were not open to any suggestion. Ka'b was at a loss: he did not know what to do.

The siege continued into the twenty-fifth day, and they requested the Holy Prophet (May God bless and cherish him) to send Abu Lubabah, so they could consult with him. They were long-term allies of Aws, and Abu Lubabah was an influential leader of that clan. The Holy Prophet gave permission. When Abu Lubabah entered their land, he confronted women and children, wailing and weeping. This scene softened his stance. Their leader, Ka'b ibn Asad, came forward and said, "O Abu Lubabah! We are glad to have you. Muhammad says we will have to submit to the judgement he passes on us, what do you say? Shall we accept his judgement?" "Yes," he said, but at the same time he pointed to his throat, which meant slaughter. His gesture was in contradiction with his assent, and it might have prolonged the siege till later. When he realized his mistake, he was overwhelmed with a sense of guilt. He regretted it and could hardly walk. As soon as he was aware that he had betrayed the Messenger of Allah, his face changed color, and he recited, "Verily, we are for God, and verily unto Him are we returning." Ka'b was looking at him and said, "What is bothering you?" "I have betrayed God and His Messenger," he said. With tears flowing from his eyes, he went through the back door, avoiding facing his friends who were waiting for him. He went straight to the Mosque and bound himself to one of the pillars, saying, "I will not move from this place until

God relents unto me for what I did." (Waqidi)

The news of Abu Lubabah spread among the believers, and it also reached the Holy Prophet (May God bless and cherish him). He said, "Leave him alone until Allah the Almighty passes His judgment on him. Had he come to me, I would have prayed to God to forgive him, what he has done, it is not for me to free him until God decrees." Gabriel descended and brought the following revelation,

"O you who believe! Do not betray Allah and His Messenger or betray the trusts while you know." (Quran 8:27)

He remained tied to the pillar for ten to fifteen days. His wife and daughter took turns coming to him and untying his ropes for a short time so that he may make ablution and pray. Then, after he had prayed, he would tell them to bind him once more.

One morning, when the Holy Prophet (May God bless and cherish him) was at the house of Umm Salamah, Gabriel brought the verses that spoke about the repentance of loyal people like Abu Lubabah. At this, the Holy Prophet (May God bless and cherish him) smiled. Umm Salamah, who saw him smiling asked for the reason for his smile. "The repentance of Abu Lubabah has been accepted," said the Holy Prophet (May God bless and cherish him).

THE JUDGEMENT OF SA'D IBN MUADH

The next day, despite Abu Lubabah's warning, the Bani Qurayzah opened the gates of their fortress and submitted to the Holy Prophet's (May God bless and cherish him) judgement. The men were led out with their hands bound behind their backs and were grouped together in a space near the trench. Muhammad Ibn Masalmah was leader of them. Abdullah Ibn Salam (who was a Jewish scholar and had accepted Islam) had been given the job of seeing to women and children.

When the Muslims entered the fortress, they saw what the Jews owned. They had one thousand five hundred swords, three hundred sets of armor, two thousand spears, one thousand five hundred shields, and much more weaponry. Too many jars and pots of wine were opened, and their contents poured away.

The clan of Aws, who had long been allies of Bani Qurayzah came to the Holy Prophet (May God bless and cherish him) and said, "O Messenger of Allah! These are our allies. We know the treatment you thought fit, for Ibn Ubay, who was the ally of Bani Qaynuqa, you pardoned seven hundred of their men and four hundred of their cavalries! Now, these are our allies, and they regret having broken their pact and forgive them for our sake this time."

The Holy Prophet (May God bless and cherish him) kept silent. The entire clan of Aws had come together, and they wanted the Bani Qurayzah to receive the same treatment as those before them. The Holy Prophet (May God bless and cherish him) turned to them and said, "Will it satisfy you, men of Aws, if one of you pronounce the judgement upon them." And they all agreed.

The Holy Prophet (May God bless and cherish him) chose Sa'd ibn Muadh who was the chief of Aws. The people of Aws went to Medina to get hold of Sa'd, who was being treated for a wound he had sustained in the trench near the Mosque. The Holy Prophet (May God bless and cherish him) had placed him there so that he could visit him more often. (Ibn Hisham). They mounted him on an ass and brought him to the camp. On the way, they requested him; "O Abu Amr! The Messenger of Allah has appointed you to pass judgement upon Bani Qurayzah. So be kind to them, you know how Ibn Ubayy acted concerning his own allies. Please treat them with compassion." Sa'd was an upright person and man of justice. Like Hazrat Umar he had been against sparing the prisoners at Badr, and their opinion had been confirmed by the revelation. Many polytheists who had been ransomed on that occasion had come out against them at Uhud and at the trench. In this recent campaign, the strength of the invaders had been largely due to the conspiracy of the Jews of Bani Nadir. Moreover, Sa'd Ibn Muadh was himself one of the envoys to Bani Qurayzah and had seen the ugliness of their conspiracy.

Sa'd remained silent and determined, and he knew that if he gave a severe judgement, the people of Aws would blame him forever. Therefore, he said to them, "The time has come for Sa'd in the cause of Allah, to give no heed unto the blame of the blamers." Hearing these words, Dahhaq Ibn Khalifa said, "Woe unto that tribe," and he started to cry.

When Sa'd reached the place where the Holy Prophet (May God bless and cherish him) was stationed, the Holy Prophet (May God bless and cherish him) called to his companions and said, "Stand up and greet your master." All the Companions stood up in two rows and began to greet Sa'd ibn Muadh until he came beside the Messenger of Allah.

After he had rested for a while, the Holy prophet (May God bless and cherish him) told him, "Pass your judgement over them, O Sa'd." To which Sa'd replied, "The real authority to judge lies with Allah and his Messenger." The Holy Prophet (May God bless and cherish him) said to him, "Allah has ordered that you should pass judgement on them." The Aws surrounded Sa'd once again and said, "O Abu Amr, the Holy Prophet (May God bless and cherish him) has conferred upon you the job of passing judgement on your allies, be clement with them." Upon which he turned to them and said, "Do you then swear by God and make by Him your covenant that my judgement shall be the verdict upon them." "We do," they answered. "And is it binding upon them who are there?" He glanced in the direction of the Holy Prophet (May God bless and cherish him), but not mentioning his name out of respect. "It is so," said the Messenger of Allah.

Now was the time to pass judgement, and he started to say the following words slowly and clearly, "My judgement is that their men who reached puberty shall be slain, their women and children should be taken captive, their land should be distributed among the Muslims." The Holy Prophet said to him, "O Sa'd, you have judged with the judgement of Allah from above the seven heavens."

The women and children were taken away to the city where they were lodged, and the men spent the night in the camp, where they exhorted one another to be patient and firm. In the market of Medina, long and narrow trenches were dug. The men of Bani Qurayzah, about seven hundred in all were taken in small groups and every group was made to sit alongside the trench that was to be his grave. Then, the younger Companions cut off their heads, each with a strike of the sword.

When Huyay was brought into the market, he turned towards the Holy Prophet (May God bless and cherish him) and said, "I blame not myself for having opposed thee, but whoso have forsaken God, the same shall be forsaken." Then he told his fellow Jews, "The command of God cannot be wrong - a writ and a decree and a massacre that God hath set down in His Book against the sons of Israel." Then he sat down beside his grave, and he was beheaded.

The judgement passed by Sa'd ibn Muadh did not apply to all the Bani Qurayzah. There were young men such as Atiyyatu-i-Qurazi, Rifa'a ibn Shawwal, Amr ibn Suda, Ibn Saya's sons Salaba and Usayd and their cousin Asad ibn Ubayd. These men were forgiven.

Zabir ibn Bata had done a great favor for Thabit ibn Qays ibn Shammas during the times of the Buath wars. Though Zabir was a strong opponent of Islam, Thabit ibn Qays wanted to repay his favor. Therefore, he went to the Holy Prophet (May God bless and cherish him) and said, "I owe Zabir a favor from the day of Buath, he had held my hand and saved me! That is why I speak of this favor, and I ask you to release him for my sake." The Holy Prophet (May God bless and cherish him) replied, "He is yours." When Zabir was told of his reprieve, he said to Thabit, "And old man, without wife and without children, what will he do with life?" so Thabit went back to the Holy Prophet (May God bless and cherish him), who gave him Zabir's wife and children. But Zabir said, "A household in the Hijaz without property, how can they survive?" So Thabit went again to the presence of the Holy Prophet (May God bless and cherish him) and interceded for him, and the Messenger of Allah granted Zabir his possessions except his arms and armor.

Zabir asked about the fate of Ka'b ibn Asad, Bani Ka'b and Bani Amr, and he was told that they all were killed. Their deaths overwhelmed him, and he said, "By God, I ask you, Thabit, by the claim I have on thee, that you should join me with my people, for now that they are gone, there is no good in life." At first Thabit was surprised, but when he saw that Zabir really meant it, he took him to the execution place where he was beheaded. His wife and children were set free, and their property was returned to them under Thabit's guardianship.

RAYHANA BINT ZAYD

Women and children were divided, together with the property, amongst the men who had taken part in the siege. Many of these captives were ransomed by Bani Nadir of Khaybar. Rayhana bint Zayd ibn Amr was among the captives, and she had fallen to the lot of the Holy Prophet (May God bless and cherish him). The Holy Prophet (May God bless and cherish him) offered her Islam, but initially, she did not accept it. At first, he put her with her aunt Salma, in whose house Rifaah had already taken refuge. Later, Rifaah talked to her about Islam, and she entered Islam, which made the Holy Prophet (May God bless and cherish him) happy.

THE DEATH OF SA'D IBN MUADH

Sa'd ibn Muadh was a heavy-built and tall man. He was handsome and majestic in appearance. A month had passed since he had been wounded, but his wound never healed. After he had passed his judgment on Bani Qurayzah, he returned to his sick bed. He had prayed to Allah to let him live if he had to do any more fights against the enemies of God in the future. And if not, would he let him die? His condition worsened, and he became unconscious. The Holy Prophet (May God bless and cherish him) was at his bedside, he put his head on his blessed chest and prayed,

"O Lord, Sa'd had striven upon the Thy path and had full faith in Thy Messenger. He did all that he could do. When You take him to Your presence, please take his soul like the souls You have taken with ease."

Sa'd was listening to the Holy Prophet (May God bless and cherish him) and he opened his eyes, and said, "O Messenger of Allah, peace be upon you. I bear witness that you are the Messenger of Allah." After that, the Holy Prophet (May God bless and cherish him) returned home, and sometime later, Gabriel came and told him, "O Messenger of Allah! Who is the person for whom the skies have opened this evening and for whom the earth has quaked?"

Upon hearing this, the Holy Prophet (May God bless and cherish him) went to Sa'd's house along with his Companions. When they lifted his bier and took it to al-Baqi, the bearers were amazed at the lightness of his body, for Sa'd was a heavy man. When they told the Holy Prophet (May God bless and cherish him), he said, "I saw angels carrying him." It was as if the whole of Medina was present at the cemetery. When they lowered the body of Sa'd into the grave, the Messenger of Allah's face changed color and became pale, and he said three times, "*Subhanallah*" (Glory be to God). All the Companions repeated it and the cemetery resounded with glorification. Then, after some time, with tears in his eyes, the Holy Prophet (May God bless and cherish him) said, "Allah-o-Akbar" (God is most great), and the cemetery again resounded as the magnification was taken up by those who were present. When the Holy Prophet (May God bless and cherish him) was asked why he had changed color, he said, "The grave closed upon your Companion, and he felt a constriction, which if any man could escape it, Sa'd would have escaped. Then God gave him blissful relief." (Waqidi)

CHAPTER 19
UMRA EXPEDITION AND HUDAYBIA

It was already the sixth year of Hijra. The Holy Prophet (May God bless and cherish him) and the Emigrants were missing the land of the prophets, the sacred city which Hazrat Ibrahim had built. Their hearts were in Makkah, the direction they faced every time they performed prayer. Returning home was on everybody's mind. People who were tied to Makkah with birth ties were dreaming of the day they would go to the Kaaba once more.

The believers fasted in the month of Ramadan in Medina and stayed there with peace for another month. One night, the Holy Prophet (May God bless and cherish him) had a dream, and in it some of his Companions had shaved their heads, and some had their hair shortened and they were making rounds around the Kaaba in peace and safety. He had the keys of the Kaaba in his hand. The next morning, the Holy Prophet (May God bless and cherish him) shared his dream with his Companions. There was great joy and celebration in Medina and the Companions felt reassured that they would soon be going to Kaaba for pilgrimage. The Holy Prophet (May God bless and cherish him) invited his Companions to perform Umrah (the lesser pilgrimage).

In the meantime, Burs ibn Sufyan had come to Medina, and become a Muslim. When he wanted to return, the Holy Prophet (May God bless and cherish him) said to him, "O Burs! Do not make haste in returning! Maybe we will go all together! For we are planning to set off for Umrah." It was Monday in the month of Dhul-Qadah, the sixth year after Hijra. The Holy Prophet (May God bless and cherish him) went home and put on two layers of unstitched clothing, one girt around his waist to cover the lower part of the body and the other draped around the shoulders.

This time, he took Hazrat Umm Salamah on this journey. Ibn Umm Maktum was left in Medina as a deputy. The Holy Prophet (May God bless and cherish him) was accompanied by one thousand and four hundred Companions from the *Ansar* and *Muhajirin*. Two hundred of them were on horses with Sa'd ibn Zayd leading them. (Waqidi: Maghazi). Also among the pilgrims were two women of Khazraj who had been present at the second Aqabah, Nusaybah, and Umm Mani. Between them, they brought seventy camels to be sacrificed in the sacred precinct, with the intention of distributing their meat among the poor of Makkah.

The Holy Prophet (May God bless and cherish him) mounted his camel Qaswa and set off on his way. Each man took with him a sword and what might be needed. But Hazrat Umar and Sa'd ibn Ubadah came to the presence of the Holy Prophet (May God bless and cherish him) and suggested that they should go fully armed. They argued that Quraysh could not be trusted, and they might well take the opportunity of attacking them despite the sacred month. But the Holy Prophet (May God bless and cherish him) insisted, "I will not carry arms; I am going with the intention of pilgrimage."

When they reached Dul-Hulayfah, they prayed at noon. Then the Holy Prophet (May God bless and cherish him) called for the sacrificial camels, and he himself consecrated one of them, turning it to face Makkah, making a mark on its right flank, and placing a garland around its neck. Then, he called Najiya ibn Jundal to adorn the rest of the camels. He then sent ahead a man of Khazraj from the clan of Ka'b to bring him the news of the reaction of the Quraysh.

The Quraysh got the news of the departure of the pilgrims from Medina. They were faced with the dilemma, whether to stop the pilgrims from visiting the Holy Kaaba or violate the laws they respected. On the other hand, they could not allow the enemies to enter Makkah in peace and score a moral victory. They summoned an emergency meeting of the Assembly. It was decided unanimously not to let them in. "By God, this shall not happen," they said, "as long as there is a single person alive in Makkah."

The Quraysh immediately sent two hundred horsemen led by Khalid ibn Walid to the place called Kura al-Ghamim to stop the pilgrims. The Quraysh rallied the sons of Hun, the Bani Harith, the Bani Abdi Manaf, the Bani Mustaliq, and the tribes of Thaqif to join them in this fight. Busr ibn Sufyan, who was a new convert, was aware of all these activities. He came to the Holy Prophet (May God bless and cherish him) near Usfan and said, "O Messenger of Allah! The Quraysh heard about your coming, and they have taken their milk giving camels and families with them, and they are fully armed and are waiting at Dhi Tuwa. Khalid ibn Walid is stationed at a place called Kura al-Ghamim."

The Holy Prophet (May God bless and cherish him) listened to Busr intently. He then asked for a guide who could take them by another route. A man of Aslam led them towards the east and then by a difficult way until they reached the pass that led down to Hudaybiyah, an open tract of land below Makkah. In this way, they were safe from an attack by Khalid ibn Walid. However, at one point, they raised so much dust that he realized what had happened. So, he galloped back to Makkah to inform the Quraysh of their approach.

When they reached a certain point, the Holy Prophet (May God bless and cherish him) pointed to a hill far away and asked, "Can that be the hill of Dhat l-Hanzal?" Amr replied, "Yes, that is it, O Messenger of Allah." The Holy Prophet (May God bless and cherish him) said, "Whoever climbs the Hill of Mira, his sins will be forgiven, just as the sins of Bani Israel were forgiven." As soon as these words poured out of his blessed lips, everyone started to run towards the hill. The Holy Prophet (May God bless and cherish him) said, "Tonight this hill is like the door that Allah mentioned concerning Bani Israel. Go through the gate with your heads lowered and say, "Forgive, O Lord" so that your sins may be forgiven."

The pilgrims camped outside the boundaries of Haram, and for his noon prayers, the Holy Prophet (May God bless and cherish him) went a little further and entered the sanctuary area and performed his prayer there. Soon was the time for afternoon prayer, and the Holy Prophet (May God bless and cherish him) took a pail of water for his ablution. There was almost no water left for the Companions, and they were complaining of thirst. The Holy Prophet (May God bless and cherish him) told them to pour that water into a bowl, and then he placed his blessed fingers inside it and prayed. He then addressed his Companions, "There you have it, Bismillah." As the Companions watched in amazement, water was miraculously running from the fingers of the Holy Prophet (May God bless and cherish him). The Companions ran to get their waterskins. They drank from the water, made their ablution, and gave it to their animals as well. When Jabir, who was recounting the incident, was asked, "How many people were with you that day?" he said, "Had we have been one hundred thousand that water would have been sufficient." And he said that they were one thousand and five hundred. (Bukhari, Sahih: Ahmad ibn Hanbal, Musnad: Darimi, Sunan).

DIALOGUES AND DIPLOMACY

Budayl ibn Waraqa came with a delegation that consisted of people like Amr ibn Salim, Hirash ibn Umayya, Harija ibn Kunz, and Yazid ibn Umayya to the presence of the Holy Prophet (May God bless and cherish him). They were all from the tribe of Huzah. The Huzah tribe, though not Muslims were an ally of the Messenger of Allah, and they were there to help with the situation. Budayl started to speak, "We come from where the tribes of Ka'b ibn Luayy and Amir ibn Luayy are, and they have been joined by the tribes of Ahabish. They all are camped at the waters of Hudaybiyah and have sworn in the name of Allah that they will not let you reach the House of Allah even if it should cost the lives of their leaders."

The Holy Prophet (May God bless and cherish him) listened to him patiently and then said,

"We did not come to fight with anyone. We have undertaken this journey to perform our pilgrimage to the House of Allah. But we will fight whoever tries to stop us from reaching it. An armed conflict had always been detrimental to the Quraysh. If they want it, I can give them enough time to feel safe, and they should not interfere with our rituals. If those tribes they have provoked against me come victorious over me, then they will achieve what they had wanted. But if my cause wins over their tribes, they will be free to join others or Islam. They can get their swords and fight me and have their respite. But if they don't consider my proposal favorably, then I will do all I can till this head is severed from this body, and Allah, the Exalted will put His judgement to work."

After listening to the Holy Prophet (May God bless and cherish him), Budayl said, "I will convey all these you have said to the Quraysh." When the Quraysh saw them coming, they said Budayl and his friends are coming. He probably will try to get news from us. Do not ask anything?" The situation was very tense, and Budayl was aware of it. He said, "We are coming from where Muhammad is. Would you like us to give you, his news?" Ikrima ibn Abu Jahl and Hakam ibn As came forward and said angrily, "We do not need any news you may give us. But you can warn him that he cannot enter Makkah this year even if it should cost us the lives of all our men." At this, Urwa ibn Masud came forward and said, "We should listen to what Budayl has to say, and if you like it accept it, if not reject it." So, they turned to Budayl and said, "Speak then! What was it that you saw and heard." At last, Budayl got the opportunity to speak, "You are too hasty in your decision about Muhammad.

He has set off on the road not to fight but to perform his pilgrimage and pay respect to the Holy Sanctuary." Then Urwa spoke again, "Budayl has brought you a good offer that no man can refuse except for his own loss. But send me to bring confirmation directly from Muhammad, and I will keep an eye on those with him, and I will be your informer."

Quraysh accepted his proposal, but they already had sent as an envoy the man who commanded all their allies of the Bedouin tribes known as Ahabish. His name was Hulays of Bani l-Harith, one of the clans of Kinanah. It was he who had rebuked Abu Sufyan for the mutilations at Uhud. When the Holy Prophet (May God bless and cherish him) saw him approaching, he knew from his demeanor that he was a man of piety with a great reverence for sacred things. Therefore, he gave orders that the sacrificial animals should be sent to meet him, and when the seventy camels fled past Hulays with their marks of consecration and their festive ornaments, he was so impressed that he went back to the Quraysh without speaking to the Holy Prophet (May God bless and cherish him). He informed them that their intentions were entirely peaceful.

The Quraysh were exasperated and said that he was merely a man of desert and, and that he had no knowledge of the situation. This was a great mistake, and he said, "Men of Quraysh, not for this, by God, did we come to be your allies. Shall one who comes to honor the House of God be banned from it? By Him in whose hand is my soul, either you let Muhammad do what he has come to do, or I will lead away Ahabish, every one of them." "Be patient with us, Hulays," they requested, "until we reach terms that we can accept."

Meanwhile, Urwa ibn Masud of Thaqif arrived at the camp of Muslims and said to the Holy Prophet (May God bless and cherish him), "O Muhammad, I left Ka'b ibn Luayy and Amir ibn Luayy with their families and camels by the waters of Hudaybiyah. They are united against you. They swear they will not let you pass even if you crush them all. So, you must choose between two things. You will have to crush your own tribe, and no man before you have destroyed his own tribe. In that case the people around you will leave you and disapprove of you. I swear I do not see any honorable men with you. They are people you have gathered; God knows from where? I do not recognize their faces, and I know nothing of their lineage. If you should fight, they will disperse, and you will be taken as prisoner by the Quraysh. What could be worse than to be in such a situation."

All the Companions were angry, and Hazrat Abu Bakr, who was listening patiently could not contain himself and said, "You go on and lick the feet of Lat! How should we leave him and go?" The Companions were relieved when they heard Hazrat Abu Bakr say that. But Urwa was surprised and did not recognize who was speaking. So, he asked, "And who is it that speaks?" those around him said, "Abu Bakr." Urwa hesitated when he heard the name of Hazrat Abu Bakr. He remembered the help he had asked from Hazrat Abu Bakr at a time when he was having difficulty paying the blood money for a man he had killed. That day, when his closest friend helped him with two or three camels, Hazrat Abu Bakr gave him ten, and had saved him from great disaster. Urwa turned towards Hazrat Abu Bakr and said, "Had there not been this favor that I have not yet been able to pay back, I swear by Allah that I would have talked back at you."

Another thing that caught the attention of the Companions was that every time Urwa attempted to speak, he also tried to get hold of the beard of the Holy Prophet (May God bless and cherish him). Mughira ibn Sha'ba, who had become Muslim on the day of trench, noticed what Urwa was doing. He stood guard by the Holy Prophet (May God bless and cherish him) and hit Urwa's hand with the handle of his sword every time he tried to touch his beard and warned him, "Before this sword enters your guts, you should stop touching the beard of the Messenger of Allah. For the hand of a polytheist cannot touch him." Urwa refrained from any further attempts, but he stayed in the camp for several hours. He had promised the Quraysh to be their informer and was taking note of everything. But what impressed him most were things that he had never seen before. When he returned to the Quraysh he said, "O people of Quraysh! I have been sent as an envoy unto kings, unto Caesar, and Chosroes and Negus, and I have not seen a king whose men so honor him as the Companions of Muhammad honor Muhammad. If he gives a command, they almost outstrip his words in fulfilling it. When he performs his ablution, they well-nigh fight for the water thereof. When he speaks, their voices are hushed in his presence, nor will they look him in the face but lower down their eyes in reverence for him. He has offered you a good deal; therefore, accept it from him."

The negotiations were going on, and the Holy Prophet (May God bless and cherish him) sent Hirash ibn Umayya from among his Companion as an envoy and let him ride his camel, Salab. The purpose of his mission was to make it clear that his intention was not war and that he had come solely with the intention of pilgrimage. As soon as Hirash arrived, Ikrima ibn Abu Jahl drew his sword and slated the camel on the legs. He was so enraged that he almost killed Hirash. The tribe of Ahabish witnessed such an outburst of anger, intervened at once, and did not let him kill the envoy of the Messenger of Allah. They set Hirash free and let him return. "O Messenger of Allah," he said on arrival, "Send a man who is better protected than me." The Holy Prophet (May God bless and cherish him) called Hazrat Umar, to him but Hazrat Umar said that the Quraysh knew well of his great hostility to them, and that none of his own clan, the Bani Adi, were strong enough to protect him. "But I will show you," he continued, "a man who is more powerful in Makkah than me, richer in kinsmen and better protected – Uthman ibn Affan." So, the Holy Prophet (May God bless and cherish him) sent Uthman ibn Affan, and he was well received by his kinsmen of Abdu Shams and by others. But the Quraysh remained adamant to not allow the Muslims now in Hudaybiyah to visit the Holy Kaaba. However, they invited him personally to make his pilgrimage rounds, which he simply refused to do. And said, "I will not make my rounds of the House of Allah until the Messenger of Allah makes his."

The Companions were worried about the safety of Hazrat Uthman, who had gone there as an envoy and had not come back. Because the situation was tense, the Holy Prophet (May God bless and cherish him) gave orders to be vigilant and keep watch at night. Aws ibn Hawli, Abbad ibn Bishr, and Muhammad ibn Maslamah took turns to guard the camp at night. One night, while Muhammad ibn Maslamah was keeping watch, fifty men of the Quraysh led by Mikraz ibn Hafs came over to make a surprise attack on the Muslim camp. The Companions were already on alert and surrounded the enemy, and only Mikraz was able to escape. All others were taken captive. Mikraz headed towards Makkah to inform the Quraysh regarding the latest development.

On the other hand, some of the Companions, such as Kurz ibn Jabir, Abdullah ibn Suhayl, Abdullah ibn Hazafa, Umary ibn Wahb, Abu r-rum ibn Umayr, Hisham ibn As, Abu Habib ibn Amr, Abdullah ibn Abi Umayya, Ayysh ibn Abi Rabia and Hatib ibn Abi Rabia came to the presence of the Holy Prophet (May God bless and cherish him) and asked his permission to go to Makkah in secret and make their rounds around Kaaba. The Holy Prophet (May God bless and cherish him) gave them leave upon their insistence. The Quraysh became aware of their movements, whereupon they were enraged and took all of them as prisoners. They also knew that Muhammad ibn Masalmah had been taken their men prisoners as well. A group of the Quraysh stormed Hudaybiyah and started shooting arrows towards the

Muslims. The Muslims were already on high alert and were able to take twelve cavalrymen as captives from the Quraysh. Ibn Zanim, who was standing at a higher place, was shot by an arrow, and got killed.

Although neither side really wanted to fight, both parties were on the verge of war. The Quraysh consulted each other and sent Suhayl ibn Amr, Huwaytib ibn Abdul Uzza, and Mikraz ibn Hafs as envoys to negotiate a peace treaty. When the Holy Prophet saw Suhayl approaching from afar, he said to his Companions, "Your job has been made easy," for the word Suhayl came from the root easy. When Suhayl ibn Amr met the Holy Prophet (May God bless and cherish him), he said,

"O Muhammad, your friends are in prison, and some of our men attempted to raid your camp, but that was not part of our plan. These men acted in error, and we did not agree with them. So, set free our friends who have been taken as prisoners and hand over them now."

The Holy Prophet (May God bless and cherish him) listened to Suhayl and said, "I will not hand over your men until you have set my Companions free." Suhayl ibn Amr thereby sent Shuyaym ibn Abdi Manaf to the Quraysh and asked them to set free the Companions of the Messenger of Allah. The Holy Prophet (May God bless and cherish him) issued orders so that the men of Quraysh would be released. In the meantime, the news spread that Hazrat Uthman had been killed along with the ten Companions. The news of their martyrdom reached the Holy Prophet, and he said, "It seems we will not be able to part from this place without having fought the Quraysh."

Soon, there came over the Holy Prophet (May God bless and cherish him) a state that was comparable to that of receiving a revelation, but he was in full possession of his faculties. He gave instructions to one of his Companions, who went through the camp proclaiming, "Allah commands allegiance, so go forth in the name of God to make your pledge to the Messenger of Allah."

The Messenger of Allah had come to where the houses of Bani Mazin ibn Najjar were and had seated himself beneath an acacia tree that was green with spring foliage. The first man to make his pledge was Abu Sinan al-Asadi, and he said, "O Messenger of Allah, give me your hand. I swear allegiance to you." The Holy Prophet (May God bless and cherish him) said, "With What will you swear your allegiance?" Abu Sinan answered, "By whatever you like." The Holy Prophet (May God bless and cherish him) again asked, "And what is it that I want?" Abu

Sinan replied, "I will stand in front of you with my sword and fight until Allah gives us victory or until I become a martyr for Him." Then, one by one, the Companions came and pledged their allegiance to him, just like Abu Sinan.

After that, the Holy Prophet (May God bless and cherish him) lifted one of his hands and supplicated, "Verily, Uthman had gone in pursuit of Your and Your Messenger's business." Then he said, "I pledge the allegiance of Uthman," and he put his left hand as the hand of his son-in-law, and holding it with his right hand, pledged the pact. Then he turned towards his Companions and said, "You are the best on earth," and told them that the people who put their trust in him under the tree would not be touched by hellfire.

Among those who had come all the way to Hudaybiyah was Jadd ibn Qays, who had not sworn allegiance; he hid himself behind a camel not to be seen. The Holy Prophet (May God bless and cherish him) and all the Companions had donned their weapons and were ready for an ultimate encounter. Umm Ummara had taken one of the poles of the tent and tied a knife to it, thus making it into a weapon for combat.

Suhayl ibn Amr and his friends were watching all these developments very closely. They felt intimidated by the determination of the Muslims and their loyalty to the Holy Prophet (May God bless and cherish him); they returned to Makkah and spoke about what they experienced at Hudaybiyah. The Quraysh finally realized that for them, the best solution was to make peace with Muhammad on the condition that they would not visit the House of Allah but come back and do so next year. In this way, the Arabs and those who heard about his arrival here would know that we deterred him. They can come next year and stay in Makkah for three days, offer their sacrifices, and return. Then they will not have entered our land without our permission and have stayed only for a couple of days.

The Quraysh now sent back Suhayl to conclude a treaty, and with him were Mikraz and Huwaytib. Suhayl came to the Holy Prophet (May God bless and cherish him), who was sitting on the ground. He knelt. Abbad ibn Bishr and Salama ibn Aslam ibn Harith were standing guard. They spoke for a long time, and the Companions heard their voices rise and fall when a point in question was hard to agree upon or easy. When they had finally reached an agreement, the Holy Prophet (May God bless and cherish him) told Hazrat Ali to write down the terms beginning with the revealed words of '*Bismillahi ar-Rahman ar-Rahim*' (In the name of Allah, the good, the merciful). But Suhayl objected, as to Rahman, he said, "I know not what he is. But write '*Bismik allahama*' (in Thy name). some of the Companions objected, "By God, we will write naught but '*Bismillahi ar-Rahman ar-Rahim.*' However, the Holy Prophet (May God bless and cherish him) ignored them and said, "Write *Bismik Allahama*," and he went on dictating. "This is an agreement between Muhammad, the Messenger of God, and Suhayl, the son of Amr, but one more time Suhayl objected, "If we knew thee to be a Messenger of God," he said, "We would not have barred thee from the House of God, neither would have fought thee but write Muhammad the son of Abdullah." Hazrat Ali had already written "The Messenger of Allah." The Holy Prophet (May God bless and cherish him) told Hazrat Ali to erase those words. At this, he said, he could not. Therefore, the Holy Prophet (May God bless and cherish him) told him to point with his finger to the words in question, and he himself struck them out. Then he told him to write in their place "The son of Abdullah," and he did the same. The agreement stated, "The two parties agree not to engage in any conflict for the next ten years so that people will be safe and refrain from violence with one another. And whosoever comes to Muhammad without the permission of his guardian, Muhammad shall return him unto him, but whoso come unto Quraysh of those who are with Muhammad, they shall not be returned. Similarly, if any tribe wishes to enter a pact with Muhammad may do so, and any tribe who wishes to enter the bond of the Quraysh may do so as well." At that time, the leading men of Khuza'ah were present who had come to greet the pilgrims, and two representatives of Bakr had come to assist Suhayl. The men of Khuza'ah got up and announced their pact with the Holy Prophet (May God bless and cherish him) while the representatives of Bakr said they were one with the Quraysh. The treaty further stated, "Muhammad shall depart from here this year and shall not enter Makkah when we are present over there. But next year, we shall go out of Makkah so that you can enter it with your Companions and stay there for three days only. You shall not carry any arms except the arms of travelers and with swords in sheath." (Ibn Hisham)

The treaty was finally sealed, and the parties were ready to depart when suddenly a youth staggered into the camp with his feet in fetters. When he came close, they realized that it was Abu Jandal, the younger son of Suhayl ibn Amr. Suhayl had imprisoned and tortured Abu Jandal on account of his Islam and had bound him before he came to Hudaybiyah. In the absence of his father, he had managed to escape from his detention. He chose difficult paths, walking over mountains to avoid attention, and finally reached his destination to be with the Messenger of Allah. His brother Abdullah was there to welcome him. Abdullah had changed sides and gone over to the Muslim camp at the Battle of Badr. Suhayl saw his son, caught hold of the chain that was around his neck, and struck him violently in the face. Then he turned to the Holy Prophet (May God bless and cherish him) and said, "Our agreement was sealed before this man came here." "That is true," said the Holy Prophet (May God bless and cherish him). "Return him then unto me," Suhayl demanded. At this, Abu Jandal shouted at the top of his voice, "O Muslims, am I to be returned unto the idolators, for them to persecute me on account of my religion?" This was a heartbreaking situation for the Muslims. The Holy Prophet (May God bless and cherish him) took Suhayl aside and asked him, "Spare him and hand him to me, and keep him outside the terms of the agreement." Suhayl did not accept his offer and said, "I will not give him over to you and will not keep him outside the terms of the agreement." His fellow envoys Mikraz and Huwatib were so far watching and remained silent, but when they saw this situation, they felt that it was an inauspicious start for the truce. They intervened and said, "O Muhammad, we give him our protection on your behalf." Which meant that they would keep him with them, away from his father, and they held to their promise. The Holy Prophet (May God bless and cherish him) then looked at Abu Jandal with compassion and said, "Be patient and expect your reward from Allah. God will surely provide a way out. We have agreed on the terms of the truce with those people and have given them our solemn pledge. We will not break our word."

Till that moment, the Companions had no doubt that the dream of the Holy Prophet (May God bless and cherish him) would be realized. That is why they had come all the way to Hudaybiyah. They were all anticipating their own dreams of making rounds around the Holy Kaaba to come true as well. It seemed like everything had ended, and the agreement had been signed. Hazrat Umar was confused, and rising to his feet, he went to the Holy Prophet (May God bless and cherish him) and said, "Art thou not God's Messenger?" "Yes," replied the Holy Prophet (May God bless and cherish him). "Are we not on the right path and our enemies on the wrong?" The Holy Prophet (May God bless and cherish him) affirmed. "Then why should we yield to such an agreement against the honor of our religion?" said Umar. Whereupon the Holy Prophet (May God bless and cherish him) replied, "I am Allah's Messenger, and I will not disobey Him. He will give me the victory." But didn't you tell us that we should go unto the Kaaba and make our rounds?" persisted Hazrat Umar. "Even so," the Holy Prophet said, "But did I tell thee we should go to it this year?" Hazrat Umar said that he had not. "Verily, thou should go to the House of Lord and make your rounds around it." Said the Holy

Prophet.

Hazrat Umar was still not satisfied and went to Hazrat Abu Bakr to vent his frustration. He put to him the same questions he had put to the Holy Prophet (May God bless and cherish him). Even though Hazrat Abu Bakr had not heard the answers, he gave him the same exact answer to each question. And Hazrat Abu Bakr added, "Rest assured, for by God he is right."

Hazrat Umar was finally satisfied. The Holy Prophet (May God bless and cherish him) called him to put his name to the treaty, and he signed it in silence. The Holy Prophet also told Suhayl's son Abdullah to put his name to it. Other Companions who signed the treaty were Hazrat Ali, Abu Bakr, Abdul Rahman ibn Awf, and Mahmud ibn Maslamah. After the conclusion of the treaty, the Holy Prophet (May God bless and cherish him) went towards the place where all men were gathered. He said to them, "Rise and sacrifice your animals and shave your heads." But the men were so bewildered by the turn of events, and no one moved. The Holy Prophet (May God bless and cherish him) repeated his orders a second and a third time. The Companions were in shock and perplexed by the command, for according to tradition, the sacrifice had to be performed within the sacred territory, and the same rule applied to shaving the head. The Holy Prophet (May God bless and cherish him) was disappointed and went to his tent and told Umm Salamah what had happened. "Do you see what the people are doing? I order them to do something, but they look at me in the face and yet do nothing. (Waqidi, Maghazi; Salihi, Subulu l-Huda war-Rashad). Umm Salamah replied, "Go forth; and say nothing to any man until you have performed your sacrifice." So, the Holy Prophet (May God bless and cherish him) went to the camel that he himself had consecrated and sacrificed it, saying in a loud voice, so that men could hear it, "Bismillah Allah u Akbar" when the Companions heard the glorification they leaped to their feet and raced to make their sacrifices falling over each other in their eagerness to obey. The Holy Prophet (May God bless and cherish him) then called for Khirash – the man of Khuzah he had sent for negotiations to shave his head. The Companions followed and vigorously started shaving each other's heads. That worried Umm Salamah that mortal wounds might be inflicted. Some of the Companions merely cut their locks, and it was traditionally accepted. When all the rites were finally done, the Holy Prophet stood at the entrance of his tent with shaven head and said, "God have mercy on the shavers of their heads." The Companions who cut their locks complained, "And on the cutters of their hair," but the Holy Prophet repeated what he had said at first. The voices were raised again. Then, after another repetition, the Holy Prophet (May God bless and cherish him) said, "And upon the cutters of their hair."

After returning to his tent, the Holy Prophet (May God bless and cherish him) gathered his long locks from the ground and threw them over a nearby Mimosa tree. When the Companions saw it, they rushed to the tree, each one trying to take what he could for its blessing. Nusaybah was among the Companions, and she made her way to the tree and was able to snatch some locks, which she treasured until her last breath.

The ground around the camp was strewn with the hair of the pilgrims. Then suddenly, a powerful gust of wind blew that lifted the hair from the ground and blew it towards the Makkah into the sacred territory, and everyone praised Allah, taking it as a sign that their pilgrimage had been accepted by the Lord of the worlds. They now knew why the Holy Prophet (May God bless and cherish him) had commanded them to make their sacrifices.

The Holy Prophet (May God bless and cherish him) finally ordered his Companions to start their journey back to Medina. They left Hudaybiyah for Medina. On their way, they camped first at Marr az-Zahran and then at Usfan. The Companions were out of provisions, so they came to the Holy Prophet (May God bless and cherish him) to ask his permission to slaughter the camels they were mounting, and the Holy Prophet (May God bless and cherish him) agreed. They were happy but then Hazrat Umar came to the Holy Prophet (May God bless and cherish him) and said, "O Messenger of Allah, do not let them slaughter their mounts. Having more camels by our side is more important in case we are faced with an enemy. It is better than being hungry and on foot. I have an idea if you will allow me. I will ask people to bring whatever they have, and once we have all gathered, you can say a prayer, and there is no doubt Allah the Almighty will increase it and help us return home safely." The Holy Prophet (May God bless and cherish him) responded favorably to Hazrat Umar's suggestion. He spread his skin on the ground and told people to put their provisions on it.

The Companions brought all they had and placed it on the skin, and it amounted to the size of a baby goat. The Holy Prophet raised his hands and prayed over it. Then he turned towards them and told them to eat from it after pronouncing "In the name of Allah." One thousand and four hundred Companions came to this blessed banquet and ate to their fill. They also filled their bowls with leftover food. After everyone had eaten, the amount of food the size of a baby goat remained.

On their return journey, Hazrat Umar's conscience began to trouble him, and his anxiety greatly increased. He rode to the Holy Prophet (May God bless and cherish him), seeking to enter a conversation with him, but found him reserved. Therefore, Hazrat Umar rode ahead and said to himself, "O Umar, let thy mother mourn her son." He was so troubled that for having questioned the wisdom of the Holy Prophet (May God bless and cherish him), he feared there would be a special revelation condemning him.

They were now close to Kura al-Ghamim when the pace of Qaswa (the Messenger of Allah's camel) changed as if walking under a heavy load. The Companions knew that a new revelation was coming down. After some time, the Holy Prophet (May God bless and cherish him) sent a rider and summoned Hazrat Umar. His troubles vanished when he saw that the Holy Prophet's face was radiant with joy. "There has been descended upon me a Sura," he said, "Which is dearer to me than anything else beneath the sun." The new revelation was a glad tiding, announcing that the mission from which they were returning must be considered a great victory, for it opened with the words,

"Verily, We have given thee a clear victory." (Quran: 48:1). It also spoke of the recent pact of allegiance. "God was well pleased with the believers when they pledged allegiance unto thee beneath the tree. He knew what was in their hearts, and sent down the spirit of peace upon them, and rewarded them with an imminent victory." (Quran 48:18). The pledge that the Companions took under the tree is known as the pact of Ridwan. Those who fulfilled their pledge had earned divine pleasure.

The descent of *sakineh* is also mentioned in another verse, "He it is who sent down the spirit of peace into the hearts of the believers that they might increase in faith upon faith – that He may bring the believing men and women into gardens that are watered by flowing rivers, gardens wherein they should dwell immortal, and that He may take from them all guilt of evil. And ever is that, in the sight of Allah, a great attainment." (Quran 48:4-5)

The Holy Prophet's (May God bless and cherish him) vision, which prompted the expedition of Hudaybiyah, is mentioned in the Sura Al-Fath as follows,

"God hath truly fulfilled, for His Messenger, the vision; God willing, ye shall enter the inviolable Mosque in safety not fearing, with the hair of your heads shaven or cut. He knew what ye know not, and before that hath He hath given you a near victory." (Quran 48:27)

ABU BASIR'S ESCAPE

The Holy Prophet (May God bless and cherish him) and his Companions arrived in Medina after their agreement with the Quraysh in Hudaybiyah. Abu Basir of the Bani Thaqif, whose family belonged to Taif and were settled in Makkah as confederates of Bani Zuhra, had accepted Islam, but he was imprisoned and subjected to torture. Just like Abu Jandal, he had found a way to escape and, with great difficulty, had managed to reach Medina. When the Makkans found out, they asked for his return according to the Hudaybiyah agreement. Anhas ibn Sharik and Azhar ibn Abdi Awf wrote a letter for his return to the Messenger of Allah. The letter was brought by Hunays ibn Jabir, who took his slave Kawthar with him.

The Holy Prophet (May God bless and cherish him) comforted Abu Basir and told him that he was bound by the treaty to deliver him to the enemy. He reassured him that Allah the Almighty would make a way out of this situation. As Abu Basir was led by the man of the Quraysh, the Companions who were present repeated the words of the Holy Prophet, "Be of good cheer! God will surely find thee a way out."

At first halt, Abu Basir, despite his young age, managed to get the sword of the enemy and kill him. His slave, Kawthar fled in fear back to Medina. He entered the Mosque and threw himself at the feet of the Holy Prophet (May God bless and cherish him) and told him that Abu Basir had killed his master and he had to run to save his life. At the same time, Abu Basir appeared, mounted on Hunay's camel and his sword hanging by his side. "O Messenger of Allah! You did what you had to do and have fulfilled your obligation. You returned me unto them, but God had delivered me." The Holy Prophet (May God bless and cherish him) was pleased and said, "What a fine firebrand for war, had he other men with him."

The Holy Prophet (May God bless and cherish him), however, was bound by the treaty to return Abu Basir if Quraysh sent another envoy and demanded his return. Abu Basir asked the Holy Prophet (May God bless and cherish him) that the arms and armor of the dead man, along with the camel, should be treated as booty and distributed according to the law. "If I did that," said the Holy Prophet (May God bless and cherish him), "they would accuse me that I had not fulfilled the terms I agreed upon." Then he looked at Kawthar and said, "Take this man to those who sent thee." Kawthar was terrified and said, "O Muhammad, I am concerned about my own life. I am weak and unable to do so." Therefore, he refused to take custody of the prisoner. So, the Holy Prophet (May God bless and cherish him) addressed Abu Basir, "You are free; go where you will."

Abu Basir left Medina, headed towards the shores of the Red Sea, and settled in a deserted place. He was an intelligent young man, and the Holy Prophet's (May God bless and cherish him) words, "Had he but other men with him," echoed in his mind. It was a veiled instruction about what to do. Hazrat Umar also understood, and he sent a word to other Muslims in Makkah to join Abu Basir and shared his whereabouts with them. Abu Jandal, the son of Suhayl, was poorly watched, as were other young Muslims. So, Abu Jandal made his way to Abu Basir. In a very short time, around seventy Muslims joined his camp, including Walid, the brother of Khalid. They set up a post at a strategic point on the Quraysh caravan route to Syria. They made him their leader in religious affairs and obeyed his command. The Quraysh, who were now happy that they had re-established the safety of their favorite road to the north, were utterly disappointed by the attacks of this new group on their caravans, because of which many of the Quraysh traders were killed and their possessions confiscated. After sustaining heavy losses, they sent a letter to the Holy Prophet (May God bless and cherish him) asking to take these rebels into his community and promised that they would not ask for their return to Makkah. So, the Holy Prophet (May God bless and cherish him) wrote a letter to Abu Basir telling him that he could come to Medina along with his friends. When the letter reached Abu Basir, he was seriously ill and breathing his last breath. His Companions prayed over him and buried him and built a Mosque at the place of his burial. After that, they all came to Medina to join the Holy Prophet (May God bless and cherish him). (Waqidi)

When the group of Abu Basir reached the lava tract near Medina, Walid's camel stumbled, and he fell. He sustained a cut to his finger that got infected, and the wound proved to be fatal. He wrote a letter to his brother before death, urging him to enter Islam.

After Hudaybiyah, one woman escaped from Makkah and reached Medina with great difficulty. She was Uthman's half-sister, Umm Kulthum, the daughter of his mother Arwa and of Uqbah, who had been put to death on the way from Badr. During this time, God sent a revelation forbidding the return of any believing woman to the disbelievers. Her two full brothers came to Medina in her pursuit and demanded her return, but the Holy Prophet (May God bless and cherish him) refused to let them have her. In fact, there had been no mention of women in the treaty either. Later, three of the Companions, Zayd, Zubayr, and Abdul Rahman ibn Awf, asked for her hand in marriage, but she married Zayd at the recommendation of the Holy Prophet (May God bless and cherish him).

After the treaty of Hudaybiyah, a new era started in Medina. The constant danger that could come from Makkah had been averted. The people now had the opportunity to know Islam in a peaceful environment. Though soon after the treaty, Hazrat Abu Bakr and Hazrat Aisha suffered a great loss, though it led to the conversion of Hazrat Abu Bakr's son and the reunion of the family. Umm, Ruman fell seriously ill and passed away. She was buried in Baqi, and the Holy Prophet (May God bless and cherish him) prayed over her and lowered her into her grave. When the news of her death reached Makkah, her son came to hear it. This prompted him to go to Medina, where he entered Islam. He had been contemplating doing so for a while. The Holy Prophet (May God bless and cherish him) changed his name from Abdul Kaaba to Abdul Rahman. As weeks and months passed, it became evident why Allah the exalted had declared the truce a clear victory. During the next two years, people had a chance to meet freely and discuss religion. And because of that, the Muslim community was more than doubled.

AFTER HUDAYBIYAH

It was the end of the sixth year after Hijra that the Holy Prophet (May God bless and cherish him) called his Companions and addressed them, "O people, there is no doubt that Allah (Exalted is He), sent me as a mercy to all mankind. Fulfill your duty towards me so that Allah the Almighty may have mercy on you. I will send some of you as ambassadors to kings. Do not act like the children of Israel and oppose me as they opposed Prophet Jesus, the son of Mary." The Companions listened to the Messenger of Allah and said, "O Messenger of Allah, we swear by Allah that we will not contradict you on any matter, you can send us wherever you like. Without a doubt, we will obey your orders."

The Companions knew that the Holy Prophet (May God bless and cherish him) intended to write letters inviting various kings to Islam. The letters were going to be sent to Byzantines, Persians, and the Abyssinians. They suggested, "O Messenger of Allah, they do not read letters unless they are sealed." Therefore, the Holy

Prophet (May God bless and cherish him) had made a ring, and on it was written "Muhammad, Rasul Allah." From then on, this ring would be stamped at the end of all the letters to be sent.

ENVOY TO ABYSSINIA

The Holy Prophet (May God bless and cherish him) appointed Amr ibn Umayya as an envoy and sent a letter to Negus, who was the king of Abyssinia. The letter said,

"In the name of Allah, the All-Merciful, the All-Compassionate. This is a letter from Muhammad, the Messenger of Allah, to the leader of Abyssinia (Najashi). May peace and blessings be upon the believers, those who bear witness that there is no deity but Allah, that He has no peer, that He takes no partner or child, and those who verify that Muhammad is His servant and Messenger. Verily, I invite you to the peace and immensity of Islam, for I am the Messenger of Allah. Become a Muslim, accept Islam, and be part of His world peace.

"O people of the Book, come to a word common between us and you, that we worship none but God, and associate none as partner with Him, and that none of us take others for Lords, apart from God." (Quran 3:64).

Najashi, who received the letter of the Holy Prophet (May God bless and cherish him), first read it, then he kissed it and pressed it gently onto his face and eyes, and then stood up as a sign of respect and declared that he had become a Muslim. After proclaiming faith, he said, "I wish I had the opportunity to go to him. I swear, and Allah is my witness, he is the illiterate prophet that the Jews and the Christians have been expecting. Just as Prophet Moses spoke of the good news of Jesus saying, "he will be mounted on a donkey," so had Prophet Jesus spoken the good news of Muhammad, saying, "He will be mounted on a camel." Of course, the best would be to see him with one's own eye. But I have advisers among the Abyssinians, and I am waiting for their hearts to warm up to Islam."

Najashi placed that letter in an ivory box as a relic and said, "As long as this letter stays here, bounty and blessings will flourish in Abyssinia."

After the return of pilgrims from Hudaybiyah, a verse was revealed that said,

"It may be that God will establish love between you and those with whom you are at enmity." (Quran 60:7). This revelation seemed to indicate, in general, the many conversions that took place. But it was also interpreted by some as an unexpected close relationship that was now to be established between the Holy Prophet (May God bless and cherish him) and one of the leaders of the Quraysh.

Prior to that news from Abyssinia came the death of Usayd ibn Jahsh, the Holy Prophet's (May God bless and cherish him) cousin and brother-in-law. He had been a Christian before he entered Islam. After emigration to Abyssinia, he reverted to Christianity. This had greatly upset his wife Umm Habibah, Abu Sufyan's daughter, who remained a Muslim, and when four months had elapsed after the death of her husband, the Holy Prophet (May God bless and cherish him) sent a message to Najashi asking him to act as a proxy for himself and to ratify a marriage between him and the widow if she were willing. The Holy Prophet (May God bless and cherish him) did not send her any direct message. However, she had a dream in which someone came to her and addressed her as "Mother of the faithful," and she interpreted this as meaning that she would become the wife of the Holy Prophet (May God bless and cherish him). The next day, she received a message from Najashi that confirmed her vision. She, therefore, appointed her kinsman Khalid ibn Said to give her in marriage, and he and Najashi solemnized the marriage contract between them in the presence of Jafar and other Muslims. Najashi held a wedding feast in their honor in his palace and invited all Muslims.

The Holy Prophet (May God bless and cherish him) sent a message to Jafar and said that it would please him if he and the rest of the Muslim community would now return to Medina. Jafar started preparation for the return to Medina. Najashi gave them two boats. He did not want to send them alone; therefore, he sent his son Arha along with seventy guards to accompany them. However, the second boat sank in the middle of the ocean, and sixty men, including the son of Najashi, died. (Tabari, Tarikh; Ibn Hajar, Al-Isaba; Ibn Kathir, Usdu l-Ghaba)

Najashi was not the only king to whom the Holy Prophet (May God bless and cherish him) had sent a letter. At the certainty that had been given to the Holy Prophet (May God bless and cherish him) about the future spread of Islam, he was obliged to write to the Persian monarch, informing him of his prophethood and inviting him to Islam. Yemen, at that time, was under the rule of Persia. The Holy Prophet (May God bless and cherish him) sent Abdullah ibn Huzafa Sahmi to take the letter with the mediation of the governor of Bahrain, Munzir ibn Sawa. The letter began with the name of Allah and then explained that he was a prophet of Allah, inviting him to faith. But Kisra was enraged by the very first sentence. He grabbed the letter and tore it into pieces, "How can he start with his own name and not mine?" said Kisra (Khosrow). Ibn Huzafa, who had discharged his duty, tried to warn the Persians but left the court and made for Medina. In the meantime, the Persian monarch sent his men after Ibn Huzafa, but he had already reached Medina. He recounted the whole encounter to the Holy Prophet (May God bless and cherish him), who listened to him patiently and said, "Allah will tear his kingdom into pieces," and he prayed, "Dear Lord, tear his kingdom apart just as he has torn my letter apart."

Kisra sent an order to Badhan, his viceroy in Yemen, asking him to gather further information about Muhammad. Badhan dispatched two envoys forthwith to Medina so that they could see for themselves and bring his news back to him. The envoys had shaved their heads and grown moustaches. The Holy Prophet (May God bless and cherish him) did not like their appearance and asked, "Who bade you do this?" "Our Lord," they said. The Holy Prophet (May God bless and cherish him) said, "My Lord hath bidden me to grow a beard and cut short my moustache." He told them to come back tomorrow. That night Gabriel came, and told him that there had been an uprising in Persia in which Kisra has been killed. The Holy Prophet (May God bless and cherish him) told them about what had taken place in Persia. He told them to inform their master about it and added, "Tell him that my religion and my empire will reach far beyond the kingdom of Kisra, and tell him from my side, "Enter Islam, and I will confirm thee in what you have now, and I will appoint you king over your people in Yemen." They returned to Sana and informed Badhan about everything. He said, "We will see what transpires. If what he said is true, then he is a prophet whom God hath sent." He was about to send a man to Persia to find out the truth. At the same time, a messenger arrived from the new Shah, announcing what happened and asking for their allegiance. Instead of replying, he entered Islam, and so did his two envoys and other Persians who were with him. He then sent word to Medina and the Holy Prophet (May God bless and cherish him) confirmed his rule over Yemen.

LETTER TO THE BYZANTINES

The Byzantines were one of the great powers of the time. The Holy Prophet sent Dihyah al-Kalbi as an envoy to Heraclius, the king of Byzantine, and told him to deliver the letter to governor of Basra. At that time, Heraclius was in Jerusalem. The governor of Basra gave one of his men, Adiyy ibn Hatim, as a guide to take him to Jerusalem and see Heraclius. During the journey, he was told that when he met the king, he should prostrate down in front of him and not lift his head until the king said so. At this, he replied that he would not prostrate in front of anyone except Allah. Therefore, they warned him that the king may banish him. When he was brought in front of the king, the courtier said, "O king, this is a man from Arabs, and he has come to inform you about an important event that has happened where he lives." Heraclius looked at Dihyah and the letter he was carrying. Since the letter was in Arabic, a translator was called to read it aloud.

"In the name of Allah, the All-Merciful, the All-Compassionate. From Muhammad, the Messenger of Allah, to Heraclius, king of the Romans." After hearing this, the nephew of Heraclius, who was present, was enraged and struck the translator and said, "The man starts with his own name and not yours, and he does not call you Lord but just the king of Romans." "I did not know you would be so short-sighted. You want to tear the letter before it is even read. I swear by my life if he is a messenger of God as he says, then he has the right to start the letter with his own name instead of mine and to address me the king of Romans. I am not Lord over them but just a master," said Heraclius. He then ordered the translator to continue to read, "Let peace and good fortune be upon those who follow guidance (the right path). I invite you to the enormity of Islam. Be a believer and find peace so that Allah may reward you doubly. If you do not accept my invitation, know that all the sins of your people will be upon your head."

While listening to the letter, Heraclius said, "I swear, I have not heard a letter begin with "Bismillah ar-Rahman ar-Rahim" since it was used by Solomon, the son of David." Heraclius ordered his courtiers to be left alone, and called for the high priest and asked his opinion. The priest confirmed, "I swear by He apart from whom there is no deity. There is no doubt that he is the prophet that Moses and Jesus have spoken the good news of the prophet that we have been waiting for." At this Heraclius asked the high priest, "What would you advise me to do?" "I think you should follow him," said the priest.

He took the letter of the Holy Prophet, kissed it, and placed it inside a silk and velvet covering. Then he asked his assistant to bring him men belonging to the Quraysh. At that time, Abu Sufyan was leading a caravan near Gaza. So, he was brought to the court of the king. The king asked him questions, and he compared the message of the Holy Prophet (May God bless and cherish him) with the message of the previous prophets and concluded that he was indeed the awaited prophet.

He summoned the leading men of his empire to the palace. He closed the doors and stood up on a stage. He started by saying,

"O Romans, verily I have received a letter from Muhammad, and I swear that he is the prophet that Jesus spoke about and whom we have been waiting for! He is the prophet whose characteristics had been mentioned in our scripture and who's coming we had been looking forward to. Come and submit in faith to him, be his followers, and stand in rows behind him in this world and the hereafter."

All the men present in the palace were extremely furious and raised a storm of objections and disdain. They started towards the door to exit the palace. When Heraclius saw their reaction, he called out to them, "O Romans, what I said was to test your loyalty to your religion. I am glad that you have the same opinion as I have." This answer pleased the Romans, and they applauded him. The high priest was in shock as he watched all this. He could not contain himself and cried out, "I bear witness that Muhammad is the Messenger of Allah."

After a few days, Heraclius wrote a letter to the Holy Prophet (May God bless and cherish him) and gave it to Dihyah, along with many gifts to take to Medina. The letter said,

"To Muhammad, the Messenger of Allah, whose good news prophet Jesus had spoken, from the king of Romans, Heraclius. Your envoy came to me with the letter you sent. I swear that you are the messenger of Allah. We already knew about you from our scriptures, for Jesus the son of Mary had already given us the glad tidings of your coming. Although I invited the Romans to believe in you, they stayed away. Had they listened to me, it truly would have been better for them. I would have given anything to come to you, to be in your presence and wash your feet."

On his way back, Dihyah came to a place called Himsa, where a group of people from Juzam stopped him and took everything he had. He reached Medina with great hardship. He went directly to the presence of the Holy Prophet (May God bless and cherish him) and told him all that had happened. When the Holy Prophet (May God bless and cherish him) read the letter and listened to him, he said, "As long as they have my letter with them, their reign will continue."

During this period, there was an attempt to inflict harm on the Holy Prophet (May God bless and cherish him) by means of magic. Among Jews in Arabia, there were some who were expert in the science of magic, and one of them lived in Medina by the name of Labid. He was a well-known sorcerer, and he had also trained his daughter in the art of sorcery lest his own knowledge should die with him. He was given a handsome amount of money to put a deadly spell on the Holy Prophet (May God bless and cherish him). To do so, he needed some hair of the Holy Prophet (May God bless and cherish him), which he acquired through his sources. He tied eleven knots in the hair, and his daughters blew imprecations upon each knot. Then he attached it to a twig from a male date palm, which had on it the outer sheath of the pollen and threw it into a deep well. The magic could only be undone by untying the knots.

The Holy Prophet (May God bless and cherish him) became aware that something was not right. His memory was failing him, and he could not remember things. He was also feeling very weak and exhausted. He lost his appetite and could hardly eat food. He supplicated to Allah (Exalted is He), and in his vision, he saw two people, one sitting at his head and the other at his feet. He heard one of them inform the other of the exact cause of his illness and the name of the well. (Bukhari, Sahih). When the Holy Prophet (May God bless and cherish him) woke, Gabriel came to him and confirmed his dream. He then revealed to him two Suras of the Quran, Sura Falak, and Sura Nas. The Holy Prophet (May God bless and cherish him) sent Hazrat Ali and told him to recite over the well the two Suras. At each verse, one of the knots untied until all were done and the Holy Prophet (May God bless and cherish him) recovered his full strength. One of the Sura contains five verses, and the other six. The Holy Prophet (May God bless and cherish him) ordered the well to be filled, and another well was dug near that place to replace it.

MUQAWQIS: THE RULER OF EGYPT

The Holy Prophet (May God bless and cherish him) sent Hatib ibn Balta'ab as an envoy with a letter to Muqawqis, the king of Egypt and Alexandria. The letter contained similar expressions as the other ones and invited the ruler of Egypt to the Islamic faith. The Ayah (verse) sixty-four of Al-Imran was also included in the letter, "O people of the Book," Hatib delivered the letter to the king, and a series of conversations took place between them. "I want to ask you some questions to clarify certain things,' said Muqawqis. "Yes, of course," answered Hatib. "Is your master not a prophet?" "Yes, he is the Messenger of Allah." "If he is really a prophet of God, then why did he not put a curse on the people who drove him out of his homeland?" asked Muqawqis. To this Hatib replied, "You bear witness that Jesus, the son of

Mary, is the messenger of Allah, don't you? Since he is a real prophet, would it not have been more appropriate for him to ask Allah to smite his tribe rather than being raised up to the heavens by Him?"

Muqawqis was speechless and remained silent. After a while, he turned to Hatib and said, "Can you repeat what you have just said?" After listening to Hatib once again, he thought deeply and said, "You speak well, you seem to be coming from someone who has good judgment."

When the envoy of the Holy Prophet (May God bless and cherish him) saw that the king had softened so much, he said, "Before you, there were people here who said, 'Am I not your greatest Lord?' But Allah, the Almighty, punished them both in this world and the hereafter. You should take heed from it so that you don't have the same destiny." "We will not change our religion before we have found one that is better than ours," exclaimed Muqawqis. Upon that, Hatib said, "I invite you to the religion of Islam that Allah has sent, a complete religion that will not leave you wanting anything else. The Messenger of Allah invites people to the same thing. As a matter of fact, the people who oppose him most are people of Quraysh, the ones who show him most enmity are the Jews, and those who are closest to him are the Christians. I swear by my own life that Jesus brought the good news of Muhammad, and this is no different than Moses bringing the good news of Jesus. Inviting you to the Quran, the word of God is like you calling the people of the Torah to the Gospel! Whichever community a prophet had been sent to becomes the ummah of that prophet. Obeying the prophet is their duty, and now you know about the Messenger of Allah! And by calling you to the religion of Islam, we do not ask you to stray away from the teachings of Jesus. On the contrary, we invite you to follow him and live according to the commandments that he brought."

The king of Egypt was listening attentively, then he called a scribe and dictated the following letter, "To Muhammad, from the king of Egypt Muqawqis. I have read your letter, and I know what you have invited me to. I also knew that a messenger would come, but I thought he would appear in Damascus. I have treated your envoy with respect. I am sending you two slaves as a gift who are highly prized by me, Mariyah and Sirin and a mount. Peace be upon you." Later, the Holy Prophet (May God bless and cherish him) gave one of these slaves as a present to Hassan ibn Thabit and married the other one, Hazrat Mariyah. She gave him a son named Hazrat Ibrahim. The mount the Muqawqis sent as a gift was called, "Duldul." (Ibn Sa'd, Tabaqat; Tabari, Tarikh)

CHAPTER 20
THE EXPEDITION OF KHAYBAR

Amonth had passed since the agreement of the truce with the Quraysh was signed. This relieved the Muslims from the constant threat of being attacked by them for time being. This made it possible for the Holy Prophet (May God bless and cherish him) to concentrate on the dangers that the Jews of Khaybar presented. Bani Qurayzah, Bani Qaynuqah, and Bani Nadir, who had been exiled from their homeland and who now had settled in Khaybar, were preparing to launch a surprise attack on Medina. It was they who had given the Quraysh every encouragement to attack, and it was their insistence and influence that had persuaded their allies of Ghatafan to side with the Quraysh at the battle of Trench. It was also because of the Jews that Ghatafan still remained virtually at war with the Muslims. Therefore, it was obvious that Muslims could never be at peace if Khaybar remained as it was.

The leading tribesmen, such as Sallam ibn Abi l-Huqayq, Kinanah ibn Rabi, and Huyay ibn Akhtab, had decided to act quickly before the Muslims were upon them with the help of the Jews of Tayma, Fadak, and Wadi al-Qura. Usayr ibn Zarin had become their leader. Abu Rafi was at the forefront in provoking his community against the Holy Prophet (May God bless and cherish him). He had made an alliance with the tribe of Ghatafan to attack Medina.

It had long been clear that something had to be done in the direction of Khaybar, and now was the right time for this purpose. The Holy Prophet (May God bless and cherish him) was certain that the near victory promised by God in the revelation –

a victory that would moreover be rich in spoils – would be nothing other than the conquest of Khaybar. The Quran made it clear that those Bedouins who had failed to respond to his call to make the lesser pilgrimage (umrah) should not be allowed to take part in the conquest of what was, without doubt, one of the richest communities in all Arabia.

The Jews of Medina realized that the Holy Prophet (May God bless and cherish him) intended to lead a campaign against Khaybar and sent a warning to them. Even though the plans were kept secret until the last moment, it was passed from mouth to mouth. The Jews were sure of the strength of Khaybar, and they hoped the news was true because, in that case, the Muslims would sustain a crushing defeat.

The Jews of Khaybar were so confident of their own power that they refused to believe it until the news came that the holy Prophet (May God bless and cherish him) and Muslims were about to set forth. Kinanah made an emergency visit to Ghatafan to seek their help and promised them half of the date harvest if they sent them reinforcements. They agreed to do so and assembled a force of four thousand men. The Jews in Khaybar had ten thousand strong fighting men in all, and with the help of Ghatafan the total number would be fourteen thousand men.

The Holy Prophet (May God bless and cherish him) set out with a small force of sixteen hundred men only, and he left Siba ibn Urtafa as his deputy in Medina. In the mind of the Jews, the conquest of Khaybar was impossible due to its strong battlements, plentitude of provisions and the strength of their men. Among the Companions, one of the men of Aws, known as Abu Abs, came to the Holy Prophet (May God bless and cherish him). He was extremely poor; he had a camel to ride but his clothes were in rags, and he had no means to care for his family. The Holy Prophet (May God bless and cherish him) gave Abu Abs a fine long cloak, all that he had at that time. There were other men in similar circumstances. After a day, the Holy Prophet (May God bless and cherish him) noticed that Abu Abs had a much poorer cloak, so he asked him, "Where is your cloak that I gave you?" "I sold it for eight dirhams," said Abu Abs, "Then I bought two dirhams worth of dates as provision for myself, and I left two dirhams for my family and bought a cloak for four dirhams." The Holy Prophet (May God bless and cherish him) smiled, "O father of Abs, you shall have abundance of provisions and leave much for you family. You shall abound in dirhams and slaves, and it will not be good for you." (Waqidi)

On this mission, there were ten Jews with the Holy Prophet (May God bless and cherish him). There were also about twenty women Companions who were to act as nurses, cook food, and carry water. Ukkasha ibn Mihsan and Abbad ibn Bishr were sent in advance as scouts from different directions, and they had hired as guide Husayl ibn Hajira, and Abdullah ibn Noaym for a fee. (Husayl would later become a Muslim. Ibn Athir, Usdu l-Ghaba)

The believer's army was marching forward, and the Holy Prophet (May God bless and cherish him) instructed them not to utter their magnifications (Takbirs) loudly. He wanted to reach Khaybar when the people of Khaybar least expected it and wanted to catch them by surprise.

Abbad ibn Bishr came across a shepherd who was spying for the Jews of Khaybar. The man first said how the Jews were ready for war, and no force could stand against them. On further investigation, he revealed that the people of Ghatafan had indeed come to Khaybar with four thousand fighters to support the Jews. When the Muslim's army reached a place between the Khaybar fortresses of Shikk and Natat, the Holy Prophet (May God bless and cherish him) gave orders to camp, and to perform prayers. After prayers, they reached a point where they could see Khaybar and the Holy Prophet (May God bless and cherish him) instructed the army to stop. It was in the middle of the night, and they chose a place to camp there and get ready for the next day. In the meantime, Hubab ibn Munzir approached the Messenger of Allah and said, "O Messenger of Allah, this place that you have chosen as your headquarters, if this has been a command from Allah, then we have nothing to say but to obey, but if it is a choice from the point of view of warfare, then allow me to give my opinion." The Holy Prophet (May God bless and cherish him) answered, "This was just a personal choice." Hubab said, "O Messenger of Allah, this place is too close to their fortresses, and we know they have taken positions in Natat fortress. Besides, they are very expert archers, and the arrows they shoot would rain down from above and reach us easily. We will have a difficult time to shoot back at them. We should position ourselves behind these rocks so that their arrows will not reach us." The Holy Prophet (May God bless and cherish him) agreed with his suggestion and told his Companions to change their position at night. He called Muhammad ibn Maslama to find a better place for the camp. The Holy Prophet (May God bless and cherish him) moved his men into fighting position as he was riding his mount. Khaybar was the name of the fortress that spanned across a wide area. It was divided into three major parts, called Natat, Shikk, and Katiba. There were numerous fortresses of different sizes by the names of Naim, Kula, Sumra, Bari, Qamus, Watih, and Sulalim. They were all built in high places and were very strong structures. (Hamawi, *Mujmu l-*

Buldan)

It was a dark night, and the new moon had already set. They came upon Khaybar so quietly that none of the inhabitants was alerted. The Muslim army prayed in silence. As the sun rose, the increasing light revealed to them the fortresses that stood in the 'Garden of Hijaz.' When the field workers came out with their spades and mattocks, they were astonished to find themselves face-to-face with a Muslim army. They all fled back into their strongholds. The Holy Prophet (May God bless and cherish him) glorified Allah by repeating three times, "Allah u Akbar." And said, "Khaybar is crushed." And recited.

"But when it descends in their territory, then evil is the morning of those who have been warned." (Quran 37:177)

The Jews conducted an emergency war meeting. There were two camps, one whose camp was saying that they should stay inside their strong battlements and be on the defensive, and the other whose camp was saying that they should come out to the open and fight one on one. Some of the leading men, like Sallam ibn Mishkam, were in favor of fighting, they said, "Do not shy away from fighting with them here, it is better for you to die fighting than to be left alone here."

On the first day of battle, the Jews took their families and valuables to the fortress of Katiba and stocked their provisions in the fortress of Natat and were determined to fight till the last drop of blood. When the Muslims attacked, they remained inside their fortress, and no one came out. From within, they started to shower arrows at where the Messenger of Allah and his Companions were. They were shooting so fast and in such succession that by the end of the day, fifty Companions were wounded. The men of Khaybar were considered the most expert marksmen in Arabia. Hazrat Umm Salamah was among the women who accompanied the Muslim army to tend to the wounded and keep up the supply of water behind the lines. The Holy Prophet's (May God bless and cherish him) aunt Hazrat Safiyyah, Umm Ayman, Nusaybah and, Umm Salaym, the mother of Ans also participated in this expedition.

For several days fighting continued with no achievement. Then one night, when Hazrat Umar was in command of the watch, a spy was caught, and in return for his life he gave them valuable information about the various fortresses. He told them which they should capture easily and suggested that they should begin with the one that was not well guarded and that had a lot of weapons stored in its basement, including some war machines that could be used against other fortresses. The next day they easily overtook that fortress, and the war machines were taken out to be used in other attacks. They captured a ballista for hurling rocks and two tostados for bringing up men to the walls beneath an impregnable roof so they could breach an entrance. In this way, the smaller fortresses fell one by one.

The siege of Khaybar continued, and in the meantime, the Holy Prophet (May God bless and cherish him) fell ill and was unable to come out among his warriors. He called his loyal and trusted friend Hazrat Abu Bakr to his side and gave him the white standard, which meant that he was the commander of the army now against Khaybar. Night fell that day, and no results were achieved. The next day, the Holy Prophet (May God bless and cherish him) called Hazrat Umar and gave him the standard of the army. The following day the standard was given to one of the Ansar. The standard kept changing hands with no clear victory in sight.

The Holy Prophet (May God bless and cherish him) wanted to negotiate an agreement with the people of Ghatafan, who had come from outside to reinforce the Jews of Khaybar. He sent Sa'd ibn Ubada as an envoy to the commander of the Ghatafan, Uyayana ibn Hisn. Sa'd went straight to the gate of the fortress and called out, "I want to speak to Uyayna ibn Hisn." Uyayana wanted to let the envoy of the Holy Prophet (May God bless and cherish him) in the fortress for talks, but the commander of the fortress Marhab, insisted that he should go out and meet him. Therefore, Uyayana came out to where Sa'd was. "The Messenger of Allah has sent me to you," Sa'd started and conveyed the following message, "Allah the exalted had given me the good news of the conquest of Khaybar, now you should leave with your men. If you do so and when we conquer Khaybar, one year's date harvest of this place will be yours."

But Uyayana had no intention to come to an agreement, he had done the same thing on the Day of Trench. He said that he would not leave their allies in return for anything. So, Sa'd returned to the Holy Prophet (May God bless and cherish him) and informed him, "O Messenger of Allah! There is no doubt that Allah, the Almighty, will keep His promise to you, then, do not give a single date to those desert Arabs. When they see that swords are being wielded at them, they will turn back and run to their homes just as they did at the Trench." (Ibn Qayyim, Zadul - Ma'ad: Salihi, Subulu l-Huda war-Rashad)

At sunset, the Holy Prophet (May God bless and cherish him) told his Companions, "Take the standard and surround the fortress of Naim where the people of Ghatafan are." Muslim fighters gathered around the fortress and surrounded it from all sides. When they saw this new development, they were frightened and spent the night in fear. In the dark of the night, out of nowhere, they heard a strange voice that they did not know whether it came from earth or heaven. The voice loudly said three times in succession, "Your people! Your people! Your people!" whereupon the men imagined that their families were in danger. They decided to go back and started to leave the fortress. It was not only the Ghatafan who were gripped by fear that night. The Jews were also scared and regretting their decision. When the news that the Ghatafan had abandoned them reached Kinanah in the fortress of Katiba, he said, "When did we ever benefit by making an alliance with these desert Arabs? Whenever we went to them for help, they deceived us and never delivered the help they promised. I wish we had listened to Sallam, and not chosen the path of war with Muhammad."

The Muslim army was positioned opposite the fortress and watched the Ghatafan retreating home. They kept watch all night. During the night, Hazrat Umar noticed a dark shadow coming towards him from one of the fortresses. "If you give me surety for my life, I will come close to you," the person asked. "Who are you?" Hazrat Umar asked. "A man from among the Jews," said the man. He insisted on being taken to the Holy Prophet (May God bless and cherish him) because he wanted to give him some important information. They took him to the presence of the Holy Prophet (May God bless and cherish him), who was praying at that time. When he finished, he turned to the Jew named Simak and asked, "Who are you, and what information have you?" "O Abul Qasim," he answered, "Will you grant me safety if I tell you secret and important information from within the fortress?" "Yes," replied the Holy Prophet (May God bless and cherish him).

Simak gave detailed information regarding the state of fear and panic they were in, where they had their weapons and provisions, about the shelters underground, and where the catapults and weapons like dabbada were. (Dabbada was the name of a big machine that would be placed close to the wall of the fortress to make holes in the battlements. The machine top was resistant against the arrows, spears, and hot oil that might be thrown down.)

Simak's only concern was his family and his life. The Holy Prophet (May God bless and cherish him) invited him to Islam so that he could save his eternal life as well. But Simak was not ready yet, "Give me a few days to think about it," and the Holy Prophet (May God bless and cherish him) agreed. After the conquest, he returned with his wife Nufayla and children and left Khaybar having converted. However, he was not heard of again. (Waqidi)

During the entire campaign of Khaybar, the first powerful resistance they encountered was at a stronghold named Naim. Here, the Jews came out in great force, and on that day, every attack made by Muslims was repulsed. At last, the Messenger of Allah turned to his Companions and said, "Tomorrow, will I give the standard unto a man whom God and His Messenger love, God will give us victory by his hands; he is not one who turneth back in fight." All the Companions were hoping to be handed the standard and spent the entire night in anticipation. The next day, after the morning prayer, the Holy Prophet (May God bless and cherish him) asked for the standard to be brought to him. In his previous campaigns, the Holy Prophet (May God bless and cherish him) had used relatively small flags as standards. But to Khaybar, he had brought a great black standard made from the cloak of Hazrat Aisha. They called it "Eagle." The Holy Prophet (May God bless and cherish him) asked, "Where is Ali?" "O Messenger of Allah, Ali has sore eyes," said a Companion. "Call him to me." He spoke. So, Salamah ibn Akwan went to Hazrat Ali and brought him, holding his hand to the presence of the Holy Prophet (May God bless and cherish him). "Come near me," the Holy Prophet (May God bless and cherish him) said as Hazrat Ali approached. "O Messenger of Allah, I have sore eyes, and I can hardly see where I am going," replied Hazrat Ali. The Holy Prophet (May God bless and cherish him) prayed for his victory and applied a little bit of his blessed saliva to the eyes of Hazrat Ali, supplicating Allah at the same time to heal his eyes. Miraculously, Hazrat Ali's eyes healed instantly, as if they were not sore at all, and he could see clearly.

The Holy Prophet (May God bless and cherish him) gave Hazrat Ali the standard, and put his armor on him, and said, "Take this standard and advance! Fight till Allah makes you victorious, and do not turn back." Hazrat Ali went and raised the standard in front of the fortress. Someone from the Jews called, "Who are you?" "I am Ali, son of Abu Talib,' answered Hazrat Ali. One of the Jews called to his fellows, "O community of Jews, I swear by what has been revealed to Moses that your end has come, and you will be defeated today."

The gates of the fortress cranked open and a strong warrior, Harith, Marhab's brother, came out. He walked over and challenged the Companions for single combat and stood in front of Hazrat Ali. A fierce battle ensued, and in no time, he was lying dead on the ground. After that, another warrior Usayr came out, followed by Yasir. They both met the same fate as Harith. Usayr was slain by Muhammad ibn Maslamah, and Yasir by Zubayr ibn Awwam. Next, Amir came out and challenged Hazrat Ali. He had put on double armor but was cut by Hazrat Ali's sword.

The greatest warrior of Khaybar was Marhab, and he came out with his soldiers. He had double armor, and two helmets, and a sword in each hand. As soon as he came out, he shouted, "O people of Khaybar know that at times when war comes knocking on the door, and the fight is most fierce, it is Marhab who gives war its due, loaded with weapons from top to bottom." A war of words started before the swords were drawn. It was Hazrat Ali who said, "I am the one who has been nicknamed "Haider" (Lion) by his mother, and I am like the ferocious lion of the jungle, and I finish in an instant."

When Marhab heard the word "Haider," his face became pale because the night before, he had dreamt that he had been torn apart by a lion and had woken up in great fear. A fierce combat started. Hazrat Ali and Marhab drew their swords and attacked each other in violent moves. The noise of clashing swords and challenges thrown at each other was deafening. Suddenly, there was a great noise, and everyone knew that a deathly blow had been delivered. When the dust settled, they could see that it was Hazrat Ali who had been left standing. The sword of Hazrat Ali 'Dhul-fiqar' had landed with such force on the head of Marhab that it cut through the two helmets and split his skull.

When the Holy Prophet (May God bless and cherish him) saw that Marhab had been killed after Yasir, he gave the following good tidings, "Rejoice! Khaybar is easier now." During the tough battle that followed, Hazrat Ali's shield fell from his hand, and he had nothing left to protect himself with. He looked around and saw the door of the fortress. He reached for the door and yanked it and used it as his shield till the end of the battle. Jewish fighters started fleeing towards the fortresses remaining in the back. The sound of "takbir" (Allah is great) echoed throughout the Khaybar.

The Holy Prophet (May God bless and cherish him) was dressed in his armor and had put a helmet on his head. He had mounted his horse named 'Zarib' and was carrying a bow and arrow in his hand. In the meanwhile, a black man named Yasir approached him and told him that he was Amir's shepherd. He has been listening to his master Amir and his friends, "We will fight along with this man who claims to be a prophet." And hearing that, he developed a strong affection for the Messenger of Allah in his heart. So, he had come there with his sheep to find out the truth. So, he called out, "O Messenger of Allah! What do you invite people to?" The Holy Prophet said, "I invite people to Islam, to believe that there is no deity but Allah worthy of worship and to bear witness that I am His Messenger." Yasir asked, "If I bear witness and believe in Allah, what do I gain?" "If you die believing, then there is paradise for you," answered the Holy Prophet (May God bless and cherish him). Upon that, Yasir said, "O Messenger of Allah, tell me about Islam and how one becomes a Muslim?" Yasir entered Islam and asked, "O Messenger of Allah! I am black, ugly, and with bad odor, and a man with no money. If I fight against the Jews today and die, will I enter paradise?' "Yes," replied the Holy Prophet (May God bless and cherish him). It was obvious that Yasir had set his eyes on paradise. So, he asked the Holy Prophet (May God bless and cherish him), "O Messenger of Allah! These sheep and cattle have been entrusted to me. I work for the owner of these animals. What shall I do with them now?"

The Holy Prophet (May God bless and cherish him) understood his concern and said, "First, get them out of this place. Then, throw some stones at them. Allah will help you to return them to their owners." Yasir picked up some pebbles and threw them at the sheep. The entire herd started moving back to its owner's home.

Yasir joined the fighters of Hazrat Ali and entered the battlefield. Suddenly, one of the stones thrown with a catapult from the fortress hit Yasir, and he became a martyr without having performed even a single prayer. His body was brought to the Holy Prophet (May God bless and cherish him), and he prayed for him, "May Allah the Almighty beautify your face and increase your wealth of deeds." Soon, the Holy Prophet (May God bless and cherish him) was seen to turn his face away from Yasir. The Companions wondered what was happening. "O Messenger of Allah, why did you turn your face away from him?" He answered, "Two heavenly companions, two of his spouses, came by his side, wiped the dirt off his face and said, 'May Allah put the faces of those who put your face in dirt in the dirt too. May Allah kill those who killed you.' I saw two heavenly brides with him even though he did not prostrate even once." (Ibn Hisham, Sira: Waqidi, Maghazi: Ibn Athir, Usdu l-Ghaba: Ibn Hajar, Al-Isaba: Suyuti, Rawdhu l-Unf)

One of the strongholds of Khaybar was known as the citadel of Zubayr. It was impenetrable, situated on a high mass of rock with a steep approach to the gates and sheer cliff on all the other sides. Most of the Jews who had escaped from other fortresses had taken shelter within its walls. The Muslim army laid siege to it for three days. Then a Jew by the name of Gazzal from another fortress came to the presence of the Holy Prophet (May God bless and cherish him) and told him that they had a hidden source that would enable them to hold out almost indefinitely. He made a deal with the Holy Prophet (May God bless and cherish him) to tell him about the secret on the condition that his life, property, and family should be safe. The Holy Prophet (May God bless and cherish him) accepted his offer, and the man showed him where they could dig down to the water reservoir, an underground rivulet that flowed beneath the fortress. The stream was never dry, so the Jews kept no stores of water. When the Muslims cut off that underground source of water, the Jewish fighters were driven by thirst to come out and fight, but in the end, they were defeated.

The last stronghold to make any resistance was Qamus. This belonged to the family of Kinanah ibn l-Huqayq, one of the richest and most powerful clans of Bani Nadir. Some of them had long lived in Khaybar, while Kinanah himself settled there after they were exiled from Yathrib. It was Kinanah who persuaded Ghatafan to help them against Medina. But their failure to keep their promise had demoralized Kinanah. So, he sent his representative Shammah to the Holy Prophet (May God bless and cherish him) to let him know of his desire to negotiate. The Holy Prophet (May God bless and cherish him) agreed to peace talks. Therefore, Kinanah, with several of his family members, came down from the fortress. They were obviously scared for their lives, and after deliberations, the two sides agreed to the following.

1. None of the inhabitants of the fortress should be put to death or made captive.

2. The families and children of the Jews would be spared, and they would be allowed to leave Khaybar.

3. All the possessions of the Jews would become the property of the victors. They would only be allowed to take two mount loads of possessions. They would leave all their wealth and armor and arms.

4. Anyone who might try to conceal any of his possessions would be exempt from this treaty and would also risk their life.

Kinanah and other Jews agreed to this, and the Holy Prophet (May God bless and cherish him) called Hazrat Abu Bakr, Hazrat Umar, Hazrat Ali, and Zubayr, and ten of the Jews to witness the agreement.

THE LEGENDARY TREASURE

Soon it became clear to both Jews and Muslims that most of the wealth was hidden. Among the spoils they had captured so far, there was no gold or silver. And especially where was the legendary treasure of the Bani Nadir, which they had brought with them from Medina, which they had so proudly displayed in the procession through its streets. Abu Rafi, Sallam ibn Abi l-Huqayq had pointed to the camel skin in which gold, silver, and other precious metals were stored. This treasure had been accumulated by the dynasty of Abi-l-Huqayq. Initially, this treasure would fit into a sheep skin, since then it had grown, first filling a cow skin and eventually it could hardly be contained in a camel's skin.

In Makkah, the rich would go to the Jews and rent jewelry from this treasure and return it back. If they lost it for some reason, they had to pay it back as ten thousand gold coins. The Jews of Khaybar did not want to hand over this treasure. The Holy Prophet (May God bless and cherish him) questioned Kinanah and his brother about this, and he replied that since their arrival in Khaybar, the treasure had all been sold to pay for more arms, armor and fortification. The Holy Prophet was annoyed and said,

"O Sons of Abi-l-Huqayq, I know the enmity you have against Allah and His Messenger, despite that I gave protection and surety to your tribe, with the condition that you would not hide anything from me when it comes to spoils and would not conceal anything. In that case, you would have no surety of Allah and His Messenger, and it would be admissible for me to shed your blood. Now tell me, where are the skins in which you stored your precious things and gold. The skin you took away with you when you were exiled from Medina."

Even the Jews knew that Kinanah was lying and were more apprehensive because many of them deeply believed themselves to be in the presence of a prophet. One of them went to Kinanah and begged him not to hide anything, for if he lied, the Messenger of Allah would certainly be informed. Even before he could finish, Kinanah rebuked him and pushed him away. Then, a naïve Jew by the name of Salaba was brought to the presence of the Holy Prophet (May God bless and cherish him) and stated that he saw Kinanah every morning in some deserted place. Upon this, the Holy Prophet (May God bless and cherish him) turned towards Kinanah and said, "What do you say to that, if we find the treasure there, you will lose your head." Kinanah said, "Yes," and blatantly denied it. The Holy Prophet (May God bless and cherish him) sent a Companion to the place Salaba had indicated. The Companion dug that place and found part of the treasure that was brought to the presence of the holy Prophet (May God bless and cherish him). But this was not all the treasure. It appeared that he had split it into two and buried it in two different places. The Holy Prophet (May God bless and cherish him) turned towards Kinanah and asked once again, but the unfortunate man kept silent. It was clear that his wealth was more precious to him than his life. At the same time, Gabriel came to the Messenger of Allah and told him the location of the rest of the treasure. The Holy Prophet (May God bless and cherish him) sent out one of Ansar to the place Gabriel had told him and asked him to dig that place and bring out what he found. Ansar was successful in finding the treasure and brought the camel skin full of gold and jewelry. The Messenger of Allah handed Kinanah and his brother Rabi to Muhammad ibn Masalama in return for his brother Mahmud, whom they had killed. And their families were taken captive.

After the conquest of the Jewish stronghold Qamus, the remaining smaller fortresses surrendered as well. But later, the Jews of Khaybar sent a delegation to the Holy Prophet (May God bless and cherish him) and requested that since they were experts in taking care of their farms and orchards, they should be allowed to remain in their homes, and they would pay half of the entire produce. The Holy Prophet (May God bless and cherish him) was kind in this regard and agreed to their suggestion on the condition that if in the future he decided to banish them, they must leave Khaybar.

The Muslim army intended to overtake Fadak, a small but rich oasis to the northeast, and when the Jews of Fadak learned about the terms that had been imposed upon Khaybar, they agreed to surrender on the same conditions. Fadak thus became the property of the Holy Prophet, as did every other asset that had not been acquired by the force of arms.

HAZRAT SAFFIYAH

Among the people who had been taken captive was Huyayy ibn Akhtab's daughter Saffiyah, who came from the lineage of Prophet Aron. She was married to Kinanah ibn l-Huqayq before the invasion of Khaybar and when Kinanah was killed, she became a widow. Dihya al-Kalbi was one of the Companions, whom the Holy Prophet (May God bless and cherish him) had sent as an envoy to various places, who came to the presence of the Holy Prophet (May God bless and cherish him) and asked one of the captives to be given to him. He chose Saffiyah and left. One of the Companions came to the Holy Prophet (May God bless and cherish him) and said, "O Messenger of Allah! It would not be appropriate to give a lady of the Bani Qurayzah and Bani Nadir tribes, the daughter of their leader Huyayy ibn Akhtab, to Dihyah. Instead, you should take her."

The Holy Prophet called Bilal and told him to bring Saffiyah to his presence. Bilal obeyed the command and brought Saffiyah. When she came, the Holy Prophet (May God bless and cherish him) invited her to Islam and told her that if she accepted Islam, he would marry her, and if not, he would give her freedom and send her back to her tribe. Saffiyah replied, "O Messenger of Allah, I wanted to become a Muslim even before you invited me to Islam. I bear witness to your prophethood. I chose Allah and His Messenger. Allah and His Messenger are better for me than being set free and returning to my tribe." The Holy Prophet (May God bless and cherish him) made her free and took her as a wife.

ATTEMPT TO POISON THE HOLY PROPHET

After the conquest of Khaybar, the Holy Prophet (May God bless and cherish him) stayed there for a while. Zaynab bint Harith, the wife of Sallam ibn Mishkam, who had been killed in Khaybar, had also lost her father, Harith, her brother, and uncle in this conflict. And so, she wanted to avenge their deaths. She roasted a lamb in a deadly poison, with more concentration in the shoulders. She knew on inquiry that the Holy Prophet (May God bless and cherish him) was fonder of the shoulder of the lamb than the other parts. The Holy Prophet (May God bless and cherish him) prayed his evening prayer and was resting. Zaynab bint Harith came with a tray of roasted lamb that she had poisoned and presented it to the Holy Prophet (May God bless and cherish him) and said, "O Abu Qasim. This is my gift to you." Whereupon he thanked her and invited those around him to share the food.

Bishr ibn Bara was sitting close to the Holy Prophet (May God bless and cherish him); he was the one who led the Muslims of Yathrib to the second Aqabah and who had been the first to pray the ritual prayer in the direction of Kaaba. But as soon as the Holy Prophet (May God bless and cherish him) took a mouthful of lamb, he spat it out and said to others, "Hold off your hands! This shoulder tells me that it is poisoned." Bishr ibn Bara had already chewed and swallowed a piece just when the Holy Prophet (May God bless and cherish him) warned the Companions. The poison was very strong, and Bishr's face turned pale, and he died shortly afterwards. The Holy Prophet (May God bless and cherish him) called the woman and asked her if she had poisoned the lamb. "Who told you?" she asked. "The shoulder itself," said the Holy Prophet (May God bless and cherish him). "What made you do it?" asked the Messenger of Allah. She said, "You know what has befallen my tribe; you have slain my father, uncle, and husband. So, I said to myself, if he is a king, then we will have got rid of him, but if he is really a prophet, then he will somehow be informed of it and be saved." The Holy Prophet (May God bless and cherish him) nonetheless forgave the woman. But when Bishr died, she was given to the relatives of Bishr, in compensation for his blood and they would kill her.

THE ARRIVAL OF HAZRAT JAFFAR

With the fall of Khaybar, another threat against Medina was eliminated. When Makkah was the center of abuse and hatred, Hazrat Jaffar and other Muslims had emigrated to Abyssinia. But when the Muslims in Abyssinia received the message that the Holy Prophet (May God bless and cherish him) was to return to Medina, they boarded a ship that was given to them by king Najashi (Negus) and reached Arabia. They had learned that the Holy Prophet had come to Khaybar, so they arrived there to meet him. Hazrat Jaffar and his friends had not seen the Holy Prophet (May God bless and cherish him) for 15 years now. When Hazrat Jaffar walked towards the Holy Prophet (May God bless and cherish him), both were filled with emotions, and they embraced each other. The Holy Prophet (May God bless and cherish him) kissed him in between his brows and said, "I do not know what to rejoice, the conquest of Khaybar or the arrival of Jaffar?"

Hazrat Jaffar was accompanied by more than fifty Muslims, including Abu Musa al-Ashari. Among those who came to Khaybar on the first day were eighty household members from the tribe of Daws. They had become Muslims and came all the way to Medina after performing the morning prayer led by Siba ibn Urfuta. On their way, they found out that the Holy Prophet (May God bless and cherish him) was close by, so they changed their direction to Khaybar to see the Messenger of Allah as soon as possible. Among them was a man named Abdu Shams, who would later be known as Abu Hurayrah. When the Holy Prophet (May God bless and cherish him) learned his name, he said, "The sun has no slave or subject," and changed his name to Abdul Rahman. In later years, when the Holy Prophet (May God bless and cherish him) saw a kitten on his lap, he nicknamed him "Abu Hirr," and from then on, he was known as Abu Hurayrah. (Hakim, Mustadrak; Ibn Hajar, Al-Isaba; Ibn Athir, Usdu l-Ghaba)

WADI AL QURA

The siege and battle of Khaybar lasted for about two months. In this expedition, twenty-eight Companions fell martyr, and ninety-three of the Khaybar warriors were killed. Now that Khaybar was behind them, the Holy Prophet marched towards Wadi al Qura. The Jews of Wadi al Qura and Tayma, like the Jews of Khaybar, had joined forces in the event of an attack on Medina. The Muslim army arrived at sunset at Wadi al Qura, and without wasting time, the Holy Prophet (May God bless and cherish him) invited them to Islam. But they did not heed his advice and instead started showering arrows. Seeing this, the Holy Prophet (May God bless and cherish him) gave the standard to Sa'd ibn Ubayda and told his Companions to take positions for the battle. The Holy Prophet (May God bless and cherish him) invited them one more time to Islam and said that if they accepted Islam their lives and property would be under protection but that they would answer to Allah for what they harbored in their hearts. They did not accept the invitation and sent their strong warriors one by one, who were slain by Hazrat Ali, Zubayr ibn Awwam, and Abu Dujana. The Holy Prophet (May God bless and cherish him) one more time extended his invitation, but they refused. That day, eleven of the great warriors were killed.

On the fourth day, the Muslim army tightened their siege and launched a fresh attack. With the first rays of the sunlight, they eventually succeeded. The spoils were gathered and divided into five portions. Four-fifths of what was gathered was distributed among the Companions. Just like the people of Khaybar, the Jews of Wadi al Qura were given the same rights. They were allowed to remain on their land with the condition of sending half of their yearly produce to Medina. The Holy Prophet (May God bless and cherish him) appointed Amr ibn Said as their governor.

RETURN JOURNEY TO MEDINA

The Muslim army, under the leadership of the Holy Prophet (May God bless and cherish him), embarked upon their return journey to Medina. It had been a while since they left the city, and now, they were excited to be coming home again. They continued day and night, taking smaller breaks. They were so exhausted they decided to stop after midnight. The Holy Prophet (May God bless and cherish him) asked, "Can someone among you wake us up for the morning prayer? I am afraid we may oversleep." At this, Bilal volunteered and said, "O Messenger of Allah, I will keep watch and wake you up for the prayer."

Everybody was relieved and could sleep without worrying. Bilal took upon himself the duty of waking them up for the morning prayer. He started supererogatory prayers in the dark of the night. As the time went by, he felt exhausted. He sat down, leaning his back against a camel. Bilal was soon fast asleep. When the Holy Prophet woke up, he saw that all the Companions, including Bilal, were sleeping. The sun was coming up, and they all were still in a deep sleep. The Holy Prophet (May God bless and cherish him) looked for Bilal and said, O Bilal, what have you done." Bilal woke up to the voice of the Holy Prophet (May God bless and cherish him) and was embarrassed. They all had missed the morning prayer. He first told them, "This is a valley where the devil roams," and gave orders to march. After some time, the Holy Prophet (May God bless and cherish him) told them to stop. He then made his ablution and told Bilal to make the call of prayer. The Holy Prophet (May God bless and cherish him) led all the Companions in prayer and said, "The soul of each one of us is in the hand of Allah. He can take it at any time. He is the one with power and might. So, when you forget your prayers, perform them as soon as you remember them. For God says, "Perform the prayer in order to remember Me."

As they approached Medina, the Companions were overjoyed both because of the victory they had had at Khaybar and because they were back safely. Suddenly, the mountains and valleys of Medina were resounding with their takbirs (magnification of Allah's name). The Holy Prophet told them, "Remember Allah quietly, for you are not praying to one who is distant from you, nor to one who cannot hear you. Allah is the one who hears all, whether a loud call or the heart's secret, and who is closest to you all. And He is with you all the time."

Then he turned towards Abu Musa al-Ashari, who was close to him, and said, "O Abdullah ibn Qays," Abu Musa responded, "Let my mother and father be sacrificed to you, o Messenger of Allah!" the Holy Prophet (May God bless and cherish him) continued, "Shall I tell you something that is the treasure of paradise?" "Of course, O Messenger of Allah," The Holy Prophet (May God bless and cherish him) said, "*La hawla wala quwwata illa billah*" (There is no power except with Allah). The Companions who heard these words from the blessed lips of the Holy Prophet

(May God bless and cherish him) had stopped saying takbirs and were reciting this sentence, which they just learned to be the treasure of paradise.

AFTERMATH OF KHAYBAR

After the campaign of Khaybar, the spoils were distributed among the warriors. It also enabled the Holy Prophet (May God bless and cherish him) to do two things. Firstly, he told the Emigrants to give back the property that the Ansar had given them when they had left Makkah and their properties. This included a date grove that Anas's mother, Umm Sulaym, had gifted the Holy Prophet (May God bless and cherish him), which he had granted to Umm Ayman to live on after Hijra. Thus, this property was returned to its original owner. At the same time, Makkah was suffering from a great drought and both her people and animals were facing famine. The Holy Prophet (May God bless and cherish him) sent aid via Amr ibn Umayya to the leaders of the Quraysh, such as Abu Sufyan, Suhayl ibn Amr, and Safwan ibn Umayya to be distributed among the poor of Makkah. But Suhayl ibn Amr and Safwan ibn Umayya rejected the offer, as they could not bring themselves to accept help from people who they had shown great enmity until yesterday. However, Abu Sufyan acted on the contrary and said, "May Allah reward the son of my brother with goodness, for he has done what becomes kinship and helped us." He then distributed the help among the needy of Makkah.

It was during this time that Abu Hurayrah came to Medina with the people of Daws. He joined the people of the bench (Ashab e Suffa) and lived in the Mosque (Masjid e Nabawi). He was happy to serve Allah and His Messenger and devoted himself to the path. His mother had also come with him to Medina, but she did not enter Islam. Abu Hurayrah was very concerned about his mother. So, he decided to speak to the Holy Prophet (May God bless and cherish him) and said, "O Messenger of Allah! I invited my mother to Islam many times, and each time she has refused, and cursed me. I made her the same request today and she uttered words against you, and I did not like it. Will you pray to Allah for my mother to become Muslim?"

The Holy Prophet (May God bless and cherish him) listened to his sincere request that came from his heart. He lifted his hands and prayed for Abu Hurayrah's mother. He was extremely happy, for he knew that the supplication of the Holy Prophet (May God bless and cherish him) would surely be answered, and as a result his mother would be saved, both in this world and the hereafter. He left the Mosque and hurriedly went home to see his mother. When he reached home, the door was closed. He knocked at the door, and his mother called out to wait as she was making an ablution and getting on clean clothes. When she came out, she looked at Abu Hurayrah with a smile and said, "I bear witness that there is no god, but Allah and that Muhammad is His Messenger."

Abu Hurayrah was ecstatic as if the entire world had been given to him. With a heart full of joy, he ran back to the Mosque and said, "O Messenger of Allah! Allah has accepted your prayer, and my mother has accepted Islam." This made the Holy Prophet happy as well, and he said, "Dear Lord! Put love into the hearts of your believing subjects for Abu Hurayrah and his mother and put love into their hearts for the believers as well."

Khaybar was followed by six other campaigns, which were relatively smaller, two of which under Hazrat Umar and Hazrat Abu Bakr respectively, were against the clans of the tribe of Hawazin, whose territory blocked the main route to Yemen. The others were to the east and north against the clan of Ghatafan. Two of the campaigns were against the Bani Murrah, who lived close to Fadak, which now belonged to the Holy Prophet (May God bless and cherish him). The Jews of Fadak were now working for the Holy Prophet (May God bless and cherish him), and they needed protection. Initially, the Holy Prophet (May God bless and cherish him) sent a small force of thirty fighters to deal with the situation, but most of them were killed by the rebels. The Holy Prophet (May God bless and cherish him) immediately dispatched a force of two hundred men to deal with the enemy. The enemy was put to flight, and a good number of them were slain.

On this campaign, Usama, a seventeen-year-old youth, was also sent. He had participated in the Battle of Trench, but this was his chance to show his steel. During the night, a man of Murrah mocked him for his young age. Usama was enraged and followed the man deep into the desert, though he was commanded to stay close to other fighters. He eventually got hold of the man and injured him. And at the same time the man recited '*La Ilaha Illallah*' (There is no god but God). Usama heard his testification but despite that he dealt him a fatal blow. Ghalib ibn Abdullah was the commander of the Muslim force. That night, Usama returned late, and the commander was angry at him. Usama explained, "I followed a man who laughed at me, and I caught and wounded him, then he recited '*La Ilaha Illallah*.' "Did you leave him then?" asked the commander. "Nay, not until I dealt him a death blow." At this, all the Companions bellowed at him, and he realized his mistake. He was so remorseful that he did not eat or drink on the way back to Medina. A revelation had come earlier regarding one or two incidences where a believer had been about to kill a disbeliever, who had then accepted Islam and recited '*La Ilaha Illallah*' and motivated by the idea of losing the spoils of war, the victor had said, "You truly are not a believer," and had therefore killed him.

"O you, who believe, when you fight in the way of Allah, discriminate, nor say unto him who gives you a greeting of peace, "you are not a believer," aspiring for the goods of worldly life, for with Allah are goods in plenty. You were like that before, but God had sent down His grace upon you. Therefore, discriminate. Verily, God is informed of what you do." (Al-Nisa 4:94).

When Usama reached Medina, he went straight to the Holy Prophet (May God bless and cherish him). The Holy Prophet (May God bless and cherish him) welcomed and embraced him and asked about his mission. Usama told us everything that had happened during that campaign. When he reached the point where he had killed him after he had recited '*La Ilaha Illallah.*' The Holy Prophet (May God bless and cherish him) was upset and said, "Did you slay him after he accepted Islam?" "O Messenger of Allah!" he answered, "He did say that only to escape his death." The Holy Prophet (May God bless and cherish him) said, "Did you open his heart to know whether he spoke the truth or he lied?" "Never again, I will slay anyone who proclaims faith," he said. He felt guilty and wished that he had only entered Islam that day because the Messenger of Allah affirmed that entry into the religion effaces the guilt of all past sins.

CHAPTER 21
UMRAH: THE LESSER PILGRIMAGE

It was Dhul al-Qadah, the seventh year after Hijra, that Gabriel brought the verse.

"The prohibited month for the prohibited month, and so for all things prohibited, there is the law of retribution. If anyone transgresses the prohibition against you, transgress ye likewise against him. But fear God and know that God is with those who restrain themselves." (Quran 2:194).

This was a reminder for the Holy Prophet (May God bless and cherish him) that it was time for the lesser pilgrimage that he could not perform last year should be undertaken now. Hence, the Holy Prophet (May God bless and cherish him) instructed his Companions to prepare to perform the rites of lesser pilgrimage. He also stressed that except for those who fell martyr or died, no one from those who had been at Hudaybiyah should stay behind. There were around two thousand pilgrims in all, including Abu Hurayrah, who had not been to Hadaybiyah. He had arrived in Medina with other members of his tribe during the campaign of Khaybar, and because of extreme poverty, had joined the people of the Bench.

The Holy Prophet (May God bless and cherish him), dressed in *Ihram,* stood at the door of the Mosque and started reciting the *Talbiya*; everyone who heard him began to recite the same. Medina was echoing with the sound of,

"Labbayk allahumma labbayk, labbayka la sharika laka labbayk, innel hamda wan nimata laka, wal Mulka la sharika lak."

The Muslims were taking sixty camels with them for sacrifice. The Holy Prophet

(May God bless and cherish him) had prepared his own camel and had marked it on its neck. He appointed Najiya ibn Jandal and five others to take the camels on a route with abundant greenery to graze upon until they reached Makkah. As a precautionary measure, the Holy Prophet (May God bless and cherish him) appointed Muhammad ibn Maslama, a leader of one hundred horsemen, and instructed them to take weapons and store them outside the Holy Precinct. When this advance party reached a place called Marr az-Zahran, they encountered several people from the Quraysh, who were worried to see them with a huge number of weapons. They immediately returned to Makkah and informed their leaders. "How can it be?" they questioned. "We did not violate the terms of the agreement, so why is Muhammad advancing with his friends toward us with their weapons?" So, they sent a delegation under the leadership of Mikraz ibn Hays to the Holy Prophet (May God bless and cherish him). He reassured them that the pilgrims would not enter Makkah with weapons.

When the pilgrims reached the sacred territory, the Quraysh vacated the entire city of Makkah and withdrew to the top of the surrounding mountains. The leaders of the Quraysh were gathered on Mount Abu Qubays, from where they could easily watch the Mosque. From the mountain top, they could also see the entire Makkah and the roads leading to it. Soon, the pilgrims poured into Makkah from the northwestern pass just below the city. Their indistinct humming voices were getting louder as they came close. They were chanting, *"Labbayk Allahumma Labbayk"* (here I am, O Lord, at Thy service). The Holy Prophet (May God bless and cherish him) was riding Qaswa, with Abdullah ibn Rawaha in front, holding the bridle. He was leading the bare-headed pilgrims in ihrams, of which some were on camelback and some on foot. As Abdullah ibn Rawaha was walking in front of the Holy Prophet (May God bless and cherish him), he was reciting poetry that spoke about the changes in circumstances from yesterday to today. Hazrat Umar found it inappropriate and warned him to stop singing. But the Holy Prophet (May God bless and cherish him) intervened and told Hazrat Umar to leave him alone. Then he turned to Abdullah and told him to chant the following as they entered Kaaba,

"He is Allah, the Mighty and Majestic. There is no deity but Him. He grants His servant's victory; He makes his army triumph and destroys those that stand in front of him."

Every pilgrim was wearing his upper garment as a cloak, but the Holy Prophet (May God bless and cherish him) adjusted his garment by passing it under his right arm, leaving the shoulder bare and crossing the two ends over the left shoulder so that they hung down back and front. All the believers followed his example. Still riding Qaswa, the Holy Prophet (May God bless and cherish him) went to the southeast corner of the Kaaba and touched the Black Stone with his staff. Then, he made seven rounds of the Sacred House. After that he went towards the small hill of Safa and walked in between it and the hill of Marwa, completing seven laps in all. After that, he sacrificed his camel, and his head was shaved by Khirash, who had done the same for him at Hudaybiyah. This concluded the lesser pilgrimage.

The Holy Prophet then returned to the Mosque and wanted to enter the Kaaba, but its doors were locked. So, he sent someone to the person who had the keys that belonged to the clan of Abd al-Dar. His request was denied by the chiefs of the Quraysh, saying that this was not part of the agreement. Therefore, none of the pilgrims could enter the Holy House.

At noon time, when the sun was at its zenith, the Holy Prophet (May God bless and cherish him) told Bilal to go up the roof of Kaaba and make Adhan (the call of prayer). His strong, melodious voice filled the entire valley of Makkah and echoed up to the tops of the mountains. "I bear witness that there is no god but God. I bear witness that Muhammad is the Messenger of God." The leaders of the Quraysh, sitting at the top of Abu Qubays, were outraged when they saw the black slave on the roof of the holy House and making the call to prayer. At this, Ikrimah, the son of Abu Jahl, said, "I am glad God has been graceful to Abu Hakam and did not let him hear what this slave says." He was relating to the fact that his father would not have been able to bear such a sight where Bilal, once a meager slave, was standing atop of Kaaba as a free man and professing, "Allah is the greatest." Safwan ibn Umayyah said in the same vein, "Praise be to God, who took my father away before he could see this moment." Khalid ibn Asid joined in and said, "Thanks to God, who killed my father before he could see Bilal on the top of Kaaba and calling people to prayer."

The Holy Prophet's (May God bless and cherish him) tent was pitched in the Mosque. The pilgrim spent three days in place in the evacuated city. At night, those of the Makkans who had accepted Islam would come in secret and see the Holy Prophet (May God bless and cherish him). Hazrat Abbas, whose Islam was known to the Quraysh, would openly come during these days and meet the Holy Prophet. During this period, Hazrat Abbas offered the Holy Prophet (May God bless and cherish him) to marry his wife's sister, Maymunah, now a widow, and the Holy

Prophet (May God bless and cherish him) agreed to this union. Maymunah and umm al-Fadl were full sisters and with them. Living in the household of Hazrat Abbas was their half-sister Salma, the widow of Hazrat Hamzah, and her daughter Umamah.

The numbered days were up. On the morning of the fourth day, Suhayl ibn Amr and Huwaytib ibn Abdul Uzza, who was representing the Quraysh, came to the Holy Prophet (May God bless and cherish him) and said, "Your time is up, leave this place now." The Holy Prophet (May God bless and cherish him) said "How would it harm you to give me some respite, that I may celebrate my marriage amongst you and prepare for you a feast?" "We do not need your feast," they answered, "Leave us, we adjure you by God, O Muhammad. According to the agreement between us, this was the third night, and it has passed now."

The Holy Prophet (May God bless and cherish him) gave orders that all pilgrims should leave the city by nightfall. But he told Abu Rafi to stay behind and bring Maymunah with him, which he did according to his instructions.

When the Holy Prophet (May God bless and cherish him) was leaving Kaaba once again against his will, as he mounted Qaswa, he heard the feeble voice of a young girl calling out, "My dear uncle." He turned around and saw that it was Umamah, the daughter of Hazrat Hamzah, his uncle and nursing brother. It was a heart-breaking scene; eyes were filled with tears, and hearts filled with compassion. The orphaned daughter of Hazrat Hamzah ran towards the Holy Prophet (May God bless and cherish him), and Hazrat Ali was watching and ran and held her by hand. Hazrat Ali suggested that their cousin, Hazrat Hamzah's daughter, should not be left amongst the idolaters. The Holy Prophet (May God bless and cherish him) and Hazrat Abbas agreed with Hazrat Ali, and Hazrat Fatima took Umamah with her in her howdah.

After their return to Medina, the Holy Prophet (May God bless and cherish him) heard a heated argument one afternoon in the Mosque. It was Hazrat Ali, Jaffar, and Zayd, all of them were at odds with each other. The Holy Prophet (May God bless and cherish him) called them to his room and asked their dispute. They explained that it was a question of honor as to which of them had the most right to be the guardian of Hazrat Hamzah's daughter, who was currently in Hazrat Ali's home, since her arrival from Makkah. The Holy Prophet said, "I will judge between you." When they all sat down, he turned to Hazrat Ali and asked him what he had to say in this respect. "She is my uncle's daughter, and it was I who brought her here." The

Holy Prophet (May God bless and cherish him) then turned to Jafar, who said, "She is my uncle's daughter, and her mother's sister is in my house." His wife Asma was Umamah's aunt. As to Zayd, he simply said, "She is my brother's daughter, for the Holy Prophet (May God bless and cherish him) had made a pact of brotherhood between Hazrat Hamzah and Zayd when they emigrated to Medina. Hazrat Hamzah had also made a testament leaving Zayd in charge of his affairs. The Holy Prophet appreciated each of them and said, "Jafar, thou art like me in looks and in character." And he made his decision in favor of Jafar, "Thou has most right to her. The mother's sister is a mother." Jafar stood up and circled around the Holy Prophet (May God bless and cherish him) in a dancing manner. "Jafar, what is this?" said the Holy Prophet (May God bless and cherish him). Jafar replied, "It is what I have seen the Abyssinians do in honor of their kings. If ever the Negus gave a man a good reason to rejoice, that man would rise and dance around him."

KHALID IBN WALID

The treaty of Hudaybiyah was now seen by most of Quraysh to be a moral victory for the Holy Prophet (May God bless and cherish him). The leaders of the Quraysh had withdrawn from the city of Makkah, and most of them watched the pilgrims from the top of Abu Qubays in amazement. Khalid ibn Walid and Amr had gone somewhere else, but they knew that the latest development with the entry of the Holy Prophet (May God bless and cherish him) into Makkah meant the end of their hostility to him. Though outwardly, it did not look like that Khalid ibn Walid was double minded, he later confessed that he felt uneasy while returning from Uhud and the battle of Trench. Because he believed that the Messenger of Allah would triumph in the end, especially when he had avoided his squadron on the way to Hudaybiyah. With the latest victory of Muslims in Khaybar, it was evident that Islam would eventually take over the Arabian Peninsula. There were other reasons as well, such as how Khalid had a personal liking for the Holy Prophet (May God bless and cherish him). His younger brother had written him a letter before his death telling him that the Holy Prophet (May God bless and cherish him) asked about him and said, "If he would put his strength on the side of Islam against the polytheists, it would be in his favor, and we would give him preference over others." His brother wrote in the end, "Now you see my brother, what have you missed?"

Apart from this, now he had a new family relationship with the Holy Prophet (May God bless and cherish him). Khalid's mother, Asma, who had long been favorable to the Holy Prophet, had entered Islam, and now his aunt Maymunah had become the wife of the Messenger of Allah. He also had a vision, and after reflecting on that, he made up his mind. He was now looking for a like-minded person to accompany him to Medina. He could not find his friend Amr. His other comrades were Ikrima and Safwan. He approached both, but Safwan said, "Even if every other man of the Quraysh were to follow Muhammad, I would never follow him," and Ikrima said the same thing. Therefore, Khalid decided to set out alone. On his way, he came across Uthman, the son of Talha of Abd ad-Dar, the man who, years ago, had bravely escorted Umm Salamah from Makkah to Medina. He was a close friend of Khalid. Because Uthman had lost his father, two uncles, and four brothers at Uhud, Khalid was hesitant to discuss with him where he was heading. But eventually, both realized that it was impossible to hide what they were thinking. Khalid told him about his intention, and Uthman was also inclined to do so. Early next day, they both set off together for Medina.

Amr ibn Al-As, like Safwan and Ikrima, was not inclined towards Islam at all. He gathered some youth around him and went all the way to Abyssinia in the hope of finding favor with Najashi. But Najashi told him, "Do what I tell you, O Amr, and follow Muhammad. He is the truth, by God, and he will be victorious over all, just as Moses triumphed over Pharoah and his army." (Waqidi). Amr, therefore, returned and met Khalid and Uthman on their way to Medina.

In Medina, Khalid and Uthman were cordially welcomed. Khalid came to the presence of the Holy Prophet (May God bless and cherish him) and greeted him with peace. The Holy Prophet's (May God bless and cherish him) face lit up with joy. Khalid pledged his allegiance, "I bear witness that there is no god but God, and you are the Messenger of Allah." The Holy Prophet (May God bless and cherish him), "Praise be to God who has guided you. I saw great reason in you, and I hope it will bring you in the end nothing but good."

"O Messenger of Allah," said Khalid, "As you know, I fought against you in every battle and denied the truth at every turn. I ask you to pray to Allah that He may forgive me." "Islam wipes away all that went before it," the Holy Prophet (May God bless and cherish him) said and prayed, "O God, forgive Khalid for all his actions against Thy path." (Waqidi). Then Uthman and Amr testified to the unity of God and the prophethood of the Holy Prophet (May God bless and cherish him).

There were other joyful conversions in the coming months: Aqil, the brother of

Jafar and Hazrat Ali, and Jubayr, the son of Mutim. Jubayr had visited Medina to ransom captives after the Battle of Badr, and faith had taken root in his heart. And eventually, he could not resist it and submitted. When Aqil came to the presence of the Holy Prophet (May God bless and cherish him), he said, "I love thee with two loves, for thy near kinship to me, and for the love that I ever saw for thee in my uncle." (Ibn Sa'd)

After his return from the lesser pilgrimage, the Holy Prophet (May God bless and cherish him) continued sending fighters to maintain security around Medina. He dispatched a force of forty horsemen under the command of Ibn Abi l-Awja and Shuja ibn Wahb with a force of twenty-four horsemen in the direction of Hawazin. He also sent Ka'b ibn Umayr with fifteen horsemen to Bani Qada.

During this time, Hazrat Zaynab, the daughter of the Holy Prophet (May God bless and cherish him) was suffering from a chronic illness. She had a miscarriage when she was leaving Makkah for Medina, which made her extremely weak. Her husband was taken captive during the Battle of Badr but the Holy Prophet (May God bless and cherish him) freed him, on the condition that he would send Zaynab to Medina, which he did. Later Abu l-As accepted Islam and was reunited with his wife in Medina. Hazrat Zaynab died shortly afterward. The Holy Prophet (May God bless and cherish him) was with her at the end and spoke words of comfort to his son-in-law and little granddaughter. He then asked Umm Ayman, Sawdah, and Umm Salamah to wash her body and make her ready for the burial. The Holy Prophet (May God bless and cherish him) took off one of his garments and told them to wrap her in it before they shrouded her. Then he led the funeral prayer and prayed beside her grave.

CHAPTER 22
THE BATTLE OF MUTA

It was Jamadi al-Awwal, the eighth year of Hijra, and the Holy Prophet (May God bless and cherish him) sent a delegation of fifteen believers as his envoys to one of the tribes near the Syrian border. But their arrival was treated with hostility, and they were all killed but one. A similar incident happened that resulted in the death of the Companion Harith ibn Umayr, who was sent by the Holy Prophet (May God bless and cherish him) as an envoy to the governor of Basra. He was taken prisoner by the tribe of Ghassan and put to death. Ghassanides were mainly Christians and were supported by Caesar. The matter was very serious in nature. When the Holy Prophet (May God bless and cherish him) found out that his envoy was murdered, he ordered an army of three thousand men. Such a big army had been gathered only in the Trench before. He appointed Zayd ibn Harith, his freed slave, as the commander of the army and handed him the white standard. He instructed him to go all the way to where Harith ibn Umayr was killed and invite the people to Islam. Should they not accept it, then do whatever is needed. The Holy Prophet (May God bless and cherish him) told the army that if Zayd should be killed, then Jafar ibn Abi Talib should take his place. And after Jafar Abdullah ibn Rawaha should be the commander. All the Companions understood the gravity of the situation, and from his words, knew that the said commanders would fall martyr one by one. The Holy Prophet (May God bless and cherish him) specifically told them, "Fight in the name of Allah, fight against those who deny Allah, and rebel against Him in the way of Allah. But do not wrong anyone! Do not oppress anyone. Do not kill people who have devoted themselves to prayer in temples. Do not cut a single tree, do not burn a single date grove, and do not burn homes."

The Holy Prophet (May God bless and cherish him) escorted the army and saw them on their way till the hills of Wada and watched them for a long time. When the Muslim army reached the Syrian border, they heard that not only had the northern tribes come out in great numbers, but Caeser's representative had greatly reinforced them with imperial troops. Altogether, the enemy forces were more than a hundred thousand strong.

After marching, they stopped for two days at Ma'an and then continued advancing. In a place called Masharif, the two armies were facing each other. In front of the Muslim army was a sea of soldiers that seemed to have no end. Zayd decided to camp at a place called Muta and took position for the battle. The right wing was under the command of Qutba ibn Qatada, and the left wing was led by Ubada ibn Malik. Zayd nonetheless, held a counsel of war. Most of the Companions were in favor of informing the Holy Prophet (May God bless and cherish him) immediately of the impending situation. Then, he could either order them home or send more fighters to carry on the onslaught. But Abdullah ibn Rawaha was against such an idea, and he spoke vigorously, "We have before us the certainty of two good things, either victory or martyrdom, to join our brethren and be their companions in the garden of paradise. Therefore, get ready for the battle." His idea was met with approval, and the army continued its advance. They were now close to the shores of the Dead Sea, separated from its long and deep valley by the range of hills on the eastern shores. They were soon within sight of the enemy forces, and it seemed that they were outnumbered on such a big scale they had never yet experienced. The enemy forces exhibited great military splendor, with the imperial forces drawn up in the middle and with the Arab forces on either flank. After seeing the grandeur of the opposite forces, and wealth of arms and armor and the richly caparisoned horses, Zayd gave an order to withdraw southwards to Muta. The enemy was conscious of the superiority of their numbers and followed them. As they came close, instead of retreating further, Zayd gave orders to attack. Swords were drawn, and a fierce battle ensued.

At that moment, by Allah's grace, the space between Muta and Medina was open for the Holy Prophet (May God bless and cherish him) and he saw Zayd with the white standard leading his men into the fray. He saw him getting wounded multiple times until finally, he fell martyr. Jafar now took the standard and fought gallantly, until he fell. Then Abdullah took the standard of Islam, and he led the Muslim army against the enemy, and he, too, was killed. The Muslim army was driven back at this point, and they were disorganized. Tears were flowing down the radiant face of the Holy Prophet (May God bless and cherish him) as he was informing his Companions in Medina about the news of the battle, "Zayd took the standard, and he became a martyr. Then Jafar took it and became a martyr, and then Ibn Rawaha took it and became a martyr too. Now, one of God's swords took the standard and God opened the way for them."

As soon as Abdullah fell, one of the Helpers, Thabit ibn Arqam, seized the standard and handed it over to Khalid ibn Walid. From that day on, Khalid came to be called 'the sword of God.' As the Holy Prophet (May God bless and cherish him) described the battle, tears were flowing from his eyes. Then he went to the house of Jafar and said to his wife, "O Asma, bring me Jafar's sons." She fetched her three boys. The Holy Prophet (May God bless and cherish him) kissed and caressed them, and his eyes filled with tears, and he wept. "O Messenger of Allah," Asma said, "Dearer than my mother and father, what makes you weep? Have you received news of Jafar and his companions?" "Yes," said the Holy Prophet (May God bless and cherish him), "They became martyrs today!" She started crying, and the Holy Prophet (May God bless and cherish him) comforted her. The Holy Prophet returned home and told Hazrat Fatima to prepare food for Jafar's family. This became a tradition, and they cooked food for the family of martyrs of Muta for three days.

After three days, the holy Prophet (May God bless and cherish him) went to the house of Jafar and prayed for them. He also declared that he would take care of Jafar ibn Abi Talib's children himself and consoled his wife. The holy Prophet (May God bless and cherish him) then visited the house of Zayd, and when he saw his young daughter, he started crying. The Companions asked him why he was crying; he answered, "This is longing of the lover for the beloved."

That night, the Holy Prophet (May God bless and cherish him) saw in a vision that Zayd was in paradise along with Jafar, and Abdullah, and the other martyrs of the battle. He saw that Jafar was flying with wings like an angel. At dawn, he went to the Mosque, his Companions sensed that he was in a good mood, and after prayers, he turned towards them. Then he went to Asma and told her about his dream and that made her greatly consoled.

THE SWORD OF ALLAH

Khalid ibn Walid now became the commander of the Muslim army. He continued the battle with full force and deployed a new tactic in the battlefield. During the night, the ones who had been fighting in the front were pulled back to the rear, and the ones on the right exchanged with the ones on the left. The commotion that happened in the dark gave the impression that fresh troops had been added to the ranks of the Muslim army. The enemy forces noticed that now totally new men were fighting in the center of the battlefield, and fresh faces were on both flanks. The enemy commanders noted this sudden change and were now hesitant about whether to attack or not. They feared that they might be trapped by the enemy soldiers and might suffer heavy losses. So, they decided to withdraw. Khalid ibn Walid was seeking this result and wanted to bring back the Muslim army safely to Medina. They had fought relentlessly for seven days and had lost only twelve Companions, including three commanders. Khalid then gave orders to the army to return to Medina.

As the Muslim army was returning home, the Holy Prophet (May God bless and cherish him) gathered his Companions to greet the returning fighters. The Holy Prophet (May God bless and cherish him) rode on the white mule Duldul, which the Muqawqis had given him as a gift. He put Jafar's eldest son in front of him on the saddle and rode out to meet the army. People were lined up alongside the route, and as the troops passed by, they shouted, "Runaways. Did you flee from fighting in God's path?" The Holy Prophet (May God bless and cherish him) intervened and said, "Nay, they are not runaways. But by the will of Allah, those who have returned will fight again in Allah's cause."

The retreat from Muta encouraged some of the northern Arab tribes to retaliate against the new Islamic state. In the following months, men of the Bali and Quda'ah tribes were gathering in large numbers on the Syrian border with the intent to attack Medina. However, they did not have the backing of Caeser's army. As soon as the Holy Prophet received the information, he sent Amr at the head of three hundred men and gave instructions to make alliances and fight where it was needed. Amr's mother was from Bali, and this could influence the people of Bali to side with him. Amr succeeded in reaching the area in ten days without attracting attention. It was winter now, and the men were cold, so they gathered wood to light fire to keep warm, but he forbade them so that they wouldn't get the enemy's attention.

Soon, they realized that the enemy was in greater numbers than they had anticipated. So, he sent a man of Juhayrah to the Holy Prophet (May God bless and cherish him) requesting reinforcements. The Holy Prophet (May God bless and cherish him) asked Ubaydah to lead a party of two hundred men to help Amr in his campaign. Ubaydah was one of the closest Companions of the Holy Prophet (May God bless and cherish him) and had participated in every campaign with bravery and determination. The Holy Prophet (May God bless and cherish him) advised him to see that there was perfect harmony between the two forces. When Ubaydah reached the place, Amr insisted on remaining the commander of the fighters since Ubaydah was sent to help. Ubaydah said, "In my case, by God, I will obey you." Amr now led the entire force of five hundred men, and the enemy dispersed as quickly as possible. There was no resistance, and they were coming across deserted camps. So, Amr wrote a letter to the Holy Prophet (May God bless and cherish him) and claimed that he had re-established the superiority of Islam upon the Syrian border.

The influence of Islam was rapidly growing throughout Arabia. There were many reasons. The Muslims were now a formidable and incalculable force, and the Holy Prophet (May God bless and cherish him) himself was considered as a preferred, reliable, and generous ally in comparison to other parties. The message of Islam and the remarkable serenity that characterized those who practiced it, the sublime verses of the Noble Quran, the Book of God's oneness, and mercy were slowly and powerfully impacting people and winning their hearts.

CHAPTER 23
THE GREAT CONQUEST OF MAKKAH

After a two-year period of the Messenger of God's truce with the Quraysh at Hudaybiyah, it was the month of Shaban, and in the early hours of the morning the Holy Prophet (May God bless and cherish him) said to Hazrat Aishah, "O Aishah, something important had happened in the direction of Khuza'ah." Hazrat Aishah was distressed to hear such news suddenly. "O Messenger of Allah," she said. "Do you think the Quraysh would dare to violate the terms of the agreement, even though they are rendered helpless?" the Holy Prophet replied, "The Quraysh have violated the agreement because Allah wants something to happen." Hazrat Aishah curiously asked, "O Messenger of Allah! Will the results be favorable?" The Holy Prophet (May God bless and cherish him) smiled, "Yes, it will be favorable."

There was a fight between the Bakr clan, allied with the Quraysh, and the Khuza'ah clan, allied with the Messenger of God. After three days had passed, one early morning, Amr ibn Salim from the clan of Khuza'ah came to the presence of the Holy Prophet (May God bless and cherish him) along with forty horsemen. He recited a poem in the Mosque to let him know what had befallen them and asked for help from the Holy Prophet (May God bless and cherish him). The Quraysh had apparently joined forces with Bani Bakr, Bani Nufasa, and Watir and had launched an attack on Khuza'ah, in which twenty-three people were killed, mostly children, women, and elderly. The leading men of Quraysh such as Safwan ibn Umayya, Ikrima ibn Abu Jahl, Huwaytib ibn Abdi l-Uzza, Shayba ibn Uthman, and Mikraz ibn Hays had taken part. The Quraysh not only participated in the act of aggression but had also provided logistical support, arms and mounts. The attack was carried out at night because the Quraysh did not want to appear to be violating the Hudaybiyah openly. (Waqidi, Maghazi; Ibn Sa'd, Tabaqat; Salihi, Subulu l-Huda war-rashad)

The next morning when the gravity of what had happened came to light, the Quraysh regretted what they had done, because they clearly violated the agreement. The holy Prophet (May God bless and cherish him) listened to Amr ibn Salim and said, "O Amr, you will be helped." He told him that they could rely on him. When they had gone, the Holy Prophet (May God bless and cherish him) went home and told Hazrat Aishah, "May I not be helped, if I help not the sons of Ka'b."

The Holy Prophet (May God bless and cherish him) called a Companion named Damra and asked him to go to Makkah. Damra went to Quraysh with three options,

1. Paying the blood money to the clan of Khuza'ah and be absolved.
2. Cancelling their agreement with Bani Nufasa; this meant that Bani Nufasa would be free to decide their relationship with Messenger of Allah.
3. Annulling the pact of Hudaybiya, which would mean declaring war on the part of the Quraysh. (Waqidi, Maghazi; Salihi, Subulu l-Huda war-Rashad).

Although the Quraysh denied committing the act, they were extremely worried and wanted to find a way out of this situation. So, they went to Abu Sufyan, especially Ibn Hisham, and Abdullah ibn Rabia and said, "This is wrong and that you must make it right. Suppose you can't, then find some other reason for peace. Otherwise, Muhammad will come here with his Companions and will hold us accountable for it." Abu Sufyan turned towards the Quraysh and said, "You cannot put this responsibility solely on me. I was not consulted on this matter. I did not know about it, and I did not authorize it. I swear by Allah that if I am not wrong, Muhammad will surely declare war on us. Currently, I do not see any other option but going to Muhammad and ask him to renew and extend the agreement."

Abu Sufyan had recently returned from Syria. The Quraysh sent him to Medina to see the Holy Prophet (May God bless and cherish him) and renew the agreement. On his way he saw the men of Khuza'ah returning from Medina and he feared that he was too late. He went to the Holy Prophet (May God bless and cherish him) and said, "O Muhammad, I was absent at the time of the truce of Hudaybiyah, so let us now strengthen our pact and extend its duration."

The Holy Prophet (May God bless and cherish him) briefly replied, "Have you broken the agreement on your side?" "God forbid," Abu Sufyan answered. "We have not either," said the Holy Prophet (May God bless and cherish him). "We are keeping to the pact for the period agreed upon at Hudaybiyah. We will not modify it, and neither will we accept another in its place." The Holy Prophet (May God bless and cherish him) did not say anything else. Abu Sufyan was disappointed. So, he went to see his daughter, Umm Habibah, hoping that she might intervene on his behalf. He was seeing his daughter after a period of fifteen years. When he wanted to sit upon the Holy Prophet's rug, she hastily rolled it up from underneath him. He was surprised by her action and said, "Little daughter, you do not think me worthy of sitting on this rug?" "It is a prophet's rug," she said, "And you are an idolator, hence an unclean person." Then she addressed him, "O father, you are lord of the Quraysh and their leader. How is that you have failed to recognize the truth and failed to enter Islam? You have been worshiping stones that can neither see nor hear."

"O my Lord, am I to forsake what my ancestors worshiped to follow to Muhammad?" He was disappointed and realized that no help was to be expected from her. So, he went to Hazrat Abu Bakr and some of the other Companions to request help on his behalf for renewal of the agreement. He also requested general protection between man and man, but Hazrat Abu Bakr merely answered, "I grant protection only within the scope of protection granted by the Messenger of Allah."

That day, Abu Sufyan went to Hazrat Ali ibn Abi Talib and said, "Wouldn't you like to be lord over the Arabs and, in a gracious gesture towards your tribe, grant them protection and renew the treaty with them?" Hazrat Ali replied, "Far be it from me to act contrary to God's Messenger in a matter." Then Abu Sufyan went to Hazrat Fatima and said, "Wouldn't you like to be the finest queen of the Arabs and offer protection among your people?" Indeed, your sister protected her husband Abu al-As ibn al Rabi from God's Messenger, and that was not overruled." Hazrat Fatima replied, "Far be it from me to act contrary to God's Messenger in a matter." Then he said the same to Al-Hassan and Al-Hussayn, "Grant sanctuary among the people, just say, 'Yes.' But they said nothing. Looking to their mother, they said, "We stand by what our mother says." Thus, Abu Sufyan gained nothing.

Abu Sufyan turned back to Hazrat Ali in desperation and said, "O Abu Hassan, I see that I will not be able to manage this business. Show me a way out of this." Hazrat Ali replied, "I see nothing that can help you today." Then he asked him whether he was the lord of Kinanah. "Yes, I am their lord," Abu Sufyan said. "Then you should rise and announce that the Bani Kinanah is now under your protection and then return to your land." "Do you think this will really benefit me?" asked Abu Sufyan. "Not really, but there is nothing else you can do," answered Hazrat Ali. Therefore, Abu Sufyan went to the Mosque and said, "O people, I grant protection between man and man; I have taken them under my protection. I do not think anyone will break the promise that I have made on this matter." Then he went to the Holy Prophet (May God bless and cherish him) one last time, "O Muhammad, I have taken them under my protection. I do not think you will renounce my protection." The Holy Prophet (May God bless and cherish him) merely answered, "This is what you think." And the Umayyad chief returned to Makkah and told them about the developments in Medina.

After Abu Sufyan left for Makkah, the Holy Prophet (May God bless and cherish him) began to prepare a campaign. He came home and asked Hazrat Aisha, "Make preparation for the campaign but keep it secret." After learning about the new campaign, Hazrat Abu Bakr came to see Hazrat Aisha and asked her the reason for the preparation, as he wanted to know whom the Holy Prophet (May God bless and cherish him) was intending to fight. But Hazrat Aisha did not reveal the target. So, Hazrat Abu Bakr came to the Holy Prophet (May God bless and cherish him), and he told him that they were going against the Quraysh. "Should we not wait for the time of the agreement to expire?" asked Hazrat Abu Bakr. The Holy Prophet (May God bless and cherish him) answered, "They have broken the agreement, and I should attack them. But this is a secret; let people speculate that God's Messenger is for Syria or Taif or for Hawazin. O Lord, let the Quraysh be in the dark and not know or hear about our plans. So that we may surprise them in their land."

The Holy Prophet (May God bless and cherish him) gave instructions that all important routes should be controlled so that their movements would not be known to anyone else. The believers already knew that they were preparing for an attack and were considering different possibilities as to whom they would be fighting. After it was widely presumed that the Holy Prophet (May God bless and cherish him) was going to march on to Makkah, Habib ibn Abi Balta'ah gave a letter to a woman of Muzaynah and asked her to take it to his relatives in Makkah to warn them of the impending attack. He had given it to a woman of Muzaynah who was travelling to Makkah, and she hid the letter in her hair. In the meantime, Gabriel came to the Holy Prophet (May God bless and cherish him) and informed him about the letter. The Holy Prophet (May God bless and cherish him) immediately called Hazrat Ali and Zubayr and said to them, "Intercept that woman who is taking the letter given to her by Habib that warns the Quraysh about our campaign."

Both carried out the orders and searched the baggage of the woman but did not find the letter. They threatened to conduct a search if she did not produce it. So, she gave them the letter, and it was taken to the Holy Prophet (May God bless and cherish him). The Holy Prophet (May God bless and cherish him) sent for Habib and asked, "O Habib, what made you do such a thing?" "O Messenger of Allah, I swear by Allah that I have faith in Allah and His Messenger. I have not changed my religion, nor am I after something else. I am a man without standing among the people of Makkah, without kinsmen of influence, and for the sake of my son and my family, I sought to win their favor." Hazrat Umar was there, and he was enraged and said, "O Messenger of Allah! Allow me to strike off his head for he is a hypocrite." But the Holy Prophet (May God bless and cherish him) responded, "How can you do that, O Umar? Has God not looked upon the men of Badr and said, "Do what you will, for I have forgiven You?" Habib was one of the combatants in the Battle of Badr.

The Holy Prophet (May God bless and cherish him) sent Abu Qatada ibn RabI with a sizeable unit to a place called Bantal Izam towards Damascus, thus giving the impression that the Muslim army was heading that way. At the same time, he sent messengers to all tribes whom he felt would comply with his summons to be gathered in Medina at the beginning of the next month, which was Ramadan. A headquarters was set up by the well of Abu Inaba, and Muslims were coming in droves, ready to obey the command of the Messenger of Allah. Everyone who had entered Islam had responded to the call of the Holy Prophet (May God bless and cherish him). It was Wednesday, the first day of Ramadan, and everyone was fasting. The Holy Prophet (May God bless and cherish him) announced, "Those who want to may continue their fasts; those who want to may break their fast." Then he sent a force of two hundred under the command of Zubayr ibn Awwam to scout the area. The army prayed the afternoon prayer behind the Holy Prophet (May God bless and cherish him) and started their march.

The surrounding tribes gathered on the appointed day, and no able-bodied Muslim stayed behind. The Emigrants were seven hundred, with three hundred horsemen; the Helpers were four thousand with five hundred horsemen; and the tribes, including those who joined them on the way, brought the total number of soldiers up to nearly ten thousand men. The Muslim army was the largest that had ever set out from Medina, and except for a few close Companions, no one knew who the enemy was.

On their way, the weather was extremely hot, and the Holy Prophet (May God bless and cherish him) saw a dog lying by the side of the road with a litter of recently born puppies that she was nursing. The Holy Prophet (May God bless and cherish him) was afraid that she might be harmed by one of the men. So, he told Juayl of Damrah to stand beside her until everyone had passed and make sure the dog and its puppies were safe.

When the Muslim army was about half the way, they saw that Hazrat Abbas and Umm al-Fadl and their sons were coming to Medina. They had decided that it was now time to make Hijra to the city of the prophet. The Holy Prophet (May God bless and cherish him) was very pleased to see them and invited them to join the campaign. Hazrat Maymuna was also overjoyed by their arrival, who had accompanied the Holy Prophet (May God bless and cherish him) on this expedition.

When they reached Qudayl, the fighters from Bani Sulaym, a troop of cavalry nine hundred in number, joined the Muslim army. One of their leaders addressed the Holy Prophet (May God bless and cherish him), "O Messenger of Allah! We are your maternal uncles. (He was referring to Hashim's mother, Atikah, who was a woman of their tribe). We have come to fight along with you. We are steadfast in battle and firm in the saddle." Bani Sulaym had brought their standards and their pennants with them. They requested the Holy Prophet (May God bless and cherish him) to mount them and give them to men of his own choice. But it was not yet time for flying the flags. Now, everybody knew where they were heading.

When the army reached a place called Marr-az-Zahran, the Holy Prophet (May God bless and cherish him) himself and many others who fasted until they reached the Holy Precinct broke their fast. Earlier the Holy Prophet (May God bless and cherish him) had proclaimed that it was permissible to break the fast during travel. However, the full number of days missed was to be fasted later. The reason for breaking the fast at Maa az Zahran was to gather up their strength to face the enemy. This aroused curiosity because they were close to Makkah, but at the same time other hostile tribes were also nearby. The southern territory could also be the target because it was the center of worship of Al-Lat. The question of who the enemy was on everyone's mind. Ka'b ibn Malik volunteered to go to the Holy Prophet (May God bless and cherish him) and find out the answer. But the Messenger of Allah smiled at him, and Ka'b had to return without any clue.

The Quraysh and Hawazin were also eager to know which one of them was at risk of attack. The tribe of Hawazin was spread through the entire slopes of the mountains that lay on the southern extremity of the plain of Najd. Taif was on one of these slopes, inhabited by Thaqif and the guardians of the temple of Lat. They sent messengers to the neighboring clans that an enemy of ten thousand was rapidly approaching them from Yathrib. They began to assemble near Taif and prepared themselves for the worst.

The Quraysh were in a great dilemma; they knew that it was them who had broken the agreement and that the Holy Prophet (May God bless and cherish him) did not renew it. At sunset, the Holy Prophet (May God bless and cherish him) gave orders to the army to relax. He told them to collect brushwood, spread out, and each man to light a fire after dark. From a distance, the ten thousand campfires could now be seen burning. The news quickly reached Makkah that Muhammad's army was far larger than they had feared. The Quraysh convened an urgent meeting and designated Abu Sufyan to go out to speak to the Holy Prophet (May God bless and cherish him) once more. On this mission, Hakim, Hazrat Khadijah's nephew, accompanied him, who had done his best to stop the Battle of Badr. Budayl ibn Waraqa of Khuza'ah also joined him, who had helped the Holy Prophet (May God bless and cherish him) at Hudaybiyah. When they reached a place called Arak, located in Marr az-Zahran, they were awestruck to see an army as big as a sea, camped with thousands of fires burning in front of the tents. The neighing of the horses and bellowing of the camels were frightening, and they were struck by fear.

After some time, Hazrat Abbas slipped out of his tent, hoping to find someone to send a message to the Quraysh to send a deputation to the Holy Prophet (May God bless and cherish him) before it was too late. When he met Abu Sufyan and his friends, he took them to the tent of the Holy Prophet (May God bless and cherish him). Abu Sufyan looked at the Holy Prophet (May God bless and cherish him) and said, "O Muhammad, you have come with a great army composed of many different tribes against thy kindred." The Holy Prophet (May God bless and cherish him) intercepted him, "It is the Quraysh who are the transgressors. You have broken the agreement of Hudaybiyah, helped and designed the attack on Bani Ka'b, and shamelessly violated the Holy Precinct of God and His Sanctuary."

Abu Sufyan wanted to change the topic and said, "You should turn your anger and power against Hawazin, for they are your staunch enemies and further from thy in kinship." The Holy Prophet (May God bless and cherish him) replied, "My Lord will grant me victory over them too, after victory and establishment of Islam in Makkah. Allah will enrich me with their goods as spoils and their families as captives."

Most of the leaders of the Quraysh, Abu Sufyan, and the other two men were very impressed by the military power of the Holy Prophet (May God bless and cherish him), the obedience of the Companions, and their practice of worship. The Holy Prophet (May God bless and cherish him) invited them to Islam and told the three men, "Bear witness that there is no god but Allah, and that I am the Messenger of Allah." Hakim and Budayl, therefore, made their profession of faith. A change was taking place inside Abu Sufyan, but he only said, "There is no god but God" and kept silent. Then he said to the Holy Prophet (May God bless and cherish him), "O Muhammad, there is still a little doubt in my soul; give it a respite." The Holy Prophet (May God bless and cherish him) told Hazrat Abbas to take him to his tent for the night.

Abu Sufyan was still debating the issue with himself, and for a moment, he had the idea to go to the surrounding tribes and gather an army to attack the Messenger of Allah. While he was deep in his thought, someone placed a hand on his shoulder and said, "Then Allah will humiliate you and we will triumph once more." Abu Sufyan was startled, and he turned around to see who it was. He was so embarrassed to see that it was none other than the Holy Prophet (May God bless and cherish him). He immediately uttered; I bear witness that you are the Messenger of Allah." It was something that only he knew about, and he had not spoken it out loud either. Only the knower of the unseen, Allah, must have informed His Messenger. Abu Sufyan continued, "I ask Allah to accept my repentance; I seek His forgiveness. I had certain doubts about you being the Messenger of Allah till now. But all those doubts are gone. I swear by Allah that what made me think that way was nothing but whispers of the devil and my carnal soul." (Salihi, Subulu l-Huda war-Rashad)

Abu Sufyan and his friends had experienced surprise after surprise while they were in the camp. At dawn, the call to prayer was made throughout the camp, and they were greatly shaken by the sound of it. "What are they doing?" Abu Sufyan asked. "The prayer," said Hazrat Abbas. "And how many times do they pray each day and night?" Abu Sufyan asked. Hazrat Abbas told him that it was five times. Then he noticed that the believers eagerly crawled and jolted each other, that they might be splashed with water from ablution of the Holy Prophet (May God bless and cherish him) or have some drops of what was left from it. Abu Sufyan was amazed and said, "O Abbas, I have never seen such sovereignty as this," then he took him to the presence of the Holy Prophet (May God bless and cherish him) and said, "O Messenger of Allah, you know well the love of Abu Sufyan for honor and glory grant him therefore some favor." "I will," said the Holy Prophet (May God bless and cherish him). He turned to Abu Sufyan and told him to return to the Quraysh and tell them, "Whoso entered the House of Abu Sufyan shall be safe, and whoso locked upon himself his door shall be safe and whoso entered the Mosque shall be safe." (Waqidi)

Abu Sufyan and his friends asked permission to return to Makkah, but this time, Hazrat Abbas suggested to the Holy Prophet (May God bless and cherish him),

"O Messenger of Allah! I am not sure that Abu Sufyan would not turn back on his heels. It would be better if you keep him by your side for a while so that he may see the size and grandeur of the Muslim army and get a better grip of the situation."

Hazrat Abu Bakr was of the same opinion, so he asked his Companions to go after Abu Sufyan. It was again Hazrat Abbas who caught up to him. When Abu Sufyan saw him, he asked, "Is this a betrayal, O sons of Hashim?" Hazrat Abbas was not late in answering, "Know that those who stand in prayer behind the Holy Prophet (May God bless and cherish him) never betray people. In fact, we want you to wait until morning and see for yourself the army of Allah and what He is preparing for the Makkans."

THE PARADE AND THE CONQUEST

The next morning, the Holy Prophet (May God bless and cherish him) issued orders for the final advance towards Makkah. He called for the standards and pennants to be brought to him. These were mounted one by one and given to the different tribes. All the men gathered under their standards and started their historic march. Abu Sufyan was accompanied by Hazrat Abbas as far as the narrow end of the valley. There, they stood on a rock so that they could see the size of the army as they passed. The sight was magnificent. There would still be enough time for Abu Sufyan to return to Makkah and describe what he saw and to deliver his message.

The first to pass by Abu Sufyan was Khalid ibn Walid, leading a force of one thousand horsemen of Sulaym. When he came close, he uttered three magnifications: Allah u Akbar. They were followed by yellow turbaned Zubayr at the head of five hundred horsemen (of Emigrants). He likewise uttered three magnifications as he passed by Abu Sufyan. The entire valley resounded with their magnification. Troops after troops went by, after Zubayr, Abu Dharr passed with three hundred, Aslam with four hundred, Bani Ka'b with five hundred, Muazayna with one thousand, Juhayna with eight hundred, and Kinanah with two thousand. Finally, the Ghatafanite clan of Ashja passed by Abu Sufyan, one of whose standards was carried by Nuaym, the former friend of him and Suhayl. "Of all the Arabs," said Abu Sufyan, "These were Muhammad's bitterest enemies." "Allah caused Islam to enter their hearts," said Hazrat Abbas, "This is evidently by the grace of God."

The last of the groups of fighters belonged to the Holy Prophet (May God bless and cherish him), consisting entirely of Emigrants and Helpers. The Holy Prophet (May God bless and cherish him) had given the standard to Sa'd ibn Ubaydah, who was leading the fighters to Makkah. The fighters were fully armed and dressed for battle in their armor, with only their eyes being visible. As they passed beside Abu Sufyan, Sa'd ibn Ubaydah said in a loud voice,

"O Abu Sufyan! Today is the day of slaughter! The day when the inviolable shall be violated. The day of God's abasement of the Quraysh."

The Holy Prophet (May God bless and cherish him) was mounted on Qaswa; on his right side was Hazrat Abu Bakr, and on his left was Usayd ibn Khudayr. When he came close, Hazrat Abbas excitedly said to Abu Sufyan, "Here is the Messenger of Allah." Abu Sufyan replied, "The affair of the son of your brother has reached a climax. He is a mighty king now." Hazrat Abbas said to him, "O Abu Sufyan, this is not sovereignty but prophethood."

As the Holy Prophet (May God bless and cherish him) was close enough, Abu Sufyan cried, "O Messenger of Allah, have you ordered the killing of your tribe? Have you not heard what Sa'd has said." Then he requested, "I beg thee by God, on behalf of thy people. Out of all God's creation, you have the greatest piety, the most merciful, and the most beneficent."

The Holy Prophet (May God bless and cherish him) said, "O Abu Sufyan, Sa'd is mistaken. Today is the day of mercy. The day on which God has exalted the Quraysh." Abdul Rahman ibn Awf and Hazrat Uthman, who were close to the Holy Prophet (May God bless and cherish him) were worried that Sa'd might launch a violent attack upon the Quraysh. Therefore, the Holy Prophet (May God bless and cherish him) sent a message to Sa'd to give the standard to his son Qays, who was a man of relatively milder temper, and to let him command the fighters. To honor the son was to honor the father, but Sa'd refused to hand it over to his son without a direct command from the Holy Prophet (May God bless and cherish him). The Holy Prophet (May God bless and cherish him) unwound his red turban and sent it as a token to Sa'd. He immediately gave the standard to Qays. (Waqidi)

The Muslim army had started their march towards Makkah. Meanwhile, Hazrat Abbas approached the Holy Prophet (May God bless and cherish him) and asked his permission to go to Makkah and invite them to Islam and give them the surety. At first, the Holy Prophet (May God bless and cherish him) agreed to allow him to go to Makkah and gave him his mule to ride. But then he said, "I fear that Quraysh will mistreat you like the tribe of Thaqif mistreated Urwah ibn Masud." He then called Hazrat Abbas to stay with him.

Abu Sufyan, however, went back to Makkah with all speed, stood outside his house, and shouted at the top of his voice. People gathered around him in large numbers. He said, "O people of Quraysh, Muhammad is here with a great army that you cannot fight against. Muhammad is here with ten thousand strong fighters. He has granted me that whoso enter my house shall be safe." The crowd asked, "For God's sake, how many people can enter your house?" Abu Sufyan continued, "And whoso closes his door and seeks refuge in his house shall be safe. The people who take refuge in the Mosque shall be safe as well."

Hind now came out of the house and seized her husband by his beard, "Kill this husband of mine who is good for nothing. What a terrible guardian and leader he is for his people." Abu Sufyan shouted back, "O people, let not this woman deceive you against your better judgement, for you are facing a mighty force beyond your power."

It was Friday, the thirteenth of Ramadan, and the entire army was gathered at Dhu Tuwa near the city of Makkah. There was no sign of resistance as if the city was empty. The Holy Prophet (May God bless and cherish him) was riding Qaswa, and when the camel halted, the Holy Prophet (May God bless and cherish him) bowed his head until his beard touched the saddle in gratitude to Allah. The Holy Prophet (May God bless and cherish him) had given command of the right-wing to Khalid and left-wing to Zubayr. The main body of the troops was divided into two; half of it was led by Sa'd and his son Qays, and the other half by Abu Ubaydah. The army was instructed to enter the city from below and others through three different passes.

The Messenger of Allah gave orders to fight only those who resisted them. As he was entering Makkah from the upper part, the women were throwing their scarves they had towards the necks of the horses, thus showing their respect and joy. When the Holy Prophet (May God bless and cherish him) saw this, he turned towards Hazrat Abu Bakr and said, "What had Hassan said?" Hazrat Abu Bakr understood and started reciting a poem that described the scene they were experiencing. This was a poem that Hassan ibn Thabit had composed and read even before the conquest of Makkah, describing the way that the women of Qada would hit the necks of the horses with their scarves as they entered Makkah. That is why the Holy Prophet (May God bless and cherish him) told his Companions to enter Makkah from the place that Hassan had pointed out.

When the news of the Muslim army reached Makkah, most of the Quraysh retreated to the mount of Abu Qubays. Among them was an old man with a staff, helped by a woman. They were Abu Quhafah and Quraybah, the father and sister of Hazrat Abu Bakr. That morning, when they heard that the army was at Dhu Tuwa, the blind man asked her daughter to take him up the mountain and describe to him what she saw. It was he who had climbed the same mountain when he was young to watch the army of Abraha and his elephant. Now, he was old and blind; therefore, he asked his daughter to describe the scene for him. Quraybah described what she could see as a dark mass of black, and he said that those were horsemen drawn up in close formation, waiting to invade. Then, she described the black mass spreading out until it became four distinct divisions. Abu Quhafah hurriedly told her to take him home with all speed. They were still on their way when a troop of horses swept past them. One of the horsemen snatched the necklace Quraybah was wearing, but otherwise, they reached home safely.

Ikrima, Safwan, and Suhayl had gathered their forces on Mount Abu Qubays together with some of their allies from Bakr and Hudayl, and they were planning to attack the Muslim forces. When they saw horsemen entering the lower part of

Makkah, they attacked them. These horsemen were under the command of Khalid. A fierce fight started, and thirty of the attackers were killed, along with two losses on the Muslim's side. The enemy forces scattered. Ikrima and Safwan escaped on horseback to the coast. Suhayl went to his home and locked himself.

When the Holy Prophet (May God bless and cherish him) came to a place called Adhakhir, he saw the flash of drawn swords. He said, "Did I not forbid fighting?' But when they explained that the fighters of Khalid ibn Walid were attacked, they only fought back. The Holy Prophet (May God bless and cherish him) said that God had ordained it for the best.

When he saw the dwellings of Makkah as he passed Adhakhir, he stopped and thanked Allah. Then he turned to Jabir and said, "O Jabir, this is the place where we will settle." It was right here that the Quraysh had gathered and formed an alliance against the Holy Prophet. (Waqidi). The Holy Prophet (May God bless and cherish him) went towards the red leather tent which Abu Rafi had now pitched not far from the Mosque. Hazrat Umm Salamah, Hazrat Maymunah, and Hazrat Fatima were waiting for him in the tent. Umm Hani had also arrived; her husband Hubayrah, who was an idolator, had foreseen the fall of Makkah and had gone to live in Najaran. But two of her kinsmen by marriage, one of them the brother of Abu Jahl, had taken part in fighting against Khalid and had come to her house for refuge. When Hazrat Ali came to her house, he saw the two Makhzumites, so he drew his sword to kill them. But she said that she had given protection to them. Whereupon Hazrat Ali left the house. And now she locked them in her home and came to the presence of the Holy Prophet (May God bless and cherish him) to intercede on their behalf. He greeted her and listened to her and said, "It shall not be whom thou make safe, him we make safe; whom thou protect, him we protect."

Makkah had surrendered, and the people were quiet. The Holy Prophet (May God bless and cherish him) took ablution in his tent, and as an expression of gratitude to Allah, he performed eight cycles of prayer. Then he asked for his camel. Qaswa was brought to the door of the tent. The Holy Prophet (May God bless and cherish him) re-entered his tent and put on his helmet and armor. He also donned his sword and started towards Kaaba. On his way, children of Quraysh had lined up on both sides and were welcoming the Messenger of Allah. The female children had taken their scarves and were waving them at the horses that passed by them.

As soon as the Holy Prophet (May God bless and cherish him) saw the Kaaba, he shouted, "Allah o Akba.r" Whoever heard his voice, shouted 'Allah o Akbar' as if the entire Makkah was echoing with the words "God is Greatest." The Holy Prophet (May God bless and cherish him) gestured to remain silent, and he started his rounds around the Kaaba. Muhammad ibn Maslama was holding the reins of Qaswa. First the Holy Prophet (May God bless and cherish him) came close to the Black Stone, and after saluting it with his hand, he started his Tawaf (rounds).

That day, the Kaaba was home to three hundred and sixty idols, including Hubal, Isaf, and Naila. The Holy Prophet (May God bless and cherish him) pointed to each one of them with his finger, and they all fell on their faces to the ground. At the same time, the Holy Prophet (May God bless and cherish him) was reciting,

"The Truth has come, and falsehood has vanished; surely falsehood is ever bound to vanish by its very nature." (Al-Isra 17:81)

He then dismounted Qaswa and prayed at the Station of Ibrahim (Maqam e Ibrahim), which was at that time adjoining the Kaaba. Then he went towards the well of Zamzam. Hazrat Abbas pulled a bucket of water and offered it to the Holy Prophet (May God bless and cherish him). He drank from it and took ablution with it. The Companions flocked around him to get a drop of his ablution water and to rub it on their faces and eyes. Then, he confirmed forever the traditional right of the sons of Hashim to water the pilgrims. At the same time, Hazrat Ali brought the key to the Kaaba, upon which Hazrat Abbas requested him to give their family also the right of guarding it. But the Holy Prophet (May God bless and cherish him) said, "I gave you only that which you had lost, not that which would be a loss to others." Then he called Uthman ibn Talha, a man of Abd ad-Dar who had come to Medina with Khalid and Amr and handed him the key, and he confirmed his Clan's traditional right of guardianship.

The Holy Prophet (May God bless and cherish him) gave orders to destroy Hubal, the largest of the idols and it was broken into pieces on the ground. He also ordered that all the idols should be burned. He called Hazrat Ali to come next to him and told him to kneel. Hazrat Ali at once knelt where he was told to do so. The Holy Prophet (May God bless and cherish him) climbed on the shoulders of Hazrat Ali and told him to stand up. Hazrat Ali did exactly what he was asked. As soon as Hazrat Ali was getting up to stand, the Holy Prophet (May God bless and cherish him) commanded him to sit down. Hazrat Ali obeyed the instruction. Thereupon, the Holy Prophet (May God bless and cherish him) himself knelt and said to Hazrat

Ali, "Now, you mount on my shoulders." This was a prophetic order that Hazrat Ali complied with, and he stood on the shoulders of the Holy Prophet (May God bless and cherish him). Hazrat Ali was now at the top of the Kaaba, and the Messenger of Allah said to him, "Throw down all the idols that the polytheists had put there." One of the idols was fixed with iron rods, so the Holy Prophet (May God bless and cherish him) told him to yank it and pull it down. Hazrat Ali did the same with much ease.

INSIDE KAABA

Afterwards, the Holy Prophet (May God bless and cherish him) called Bilal and told him to go to Uthman ibn Talha and bring the key to the Kaaba. After much persuasion, Uthman was able to get the keys from his mother and came to the presence of the Holy Prophet (May God bless and cherish him). He opened the door of the House of Allah for the Holy Prophet. The Holy Prophet (May God bless and cherish him) stood at the threshold of the Kaaba, and he proclaimed, "Praise be to Allah, who has fulfilled His promise and helped His slave and routed the enemies." He then entered the Kaaba. Usama and Bilal followed behind him. He then told Uthman to lock the door behind them. The walls inside Kaaba had been covered with pictures of pagan deities. There was a picture of the virgin Mary and baby Jesus and a painting of the prophet Ibrahim. The Holy Prophet (May God bless and cherish him) told Uthman to remove all pictures and clean the inside of the Kaaba. The Holy Prophet (May God bless and cherish him) went around inside of the Kaaba constantly reciting 'Allah o Akbar,' then he stopped and performed two cycles of prayer between two pillars.

Outside in the Mosque, the Companions were waiting in curiosity. They wondered what the Holy Prophet (May God bless and cherish him) was engaged inside the Kaaba. Most of the Makkans, who had taken refuge in their homes, had now joined those who were in the Mosque and were sitting not far from the Kaaba. The Holy Prophet emerged from the House of Allah and addressed the crowd, "O Quraysh, what kind of judgement do you expect me to pass onto you today?" There was complete silence, and then a voice was heard, "We say well, we think well, you are a noble and generous brother and son of a noble and generous brother. It is for you to decide." It was none other than Suhayl ibn Amr, the famous poet of the Quraysh. His son Abdullah had told him that the Holy Prophet (May God bless and cherish him) had given him protection. Therefore, he had come out to witness the new beginnings. The Holy Prophet (May God bless and cherish him) understood what Suhayl meant by these words. Then, he spoke to Quraysh in words of forgiveness that, according to the Quran, Joseph spoke to his brothers when they came to him in Egypt. "Verily, I say as my brother Joseph said, 'No reproach this day shall be on you. May God forgive you. Indeed, He is the Most Merciful of the Merciful." (Yusuf 12:92)

The Holy Prophet (May God bless and cherish him) had it proclaimed throughout the city that everyone who had an idol in his home must destroy it. He then withdrew to the Hill of Safa, where throngs of people paid homage to him and entered Islam. People were submitting in faith to Allah and swearing their allegiances to the Holy Prophet (May God bless and cherish him). In the past, one of the conditions for allegiance was Hijra (Emigration), but now it was no longer needed to leave Makkah. After the conquest of Makkah, there was no need for emigration, but it was now based on purity of intention and Jihad. The Holy Prophet (May God bless and cherish him) said, "Keep your intentions pure, and when you are called to jihad on the path of Allah, you must respond to that call and be quick to respond on the path of Allah."

When the men had pledged their allegiance, it was time for the women to pledge their allegiance. The Holy Prophet (May God bless and cherish him) was standing on the Hill of Safa and accepting the allegiance from women. Hind, the wife of Abu Sufyan and the daughter of Utba ibn Abu Rabia, who had been killed in Badr, was among the women pledging her allegiance to the Messenger of Allah. She approached him and said, "Praise be to God, who has exalted the religion, He has chosen for Himself, so I may benefit from the grace that you have brought. O Muhammad! I am a woman who believes in Allah and swear by His existence." Her face was still covered, and the Holy Prophet (May God bless and cherish him) did not know who she was. Then she lifted her veil and said, "I am Hind, the daughter of Utba." The Holy Prophet (May God bless and cherish him) said, "Welcome."

Another of the women who came to see the Holy Prophet was Umm Hakim, the wife of Ikrima. When she accepted Islam, she requested the Holy Prophet (May God bless and cherish him) to give her husband immunity. The Holy Prophet (May God bless and cherish him) gave her his word, although Ikrima was still at war with him. Umm Hakim found out whereabouts of her husband and went after him to bring him back.

Hazrat Abu Bakr went to see his father in his house. His father and sister were expecting him. He returned to the presence of the Holy Prophet (May God bless and cherish him) with his father and sister Quraybah. When the Holy Prophet (May God bless and cherish him) saw that Hazrat Abu Bakr was leading Abu Quhafah by the hand, he said, "Why did you not leave the old man in his house for me to go to him there?" "O Messenger of Allah," said Abu Bakr, "It is more fitting that he should come unto thee than that you should go unto him." The Holy Prophet (May God bless and cherish him) took him by the hand, and made him sit in front of him, and invited him to Islam, which he readily accepted.

ADDRESSING ANSAR

Later, the Holy Prophet (May God bless and cherish him) walked up the Hill of Safa, and, from there looked at the House of Allah. He raised his hands, praised and exalted Him, and prayed to his Lord. As he continued his whispered prayer, he felt the signs of revelation upon himself. When the revelation had ended, the Holy Prophet (May God bless and cherish him) called out, "O people of Ansar!" He was addressing Ansar directly. At that time, most of the Ansar were sitting below and discussing among themselves, wondering whether the Holy Prophet (May God bless and cherish him) would return to Medina with them. When they heard his call, they ran towards him and said, '*Labbayk ya Rasul Allah.*' The Holy Prophet said, "You wonder, this man has come back to his homeland, and will he return to us? Or instead, he will join his friends and relatives and stay here?" This was indeed their real concern, especially after the conquest of Makkah. They thought he might stay in his homeland. They did not want to part with the Holy Prophet and return to Medina alone. With their head bowed, they said, "Yes, we said that O Messenger of Allah."

"Do I not have a name that you should speak of me as this man? I am the servant of Allah and His Messenger, and I emigrated for Allah to your land. Then my life is your life, and my death is your death." These words had a deep impact on their hearts, and they started sobbing with tears flowing down their faces. They came close to him and said, "We swear, O Messenger of Allah, we said that only because of our deep love for Allah and His Messenger." Upon this, the Holy Prophet (May God bless and cherish him) said, "There is no doubt that Allah and His Messenger see and understand your situation and verify what you say."

The holy Prophet (May God bless and cherish him) looked towards his uncle Hazrat Abbas and said, "O Abbas, where are the sons of your brother (Abu Lahab)

Utba and Muattib? I don't see them." These were the sons of Abu Lahab. And it was Utba who, under the pressure of his father, had divorced Hazrat Ruqayyah (the Holy Prophet's daughter). Therefore, he was afraid to confront the Messenger of Allah. But today was a Day of Reconciliation. The Holy Prophet (May God bless and cherish him) asked Hazrat Abbas, "Bring them to me." Hazrat Abbas said, "They have gone to stay out of sight." Later, Hazrat Abbas mounted his horse and went after them. He found them and told them what the Holy Prophet (May God bless and cherish him) said about them and invited them to Islam. Their hearts had already opened to faith. They went to the presence of the Holy Prophet (May God bless and cherish him) along with their uncle. When the Holy Prophet (May God bless and cherish him) saw them, his face lit up. He stood up and greeted them. Then, holding their hands, he came all the way to Multazam, which is that part of the Kaaba wall that lies between Black Stone and the door. There the Holy Prophet supplicated for a long time. Seeing the joy on his face, Hazrat Abbas asked the reason for it. He replied, "I asked the Lord to spare the two sons of my uncle for me, and He responded favorably to my request. He has given them to me." (Waqidi)

During this time, most of the Makkans had converted to Islam and had pledged their allegiance to the Holy Prophet (May God bless and cherish him). Safwan's cousin Umayr had pleaded with the Messenger of Allah and obtained a two-month's respite. However, Safwan intended to leave Makkah and found a boat to deport. Before he was able to leave, Umayr went after him and found him. He told him about his immunity, but he was afraid and did not agree. Umayr went back to the Holy Prophet (May God bless and cherish him), whereupon he gave his turban of stripped Yemeni cloth as a token of his safety. This reassured him, and he came to the presence of the Holy Prophet (May God bless and cherish him) and said, "O Muhammad, Umayr told me that if I agreed to enter Islam, I will be safe, but if I did not, you will give me two month's respite." "Stay in Makkah," the Holy Prophet (May God bless and cherish him) said. "Not until you give me a clear answer," replied Safwan. "You shall have four months' time." The Holy Prophet (May God bless and cherish him) extended the time, and Safwan agreed to stay in Makkah.

On the day of the conquest of Makkah, many of the Quraysh, who were staunch enemies of the Holy Prophet (May God bless and cherish him), had fled the city. This included Abdullah ibn Ziba', Ikrima ibn Abu Jahl, Safwan ibn Umayya, Wahsi ibn Harb, Dhu al-Jawshan, Harith ibn Hisham, Saib ibn Sayfiyy, Adiyy ibn Khiyar, Uqba ibn Harith and Muawiya Ibn Abu Sufyan. Nevertheless, they all had returned one way or the other and accepted the religion of Islam.

After the victory of Makkah, Ikrima decided to take a boat from the coast of Tihamah to Abyssinia. As he was stepping on board, the captain announced, "Make good thy religion with God." "What shall I say," asked Ikrima. "Say, there is no god but God," was the answer by the captain. He further explained that due to fear of shipwreck he would not accept a passenger who did not testify. The words of 'La Ilaha illallah' entered the soul of Ikrima. He knew in his heart the truth of it. He said to himself one can accept the truth on board; one can accept it on land. The entire message of the Holy Prophet (May God bless and cherish him) was summed up in 'La ialha illallah.' At the same time, his wife arrived and told him that the Holy Prophet (May God bless and cherish him) had granted him safety in Makkah. Therefore, they returned. He went straight to the presence of the Holy Prophet (May God bless and cherish him). The Messenger of God knew that he was coming and told his Companions "Ikrima, the son of Abu Jahl, is on his way as a believer. Therefore, do not revile his father, for reviling the dead make the living upset and do not reach the dead." The Holy Prophet (May God bless and cherish him) greeted him with a face full of joy, and he readily accepted the faith. Ikrima requested the Holy Prophet (May God bless and cherish him), "O Messenger of Allah, please pray to God to forgive me for all my enmity against you." The Holy Prophet (May God bless and cherish him) prayed to Allah as he requested. Then Ikrima said that he spent money and fought against the truth, but henceforth, he would spend double of it and fight with more vigor in the path of Allah, and he kept his word. (Waqidi).

After the victory of Makkah, the Holy Prophet (May God bless and cherish him) entered the House of Allah and cleaned out from the Kaaba all idols. In Arabia, there were three main shrines of paganism near Makkah, and one of them was the temple of al-Uzza at Nakhlah. The Holy Prophet (May God bless and cherish him) gave orders to Khalid ibn Walid to destroy this temple of idolatry. When his fighters reached the place, the caretaker of the temple hung his sword on the statue of al-Uzza and called upon the goddess to defend herself and kill Khalid. Khalid destroyed the temple and the statue of al-Uzza, and he returned to Makkah. Upon his arrival, the Holy Prophet (May God bless and cherish him) asked, "Did you see anything?" "Nothing," replied Khalid. "Then you have not destroyed her," the Holy Prophet proclaimed, and he insisted to go back and destroy it. Therefore, Khalid ibn Walid went back to Nakhlah, and he saw that out of the ruins of the temple, a black woman came, who was entirely naked with long, disheveled hair. Later, Khalid narrated, "I was terrified, and my spine was seized with shivering." At that moment, he shouted, "Uzza, denial is for thee, not worship," and he drew his sword and cut her down. He came back to the Holy Prophet and informed him what he saw and did.

CHAPTER 24
THE BATTLE OF HUNAYN

More than two weeks had passed since the conquest of Makkah, and during this time, the Holy Prophet (May God bless and cherish him) was praying short prayers because he did not intend to stay longer in the city. He wanted to consolidate the rule of Islam over Makkah and then return to Medina. During this period, the Hawazin were preparing their army to confront the Holy Prophet (May God bless and cherish him). They feared that they were the next target. Their concern was genuine after the destruction of the temple of al-Uzza, which had been the sister shrine to their own temple of al-Lat. With the help of the neighboring tribes, they had gathered an army of some twenty thousand men to the north of Taif at a place called Awtas.

The Holy Prophet (May God bless and cherish him) sent Abdullah ibn Abu Hadrad to collect information and bring him the news of Hawazin. He immediately embarked on his mission and visited the tribes of Hawazin. He saw that they were ready for a war on a very large scale and had assembled their forces. They were worried and said, "Muhammad has now conquered Makkah. There is no reason that he should not attack us next. Therefore, it would be better if we attacked him first. We swear he has always fought with people who do not know how to fight. Let us join forces and attack him first before he comes to us."

Hawazin had won the support of the tribes of Thaqif, Nasr, and Jusham. The tribes of Sa'd ibn Bakr and Bani Hilal did not support them. The clans of Ka'b and Kilab told them, "We swear that should you get the support of everyone from the east to west and fight Muhammad, he would still defeat you."

The Holy Prophet (May God bless and cherish him) appointed a man of Abdu Shams as a caretaker of Makkah and nominated Muadh ibn Jabal as an instructor to teach the tenets of Islam to the new converts. The Holy Prophet (May God bless and cherish him) marched out with his army now consisted of twelve thousand men. He was also accompanied by Safwan and Suhayl. Safwan had not yet entered Islam but was defending Makkah against the invaders. The Muslim army needed more armor and weapons. Therefore, the Holy Prophet (May God bless and cherish him) sent for Safwan to have a word with him. When Safwan came, the Holy Prophet (May God bless and cherish him) said, "O Abu Umayya, will you loan us weapons against our enemies?" "O Muhammad," said Sawan, "Is it a question to give or I will take?" But the Holy Prophet (May God bless and cherish him) requested him and said, "It is a loan to be returned. "Safwan supplied the Muslim army with more than a hundred coats of mail, shields, and other weapons that went along with it. He also agreed to provide camels to transport the weapons to their final camp. In a similar way, the Holy Prophet (May God bless and cherish him) also borrowed more than three thousand spears from his uncle's son Nawfal ibn Harith, and when taking them, he complimented, "I see that your spears can break the backs of the enemies."

The Hawazin had chosen a young man named Malik ibn Awf as their commander, who was famous for his bravery and charismatic personality. As a strategy of war, he had ordered his men to bring their women, children, and cattle along with them. He thought having all their possessions and family in the rear of the army would make the men fight more valiantly, even though the elderly men did not like his idea. Malik sent three men to collect information about the Muslim army and to report it to him. After a short while, all three men returned in a state of exhaustion. They looked bewildered and fear-stricken. When one of them regained his senses, he said, "We saw white men on piebald horses and all of a sudden were smitten by an unseen force." 'We are not fighting people of the earth," said another one, "But people of heaven. We strongly advise you to return to the army. If our men see what we saw, they will suffer and flee." Malik was furious and said, "Shame on you. You are a bunch of cowards." He ordered that they should be locked up in the rear so that they would not spread panic throughout the army. Then, he asked his commanders, "Bring me a courageous man." So, he sent another scout to bring the news of the Makkan forces. He also returned in the same shaken state. He had also seen terrifying horsemen in front of the Muslim army.

Malik did not pay any attention to his warning. He issued orders after the dark to advance towards the valley of Hunayn because he knew that the Muslim army would have to pass through it. He halted his army at the end of the valley. He positioned a large number of horsemen on either side of the valley on the land that began to slope down. The horsemen were stationed in a way that they could not be seen from below. He told them to charge upon the enemy when he gave the signal. They were backed up by the main body of the army near the top of the gorge.

During the night, the Muslim army was encamped at the other end of the valley. At dawn, the Holy Prophet (May God bless and cherish him) prayed and gave them the standards. The Holy Prophet (May God bless and cherish him) had two armors, a helmet and a shield. He encouraged his fighters and gave them good tidings of victory if they remained steadfast. It was still dark, and the army descended into the valley. Khalid ibn Walid was leading the fighters of Sulaym and others. Behind him were the newly converted Muslims from Makkah. The Holy Prophet (May God bless and cherish him) was riding his horse (Duldul) amid the Helpers and Emigrants. This time, he was also surrounded by his own family members, including Abu Sufyan and Abdullah, who had joined him on this expedition. With him were the two eldest sons of Hazrat Abbas, Fadl and Qitham, and the two sons of Abu Lahab.

It was still early morning; the sky was overcast, and the front portion of the army had entered the valley. The body of Hawazin horsemen came into view above them on the opposite slope. The huge mass of the Hawazin army was at the other end of the valley, blocking that end. The Muslim army was trapped. Without losing time, Malik gave his signal to attack. Thousands of enemy horsemen swept down upon Khalid and his men.

The enemy's onslaught was sudden, fierce, and so overwhelming that the Bani Sulaym could not stand and resist it. They were not ready for the battle yet and had not even drawn their swords. They simply turned around and fled, creating mayhem and panic among the ranks of Makkans who were behind them. They ran up the slope which they had just descended. It was like doomsday. The Holy Prophet (May God bless and cherish him) was in the middle of the army but was able to withdraw to the side of the road and stand firm over there. He was surrounded by the small group of those who were riding with him – it was Hazrat Abu Bakr, Hazrat Umar, some of the Emigrants and Helpers – and all the men of his family were with him. Harith's son Abu Sufyan stood close to him and took hold of Duldul's bridle.

The Holy Prophet (May God bless and cherish him) called to his Companions,

"O people, come towards me! I am the Messenger of Allah. I am Muhammad, the son of Abdul Muttalib." But his voice was drowned in the noise of the battle. So, he told Hazrat Abbas, who had a strong and powerful voice, to shout, "O Companions of the tree, O Companions of the Acacia!" Those who heard the call immediately responded and started shouting "Labbayk," (here at thy service). In a short time, Helpers and Emigrants rallied around him. The Holy Prophet (May God bless and cherish him) now had a hundred men around him, and he spread them out across the field, and they were able to momentarily check the onslaught of the Hawazin. At the same time, Hazrat Abbas continued to shout and as a result many of the fighters who had fled returned to the fight.

As the Hawazin were preparing a fresh attack, the Holy Prophet (May God bless and cherish him) stood up in his stirrups, raised his hands, and prayed, "Dear Lord, come to our side and give us victory that you have promised. Otherwise, there would be no one left on earth who would worship you. Praise belongs to you, and help can only be asked of you." Then he turned to his foster brother and told him to give him some pebbles. He took them in hand and threw them in the faces of the enemy as he had done in Badr. Suddenly, the tide of the battle turned. It seemed to the enemy that they were against the heavenly fighters as had been previously experienced by their scouts. Soon after, Gabriel brought the following revelation:

"God had helped you on many fields, and on the day of Hunayn, when you exulted in your numbers, and they availed you naught, and the earth for all its breadth was straightened for you, and you turned back in flight. Then God sent down His spirit of peace upon His Messenger and upon the faithful, and sent down hosts that you saw not, and punished those who disbelieved. Such is the wage of the disbelievers, and afterwards God relents unto whom He will, for God is Forgiving, Merciful."

That day, the Companions charged on the enemy with great valor once again. The Holy Prophet (May God bless and cherish him) himself was fighting valiantly on the front line. Divine peace descended upon the believers, and they forgot all the turmoil of the battlefield. At the same time, there was a great thunder in the sky that rattled the hearts of the enemy forces and caused tremors in them. God's help had arrived from heaven, and five thousand angels had descended in legions. Those warriors had the ends of their turbans hanging from their shoulders. The Hawazin forces were routed, and they fled in haste. Malik, who fought with much bravery, finally retreated with the men of Thaqif to their walled city of Taif. The Muslim army pursued the Hawazin as far Nakhlah and killed most of them. The enemy forces retreated to their camp at Awtas, but the Muslim fighters dislodged them, and they took refuge in the mountains.

The Hawazin had brought their women and children behind their army. Some of the women had swords and were wounded by Muslim fighters. When the Holy Prophet (May God bless and cherish him) saw that a woman was killed, he sent a command to Khalid ibn Walid not to touch women and children ever during a battle. Usayd ibn Khudayr, who heard the Holy Prophet (May God bless and cherish him), asked, "O Messenger of Allah, are they not the children of the polytheists?" The Holy Prophet (May God bless and cherish him) got angry and said, "Are not the best among you the children of polytheists."

A fatally wounded man, whose courage on the battlefield was highly praised, was brought to the Holy Prophet (May God bless and cherish him). He said, "He is from the inhabitants of the Hell." The Companions were astonished but soon remembered Quzman, who had committed suicide on the day of Hud. So, the Companions kept an eye on him, and he, like Quzman stabbed his belly with an arrow, when the pain became too much for him to bear. The Companions informed the Holy Prophet (May God bless and cherish him) about it. He called Bilal and said, "Only believers will go to paradise."

The Muslim army had lost many men in the initial onslaught of the battle, and most of them were from Bani Sulaym, because they were in the forefront and had born the heavy losses. After that, few Muslim fighters had been killed. One of the martyrs was Ayman, Usama's elder brother.

The war had ended, and the great majority of the enemy forces had fled. But many were taken captive, including the women and children who had accompanied the troops. The enemy had left a fortune. The spoils that were left on the battlefield included twenty-four thousand ounces of silver. Six thousand men and women were taken as captives. The Holy Prophet (May God bless and cherish him) gave orders that women and children should not be touched, and pregnant women should be left alone and cared for. He appointed Abu Sufyan to be responsible for the captives. The Holy Prophet (May God bless and cherish him) put Budayl ibn Waraqa in charge of the spoils and instructed him that it should all be taken, including the captives, to the nearby valley of Jiranah, close to Makkah. Then he turned to his Companions and said, "O people! It is not permissible for me to take anything – not even a pin –

other than one–fifth of what Allah has given me as spoils, and this one-fifth will eventually return to you. Therefore, bring me whatever you have by way of spoils. Do not make spoils your personal property; otherwise, you will account for it on the Day of Judgment."

The clan of Sa'd ibn Bakr were allies of Hawazin against the Muslim army. The Holy Prophet (May God bless and cherish him) had spent his infancy and childhood in that clan. One of the elderly ladies, who was among the captives, came forward and said, "By God, I am the sister of your chief." The Companions did not trust her claim but nonetheless brought her to the presence of the Holy Prophet (May God bless and cherish him), "O Muhammad, I am thy sister," she proclaimed. The Holy Prophet (May God bless and cherish him) looked at her intently; she was an old woman of seventy or more. "Do you have any proof?" he said. She at once showed him the mark of a bite, "You bit me when you were young," she continued, "I was carrying you in the valley of Sarar. We were there with the shepherds. Thy father was my father, and thy mother was my mother." The Holy Prophet (May God bless and cherish him) knew that she was telling the truth, and it was indeed Shayma, one of his foster sisters. He spread out his rug for her and asked to sit. He asked her about her parents, Halimah and Harith, and tears flowed from her eyes when she told him they had died years ago. They talked for a while. The Holy Prophet (May God bless and cherish him) offered her to stay, or she could return to her clan. She said that she wished to enter Islam but would like to return to her clan. The Holy Prophet (May God bless and cherish him) gave her valuable gifts and told her to remain with her people in the camp.

The fleeing Hawazin and the Thaqif retreated to their stronghold Taif and enclosed themselves in the fortified walled city. They had enough provisions in their city to last them for a year. They had ample weapons and means of resisting an attacking army. They were also expert archers. The Holy Prophet (May God bless and cherish him) set out with his army for Taif. The Messenger of Allah sent Khalid ibn Walid as the commander of a pioneer force consisting of one thousand fighters. Khalid came all the way to the enclosure and went around it. He did not find anybody to speak to. He then went to the main gate of the castle and shouted, "Let one of you come down so that I can speak to him. I guarantee his safety until he goes back or give me the surety that I may come to you so that we can speak." They answered, "No one from us will come to speak to you, nor will we let you come here, O Khalid, your friend had always fought men who did not know how to fight until this day."

When the Muslim army reached Taif, they laid siege to the city. There were many fierce exchanges of arrows, because of which twelve Companions were killed. The Holy Prophet (May God bless and cherish him) set up his camp further away from the castle. No one dared to come outside the castle and fight face-to-face with the Muslim fighters. Khalid would call out frequently, "Is there no one who will come out and fight like a man." Finally, a man called Yalyal said, "No one from us will confront you this day. We will continue to wait inside. We have enough provisions that will last us for years. If you wait until you run out of your supplies, then we will draw our swords and fight you to the last breath."

Half a month went by, and the Muslims were no more near capturing the town than they had been on the first day. At this juncture, Salman Farsi suggested setting up catapults in front of the walls and throwing bigger stones to breach the walls. The Muslim army also constructed two dabbabas, machines that protected the fighters from arrows and hot oil that could pour down from the castle walls. The attack did not result in any success.

The Holy Prophet (May God bless and cherish him) one day announced by means of a crier that any slave of Thaqif who came down and joined the Muslims would be set free. About twenty slaves managed to make their way out of the city and came to the Holy Prophet (May God bless and cherish him) and pledged their allegiance. Hence, they were all set free.

The enemy had enough provisions in their city and had also ample means to resist any breach of the walls. The Muslim army was encamped outside the city for almost fifteen days. The Holy Prophet (May God bless and cherish him) had a dream in which he was given a bowl of butter, and a cock came and pecked at it and spilled it. The next morning, he told Hazrat Abu Bakr his dream and asked his opinion. Hazrat Abu Bakr said, "I don't think that you will be able to attain the goal concerning the Taif today." The Holy Prophet (May God bless and cherish him) then turned to Nawfal ibn Muawiya and said, "O Nawfal, what do you think about continuing or lifting the siege?" Nawfal said, "O Messenger of Allah! They are like a fox stranded in its den. If you chase after it, you will catch it. If you let it go, it will not be able to cause any harm." The Holy Prophet (May God bless and cherish him) had already made up his mind because the siege was not the best way to overcome them. So, he told his Companions in the early hours of the morning that the siege was going to be lifted and that they would go home. He mounted his camel, and people, including Jabir, came to him and asked to curse the people of Thaqif, who had caused so much trouble. The Holy Prophet (May God bless and cherish him) raised his hands in supplication and said, "O God, guide Thaqif and bring them to us." Among those who were killed beneath the walls of Taif was Umm Salamah's half-brother, the Holy Prophet's (May God bless and cherish him) cousin, Abdullah, who had recently converted to Islam.

WINNING HEARTS

The holy Prophet (May God bless and cherish him) mounted on his camel and travelled through Qarna l-Manazil and Nahla from Taif to Jiranah. While the army was on the way, the camel of one of the Companions, Abu Ruhm, had come so close to the mount of the Holy Prophet (May God bless and cherish him) that his rough boots hurt the leg of the Holy Prophet (May God bless and cherish him). He looked at him, stroked him lightly with his whip, and said, "Take your feet away, you just hurt me." When they reached Jiranah, although it was not his turn to graze the camels, Abu Ruhm volunteered to do so. He was feeling guilty for having hurt the Holy Prophet (May God bless and cherish him). At the same time, the Holy Prophet (May God bless and cherish him) was looking for him. When he was told about it, he immediately came to the presence of the Holy Prophet (May God bless and cherish him). His heart was full of anxiety, and he felt shame. As soon as the Holy Prophet (May God bless and cherish him) saw him, he said, "You had hurt my foot, and I hit you with my whip. Take these sheep in return for that." The Holy Prophet gave him eighty sheep in compensation. Abu Ruhm breathed a sigh of relief. He had never witnessed such great generosity.

On their way to Jiranah, a man approached and tried to come close to the Holy Prophet (May God bless and cherish him). The Companions intervened to keep him away because they did not know who he was. At last, the man raised his voice so that the Holy Prophet (May God bless and cherish him) could hear as well. He was holding a letter in his hand and said, I am Suraqa ibn Jushm, and I have this letter. Suraqa was the man who had followed the Holy Prophet (May God bless and cherish him) during his Hijra to get his prize put on the Messenger of Allah's head. He had returned as a Muslim from that encounter, and the letter he was holding was the letter he had received from the Holy Prophet (May God bless and cherish him) that day. (Ibn Kathir, Al-Bidaya wan-Nihaya; Sira ibn Hisham; Salihi, Subulu l-Huda war-

Rashad)

The Holy Prophet (May God bless and cherish him) heard his voice and said, "Today is the day of loyalty and kindness; bring him to me." Suraqa came to the Holy Prophet (May God bless and cherish him) and greeted him with peace and presented the Holy Prophet (May God bless and cherish him) his due of Zakat. During his conversation, he asked, "O Messenger of Allah, if camels that have no owners come and drink from the pool that I have made for stray animals, can I benefit from them as well?" "Yes," replied the Holy Prophet (May God bless and cherish him), "It is a good deed to give water to any living thing that has a liver."

When the Holy Prophet (May God bless and cherish him) reached Jiranah, there were six thousand slaves, mostly women and children, in a large enclosure, sheltering from the sun. They were all poorly dressed in either tethered clothes or not enough to cover them. The Holy Prophet (May God bless and cherish him) sent a man of Khazraj to Makkah to purchase new clothes for each one to be paid out of the silver that was part of the spoils. The spoils consisted of about twenty-four thousand camels and more than forty thousand sheep and goats. The Holy Prophet was deliberately delaying his decision about slaves and the spoils of war because he anticipated that Hawazin would send him a delegation requesting forgiveness and generous treatment. More than ten days had passed since they had left Taif, and there was no delegation sent by the Hawazin. Most of the fighters were eager to receive their share of the spoils and slaves. However, the Holy Prophet (May God bless and cherish him) did not want to delay his fifth of spoils that he used for the common good. In fact, a recent revelation has stressed a new category of people to benefit from such spoils. The Quranic verse said,

"The alms are for the poor and the needy, and for those who collect them, and those whose hearts are to be reconciled, and to set free slaves and captives, and for the relief of debtors and for the cause of God and for the wayfarer – an obligation enforced by God. And God is Knowing and Wise." (Al-Taubah 9:60)

And now it was time to distribute the spoils of war. Before it was done, one-fifth was put aside, as was the command of Allah. All the fighters were wondering who would get how much. The Holy Prophet (May God bless and cherish him) started distributing the spoils according to the new revelation among some of the prominent men of the Quraysh who had recently accepted Islam to win their hearts. Salihi numbered them fifty in his book Subulu l-huda war-Rashad. For example, Abu

Sufyan was given a hundred camels, but he reminded the Holy Prophet (May God bless and cherish him) that his two sons, Yazid and Muawiyah, should also be given a hundred each. In this way, he received three hundred camels. But it created discontent among the army. When the Holy Prophet (May God bless and cherish him) gave Hakim ibn Hizam one hundred camels, he asked for two hundred more, which the Holy Prophet (May God bless and cherish him) allotted him right away. But he said to Hakim,

"O Hakim, the worldly goods are like a green pasture, whoso takes them with sincerity of the heart shall be blessed therein, but whoso takes it for the desire of his soul shall not be blessed therein, and his example is like the one who does not feel satiated although he eats all the time. The upper hand is better than the lower hand, and so when it comes to giving, give first to those who are close to you."

Hakim ibn Hizam felt great shame, and he turned pale, and he could not look the Holy Prophet (May God bless and cherish him) in the eye and said, "By Him, who sent you with the truth, I will not ask anything from anyone after this." He took only a hundred camels and refused to take the rest. (Waqidi)

Safwan ibn Umayyah received a gift of one hundred camels even though he had not entered Islam, but his admiration for the Holy Prophet (May God bless and cherish him) grew even more. He had taken part in the battle of Hunayn, and when one of the Makkans in the rear expressed happiness at the initial flight of Muslims, Safwan rebuked him and said, "I would rather submit to a man of the Quraysh than a Hawazin."

Safwan was riding alongside the Holy Prophet (May God bless and cherish him) during the distribution of the spoils. As they rode through the valley of Jiranah, in one of these, the pasture was remarkably luxuriant and full of camels and sheep. Safwan was amazed by the sight. The Holy Prophet (May God bless and cherish him) said to him, "O Abu Wahb, I think you like this valley very much." Safwan turned back and said," Yes." The Holy Prophet (May God bless and cherish him) said, "It is yours with all that is in it." Safwan was not expecting such generosity. He was rather shocked and gathered himself and said, "I bear witness that there is no god, but God and you are His Messenger, because such greatness can only be found in a prophet."

Suhayl was also one of those whose final doubts were overcome in Jiranah through his relationship with his son Abdullah, along with his witnessing of the miraculous victory at Hunayn and his close experience of the Holy Prophet's (May

God bless and cherish him) presence and nobility. He accepted Islam sincerely and remained steadfast. A few years later, when his son Abdullah was killed in a battle, and Hazrat Abu Bakr confronted him, he said, "I have been told that God's Messenger said, "The martyr shall intercede for seventy of his people, and I have hopes that my son will not begin with anyone before me."

Among others who accepted Islam in Jiranah were some leading men of Makhzum. Two brothers of Abu Jahl, Khalid's half-brother Hisham, the full brother of young Walid who had died, and a second son of the Holy Prophet's aunt Atikah, Zubayr. It was Zubayr, who some ten years previously, in defiance of Abu Jahl, who had been the first to speak in the assembly in favor of the annulment of the ban on Bani Hashim and Bani Abdul Muttalib. His mother, Atikah had already become a Muslim before either of her sons.

When Abbas ibn Mirdas was given less of a share compared to others, he was disappointed and expressed his discontentment by reciting a poem openly criticizing the Holy Prophet (May God bless and cherish him). He said that Safwan ibn Umayyah, Aqra ibn Habis, Uyayna ibn Hisn, and Hakim ibn Hizam had been given one hundred camels each, whereas he had received forty. In fact, Aqra and Huyayna were given more to make their entry into Islam easier. It was Allah, who in a recent revelation, had commanded that a share should be given to those whose hearts were to be warmed to Islam.

HAWAZIN DELEGATION

The Holy Prophet (May God bless and cherish him) had spent several days in the valley, but still no delegation had come from Hawazin. Therefore, the Holy Prophet (May God bless and cherish him) allocated each man his share of the spoils. Then, one day, the Hawazin delegation arrived with Zuhayr ibn Surad leading them. The Holy Prophet's (May God bless and cherish him) nursing uncle, Abu Burqan, was among them. They all had become Muslims and pleaded with him that the entire tribe of Hawazin should be considered as his foster kinsmen and asked for his generosity. They said, "O Messenger of Allah, we are a deeply rooted and noble people, as you know calamity befell on us, be good to us and be generous to us so that Allah may be generous to you in return."

After that, the poet Zuhayr ibn Surad took his turn to speak and said, "O Messenger of Allah, some of the slaves present here are your nursing aunts and the family of those who nursed and looked after you. Had we been a family who had nursed the king of Iraq, Numan ibn Minzir, and had we been put into a similar situation with them, we would expect mercy and good treatment from them. We hope to be saved from this difficult situation. O Messenger of Allah! You are the best among those nursed and brought up; be kind and generous to us." Zuhayr expressed his mind eloquently through his poetic prowess.

The Holy Prophet (May God bless and cherish him) told them that he waited for them until he thought they were not coming, and the spoils had already been distributed. Then he asked them which were dearer to them, their sons and their wives, or their possessions, even though he knew the answer. They said, "Give us back our sons and our wives." The Holy Prophet (May God bless and cherish him) replied, "As for those that have fallen unto me and unto the sons of Abdul Muttalib, they are yours. I will plead with other men on your behalf when I have led the congregation in the noon prayer, then say, "We ask the Messenger of Allah to intercede for us with the Muslims, and we ask Muslims to intercede for us with the Messenger of God," (Ibn Ishaq)

Then, after the noon prayer, the Hawazin delegates addressed the congregation and made a very strong case for the release of the prisoners. In response to their plea, the Holy Prophet (May God bless and cherish him) turned to the people, thanked Allah, and exalted Him, and said, "There is no doubt that they are your brothers; they have come here having repented. There is no doubt that I believe it would be appropriate to give back the prisoners that are my share, and whoever among you feels the same, let him do likewise. And whoever thinks he needs to hold onto his share of the slaves that Allah has given, let him do so."

The Emigrants and Helpers immediately presented their captives to the Holy Prophet (May God bless and cherish him). As for the tribes, some of them did the same, and some refused. When the Holy Prophet (May God bless and cherish him) promised six camels from the spoils for every prisoner that was set free, the majority agreed. In this way, they were all returned to their people except one young woman who had fallen to the lot of the Holy Prophet's (May God bless and cherish him) maternal cousin, Sa'd of Zuhrah, and who wished to remain with him.

Before the delegation left, the Holy Prophet (May God bless and cherish him) asked them about their leader Malik ibn Awf. They told him that he had joined Thaqif in Taif. The Holy Prophet (May God bless and cherish him) said to them, "Send him word that if he came to me as a Muslim, I would return his family and his possessions, and I will give him a hundred camels." He had sent Malik's family to his aunt Atikah in Makkah and had withheld his property from being distributed. The Hawazin conveyed the message of the Holy Prophet (May God bless and cherish him) to their leader, Malik ibn Awf, telling him that he should come and benefit from this offer of safety. Malik feared that if the people of Thaqif learned about this offer, they would imprison him in the castle.

So, he secretly prepared a camel and sent it with a slave. He told him to wait for him until he arrived at a place called Danha. He got on a horse in the middle of the night and made his way straight for Danha. No one had realized that Malik had left. Malik came to Danha and mounted his camel and went to the presence of the Holy Prophet (May God bless and cherish him) in Jiranah. The Holy Prophet (May God bless and cherish him) was pleased to see him and gave back to him his family, his possessions, and a hundred camels. The holy Prophet (May God bless and cherish him) also put him in command of the already large and increasing Muslim community of Hawazin with instructions to give Thaqif no peace.

The Holy Prophet (May God bless and cherish him) used the principle of giving to those whose hearts were to be reconciled, as was revealed in a recent revelation. He gave rich gifts to prominent Bedouins whose Islam was highly questionable, whereas many deserving men of the desert were left behind. That is why Sa'd of Zuhrah asked the Holy Prophet (May God bless and cherish him) why he had given a hundred camels each to Uyaynah of Ghatafan and Aqra of Tamim and nothing to Juayl of Damarah, who was also exceptionally poor. The Holy Prophet (May God bless and cherish him) replied, "By Him in whose hand is my soul. Juayl is worth more than a world full of men like Uyaynah and Aqra, but their souls, I have reconciled that they might better submit unto God. Whereas, I have entrusted Juayl unto the submission he had already made." (Waqidi)

At the same time, there was a growing discontentment among four thousand Helpers. Someone from the Ansar said, "This distribution of spoils is not fair. Allah's will have not been considered." Ibn Masud, who heard this said, "I swear I will report this to the Holy Prophet (May God bless and cherish him)," so he went directly to the presence of the Messenger of God and informed him of the situation. The Holy Prophet (May God bless and cherish him) was greatly dismayed, and he said, "Who can act justly if not Allah and His Messenger?"

When feelings rose high among the Helpers, Sa'd ibn Ubaydah went to the Holy Prophet (May God bless and cherish him) and told him what was in their minds and their tongues. The Holy Prophet (May God bless and cherish him) listened to Sa'd and asked Sa'd about this issue. "When distributing the spoils, you gave them away to your own tribe and other Arab tribes, and gave Ansar nothing," replied Sa'd ibn Ubaydah. "And what do you think about it?" asked the Holy Prophet (May God bless and cherish him). "O Messenger of Allah," he answered, "I am like one of them." The Holy Prophet (May God bless and cherish him) told him to gather all the Ansar (Helpers) in one of the enclosures that had been used to shelter the captives, and some of the Emigrants also joined them, with Sa'd's permission. When all of them were gathered, Sa'd went and informed the Holy prophet (May God bless and cherish him).

The Messenger of Allah first thanked Allah and then began to speak, "O people of Ansar! I have been informed that you are deeply dismayed with me in your souls. When I came to you, you were lost, and did not Allah, the Almighty, provide you with guidance through me? You were all poor, and did not Allah make you rich through me? You were enemies of each other, and did not Allah make your hearts one and abolished all enmity?" "Yes, Indeed," they answered. "Allah and His Messenger are most bountiful and generous." The Ansar were silent with their heads bowed down.

The Holy Prophet (May God bless and cherish him) continued talking, "I swear that you may say the following if you like, "You came to us as an exiled man, we housed you! You came to us needing, and we helped you! You came to us in fear and anxiety, and we protected you! You came to us abandoned, we supported you, and you came to us denied and we believed in you!" then you will have told the truth. I will verify what you say. O people, you are stirred in your souls about the things of this world, whereby I have reconciled men's hearts that they may submit unto God. I have entrusted you unto your Islam. O people of Ansar! Are you not happy that while people return to their homes with camels and sheep, you go to your homes with the Messenger of Allah? I swear that the thing you return home is much more auspicious than what they go home with. I swear by Him who holds my life in His hands that if all men, but the Helpers went one way, and the Helpers another, I would go the way of the Helpers. God have mercy upon the Helpers, and their sons, and on their son's sons."

Having listened to such heart-melting words, the Helpers were moved deeply, and they wept until their beards were wet with tears. And they unanimously said, "We are well content with the Messenger of Allah as our portion and our lot."

LEAVING JIRANAH FOR LESSER PILGRIMAGE

It was now three months since the Holy Prophet (May God bless and cherish him) had left Medina. He stayed in Jiranah for thirteen days and one Wednesday evening, he decided to perform the lesser pilgrimage. He put on his ihram in the lower part of the valley of Jiranah and embarked on his journey to Kaaba. He made his rounds around the House of God and walked between the hills of Safa and Marwa. He then shaved his head and completed the Umrah (lesser pilgrimage). The Holy Prophet (May God bless and cherish him) returned to Jiranah. On his way, he met Urwah of Thaqif, the man who was present at Hudaybiyah and had noticed the love of the Companions towards the Holy Prophet (May God bless and cherish him). Urwah was absent during these last conflicts but was so impressed by the miraculous victory of Hunayn that he entered Islam and pledged his allegiance to the Holy Prophet (May God bless and cherish him). He then wanted to return to Taif and preach Islam to the people of Thaqif. But the Holy Prophet (May God bless and cherish him) advised him not to go and told him, "They will slay you." "O Messenger of Allah," said Urwah, "I am dearer to them than their firstborn." "They will kill you," the Holy Prophet (May God bless and cherish him) reiterated. But Urwah was insistent on going to Taif and asked for permission a third time. Upon this, the Holy Prophet said, "Then go if you will."

When he returned to Taif, his house was surrounded by archers, and he was mortally wounded by an arrow. When he was dying, his family asked him about his death, and he replied, "It is a grace which God in His bounty has given me." Then he told his son to bury him outside Taif with the martyrs. When the Holy Prophet (May God bless and cherish him) was informed of his death, he commented, "Urwah is like the man of Yaseen. He called his people unto God, and they slew him." (Waqidi)

A man named Habib, who was a carpenter in Antioch, called upon his people to accept the message of Jesus after they had rejected the Companions of Jesus, Peter, and others. They killed him, and it is mentioned in the Quran.

"It was said to him: enter Paradise. He said: I wish my people knew how God has forgiven my sins and lavished upon me His Bounty." (Yaseen 36:26-27). After his death, his son and nephew went to Medina and lived with their cousin Mughirah, who was one of the Emigrants.

The Holy Prophet (May God bless and cherish him) left the valley of Jiranah and passed through Saraf and Marr az-Zahran and arrived in Medina in three days before the month of Dhu al-Qadah had ended. The time that passed between his departure from Medina to the conquest of Makkah and his return was around three months. During this time, much was accomplished; Makkah had been conquered, Hawazin had been defeated, and victory at Hunayn achieved. Similarly, Taif had been laid siege to and the lifted and left alone until the day they would open doors and come out of their own volition. Thousands of people who were strong enemies of Muslims, chiefly Makkans, became Muslims. Those who took part in this campaign returned with large spoils. The Holy Prophet (May God bless and cherish him) entered Medina after a long absence and made straight for the Mosque. First, he thanked and praised his Lord for His bounty.

Before returning to his home, the Holy Prophet (May God bless and cherish him) went to the door of his beloved daughter, Hazrat Fatima al-Zahra, to see her first after a long separation. It was Hazrat Fatima who opened the door and saw her beloved father at the threshold. She was overjoyed, and looking at Father with love and affection, she kissed his hands. The Holy Prophet (May God bless and cherish him) kissed her forehead. Tears of joy were flowing from her eyes, and she hugged her father while sobbing. The Holy Prophet consoled her, "What is it that makes you cry, O Fatima? Why is it that you are crying?" He asked. She sobbed for a while and tried to calm down and said, "I can't see you like this, O Messenger of Allah. You have been through so many hardships; your hair is disheveled, you are covered with dust, your color is gone, and the dress you wear is in tethers. I just can't see you like this, my beloved father." The Holy Prophet (May God bless and cherish him) caressed her head and said,

"Do not cry, my dear daughter! Allah has sent me with a message that the day will come when this message reaches the entire world like day and night. There will not be a house in the world, made of mud brick or stone that Islam has not entered. There will not be a tent made of camel hair, sheep wool of goat hair that Islam will not enter it."

THE CENTER OF CIVILIZATION

Medina had now become the hub of civilization and peace. The period of *Jahiliyah* and chaos had finally come to an end, and a new era of justice and equality had dawned on the face of the Arabian Peninsula that would soon envelop the entire world. The Holy Prophet (May God bless and cherish him) assigned duties to his Companions. Some for teaching people the subtleties of Islam and others matters of the religion; some Companions were sent as envoys to invite tribes and groups to Islam. Some were charged with forming alliances with formidable forces as a measure of security and peace, while others were assigned to collect *Zakat* (Alms) from Muslims and *Jizyah* (Tax) from non-Muslims as a tax for their protection.

After returning to Medina, the Holy Prophet (May God bless and cherish him) sent Uyayna ibn Hisn to the tribe of Bani Tamim, Yazid ibn Husayn to the tribes of Aslam and Ghifar, Abbad ibn Bishr to the tribes of Sulaym and Mayzayna, Rafi ibn Maqis to the Juhayna, Amr ibn al-As to the Bani Farzana, Dahhaq ibn Sufyan to Bani Kalb, Bashir ibn Sufyan to the Bani Ka'b, Ibn Lutaybiyya to the Bani Zubayr, Muhajir ibn Abi Umayya to the city of San'a, Zaid ibn Labid to Hadramawt, Adiyy ibn Hatim to Tayy and Bani Asad, Malik ibn Nuwaira to Bani Hanzalah, Qays ibn Asim to Sa'd, Ala ibn Hadrami to Bahrain and Hazrat Ali to Najaran. The Holy Prophet (May God bless and cherish him), thereby, was spreading the word of Allah to the vast areas of the Arabian Peninsula.

During his stay in Medina, the Holy Prophet (May God bless and cherish him) also sent out several small expeditions. One of these was under the leadership of Hazrat Ali. It was against the tribe of Tayy, whose territory lay to the northeast of Medina. The Holy Prophet (May God bless and cherish him) had previously sent Hazrat Ali to destroy the shrine of Manat at Qudayd on the Red Sea, and thus, the main centers of idolatry were destroyed except for the shrine of al-Lat at Taif. But the people of Tayy had a temple and worshiped an idol there, and the aim of Hazrat Ali's campaign was to destroy that temple. Tayy was the tribe of Hatim, who was a famous poet. His son Adiyy was a Christian like his father and had succeeded him after his death as the chief of the tribe.

When Hazrat Ali ambushed the tribe of Tayy, Adiyy fled with his immediate family except for one of his sisters, who was taken captive with many others. She was brought to Medina to the presence of The Holy Prophet (May God bless and cherish him). She threw herself at the feet of the Holy Prophet (May God bless and cherish him) and begged for mercy. She said, "My father would always free the captives, take care of the guests, feed the hungry, and comfort the distressed. He would never turn away who asked for help. I am the daughter of Hatim." The Holy Prophet (May God bless and cherish him) comforted and reassured her and told his Companions to let her go, for her father loved noble ways, and Allah loves those who are generous and kind.

During this time, a man of her tribe had come and asked for her release. The Holy Prophet (May God bless and cherish him) put her in his custody and gave her a camel and some fine gifts. Upon her release, she went in search of her brother and persuaded him to go to the presence of the Holy Prophet (May God bless and cherish him) and ask for forgiveness. He did so and accepted Islam and thereby pledged his loyalty to the Messenger of Allah. The Holy Prophet (May God bless and cherish him) appointed him as the chief of Tayy, and he sincerely propagated Islam and proved to be a valuable ally.

BIRTH OF HAZRAT IBRAHIM

The mother of the faithful Hazrat Mariyah was expecting a baby soon. An elderly lady named Salma, who twenty years early had attended Hazrat Khadijah at the birth of all her children, was living in Medina. She was also the midwife who had helped to bring Hazrat Fatima into the world. She insisted that she should deliver this baby as well. The Holy Prophet (May God bless and cherish him) agreed to her request, and she went to the place where Hazrat Mariyah lived in the upper part of Medina.

A baby boy was born at night. Soon after his birth, Gabriel came to the Holy Prophet (May God bless and cherish him) and said, "O father of Ibrahim," and in the meantime Salma sent her husband Abu Rafi to tell the Holy Prophet (May God bless and cherish him) that he had a son. The Holy Prophet (May God bless and cherish him) was happy, and the next morning after dawn prayers he announced to his Companions that Allah had granted him a son. "I have named him," he said, "By the name of my father Ibrahim." The people of Medina celebrated the birth of this child, and women of Ansar volunteered to be the foster mother. The wife of a blacksmith, Umm Sayf, was selected to suckle the baby. The Holy Prophet (May God bless and cherish him) visited his son every day and spent much of his time over there.

But Hazrat Ibrahim fell ill during his infancy and was moved to a date orchard near the house of her mother under his mother and aunt's care. The Holy Prophet

(May God bless and cherish him) was informed about his condition. He was deeply saddened by the news, and he felt that he could no longer carry himself, and asked Abdul Rahman ibn Awf to give him his hand to lean upon. He reached in time to say farewell to his infant son in his mother's lap. The Holy Prophet (May God bless and cherish him) lifted his son and placed him in his own lap. His face reflected sorrow, and his heart was full of grief. Tears were flowing from his eyes, and he said to his son, "O Ibrahim, against the will of Allah, we cannot do anything," and then he fell silent. As Hazrat Ibrahim surrendered his soul, his mother and aunt watched and cried loudly. The Holy Prophet (May God bless and cherish him) once again said, "Were it not true that the last of us will join the first, we would have mourned you even more. The eyes send tears, and the heart is saddened, but we do not say anything except what pleases the Lord. Indeed, O Ibrahim, we are bereaved by your departure from us." The body of Hazrat Ibrahim was carried by a little bier by the Holy Prophet (May God bless and cherish him) and his uncle Hazrat Abbas. The funeral prayer was led by the Holy Prophet (May God bless and cherish him). The Messenger of Allah then filled the grave with sand and sprinkled water over it and placed a landmark on it.

It was during the same time, at the beginning of Rajab, that the news of the death of Negus (Najashi) came to the Holy Prophet (May God bless and cherish him). When the Holy Prophet (May God bless and cherish him) had finished the next ritual prayer, he ascended the pulpit and announced, "Today, a righteous person has died. Therefore, O Muslims, arise and pray for your brother Ashamah." Then, he performed the funeral prayer. Later, it was reported that a light was seen that was constantly shining on his grave. (Ibn Ishaq)

TABUK

While the Holy Prophet (May God bless and cherish him) was busy in Medina taking care of a vast array of issues, some concerning news arrived from Damascus. Rumors were spreading that the Byzantine army was marching towards Syria to invade the north of Tabuk near the Gulf of Aqaba. Byzantine emperor Heraclius had defeated the Persians and had taken control of the land of Jerusalem. This victory had been predicted by the revelation, which said that the day the believers will rejoice. (Quran 30:84). As a result, the Persians were forced to evacuate their forces from Syria and Egypt. However, the Persian forces were replaced by a Christian army. This was a formidable threat to the newly established Islamic state in Medina.

The Christian Arabs of the region had written a letter to Heraclius to persuade him to act against the Holy Prophet (May God bless and cherish him). They wrote, "The person who claims to be a prophet has died, and his Companions are also dying of hunger. Their resources are scarce, and they have lost everything. If you want to convert them to Christianity, it is just the right time." Meanwhile, the Arab tribes of Lakhm, Judham, Ghassan, and Amilah revolted and announced that they would support the Byzantine army if they were to attack the Muslims.

At the same time, the Ghassanid leader Shurahbil ibn Amr, who had killed the envoy of the Holy Prophet (May God bless and cherish him) and fought against the Muslim army in Muta, was waiting for an opportunity to invade Medina. It was also said that the Byzantine contingent had already marched south as far as Balqa. These reports were not reliable but were, in a way, exaggerated. The Byzantine emperor was not preparing for war. In fact, he suggested to his generals that a treaty should be made with the Holy Prophet (May God bless and cherish him), giving him the province of Syria on the condition that the Muslims would not advance any further. However, his generals did not agree with him and were extremely averse to this idea.

The Holy Prophet (May God bless and cherish him) was certain that Allah would make him victorious and open Syria to his army. Whether the time had come for the divine promise, or he wanted to prepare his Companions for the inevitable northern campaign, the Holy Prophet (May God bless and cherish him) gave orders to prepare for war. He sent word to Makkah and to the tribes around Medina that they must send at once all their available armed and mounted men for the Syrian campaign. The Holy Prophet (May God bless and cherish him) used to keep his true intentions as secret as possible, but in this case, there was no secrecy.

It was the beginning of October in the year AD 630. The season at that time of the year was exceptionally hot, and Medina was experiencing one of its most arid seasons. The fruits were ripening and ready to harvest. People could not dare to come out in the burning sun. Some people were not willing to take part in this expedition due to the adverse seasonal conditions and the other reason being the powerful and mighty forces of the enemy. Therefore, hypocrites and less devoted Muslims came to the Holy Prophet (May God bless and cherish him) with various excuses.

Jadd ibn Qays, with a group of his followers, came to visit the Holy Prophet

(May God bless and cherish him) in the Mosque. He requested of him saying, "O Messenger of Allah, I am a poor old man. These are my excuses. So, please allow me to stay behind." The Holy Prophet (May God bless and cherish him) listened to him and then said, "Get ready for the expedition, for you have the means." Jadd was unwilling to go, so he said, "You should allow me to stay so I don't fall into temptation. As my tribesmen know, I am very fond of women – the fondest among my people. If I go there and come across the women of the Bani Asfar tribe, I cannot promise to be patient." The Holy Prophet (May God bless and cherish him) turned away his face and said in a disapproving voice, "You are excused."

When the son of Jadd ibn Qays heard what his father had said to the Holy Prophet (May God bless and cherish him), he admonished him, "How can you oppose his orders? Is there a richer person than you among the Bani Salima? Why haven't you started preparing for the expedition.?" His father tried to explain, "O my son! In this hot weather and burning winds, I cannot leave for that region. I fear those people even when I am sitting in my home. I do not have the courage to oppose them in the battlefield. And I already know the outcome of this war." His son was not satisfied and continued to argue with him. Jadd slapped him in the face violently to silence him.

The number of people who made various excuses and asked permission to stay away from the battle was around eighty. There were also four men of good faith, Ka'b ibn Malik, and two other Khazraj, and a man from Aws, who did not deliberately decide to remain at home, nor did they make any excuses. However, they procrastinated from one day to another until it was too late, and the troops left the city. But most believers got ready with all speed, and the well-to-do Companions contributed generously with their money and resources.

The situation was dire, the enemy formidable, the road was long, and the resources were scarce. The Holy Prophet (May God bless and cherish him) ascended the pulpit in the Mosque and appealed to his Companions to offer help to those who needed much help, and then he supplicated, "Dear Lord! If something harmful fell upon my people and destroyed them, on this earth, there would be no one to worship you." Then he prayed to Allah for the success of these people whose hearts were filled with faith even though their resources were meager. There were people who wished to join the campaign wholeheartedly but could not do so because they lacked the means. They came to the Holy Prophet (May God bless and cherish him) and requested help. The Companions already started to give away their wealth and possessions for the cause of Allah.

Hazrat Abu Bakr went to his home, took all his possessions, and brought them to the Holy Prophet (May God bless and cherish him) in the Mosque. When he saw him, he asked Hazrat Abu Bakr, "Have you left anything for your family?" Hazrat Abu Bakr replied, "I left them Allah and His Messenger." He was so sincere, and his faith was so strong that he did not fear poverty would befall him. Soon after, Hazrat Umar brought his possessions and donated them for the cause of Allah. That day leading Companions such as Hazrat Uthman, Talha, Abbas, Sa'd ibn Ubaydah, and Ibn Adiyy contributed generously to equip the Muslim army.

One day, Hazrat Abu Bakr came to the Mosque into the Holy Prophet's (May God bless and cherish him) presence draped in a white blanket with a pin of date palm sticking out from the front of the blanket. Gabriel descended and said, "O Muhammad, God sends you His greetings and says, "What is with Abu Bakr that his cloak is pierced by a pin?" He said, "O Gabriel, he spent all his possessions before the conquest."

Gabriel said, "God says, 'Give him My greeting and ask him if he approves of Me in this poverty of his or he is angry?"

He said, "What shall I be angry with my Lord? I approve of my Lord."

"Those who have faith in the unseen and perform the prayer and spend of what We have provided them." (Quran 2:3)

Hazrat Uthman alone donated mounts and equipment for ten thousand men, that was one-third of the entire army. Seeing Hazrat Uthman coming to his presence with his contribution, the Holy Prophet (May God bless and cherish him) raised his hands in prayer and said, "Dear Lord! Be pleased with Uthman as I am pleased with him." He looked at the gold and silver that was brought by Hazrat Uthman; he turned to his Companions and praised Uthman, "From now on, whatever Uthman does will not hurt him."

Witnessing the wealthy people of the community donating their wealth, the rest of the community also brought their possessions. People even shared their only camels and gave away their daily provisions to the army. The women Companions were also at the forefront, donating their earrings, bracelets, anklets, and other golden jewelry for the sake of Allah and His messenger. Hazrat Aishah displayed the donated jewelry in her quarter to encourage the women to participate.

On the day of Tabuk, Wasilla ibn Asqa was shouting on the streets of Medina, "Is there anyone who would offer me his riding animal so that I can go to war? I would share of my spoils with him." Upon hearing his call, Ka'b ibn Ujra who was an old man agreed to lend his animal. Despite all this, there were those not able to find a sword to fight or a camel to ride. They did go before the Holy Prophet (May God bless and cherish him), but nothing was left of the donations. Many were disappointed; their desire to fight for Allah ended in nothing, and they shed streams of tears. A subsequent revelation has mentioned "The seven weepers"—five needy Helpers and two Bedouin of Muzaynah and Ghatafan, who were turned away due to lack of resources.

"Nor (is there blame) upon those who, when they came to you that you might give them mounts, you said, "I can find nothing for you to ride upon." They turned back while their eyes overflowed with tears out of grief that they could not find something to spend for the cause of Allah." (Al-Taubah 9:92)

When all the fighters from the surrounding tribes had arrived, the Muslim army was thirty thousand strong with ten thousand horsemen. A camp was set up outside Medina to lodge all the forces and Hazrat Abu Bakr was put in charge of them to look after the affairs until the army was ready for the march. It was Thursday, in the month of Rajab, and the Holy Prophet (May God bless and cherish him) himself rode forth and took the command. He left Hazrat Ali to look after his family and was in charge of Medina. But the hypocrites started gossiping that the Holy Prophet (May God bless and cherish him) had found him a burden and left him behind. Hazrat Ali heard the rumors and was so distressed that he put on his armor and overtook the Holy Prophet (May God bless and cherish him) at the first halt. He begged his permission to join the army, and he told him what the people were saying. The Holy Prophet (May God bless and cherish him) comforted him and said,

"They lie; I made you stay for the sake of what I had left behind me in Medina. So, return and represent me in my family and in thine. Are you not content, O Ali, that you are to me as Aron was unto Moses, save that after me there is no prophet." (Ibn Ishaq)

It was about ten days after the Holy Prophet (May God bless and cherish him) and his army had left Medina; one of the believers who had stayed behind, Abu Khaythamah of Khazraj, went out into his orchard on a hot day. His wives had cleaned and sprinkled the two huts in the shade and had prepared a meal for him.

Cool water was poured out for him in an earthenware jar. While standing at the door of the hut, he felt guilty and said to himself, "The Messenger of Allah is under the scorching sun, blown by hot winds, while Abu Khaythamah is enjoying cool shade with delicious food made ready for him, accompanied by his mates and resting in his orchard." Then he turned to his wives and said, "By Allah, I will not rest in the shade until I have overtaken the Messenger of Allah, so make ready my mount and provisions." His wives did what he asked, and he hurriedly saddled his camel and set off after the army.

Abu Dharr had also stayed behind but said that he would catch up with the army as soon as he got ready. After many days, he had not been able to catch up with the rest of the army. The Companions reminded the Holy Prophet (May God bless and cherish him), "O Messenger of Allah, Abu Dharr had not been able to join us." The Holy Prophet (May God bless and cherish him) responded, "Leave him to himself; if there is some good in him, Allah the Mighty and Majestic will make him catch up with us." And thus, made it clear that he was expecting him to come somehow. Abu Dharr had not been able to set out with the army, instead, he stayed behind to feed his camel that was very weak and not suitable for the long and arduous journey. Abu Dharr started his journey, nonetheless. When he reached the place called Dhi al-Marwa, his camel could no longer walk. He waited for a day, hoping his camel would get some strength and be able to move. However, when he lost hope, he put his load on his back and tried to catch up with the rest of the Companions. He had become weak and exhausted in the hot desert. His lips were dry and cracked with thirst, and he had no energy left in him because of hunger. But he was strongly determined and finally was able to catch up with the Holy Prophet (May God bless and cherish him). The Companions saw someone from afar coming in the middle of the day. "O Messenger of Allah, there is someone who has made his way here all alone," one of the Companions reported. The Holy Prophet (May God bless and cherish him) looked in the direction where they were pointing and said, "It must be Abu Dharr." And indeed, it was Abu Dharr. The Holy Prophet (May God bless and cherish him) then said to his Companions. "May Allah treat Abu Dharr with mercy; verily he will walk alone, die alone, and will be resurrected alone in the hereafter."

Having endured the difficulties of the road, Abu Dharr came to the presence of the Holy Prophet (May God bless and cherish him) and told him of all that had happened on the journey. The Holy Prophet (May God bless and cherish him) comforted him and said, "May Allah embrace you in His mercy, O Abu Dharr! Do not forget that each step that you took to reach me is a good deed, and each step that you have taken has erased one of your bad deeds."

While the Muslim army was marching northward, one day at dawn, the Holy Prophet (May God bless and cherish him) was late in making his ablution. The Companions were waiting in lines to pray, and they waited for him until they feared that the sun would rise soon before they had prayed. Then they decided that Abdul Rahman ibn Awf should lead them in prayer, and they had already performed one of the two prayer cycles when the Holy Prophet arrived. Abdul Rahman was about to draw back, but the Holy Prophet (May God bless and cherish him) pointed him to stay where he was. The Holy Prophet (May God bless and cherish him) joined the congregation led by Abdul Rahman ibn Awf. When they had offered the greeting of peace, the Holy Prophet (May God bless and cherish him) continued and prayed the cycle he had missed. After his prayer, he said, "You have done right, for verily a prophet does not die until he had been led in prayer by a pious man of his community." (Waqidi)

When the Muslim army was a day away from Tabuk, the Holy Prophet (May God bless and cherish him) told his Companions, "By the grace of Allah, tomorrow we will reach the spring of Tabuk. The sun will be very hot when you reach it. If any of you reach it before me, let him not drink from that water." But two of the first men to reach it drank from the spring, and when the rest of the army arrived, the water had become less than a trickle. The Holy Prophet (May God bless and cherish him) was upset because he had warned them not to touch the water. The spring had dried up, and only a little water was available. The Holy Prophet (May God bless and cherish him) told some of the Companions to scoop up whatever water they could in their hands and pour it into a water skin. He washed his hands, face, and mouth and poured the rest of the water over the rock that covered the mouth of the spring. He turned towards his Lord and prayed. As soon as, he finished his prayer, the water gushed forth with a sound of thunder and continued to flow until all the men had satisfied their needs. The Holy Prophet (May God bless and cherish him) turned to Muadh, who was beside him, and said, "It may be, O Muadh that you should live to see this place as a valley of many pastures." And it was as he had prophesized.

One of the Emigrants named, Abdullah ibn Dhu l-Bijadayn, died while he was with the Muslim army in Tabuk. He was a Companion who badly wanted to become a martyr. He had expressed his desire to the Holy Prophet (May God bless and cherish him) as well. The Holy Prophet (May God bless and cherish him) gave him the good news that he would be a martyr even if he should die in his bed, and now that tiding had been fulfilled in Tabuk. The Holy Prophet (May God bless and cherish him) was grieved by the news of his death and came to where his grave had been dug. He prayed for him, "Dear Lord! I was content with him as long as he lived, and You be content with him as well." When Abdullah became a Muslim, his entire property was confiscated by his family. His uncle was very tough on him and even took his clothes off his back. He found a piece of cloth with the help of his mother, cut it into two, and wore one piece on top and one below and, in such a state, emigrated to Medina. The Holy Prophet (May God bless and cherish him) had given him this name while seeing him wear this cloth of two parts. He used to read the Quran too loudly, and Hazrat Umar once rebuked him. But the Holy Prophet (May God bless and cherish him) told him to leave him alone and said that he had come on Hira there to Allah and His Messenger. (Waqidi, Maghazi; Ibn Athir, Usdu l-Ghaba; Ibn Hajar, Al-Isaba)

The Muslim army waited at Tabuk for almost twenty days but could not see an army or any evidence of any impending danger. The reports and news that had reached the Holy Prophet (May God bless and cherish him) were exaggerated and unfounded. On the other hand, it was not yet time for the conquest of Syria. Therefore, the Holy Prophet (May God bless and cherish him) sent Dihyah al-Kalbi as an envoy to Heraclius, who had done this before. In a letter he gave him, the Holy Prophet (May God bless and cherish him) gave him three options; embracing Islam, staying in their own lands by paying annual tribute, or to fight. As soon as he received the letter of the Messenger of God, he called a counsel of his high-ranking officials and reminded them that the new prophet would one day rule his lands. But his officials were averse to his ideas. Heraclius chose not to fight.

Next, the Holy Prophet (May God bless and cherish him) made a treaty of peace with Christian and Jewish communities, who lived at the head of the Gulf of Aqabah and along its eastern coast. In return for a yearly tribute, they were guaranteed protection by the Islamic State. The holy Prophet (May God bless and cherish him) sent Khalid ibn Walid with four hundred and twenty horsemen to Dumat al-Jandal, to the northeast of Tabuk. This important stronghold was on the road to Iraq from Medina, as well as one of the roads to Syria. The Holy Prophet (May God bless and cherish him) ordered Khalid to take the king of Bani Kinda, Ukaydar ibn Abd al-Malik prisoner, and return. Khalid ibn Walid told the Holy Prophet (May God bless and cherish him) that the number of fighters he had would not be enough for this mission. At this, the Holy Prophet (May God bless and cherish him) replied, "You will find him hunting wild bulls outside his fortress and surprise him, but do not kill him. Bring him to me." Indeed, it was so, the day Khalid arrived, Ukaydar was hunting wild bulls. He was accompanied by his brother Hassan and some other men. Khalid took all of them captives and brought them to Medina. The Holy Prophet (May God bless and cherish him) invited them to Islam. They made an alliance with the Messenger of Allah and agreed to pay the yearly tribute.

In the meantime, the leader of Ayla, Yuhanna ibn Ruba, came to the presence of the Holy Prophet (May God bless and cherish him) with gifts and made an agreement to pay the tribute. Among the gifts that were brought was a beautiful white horse. The Holy Prophet (May God bless and cherish him) gave him a cloak as a present. (Bukhari, Sahih; Abu Dawood, Sunan)

Similarly, the Jewish tribes of Jarba and Azrush had also come and made a peace treaty with the Messenger of God. According to this treaty, they would pay a tribute of a hundred dinars to be collected in the month of Rajab and hence entered the protection of Islam. The people of Makna made a deal with the Holy Prophet (May God bless and cherish him) to give one-fourth of their fruit produce and one-fourth of the cloth they wove as a tribute in return for the protection of their lives and property. Even though there had been no direct contact with the Byzantines in Tabuk, this expedition had thus achieved far-reaching results. The Holy Prophet (May God bless and cherish him), after consultation with his Companions, decided to return to Medina.

CHAPTER 25
BACK IN MEDINA

When the Holy Prophet was about to enter Medina, he turned towards his Companions and said, "There are some people in Medina that are always with you at every step, in every valley you go." It meant that not all who stayed in Medina were hypocrites, for among them were Ka'b ibn Malik, Murara ibn Rabi, and Hilal ibn Umayya. They were sincere believers and yet had not been able to come due to personal reasons. And so, there was a difference between those who did not come to Tabuk by making excuses and those who had legitimate excuses. While passing by the mountain of Uhud, the Holy Prophet (May God bless and cherish him) looked towards it and said, "Uhud is such a mountain that we love it, and it loves us." Then he turned towards Ansar (Helpers) and said to them, "Do you want me to tell you the most auspicious of the Ansar houses?" "Yes, O Messenger of Allah,' they replied. The Holy Prophet started to count, "Among the houses of Ansar, the most auspicious are the Bani Najjar and then the sons of Abdullah ibn Aswad, and then the houses of Bani Saida."

The return from Tabuk was also fraught with grief. Another daughter of the Holy Prophet (May God bless and cherish him), Hazrat Umm Kulthum, had passed away during his absence, and this time, Hazrat Uthman had also been absent. The Holy Prophet (May God bless and cherish him) prayed at her grave, and he said to Hazrat Uthman that if he had another unwedded daughter, he would have given her to him in marriage.

All the hypocrites who remained behind and did not take part in the Tabuk expedition went to the Holy Prophet (May God bless and cherish him) and made their excuses, which he accepted. But he reminded them that God knew their most secret thoughts. He also told the three believers who stayed behind in Medina to depart from him and gave instructions that no one should talk to them until God decided their case. The three men lived as outcasts for almost fifty days. On the fiftieth day, the Holy Prophet (May God bless and cherish him) announced in the Mosque that God had generously forgiven them.

"And (He also forgave) the three who were left behind (And regretted their error) to the point that the earth closed in on them despite its vastness. And their souls confined them, and they were certain that there was no refuge from Allah except Him. Then, He turned to them so they could repent. Indeed, Allah is the accepting of repentance, the Merciful." (Al-Taubah 9:118)

The entire congregation was happy, and some of them ran to inform them about the good news. Ka'b ibn Malik was the youngest of the three, and he had left town out of shame and had pitched a tent in the desert outside of Medina. Later, he said that he had heard a horse galloping towards his tent and a voice that shouted, "Glad tidings, Ka'b," so, immediately prostrated to Allah, for there could be no good news except one. Then he went to Medina and entered the Mosque. "When I greeted the Holy Prophet," he said, "His face showed with gladness as he said to me, "Rejoice, the best day that had come upon you since your mother born you." Ka'b asked, "Is this from you, O Messenger of Allah, or is it from Allah?" "Nay, it is from Allah," he said. "When the Holy Prophet (May God bless and cherish him) was happy on account of good tidings, his face would light up like the brightness of a moon." (Ibn Ishaq)

THE YEAR OF DELEGATION (SANAT AL-WUFUD)

Delegations had been coming to Medina after the conquest of Makkah and more so after the Holy Prophet (May God bless and cherish him) returned from Tabuk. It seemed like a new delegation arrived every day. After seeing the success of the Messenger of Allah in Makkah, Hunayn, and Tabuk, Arab tribes were coming to submit. There were those who came on their own and became Muslims and those who came to Medina in delegations and were introduced to the message of Islam. It is narrated that three hundred and fifty delegations came to Medina in one year with the purpose of entering Islam. The flow of delegations had started after the Hijra, with Muzaynas, in the eighth year.

(This process had gained momentum, and in the ninth year, it reached its zenith.

This process continued until the death of the Holy Prophet (May God bless and cherish him), and a total of three hundred and forty-three delegations had come to Medina. Ibn Ishaq reported that the number of these delegations was fifteen, and historians such as Ibn Sa'd narrated to be sixty. Scholars such as Ibn Qayyim and Qastalani have written this number to be three hundred and thirty-two. The reason behind this difference is probably that they did not consider groups under a certain number to be a delegation or that they counted only the visits that happened in the ninth year.)

THE DELEGATION OF THAQIF

After Malik, the young leader of Hawazin, converted to Islam, he was confirmed by the Holy Prophet (May God bless and cherish him) as the chief of his tribe and was given the task of relentlessly engaging the people of Thaqif. The city of Taif was impenetrable but surrounded by the Muslim community on all sides. They could not do any business outside, and any caravan they sent was also in danger of attack and being despoiled. They could not even take their camels and sheep to pasture without the risk of being captured by Malik's men. Malik also had warned them that he would kill any man of Thaqif who fell into their hands unless they abandoned idol worshiping. After a while, they felt extreme pressure and had no choice left but to submit. They sent a delegation to the Holy Prophet and said that they would enter Islam and requested a document that would guarantee the safety of their people, property, and land. The people of Thaqif went to Abdi Yalyal ibn Amr to act as an envoy on their behalf, but he said that he alone would not be able to do so. Therefore, they sent two men with him to Medina.

It was Ramadan, and they were received well, and a tent was set up for them close to the Mosque so that they could hear the word of Allah and take heed and observe how Muslims prayed to their Lord. It was agreed that if they entered Islam, their territory and property would be under the protection of the Islamic state. However, they had some reservations. They wanted to be exempt from the daily prayer. The Holy Prophet (May God bless and cherish him) insisted that they should pray and said, "There is no good in a religion that has no communal prayer." They also wanted exemption from some prohibited acts in Islam. Abdi Yalyal asked the Holy Prophet (May God bless and cherish him) about adultery. He replied, "That is a sin, and Allah has forbidden it for believers and recited,

"Do not draw near to any unlawful sexual intercourse; surely it is a shameful, indecent thing, and an evil way." (Al-Isra 17:32). Then Abdi Yalyal asked about the interest. The Holy Prophet (May God bless and cherish him) said, "Interest is also forbidden," and read the revelation, "O you who believe! Fear Allah and give up what remains (due to you) of interest, if you are (in truth) believers." (Quran 2:278)

The delegation of Thaqif did not stop there and asked, "What do you say about alcohol? We squeeze our grapes and drink the juice; we can't help not to drink." The Holy Prophet (May God bless and cherish him) responded,

"Allah has verily prohibited it and recited, "O you who believe! Intoxicants, gambling, sacrifice on stone alters (to other than Allah), and divining arrows are but defilement from the work of Satan, so avoid it that you may be successful." (Al-Maedah 5:90)

The Holy Prophet (May God bless and cherish him) did not agree to their requests. They asked him to let them keep their idol al-Lat undestroyed for three years, and when the Holy Prophet (May God bless and cherish him) refused, they asked for two years and then one, until finally, they asked for only one month's respite, which the Holy Prophet (May God bless and cherish him) did not agree with. Then, they begged him not to let them destroy their idols with their own hands. However, he agreed to excuse them from destroying their idols with their own hands. Later, he sent Mughira ibn Shuba and sent Abu Sufyan with the mission to destroy the idols. It was Mughira who single-handedly destroyed al-Lat and no none sought to stop him.

When the Holy Prophet (May God bless and cherish him) conquered the city of Makkah, Abu Amir, the father of Hanzalah, and Wahshi, the killer of Hazrat Hamzah, had both taken refuge in Taif, which seemed to them as a very secure place. When the people of Thaqif submitted to Islam, Abu Amir fled to Syria, and it was there that he died lonely and homeless, fulfilling the curse he had unconsciously laid upon himself. But Wahshi had no place to hide. Someone told him that the Messenger of Allah would put no man to death who accepted Islam. So, he came to Medina and entered Islam. One of the believers recognized him and told the Holy Prophet (May God bless and cherish him), "O Messenger of Allah, this is Wahshi." The Holy Prophet (May God bless and cherish him) said, "Let him be, for one man's Islam is dearer to me than killing of a thousand disbelievers." Then he looked at the face of Wahshi and asked, "Are you indeed Wahshi? And then he said, "Tell me how you killed Hamzah?" when Wahshi finished his account, the Holy Prophet (May God bless and cherish him) said, "Alas, take thy face from me, let me not look upon you again."

THE DELEGATION OF NAJARIAN

Thaqif was not the only tribe to send a delegation to the Holy Prophet (May God bless and cherish him). Many other envoys came to Medina from all over Arabia. However, the delegation of Christians of Najaran attracted attention among all the other ones. They were affiliated with the Byzantine in the past. There were sixty people, and fifteen of them were noblemen. The Holy Prophet (May God bless and cherish him) had written to them in a letter, "I ask you to stop worshiping subjects and invite you to come and worship Allah. Stop relying on the help of people and entrust all your affairs to Allah. If you do not agree with this, you can choose to pay an annual tribute. And if you do not accept this either, know that it would mean a war." After receiving this letter, the people of Najaran sent their delegation. They were received by the Holy Prophet (May God bless and cherish him) in the Mosque. When the time of prayer came, they were allowed to pray there, which they did facing east. After they had prayed, the Holy Prophet (May God bless and cherish him) invited them to Islam, but they said, "We are Muslims even before you," and declined his invitation. The Holy Prophet (May God bless and cherish him) said to them, "There are three things that do not make you Muslims, that is you pray to the Cross, that you eat pork, and that you attribute a son to Allah." There was much disagreement between them and the Holy Prophet (May God bless and cherish him) concerning the person of Jesus. They objected, "How can you say this about Jesus that he is not the son of God? Can you show us a person without a father if you say the truth?" Then came the revelation.

"Verily, the likeness of Jesus with God is as the likeness of Adam. He created him from dust, then God said to him 'Be,' and he was. This is the truth from the Lord, so be not of the doubters. Then whosoever argues with you about it after (this) knowledge has come to you say, 'Come let us call our sons and your sons, our women, and your women, ourselves and yourselves, then supplicate earnestly (together) and invoke the curse of Allah upon the liars (among us)." (Al-Imran 3: 59-61)

The Holy Prophet (May God bless and cherish him) recited these verses to them and invited them to Islam, but they strongly disputed the revelation. Then the Holy

Prophet (May God bless and cherish him) invited them to meet him and his family and to settle their disagreement in the way suggested by the divine revelation. They replied they would think about it. So, the next day, the Holy Prophet (May God bless and cherish him) gathered the People of his House. Hazrat Ali was with him, and behind them were Hazrat Fatima, Hazrat Hassan, and Hazrat Hussayn. The Messenger of Allah was dressed in a large cloak, and he spread it wide enough to envelop them all in it, including himself. This is why the five of them are reverently called "The People of the cloak." He told them, "When I pray, say Amin."

When the delegation arrived, they were scared, and one of them said, "Do not proceed to imprecation, for if he is truly a prophet, when you start cursing, neither we nor those who come after us will be saved." They surrendered and agreed to pay the yearly tribute in return for full protection of the Islamic state for themselves and their churches.

Delegations kept pouring into Medina. Delegations from Abdi Qays, Uzra, and Baliyy had come and returned after accepting Islam. There were twelve people in the delegation of Uzra, and they informed the Holy Prophet (May God bless and cherish him) that they were related to him through his grandfather Qusayy from their mother's side. The Holy Prophet (May God bless and cherish him) gave them the tidings that Damascus would soon be under the banner of Islam. He forbade them to take money for soothsaying and to eat the flesh of the sacrifice made to exalt people.

The delegates from the tribe of Fazara came to Medina and complained to the Holy Prophet (May God bless and cherish him) about the drought and famine they were facing. They asked him to pray for them, and the Holy Prophet (May God bless and cherish him) prayed for rain and invoked the mercy of Allah. Another delegation that drew attention was the delegation of Bani Hanifa, and it included Musaylimah ibn Habib (Al-Kadhaab) who would later claim to be a prophet. They had come from Yamama and entered Islam. The tribes kept coming from Yemen, Azd, the Bani Sa'd, Bani Amir ibn Qays, the Bani Asad, Bahra, Halwar, Muharib, Bani Harith ibn Ka'b, Bani Mustaliq, Bani Abbas, Muzayna, Murad, Zubayd, Kinda, Dhi Murra, Ghassan, and Bani Iysh.

Among others were four Himyarite princes who accepted Islam and renounced polytheism and its adherents. They wrote letters to the Holy Prophet (May God bless and cherish him), and he replied to them. The Holy Prophet emphasized the obligation of Islam, bidding them to treat well his envoys, who he would send to collect the yearly taxes and tribute incumbent upon Muslims, Christians, and Jews. He also made clear that "A Jew or Christian who adheres to his religion shall not be turned away from it but shall pay Jizya (tax) and shall have the protection of Allah and His Messenger." Allah, in a recent revelation, said, "For each of you we have prescribed a law and a path, and if God had willed, He would have made you one people, but He intended to test you in what He has given you. So, vie with one another in good works. Unto God, you will be brought back, and He will then inform you of those things wherein you differed." (Al-Maeda 5:48)

Ibn Ubayy ibn Salul, who was one of the leading hypocrites, fell seriously ill after one month of the Tabuk expedition. It was obvious that he would not survive this illness. His son Abdullah was a sincere believer, and he knew about his father being a hypocrite. However, after his father died, he came to the presence of the Holy Prophet (May God bless and cherish him) and requested him to lead his father's funeral prayer. The Holy Prophet (May God bless and cherish him) responded favorably to his petition. In what state of soul Ibn Ubayy died is not known, but the Holy Prophet (May God bless and cherish him) led the funeral prayer for him and prayed beside his grave. As soon as Hazrat Umar knew about it, he rushed to the Holy Prophet (May God bless and cherish him) and objected against the bestowal of such grace upon a hypocrite. The Holy Prophet (May God bless and cherish him) smiled and answered,

"O Umar, stand alongside me. God has given me the choice, and I have chosen." It was revealed to the Holy Prophet (May God bless and cherish him), "Ask forgiveness for them (O Muhammad) or do not ask forgiveness for them. If you should ask forgiveness for them seventy times, never will Allah forgive them. That is because they disbelieved in Allah and His Messenger, and Allah does not guide the defiantly disobedient people." (Al-Taubah 9:80). The Holy Prophet (May God bless and cherish him) then continued, "And did I know that Allah would forgive him if I prayed more than seventy times, I would increase the number of my supplications." (Ibn Ishaq)

The Holy Prophet (May God bless and cherish him) finished the funeral prayer. But before he finished, Gabriel revealed the following verse concerning the hypocrites.

"And never pray the funeral prayer over one of them who had died, nor stand beside his grave, for verily they disbelieved in Allah and His Messenger, and died when they were defiantly disobedient." (Al-Taubah 9:84)

It is also narrated in one of the traditions that the Holy Prophet (May God bless and cherish him) had visited Ibn Ubayy during his illness and realized that the impending death had changed him. He requested the Holy Prophet (May God bless and cherish him) to give him a garment of his own in which he could be shrouded and to accompany his body to the grave, and the Holy Prophet (May God bless and cherish him) graciously agreed to do so. Then again, Ibn Ubayy begged the Holy Prophet (May God bless and cherish him), "O Messenger of Allah! I hope that you will pray beside my bier and ask forgiveness of God for my sins." His son Abdullah was present as well, and the Holy Prophet (May God bless and cherish him) assented to his request.

Amir ibn Tufayl, who was now the chief of Bani Amir, came with a delegation to Medina. He was the one responsible for the massacre at Bir Maunah, and he came with his own agenda. He proposed that in return for his Islam, the Holy Prophet (May God bless and cherish him) should name him his successor. The Holy Prophet (May God bless and cherish him) denied his request and said, "It is not for thee nor for your people." He then asked, "Give me the tent-dwellers and keep thou the villagers." Again, the Holy Prophet (May God bless and cherish him) said, "Not so," "But I will make you the commander of the cavalry because you are an excellent horseman." Amir ibn Tufayl was arrogant and said annoyingly, "I will fill the land with horsemen and footmen against you." When he departed, the Holy Prophet (May God bless and cherish him) supplicated, "O Lord, guide the Bani Amir, and rid Islam of Amir, the son of Tufayl." Amir was afflicted by a sore that got infected, and he died even before he reached home. His tribe was keen on entering an alliance with the Holy Prophet (May God bless and cherish him) and sent another delegation to Medina. The famous Arabian poet Labid was one of the envoys, and he accepted Islam. He stopped composing poetry and remarked that after Quran, the word of God there is no room for his poetry. However, he continued praising Allah and His Messenger through poetry.

In the month of Dhu al-Qadah of the ninth year of Hijra, the following verses were revealed to the Holy Prophet (May God bless and cherish him), "It is Allah's due that all who have the means to visit it should visit the House of Allah." Thus, pilgrimage or Hajj was made an obligation. After receiving the divine command and with the approach of the pilgrimage season, the Holy Prophet (May God bless and cherish him) appointed Hazrat Abu Bakr as the leader of the caravan to perform the Hajj. There were three hundred Companions in that caravan, and it set off from Medina. When they were on the road, revelations kept coming, and it was important that all pilgrims in Makkah (both Muslims and polytheists) should hear those divine rules. The Holy Prophet (May God bless and cherish him) made it clear that it should be a man from his own family who will transmit these commands. So, he told Hazrat Ali to get ready as soon as possible and set out with all speed before the pilgrims reached Kaaba. Hazrat Ali was given the task to recite the verses in the valley of Mina and to make it clear that after that year, no one would be allowed to go around the Kaaba naked, and most importantly the idolators would not be allowed to make pilgrimage after that.

Hazrat Ali took the instructions and caught up with the pilgrims at a place called Arj. Hazrat Abu Bakr was concerned to see him and asked if he had come to command the caravan, but Hazrat Ali replied that he was under his command and had come for a task. So, they proceeded together, and Hazrat Abu Bakr led the prayers and preached the sermons.

The pilgrims performed the rites of Hajj, went around the Kaaba, and walked between Safa and Marwa. On the day of the feast, all pilgrims were assembled in Mina to offer their sacrificial animals. Hazrat Ali stood next to Jamra and announced the divine message. In this message, the idolators were given four months' time to come and go in safety, but after that Allah and His Messenger would have no obligation towards them. These idolators who had made a special treaty with the Holy Prophet (May God bless and cherish him) were exempt from this until its term ran out. This recent revelation also addressed the concerns of the newly converted Makkans, who feared that the exclusion of the idolators would deprive them of trade opportunities. It said, "O you who believe, indeed the idolators are unclean, so let them not approach the Holy Sanctuary after this year. And if you fear poverty, Allah will enrich you with His bounty. Verily, God is All-Knowing, Infinitely Wise." (Quran 9:28)

THE LAST PILGRIMAGE

During the month of Ramadan, the Holy Prophet (May God bless and cherish him) used to sit in the Mosque for a special retreat (*itekaf*) during the middle ten days of the month, and some of his close Companions would accompany him. But this year, after having finished the ten appointed days, he decided to remain in retreat for another ten days, that is, till the end of the month. His Companions followed suit. Gabriel would visit him frequently in the month of Ramadan. And he would recite the entire Quran from the beginning to the end for the Holy Prophet (May God bless and cherish him). The Holy Prophet (May God bless and cherish him) would also recite the Quran in its entirety back to Gabriel to make sure that nothing of the revelation has been forgotten. In this way, the exact place of which verse would be in which section of what Sura was determined. Similarly, the sequence of the Quranic chapters was set for certain. After the retreat, the Holy Prophet (May God bless and cherish him) told his daughter Hazrat Fatima as a secret not to be told to others, "Gabriel recited the Quran unto me and I unto him once every year, but this year he has recited it twice with me. I cannot but think that my time has come." (Bukhari, Sahih)

The Holy Prophet (May God bless and cherish him) had accomplished his mission, proclaimed the divine message, and established a society based on, "There is no god but God" (*La ilaha illallah*). The House of Allah had been cleaned of idols and from polytheism, and its original dignity and sanctity had been restored. The Holy Prophet knew that his stay in this world was about to end. It was obvious from his conversation with Muadh, whom he had dispatched to Yemen in the tenth year of Hijra. He told him, "O Muadh! You may not see me after this year. You may even pass by my Mosque and my grave." When Muadh heard these words, he wept bitterly, knowing that he would part with the Messenger of Allah.

It was in Dhu al-Qadah when there were only five days left till the end of the month when the Holy Prophet (May God bless and cherish him) declared to his Companions about his intention to perform the pilgrimage. It was announced throughout Medina that the Holy Prophet (May God bless and cherish him) would lead the pilgrimage himself. This news was sent to all Arab tribes. Large numbers of people flocked to the city of Medina from all over the desert to accompany the Messenger of Allah on every step of the way. This pilgrimage would be totally different than any other in the past hundreds of years because this time, all the pilgrims would be worshippers of One God, and no idolator would be present to perform any heathen rites.

On a Saturday, at the end of the Dhu al-Qadah, right after the noon prayer, the Holy Prophet (May God bless and cherish him) embarked on his journey. He combed his hair, applied some perfume, put on his clothes, saddled his camel, and set off on the road. He passed through Shajara and arrived at Dhul-Hulaifah before the afternoon prayer. He performed two Rakkah (cycles) and spent the night there. In the morning, he addressed his Companions and said, "Someone, sent by my Lord, has called on me tonight and said, pray in this blessed valley and say, I intend Umrah combined with Hajj." (Bukhari, Sahih)

He, therefore, told his Companions that his intention for the journey was both Hajj and Umrah. He took a bath and put on his ihram. Hazrat Aisha perfumed him with her hands on both body and head with musk. He had brought with him around one hundred animals as sacrifice and had marked them all to make them known that they were sacrificial animals. The Holy Prophet chanted, "*Labbayk Allahuma Labbayk*" (I am at Your service, O Lord, I am at Your service). Then he came out and mounted his camel Qaswa. And said "*Labbayk*," and when he moved into the open field, he said "*Labbayk*" again. All the Companions joined in his talbiya and said, "*Labbayk Allahuma Labbayk*, here are we O Lord, *Labbayk la sharika laka Labbayk*, here we are O Lord, and You have no partner, *Innal hamda wa'n ni mata laka wal Mulk*," praise and richness and dominion are all Yours, *La sharika lak*," "You have no partner." These chants were echoing in the atmosphere.

The huge caravan of pilgrims under the leadership of the Holy Prophet (May God bless and cherish him) went through Bayda, Malal, Rawha, Arj, Abwa, Juhfa, Kudayl, and Ghamim, and reached Dhi Tuwa. The Holy Prophet (May God bless and cherish him) spent the night there. After morning prayer, he took a bath and then walked to Makkah. The entire journey took a week. He entered Makkah when the sun was at its zenith, and his entry was from the upper region of the city. It was Sunday morning, the fourth day of Dhul-Hujjah in the tenth year of Hijra. As soon as he entered the Holy Sanctuary, he circumambulated the Kaaba. In the first three rounds, his steps were quick. In the remaining four, he was slower and thus completed his seven rounds. Then he turned to the place of Ibrahim (Rukn Istilam) and read the following verse,

"We made the House (Kaaba in Makkah) a place of return for people and a place of security. And stand in prayer (O believers, as you did in earlier times) in the station of Ibrahim. And we charged Ibrahim and Ismael, saying, "Purify My House for those who go around it as a rite of worship, and those who abide in devotion, and those who bow and prostrate." (Quran 2:125)

The Holy Prophet (May God bless and cherish him) performed two cycles of prayer and recited Sura Al-Kafirun and Al-Ikhlas. Then he came back to Rukn and walked towards Safa, when he came close to it, he recited.

"Indeed, al-Safa and al-Marwa are among the emblems of God. So, whoever makes Hajj to the House or performs Umrah, there is no blame on him for walking between them. And whoever does a good work voluntarily, surely, God is All-Responsive to thankfulness, All-Knowing." (Al-Baqarah 2:158)

After that, the Holy Prophet (May God bless and cherish him) went to Safa and Marwa and started walking between them. When he went to the top of Safa, he turned towards Kaaba and said the takbir, then raised his hands and prayed. He then turned towards Hajun; this was the place where he had spent the three most difficult years of his life with his Companions. His beloved uncle Hazrat Abu Talib, who was his great supporter, had died there. His beloved wife and life partner of twenty-five years, the mother of faithful, Hazrat Khadijah, had passed to the mercy of Allah and is buried here.

ARAFAT

The Holy Prophet (May God bless and cherish him) returned to the Mosque; he then entered the Kaaba with the keeper of the keys 'Uthman add al-Dar, along with Usamah and Bilal as before. That evening, when he visited Hazrat Aishah in her tent, she noticed that the Holy Prophet (May God bless and cherish him) was sad and asked him why. "I have done a thing today," he said, "that I wish I had not done. I entered the Kaaba, and it may be that people (in years to come) would not be able to enter it and, it would make them sad. They would say we were only ordered to go around it and not ordered to enter it."

The Holy Prophet (May God bless and cherish him) stayed in Makkah for four days. On Thursday, he went to Mina with his Companions at noon. A tent was set up for him in the place called Namira and there he prayed his five daily prayers. Having spent the night, he rode to Arafat after daybreak. It is a valley about thirteen miles away from Makkah, just outside the Sacred Precinct. Arafat is on the way to Taif and is bordered on the north and east by the mountains of Taif. A hill that is also named Arafat on the Mount of Mercy is situated there. The Holy Prophet (May God bless and cherish him) set up his station there that day. Some of the Makkans were surprised that he had gone so far. But he said that Prophet Ibrahim had ordained the day on Arafat as an essential part of the pilgrimage. He was surrounded by his Companions, almost one hundred and twenty in number. The Holy Prophet (May

God bless and cherish him) delivered a very important sermon, and all were listening to him with great attention.

"O people!" he said with conviction, "Listen well to my words. For I do not think I will be able to meet you here after this year." No one among the Companions even thought that one day, the Messenger of Allah would leave this world. But it was he himself who reminded people of this fact. There was an atmosphere of sadness, and the Companion's hearts were full of pain. The Holy Prophet (May God bless and cherish him) continued, "Your blood, your property, and your honor are as sacred as this day, this month, and this land (city). Take heed! I have abolished all practices of paganism and ignorance (Jahiliya) before Islam. The first claim on blood I abolish is that of Ibn Rabia bin Harith ibn Abdul Muttalib, who was being nursed in the tribe of Bani Sa'd and who was killed by the tribe of Hudayl. It was the first blood feud from the time of Jahiliya that I annul it. Usuary is forbidden, and I make a beginning by remitting the amount of interest which Abbas ibn Abdul Muttalib is supposed to receive; it is forgiven. Take heed concerning women and fear Allah, for you have taken them as trusts from Allah and made them your lawful companions with the words of Allah. It is incumbent on you and upon them to honor their conjugal rights and not to commit acts of impropriety, which, if they do, you have authority to chastise them without going too far. If your wives remain from impropriety and are faithful, it is your duty to provide for their sustenance and provide them with suitable clothes. Verily, I have left among you the Book of Allah; if you hold fast to it, you shall never go astray." (Muslim; Sahih)

"O people, I am not succeeded by a prophet, and you are not succeeded by any nation. So, I urge you to worship your Lord, to pray five times, to fast Ramadan, and to offer charity of your provisions willingly. I recommend you perform the pilgrimage of the Holy House of your Lord and obey those who oversee you; then you will be awarded to enter paradise of your Lord."

He then imparted to them a revelation that he had just received, and that completed the Quran,

"This day, those who disbelieve have despaired of (defeating) your religion, so fear them not, but fear Me! This day, I have perfected for you your religion and completed My favor upon you, and it hath been My good pleasure to choose Islam for you as your religion." (Al-Maedah 5:3)

Safwan's brother Rabiah ibn Umayya, who had a powerful voice, was told by the Holy Prophet (May God bless and cherish him) to repeat his words and convey them to others. The Holy Prophet (May God bless and cherish him) then asked, "And you will be asked about me. What are you going to say?" the people replied with one voice that filled the entire valley, "We bear witness that you have conveyed your message and fulfilled your mission." The Holy Prophet (May God bless and cherish him) raised his forefinger towards the sky and said, "O Lord, bear witness." He said that three times. (Ibn Ishaq)

Hazrat Bilal recited the call for prayer after the sermon and made the second call as well. The Holy Prophet (May God bless and cherish him) performed the noon prayer, then Bilal again proclaimed *iqamah* (second call) and the Holy Prophet (May God bless and cherish him) performed the afternoon prayer, and there was no prayer in between the two. He spent the day in supplication. But when the sun had set, he mounted his camel Qaswa, and having Usama mount behind him, he rode down the hill towards Makkah, followed by all the pilgrims. It was the tradition to ride quickly at this point, but as they gathered speed, he said, "Gently, gently! Let the strong among you have a care for the weak." They spent the night at Muzdalifah, which is within the sacred precinct.

Then, he performed the *Maghrib* and *Isha* prayers with one Adhan and two *iqamahs*. He did not offer any prayer in between the two prayers. Then he rested till it was time for *Fajr* (morning) prayer. After the prayer, he mounted Qaswa and rode towards *Al-Mash ar al-Haram*. He shouted, 'Allah o Akbar' and '*La ilaha illallah.*' He collected pebbles to stone Satan, who is represented by three pillars at Aqabah in the valley of Mina. Hazrat Sawdah had asked the Holy Prophet to allow her to leave Muzdalifah in the early hours so that she could perform the rite of stoning before throngs of people arrived. So, he sent her ahead in the company of Umm Sulaym, escorted by Abdullah, one of the sons of Hazrat Abbas.

Before the sun was high, the Holy Prophet (May God bless and cherish him) made his way to Mina. This time, he mounted Fadl ibn Abbas behind him. He stopped at the Jamrah and pelted seven stones at the Satan and proclaimed, "Allah is most great" each time. Then he set off to the sacrificial place, and the animals were sacrificed. The Holy Prophet (May God bless and cherish him) called someone to shave his head. All the Companions gathered around him in the hope of getting some locks of his hair. In the meantime, Khalid ibn Walid approached him and said, "O Messenger of Allah, my father and my mother be thy ransom! Thy forelock, give it unto none but me." The Holy Prophet (May God bless and cherish him) gave it to him, and he reverently pressed it against his eyes and lips.

The Holy Prophet (May God bless and cherish him) then told the pilgrims to visit Kaaba and make their rounds but he returned to spend the next two night in Mina. He waited until late afternoon, and he took his wives with him to the House of God.

GHADIR AL-KHUMM

In the month of Ramadan, before embarking on the pilgrimage journey, the Holy Prophet (May God bless and cherish him) commanded Hazrat Ali to head a campaign in Yemen with a troop of three hundred horses. And now they were returning to Makkah from the south. Hazrat Ali rode ahead of his men, eager to meet the Holy Prophet (May God bless and cherish him) as soon as possible and join him in the pilgrimage rites. After performing his pilgrimage, he had allocated one-fifth of the spoils as the Messenger of Allah's share. There was enough linen in the spoils to clothe the entire army, but Hazrat Ali decided that the spoils be handed over to the Holy Prophet (May God bless and cherish him) untouched. However, in his absence, the caretaker of the spoils was persuaded by the fighters to lend each man a new change of clothes out of the linen. They had been away from home for almost three months, and a change of clothes was very needed. When the fighters were close to Makkah, Hazrat Ali rode out to meet them but was surprised to see the entire army in new clothes. His commander explained, "I gave them the garments that their appearance might be more pleasing as they mingle among people." All of them anticipated that everyone in Makkah would be dressed in their finest clothes on pilgrimage. Naturally, they also wanted to look their best as well. But Hazrat Ali disagreed and felt that such a liberty was not appropriate. He ordered them to put on their old clothes and return the new ones to the spoils. This caused great resentment throughout the army, and the news reached the Holy Prophet (May God bless and cherish him). He said, "O people, do not blame Ali, for he is too diligent in the path of Allah to be blamed." But perhaps everyone did not hear these words, and the discontent continued.

It was the eighteenth of Dhu al-Hijjah, and the Holy Prophet (May God bless and cherish him) started his return journey to Medina. Some of the troops that were under the command of Hazrat Ali during the campaign of Yemen continually showed resentment against Hazrat Ali. The Holy Prophet (May God bless and cherish him) was deeply hurt, and his face changed color. On his way back, when the pilgrims had halted at Ghadir al-Khumm, the Holy Prophet (May God bless and cherish him) gave orders to bring all the people together, and he delivered a sermon,

"O people! There is no doubt that I, too, am a human being, and I believe before long the messenger of my Lord will come, and I will respond to his call. I leave you with two important things; the first is Allah's Book. There is guidance and light in it, and you must hold firm to it. The second is the people of my house."

Then he took his son-in-law Hazrat Ali by the hand and raised it and proclaimed,

"Whoever acknowledges (takes) me as his master (Wali), Ali is his master." And he repeated it three times. Then he raised his hand and prayed,

"Dear Lord! Put your trust in him who puts his trust in him (Ali). And whoever turns his face away from him and declares him as enemy, turn your face away from him and declare him an enemy." (Ibn Kathir, Al-Bidayah wan n-Nihayah)

FALSE PROPHETS

After his return from the last pilgrimage, the Holy Prophet (May God bless and cherish him) continued to receive delegations in Medina and sent envoys inviting people to the path of Allah and Islam. During the lifetime of the Holy Prophet (May God bless and cherish him), several imposters arose who claimed to be prophets and started gathering followers around them. One of them was from Yemen, a man called Aswad ibn Ka'b. He had successfully attained followers by showing certain illusions and had gained control over a wide area of the desert. The Holy Prophet (May God bless and cherish him) sent Jarir with a letter addressed to him, but he was an arrogant person. He claimed that two angels, Sahik and Sharik, came to him and brought him revelation, and they informed him news about what would happen to the people. However, his pride turned away from him many of his followers, and after some time he was murdered.

Another person who claimed to be a prophet was Tulayhah, a chief of Bani Asad. He was defeated by Khalid ibn Walid and was taken as a prisoner. Thereupon, he renounced all his claims and became a devoted Muslim, and he became a strength for Islam.

Bani Hanifah in Yamamah were Christians by faith. They had sent a delegation to Medina last year. Their lands lay along the eastern side of Najd. A man called Musaylimah was among the delegates, and seemingly, he accepted Islam and returned to his tribe. Later, he claimed to be a prophet too and was able to gain a considerable following for himself. After the pilgrims returned from Hajj, he sent two envoys to Medina with a letter that said, "From Musaylimah, the messenger of God to Muhammad, the Messenger of God. Peace be on thee! It has been given to me to share with thee the authority. Half the earth is ours, and half belongs to the Quraysh, although they are people who transgress." When the content of the letter was known to the Messenger of Allah, he asked the envoys what they thought of this matter. They replied, "Our opinion is as of his." The Holy Prophet (May God bless and cherish him) was furious and said, "By God, if it were not that envoys may not be slain, I would cut off your heads." Then, he called Hazrat Ali to his side and dictated a letter for them to take to their master. The Holy Prophet (May God bless and cherish him) said in the letter, "From Muhammad, the Messenger of Allah, to Musaylimah the liar. Peace be upon him who follows the guidance! Verily the earth belongs to Allah, He bestows it to whom He will of His slaves to inherit it, and the end is superior for the pious." (Ibn Ishaq). In the later days, Musaylimah was killed by a javelin from the hand of Wahshi, while Abdullah, the son of Nusaybah, struck him a mortal blow with his sword.

All these imposters posed a potentially serious threat to Islam in the eleventh year of Hijrah. Among them was a woman by the name of Sajah from Tamim, who claimed to be a prophetess. But nobody took her seriously and she did not amount to anything.

THE LAST CAMPAIGN

The last campaign was against the Byzantine state near Syria. The Muslims living in that area were subject to great pressure and torture. The Romans were so emboldened that they even killed the envoy of the Holy Prophet (May God bless and cherish him), Farwa ibn Amr al-Judhani, who was the representative of the state of Medina at Ma'an.

Four days were left until the end of the month of Safar. It was a Monday in the eleventh year of al-Hijrah, and the Holy Prophet (May God bless and cherish him) mobilized a great army and appointed a young commander, Usama bin Zayd bin Harith, to attack the lands bordering Al-Balqa and Ad Davus. The goal of the expedition was to show the power of Islam to the Byzantines and to reassure the Arab tribes who were settled at the border of Byzantine that their security was the duty of the Islamic state. The Holy Prophet (May God bless and cherish him) gave

Usama the standard of the army with his own hands. Usama took the standard and gave it to the standard bearer, Burayda ibn Husayb, and went to Juruf where the army was waiting for his orders.

CHAPTER 26
THE ILLNESS OF THE HOLY PROPHET (MAY GOD BLESS AND CHERISH HIM)

It was Wednesday, and the Holy Prophet (May God bless and cherish him) was not feeling well after he had seen the affairs of the new campaign and handing over the standard to Usama ibn Zayd. The Messenger of Allah was encouraging his Companions to make this campaign successful. In this army led by young Usama, there were senior Companions like Hazrat Abu Bakr, Hazrat Umar, Hazrat Ali, and Hazrat Uthman. It appeared that the Holy Prophet wanted to prepare the youth to lead his mission. Since Usama was the son of a freed slave and Arabs did not like to see a slave as their commander, the Holy Prophet (May God bless and cherish him) wanted to break the customs of the *Jahiliyah* period. However, many people objected to the leadership of young Usama, especially Ayyash ibn Abi Rabia, who said, "This youth had been appointed as a commander while the first Emigrants are still here." He was expressing his dissent at such a choice. It was on Saturday that the Holy Prophet (May God bless and cherish him) came to know about it. He wrapped his turban around his head, came to the Mosque, and mounted the pulpit. He addressed his Companions, "O people, I swear that just as you are opposing Usama as a commander, you opposed his father as well and raised your objections to his leadership. By Allah, he is the one best suited to command. It is also a fact that his father was the dearest of people to me, and after him, the dearest is Usama. Do not leave the army of Usama behind at any cost, and make sure it succeeds."

Therefore, all the Companions rushed towards Juruf, and they spent Sunday there. Usama came back again on Sunday. The Holy Prophet was running a high fever, and his wives were giving him medicines to relieve his pain. Usama bent down and kissed the Holy Prophet (May God bless and cherish him). The Holy Prophet (May God bless and cherish him) was unable to speak. He lifted his hands towards the sky for a while and then put them on Usama. He prayed for the young commander. Usama returned to his camp in Juruf that day but came back on Monday. The Holy Prophet (May God bless and cherish him) was feeling slightly better; seeing him in that condition, Usama returned to the army to fulfill his mission.

RETURN TO ALLAH

The Holy Prophet (May God bless and cherish him) understood that his divine mission on earth was now complete. The revelation of Sura An-Nasr in the days of al-Tashreeq was a clear indication that his farewell was forthcoming. In his statements and deeds, the Holy Prophet (May God bless and cherish him) was somehow conveying this message to his Companions. During the month of Ramadan, in the tenth year of Al-Hijrah, he secluded himself in the Mosque for twenty days instead of his usual practice of ten days. During this time, Angel Gabriel recited the Noble Quran twice with him.

In the farewell pilgrimage, he announced, "I do not know whether I will ever meet you at this place after this year." One night, after he had ordered preparations for the Syrian campaign under the leadership of young Usama, he called his freedman, Abu Muwayhibah and said, "I have been ordered by Allah to ask forgiveness for the people of Baqi (cemetery). So, come with me." Both went to Baqi. As soon as the Holy Prophet (May God bless and cherish him) approached the cemetery he said, "Peace be upon you, O people of the graves. Rest in peace, how much is your state better than the state of the people still living? This world is full of dissension like a dark night, one following another, each worse than the last." Then he looked at Abu Muwayhibah and said, "The Lord has offered me the keys of the treasuries of this world and immortality therein followed by paradise, and I have been given the choice between that and meeting with my Lord and paradise."

Abu Muwayhibah was excited and said, "O Messenger of Allah, my mother and father be your sacrifice, take the keys of the treasuries of the world and immortality therein, followed by paradise." At this the Holy Prophet (May God bless and cherish him) answered, "I have already chosen the meeting with Allah and paradise." After that, he prayed for the people of the graves in Baqi. (Ibn Ishaq).

One day, the Holy Prophet (May God bless and cherish him) was sitting in the Mosque, and he suddenly extended his hand as if to take something, but then he withdrew his hand. The Companions noticed this action and were curious to know about it. The Holy Prophet (May God bless and cherish him) said, "I saw paradise, and there were branches loaded with grapes. I reached out for a cluster of it. Had I taken it, you would have eaten of it as long as the world existed." (Bukhari, Sahih). Recently, the Holy Prophet (May God bless and cherish him) spoke of paradise and the afterworld frequently as if to remind his Companions about his death that it might be imminent.

Although the Holy Prophet (May God bless and cherish him) was sixty-three years of age, he looked remarkably younger in appearance. His eyes were full of brightness, and there were only a few white hairs in his black hair. It was obvious that the holy Prophet (May God bless and cherish him) had already started to say his farewell to his Companions. He had an earnest desire to be united with his Exalted Friend (Al-Rafiq al-Ala). He had been giving signs of his departure for a year now, such as what he had said when he sent Muadh to Yemen and the way he asked for his follower's good acclamation during the farewell pilgrimage.

He visited Uhud, where his most beloved Companions were laid to rest. He said farewell to those who accompanied him at that time but also to those who were buried there.

On Monday, the twenty-ninth of Safar, in the eleventh year of Al-Hijrah, the Holy Prophet (May God bless and cherish him) attended a funeral prayer in Al-Baqi. On the way back, he suffered from a severe headache and ran a high fever. His temperature was so high that it could be felt from the outside of the turban he had wrapped around his blessed forehead. Despite that, he went to the Mosque and led his followers in prayer. After prayer, he mounted the pulpit and addressed his congregation,

"There is a slave amongst the slaves of Allah unto whom Allah had given him a choice to choose between this world, and that which is with God, and the slave has chosen that which is with Allah." When Hazrat Abu Bakr heard these words, he wept, for he knew that the Holy Prophet (May God bless and cherish him) was speaking of himself and that his life on earth was coming to an end. The Holy Prophet (May God bless and cherish him) saw him and knew that he had understood. He told him not to weep and said, "O people! The most generous of men unto me in his companionship and what his hand bequeathed is Abu Bakr. If I were to make any friend other than Allah, I would have chosen Abu Bakr. But companionship and brotherhood of faith is ours until Allah unites us in His presence." It was also on this occasion that the Holy Prophet (May God bless and cherish him) looked around the Mosque and, pointing to the many doors that opened into the Mosque, said, "Let them be closed except the door of Abu Bakr."

Then he continued and said, "I go before you, and I am your witness; you will meet me at the "Pool," which I can see from here, where I stand. I fear not for you that you will set up gods beside Allah, but I fear for you this world, lest you seek to compete with one another in worldly gains." (Bukhari, Sahih)

Despite his constant illness, the Holy Prophet (May God bless and cherish him) led his Companions in prayer for eleven days. His sickness lasted for a total of fourteen days. As the sickness got worse, he could only pray in a sitting position, and he told his Companions that they should also pray in a sitting position. During the last week of his life, he used to ask his wives, "Where shall I stay tomorrow?' and they would name the wife to whom he would go. But the Holy Prophet (May God bless and cherish him) continued to ask, "And where the day after?" until his wives understood that the Holy Prophet (May God bless and cherish him) was impatient to be with Hazrat Aisha. Whereupon, all the wives came to him and said, "O Messenger of Allah! We have given our days with you to our sister Aisha." He accepted their offer but was too weak to walk himself. Therefore, Hazrat Abbas and Hazrat Ali helped him to Hazrat Aisha's room. (Ibn Sa'd)

It was Thursday, four days prior to his departure from this world, that the Holy Prophet (May God bless and cherish him) summoned his Companions, even though he was suffering from severe pain. He said,

"Come near me, and I will dictate you to write something so that you will never fall in error."

There was discussion among the Companions. Hazrat Umar ibn Khattab said, "The Messenger of Allah is suffering from debilitating pain, and you have the Book of Allah with you. The Noble Quran is sufficient unto you." Some other Companions, however, insisted the writing be made. When the Holy Prophet (May God bless and cherish him) heard them debating over this issue, he commanded them to go away and leave him alone. (Bukhari, Sahih).

According to tradition, the Holy Prophet (May God bless and cherish him) recommended three things.

1. Jews, Christians, and polytheists should be expelled from Arabia.
2. The delegations should be respected and treated well in a way like his custom.
3. As for the third recommendation, the narrator said that he had forgotten it. It could have been adherence to the Book of Allah and Sunnah. It could possibly be related to the success of Usama's army, or it could be related to performing prayers and treating slaves compassionately.

Later that evening, his illness got worse, and he could no longer lead the prayers, even in a sitting position. The Holy Prophet (May God bless and cherish him) asked Hazrat Aisha, "Have the people performed the prayer?" "No, they have not. They are waiting for you," said Hazrat Aisha. So, he asked her to put some water in the pot, and he washed himself. He wanted to stand up, but he was too weak. When he regained some strength, he asked again, "Have the people performed the prayer?" He then asked for water and washed himself again but was still unable to go out and pray with his Companions. So, he asked Hazrat Aisha, "Tell Abu Bakr to lead the people in prayer." But Hazrat Aisha feared that it would greatly pain her father to take the place of the Messenger of Allah. So, she said, "O Messenger of Allah, Abu Bakr is very soft-hearted, not strong of voice and much given to weeping when he recites the Quran." "Tell him to lead the prayer," The Holy Prophet commanded. She tried again, this time suggesting Hazrat Umar should lead the prayer. The Holy Prophet (May God bless and cherish him) strongly reiterated, "Tell Abu Bakr to lead the Companions in prayer." Hazrat Aisha turned towards Hazrat Hafsa with an appealing glance, who now began to speak. But the Holy Prophet (May God bless and cherish him) silenced her, saying, "You are even as the women that were with Joseph, tell Abu Bakr to lead the prayer." (Ibn Sa'd)

For the rest of his illness, Hazrat Abu Bakr then led the companions in prayers. There were seventeen prayers he led during the life of the Holy Prophet (May God bless and cherish him). (Bukhari, Sahih)

The Holy Prophet (May God bless and cherish him) spent most of his time leaning against Hazrat Aisha's breast or on her lap. During the day, he called Hazrat Fatima to himself. At this, Hazrat Aisha withdrew a little to allow some privacy between the father and the daughter. Hazrat Aisha noticed that the Holy Prophet

(May God bless and cherish him) whispered something into his daughter's ear, who then wept with tears rolling down her cheeks. Then, after some time, he whispered another secret, and this time, she smiled while tears were still in her eyes. Hazrat Aisha was curious to know what he had told her. So, at the time of her leaving, she asked her about it. Hazrat Fatima later told her, "The Messenger of Allah told me he would die in this illness, and therefore, I wept. Then he told me that I will be the first person among his household to join him, and therefore, I laughed." (Bukhari, Sahih). The Holy Prophet (May God bless and cherish him) also gave her the glad tidings that she would be the queen of all the women of the world. He then asked that Al-Hassan and Al-Husayn be brought to him. He kissed and caressed both and strongly recommended that they should be looked after well. Hazrat Fatima was aware of the great pain the Holy Prophet (May God bless and cherish him) was experiencing. So, she said, "What great pain my father is in." Whereupon the Holy Prophet (May God bless and cherish him) said, "He will not suffer anymore, when today is over."

During his illness, he used to place a cloak over his face. Whenever he felt severe pain in his body, he would remove the cloak from his face and declare, "God's curse be upon the Christians and the Jews, for they have adopted the graves of their prophets as places of worship." Hazrat Aisha later related that the Holy Prophet (May God bless and cherish him) was warning us against the like of what they did.

As his illness got worse, his fever rose high, and he almost fainted. He said to his wives, "Pour over me seven skins of water from different wells that I may go out unto the men and advise them." Hazrat Hafsah brought a copper tub to Hazrat Aisha's room, and the other wives brought water. When he sat down, they poured water over him. Then, they helped him to dress and bound up his turban. Two men helped him to go to the Mosque. The Holy Prophet (May God bless and cherish him) said, "O people, come close to me." He first spoke of the wrongs that the previous ummahs had fallen into and then said, "Do not turn my grave into an idol's house where people come to worship." After that, the Holy Prophet (May God bless and cherish him) announced, "Whosoever I have hurt among you, here is my back, let him come and take his due. Whomever, I said a hurtful word to and broke his heart, let him come and say what he likes and take his due." No one came forward. But the Holy Prophet (May God bless and cherish him) repeated his words after the noon prayer. Someone stood up and said that he owed him three dirhams. The Holy Prophet (May God bless and cherish him) called his cousin Fadl and said, "Give it to him."

The same day, the Holy Prophet (May God bless and cherish him) stood up and addressed his Companions. He offered praise to God and extolled His glory. Asking God to forgive those martyrs slain during the Battle of Uhud. He then said,

"You, O assembly of Emigrants, you shall continue to increase, but the Ansar (Helpers) shall not increase. They are like salt in a dish. The Ansar are my trusted Companions in whom I found refuge, so exalt their noble deeds and overlook their misdeeds." (Al-Zuhri)

On Monday, the Messenger of Allah was feeling a little better. He stood up, pulled the veil of his chamber aside, and watched Hazrat Abu Bakr lead the believers in prayer. Anas said, "I looked at his countenance as though it were the page of the Book, and he smiled." Anas continued, "We were almost tempted to abandon our prayer because of the joy we felt upon seeing the Holy Prophet (May God bless and cherish him). Even Abu Bakr turned, thus delaying his prayer. But the Holy Prophet (May God bless and cherish him) gestured him as if to say, 'As you are.' The worshipers were standing in orderly rows when they sensed that the Holy Prophet (May God bless and cherish him) was approaching. They gave him way. He came all the way behind Hazrat Abu Bakr and put his hand on his shoulder. Hazrat Abu Bakr wanted to step back, but the Holy Prophet (May God bless and cherish him) joined the prayer. When the Imam had finished, he prayed for the cycle he missed. As he was leaving, he commented, "A prophet does not die until someone from his congregation has led him in prayer."

On Sunday, the day before his union with his Exalted Friend, he set his slaves free. He told Hazrat Aisha that she should give away the seven dinars she had in her possession as charity. He was overcome by weakness. When he recovered, he asked whether it had been distributed, and they were not. So, he asked for it and counted it in his palm. Then, he sent it to Hazrat Ali to distribute it among the needy. "How can Muhammad go to the presence of his Lord while he still has these with him?" he asked. The Holy Prophet (May God bless and cherish him) gifted his weapons to the believers. So, when the night fell, Hazrat Aisha had to borrow some oil from her neighbor to light her oil lamp. Even his coat of mail was deposited as collateral to a Jew for thirty Sa' of barley.

(Mamar ibn Rashid said Ayyub related to him on the authority of Ikrima) Al-Abbas ibn Abdul Muttalib said, "I said to myself, 'By God, I must know for certain how much longer the Messenger of Allah will remain among us.' So, I said to him, 'O Messenger of Allah, if only you were to take a chair to sit upon, then Allah would spare you the dust and keep petitioners away!" "I will let them contend with me over a spot to sit on my robe (Rida) even if they tread upon my heels," the Holy Prophet (May God bless and cherish him) replied. "Their dust shall cover me until Allah grants me respite from them." Then, I knew his time with us was short."

Al-Abbas and Hazrat Ali were coming out of the Holy Prophet's (May God bless and cherish him) home while he was still ill, and a man encountered the two and asked, "O Abul Hassan, how fares the Messenger of Allah, this morning?" "The Messenger of Allah has recovered," Hazrat Ali replied. Then Al-Abbas said to Hazrat Ali, "After three days, you will be the servant of the staff." (Al-Zuhri). Al-Abbas then said to Hazrat Ali, "I have this sense that I can perceive death in the faces of Abdul Muttalib's progeny, and I fear that the Messenger of Allah will not recover from this affliction of his. Come with me to him that we may ask him. For if the right to rule is to be ours, then we will know for certain, and if it is not to be ours, then we will ask him to grant us his blessings." But Hazrat Ali replied to him, "What would you think if we were to go to him and he did not give it to us? Do you believe that the people will then give it to us? By God, I will never ask it of him." (Ibn Ishaq)

The Holy Prophet (May God bless and cherish him) had now returned to his couch and was lying with his head upon Hazrat Aisha's chest and was so exhausted as if all his strength was drained. At the same time, her brother Abdul Rahman ibn Abu Bakr entered the room with a *siwak* (root of a desert plant used for brushing teeth) in his hand. Hazrat Aisha said that while the Holy Prophet (May God bless and cherish him) was leaning against me, he was looking at the *siwak*. So, I asked him because I knew that he wanted it. "Would you like me to take it for you?" He nodded in agreement. I took it and gave it to him. As it was too hard for him, I asked him, "Shall I soften it for you?" He nodded again. So, I chewed on it to make it soft. Then I gave it to the Messenger of Allah, who brushed his teeth with it despite his weakness. There was a water pot nearby. He put his hand in it, wiped his face with it and said, "There is no god but God, death is full of agonies." (Bukhari, Sahih)

Soon after, the Holy Prophet (May God bless and cherish him) lost consciousness, and Hazrat Aishah thought it was the onset of death, but after some time, he opened his eyes. She then remembered that once he told her, "No prophet is taken by death until he has been shown his place in Paradise and offered the choice to live or to die." She, therefore, realized that the Messenger of Allah had been shown the vision of the hereafter. "He will now choose us." She said to herself. Then he raised his finger up, looked towards the ceiling, and moved his lips. Hazrat Aisha came close to him and listened. She heard him say,

"With the supreme communion in Paradise, with those on whom You have showered Your grace, with the prophets, the truthful ones, the martyrs, and the good doers. O Allah, forgive me and have mercy upon me, O God, with the supreme communion." (Ibid). Then he repeated the last words three times, "In the most exalted company." He then went limp. His blessed head grew heavier upon Hazrat Aisha's chest until other wives began to lament. Hazrat Aisha laid his head on a pillow and joined them in weeping.

This happened in the morning on Monday, the twelfth of Rabi ul-Awwal, in the eleventh year of Al-Hijrah. The Holy Prophet (May God bless and cherish him) was sixty-three years and four days old when he attained his union with the Divine Beloved.

Al-Zuhri said, Anas ibn Malik related to me when the Messenger of Allah was taken from us on Monday, we were in the Mosque. Hazrat Umar stood up and said,

"Verily, the Messenger of God has not died! Rather, his Lord had sent for him as He sent for Moses for forty nights! Thus, Moses stayed away from his people for forty nights. By God, I expect the Messenger of Allah to live long enough to cut off the hands of the hypocrites and to cut out the tongues of those claiming that the Messenger of God had died."

Ibn Al-Abbas reported that Hazrat Abu Bakr entered the Mosque while Hazrat Umar was speaking to the people. He went straight to the chamber of Hazrat Aisha, where the Holy Prophet was lying on the bed. He pulled back the *hibarah* (cloak) in which the blessed body of the Holy Prophet (May God bless and cherish him) had been shrouded. He looked at the radiant face of his beloved friend, leaned over him, and kissed him. Then he said, "By God, God will not cause you to suffer two deaths. You have already died the death after which you shall never die again."

After that, Hazrat Abu Bakr went out to the Mosque, where Hazrat Umar was still talking to the people. Hazrat Abu Bakr said to him, "O Umar, sit down!" but he refused to sit. He reminded him two or three times but did not listen. Then Hazrat Abu Bakr stood up and affirmed the oneness of God, and the people turned towards him and left Hazrat Umar. When Hazrat Abu Bakr finished praising God, he said,

"Now, whoever used to worship Muhammad, truly Muhammad has died; whoever among you worshipped God, truly God lives and has not died." Then he recited the following verse.

"Muhammad is merely a Messenger before whom many messengers have come and gone. If he died or was killed, would you revert to your old days? If anyone does so, he will not harm God in the least. God will reward the grateful." (Al-Imran 3:144)

Ibn Abbas said, "By God, it was as if people had never heard this Quranic verse till Hazrat Abu Bakr recited it as a reminder. So, people started reciting it till there was no man who did not recite it."

Ibn Al-Musayyab related, "Hazrat Umar said, by God, hardly a moment passed after Hazrat Abu Bakr recited the verse, I was standing there, immediately dropped prostrate to the ground for then I knew for certain that the Messenger of Allah had died."

CHAPTER 27
SUCCESSION AND BURIAL

The news of the passing away of the Holy Prophet (May God bless and cherish him) spread like wildfire in Medina. The army of Usama was ready for the northward march. Many of the older Companions, including Hazrat Umar, were among the fighters. Umm Ayman sent a word to her son Usama that the Holy Prophet (May God bless and cherish him) was approaching death. On receiving this shocking news, he right away gave orders to return to Medina. And so, all men came to Medina to mourn the death of their beloved prophet.

Disputes about who would succeed the Holy Prophet (May God bless and cherish him) broke out even before the blessed body of the Messenger of Allah was prepared for burial. At this critical time, Hazrat Ali had withdrawn to his home, and with him were Zubayr ibn Awwam and Talha ibn Ubaydullah. The rest of the Emigrants (*Muhajirun*) were congregated in the Mosque of the Holy Prophet (May God bless and cherish him) around Hazrat Abu Bakr. Hazrat Umar was also present in the Mosque. They were joined by Usayd and many of his clan members.

In the meantime, someone came and informed Hazrat Abu Bakr and Hazrat Umar that the party of Ansar (Helpers) had assembled in the Portico of Bani Sa'ida around Sa'd ibn Ubada. After the passing of the Holy Prophet (May God bless and cherish him), they were wondering where the authority should lie. The Helpers (Ansar) were close to choosing Sa'd as their leader, and it appeared that they were going to pledge their allegiance to him. The meeting of Ansar compelled Hazrat Umar, who insisted Hazrat Abu Bakr attend the congregation, and Abu Ubaydah joined them as well. What happened at the Portico of Bani Sa'ida and how the events turned out is narrated by Ibn Abbas, who said,

"During Umar's caliphate, I used to teach the Quran to Abdul Rahman ibn Awf. Now, when Umar undertook his final Hajj, we were in Mina. Abdul Rahman ibn Awf came to see me at my residence and said, 'If only you had witnessed the commander of the faithful today! A man went to him and said, 'O commander of the faithful, I have heard so and so say, were the commander of the faithful to die, I would certainly pledge my allegiance to so and so." (The speaker is the Prophet's Companion, al-Zubayr ibn Awwam, and it is Hazrat Ali ibn Abi Talib, to whom he pledges to swear his oath of loyalty).

"I will address the people this very night!" Hazrat Umar exclaimed. "I must warn them of this group of men who seek to seize power over the Muslims by force." Ibn Abbas continued, "O commander of the faithful," I said, 'The market now is full of unfriendly mobs, and they will overwhelm any assembly you convene. My fear is that if you make a statement in their midst on the morrow, they will take your words and misinterpret it and pay no heed nor give them their due. Rather proceed carefully, O commander of the faithful, until you have arrived in Medina, for it is the abode of the Sunnah and the Hijrah. There, you can speak with the Emigrants and the Helpers alone and say whatever you wish in full command of the audience, who will heed your words and give them their due." "By God," Hazrat Umar replied, "If He so wills it, then I shall do so as soon as I set foot in Medina."

"When we arrived in Medina, the time for the Friday congregation had come. Abdul Rahman ibn Awf told me, and I rushed off to the Mosque. I found out that Saeed ibn Zyad was already seated next to the pulpit. I sat down next to him, and my knees were touching his knees. Once the sun had set, Hazrat Umar came out to meet us all, and as he approached, I said, "By God, the commander of the faithful is certain to say something the like of which has never been said from the pulpit before. This angered Said ibn Zayd, and he said, "And what exactly will he say that hasn't been said before?"

When Hazrat Umar ascended the pulpit, the muazzin began the call to prayer. Once he had finished the Adhan, Hazrat Umar stood up and praised God, as is His due, and then spoke,

"Now, I will go straight to the point. I wish to make a statement that God has ordained me to say. I know not for certain whether the hour of my death will arrive soon. Let whoever heeds, understands, and remembers my words repeat them wherever his journey may take him. But whoever fears that he shall not heed my words, let him not spread lies against me. Indeed, God sent Muhammad (God bless and cherish him) with truth and revealed through him the Scripture. One of the God's revelations was the verse of stoning. The Messenger of Allah stoned adulterers, and we stoned adulterers after him. I fear that in times to come, men will say, 'By God, stoning is not in God's Book. Then they shall go astray or neglect a command Allah has ordained. Indeed, stoning is the just punishment for the adulterer if one has married and the evidence is present, be it pregnancy or confession. We used to read in the Quran, 'Desire not for ancestors other than your own, as it is an impudence. The Messenger of Allah also said, 'Do not praise me to excess as the Christians did to Mary's son (God's blessings be upon him), for I am but a servant of God. Rather, say, the servant of God and His Messenger."

It has also reached me that a man from your ranks says, "Were the commander of faithful to die, I would certainly pledge my allegiance to so and so." But do not be deceived by a man who says, "The oath of allegiance to Abu Bakr was a hasty decision! Though it was indeed so, God dispelled its evil. And there is no one among you for whom men have risked their lives as they have for Abu Bakr. He was the best of us when the Messenger of Allah passed, even though Ali and al-Zubayr withdrew to Fatima's house and Helpers withdrew from us with their kinsmen into the Portico of Sa'ida clan. It was the Emigrants who gathered before Abu Bakr (God show him mercy), whereupon, I said, "Abu Bakr! Come with us to see our brethren, the Ansar!" Thus, we went with him leading the way, and we encountered two righteous men from Helpers who had participated in the Battle of Badr. They asked, "O assembly of Emigrants, what do you seek?" We replied we seek out these brethren of ours from the Ansar." "Return!" they said. "Settle on who will lead you among yourselves." I then replied, "Make way, for we won't be stopped." We approached them, and so they had assembled at the Portico of the Sa'ida clan, and in their midst was a man wrapped in a cloak." "Who is that?" I asked. "That is Sa'd ibn Ubadah," they answered. "What's wrong with him?" "He has taken ill," they said.

One of the Helpers rose and, after glorifying and extolling God as is His due, said, "We, the Ansars, are the legion of Islam. O company of Quraysh, you are but a troop in our ranks, a band of which wandered off the desert into our midst." By these words, did they want to take us out by the roots and take the authority from us? In my heart, I had prepared something to say and planned to say it in front of Abu Bakr so that he might help soften its harshness since his bearing was better and more dignified than mine. When I wanted to speak, he said, "Take it easy," and I was reluctant to defy him.

Abu Bakr offered praises to God, as is His due, and then he spoke. By God, he neglected not a single word that I had prepared in my heart, uttering it like or, in his insightful way, something even better. Then he said, "O company of Ansar, you have mentioned your virtues, and you deserve as much, but the Arabs will not recognize the rule of any tribe save that of the Quraysh, for they are the noblest of Arabs in lineage and abode. Indeed, it would please me to offer you either of these two men. So, pledge your allegiance to whomever you wish." Then he took hold of my hand and the hand of Abu Ubaydah ibn al-Jarrah. I did it find unacceptable, for I would have preferred to have stepped forward to be beheaded, were it not a sin, then to rule over a people in whose midst was Abu Bakr.

When Abu Bakr finished his speech, a man from the Ansar stood up and cried, "I am the stout rubbing post and the short palm heavily laden with fruit; choose a leader from among yourselves, o company of Quraysh, and we shall choose one from our own ranks lest war breaks out from our dispute and ensnare us once again."

Umar ibn Khattab replied, "Two swords cannot fit in a single scabbard; rather, the commander is to be from our ranks and the aids from yours." As the people began lifting their voices from both directions and the clamor heightened until the dispute turned dangerous, I said, "Abu Bakr! Stretch your hand so that I may pledge my allegiance to you! Abu Bakr stretched out his hand, and once I had pledged my loyalty to him, the Emigrants and the Helpers did likewise. We pounced on Sa'd until someone cried out, "You have killed Sa'd," "May God kill Sa'd," I said.

Indeed, by God, of all the things that were transcribed during these events, we saw nothing more serious than the oath of fealty pledged to Abu Bakr. We feared that if we left the Ansar to their own devices, they would have pledged their own oath of fealty immediately after our departure. In that case, we would have had to pledge allegiance to someone we could not abide, or we would have had to oppose them. In either case, chaos would have ensued. So, let not a man be deceived into saying, "The oath of fealty to Abu Bakr was a hasty decision." Though it was indeed so, God dispelled its evil, and there is no one among you for whom men have risked their necks as they have for Abu Bakr.

If someone were to pledge an oath of fealty to a man from the Muslims without consultation, neither the man nor the one who pledged allegiance should be followed. Rather, they both be put to death."

No matter what the Helpers had decided at the Portico of Sa'ida, it would have been impossible for anyone to have led the prayers in the Mosque except Hazrat Abu Bakr so long he was there. The next day, before dawn, Hazrat Abu Bakr sat down in the pulpit before the start of the prayer. Hazrat Umar stood up, bidding the congregation to pledge allegiance to Hazrat Abu Bakr, and said, "He is the best of you, the Companion of the Messenger of Allah, the second of the two when they were both in the cave." (Al-Taubah 9:40). The revelation had confirmed Abu Bakr to have been the sole Companion of the Holy Prophet (May God bless and cherish him) at that crucial juncture. At this, the entire congregation swore their allegiance to him.

Shortly thereafter, Hazrat Abu Bakr glorified God and praised Him and said, "I have been given the authority to govern your affairs, and I know I am not the best of you. If I do well, help me, and if I do wrong, set me right. Truth can only be upheld by loyalty while ignoring the truth is treachery. I am the support of the weak and poor, and it is my duty to secure their rights. The strong and rich shall be weak with me until I have restored the rights of others from them if God wills. Obey me so long as I obey God and His Messenger. But if I do, on the contrary, you owe me no obedience. Now, stand up to pray. God have mercy upon you." (Ibn Ishaq)

The Emigrants and Helpers were busy in negotiations at the Portico of Sa'ida on Monday all day till it was late at night. At the dawn of Tuesday, the blessed body of the beloved of Allah was still lying on his bed, covered with a shroud. The room was locked from the outside. After the morning prayer, the family of the Holy Prophet (May God bless and cherish him) decided that they must prepare him for the burial. But there was disagreement as to how to wash his blessed body. Allah, the Mighty and Majestic, cast a deep sleep upon all of them, and in his sleep, each man heard a voice that said, "Wash the Messenger of Allah with his garment upon him." Therefore, they went to Hazrat Aisha's room, which was vacant at that time. The members of the household of the Holy Prophet (May God bless and cherish him), Hazrat Ali, Hazrat Abbas and his two sons al-Fadl and Qitham, Usama ibn Zayd, and the freed slave Shukran took part in washing the blessed body of the Messenger of Allah. Aws ibn Khawli, a Khazrajite, begged Hazrat Ali to represent the Helpers in this auspicious act, and Hazrat Ali graciously allowed him to participate. Hazrat Abbas and his sons al-Fadl and Qitham helped Hazrat Ali to turn the blessed body from side to side while Usama poured water over it helped by Shukran. Hazrat Ali washed him while Aws propped him against his chest. The blessed body of the Holy

Prophet (May God bless and cherish him) was washed three times with water and berry leaves, while Hazrat Ali was passing his hand over his entire blessed body above the garment. He said,

"Dearer than my father and my mother, how beautiful thou art in life and in death." The Holy Prophet (May God bless and cherish him) looked as if he was merely asleep. The water for washing came from Ghars, Sa'd ibn Khaithamah's well in Quba, which the Holy Prophet (May God bless and cherish him) used to drink from. They shrouded him in three white Yemeni cotton sheets with neither a turban nor a shirt. (Bukhari, Sahih; Muslim, Sahih)

A disagreement arose about the burial place. Many of his Companions suggested that his grave should be near the graves of his three daughters and Hazrat Ibrahim and the Companions he himself had buried and prayed over in the cemetery of Baqi al-Gharqad. While some thought he should be buried in the Mosque. Then suddenly, Hazrat Abu Bakr remembered having heard the Holy Prophet (May God bless and cherish him) say, "A prophet is buried where he dies." So, Abu Talha lifted the bed on which he died, dug underneath, and cut the ground for the grave.

Then, the people came to visit the Holy Prophet (May God bless and cherish him) ten by ten. They prayed the funeral prayer individually. First came men, then the women, then the children, and then the slaves. No man acted as an imam in prayers over the Messenger of Allah. This process lasted all day Tuesday and most of Wednesday night. (Ibn Ishaq)

Those who entered the grave were Hazrat Ali, Al-Fadl, and Qitham, the sons of Hazrat Abbas and Shukran. Aws begged Hazrat Ali to let him descend, and he let him go with the others. When they were lowering the blessed body, Shukran, his freed slave, took a garment that the Holy Prophet (May God bless and cherish him) used to wear and buried it in the grave, saying, "By Allah, none shall ever wear it after you." The Holy Prophet (May God bless and cherish him) attained union with the Most Exalted One on the twelfth of Rabi ul-Awwal on the very day that he came to Medina as an Emigrant, having completed twelve years in his emigration.

BIBLIOGRAPHY

1. Abu Dawud Sulayman b. Ash'as as-Sijistani (202-275 AH); *As-Sunan*, Maktabatu'l-Islamiyya, Istanbul, Turkey.

2. Ahmad b. Abdullah at-Tabari (d. 694/1295); *Ar-Riyadu'n Nadira*, Daru'l Gharbi'l Islami, Beirut, 1996.

3. Ahmad ibn Hanbal (213-290 AH); *Musnad*, Muassasatu, Qurtuba, Egypt, 2005.

4. Al-Bayhaqi, Abu Bakr Ahmad b. al-Husayn (384-458 AH); *At-Sunanu'l-Kubra*, Maktabatu Dari'l-Baz, Makkah, 1994.

5. Al-Bazzar, Abubakr, Ahmad b. Amr b. Abdullahalik (215-292 AH); *Al-Musnad*, Muassastu Ulumil -Quran, Medina, 1409 AH.

6. Al-Bukhari, Abu Abdullah Muhammad b. Ismail (d. 256 AH); *Sahihu Al-Bukhari*, Daru'l Bashairi'l-Islamiyya, Beirut, 1989.

7. Al-Halabi, Ali ibn Burhanidin (d. 1044/1635); *As-Siratu'l-Halabiyya*, Daru'l Marifa, Beirut, 1400.

8. Al-Haysami, Ali ibn Abu Bakr (d. 807 AH); *Majmua'z-Zawaid*, Daru'l-Kitabi'l-Arabi, Cairo, 1407 AH.

9. Al-Jazairi, Abu Bakr JabirHaza'l-Habibu Muhammad Rasulullah, Daru's-Salam, Cairo, 2004.

10. Al-Qastallani, Abu'l-Abbas Shabaddin Ahmad b. Muhammad (d.923/1517); *Al-Mawahibu'l-Laduniyya bi'l-minahi'l-Muhammadiyya*, Maktabatu'l-Islamiyya, Beirut, 1991.

11. Al-Mubarak Puri Saifur-Rahman; The Sealed Nectar (*Ar-Raheequl Makhtum*); Darussalam, KSA, 2015.

12. An-Nasai, Abu Abdur Rahman Ahmad b. Shuayb (215-303 AH); *As-Sunan*, Maktabattu'l-Matbuati'l-Islamiyya, Aleppo, 1986.

13. As-Suyuti, Abdur Rahman b. al-Kamal Jalaladdin (849-911 AH); *Al-Hasais al-Kubra*, Daru'l-Kutubi'l-Islamiyya, Beirut, 1985.

14. At-Tabarani, Abu'l-Qasim Muhammad b. Ahmad (d.360 AH); *Al-Mu'jamul-Awsat*, Daru'l-Haramayn, Cairo, 1415.

15. At-Tabari, Muhammad b. Jarir b. Yazid b. Halid (224-310 AH); *Al-Jamiu'l-Bayan*, Daru'l-Fikr, Beirut, 1405.

16. Az-Zarqani, Muhammad Abdul Azim; *Manabilu'l-Irfan fi Ulumi'l-Quran*, Daru Ihyai'l-Kutubi'l-Aarabiya, Cairo, 1943.

17. Az-Zuhri, Abu Bakr ibn Shihab Muhammad b. Muslim b. Ubaydullah

(124/742); *Tanzilu'l-Quran*.

18. Eaton Charles Le Gai; Islam and the Destiny of Man, State University of New York Press, Albany, NY 1985.

19. Ibn Al-Athir, Abu'l-Hassan Izzaddin Ali b. Muhammad, (d. 630/1233); *Al-Kamil fi't-Tarikh*, Daru'l-Kutubi'l-Islamiyya, Beirut, 1995.

20. Ibn Aljawzi, Abdul Rahman b. Ali b. Muhammad, (508-597 AH); *Sifatu's-Safwa*, Daru'l-Marifa, Beirut, 1979.

21. Ibn Athir, Abu'l-Hassan Izzaddin Ali b. Muhammad (d. 630/1233); *Usdu'l_Ghaba fi Mar'rifati's-Sahaba*, Darru'sh-Shaab, Cairo, 1970.

22. Ibn Hajar, Ahmad b. Said az-Zahiri (d. 456 AH); *Jawaminu's-Sira wa Hamsu Rasail li Ibn Hazm*, Daru'l-Ma'arif, Egypt, 1900.

23. Ibn Hisham, Abdulmalik ibn Hisham ibn Ayyub al-Himyari (d. 213/828); *At-Siratu'n Nabawiyya*, Daru'l-Jil, Beirut, 1411.

24. Ibn Ishaq, Abu Abdullah Muhammad b. Ishaq b. Yasar (150/76) *Siratu Ibn Ishaq*, The Life of Muhammad, Oxford University Press, New York, 2003.

25. Ibn Kathir, Abu'l-Fida Ismail ibn Umar ibn Kathir ad-Dimashqi (d.774 AH); *Al-Bidaya wa'n-Nihaya*, Daru'l-Ma'arifa, Beirut; As-Siratu'n-Nabawiyya, Daru'l-Ma'arifa, Beirut, 1976.

26. Ibn Kathir, Abu'l-Fida Ismail ibn Umar ibn Kathir ad-Dimashqi (d.774 AH); *Tafsiru'l Qurani'l Azim*, Daru'l-Fikr Beirut, 1401.

27. Ibn Maja, Muhammad b. Yazid al-Kazwini (207-275 AH); *As-Sunan*, Daru'l-Fikr, Beirut.

28. Ibn Sa'd, Abu Abdullah Muhammad b. Sa'd al-Mani (168-230 AH); *At-Tabkatu'l-Kubra*, Daru's-Sadir, Beirut.

29. Lings Martin: Muhammad, his life based on the earliest sources, Inner Traditions, Rochester, Vermont, 2006.

30. Maybudi Rashid ad-Din; *Kashf al-Asrar* (The unveiling of the mysteries); Royal ahl al-Bayt Institute for Islamic Thought, Amman, Jordan, 2015.

31. Muslim, Abu'l-Husayn al-Hajjaj an-Naysaburi (206-261 AH); *Sahih Muslim*, Daru Ihyai't-Turasi'l-Arabi, Beirut.

32. Qadi Iyad ibn Musa al-Yahsubi; Muhammad Messenger of Allah (*Ash-Shifa of Qadi Ilyad*); Madina Press, cape Town, South Africa, 2014.

33. Schimmel, Annemarie: And Muhammad is His Messenger; The University of North Carolina Press, Chapel Hill, NC, 1985.